Academic Writing

Genres, Samples, and Resources

Mary Kay Mulvaney
Elmhurst College

David A. Jolliffe
DePaul University

PEARSON
Longman

New York   San Francisco   Boston
London   Toronto   Sydney   Tokyo   Singapore   Madrid
Mexico City   Munich   Paris   Cape Town   Hong Kong   Montreal

Vice President and Publisher: Eben W. Ludlow
Senior Supplements Editor: Donna Campion
Production Manager: Donna DeBenedictis
Project Coordination, Text Design, and Electronic Page Makeup:
    Elm Street Publishing Services, Inc.
Senior Cover Design Manager/Designer: Nancy Danahy
Cover Photos: © Corbis, Inc.
Photo Researcher: Julie Tesser
Manufacturing Manager: Mary Fischer
Printer and Binder: RR Donnelley & Sons Company/Crawfordsville
Cover Printer: Coral Graphic Services, Inc.

For permission to use copyrighted material, grateful acknowledgment is made to the
copyright holders on pp. 526–528, which are hereby made part of this copyright page.

Library of Congress Cataloging-in-Publication Data
Mulvaney, Mary Kay.
  Academic writing: genres, samples, and resources / Mary Kay Mulvaney, David A.
Jolliffe.
      p. cm.
    Includes index.
    ISBN 0-321-17974-9
    1. English language--Rhetoric--Problems, exercises, etc.   2. Academic writing—
Problems, exercises, etc.   I. Jolliffe, David A.   II. Title.
PE1408.M744 2005
808' .042--dc22
                                                              2004020960

Please visit us at http://www.ablongman.com

ISBN 0-321-17974-9

1 2 3 4 5 6 7 8 9 10—DOC—07 06 05 04

To the countless dedicated composition instructors who labor long and hard to foster student opportunities for intellectual inquiry and growth through academic writing

BRIEF CONTENTS

PART III ACADEMIC WRITING
STRATEGIES FOR SUCCESS

PART IV ACADEMIC WRITING
READINGS FOR RESPONSE

DETAILED CONTENTS

PART III ACADEMIC WRITING STRATEGIES FOR SUCCESS

PART IV ACADEMIC WRITING
READINGS FOR RESPONSE

PREFACE TO INSTRUCTORS

Near the beginning of his often-quoted 1985 article in *College Composition and Communication,* "Inventing the University," David Bartholomae offers the following observation: "Every time a student sits down to write for us, he has to invent the university for the occasion—invent the university, that is, or a branch of it, like History or Anthropology or Economics or English." During a typical evening at the word processor, in other words, a student may need to write himself or herself into the position of a budding historian writing an informative report on the Trail of Tears relocation of the Cherokee in the early nineteenth century; a novice anthropologist writing a field observations paper about a visit to an archeological dig; a would-be economist writing a social science research report on the effect of a new parental voucher system on school funding in a certain state; or an incipient literary critic writing an analysis of the devotional poetry of John Donne.

This book is designed to help students like these, both at the start of their college and university careers and as they proceed through them. *Academic Writing: Genres, Samples, and Resources* is based on three assumptions: First, faculty in fields and disciplines throughout the university are realizing that students ought to be writing in their classes. These faculty members realize that students learn material more effectively and thoroughly if they write about it, both while they are learning it and after they seemingly have mastered it. Next, the writing that students do in their classes always assumes the form of some genre. Genres, as composition scholarship in the past two decades has been arguing, are not simply empty templates—shells into which content can be "poured" robotically. Instead, they are "tools" that writers—both scholars and professionals—in different disciplines use to accomplish knowledge work, address audiences, and achieve goals and purposes in their fields. As tools of disciplinary activity, genres shape writers' identities and behaviors, influence their selection of topics and evidence, direct their choices of organizational patterns and formats, and even affect their decisions about style. Finally (and we suspect this is more and more the case), students learn by studying models. Faculty members can lecture, explain, cajole (and so on) at great length about the type of paper they hope students will produce in response to a certain assignment. It is our opinion, though, that nothing is a better teaching tool than a clear model—even if the model does not *exactly* match the kind of paper a faculty member is seeking. If it does match, the faculty member can say, "Here, this is the kind of paper people in this discipline write." If it doesn't match, then the faculty member can say, "Look at this model. It's *almost* what we have in mind in this field. Take this paper as your model, and do just a few things differently."

Academic Writing can be used in any course, at the first-year or more advanced levels, that aims to introduce students to the many types of papers students need to write in the course of their studies. In addition, we hope *Academic Writing* will provide a valuable resource for students throughout their college years, even if they are not enrolled in a class specifically designated as a writing course.

The book is organized into five sections. Using two "real-life" scenarios, Chapter 1 illustrates for students how understanding genre as a concept will help them become better students and more effective writers in college. Chapter 2 demonstrates more generally how writing in college requires students to develop productive habits, insights, and attitudes about writing acts, writing processes, and their own "writerly" voice. Chapter 3 is the centerpiece of the book. In this chapter, we offer explanations and 30 annotated samples of 15 different genres, representing student writing in 18 academic fields and disciplines. We hope these samples, which we gathered from students at numerous colleges and universities throughout the United States, provide effective models for teaching and learning writing. The papers are genuine student work, as submitted in response to an assignment—not "doctored up" for excellence. We hope faculty members will teach these models not as templates that students should follow slavishly but as examples from which students can learn and, in some cases, upon which they can improve. Chapter 4 introduces students to concepts of information literacy—that is, principles and practices they will need to follow to acquire the resources they might need to write the kinds of papers explained in Chapter 3. Finally, Chapter 5 presents four units of readings and images on compelling contemporary issues of interest to today's college students: music, work, America's image, and the Internet. Faculty and students can use these units as background material and springboards for writing papers in many different genres.

It is our belief that this textbook presents a unique discussion of the multifaceted experience of academic writing. We hope it will provide you and your students some thought-provoking insights and useful resources as you jointly "invent" your experience of the world of higher learning.

Instructor's Manual

The Instructor's Manual by Michaela Lawrence and Nadya Pittendrigh, both of the University of Illinois at Chicago, is a useful tool that makes teaching from *Academic Writing* easier by providing a detailed overview and outline for each chapter, answers to many of the text's questions, two sample syllabi, and a list of recommended background readings. The manual helps instructors spend less time figuring out what parts of *Academic Writing* to use and more time creating meaningful discussion and writing sessions.

Acknowledgments

First of all, we wish to thank all of the students who granted us permission to use their work for publication here and our many colleagues from across the nation who helped us locate some of the best student papers available. Without them, this book would have been impossible.

We would also like to thank the hundreds and hundreds of students and instructors with whom we have shared the trials and tribulations of academic writing for decades. It is you who have informed this work in countless ways and inspired us to share insights we hope make some contribution to your efforts.

We're especially grateful to those colleagues who reviewed our manuscript for Longman and so generously offered us helpful suggestions and encouragement: Thomas Amorose of Seattle Pacific University; Dominic Delli Carpini of York College of Pennsylvania; Kathryn Evans of University of San Francisco; and Stephen W. Wilhoit of the University of Dayton.

Special thanks go to the wonderful reference librarians of Elmhurst College, especially Jennifer Paliatka, who graciously and patiently shared her wealth of knowledge about electronic and print resources, and Ayanna Gaines, who provided helpful and interesting leads for the visuals included here. And special gratitude also goes to Helen Marlborough of DePaul University for her kind support of this project.

We want to thank our editor, Eben Ludlow, for his patience, encouragement, and insights; thanks, also, go to his editorial assistant, Liliana Kim, for being so timely in response to questions and most helpful with many never-ending details.

MARY KAY MULVANEY
DAVID JOLLIFFE

Finally, I wish to especially thank my extremely patient husband and children for their endless support throughout this project.

MARY KAY MULVANEY

INTRODUCTION

If you're like most college students, two questions people ask you regularly are these: "What are you going to major in?" and "What kind of job do you think you're going to get after you graduate?" Questions like these—which some students can answer more definitively than others—justifiably lead you to assess what you might call your "skill set": the things you're good at doing, the areas where you have developed successful, and perhaps even marketable, abilities.

One aspect of that skill set might be writing. If you like to write and think you're pretty good at it (and getting better as the years go on), you might think that there are just a few majors and career fields that would really capitalize on this part of your skills and abilities. Conversely, if you are not keen on writing, you might think you can select a major in which you will hardly have to write at all, and perhaps you can get a job that doesn't involve writing. Actually, neither of these outlooks is completely accurate. In colleges and universities today, students in all kinds of courses and majors are discovering that they need to work on their writing abilities in order to succeed, and in the job market of the twenty-first century, workers in all high-quality jobs will need to be proficient writers and be willing to work on improving their writing on the job.

Such was not always the situation in higher education and the world of work. In the past, students who were "good writers" would become English majors (or perhaps journalism or communications majors); these students would write lots of papers of many kinds—stance or position papers about literary periods, themes, and techniques; reviews of books (and perhaps plays, concerts, and art exhibits); newspaper articles and magazine features; sometimes even fiction, poetry, and drama of their own. Similarly, in the past, the businesses, industries, organizations, and corporations in which you might get a job after you graduated had people on their staffs who were seen as the "good writers." These were the people who wrote the reports, the proposals, the memorandums, and the letters that enabled the business, industry, organization, or corporation to function and prosper.

This situation began to change around 30 years ago. College-level faculty and administrators began to recognize three things about the role of writing in higher education: First, they realized that students learn the material they study in college courses more thoroughly and effectively if they write about what they are learning, both while they are learning it and after they have learned it. This realization suggested to faculty and administrators that students in most classes should write extensively about the course material—for essay examinations demanding considerable writing or in substantial papers they write for the class. By writing extensively about a content area, the faculty and administrators came to understand that students master the content area material more thoroughly. Second, these faculty and administrators began to understand that the *process* of writing extensively in academic fields and disciplines is every bit as important as the *product* that students produce. Consequently, a great many instructors not only decided it would be a good thing to require their students to write regularly in their courses but also began to ask their students to submit first drafts of their papers, to consult with somebody (the instructor, the teaching assistant, a tutor in a writing center, a classmate, and so on) about the draft, and to consider this feedback as they revised their work for final submission.

Three reasons supported this decision to build "the writing process" into courses throughout the disciplines: Students learn more from their writing if they process a piece fully; students need to learn to work collaboratively on their writing projects since such collaboration is commonplace in most fields of professional work; and, time and again, students reported that one of the most valuable parts of an undergraduate education was the supportive, formative feedback they got from their professors.[1] Finally, college faculty and administrators began to realize the vital importance that writing plays in *all* academic and professional disciplines. Knowledge isn't simply reported by scholars and teachers in universities: Knowledge is created. And the prime location of this knowledge creation, faculty and administrators came to understand, is not so much the laboratory or the library or the research site in the field—the prime location of knowledge creation is the word processor, the legal pad, the page. Since professionals in all fields use writing to help create knowledge and make it visible, you, as students, should be writing in all disciplines throughout your college years.

These three ideas about writing in college—that students learn more effectively by writing, that writing is a valuable educational process in its own right, and that writing aids the creation of knowledge in all fields—helped give birth to a movement that goes by the name of *Writing Across the Curriculum* (WAC), *Communication Across the Curriculum* (CAC), or *Writing in the Disciplines* (WID) at different institutions. Whatever the movement is labeled, it calls for students to be active writers, readers, speakers, and listeners in many, if not all, of their courses.

About the same time that higher education was forging the new WAC/CAC/WID movement, businesses, industries, not-for-profit governmental organizations, and corporations were changing with regard to writing as well. These work sites, which employ many college graduates, were moving away from an organizational structure in which one or two people were seen as the "good writers" and did the bulk of the important writing for the entire operation. Instead, many of these work sites organized their workers into collaborative teams, all the members of which would be responsible for some portion of a project involving writing. Major proposals and undertakings by these organizations often required these teams to write many documents that would be addressed to varying audiences—some readers were specialists in the field; some were generally educated "lay" readers, some were governmental officials; some were funding agents, and so on. Beginning about the early 1980s, therefore, the workplace became a highly literate site that required employees in all fields to read critically, write clearly and correctly, and, in general, communicate both efficiently and effectively.

---

[1] See Richard J. Light, *Making the Most of College: Students Speak Their Mind* (Cambridge, MA: Harvard UP, 2001).

This book is designed for students who want to succeed in this new world of writing in college and the workplace beyond—students like you. We begin with two chapters designed to orient you to participating in these worlds—Chapter 1 talks about understanding the notion of genre and exploring the different genres one might write in classes or work settings, and Chapter 2 talks about writing in college in general—and we conclude with a chapter of guidance about conducting research (Chapter 4) and several units of readings that might lead to interesting writing (Chapter 5). The centerpiece of the book is Chapter 3, an annotated catalogue of 15 genres, representing 18 different academic disciplines, which students most frequently have to produce in their college courses. They come from students just like you who were given specific assignments in their courses at actual colleges and universities throughout the country. We envision *Academic Writing* as a resource that will occupy a valuable place on your bookshelves throughout your undergraduate years and will go with you to whatever location awaits you after college.

Exploring Genre

A College Writer's Tool for Understanding Writing

As a college writer, you need to work with a robust and productive writing process; read carefully and critically, to integrate what you read into your writing; and develop an appropriate writer's voice. No doubt you are already somewhat familiar with many of these aspects of writing. We will discuss them in much greater detail in the next chapter. For now, we focus on an exciting feature of writing that you have probably paid little attention to in the past. It is something that you need to carefully attend to in all of your college courses—the power of *genre*.

Almost all of the writing you must do in your courses is influenced, directly and strongly, by the *type of paper* you must write. The special term people use to refer to the way types of papers shape writing is *genre*. (It's a French term, so learn to say it correctly. It's pronounced *zhahn-ruh*, with the accent on the first syllable.) We will use the term in two ways. First, we will use it to refer to specific types of papers: A lab report is a genre. So is a case study, and a journal entry, and a Web page. Second, we will use the term to name a concept: We will talk about the *power of genre* to influence the decisions you must make as a writer in your different courses. As you become more aware of the influence of genre, and more familiar with the genres your courses require you to produce, you will find that understanding genre helps you make decisions about what kinds of topics to write about, how you should portray yourself as a writer to your readers, what "counts" as good ideas and evidence in a paper, what kinds of organizational patterns and formatting conventions you are supposed to use, and even what kinds of style—sentences and words—are appropriate.

Genre: It's More than the Form or Structure of a Paper

When you are faced with the prospect of writing a substantial paper for one of your courses, your first questions might be about its form, shape, and structure: How long does the paper have to be? Is it supposed to have an introduction, body, and conclusion? Is it supposed to have a title? Are you allowed to refer to yourself as "I"? Are you allowed to use informal language—contractions, for example? Do you have to incorporate research into the paper? If so, are you supposed to cite your sources using some specific style? These are all important questions, but unfortunately, the answer to each of them is, "It depends." "Depends on what?" you might ask. In some cases (such as the one described in the second scenario below), it might depend on the professor who assigns the paper. In other cases, it might depend on the academic field of your class. Papers in the sciences, for example, usually have a different form and structure than papers in the humanities. But there is one overarching answer to this "Depends on what?" question, an answer that encompasses individual instructors' preferences and the conventions of particular academic fields: It depends on what genre you are being asked to produce in your writing; answering *that* question requires that you understand a basic definition of genre.

While a certain genre often *has* a distinctive form or structure, you need to think about the concept of genre as something broader. A genre is not simply an empty shell, a formal template into which you can "pour" the content, and *voilà,* you've got a paper. A genre is, instead, *an appropriate response to the rhetorical situation that you, the writer, are in.* You, the writer, are faced with a problem that needs solving, an issue that needs addressing. You have a reader or a community of readers—an *audience*—with whom you want your composition to interact, with whom you want to "do business." (Note: You may think the only real audience for your composition is your instructor or teaching assistant, but think again. These people are rarely isolated, idiosyncratic, individualized readers. These people are readers who *represent* the community of scholars and teachers in their field. You're not simply writing to them; you're writing to them and others like them.) You have a purpose to accomplish with these readers: You want to inform them about your ideas or perspectives; you want to present a complex proposition to them and convince them to accept it; and you want to move them to new levels of thought, belief, or action.

In sum, when you have a need to write, an audience to write to, and a purpose to accomplish, you have a rhetorical situation. Once you realize what the rhetorical situation is, then you can ask yourself, "What is the *most appropriate* type of composition I can produce in such a situation?"

- Consider: In your home, apartment, or dorm room, you're getting lousy service from the electric company. Your electricity keeps going on and off for no good reason. Do you write a poem about the situation and send it to your grandmother? Of course not. You might call the electric company and register your complaint, and you might follow up that call with a letter detailing your problem and asking for a solution.
- Consider: In your financial aid office, you see an announcement of a new scholarship being offered by a local service organization. Do you compose a song about your qualifications, record it, and send it in to the organization? Of course not. You write a cover letter and an essay explaining why you deserve to get the scholarship, just as the announcement asks you to do.

- Consider: You have conducted some independent research in a biochemistry lab. Do you write a short story in which the fictitious central character is a budding scientist? Of course not. You write a lab report, following all the conventions your biochemistry instructor and lab assistant have taught you.

In each of these instances, you make a decision about what genre to produce based on the rhetorical situation you are in. You recognize a motivation for writing; you know the audience you are writing for; and you ascertain a purpose you want to accomplish. With all these considerations in mind, you produce the appropriate genre.

To make these ideas more concrete, let's examine two scenarios that will show how understanding genre as a principle and specific genres in particular will help you become a better writer.

The Case of Casey and the Writing Demands of a Five-Course Load

Casey is a typical second-year student at a large university. Take a look at the types of papers she will need to produce in her first-semester courses so that you can initially see how the power of genre will shape her writing and later examine how genre will influence your own work as a writer.

In her first year, Casey took mostly general education courses, but now she's ready to begin working on her major as well. After taking introductory psychology as a first-year student, she is pretty sure she's going to declare psychology as her major. For the first semester of her sophomore year, she registers for a full load (five courses at her school): one course in her major, two more general education courses, a course for her minor, and an elective. Here is Casey's schedule:

- Psychology 242, Research Methods—This course introduces psych majors to the methods of conducting both quantitative and qualitative research in their field. The course has a reputation as being a "rite of passage"—difficult, but ultimately very worthwhile.
- Philosophy 230, Contemporary Issues in Ethics—This course fulfills a general education requirement in philosophy. By reading the course abstract before registering, Casey learns that a unit of this course will deal with ethical issues related to mental health. Since Casey would eventually like to get a job as a mental health professional, she looks forward to this potentially difficult but useful course.
- Physics 208, Sound and Acoustics—This course fulfills a scientific lab requirement, something that Casey is not relishing. Having taken general biology, general chemistry, and general physics in high school, Casey thinks a physics course about sound will at least be new territory for her. Feeling a sense of adventure, she signs up.
- Management 300, Management Concepts and Practices—While she's relatively certain she wants to find a mental health job related to her psychology

major, Casey thinks it might be wise to have some background in business as well. She's thinking of declaring management as her minor, and this course would count toward it.

- Communications 206, Introduction to Film—This course fulfills an arts and literature general education requirement. Casey considers herself an avid movie fan, and she feels fortunate to get into this course, which always fills and closes quickly at her school. This, she thinks, is going to be her fun course.

A careful student, Casey spends some time early in the semester reading the syllabi for her courses and making notes about the major assignments she will need to complete for each course. Here is a summary of Casey's workload:

- For Psychology 242, Research Methods, she will take a midterm and a final examination, write three brief (two-page) reviews of the methodology presented in articles published in psychology journals, and, for the major project, write a 10-page proposal for a psychology study or experiment that she might conduct herself. She will not be required actually to conduct the study or experiment, just to propose it.
- For Philosophy 230, Contemporary Issues in Ethics, she will take three one-hour examinations, write two two-page response papers based on the assigned readings, and write a substantial (15 to 20 pages) researched argumentative paper on an ethical issue currently being debated. On the days Casey's response papers are due, she will bring copies for everyone in the class, and the session will begin with a brief discussion of her response. She hopes to write her researched argumentative paper on some ethical issue involved in the treatment of Alzheimer's disease.
- For Physics 208, Sound and Acoustics, Casey will take two one-hour examinations and a comprehensive final examination, and she will also complete four laboratory reports. There is no final paper required.
- For Management 300, Management Concepts and Practices, Casey will take a midterm and a final examination, write a proposal for a case study of a business or not-for-profit organization, and then conduct and write up the case study, which will describe, analyze, and evaluate the management practices of the business or organization. The case study will be about 20 pages long.
- For Communications 206, Introduction to Film, Casey will write four relatively brief (three to four pages) film reviews, take a final examination, and write a longer (12 to 15 pages) review essay, examining at least three films directed by the same person.

Notice two things about Casey's workload for the semester: First (and this should be obvious), Casey is going to be quite busy. If you consider a major paper to be one that is longer than 10 pages, she will write four major papers. In addition, she will write 13 shorter papers and reports, plus take midterm and final examinations. Second (and this is the major point of this chapter), Casey will do her best work with these writing assignments if she understands each of the tasks as calling for a specific genre.

How Casey Will Produce Different Genres for Different Rhetorical Situations

One thing Casey will discover in this very challenging semester is this: As she produces each of these papers, the power of genre will strongly influence both her as a writer and the type of academic work she does. To see this influence at work, let's consider how Casey might have to proceed on the four major papers and the lab reports. In each case, she will be faced with a different rhetorical situation: a motivation to write, an audience with whom she needs to interact, and a purpose to accomplish with her writing. Accordingly, Casey's decisions about what genre to produce will influence her as a writer in the following five ways:

- *The definition of "the writer":* The genre she chooses to produce will help define what kind of person she portrays herself as. What kind of person can a particular genre suggest the writer is? Strong? Well-educated? Discriminating? Forward? Passive? Calm?
- *The purpose of the text and the relationship between the writer and the reader:* The genre she chooses will have some informal guidelines about how the writer interacts with the reader. Is it the writer's role to teach the reader? To please the reader? To move the reader to some action? Does the writer expect that the reader will agree with the major points being made? Disagree? Interact and "talk back" in any way?
- *The selection of a good topic and appropriate evidence:* The genre she chooses will help her both select a topic and find appropriate evidence. What would be a good topic to write about in each case? Why would that topic be a good idea to set before readers? What counts as evidence in this kind of paper? Does the writer need to draw upon research? Observation? Experimentation? His or her own experiences and ideas? Interviews with other people?
- *Organization and format:* Because genres often do have some particular formal and organizational features, the choice of genre will help Casey make choices about form and structure. In each of these papers, what comes first, second, third, and so on? Are there distinct parts of the papers? Are these parts labeled? Does the paper have a title? Headings? Subheadings? Is there a Works Cited or bibliography section? If so, what format does it follow?
- *Style:* The choice of genre also suggests some choices about words, phrases, and sentences. Should the style be formal, informal, or somewhere in between? Are there special words and phrases—the professional language of a specific discipline—that the writer should use in this kind of paper? Is it okay to use "I"? Is it okay to use contractions?

Casey's Genres and Their Influence on Her as a Writer

Psychology 242, Research Methods

- *The writer:* In writing the proposal for a study, Casey will need to portray herself, the writer, as dispassionate and detached. She will strive to be seen as a novice social scientist, one who is going to study a psychological issue in a controlled fashion.
- *Purpose and writer-reader relationship:* Since she will not actually conduct the study, but only propose it, her goal will be to teach her reader—the professor, who will read the paper not as an isolated, idiosyncratic individual, but instead as a representative of the experimental psychology community—that she knows how to define a psychological problem, research its background, and set up a procedure to study it. She should anticipate that her reader will scrutinize most closely the "Methods" section of her paper, looking for ways that the proposed study will either adhere to or violate the field's conventions of gathering and analyzing data.
- *Topic and evidence:* She will have to choose a topic that is open to experimental examination in the social sciences, one that will enable her to randomly divide her research subjects—that is, the people she will study—into a control group and an experimental group, and one that will enable her to treat the two groups in precisely the same fashion except for one experimental variable. The proposal will have to provide evidence that the study would draw upon only those sources of evidence that come from the actual study itself; Casey's own experiences, observations, outside reading, and ideas would not be acceptable evidence.
- *Organization and format:* She will have to organize the paper by providing a descriptive title of the proposed experiment, succinctly focusing on the problem at hand by writing a brief "literature review" of previous studies on the same topic, setting out the hypothesis that the study will either confirm or refute, describing the selection and division of her subjects and the experimental treatment in some detail, and listing all the sources she has cited in the paper. This listing will appear in a section labeled "References" and will follow a format prescribed by the American Psychological Association.
- *Style:* The style will be very straightforward. The proposal will need no elaborate, attention-grabbing introduction. There will be no need for ornate language or fancy vocabulary although she will have to use the terms generally found in psychological research—terms such as *random sampling, reliability, validity,* and so on. Many of her sentences, particularly in the section that describes her proposed methods, will be in the passive voice. She will probably not use "I" in the paper, and neither will she use contractions.

Philosophy 230, Contemporary Issues in Ethics

- *The writer:* For the researched argument about some ethical issue related to Alzheimer's disease, Casey will need to come across as a scholarly, well-read person who is capable not only of researching a topic but also of synthesizing what she finds, comparing and contrasting it to her own experiences and ideas, thinking through the implications of her research findings, and creating a sharp, refined perspective that grows out of both her research and her own thoughtful considerations.

- *Purpose and writer-reader relationship:* Her primary goal will be not so much to teach the reader facts and perspectives about the treatment of Alzheimer's disease as it will be to convince the reader to adhere to—to buy into and accept—the perspective on its treatment that Casey puts forward in her paper.

- *Topic and evidence:* Since the class will cover, among other topics, ethical issues related to health care, Casey's topic will be quite appropriate. Her paper will probably not be successful, though, if she relies solely for her evidence on material she finds by reading academic articles, chapters in books, and Internet sites. A researched argument must do more than simply summarize research findings, so Casey needs to show her reader how she has reasoned her way through the material she has found and come up with her own take on the issue. In the summer after her freshman year in college, Casey worked as an aide in an assisted-living facility for the elderly, and she got to know several residents who had Alzheimer's. Depending on whether her professor allows it, she may be able to draw on those experiences in the paper. She thinks she might be able to get an interview with one of the medical directors of the facility, and material from that might be useful evidence in support of her claims. Casey's personal opinions and biases about how Alzheimer's patients are treated are not the most important kind of evidence she could use in this paper, but she shouldn't overlook them completely—they might be a valuable springboard into discussing a point she wants to make in support of her thesis.

- *Organization and format:* The paper will have a title; an introduction with a thesis statement at the end of it; several paragraphs in which Casey will develop and support her thesis, drawing on her synthesis of the research and her own thinking; and a conclusion. None of these sections will be labeled with a heading—they will just come one after another. Throughout the paper, Casey will need to weave references to and discussions of the research material into her own writing, and she will need to cite references to the research material using the citation style prescribed by the *Chicago Manual of Style*. At the end of the paper, she will need to incorporate her references in endnotes, once again following the *Chicago Manual*.

- *Style:* The style of this paper will be relatively formal. She will need to use many key terms from the fields of ethics and health care, and she should define any of these terms the first time she uses them. If her professor approves her plan to refer to her work experience in elderly care, Casey will be able to use "I" in part of the paper, but in most sections of the paper, the emphasis will be on the argument and the research, not on her own personal reactions to it, so first-person references will be scarce. She will not use slang expressions or contractions.

Physics 208, Sound and Acoustics

- *The writer:* For her laboratory reports, Casey will need to write like a scientist. She must keep herself as an individual writer in the background and put in the foreground what she has done in her labs. Though she will probably never refer to herself as "I" in the reports, she (the voice behind the writer) needs to come across as someone who is careful, measured, and in control.
- *Purpose and writer-reader relationship:* The purpose of each of the four documents is the same: to report, as clearly as possible, what was done in each laboratory experience, and to explain how the discoveries that Casey and her classmates make in the lab experiences relate to the material they are reading in their textbooks about acoustics and sound.
- *Topic and evidence:* For each of the four reports, the "topic" will be given—it will grow out of the instructor's specific instructions for how to complete the lab work—and the evidence cited will derive from the actual lab work.
- *Organization and format:* The format for each report will be the same. Casey will use the title for the report provided by her instructor. Drawing on the textbook and course lectures, she will write a brief introduction of the problem studied in the lab. Next, she will describe her laboratory materials and methods as clearly as possible, list her results (frequently accompanying the list with a graph or table), and then provide a discussion of what the results show in relation to the theoretical material in the textbook. She will label each of these sections with the headings "Introduction," "Materials and Methods," "Results," and "Discussion." Since she will not be reading any background information in order to produce the lab report, she will not need to cite secondary sources in footnotes or a reference list.
- *Style:* The paper will be written mostly in the passive voice ("The sound was measured . . . ") rather than the active voice ("I measured the sound . . . "), since the laboratory reports emphasize what is done, rather than who does it.

Management 300, Management Concepts and Practices

- *The writer:* The case study of a business or not-for-profit organization for Management Concepts and Practices will be Casey's first experience with producing a real-world genre, in contrast to a paper that is designed solely to be read by a professor or her classmates. Consequently, as a writer, Casey needs to show evidence that she has immersed herself in the business or organization she has chosen to study—that she has talked to its employees, visited its locations, studied its documents, and so on.
- *Purpose and writer-reader relationship:* She needs to show her readers (her professor, but also, by implication, the management and employees of the business or organization) two things: first, that she has studied the situation thoroughly and not missed any important information, and second, that she has innovative, workable ideas for how the business or organization might improve.
- *Topic and evidence:* The professor for the course, Casey has learned, will suggest a number of potential businesses and organizations students might study; the professor tries to discourage students from examining small, entrepreneurial "mom-and-pop" organizations, and instead wants students to look at

more substantial businesses. For evidence, Casey has also learned that the professor urges the students to use all the information they can find: interviews with clients and workers at all levels, site visits, and document analysis.

- *Organization and format:* The professor also keeps a file of case studies that students have written in previous semesters so that Casey and her classmates can examine effective models of the genre. The case study will have four parts, one of which will be subdivided, and each of which will be labeled with headings and subheadings. The section labeled "Introduction" will describe the business or organization and its mission and lay out the problems it is facing that the case study is designed to address. The section labeled "Descriptions" will set out in extensive detail all the aspects of the business or organization—its structure, its modes of operation, its personnel, and so on—that are pertinent to dealing with the problems laid out in the introduction. The section labeled "Proposals" will describe and argue for specific plans for dealing with the aforementioned problems. Within this section, for each proposal Casey offers, she will write subsections labeled "Budget," "Personnel," and "Timeline." The case study will end with a section labeled "Conclusion," which summarizes the entire document and argues for the value of the proposals developed in the previous section.

- *Style:* The style can be personal. It should not use slang or contractions, but it may use the word "I" and it may include narratives of the writer's personal experiences with studying the organization.

Communications 206, Introduction to Film

- *The writer:* In writing a review essay of three films by the same director, Casey will need to come across as someone who not only watches lots of movies but also views films with a critical, comparative eye.

- *Purpose and writer-reader relationship:* Her goal will be to demonstrate three things to her readers (the professor and the other members of the class, whom the professor likes to refer to as her "seminarians of criticism"): first, that there is some unifying feature in all three films that distinguishes them as bearing the marks of that particular director (What makes a Robert Altman film distinctive? What is a Coen brothers' movie?); second, that the director's (or directors', in the case of the Coen or the Farrelly brothers) work has some identifiable artistic merit; and third, that the films contribute in some way to the cultural and social fabric of the times during which they were made.

- *Topic and evidence:* The professor, Casey finds out, will provide a large list of directors whose work students can choose to examine in this review essay, but to provide evidence for claims, Casey and her classmates will need to draw upon published reviews of the films when they were originally screened, books and articles written about the directors by film scholars, background information on the history of film, and the writer's personal responses to the movies.

- *Organization and format:* While not as strictly prescribed as the lab reports, the organization of this paper will nonetheless call for distinct sections labeled with headings. The review essay will have a descriptive, attention-grabbing title. Its introduction will not be labeled as such with a heading. Its function will be to provide background information about the directors—biographical information, filmography, and so on—and to provide a carefully constructed thesis that makes a commitment to the reader about the three aforementioned goals of the paper. Each of the three sections following the introduction will be labeled with the name of the film to be discussed in that section. (For example, in a review essay about the films of Robert Altman, sections could be labeled *Nashville, A Wedding,* and *M*A*S*H.*) The concluding section will not have a heading, but will simply draw together everything that has come before in a way that highlights why the educated, artistically informed public should appreciate the work of the particular director.

- *Style:* Casey as an individual writer can be very present in the paper. She may refer to herself as "I"; she may use informal diction and contractions as she describes seeing the films; and she may offer rhetorical questions and perhaps even some exclamations to her readers.

MEETING THE CHALLENGE

Determine your *own* writer demands.

- Look over all the courses you are taking during the current academic term or speculate about the courses you will take next term.
- List all the major papers you will write, noticing carefully what *name* or *label* a professor gives to a paper.
- Finally, take notes about how the genre of each major paper influences the way you must define yourself as a writer; the way you must interact with your readers; and the organization, format, and style you must use.

Dana's Dilemma: Genre Decisions Usually Must Be Made by Writers Themselves

Dana faces a challenge that is the converse of the one confronting Casey. Rather than writing several papers that go by different names for the genre, Dana must write several papers that go by the same label.

Dana is a very thoughtful student. He's particularly interested in understanding the subtleties, the shadings, and the nuances of the meanings of words. As a government major, he finds himself giving lots of thought—while he works out at the gym or watches the news or lies awake at night ruminating—about what people mean when they use the word *politics* or invoke the term *culture* or debate issues of *public policy.*

Because he wants to do well in his classes, Dana listens carefully to what his professors say they are looking for in a writing project; and he reads their assignment sheets carefully and keeps the directions beside him at his desk while he's writing the papers. This level of attention has led Dana to conclude that there is one word many professors use to describe the genre they want their students to produce, and he has realized that the term can have a very different meaning from one professor to the next. The word is *essay.*

Dana has been in college long enough to realize that professors operate on the principle of academic freedom—each of them usually makes his or her own decisions about what material to teach in class, what kinds of tests and papers to assign, and so on. It probably would not be a good idea, therefore, for Dana to go to each of his professors and say, "Would you all kindly mean the same thing when you ask students to write an *essay!*" It's up to the students, he has concluded, to learn what each professor means by that term, so Dana (like Casey in the first scenario) decides to do a little detective work in advance of starting a semester with four courses that require writing. He talks to students who have taken each of the courses before. He talks to teaching assistants who lead discussion sections and work as writing tutors for some of the courses. He even gets bold and decides to ask the professors to describe what they mean by the term *essay.* Here is what he finds out:

- In English 300, Composition and Style, when Professor Dillon asks the students to write an essay, she wants students to write something that is akin to a short story. A good essay, she says, contains a vivid, graphic narrative, but it does so not simply to tell a story but instead to suggest a point, a generalization, or a conclusion that grows out of the story. The writer must be careful, Professor Dillon explains, not to belabor the point he or she is trying to make or be too obvious about it. Thus, in this section of Composition and Style, an essay should not have a distinct thesis statement. Writers of these essays need to tell their stories from a distinctly personal perspective—they are encouraged to refer to themselves as "I" and to draw upon their own observations, ideas, experiences, and reading—and the point, conclusion, or generalization they are trying to make grows out of the narrative.
- In Political Science 200, Political Inquiry, when Professor Sarjahn assigns an essay, she expects students to produce a genre that succinctly introduces the general topic they are writing about, states a thesis clearly in the first paragraph of the essay, provides a "mapping" statement (often beginning, "In this essay, I shall demonstrate . . . ," or words to that effect) about what the reader can expect to find in the composition, and then sets out a topic statement and support for each conclusion or generalization suggested by the thesis and the mapping statement. The support—that is, the evidence writers cite as examples of the points they make—can come only from the readings assigned for the course or found by the students in independent research projects. Personal examples and anecdotes are not acceptable evidence.
- In Religious Studies 206, Social Ethics, when Professor Rulondo asks students to write an essay, he is looking for a genre that falls somewhere between the one that students produce in English 300, Composition and Style, and the one called for in Political Science 200, Political Inquiry. Professor Rulondo expects an essay to have an introduction and thesis statement, but he does not want students to write the mapping statement ("In this essay, I intend to show . . . ," etc.). He simply wants students to make their points with strong topic sentences at the beginning of each section that develops their thesis. Moreover, he hopes students will draw on a variety of sources for their evidence—both the readings they do for the course and their own personal ideas, observations, and experiences.
- In Biological Sciences 121, Infectious Diseases and Immunity, when Professor Abrams assigns an essay, he expects students to read several pieces of published research ("the literature," as he refers to it) on a subject related to the general course topic and to identify common concerns or issues evident in each of the

published pieces. Professor Abrams wants no contextualizing or attention-grabbing introduction and he urges students to begin their essays with a simple declarative sentence (for example, "Infectious diseases are often spread by food-handling practices in small restaurants") and then to follow this straightforward introduction with a substantial paragraph about each source they read. Each of these paragraphs, the professor urges, should begin by citing the source: "Jones, Schmitt, and Schwartz in a 1997 study found that . . ." Professor Abrams insists that there be a raised endnote number 1 after Schwartz's name (and, obviously, raised numbers 2, 3, 4, and 5 after the author's name, or authors' names, in the following paragraphs) and that these numbers correspond to actual endnotes in which the writer cites his or her sources, using the Council of Science Editors style. In an essay for Professor Abrams' class, no conclusion is necessary—when the writer has reviewed the major findings in the five sources, the essay is done.

What Dana's experience shows is this: It is the rare case when an instructor or teaching assistant explains clearly and completely what genre he or she expects the students to produce and provides explicit instructions for writing that genre. Student writers must take it upon themselves to find out how individual instructors define the genres they assign. Once again, a good starting point for students' investigations in this realm is the rhetorical situation, but this time perceived through the eyes of the instructor. As a writer, ask yourself the following questions:

- What does the instructor perceive as the students' motivation for writing this assignment? Why exactly should a student invest his or her time and energy in this project?
- Who are the readers with whom the instructor thinks the student writers must interact?
- What purpose does the instructor believe student writers will accomplish with this composition?

Given all these considerations, how does the instructor suggest definitions of the writer, the writer-reader relationship, the nature of good topics and good evidence, and principles of organization, format, and style? In answering these questions, you will be identifying more specific genres than the "essays" described above, and you will be using the concept of genre as a means of organizing your thoughts as well as your writing activity.

MEETING THE CHALLENGE

Assess your *own* experience with genre.

- Identify two (or more) classes you are taking in which instructors or teaching assistants ask you to produce a genre that they call by the same name.
- Define what each instructor means by the term and then describe what the genre in each class suggests in terms of the definition of the writer; the dimensions of the writer-reader relationship; the nature of good topics and evidence; and the principles of organization, format, and style.

Writing-to-Learn and Learning-to-Write Through the College Years

Writing Within College

Writing will no doubt play a significant role in your academic career. Not unlike Casey and Dana, as we saw in Chapter 1, you will find writing to be a demanding, challenging, and, hopefully, exciting dimension of your college experience. It's important that you understand *why* writing is so central to most students' college experience—not because it is something you are "required" to do, but rather for two main reasons:

1. Writing is a powerful way *to learn*—anything!
2. Writing is crucial to becoming a significant participant in any specific discipline or career area—to become part of a particular field or profession. It is the way to learn what information is important in a field and how to think and use language like other scholars and/or practitioners in a field.

Researchers often call this two-dimensional view of writing "writing-to-learn" and "learning-to-write." Writing-to-learn has emerged from the work of educators, psychologists, scholars, and researchers of all kinds who have found that writing is a powerful way to learn, but not only to learn specific material or content in your courses. More importantly, writing helps us learn how to think in depth, and to think critically and analytically about our own ideas and the ideas of other people. Learning to write, of course, might refer to specifics of organization, content, style, voice, grammar, and mechanics. But it also encompasses learning conventions of specific fields, such as formats and styles unique to certain disciplines, and learning features of specific writing communities, such as ways of prioritizing information or methods of creating knowledge. In short, *how and why* a biologist writes is very different from *how and why* an historian writes or *how and why* an accountant writes and so forth.

There is a significant scholarly movement that has been in existence for nearly three decades, now called the Writing-Across-the-Curriculum Movement (WAC). Sometimes it is alternately called "WID," meaning Writing-in-the-Disciplines, or even more recently, "CAC," meaning Communication-Across-the-Curriculum. Though the emphasis in each is slightly different, all essentially focus on the importance of writing as central to the academic experience. You may be familiar with such a movement at your college or university. Perhaps you have a WAC or WID requirement for graduation or need to take a certain number of WI (writing-intensive) courses in order to fulfill your degree requirements.

Despite institutional differences, writing will no doubt play a significant role in your college career, and learning to write effectively will clearly aid in your success on campus and throughout your future. It is important to keep in mind that writing is not ONE thing that can be easily learned with a little practice and then considered "accomplished." Of course, all writing involves using some language system, combining words in certain prescribed combinations, and selecting a medium for production (a pencil and paper or a computer, most likely); but when viewed closely, writing is a *very* complex phenomenon that deserves your serious attention.

Writing Surrounds Us

Think of the kinds of writing you encounter every day: newspaper stories, ads, editorials, letters from friends, e-mails from friends, television and movie scripts (that you may "read" by simply viewing), novels, magazine articles, movie reviews, junk mail letters, catalogue descriptions, textbooks, course packets, operation manuals for your cellular phone, VCR, or new computer software—the list could go on and on.

Think for a minute of the kinds of writing you personally have produced to this point both within and outside of school—essays for entrance to your college, reports or papers for courses, e-mails to friends, letters to potential employers, letters to the editor of a local or campus newspaper, personal journal entries, class notes, poems or short stories. Maybe as part of your job or for a campus organization you're involved with you write reports to your supervisors or invitations or flyers for clients; record inventory; write recommendation letters for coworkers or summaries or outlines of information for clients; take notes at meetings; produce a memo about a meeting; etc., etc. In short, writing, in a myriad of forms, surrounds us!

Why do we write? For many different reasons, to be sure:

- To record information
- To help retain information
- To deal with processes
- To communicate facts or ideas to someone else
- To explore feelings
- To figure out what we really mean or think about a subject
- To demonstrate knowledge to others
- To share information with others
- To persuade others to accept, or at least to understand, our ideas and perspectives
- To present the formal arguments or reasons for a particular course of action or decision
- And often, whether we realize it or not, to create *new* knowledge

Differences Between College and High School Writing

Perhaps you are wondering what is different about college writing. After all, you have been writing, at least by one definition of that term, since first grade and no doubt you wrote in some high school classes. Perhaps you even wrote extensively in high school, frequently being assigned short reports for various classes and/or having to produce a 10-page, fully documented research paper in junior or senior year. Even so, you are likely to find the experience of academic writing in college to be quite different, primarily in four ways: the expected level of quality, the variation in types and frequency of writing, the difference in instructional detail, and the disparity between an "assignment" and a "project."

Most students will find that the level of expectation between high school teachers and college professors is considerably different. Most college professors are *very* familiar with the writings within their subject areas; most are also continuing to write and to publish academic journal articles and reports within their fields. They are generally far removed from the world of high school, and many have had little or no "teacher" training and may insist that you immediately begin functioning like junior scholars in training. They will assume that you are competent writers regarding certain basics such as the proper use of the conventions of Standard Written English (that is, conventional use of spelling, punctuation, and grammar rules). They will probably also assume that you know what it means to formulate a thesis and defend it. They may further assume that you already know how to locate and evaluate appropriate research materials within their fields. Some of these expectations may be unfair, depending upon your position within your academic career, but nonetheless, they often exist and they must be addressed.

Chances are, long-term writing tasks will be assigned much more frequently in college than they were in high school. You may find yourself facing a semester with one or more *major* writing projects in each of the four or five courses you are taking (all within different disciplines) in addition to shorter, short-term writing tasks. Perhaps in your high school years, you did most of your writing for your English teacher. Now, at many colleges, with increasing scholarly evidence of the value of writing as a powerful way of learning, writing projects are assumed to be an integral part of your scholarly training in *all* fields. So in a given semester, you may be producing a social science research project accompanied by a detailed written report, critical reviews in a fine arts class, a field report in your education or nursing preservice course, and a heavily researched analysis paper for your composition class at the same time that you are expected to keep an observational journal in your chemistry class, a reading log in your literature class, and/or a double-entry notebook in your anthropology class.

Keep in mind that, unlike in high school where teachers are often in frequent contact with each other and may even know, for example, to avoid giving a big exam on a given day in their math class because the semester research paper outline is due in everyone's English class, in college your professors will most often have no idea what other courses you are taking, what other assignments you have pending, or what expectations other departments may have in place. Consequently, you need to be able to handle the time demands of doing a great deal of writing, as well as to begin to understand some of the disciplinary differences from one field to another, and, hopefully, to take advantage of the learning opportunity each of these occasions to write affords you.

One thing you may clearly notice as a difference between high school and college writing assignments is the seeming lack of step-by-step instruction provided by your professor, particularly outside of your English classes. Frequently, a professor will simply state on the syllabus that a critical literature review or a scientific research paper is due on X date. There may be a few details about length or topic choices, but there may be next to nothing regarding procedures. (Fortunately, this text can help fill in that gap!) Chances are, when you did your big research paper project in high school, the teacher walked you through the steps. For example, you were probably required to get topic approval, and perhaps you were shown specifically how and where to locate source materials and were required to take notes in a very prescribed system—maybe on four-by-six-inch cards—with specific due dates for each stage of the paper. Most likely, first a draft was due and then it was peer and/or instructor reviewed, etc.

Now, however, you may simply be given the project and the due date, so a lot more is up to you. You must be self-motivated about figuring out a realistic time schedule for thinking about a topic; doing some early reading to get a handle on the basics of the topic; allowing yourself enough research time for fits and starts, for missing materials, for interlibrary loan requests, and so forth; as well as allowing time to take notes, to read and reread, and to think and rethink about your project thesis or focus. A major lesson to learn is that academic writing *takes time.* You need time to read, to research, to think, to compose, to revise, and to polish a final draft. Leaving a major writing project for a night or two before it is due is *a big mistake*—one that many a first-year college student has made and regretted.

Another major difference between high school and college writing—besides the expectation levels, the time factors, the frequency and variety of assignments, and the lack of specific direction—may be evident in an exploration of the difference between an "assignment" and a "project." While many people use these terms in school contexts interchangeably—i.e., both are tasks given by an instructor to be completed by a given time in order to receive credit for a course—there are some essential differences that may be useful to keep in mind as you advance in your academic career. For our purposes here, we would like to use the word *assignment* as a descriptor of most high school tasks (and perhaps of some entry-level or routine college tasks). Generally speaking, assignments have some fairly prescribed limits and fairly specific directions, and most importantly, they tend to be about situations that have right and wrong answers that all participants can mutually arrive at in a limited period of time. So, for instance, if you get "assigned" 20 algebra problems in your textbook, all students in the class compute the same 20 problems, and ostensibly all will arrive at the same answers in approximately the same amount of time. Perhaps in your English class you may have been "assigned" to write a two-page composition summarizing the significant actions of the main character of a novel you read for class discussion. Basically, all class members (assuming they have read the text) may essentially produce a very similar product. Even when you were assigned "projects" in high school—let's say for a science fair or a history class—very often they basically involved gathering facts and regurgitating them, and little or no personal analysis of those facts. Thus, most students were capable of producing very similar projects, sometimes differentiated only by how much time and care they took in finding "enough" material to recap.

College writing projects usually present a far different scenario. Think back to the case studies presented in Chapter 1. Generally speaking, college projects are far less prescribed. For instance, rather than containing very specific parameters, perhaps even such things as, "You must have three body paragraphs with two detailed examples in each one," the directions may be much more open-ended. You may be given multiple options or be expected to create your own options. Ultimately, the results may look extremely varied because of the expectation that students provide considerable personal input. It is possible that your professor has no particular preconceived result for the project at all, but rather wants to see evidence of originality and academic rigor on your part. Most often, projects do not have simple "right" answers and are not things that can be completed in nearly identical ways by multiple participants, because they assume more unique contributions on the students' part. Furthermore, they assume more time and energy, they are long term, and they clearly cannot be completed in single sittings as one evening's "homework assignment."

Perhaps the most useful way of looking at the difference between assignments and projects at the college level is to consider that college-level projects anticipate a far greater level of personal scholarly involvement—that is, they demand an engagement on your part that includes original, personal analysis. Simply put, your professors want you to process and then create, not regurgitate. They want to see evidence of original, critical thinking on your part that has enabled you to "create again something new."

In the language of rhetoric and language scholars, one might say that the projects are epistemic or "knowledge-creating" rather than simply reproductive or "knowledge-recording," as many high school assignments are. It is up to you to begin to create new knowledge—to question existing ideas, to make connections with various theories and forge new ground—to not be content to simply identify and then mimic what others have already said and thought. Of course, that certainly doesn't mean that you should ignore what is available and simply formulate everything from your own mind and experience—quite the contrary. In order to generate informed opinions of your own—in order to generate new ideas—you must know what the current thoughts are on a topic. True academic writing is never done in isolation; rather, it is part of a conversation—a conversation with other scholars who are also continually questioning, exploring, and stretching the boundaries of existing theories and thought, trying to create new perspectives to understand aspects of our human experience.

One of the best explanations of the differences between high school and college writing is offered by a first-year college writer. When asked about the differences, Richard Rohatsch responded:

> The biggest difference between college and high school writing has been the expectations. In high school I became used to writing research papers where my opinions were only evident in the opening and closing paragraphs. All the

support for my position was in the words of the sources I had used. However, in college, research papers became primarily my own work and I used sources to support my thesis and views as opposed to using sources as the main source of all ideas.

The other major difference I have noticed is the renewed emphasis on things typically overlooked in high school. College writing seems to be much more focused on things like grammar, sentence structure, and transitions than high school writing. I have learned that simply by using effective transitioning, keeping various styles for each sentence, and focusing on punctuation, my writing has become much more mature and professional.

The final difference I have noticed has been how much feedback is needed before turning in a paper. In high school I was used to skimming through my paper briefly to find any major mistakes before handing it in. However, in college I have found it valuable to have someone else read my paper to get some feedback. Oftentimes, something will make perfect sense to you but will require more details to another person. I have never turned in a college paper without having at least two people look at it and I have even gone so far as to have five other people look at my paper. It is a great way to get some feedback from your peers because each person will have a different perspective on what needs to be fixed.

MEETING THE CHALLENGE

Consider the differences within your own writing experience.

- Reflect on your experiences as a high school writer and thus far as a college writer.
- Explain some of the differences in a 100-word paragraph.
- Now reflect on and record the changes you are making as a writer to accommodate those differences.
- Compare your responses with your writing partner.

Developing a College Writer's Voice

Developing a "voice" is another important aspect of becoming an effective college writer. Every piece of writing has a voice. Voice is that elusive, ever-present stamp of "self" on a text. Voice may be thought of as a combination of the personality of the writer that comes through to the reader; the perspective the writer assumes, often influenced by the audience being addressed as well as by the purpose and previous level of knowledge, and so forth; and the tone of the passage. For example, when you read a text, consider whether it sounds authoritative, confused, speculative, self-assured, angry, sympathetic, etc. Determine whether it sounds informed or naïve, complex or simplistic, sarcastic or sincere, decisive or questioning, and so forth. Does it seem credible? Why or why not? In analyzing the voice of a passage, sometimes it is useful to close your eyes after reading a short section and literally imagine hearing the text as if it were being given as a speech. Envision the speaker and his or her attitudes. Then articulate how the image is created for the reader.

MEETING THE CHALLENGE

Analyze a passage for voice.

- Read the passage below (a brief excerpt of a report on Native Americans written by a sociology student, Rachel Hartman).

  Without the Native Americans' generosity the Pilgrims would have surely died in their first months in the "New World." They knew little about agricultural techniques and successful crops and used the Native Americans to their advantage. By the 16th century, the Pilgrims had become the epitome of every reason behind leaving their homelands. The Pilgrims began encroachment on the native's land and their society. "The Pilgrim Fathers fell on their knees, and then, as the saying goes, fell on the aborigines" (Davis 1972:18). The Pilgrims felt that if the Indians were not Christians they must be Devil-worshippers. The Pilgrims felt that instilling their beliefs and culture on the savages was a blessing. Through this delusion the crimes against Native Americans, the violation of property rights, began unremittingly for three centuries and continues even today.

- Analyze the passage for features of voice.
- Write a paragraph describing the voice, pointing to specific items in the passage for evidence to support your assertions.
- Compare your analysis with a writing partner. Discuss similarities and differences.
- Reassess your analysis based upon your discussion and then redraft your paragraph.

Whenever you write, a certain "voice" is revealed. Now your challenge is to begin to develop an academic voice. Does that mean to use big words that sound artificial and that perhaps neither you nor many others understand? *Absolutely not.* However, acquiring some new vocabulary within the fields you are studying is surely part of developing an academic voice. You need to understand the basic language of people in the field and learn to use the terms in a comfortable, natural-sounding manner.

Several scholars have studied college students in various stages of learning and development of voice (notably Mary Belenky and her colleagues). They have studied the stages that we might find useful in considering the development of voice in college writers.[1]

Often, beginning college students have a very simplistic voice; then as awareness and knowledge increase, a desire to imitate more sophisticated and authoritative voices in a field may grow. Imitation is often very stiff and artificial because no process of internalization has occurred. Rather, they are simply trying to "puppet back" what

---

[1] Belenky, Mary, et al. *Women's Ways of Knowing: The Development of Self, Voice and Mind.* New York: Basic Books, 1986.

they have read, even if they paraphrase slightly in their own words. Sometimes there is a readiness to immediately adopt everything they read as "truth," assuming the mentality that "if it says it in a textbook or a printed source, it must be true," and thus, they assume that simple "transfer" of information is all that is necessary to create a strong piece of academic prose. Other students go to the other extreme and reject nearly all professional information and feel that anything they personally think and write must be right, insightful, and above challenge. They argue that it "feels right" or "it's just what I think," and maintain that no one else need question it.

Gradually, a balance must occur in order to develop a genuine academic voice. It must be a combination of established knowledge in a field and personal analysis and response to that knowledge. In other words, it must be highly informed opinion that reflects internalization of the facts, theories, and questions in a given field and then evidences personal interpretation of them. Interpretation must be based upon connections that you begin to make between experience in your own personal sphere and the academic sphere you are encountering. One group of scholars has talked of a level of "connected knowledge" that begins to take place when a personal authoritative voice is formed. This is clearly your goal as a college student. Ultimately, you are moving along the path to an even slightly higher level of voice, by not only making connections but by actually "constructing" knowledge in your *own* voice. This newly "constructed" knowledge is very aware of the other "voices" and ideas within the field you're exploring, and yet, is truly your own.[2]

How can you begin to gain a credible academic voice? Here are some suggestions:

- Read critically and widely.
- Gain an understanding of academic materials, which includes reading closely enough to understand concepts and to begin to internalize specialized vocabulary.
- Observe textual features that vary by discipline, including conventions such as style preferences for writing in first or third person and for using subheadings, charts and graphics, and specific formats to meet prescribed requirements.
- Examine certain priorities within a specific discipline. Are the readings based primarily on field experiences, on theories, on close textual analysis, or on personal interviews, etc.?
- Note comparisons that occur within a field between other people's theories or contributions as you read within that field.
- Notice names that continually surface like "Einstein" in physics or "Picasso" in art and understand their contributions to the field.
- Follow current topics that appear to be "cutting edge"—conversations that surface repeatedly in various disciplines, such as the prevalence of increased globalization with the rise in technology and the need for greater Western understanding of Islamic culture since September 11, 2001.
- Try to make connections between topics that arise across disciplines—within your different courses in different departments. In other words, determine the

---

[2] Ibid.

"conversations of scholars" across academia so you can "eavesdrop" and begin to contribute.

- Experiment with developing a personal voice that is sincere and unique, yet simultaneously highly informed and knowledgeable.
- Learn general rules of academic voice such as, "Be polite and respectful of other's opinions"; no matter how much you disagree, be respectful of other perspectives and deliver your counterarguments in a civil manner, never insulting the personhood of another "voice."
- Establish your credibility by doing your homework—reading enough to have substance for your arguments and avoiding broad, sweeping generalizations and faulty reasoning.
- Ask other people for input on your work. Scholars don't write in a vacuum—get feedback on drafts. Visit the Writing Center on your campus. Share your writing informally with friends and ask for honest feedback.
- Read other model texts if available for ideas.
- Revise, revise, revise—don't be content with just getting something done. Rather, work on it, rework it, and continue to look for ways to improve your writing.
- Take your work seriously. To truly succeed as a college writer and to begin to fully participate in the academic community you have selected require major effort on your part.

Keep in mind that while you are learning to become a more effective writer in college, you will also be using writing as a powerful means to be a better learner for the rest of your life. You will be developing your own academic voice as you move through your academic career, a voice that you can continue to build on within your chosen career field.

Reading's Role in Writing

Another major component to being an effective college writer involves understanding the relationship between writing and reading. Writing in college is very closely linked to reading. Rarely will you be asked to write about something without first reading appropriate texts. Even a personal-response essay assignment will often first involve reading other essays or short stories or news articles about a topic and then writing in response to them. And, of course, many college-level writing assignments will hinge upon extensive reading assignments. That is, the assignment will require designated readings as the basis for a particular type of writing task such as a literature review or a critical analysis. Or you may be directed to locate readings yourself that are appropriate to a given topic or concern in order to gain background knowledge on a topic or to write a synthesized report of multiple viewpoints. The writing possibilities are nearly limitless, but nearly always, academic writing demands careful reading as a significant part of the process.

When faced with all of this reading, it is important to keep in mind that reading is *not* a singular activity done in exactly the same way all of the time. In fact, there are many variables in reading, as in any other activity. Reading can mean different things at different times depending upon its purpose or depending upon the expectations linked to the assignment, for example. At any rate, it is important to remember that reading is not nonvariable. Let's examine some different types of reading.

Types (or Styles) of Reading

- Preview reading—Often it is appropriate to conduct preview reading to determine if a given text might be useful for a task. This includes quickly surveying the book or article, noting the title, the author, the publisher and date of publication and any subheadlines or distinctive quotes set off in boxes that provide a glimpse into the content and even the perspective. It includes checking for illustrations or graphs that may provide valuable clues to the nature and focus of the text.
- Skimming—Sometimes it is appropriate to skim the entire text simply to get the gist of it. Frequently, this saves a great deal of time if you must tackle a great number of texts for an assignment. Skimming will allow you to gain a bit of overview knowledge, begin to recognize repeated terms and key contributors, for instance, and to sort which readings will require close attention at another time and which have served their purpose with merely a skimming.
- Casual reading—Sometimes you will want to do more than skim and instead read the entire article, but probably not take the time to write out notes or "doctor" the text in any way for future examination. This kind of reading should allow you to gain at least a passing understanding of the key points, while not be focused enough to absorb the details.
- Close—Often with the reading required in an academic context, you must do a close reading of a text. This type of reading takes more time and focused attention as it assumes that your intent is not merely to get the gist or gain a passing understanding, but rather to gain an in-depth understanding of the text. This kind of understanding is needed for both recall and application of the content—usually the expectation in an academic setting.

MEETING THE CHALLENGE

Practice your college-level reading skills. The following is an excerpt from a journal article entitled "The Agony of Ecstasy: Responding to Growing MDMA Use Among College Students," which appeared in a 2002 issue of *Journal of American College Health*.

- Read the passage below in three different ways: **preview, casual, close.**

  Ecstasy is a drug like no other. This simple statement is borne out in the somewhat unusual history of ecstasy and in the myths surrounding its use and effects. "Pure" ecstasy is MDMA (3.4-methylenedioxymethamphetamine)—not a difficult substance to make. However, most ecstasy purchased on the street or in clubs is nothing close to pure. Other chemicals, such as ephedrine, codeine, caffeine, and ketamine (a general anesthetic) are frequently added or passed off as ecstasy. ("Herbal" ecstasy, which can be purchased legally, is mostly ephedrine and caffeine, and contains no MDMA.)

The pharmaceutical company E. Merck in Germany first developed MDMA in the early 1900s. It is chemically related to both hallucinogens and stimulants in the way it induces euphoria and enhanced self-awareness, but it does not seem to produce psychotic effects or visual distortions. As a serotonin agonist, it works on the same system as antidepressants such as fluoxetine (Prozac™), paroxetine (Paint™), and sertraline (Zoloft™), with which it is sometimes taken in combination. Whereas these substances influence mood through inhibiting the reuptake of serotonin, MDMA substantially boosts serotonin release, producing many times the effect.

- Compare your readings each time. Record what you did differently. What did you learn with different approaches to reading?
- Compare your reading with a writing partner, discussing the content and determining if you drew the same or different conclusions about the passage.

In addition to these different types of reading, there are variables within the activity of reading. Reading can vary greatly depending upon the nature of the material itself and your specific focus. Let's examine some focus possibilities. Your reading focus may be:

- To understand content—Sometimes you want to read solely to comprehend the "what" of a given text; with this kind of reading you want to be able to restate, in your own words, the main ideas of a text—not pass judgment on it, but merely understand it enough to be able to mimic it.
- To determine style—Sometimes you want to read a passage to get a feel for the style of the author: the "how" of an author's writing, looking at ways he or she uses language to create a certain mood or establish a certain tone—serious or sarcastic, flippant or scholarly. Of course, style impacts content and vice versa, but you can make a decision to pay close attention to style while you read.
- To identify and clarify opinion—Sometimes you read to intentionally uncover the opinion of the author and/or to form your own opinion. To do this, you need to be very sure of the author's opinion on an issue and then to want to determine your own, agreeing or disagreeing (or perhaps a little of each) with the text you've read.
- To evaluate or assess the reliability and/or credibility of a text—For this, it is helpful to look at certain features. You should determine something about the credentials of the author—whether he or she is considered an expert in the field, for instance. Does the author have other publications on the same topic? If you are reading for scholarly research, check the references of the text. Does the author draw from several different sources? Are the sources academic journals or books published by university presses? Consider the date of publication if timeliness is a factor in your research. If you have questions about these features, check with your professor and/or your reference librarian.
- To examine the context—Why was this text written? What was this written in reaction to? What has been occurring lately to stimulate interest in this topic?

Have you heard this subject discussed in everyday conversations or ordinary newspapers? Often, reading materials are produced in relation to actual historical happenings. For example, readings published on Islamic culture have been much more prevalent since September 11, 2001.

- To connect with other readings—Sometimes reading, especially for academic tasks, demands a very conscious process of articulating connections—of specifying intertextuality, if you will. For example, you have been directed to acquire 10 sources for a critical research paper. In this situation, you want very much to know how they interrelate—which authors repeat essentially the same information, which agree with each other on controversial issues, which disagree, which seem to be presenting something from a new angle, etc. In other words, you intentionally conduct a "connected reading" of a sort. An exercise we sometimes promote in guiding students through the research process is the use of a source focus chart (an idea adapted from a composition scholar, Ann Feldman). This chart makes visible the connective threads in your research process. Students usually find it useful to articulate in this manner the connections between sources for a given topic. An *excerpt* of a source focus chart prepared for a critical report on Chinese perceptions of contemporary U.S. culture would look something like this:

Text[a]	Key point(s)	Personal comments/ responses	Relationship to other texts	Relationship to paper outline/plan
Smith	• China remains skeptical of U.S. motives • China rejects U.S. diet	Highly passionate; flimsy reasons	Disagrees with Jones	Use in section I.A.2
Jones	• Western influences apparent in China on multiple fronts	Sound resource; strong references	Supports Thompson	Use in section II.B.3
Thompson	• China points to weak morals in U.S. • China admires aspects of democracy/ fears others	Vivid examples; balanced view	Clarifies Smith's position with detailed examples	Use in section I.C.4

[a]*Identify text by author and title to cross-reference bibliography.*

The Activity of Reading: An Act of Composing

To really make reading a useful process, you need to "take ownership" of your reading. It can be useful to think of reading as an act of composing! Thinking of reading as writing may sound strange to you, but it's not really. Let's examine this.

Often it may seem that you are reading a single text, in relative isolation. Actually, this is never really the case. Even with reading single texts, your experience of them is never one-dimensional. That is, you always bring your previous thoughts and experiences, both previous reading experiences and other types, to each text you encounter. In other words, there is a certain "intertextual" process that always accompanies the activity of reading. Furthermore, since no two people read the same text in exactly the same way, some scholars have argued that, in fact, no single version of a text ever exists—even for a course with an assigned text—because of the various readings that each student and instructor "create" along the way.

So, reading at some level is never an isolated process because of the inherent intertextuality of the very activity of reading. However, sometimes we do choose to focus at a given moment on a single text. Yes, it will be an intertextual experience because of our often unconscious, or at least nondeliberate, input while reading. However, it may require an attempt to interpret it in similar ways to other readers in order to arrive at points of common understanding for discussion.

MEETING THE CHALLENGE

Reflect upon connections.

- Consider the brief reading assignment in the previous section that discusses the drug ecstasy.
- Reflect upon the mental associations you made with other readings and/or experiences you had while in the act of reading. Record them briefly.
- Ask your writing partner, who read the same text, to share his or her connections.
- Write a short paragraph comparing your thoughts and his/hers on the meaning of the text.

In overlooking the intertextual nature of texts, readers often misconstrue the act of reading to be a passive process; after all, it doesn't look like you're "doing" anything in particular when you are reading. In fact, reading, particularly academic reading, should be anything but a passive process. Reading at the college level is ***not*** a passive activity; it demands steady engagement on your part as a reader. What exactly does that mean?

Let's examine ways to become a strong academic reader.

Approach the text as something that needs a response, a reaction from *you!* First of all, you need to understand what the text is communicating, to clarify the "what"—to break it down or dissect it, if you will. If you simply "read" the text without marking anything significant, underlining key terms, or writing any margin notes, chances are that when you return to the unannotated page a few days later during a class discussion, you'll find that your mind is a "blank" as well.

One way to significantly engage with a text is to "gloss the text." This can be done in a variety of ways. Many students are quick to grab the ever-present fluorescent highlighters (available in a wide variety of types these days). While they can be useful for drawing your attention to certain items, be careful not to *overuse* them. Many students find they highlight nearly everything when they read, only to discover later that they once again have a block of text that means very little to them, only now it is a pleasant lemon yellow version of meaningless text.

It is more useful to mark the text in very specific ways. Here are a few hints for active reading—to determine and to be able to reclaim the "what."

- Underline the key idea or topic sentence in each paragraph.
- Use colored highlighters sparingly; reserve them for really significant points. Perhaps use a couple of colors to indicate related points in different sections of a text.
- Circle subheadings or key terms in a passage to bring visual attention to them.
- Number arguments or distinct points of a section with numerals in the margin of the text, clearly indicating that four subpoints substantiate a particular main point, for example.
- Draw arrows or connecting lines in the margins to indicate relationships between parts of the text.
- Place question marks to indicate points of confusion, and later attempt to clarify them or bring them up during class discussions.
- Annotate a passage with an asterisk to indicate its special importance.
- At the end of a chapter or section, sketch a simple outline of the key arguments or subpoints of the section.
- Compose endnotes or frontal notes at the end or beginning of each chapter or essay assignment that summarize in a sentence or two the main point of the text, the position of the author, and the way that position is communicated.
- Try to write a paraphrase of a section—with the book closed! You will soon discover whether or not you really know what an author has said, if you try to restate it in abbreviated form in your own words.

Once you grasp the "what" of a text, it is equally important—actually more important for college students—to formulate your response to the "what." Do you agree or disagree with the information you encountered? Is it significant or not? Why or why not? Does it remind you of other things you've read or heard about? If so, how does it relate to that information? Does it offer more detail? Rehash the same things? Offer new insights, etc.?

It is important to take time to process and interpret the text. It is usually not enough to simply comprehend it; rather, in order for it to be really useful to you,

you must integrate it within a personal frame of reference. So take the time to annotate the text further. For example:

- Indicate your own response to the "what" of the text.
- Sometimes it is useful to keep a reading log, a kind of journal on key readings. Briefly summarize the key points and then react to them; indicate connections between sections and to other readings or experiences you have had.
- Some teachers may require you to keep a double-entry notebook in which you take notes on a given reading in two columns. In the first column, create a summary of the key points and in the second column, take notes on your notes—indicate your own personal reaction, ask questions, make connections to other key points. You might make statements such as "agrees with author X" or "extends the argument raised by author Y," etc.

Attending to some of these tips will improve your critical reading skills and also your writing skills.

Remember that just as audience and purpose have a tremendous impact on different writing activities (as we have discussed above), there are multiple reasons to read; and once again, audience and purpose make a difference. You might read different texts, or even read the same text more than once, for different reasons. Sometimes you read entirely for pleasure, with little concern for retention and no sense of accountability to anyone else. Sometimes you read to satisfy a vague curiosity about something, something you want just a passing knowledge of because you've heard conversational references to it lately. But often in your role as a college student you are reading texts to complete some specific academic activity. This kind of reading is different. And even "assignment" reading is not one singular, universal thing—it can vary tremendously. Surely, you read texts in different stages of an assignment, for instance:

- To help locate an initial idea for a topic
- To locate background information
- To find comprehensive sources
- To fill in holes regarding something you are in the process of researching
- To answer specific questions
- To add current readings to established key past readings
- To help summarize or conclude a project

The bottom line is: Don't simply "read." Rather, approach your reading as an activity that ***demands and commands your interaction.*** Assume that when you read, you are being challenged to create a new reading of the text. You should take ownership of the text and not simply transfer to your eye and brain what someone else has written. You must, in essence, compose a new text as you read—that is, "write a new reading"—if you are to really succeed in an academic environment.

MEETING THE CHALLENGE

Gloss a text, composing a meaningful version of it.

- Read the passage below, which is excerpted from a student paper on the history of Native Americans.

Without the Native Americans' generosity the Pilgrims would have surely died in their first months in the "New World." They knew little about agricultural techniques and successful crops and used the Native Americans to their advantage. By the 16th century, the Pilgrims had become the epitome of every reason behind leaving their homelands. The Pilgrims began encroachment on the native's land and their society. "The Pilgrim Fathers fell on their knees, and then, as the saying goes, fell on the aborigines" (Davis 1972:18). The Pilgrims felt that if the Indians were not Christians they must be Devil-worshippers. The Pilgrims felt that instilling their beliefs and culture on the savages was a blessing. Through this delusion the crimes against Native Americans, the violation of property rights, began unremittingly for three centuries and continues even today.

    The Pilgrims brought with them alcohol and disease. Disease, poverty, and starvation, in addition to having their land taken and thus breaking their ties with the earth, gods, and spirits, added to the demise of the Native Americans. The settlers brought with them diseases the Indians had never known and were powerless to resist; more died from disease than warfare. Epidemics of smallpox, measles, dysentery, typhoid, tuberculosis and cholera ravaged their population and in some cases whole tribes were wiped out (Davis 1972:28). And the white man also brought with him one final blow to the Indian population, alcohol; the resistance of the Indian was pathetically low (Josephy 1991:24). The settlers would use liquor to squander the Indian's land and goods, and when he had finally lost his wealth and his freedom, he turned to alcohol, but this time as a means for oblivion (Davis 1972:30).

    In the beginning the odds between the Native Americans and the settlers were relatively equal. The natives were familiar with the terrain and the white men had guns. The white men believed in Manifest Destiny, that the land was theirs for the taking and they possessed the divine right of conquest (Wallace 1993:38). The natives struggled to hold their land, but eventually the white men became more numerous and powerful. The people were sold into slavery and raped of their land and goods. There were more men coming to the New World at a feverish pace, which meant less hope for the Native Americans, fewer rights and more land to be repossessed.

- Now reread the passage, glossing it carefully.
- Compare your glossing with a writing partner's. Note similarities and differences in what you highlighted and in how you emphasized certain points. Discuss different ways to create a mini "rereading" of the text to make it meaningful for you.

The Activity of Writing: A Multifaceted Challenge

Just as college-level reading is a demanding activity, so is writing. In fact, for most people it is even more demanding. Indeed, writing is often a *very* difficult thing—it can be frustrating, tiring, and enervating, even as it is fulfilling and exhilarating. One thing is sure: it is *not* passive. It demands a lot from you, the writer! Taking a close look at just what writing entails can sometimes ease the challenge.

Think for a moment about a time you had a writing task—maybe for school, for work, or simply for yourself, something like writing a letter to a company as a dissatisfied consumer. The writing activity itself will vary greatly, largely depending upon three factors: the **writer,** the **task** itself, and the **audience** for the task. Let's examine these separately for a moment.

1. **The writer**—To understand yourself as a writer, think of the four primary things that affect that role:
   a. your "writer personality";
   b. your level of experience or degree of familiarity with the task;
   c. your knowledge of the specific content; and
   d. your motivation for accomplishing the task at hand.

   a. Many factors about the writer him- or herself impact the activity of writing. One variable is simply **the personality** of the writer. Think of the way you approach any task that needs to be done. Do you spend a long time preparing for it, assembling necessary materials, determining about how much time you need to complete the task, and finding models, samples, or instructions to guide you? Or do you tend to "plunge in" and determine along the way when you need to stop and gather more information or aids? Do you tend to procrastinate about tasks and feel you work best under pressure from tight deadlines? Or do you have to work ahead because you tend to panic if the deadline is approaching too quickly and you feel you will not have adequate time to finish? Are you good at "multitasking"? Or do you have to focus on *one* thing at a time, with little or no distractions? What kinds of work conditions are best for you? Can you function with background noise or activity? Or do you have to have absolute quiet to really concentrate on a challenging task? Do you like to organize your time to allow for false starts or unanticipated delays, or can you simply eliminate all other distractions and work continually on one project?

   Understanding some specifics about your "task personality" in general and yourself as a writer in particular, can go a long way in easing your academic career and ensuring your academic success.

MEETING THE CHALLENGE

Determine your *own* writer personality.

- Reflect on your last major academic writing activity. In a 10-minute writing session, explain the procedure you followed, considering the conditions, the timing, the materials, and so forth.

- Now in another five-to-ten-minute writing session, evaluate the positives and negatives of the activity. What was most challenging? What was most successful? Least successful? What, if anything, would you do differently, if you had the time?
- Finally, write a detailed paragraph describing your writer personality.

b. Besides understanding something of your writer personality, another key factor that can impact your success with accomplishing a task concerns your level of **experience or familiarity with the task** required. Writing a specific type of text gets easier with practice just like anything else does. So, for instance, let's assume that in your summer job you had to routinely write a weekly progress report on department goals. Surely the first one took you much longer than one you did eight or ten weeks later. The same will be true with academic writing assignments. Your first summary essay, lab report, or critical review will probably be more time-consuming than your fifth essay, report, or review.

c. Your specific **content knowledge** for a given activity will also impact you as a writer. If you are very familiar with the subject matter for an academic writing assignment, it will be much easier to assemble and evaluate sources, to comprehend the reading material on a given topic, and to recognize the terminology or prominent names in the field. Just consider your reaction to your very first exposure to an entirely new topic; you're trying to get a sense of what is being discussed, to understand the very language used, to make a connection to previous knowledge, and to place the new topic in some kind of relationship to that knowledge. Then think for a moment about some topic you know well, perhaps details of a sport you play or enjoy watching or a favorite place you've visited repeatedly. If asked to write a brief description of that activity or place, it may be relatively simply for you, whereas if asked to do the same thing about a different sport or place of which you have no knowledge, it would be a much more demanding task. In other words, knowledge of the topic is an extremely important factor in influencing your attitude, your level of confidence, and your game plan as a writer.

MEETING THE CHALLENGE

Assess your content knowledge for a writing activity.

- Recall some writing activity you're currently working on (or recently completed).
- Write responses to these questions: Have (had) I done something like this before? If so, when? How long did it take? Did I need outside help? Am I familiar with basic terms, names, and procedures for this assignment, or is this a brand-new experience in every respect? What resources will I need?
- Now write a brief a work plan (outline or bulleted list format is probably best) itemizing information you need to know and/or acquire to complete this activity.

d. Another factor that plays a part in your performance as a writer is your **motivation** for performing a given writing task. If you are personally committed to the outcome of the task, no doubt you will be more willing to begin it and to stay focused on it until completion. In other words, *internal motivation* is almost always the best assurance of success. For example, if you are personally committed to wanting to secure a refund for an erroneous charge on your credit card bill, you will probably not delay in writing the necessary letter to the credit department.

Quite often the motivation may appear to be more external. For example, writing a research report in order to meet course requirements and to obtain credit for a given course needed for your degree may appear externally motivated. In other words, you're completing the writing assignment simply for a grade. However, the reality is that most often a successful academic experience combines *internal* and *external motivation.* It may seem that you are writing that lab report strictly for a grade or to honor a professor's request, but if grades are important to you personally—partly for academic and/or career advancement, perhaps partly to please your parents or sponsor, and partly for sheer personal satisfaction as a measure of accomplishment—that external motivator of "grade" actually becomes an internal motivator as well.

Furthermore, if you invest yourself personally in the actual activity and content of the writing task, you will find yourself more and more internally motivated. In other words, try to pursue a subject of interest when at all possible. If you commit yourself to learning something for *you,* not simply for a grade, the writing task will go much smoother. One thing is for certain: if you don't really have to and/or want to perform a writing task, it will be extremely difficult to succeed at it. Motivation does make a difference! Now that we've surveyed you as a writer, let's focus on the writing task itself.

2. The **writing task**—Besides facets regarding you as a writer (your personality, your level of expertise, your knowledge, and your motivation), the nature of the task itself greatly impacts the activity of writing. Your approach to a writing project will vary depending upon the complexity of the project itself. For example, are you trying to write a one-page letter to acknowledge the delivery of an order, or are you trying to write a 10-page comprehensive analysis of an economic theory? Those writing tasks certainly cannot be accomplished in exactly the same way.

Some academic writing tasks can be relatively straightforward, such as preparing a one-page summary of a lecture presentation, while other academic writing assignments, such as preparing a 12-page field report recording observations and then analyzing their significance relative to specific sociological theories, may be daunting indeed. From a more positive perspective, however, the second task will be much more stimulating and challenging and, ultimately, more beneficial and satisfying as well. But, clearly, writing tasks themselves vary in their demands on you in terms of time and mental and physical energy. Therefore, they cannot all be treated equally. Academic success has much to do with adequately assessing the expectations of your varied writing assignments and planning your time accordingly.

MEETING THE CHALLENGE

Assess the task itself.

- Recall any *two* writing assignments in any classes in the previous semester (or in high school, if necessary).
- Write a brief description of the assignments: summarize the task, the goals, and basic procedures. Estimate the time it took to complete them and comment on your level of success with each project. Reflect on your expectations before and after the task. Consider whether you would do anything differently now. If so, what?
- Write a brief comparison-contrast of the two writing tasks. How were they similar or different in degrees of complication? Did the audience differ considerably? If so, how did that impact your writing? How much time did you allow for each? How much previous knowledge did you bring to each task? Which was more successful for you? Why?

3. The **audience**—There is one other significant factor that impacts the activity of writing: the audience for which you are writing. Perhaps you haven't thought about that before, but you **always** write for some kind of an audience—even if that audience is *you,* in a private journal. (In fact, sometimes that private audience of self can be the most demanding.) Sometimes the audience demands are informal and casual, as with writing a quick e-mail to a friend. More frequently, academic tasks are written for an audience of your college peers and your professor. Sometimes, however, you are assigned another audience, imaginary or genuine. For example, you might be assigned an audience of a board of directors of a large endowment to whom you are asked to write a grant proposal for funding a theater festival on campus or a local environmentalist group with whom you are sharing the results of your scientific research project on chemical waste. In the case of *any* audience, you need to assess the characteristics of the audience itself and its expectations in order to successfully complete the writing task.

There are numerous characteristics of any audience that may significantly affect your writing activity. Some of these audience variables include age, gender, experience/knowledge level, interest, and motivation. Any of these factors may significantly impact just how much you need to share with your audience by way of background or groundwork in your report. Consider, for example, explaining the function and lingo involved with "IM-ing" to a group of middle school students versus a senior citizen group. Or imagine the difference between writing a marketing plan for your professor who has published widely in the field of marketing theory versus a group of friends with an idea for a start-up company distributing a new type of CD burner to college students. The social characteristics (age, gender, ethnicity) of your audience, as well as the level of knowledge and experience your audience possesses, can significantly impact how you organize and complete your writing task.

Similarly, audience motivation can make a major difference in how you approach a given writing task. Consider whether your audience really wants this information. If so, for what purpose? If they do, you probably can concentrate on informative techniques and clarity issues. Or if you think they need or should want this information, persuasive techniques will be much more important in your report, in addition to accurate and comprehensive information.

To further complicate the picture, often there is more than one audience involved for a single writing task. Frequently, there may be a primary audience, such as that board of directors viewing the grant proposal. However, at the same time, there may be numerous secondary audiences such as your peer group, your immediate supervisor, a peripheral interest group, and so forth. Assessing as many audiences as possible will increase the effectiveness of your work as a writer.

Most college students quickly learn that audience expectations can vary from one professor to another. Some professors are very concerned with detail, some with creativity, some with accuracy, some with "big-picture" implications—and some with all of the above. Be sure to obtain as much information as possible from your professor regarding his/her expectations. Regardless of their criteria, audience factors undoubtedly affect you as a writer—indeed, they can be overwhelming! Adequate assessment of those factors before *and* periodically during the activity of writing can significantly impact your success in completing a writing task.

MEETING THE CHALLENGE

Conduct an audience analysis.

- Recall a recent writing task for an audience other than your professor. Perhaps you wrote an application letter, a consumer complaint letter, a note to a friend, or a memo for your boss at work. List as many factors as you can about the potential audience(s) for that text. Do you know (or can you imagine) anything about their gender, age, ethnic/religious background, level of experience, personal involvement with the issue, and so forth?
- Write one paragraph of your text with any three specific factors of the audience clearly in mind.
- Rewrite the same paragraph with an entirely different audience in mind. For example, shift your factors from middle-age male marketing representatives to teenage female consumers or to a mixed-age-and-gender group of professors visiting from overseas.
- Discuss the variances with a writing partner.

With all of these variables, how can you ever begin to function as a writer—especially as an academic writer—and succeed? It is a challenge, but it is also very possible! No matter how differently you function as a writer, how complex the task at hand, how challenging the audience(s), some things about the writing process will be similar, and there are many skills and strategies you can work on mastering that will assist you. To begin with, understanding the various aspects of writing as an activity can certainly help a great deal. Let's examine those.

The Activity of Writing: Specific Actions

The activity of writing is a complex combination of multiple actions. Frequently, the actions overlap, and they essentially defy isolated definition. Nonetheless, it is useful to attempt to analyze them as singular actions, if only to then recombine them during an actual writing task. Essentially, there are four key actions involved in any writing task:

- Planning or prewriting
- Drafting or composing
- Revising
- Proofreading

(Note: Sometimes these last two are combined; however, there are important reasons to think of them separately, as you'll see in the following discussion.)

First, a word of caution regarding these writing actions: Some people equate identifying actions with delineating steps or stages, which implies that they are necessarily sequential and, indeed, must be followed in a specific order. In reality, writing is not a linear process conducted in neat, sequential steps, like following a recipe for making a cake. Rather it is "recursive"—meaning that the actions of writing are more like "places" at any given moment and it is very possible to revisit them in random order. Furthermore, it is very possible, even while conducting one action, to be thinking of a different action. Aspects of writing inevitably overlap and double back upon themselves. Nonetheless, while you are working on one aspect you need to focus on particular demands of the action. Another danger of describing a writing process is that students may think it is the *only* way to complete a writing assignment or that *every* writing task must be approached the same way.

Recently, some scholars have argued that discussing writing as a process encourages students to think of writing as a fixed, predictable, and/or absolutely controllable thing, when in reality, it is always a context-driven, extremely variable activity. Despite these theoretical debates, the reality is that to write anything (just as we are discovering now), you need to do some planning and thinking as you do some drafting and composing—frequently stopping and starting and blending those two. Only after at least some planning and/or composing can you revise. And, if you are invested in the final quality of your text, you eventually need to conduct final proofreading.

So, let's examine these activities or "places" a bit further.

Planning Actions

Every writing task needs some degree of planning. All of the factors of the writing activity—your writer personality, the task itself, and the audience as discussed above—will influence how you structure your planning. For some college students, the first "step" in planning may be to delay the task at hand. Of course, that is dangerous if you postpone the inevitable too long. However, delay isn't *always* a bad thing, if you're thinking constructively, that is. Some writers do a lot of mental prewriting. However, most often, failure to begin the planning or prewriting stage is merely useless procrastination. You will most likely be more successful as a writer if you adopt one of the various methods of prewriting discussed below.

To begin writing, you need to make a few basic decisions. Find a way to plan— that is, find a place that is conducive to writing for *you*. For some, it will be a private study carrel in a research library; for others, it will be a crowded coffeehouse that has lots of background noise that forms a kind of droning cocoon. Estimate a time schedule for the writing task. For a very large project like a research paper that you're given months to write, consider making a specific schedule of steps. Have the proper materials when you begin the writing task, such as a computer disk, extra paper, pencils, etc. Also, plan some time to simply "muse over" the topic, talk with friends, look at models, or jot down notes as they randomly occur to you.

The suggestions above are all part of the prewriting process. Additionally, there are several formal prewriting activities that many students find helpful. Let's examine those briefly.

Brainstorming

- Allow and encourage yourself to think of *any* possible terms, ideas, phrases, ways to approach the topic.
- Randomly say them aloud with someone recording you, or simply discuss ideas aloud and then gradually try to generate a list of key ideas and then a rough working plan to begin your writing task.
- Brainstorm alone or with a friend or a small group.

Freewriting

- Think of your topic or task and simply force yourself to sit down and write for five to ten minutes about absolutely anything that comes to your mind.
- Try to stay focused on the topic, but if nothing comes, simply write, "I can't think of anything to write right now, but I will not stop writing because I have to work on project X."
- Keep writing down one or two key terms or phrases from the assignment sheet you received and see if some ideas begin to form.
- At the end of the 10 minutes, look back over your notes and see if there are any consistent threads.
- Now freewrite again using those threads.
- If your project involves significant outside research, you will have to do extensive searching and reading first. Keep notes from that process in front of you and work back and forth from them to generate ideas for your text.

Clustering

- After a brainstorming session in which you've recorded everything you can think of, return to your notes and pick out a key concept or two.
- Literally create a kind of diagram for yourself placing the key idea or topic in a circle in the center of the page. Play word association for a few minutes and list all sorts of related terms around the center word.
- Then analyze your random notes and begin to cluster them under related subtopics or key units.
- Keep refining your clusters until you have some working points for early drafting.

Outlining

- Some people find it useful to create a "working outline" early on, listing subtopics in some related order. This gives you mini sections to approach at different drafting periods. It often makes the overall task seem less daunting, as it gives you a reasonable chunk to focus on a little at a time.
- Remember to continually revise the outline as you move through the writing activity.
- Keep in mind that a complete "formal" outline is really more like a table of contents, which can usually only be finalized when the text is completely drafted. (In fact, this can be a very useful revising tool to check the organization and flow of your report or paper.)

Sharing with a Writing Partner

- Many people find it useful to attempt to explain a writing project to a friend or colleague or professor—anyone willing to listen. Often they can help you think through your focus or make some connections between sections and so forth.
- The mere process of trying to articulate your thoughts to another person often enables you to crystallize some random ideas and/or see connections that are invaluable for producing the drafted text.

Explaining Aloud to Yourself

- You can even try the above process on yourself. Go ahead—talk to yourself aloud (you might want to pick a private space for this), and simply try to explain to yourself what you are trying to compose. Force yourself to think about your audience, your purpose, your overall scope, your resources, etc.

Asking the "W" Questions

- Some students find it helpful to approach a topic or writing task by using the *W* questions—the so-called "journalistic *Ws*": who, what, when, where, why (and sometimes how).
- Simply stating your topic at the top of a page and then listing *any and all* answers to each one of these questions can be a useful way to generate information, starting points, and other valuable questions that lead you further on your search for information or to stimulate more written text.

Sometimes, the planning process involves doing research. Of course, research demands will vary tremendously depending upon the nature of the writing task. If you are writing a journal observation of a classroom visit for an elementary education class, the research will be the visit and the writing may take place simply from your own observation notes. Or if you are directed to write a summary of a journal article, your only research involves locating the article and reading it carefully. If you are writing an opinion piece on the current campus debate about computer facilities, your research might include interviewing campus personnel and fellow students or visiting other, comparable campuses and observing their approach to the problem. It may include getting quotes from hardware and software providers for expanding the number of terminals, and so forth.

Of course, if your writing activity involves producing a scientific research paper, you will have to conduct laboratory research and analyze the results and/or read about others' experiments and synthesize the results of their experiments. Later in this text, numerous types of academic writing will be examined in detail, indicating more about research demands in specific cases.

MEETING THE CHALLENGE

Try a prewriting action.

- Recall a recent or pending writing assignment. Or think about this topic: college students' writing habits.
- Select one of the above prewriting activities. Use it for this (or another) topic.
- Compare your outcome with a writing partner's.
- Select a different prewriting activity and repeat the process.
- Now write a short paragraph reflecting on the usefulness of the process. What might you do differently next time? If you have to actually write a paper on this topic now, what do you need to do now? Will you need to conduct formal or informal research?

Drafting or Composing Actions

After conducting some of the prewriting actions, doing some preliminary research (formal or informal) as dictated by the writing activity, assessing your audience, generating some basic ideas and starting points, and/or devising a full-scale working outline, you will need to move to the next "place" in your writing activity—the action of drafting or composing.

Again, you'll have to decide upon the best place to work, the best time to work, and the best medium to use. Many college students find they are simply not "morning people," and need to find time later in the day to write at their best. However, many report that forcing themselves to rise early and work when the dorm or apartment is quiet can be the most productive writing time. Some writers still report needing to draft by hand in pencil and then type on the computer later. If you can get used to drafting at the computer, your revising time can be much easier, and the time you save in not retyping can be invaluable. If you tackle drafting at the computer, don't be fooled into thinking that you need to write it perfectly the first time, simply because it may appear neat on the screen. Rather, feel free to simply jot down notes or phrases, to leave blanks or insert a series of question marks, or to have several windows open simultaneously with different sections of drafts or valuable research notes available. Make the computer work for you as a valuable drafting tool.

When facing a draft of a large project, acknowledge the fact that you won't be able to write it all in one sitting. Learn to draft in chunks. Break down the project into doable segments. For example, if you're assigned to write a 10-page critical research paper, design your working outline such that you create a breakdown of four different two-page segments, plus an introduction and conclusion and eventually strong transitions. Tackle any one of the four two-page segments at a time. They need not be in any specific order. Begin with the segment you feel most confident about at first, and save the more complex segments for when you're "on a roll" and/or very well rested. Give yourself breaks, but stay with a certain schedule, if at all possible. Remember that the drafting or composing process is not without lots of fits and starts—it is not a smooth process.

Produce a working draft *before* you try to envision major revisions. You usually cannot effectively revise until you have produced a fairly substantial first draft. However, you may find yourself revising wording or organizational plans as you draft. Certainly, you shouldn't worry about copyediting concerns like spelling, punctuation, and formatting while drafting. Research has shown that very young and/or inexperienced writers tend to stop themselves frequently to "fix things." Generally, that is a waste of time and an unnecessary interruption to your composing process. Your brain can only process so much at any one time. So remember that while you are composing that first draft, the primary task is creating text, not perfect text, but rather language to work with—language that represents some of your existing ideas and language that prompts creation of new ideas while in the act of writing. The reorganization of text, the transitions between texts, and the attention to surface-level features of text like spelling and punctuation or format concerns come much later. Right now, in the drafting stage, that's not your main focus. Does that mean that some writers won't stop to make corrections or to move things around? Of course not, and if that is useful for you, do it. But don't be a slave to it. That's the beauty of computers—much can be easily fixed later.

If you find you are stuck at a certain point in attempting to produce a first draft, sometimes it is helpful to simply write a parenthetical note such as "need more info on X" or to jot down a few questions or to list a string of reminder terms, and then to keep on going with what you do know or feel inspired about at the time. Sometimes you will need to move to a different section altogether.

A word about introductions and conclusions: Many writers report that it is very difficult to get started with that perfect introduction. Often it is useful to skip the introduction until the end—actually, once you have the body of your paper or large sections of a report drafted, it is often much easier to determine what constitutes a valuable lead into it or an appropriate "audience hook." Similarly, the conclusion probably cannot be fully fleshed out until you've completed the project.

However, in some cases you actually begin with the conclusion. For example, in a thesis-driven essay, your thesis (or controlling) statement that is usually in the opening paragraph is actually the conclusion that you've reached about a given topic, which you are now attempting to convince your reader to accept or at least to demonstrate how you arrived at it.

The main thing to remember about the drafting or composing stage is that drafting is *not* a smooth, contiguous process. You will be juggling numerous tasks simultaneously, and the writing process will not work in exactly the same way for any two people or for any two different writing tasks.

Revising Actions

Once you've composed a first draft or at least a substantial segment of it, you will probably begin the process of revising. Revising is *not* about fixing typos! Revising is quite literally "re-visioning"—looking again at your assignment, at what you've already written, and at what you've thought about while you drafted or even after that point. You will need to look at your draft as a working unit. Ask yourself again about the purpose of the writing activity, paying attention to the level of comprehensiveness required as well as to assignment particulars, and about the audience: Are you reaching them? Meeting their needs? Also, consider the nature of your authorial voice, the tone that comes through, and the appropriateness of the diction you selected. Are you projecting the persona that you intended? Revising also includes attention to features like overall organization, transitions between sections, stylistic enhancements like varying sentence patterns, and/or conformity to conventions of a particular genre. (See Chapter 3 for detailed models of different genres and their conventions.)

Some researchers claim that most good writers spend the longest time on the revising stage—in actuality, it is still a composing or drafting stage, just at a more focused level. Often, effective revising takes longer than producing the first draft. Certainly, it varies with the nature of the project, the pre-research demands, your familiarity with the topic, time deadlines, and also the amount of mental revising you do along the way during the initial composing.

Proofreading Actions

Once you've completed the really challenging work of producing a written product, with all of the demands of planning and drafting and revising, remember that there is one final activity you must perform: This final activity involves proofreading. This is often a tedious action that college students—and indeed all writers—frequently may want to ignore. However, that is really a bad decision! Some of your best writing in terms of its intellectual content, interesting phrasing, and audience engagement can be seriously diminished if the appearance of the final product lacks "finish." Your credibility as a writer is partially dependent upon your willingness to attend to final details.

Here are a few useful tips for proofreading:

- Try proofreading aloud—you will often hear errors or inconsistencies that you don't see in a quick silent read.
- Proofread your document backward. In other words, begin at the end and read it sentence by sentence moving to the start. Obviously, this is not reading for content, but because you won't be following the content and assuming you know what the text says, you can focus on surface-level features.
- Solicit another pair of eyes—i.e., have a friend proofread your work. It is often easy to look past the same errors over and over again because you assume the page says what you intended it to say when composing.
- Allow a cooling-off period. Never try to proofread when the text is immediately fresh in your mind. Give yourself at least a few hours, if not a day or more, between final revision of the text and your proofreading session.
- Acquaint yourself with at least a few of the commonly used proofreader's marks, such as ¶ (for paragraph) or ∧ (for insert). They are listed in most good dictionaries and grammar handbooks. Some professors will use them faithfully and you will need to recognize them to make corrections on your drafts.

When conducting your final proofreading, consider the following list of reminders:

- Edit carefully for compliance with all expectations of Standard Written English (SWE) regarding rules of grammar and mechanics—everything from subject-verb agreement to the proper use of the semicolon. Use a grammar handbook whenever necessary.
- Employ spell-check, but don't depend on it exclusively—it cannot make contextual judgments like the appropriateness of "their" versus "there" versus "they're."
- Use your software's grammar-check, but don't be overly dependent upon it. There are *frequently* mistakes within systems.
- Check for format consistencies and appropriateness in your use of subheadings, font choices, bold or italics, etc.
- Proofread for overly repeated word choices; sometimes the "find and replace" function on your computer can be extremely useful here.
- Make certain the final project is neatly presented on clean paper and stapled or in a binder if appropriate.

Looking Ahead

Now that you have a clearer understanding of genre as a means of organizing learning and creating texts (as discussed in Chapter 1) and an understanding of the nature of academic writing, its sources, its purposes, its demands, and its complexities, you are ready to explore more of the specifics of academic writing. Chapter 3 will examine 15 different genres of academic writing by describing genre characteristics and then presenting 30 different examples. All of the examples are actual student essays written for courses from a wide variety of disciplines that are taught at colleges and universities across the nation. These annotated samples can serve as models for you as you approach varied academic writing tasks throughout your college career. Chapter 4 explores strategies for successful academic writing, including acquiring information literacy skills; developing specific writing techniques such as summarizing, quoting, analyzing, and synthesizing; and learning documentation procedures. Chapter 5 concludes the text with four Readings Units. These readings, which cover vastly different, though all highly relevant, contemporary issues, provide content and context for the *practice* of academic writing.

Understanding Types of Academic Writing

Writers of all kinds—student writers and professional writers, novices and experts, beginners and old hands—benefit from models. When you need to write a document of any kind, think how valuable it is simply to be able to see how some other writer has tackled the task and how this other writer has envisioned the scope of a similar project, along with its structure, organization, format, and style. You do not want to consult the model to copy from it, of course—you simply want to see how another writer has handled the job.

Our goal in this chapter is to present you with a catalogue of useful models. We focus on 15 genres that students are often asked to produce in their college and university classes and in their professional lives beyond academia; and for each of these genres, we present two different examples. In each model paper, we offer marginal notes that explain how the writer is organizing the paper, presenting and developing ideas, and effecting an appropriate style according to accepted conventions of the particular genre. We present 15 genres, but there are certainly others we could have chosen. We selected these particular genres because of the frequency with which we encountered them on our campuses and in talking with dozens of students and colleagues across the country. Some are primarily written from personal experience, while others require close reading of print and electronic sources, and still others are dependent upon empirical data or specialized interaction with the World Wide Web. Some texts, of course, combine several of these features.

Keep in mind that *all* of these papers are actual student papers, written at actual institutions of higher education, to satisfy actual assignments. While all of them are of good quality, they are the work of students who are just entering or even just sampling particular disciplines, not professional scholars. Many of them could no doubt be improved with further revisions. (Perhaps your instructor will assign you to try your hand at that very task.) Indeed, keep in mind that *all* writing, even the work of a polished professional, can be revised. The challenge of producing good writing is a never-ending task!

In this chapter you will find genres from an array of academic fields and disciplines: nursing, women's studies, philosophy, composition, marketing, geography, sociology, literary studies, biology, chemistry, library science, education, communication studies, history, journalism, psychology, and business. The student writing we share from this wide range of fields supports a point we make in Chapter 2: In all disciplines, writers make their knowledge visible by writing about it. To know how to create knowledge in a field—to know how to participate in its intellectual discussions and its important work—one needs to know something about how writing works in the field. The models provided in this chapter bring this knowledge to life.

PERSONAL ESSAYS

Personal essays have long been a common assignment in composition and journalism classes. They also appear widely in popular magazines. However, until fairly recently they were not widely assigned outside of "English" classes where story or narrative, a common element of personal essays, was traditionally valued. Narrative is now being widely studied by psychologists, linguists, health and business professionals, and so forth. Increasingly, narrative as a writing genre is gaining more and more academic and public attention as a valuable way for us to learn about ourselves, about each other, and about the principles and priorities of academic communities. Consequently, personal essays, which are frequently in the form of a narrative or include the narration of events or circumstances, are being assigned in numerous disciplines across the curriculum. So, you may find yourself assigned to write a personal essay for any number of classes. Let's examine personal essays' characteristics, goals, and strategies in some detail and then look closely at two student-written personal essays as examples of this genre.

An essay, strictly speaking, comes from the French verb *essayer*, meaning "to try." A writer who undertakes to produce a personal essay, therefore, takes a "try" at understanding some intellectually or emotionally challenging fact, setting, idea, or phenomenon. A personal essay is generally exploratory and does not necessarily come to closure. Instead, a personal essay represents a visible manifestation of the writer's contemplating, using, or thinking through the topic selected. "Personal" essays, as the name implies, generally offer the writer the chance to contemplate the influence of people, events, or configurations of ideas on his or her personal life.

In other words, essayists are generally attempting to clarify for themselves their thoughts and reactions to these experiences. Through the act of writing about their experiences, they often come to new interpretations or insights that enable them to understand significant aspects of their own past, motivations, relationships, etc. So personal essays can definitely serve the writer's "self." Additionally, the writer of the personal essay, unlike an individual who is keeping a private diary, attempts to effectively share his or her experiences, interpretations, and insights with their readers, thereby expanding the notion of "personal" to other persons as well. Readers will respond in their own ways to the details of the story, perhaps identifying with aspects of it and translating it relative to their own personal experiences. Thus, the adjective "personal" refers both to the author and to the audience.

Some personal essays, especially those for a typical academic audience, are structured as thesis-driven papers. That is, the central idea being explored or mused upon is clearly expressed (usually in the form of a thesis statement) most commonly found near the end of the opening paragraph of the personal essay. In other words, unlike in most stories or narratives, often the ending or conclusion of a personal essay is actually revealed up front in the form of the thesis statement. Personal essays written for popular magazines often do not explicitly state a thesis. Nevertheless, the attentive reader can still deduce a central idea that the effective essayist continually hovers around, if not overtly states. Regardless of whether the writer chooses to explicitly state or simply imply a thesis or controlling idea, the personal essay generally unfolds in a relatively informal, almost conversational manner—in a "personal" way, in other words. Thus, in a sense the adjective "personal" refers not only to the author and the audience, but also to the text itself.

If you are assigned to write a personal essay in an academic setting, you should clarify two points with your instructor: whether an explicit thesis is necessary and whether you should use first or third person in the paper. As mentioned above, often a personal essay for academic purposes is expected to posses an explicitly stated thesis even though personal essays in well-respected magazines such as *Harper's* or *The New Yorker* will frequently not be structured that way. Keep in mind, however, that in most essays written for the humanities, thesis statements are not specifically signaled, as you will see in scientific reports later in this textbook. In fact, theses like, "This paper is about X" are generally frowned upon as being uncreative and/or nonengaging. Regarding the issue of person, some instructors may still insist upon the use of third person (i.e., using "he" or "she" and avoiding all direct references to "I") as the only acceptable form of "academic" writing. This view long dominated within academia and still lingers today. However, most often you will not only be given permission to use first person throughout your paper but, in fact, will be expected to do so. Clearly, that would be the logical assumption for a personal essay.

Writers of personal essays typically employ certain strategies for their exploration of an idea or experience. There are four major ways to develop personal essays. First, writers may narrate, telling stories from their experiences to make their central ideas concrete. Second, they may provide descriptive details, sharing with their readers specifics of the sights, sounds, smells, tastes, or feelings of a given setting or phenomenon. Third, they may decide to divide and classify the central fact or situation into component parts in order to make observations on the whole. Finally, they may engage in explanatory writing, sometimes called "exegesis," to offer explicit generalizations regarding the details. In essence, the writers are saying, "Here is what this narrative or description leads me to think. I hope you, the reader, can at least provisionally think this way, too."

As an academic genre, the personal essay does not insist on any one format, unlike, say, the formal scientific research report that we will examine later. Your audience will typically not only accept but actually invite a variety of approaches to the personal essay. Essentially, the only consistent audience assumptions for the personal essay are a personal tone; an honest sharing of specifics of the individual writer's ideas, circumstances, or experiences; and an engaging text.

The two personal essays included here exemplify many of the characteristics discussed above. The first one, entitled "The Gift," was written by a freshmen composition student. Typical of the genre of the academic personal essay, the thesis or central idea is stated within the first paragraph. The author develops his personal insights primarily through: 1) narrating events and experiences, 2) providing descriptive details, and 3) engaging in explanatory writing or exegesis. Through these methods, he explores and explains his thoughts on the experience, attempting to lead the reader to share in the personal experience.

The second personal essay, an assignment for a journalism class, also states the thesis or central idea within the first paragraph, and then proceeds to develop the essay by narrating events and experiences, providing descriptive details, and engaging in explanatory writing (exegesis). Notably in this essay, the writer also makes use of another technique, namely, dividing the topic into components and offering comments on each of them. The essay might be outlined rather easily into five parts: 1) time in class with Miss Tobias, 2) time outside of class with Miss Tobias, 3) class without Miss Tobias, 4) post-class visits with Miss Tobias, and 5) the death of Miss Tobias. After sharing each part, the writer engages in explanatory comments, moving the reader toward a greater understanding of the writer's ultimate realization.

PERSONAL ESSAY 1

Composition

The Gift

Duane Smith
Saint Xavier University

The Gift

There have been many gifts given to me in my life that I treasure, but there is one in particular that has more meaning than the rest. This gift is a baseball jersey that was given to me by my father. It is a very special gift because my father and I have a very special relationship built around baseball. It was given to me on vacation in Cooperstown, N.Y., the birth town of baseball.

The rare jersey now hangs calmly from the ceiling in my bedroom above everything else. It is rare because you can only get it from the

Thesis statement— an early focus is provided in this essay, enabling the reader to begin to immediately connect with the personal revelations of this author.

Extensive use of descriptive details describing the location and appearance of the jersey helps set the emotional tone of this essay.

Note the extensive use of detail in explaining the feelings the jersey produces; the author is using this strategy to clearly establish his "personal" stance. This is crucial in the genre of the personal essay.

Here the author adopts a slightly different strategy. He develops the essay through narration, relating stories of the father-son relationship built around baseball.

This section might be labeled "explanatory writing" or "exegesis," discussing the meaning of the shared times.

Cooperstown Collection in New York. The big orange and blue lettering displaying "Knights" lights up the front of the blue pin-striped jersey, giving it a look of greatness. The name stands for a baseball team, from New York, whose hopes and dreams are made a reality by one man, a natural. On one sleeve is the baseball centennial patch displaying the American colors of red, white, and blue. On the other, a blue patch with a gold bolt of lightning shows the natural power it contains. The back displays the number nine, in orange and blue, with a rare sense of pride. The thick fabric has a warm feeling and it fills that empty feeling inside. It gives you a feeling of power and dominance. The jersey was given to me by someone very special in my life. Someone with whom I cherish the game of baseball. This person is my father.

My father and I have loved the game for as long as I can remember. I can remember playing catch with my dad in those late summer afternoons when I was younger. We played in the middle of the street until the warm summer sun started to set. My father taught me the facts of life while we were out there experiencing those rare father-son moments. He taught me most of those facts through baseball. I guess he wasn't too good at those modern father-son talks. We shared all of our hopes and dreams that were yet to come while we were out there. Those moments with my father were ones that I'll never forget.

My father is a fairly built man whose true personality and desire to succeed is brought out by baseball. The only two things that seem to interest him are baseball and cars, which can explain why he is a mechanic. His light gray and brown hair and fully grown beard show the many experienced years of life in him. He was always a caring and sensitive father who wanted nothing but the best for his children. He always made sure that we (my sister and I) were headed in the right direction. He always pushed us to do the best we could do and to never give up in life or anything. I can remember being so frustrated with baseball once that I just wanted to quit playing. The night that I told him that, we talked on the baseball field all night. He told me how life gets hard for everyone, but you can't just quit.

"These challenges that you are facing now are what separates the men from the boys," he said. "You decide what you want to do."

He taught us to enjoy life and appreciate everything that we have. I have been very fortunate in my life so far to have everything that I have. I have a lot of things that my father never had, and I have him to thank for that. I know that my father knows he's very fortunate to have a job and a loving family. He doesn't take it for granted at all.

"You see these hands, son?" he asked me once, showing the wear and tear on his hands from being a mechanic. "I don't want your hands to look like these when you're older. I'm doing this now so you don't have to when you're my age. I want you to enjoy what you are doing when you're my age. My father did the same for me, but I turned away from it. Hopefully, you'll be smart enough to take baseball as far as you can."

"Why did you turn away from Gramps?" I asked.

"I didn't realize what he was trying to do for me," he said sadly. "I didn't realize that I only had one chance in life to do what I always dreamed."

"Don't worry," I said. "I'll never give up. When I'm a professional baseball player I'm going to get you everything you deserve."

I said this because I was able to see the sadness inside him. I knew he was sorry that he gave up on certain dreams in life. Even though he doesn't fully enjoy his job now, he still works hard every day just so I can have a bright future.

After playing catch in the afternoons and hearing that fatherly advice, he said something that he still says to me this day.

"You have a gift. Don't let it go to waste. There is nothing worse than a waste of talent," he said.

Further descriptive details are used to sketch a picture of his father. This is a crucial element of the essay because the father-son relationship and the son's insights into the father's character are essential to the reader's understanding the significance of the "gift."

This narrative of a significant event of the past provides further build up of emotion and suspense for the reader. In this genre, this layered use of narrative, example, and detail is especially important.

Here he narrates another significant conversation with his father.

"Don't worry," I said. "I won't give up."

Then came those final words every boy wishes to hear from his father.

"I'm proud of you," he said.

Since my family is so big on baseball, we decided to take a vacation to the birth town of the sport one summer. The trip itself was incredible. I couldn't imagine anything else being better than being in Cooperstown. I was soon to find out, though, that there are some things.

It was induction weekend in Cooperstown, N.Y. Five baseball players were going to be inducted into *The National Baseball Hall of Fame*. Many great baseball players of the past were in town that warm weekend of July to sign autographs and witness the event. It was a special weekend for baseball, and I was there.

The author returns to his effective use of descriptive detail to build the anticipation for the reader.

The streets were filled with people. The atmosphere of baseball was everywhere. Everyone was so anxious to meet the players and get autographs. People were running around everywhere like little kids in a candy store. All the stores on the Main Street were full of people, too. My family and I had to walk in a single file line around the stores because of all the people. The stores had many authentic pieces of baseball history. Although the prices were very high, it was a great feeling being in the presence of some of that historical past. You could feel the history make its way into your memory. I really didn't think that things could get much better, but there was a moment to come that weekend that was even more special.

This passage provides further exegesis, explaining the author's emotional interpretation of the conversation being foreshadowed here.

Details of explanatory writing provide more context for the reader.

After eating lunch, my family and I decided to walk the main strip of town (Main Street) to see if we could meet some of the old baseball players. I eventually met Pete Rose, Whitey Ford, Larry Dolby, and Lou Brock. Those players were some of the greatest to ever play the game. It was a great experience to meet them. When I shook hands with them, I felt a special feeling inside. It was very special. I did not think anything could top meeting them, but there was one thing. Moving along down the strip, my father stopped in front of a store called "National Pastime." He asked if I wanted to go in and look around. We went inside while my mother decided to stay outside to enjoy the warm weather. The store was magnificent. I was overwhelmed with all the authentic things that were in there. Everywhere I turned, there was a piece of baseball history staring me in the face. They had original bats, signed baseballs, authentic mitts, pictures, pennants, and other different types of sports memorabilia. Whatever came to mind, they had it. There was one thing that stuck out from the rest, though. On the wall, I saw hanging the jersey that Robert Redford wore in the movie *The Natural*. It was one of my favorite baseball movies. I used to watch it a lot with my father when I was a kid. It looked just like it did in the movies. I always dreamed about having that jersey ever since I was little. I showed my father the jersey, and he loved it too. I asked him if we could buy it, but he said it was too expensive. I wasn't disappointed or mad to hear that from my father because I didn't go to Cooperstown to buy things. I went because I wanted to experience the history of baseball. I put the jersey back on the wall so I could finish looking around the store. I waited outside with my mother until my father was finished looking. When he came out of the store, he was carrying a bag. As he approached me, he handed me the bag. He said it was a surprise. I opened the bag and saw the jersey in there. I couldn't believe it. My father bought the jersey for me. It meant so much to me. I was so happy, but at the same time, I was a little confused, too.

"Why did you buy this?" I asked. "I'm not complaining or anything, but you said it was too expensive."

"I wanted you to have something special to remember this weekend," he said.

The writer narrates the important vacation that leads to the possession of the jersey.

More descriptive details used, building the emotional intensity.

Keep in mind that in a personal essay, the writer is essentially making an argument to convince the reader of the value of the writer's "personal" view or experience.

An important sharing of feelings occurs, explaining the climatic event. It is those feelings that are, of course, the focus of this personal essay genre, not the event itself.

"This trip is special to me just being here with you guys," I said. "Some people don't even get to come here or even spend time with their family. You really didn't have to spend all that money."

"You never know if you'll ever be back here again," he said. "Plus, you have always wanted that jersey ever since you were little, and now it's yours."

Here the explanatory writing (exegesis) includes his adult reflections on the childhood experience. This element of personal reflection is a significant aspect of this genre, since it is often only through retrospection that we determine the personal value of things, persons, or events.

I can remember the look on my father's face that afternoon. He knew that he did something good. He was happy to see me happy. This gift has a lot of importance to me. It is from someone whom I love very much and with whom I have shared many experiences of baseball. It is something that will always remind me of the precious father-son moments we had while enjoying the game of baseball. It will also remind me of being in Cooperstown with my family enjoying the past. The gift is a constant reminder for me today to never give up in life. No matter how hopeless things get, always work hard because it pays off in the end. It also keeps me striving for my dream to play professional baseball.

INVESTIGATING THE GENRE SAMPLE

1. Why is it that the genre of the personal essay so often uses material objects, such as a baseball jersey, as the subject matter as in the case of "The Gift"?
2. In the fourth paragraph, Duane Smith offers a detailed description of his father's appearance and character. What function do you think that paragraph serves in the essay as a whole?
3. Near the end of the essay, Smith provides a specific list of items that suggest "baseball history staring me in the face." Some writers producing a personal essay might be tempted to make this list of items *more specific*. How could that be accomplished?

PERSONAL ESSAY 2
Journalism

The Untold Story of an Unsung Hero

Chris Welch
Northern Kentucky University

The Untold Story of an Unsung Hero

In life, there are a few special people who stand out in our memory. Maybe it is someone who saved a life, or was a great inspiration. Or, perhaps, this special person is one who was simply admired, a strong or selfless person who put others before him- or herself. Sometimes, we never come to appreciate the people like this until it is too late. Other times, however, we know all along that we are dealing with a truly amazing person. This was the case for me during my high school years. I had taken one year of Spanish in my freshman year and liked it enough to sign up for Spanish II for my sophomore year. I never really gave much thought to who the instructor would be, but I can remember how I felt when I saw my sophomore year schedule for the first time. Right after "Spanish II" was the name: "Tobias."

I can also remember the dread I felt when I saw that name. I had heard about Miss Marilyn Tobias. Everyone told me that she was one of the strictest and most challenging teachers in the school. They were right. Classes were tough. She was so intimidating that I was humiliated on a semi-daily basis whenever I couldn't conjugate a verb correctly or answer a question. Soon, however, I began to understand and come to love her dry sense of humor. Even more importantly, I began to realize how much I was learning. The humiliation soon became less frequent and not quite as harsh. I'd spent almost the entire year afraid of such an intimidating teacher, but I finally saw through that to the truth: she cared

Note the engaging opening line, typical of a strong personal essay.

The thesis statement provides the focus for the reminder of the essay.

Explanatory writing, or "exegesis," which recalls emotions is consistent with the intent of a personal essay.

The writer narrates the class beginnings to provide a context for the reader. We are being "drawn in" by the writer to share in the personal experience.

Descriptive details continue to heighten the personal nature of this essay.

Notice the shift in perspective here, which is common in personal essays. Here the explanatory writing is reflecting back with a mature perspective on the high school experience.

so much about our learning that she was willing to sacrifice her own popularity with the students for it. These days, that is extremely rare.

I began to truly enjoy the class, and went on to Spanish III the following year. That year, the Foreign Language Department bought new textbooks for all the Spanish classes, but Miss Tobias, claiming they were too easy, refused to use them. For the entire year, they sat in a stack in the back of the room while we continued to use the older, more difficult books. Also during the year, the school began a campaign of "zero tolerance" of gangs and gang activity. One day, a classmate and I, jokingly, thought it would be funny if there was a "gang" of Spanish students. Suddenly, an idea had sparked. Within a month, almost all of the students in our class, as well as some from other classes, had joined "Los Espanoles," a "gang" of students who studied and loved Spanish. We often went on outings to Mexican restaurants and even made T-shirts with our logo on them. Once, a student invited the entire group (and Miss Tobias, of course) to her house for an authentic Mexican meal. Our love for the language, thanks to Miss Tobias, had brought us together.

Descriptive details can reinforce the personal nature of the essay.

Narrative description of the formation of the Spanish "gang" emphasizes that the group is clearly bonding. This is an aspect of this personal experience that the writer wants to highlight.

Descriptive details reinforce the heightened emotion.

Then, suddenly, Miss Tobias began missing days of school. The woman who had been out sick for only four or five days in her thirty years of teaching missed a day here, a day there, and finally stopped coming to school all together. Eventually, our substitute told us the reason. Miss Tobias had cancer. She was being treated, and her chances were so good that she would most likely return to teach for the next school year. Our hopes were up, and we were confident that she would be back.

Narration of the change in events is followed by the writer's emotional reaction to the change, crucial to establishing his personal message here.

However, when the next year rolled around, she wasn't there. Our new teacher told us that she was doing O.K., but was still too weak to start teaching again so soon. The Spanish IV class was cold and boring. Instead of learning more of the language we'd grown to love, we learned about Spanish art and culture. The new teacher didn't really care about our learning, but more about how she was going to fill up each class period. It stung to have such a poor teacher and to be learning so little. "Los Espanoles" still did things, often with Miss Tobias. When we went to her house one evening, we complained about the class, and, although she hid it well, we could see the hurt in her eyes. She felt like she had failed us.

We asked how she was doing, and she told us that this was not her first battle with cancer, but her second. Sixteen years before she had had the same ovarian cancer. Every Friday after school she would go to the hospital for chemotherapy treatments. She spent most of the weekend violently ill, and sometimes even threw up on Monday mornings before she left her house. A few times, she said, she had to pull off the road and get sick on the way to school. Even so, she never missed a single day of school the whole time, and overcame the cancer. I was awed by her incredible willpower and dedication. Her strength was incomprehensible to me.

However, sometimes even heroes can fall. In a hospital room on a warm Sunday morning in July, Miss Tobias died. Another student and I, having visited her the night before, returned, only to find that we were fifteen minutes too late. I left the hospital, got in touch with a few other members and told them, and then drove off. I went to a park and sat down, looking through the scrapbook of "Los Espanoles." It was filled with photos of different outings, stories, and memorable events. I slowly realized that Miss Tobias was the only reason we ever became friends and started the group. Every story and picture illustrated something Miss Tobias had given us. The pictures of us in the restaurants showed our dedication to the language. Our stories showed our love of the class and of her. Stories and nasty comments about our Spanish IV class with the other teacher captured how great was our desire to learn. We are

Explanatory writing with personal commentary on his student experience and reflection on the emotions of the situation are the essence of this piece as a personal essay.

Note the impact of the descriptive details.

Descriptive details help relay the emotions of the writer.

The essay concludes with an extended section of explanatory writing. Here the writer is clarifying the impact of this personal experience.

The final sentence recalls the opening and the thesis. It is now accompanied by a reflective explanation—often the key feature of a personal essay.

living proof of Marilyn Tobias's dedication and strength. She is that special person, that hero in each of our lives, not because she taught us the Spanish language, but because, thanks to her, we know a little more about how to live—and how to die.

INVESTIGATING THE GENRE SAMPLE

1. Chris Welch calls his essay about Miss Tobias an "untold story of an unsung hero." What do those words suggest about the type of memorable characters that people frequently write essays about?
2. The first word in the second sentence of this essay is "Maybe." The third sentence begins "Or, perhaps." What do these words suggest about the personal essay as a genre? What is the effect of these words on the reader as he or she works to understand the focus of this essay?
3. Look at the fourth sentence in the paragraph that begins "Then, suddenly, Miss Tobias began missing days of school." How many words does the sentence have? How would you describe the structure of the sentence? How does the impact of this sentence relate the meaning, purpose, and effect of the whole essay?

JOURNALS

The use of **journals**—sometimes called *reading journals*, *response journals*, *dialogue* or *dialectical journals*, or *conversation journals*—has become widespread in college courses. In many fields throughout the college and university curriculum, instructors ask students to write regularly in their journals, offering responses to readings, observations, or experiences; raising questions that the writer thinks merit further examination; and doing a considerable amount of "thinking on paper" about the writer's progress so far in the course and plans for the remainder of it. Some instructors ask that students keep a separate notebook for their journals; other instructors allow or encourage students to reserve a disk or computer file for their journal entries. Some instructors require students to write in their journals daily. (Notice that the word *journal* comes from the French word for day, *jour*.) Other instructors require students to produce a certain number of journal entries over an assigned period of time.

A journal is not a diary, in which the writer narrates strictly personal details about his or her life and speculates about their meaning. Conversely, a journal is also not a laboratory notebook, in which an experimenter makes a record of methods followed, materials used, and results tallied. A journal contains both objective and subjective writing. In a journal, the writer develops an "I–it" relationship with the material he or she is studying, saying essentially, "Here's what I have read, observed, or experienced, and here is what I make of it." In this sense, the journal might be seen as a collection of short response or reaction papers, which are explained in the next section.

The English novelist E. M. Forster once uttered a question that could be seen as embodying the major principle involved in the writing of journal entries. He asked, "How do I know what I think until I see what I say?" When writers write journal entries, they are following Forster's implied advice. They are putting their ideas on a page (or on a computer screen) so that they can examine them; consider their ramifications and implications; share them with others; think about whether they want to extend, modify, or contradict them; and so on. There's a curious, seemingly paradoxical concept involved in writing journal entries, a concept that might be labeled "temporary permanence." Is this possible, you might ask? If something is temporary, it's not permanent, and vice versa, right? Well, not exactly. When you write a journal entry, you make your ideas and observations permanent long enough to examine them and think deeply about them. What you write about in a journal entry can be seen as being open to alteration, extension, even deletion. When you write a journal entry, you're not committing yourself—you're not setting your feet in concrete or signing your name in blood. You're simply getting your ideas into visible—and, therefore, inspectable and contemplatable—form long enough to inspect them and contemplate them.

The subject of a journal entry is usually either a reading you have encountered or an experience you have had. Somewhere in the journal entry, you might be expected to summarize the text or the experience, but the most important purpose of the journal entry is not to summarize but instead to *reflect* on the reading or experience. In a good journal entry, the writer comes across as a deeply thoughtful person who takes up such questions as the following:

- How did the text or the experience make me feel?
- What thoughts, ideas, or observations did reading the text or having the experience stimulate for me?
- How did the thoughts, observations, or experiences of the characters in the text I read or the people in the event I experienced match with my own thoughts, observations, and experiences?
- What about the text or experience is personally significant for me, and why is it so?

Sometimes an instructor will supply questions like these (and this is certainly not an exhaustive list), and other times there will be no specific questions provided—the student writer in the latter case is expected to generate his or her own questions about the reading or experience. Some instructors expect students to answer any given questions in the order listed. Other instructors want the journal entry to be fluid, perhaps even alternating between passages that summarize the text or experience and those that reflect on it.

The most important audience for a journal entry is the writer himself or herself because the chief purpose of a journal entry is to allow the writer to reflect on the reading or experience. An instructor, a teaching assistant, or other students might be vital secondary audiences for a journal entry. They might read your journal entry so that they can participate in your thinking, recognize points in your entry that might be sources of further investigation and writing, identify interests and perspectives that you have in common with other members of the class, and so on. But in all cases, the secondary audiences can be seen as spectators who are slightly removed from the main "action" of the journal entry—and that is you, the writer, working out your own thoughts and ideas for your own benefit.

A typical journal entry is not very long. Many instructors ask their students to produce journal entries that are four to five handwritten pages, or two to three word-processed pages. Moreover, most instructors are looking for a simple, straightforward, informal style in a journal entry. In some journal entries, instructors expect you consciously and explicitly to use the specialized language of the field.

The following two journal entries were written for very different types of classes. The first comes from a mental health nursing class at Elmhurst College. The students were observing the interaction of clients in a group called Recovery Inc., and for each observation, the students were expected to address the following questions in a journal entry:

a. What was the most significant experience I had this week? The experience can be an incident, an encounter, or a discovery about self, a client, or the nursing profession.
b. In what ways was it important or meaningful? Try to incorporate at least one of the following concepts: family systems, role, communication, conflict, stigma of mental illness. What way did it raise questions for me personally? Professionally? (Please state these as questions.)
c. How did I react to the situation or within the experience?
d. Give an example of at least one cognitive/behavioral strategy identified in the meeting.
e. How could I use what I learned from this experience in my professional practice?

Notice that only the fourth question (letter d) invites the students to use the specialized vocabulary of mental health nursing.

The second journal entry was written by a student in a first-year seminar at DePaul University called "Empowering Chicago's Women." The students were reading Rosemary Bray's nonfiction book *Unafraid of the Dark* and were asked to write a journal entry based on each chapter.

JOURNAL 1
Nursing

Recovery, Inc. Nursing Entry

Gwen Morrice
Elmhurst College

Recovery, Inc. Nursing Entry

October 29, 2002

a. The most significant experience I had this week was when one of the group members shared about an incident that occurred at a family gathering. To make a long story short, each family at the event was to bring a dish that could be shared buffet-style for dinner. Despite the fifty plus people who attended, neither dish that this individual brought was touched, while all the other platters were picked through. Immediately this incident triggered feelings of lowered self-esteem, inadequacy, and wonder as to why they did not partake of her dishes. As her mind tried to find a way to rationalize the situation, her thoughts focused on her as the victim. Through spotting, many things were revealed to her. You cannot control the external environment; you can only control your internal environment. More specifically, you cannot control the events that occur, you can only control your reaction to the events. You do not need to know why things happen and things do not have to be right or wrong. Lastly, do not rationalize things and make them personal when they are not. The incident was important because the revelations that occurred with the spotting will help to avoid future conflicts. By realizing the event was not personal and people did not even know which dishes were hers, she arrested all her "poor me" thoughts. She is not a victim, and thus has no perpetrators to hold a grudge against. Furthermore, being in touch with one's thoughts and feelings enables one to be a more effective communicator. She realizes that she cannot control others, but her reaction to others. She has the power to suppress or express her feelings and

Initially, the writer provides a straightforward, narrative account of a significant experience in this treatment group.

Typical of this genre, the writer begins speculating on the meaning of the experience. Note how the writer begins relating the incident to content covered in the course regarding mental health issues.

Here the journal writer expands the meaning by signaling the benefit of the experience for an even broader, long-range context.

Concluding by returning to the meaning of the incident and its relation to the course content reinforces the benefit of this journal exercise for both the writer and the reader.

As directed in the assignment above, the writer casts her response to question b in the form of questions. This type of response emphasizes the open-ended nature of this genre. Often this probing, brainstorming quality is a major benefit of keeping a journal, since it stimulates exploration of multiple avenues for response.

The writer continues to answer all questions as guided on the assignment sheet for this highly structured journal.

Notice the use of specific terminology from the course underscoring the journal writer's distinct perspective.

emotions. The way in which she communicates these feelings and emotions is up to her. Lastly, I think this incident was meaningful because it reduces the stigma of mental illness. Although her anxiety condition is chronic, she has the power to control the intensity and duration of her exacerbations, or how she reacts to an anxiety-producing event. This serves to show that despite a mental illness, individuals can be extremely functional in society.

b. What preconceived feelings do I have toward people with anxiety? What areas of my life do I struggle with most? How can I benefit from what the client shared? How effective is this approach in managing anxiety? As a nurse, how can I help my clients to let go of the things that are out of their control?

c. I looked at the situation as a learning experience. I felt like I could really relate to her, and that I could have easily encountered the same experience. I know I would have been wondering why no one tried my food, and definitely taken it as a personal insult. I think the way she arrested her negative thoughts and realigned her thinking was very commendable.

d. Cognitive restructuring by monitoring one's thoughts and feelings, and refraining are cognitive/behavioral strategies that were identified in the meeting. In order to change one's cognitions, one must identify what is reinforcing and maintaining one's dysfunctional thinking and maladaptive behavior. Refraining involves focusing on other aspects of the problem and/or encouraging the individual to see the issue from a different perspective. For example with the aforementioned incident, she realized people not eating her dishes had no bearing on who she was, and there are many reasons why people may not have tried her food such as it was new and different, and many people are hesitant to try new things. This new perception of the situation prevented the aggravation of her anxiety symptoms.

e. I have a better understanding of the thought process and symptom escalation that occur with anxiety producing events. I feel like the whole idea that one can only control their internal environment, not the external environment, is very valuable and definitely worth sharing with other clients. During times of anxiety, it can be very empowering for clients to know they have the ability to control how they react to the event. Furthermore, I could definitely teach my clients how to monitor their thoughts and feelings, and reframe them when needed.

> Here the writer contemplates what courses of action could follow as a result of writing this journal entry. Again, the value of the explorative writing associated with this genre is evident.

INVESTIGATING THE GENRE SAMPLE

1. When writing a journal entry for which the instructor provides prompt questions, the writer always needs to decide how extensively to repeat or rephrase each question. What, if anything, would you encourage Gwen Morrice to do differently in this regard in her journal entry?

2. In the genre of the journal entry, the primary audience is the writer himself or herself. The instructor can be seen as an "eavesdropper," looking in to see how the student writer is doing. Where in Morrice's journal entry can you detect her inviting the instructor to peek into her mind?

3. Many journal entries do not sound nearly as certain as Morrice's does. At what point in her journal entry would you be tempted to say to her, "Are you so sure about what you say?" Why is it important to keep a spirit of questioning alive in a journal entry?

JOURNAL 2

First-Year Seminar—Women's Studies

Trials and Tribulations

Emily Ulrich
DePaul University

Not all journal entries have a title, but this one does.

The journal entry opens with a brief, personal reflection on topics that reading the chapter of *Unafraid of the Dark* brought to mind for the writer. These topics include time management, conflicts between personal life and school, and choice of major, three points of departure for discussions in first-year seminars.

Trials and Tribulations

Throughout my four years of high school, I have dealt with many trials and tribulations. One of them would be balancing social temptations and work demands at the same time. My senior year of high school I got a job at a restaurant as a hostess. I was very excited about this job because I like to work with people and I thought it would be good for me. I started in September, right in the midst of cross-country and other school-related events. At first the job was a lot of fun but I had to work every weekend, and in turn I missed out on hanging with my friends and some other events. For example, I would have to come late to basketball games for pep band. This does not sound like a big deal, but when it continues weekend after weekend, it gets old. It didn't help that my manager wasn't very understanding about my events either.

During my senior year, I felt that I missed out on a lot of different things. This wouldn't have upset me so much but this being my last year, I wanted to make the most out of it and spend as much time with friends as possible. My job with my hectic hours made it hard to do at times. At the end of the year, though, I decided to quit. It wasn't a hard decision because working there made me get very worked up and sad at the same time, because I missed doing things with my friends and family.

Another thing I have to do is hold myself back from falling for someone that I care so deeply about. He has been my best friend for the past four years and we have been through so much together. We tried being together but realized that it was just too awkward and we were just too good of friends. But to this day, I still struggle with feelings of attraction for him. It is a hard thing to deal with but I know that someday everything will work out for the better. Someone once said "I'd rather be your lover than your best friend, but I'd rather be your best friend than nothing at all." I think that quote really speaks for itself.

One more thing that I have to deal with is choosing my major. There have been moments that I have wanted to study such things as English or veterinary science. A lot of people go through different phases when they do not know exactly what they want to study. However, through all my different phases of going through my choice of a major, I have always known that I want to be in front of a camera and I want to be able to report to the rest of the world on news happenings. Current events have always interested me and I believe I am in the right city to study communications.

In reading *Unafraid of the Dark*, I am struck by Bray's strength and character that she demonstrates throughout the novel. There are several different meaningful conversations that can be discussed in the common hour. One could be talking about the points listed above. I also like to hear different people's views on race. Bray deals with a lot of issues in her memoir, and it would be interesting to hear experiences that girls in the class have had with it.

I feel very fortunate to be in a group with so many girls that have so many interests and beliefs. It seems that there is always something to talk about and therefore it makes the class even more interesting.

Note that this genre encourages "thinking on paper" as a means of working through various struggles and/or changes that life frequently brings. In other words, making thoughts "visible" promotes contemplation.

Here the writer extends the journal entry, drawing relationships between her personal experiences, discussed in the first part of the entry, and the novel that the seminar is reading. As a genre, journals promote this type of interconnection.

The writer concludes by acknowledging the intellectual and personal support she is getting from the other seminar participants.

INVESTIGATING THE GENRE SAMPLE

1. As a genre, the journal entry is particularly useful for responding to the readings in a course. Notice, though, where Ulrich's first explicit mention of the text, *Unafraid of the Dark*, comes. What does this location lead you to conclude about the differences between a response paper and a journal entry as genres?
2. In many colleges and universities, academic advisors ask students to keep journals and then read over their entries and write a brief composition before going to an advising appointment. What about Ulrich's journal entry might be useful in such a scenario?
3. What features of "Trials and Tribulations" show that Ulrich is writing a journal entry and not simply a personal diary entry?

RESPONSE OR REACTION PAPERS

A commonly assigned academic paper, in potentially all disciplines, is the **response** or **reaction paper**. Just as the name implies, this genre of academic writing seeks your response to something. It may be to a specific issue, a printed or online article, an essay, or even to an event you've attended. All of these may be referred to (using postmodern terminology) as "texts," to which you are asked to react.

This section will explain details of this genre—the general characteristics, the purpose(s), the expectations of the audience, the overall organization, and the format. It will also include two sample student-response papers with explanatory comments. The first one, written for a unique nursing/Spanish class at Elmhurst College, offers a response to a novel and the author's own immigration experience and prenursing experiences. The second one, written for a humanities seminar, responds to a live performance by a contemporary author who was participating in a campus literary festival at the University of Notre Dame.

Response papers are personal reactions that are relatively short, usually one to three pages long, and often are rather informally written. Some professors will assign a response paper with a specific "prompt" or leading question to help initiate your response, and others will make the assignment more open-ended, assuming that you will take the lead as to the nature of the response. Unlike many genres of academic writing, response papers do not require research beyond familiarizing yourself with the particular "text" to which you need to respond. Response papers showcase your ability to capture the essence of a particular text and to communicate your opinions on that text. Although some instructors still insist that all academic writing be done in third person, it is perfectly acceptable to write a response or reaction paper in first person. In fact, when you think about it, first person is really more honest and appropriate. After all, the main point of this exercise is to allow you to share *your* personal thoughts on a given text.

Generally, response papers serve multiple functions. They provide an avenue to demonstrate your understanding of a particular reading or to share your observations of a particular event with a specific audience. Secondly, they afford a platform for your opinions. In doing so, they challenge you to formulate or embellish your own ideas on a topic, to articulate your feelings on a given issue, and/or to develop your own personal voice as a writer. Thirdly, many professors assign them because these types of papers can act as an excellent discussion starter in a large group, since you have had time to preorganize your thoughts on a given assignment and have already articulated your opinions in readable prose.

In an academic setting, the audience for response papers is frequently your instructor and your classmates, who are interested in your interpretation or information. However, at times you may be asked to share your opinions with a larger audience—in a campus or local newspaper, for instance. Generally, your audience will expect a brief recap of the article or event to which you are responding and will then anticipate your personal thoughts on the topic. While the genre is relatively informal, and as such, certainly allows for a conversational tone and the use of idioms and even tactful slang, your audience will still expect this academic genre to adhere to the conventions of Standard Written English, providing for ease of readability. Finally, while you can often assume interest in the topic of your response paper on the part of your audience, it is always helpful for you as a writer to produce engaging prose. That way, even if the audience is not especially interested in the topic, they will become interested in your thoughts on the topic.

Response papers, unlike formal term papers (which are referred to in this collection as "critical papers" or "stance" or "position papers"), are somewhat unstructured. They are not necessarily organized around an articulated thesis statement in the first paragraph. However, there are certain organizational features that tend to apply to all response papers. First of all, even though you may begin your response with some striking statement of opinion, early on you must clearly identify the article or event to which you are responding. If you are writing a response paper to a published work, you will need to indicate the title, the author, and the source so that your readers will be able to retrieve the original text if they so desire. Secondly, your response should include a brief summary of the key points of the article or the significant features of the performance. Your instructor may dictate more specific requirements for the comprehensiveness of this summary. Of course, the main feature of a response paper is your response—your opinion on whatever it is to which you are reacting. Be sure to offer concrete opinions, backing up your ideas with specifics from the text under scrutiny. If possible, also try to offer some comment(s) that will link the text to others related to it or the event to some larger, future concern.

Response papers do not require specific formats, unless given by your professor. They generally appear without subheadings and without any formal documentation (except perhaps for the bibliographic citation for retrieval purposes of the article to which you're responding.). As noted, these papers might not have an articulated thesis statement; however, some focus or main point should reveal itself by the conclusion of your response.

In the two student samples that follow, you will notice two different formats, yet similar features and impacts. The first one, responding to both a literary and a personal discussion of the experience of immigration, is rather loosely structured. The writer does not focus her response with a specific thesis statement in the first paragraph, for instance. However, she does indicate the title and author of the work. As the response proceeds, she gradually summarizes the novel, essentially identifying *its* thesis. Notice how the student writer effectively interweaves a few personal comments and analytical insights throughout the response paper, and then offers a significant personal-reaction section. By the conclusion of this paper, her response to the novel and its implications for her future are clearly established.

The second student-response paper is more tightly structured. This response to a live performance, which evaluates the style and effectiveness of the speaker, clearly identifies a thesis in the first paragraph. Notice that it is also structured as a comparison-contrast response. The writer is actually responding to two different versions of the performance by the same speaker, paying close attention to "reading" the different styles adopted for different audiences. For this type of paper, the student writer chooses to offer brief summaries of each performance, interspersing his personal comments on the variables that are dictated by audience differences.

Interestingly, the second student writer adheres to writing in the third person. Do you think that perhaps his paper may have been even more engaging if he shared his opinions in first-person prose? Significantly, both of these student-response papers conclude by offering somewhat broad personal comments on the topic, expanding beyond the immediate text under examination. This expansion further engages the reader by broadening the context. Keep in mind that even though readers may not have read the same article or attended the same performance, they may still be able to closely relate to the essence of the issue at hand, especially if a wider context is provided. This is an effective way to conclude a response paper.

RESPONSE PAPER 1
Nursing/Spanish

Reflections on Alvarez's Stories and My Own

Julie L. Johnson
Elmhurst College

The writer opens this reaction paper with a striking statement of personal opinion, clearly establishing the tone of the paper; the personal tone is, of course, appropriate for this genre.

Reflections on Alvarez's Stories and My Own

As Americans, we tend to take our country for granted. We don't live in fear of our government, we don't face persecution for disagreeing with it, and overall, we enjoy the freedom to do almost anything we want. In many other parts of the world, this is not the case. In the Dominican

Republic of the 1960s, a dictator named Trujillo led the government. He was more concerned about himself than the people, and thought nothing of having his own citizens arrested or even executed for disagreeing with him. The book *How the Garcia Girls Lost Their Accents* by Julia Alvarez follows the life of a family who is forced to flee this tyrannical government. In the United States, they live safe and secure, but they are separated from family and friends and are forced to adapt to a strange new environment, one that doesn't feel much like home to them at first.

For many people who live under an oppressive government, overthrowing and deposing its cruel leader is just a dream, never to be shared with anyone. But for Carla, Yolanda, Sandi, and Fifi's father Carlos, a prominent doctor with political connections, things are different. He and his brothers, along with a CIA operative, devise a plan to assassinate the dictator—a plan that fails. Amid the growing scrutiny the "SIM," or secret police, has on the family, and the disappearances of people close to the plot, Carlos decides that moving the family out of the country is a good idea. They settle in New York City, in a small apartment that couldn't be more different than the vast estate they lived at on the "island." There they lived in a huge house that was surrounded by the houses of aunts and uncles, complete with servants, a tight-knit community of family all sharing the estate. In New York City, they don't know anyone, except for Carlos's doctor friends, who don't live anywhere near them. Their neighbors in the building are at best unfriendly, and one old woman goes out of her way to call them "Spics" and tell them to "Go back to your own country." The weather is also uninviting. It is winter when they first arrive, and it is cold and snowy outside, a climate the family has never experienced before. In the Dominican Republic, the Garcia family was wealthy and affluent. In their new land, they struggle to make ends meet, and live without the luxuries they were once accustomed to. It is a long time before the Garcias feel they belong in their new land.

Background context is provided and the novel, which is the initial focus of this paper, is identified.

The writer provides a summary of Alvarez's novel in order to create common ground with the reader before offering her personal response.

Here the writer interjects a comment of personal analysis and then offers an example.

As in many cultures, the younger generations are quicker to adapt to new surroundings than the older generations. Such is the case with the Garcia family. The girls, who spoke no English when they arrived, quickly learn it in school. Carla, who is the eldest, is forced to attend public school, and she is made fun of and picked on by a group of boys. She struggles to learn English, and to get rid of her thick accent. Eventually all the girls learn English, and they shed their thick Spanish accents so they can sound more American. Laura, their mother, already spoke some English, so even though she has an accent, she has a better grip on it than Carlos, her husband. Soon the girls start to speak only English, and their native language, Spanish, starts to sound rusty. After a while, the Garcias are allowed to return to the island. It becomes a tradition for them to go every summer, but the girls get tired of going. They are not used to the ways of the island, such as a girl not being allowed to go out without an escort, who is generally a male family member. All of their girl cousins are spoiled and prissy, planning their weddings or talking about their husbands. The Garcia girls are more concerned about college and the many political issues going on at that time, such as the women's liberation movement and the Vietnam War. The girls don't appreciate the island's simple ways any longer; instead they eagerly await their return to the U.S., to school, their friends, and their boyfriends. It is easy to see why the author, Julia Alvarez, would write about this tradition in her book. She uses it to compare the new world to the old, to show us what their lives would be like if they had never left. The girls wouldn't be the rebellious and modernized teenagers they had grown into; instead, they would be like their cousins, marrying young and not working or going to school. The return of the girls to their native environment becomes a kind of reverse culture shock, one that is beautifully described in this book.

Note how the writer interweaves personal-response comments, even within the summary section.

Like many Hispanic families, the Garcia family has a traditional structure, with the husband working outside of the home, and the mother staying at home to raise the children. The girls are very respectful of their parents, but their relationship with their father becomes difficult as the girls get older. This is because the girls start to change their ways, abandoning their traditional roles and adopting more American ones. In many instances, this is unacceptable for their father. The youngest daughter, Fifi, falls in love with a German man, and they write love letters to one another. When Carlos finds the letters, he is enraged that his unmarried daughter would do something so indecent. He is so angry that he basically throws her out, and she runs off and marries her man, forever putting a strain on her relationship with her father. Another time, the second-youngest sister, Yoyo, the writer, is to give an address to her classmates and teachers. When her father reads the speech, he becomes so angry that he tears it up, because it was not respectful enough of her teachers. Instead, she writes a speech that is more acceptable to her father, one that thanks the teachers, and one that is not true to Yoyo's feelings. Again, there is a strain put on the relationship between Carlos and one of his daughters. On the other hand, Laura, their mother, is accepting of almost everything her girls do, encouraging them to follow their hearts and dreams. She is less concerned about traditional roles than her husband, who enforces them even if it ruins relationships.

  The Garcias' immigration experience is very different from that of my family. My relatives came to the U.S. in search of opportunity, whether to own land, find work, or earn money. They were poor in their native countries, and felt that leaving was their only chance to make something of themselves. The Garcias, on the other hand, were very wealthy in their native land, almost aristocratic. They did not want to leave, and had no intention to until their lives were threatened by the dictatorship. They felt forced to go, whereas my relatives were glad to leave. One similarity in these two immigrations is that the older

The writer begins to draw comparisons of the novel to a larger context as was dictated by the assignment (or prompt) for this reaction paper.

Having summarized the novel, the writer now moves to a different section of this response paper: She relates the experience of the novel's characters to her own.

The writer lends a very strong personal voice to this response paper, overtly sharing her family experiences—ones that reflect and/or contradict the experiences of the Garcia family.

generation clings to the native traditions and culture, while the younger generation is quick to adopt the culture of the new land. Much like the Garcia girls, my grandfather forgot his native language and spoke only English for the rest of his life. Unlike my family, the girls are given the opportunity to revisit their old home, something they don't learn to appreciate until they are older. It is hard for them to readjust to life on the island when they visit, but as their lives unfold in the States, they start to yearn for the simple life they left long before.

Now the writer expands the scope of the response once more, sharing her thoughts regarding contemporary American attitudes. Note that she has moved from a discussion of the novel to a discussion of her personal family experience to a broader, more philosophical discussion of the immigrant experience in general.

Americans tend to forget that, at a certain point, nearly everyone was an immigrant to this country, or is related to someone who emigrated. That is especially the case today, where generations separate the immigrant family member from the native-born American. The immigrants of today are sometimes looked down on and hold lower positions in society. They work in low-paying jobs, face discrimination, and do not feel as welcomed by people outside of their culture. I think that if everyone were to take a walk in the shoes of an immigrant, they would be more sympathetic. This book, and this class, helped to give me an insight into what it is like to be new to this country. It has given me an in-depth look at Hispanic culture, and a new understanding of how important it is to have some knowledge of this culture as it relates to our country today. One important lesson I learned is that many of our nation's immigrants would rather be home, but they are forced to come here to find work, or to flee dangerous situations. There are many Hispanic people who will need my help as a nurse someday, and I would like to not only communicate with them effectively, but also understand where they are coming from. I will be more sympathetic to their needs, and help them adjust to American ways, which can be very difficult. If everyone who worked in social settings were to do this, it would help the immigrant population feel more at home in this strange place. I plan to respect the cultural values of the immigrants whom I will

The writer openly confesses the new insights she has gained from this reading assignment and from the class itself.

Expanding the scope of the response paper one final step, the writer reflects upon potential connections of these experiences to her future experiences as a nurse.

help, so that they will trust me more than someone who doesn't care.

There is plenty to be learned from our country's immigrants, and if we

took the time out of our busy schedules, we could open the door to

communication barriers and further our knowledge of humanity.

> The writer concludes with personal goals and a pointed advisory statement, clearly reflecting the personal-opinion aspect sanctioned by this genre.

INVESTIGATING THE GENRE SAMPLE

1. As a genre, the response paper is often used to stimulate whole-class or group discussions in college courses. What are two or three questions that Julie Johnson raises in "Reflections on Alvarez's Stories and My Own" that students could discuss?
2. One of the hallmarks of the response paper as a genre is the use of hypothetical reasoning. Where does Johnson use this type of reasoning, and what role does it play in the response paper as a whole?
3. What is the impact of Johnson's use of the first-person pronoun?

RESPONSE PAPER 2

Humanities

Michael Collins: Master of the Audience

Dan Smith
University of Notre Dame

Michael Collins: Master of the Audience

Every artist creates in order to satisfy an audience. Different audiences require different techniques of the artist. Michael Collins' performances in the recent Sophomore Literary Festival illustrate the subtle variations a speaker can use to charm an audience. In his evening performance, Collins perceived the spectators' desire for humor and obliged it. His morning workshop, though, took on a more serious tone because he noted the higher degree of sophistication and specialization of those in attendance. Although Collins' two appearances at the

> The writer must first contextualize his response for the reader—What is he responding to? Where did it occur and why? And so forth.

The writer clearly indicates the thesis of his response paper in this final sentence of the first paragraph. (Note: This is a common place-ment for the thesis in short humani-ties papers especially.)

Discussion of the evening perfor-mance, emphasiz-ing the casual tone of the event, includes an audi-ence analysis. The writer essentially restates his thesis at the conclusion of this paragraph as well.

The writer clearly develops the "ar-gument" of his re-sponse paper here, using extensive de-tail and examples to support his view that Collins could read his audience skillfully. In other words, this writer justifies his re-sponse to the reader.

Sophomore Literary Festival differed in their styles, both were effective, primarily because of his ability to "read" the audience.

The casual opening of Collins' evening reading presaged the events that were to come. The theme of the affair seemed to be "anything goes" in attire, attitude, and time of arrival. Students, wearing clothes ranging from jeans and tee shirts to coats and ties, made up the majority of the audience. Nevertheless, the professors and South Bend residents in attendance added completely different nuances to the crowd. This diverse group provided quite a challenge for the author. While some members of the audience mainly wanted an educational experience, many, perhaps because of the time of day of the performance, preferred simply to be entertained. Somehow, Michael Collins managed to accommodate both groups.

As the tentative Irish brogue began to describe the day before "The End of the World," a hush grew over the audience while each listener relished every vivid detail. Most contented themselves with listening to interesting literature, but eventually some members of the audience became tired of the extensive description and decided to look for humor in Collins' story. While some humor existed, many listeners laughed at inappropriate moments during the story. Sensing the audience's need for comic relief, Mr. Collins altered his delivery slightly in order to provide an interpretation of his work that allowed for more broad humor. Fortunately, in emphasizing the humor, Collins did not alienate those who desired a more serious literary experience, for he merely highlighted the absurdity rather than the brutality of the actions of his characters. Upon finishing the story, Collins related a few humorous anecdotes dating from his years as an undergraduate at Notre Dame and thereby further endeared himself to his audience, composed primarily of current Notre Dame students. The humor in "The Outhouse," the second story Mr. Collins read, was far more obvious than that of the first. This choice of work reflected the author's successful understanding of the audience's desires, and thus made his presentation more effective.

The morning workshop differed greatly from the evening reading, but Michael Collins again understood his audience's needs and catered to them quite well. The audience of Collins' morning workshop consisted entirely of students interested in writing. While this event also appeared casual, with students seated comfortably around a table and on the floor, a quiet intensity pervaded the atmosphere of the Sorin Room in LaFortune Student Center. Unlike those of the night before, the members of this audience primarily wanted to learn. Entertainment was not at the top of their agenda. Mr. Collins apparently sensed the students' thirst for knowledge, for he definitely catered to it. The morning's affair took on the seriousness of a classroom, with Collins teaching his students how to write. Yet, he captivated his audience through his expertise in his field and his down to earth presentation. The author discussed his methods of writing and asked the students for input into specific situations faced by a writer. For example, in writing a story about himself, an author should use the third person point of view, said Collins, for this point of view allows for a freshness of voice. If a writer wrote in the first person in this case, he would perpetrate a rather dull narrative, but by writing in the third person he can see things from a different, more interesting perspective. Collins later suggested that aspiring writers critique their own work, saying that he has criticized his own work for quite some time and has always found that his critiques improved his revisions. In sharing these tips with the audience, then, Michael Collins not only provided insights into writing that his audience greatly appreciated, but also made the audience feel more involved in the workshop by sharing intimate details of his own writing. Once again, Collins had successfully comprehended the wishes of his audience.

A detailed discussion of the second appearance is contrasted with the first. The writer notes the more academic tone of this event.

Once again, the writer offers examples to support his response to Collins's performance.

Continuing support of his thesis—that Collins aptly read his audience(s)—the writer emphasizes the particular usefulness of the advice section for budding writers.

The writer concludes by restating his personal opinion regarding Collins's success and offers a comment on the long-range implications of this author's ability to skillfully read an audience.

The patrons of the Sophomore Literary Festival truly enjoyed both of Michael Collins' presentations. While the author's approaches to the evening reading and morning workshop differed somewhat, both were quite effective. This efficacy serves as testimonial to Collins' ability to know his audience, an ability that will continue to prove invaluable to him as a writer.

INVESTIGATING THE GENRE SAMPLE

1. What "texts" is Dan Smith's paper reacting to? How are these texts both similar to and different from other texts that a college student generally encounters in courses?
2. As a genre, the response paper often tries to capture a sense of *verisimilitude*—a feeling of "actually being present" at the event the paper is reacting to. Where does Smith try to accomplish this goal, and how effectively do you think he does so?
3. Where do you see Smith trying to describe the emotional aura of the events? Why do you think such writing is appropriate in the genre of the response paper?

STANCE OR POSITION PAPERS

A great many papers a student must write in college, especially in the humanities and social sciences, can be labeled *stance* or *position papers*. Not many professors use this label, but we think it's a good one. Unless they specify otherwise, most professors expect students to write a stance or position paper when they assign projects that they refer to as "term papers," "major papers," "critical essays," or simply "essays." Because, as we explained above, the term *essay* can refer to different genres, we prefer our label because it suggests the function, purpose, and organization of the paper. **Stance** or **position paper** is a compact, meaningful name.

In this section, we define the genre of stance or position papers, and we explain their function, audience, organization, and format. Following this section, we offer two sample research-based stance or position papers: one written by a student in a philosophy class at the University of Notre Dame and the other written by a composition student at Marquette University.

In a stance or position paper, a writer assumes an analytical and discriminating stance in relation to a topic: The writer takes a position on some aspect of the topic and then proceeds to defend that position. In other words, a position paper, as we are using the phrase here, is an argumentative paper; that is, it "argues" or offers specific reasons for the validity of a thesis. For example, in a modern U.S. history course, a paper evaluating President Harry Truman's decision to order the atomic bombing of Hiroshima would be a stance or position paper. In an urban sociology class, a paper explaining the effect of storefront churches on neighborhood economic development would be a stance or position paper. And in a class on English Renaissance literature, a paper analyzing how the Great Chain of Being principle helps explain conflict and characterization in drama would be a stance or position paper.

Notice that most papers that are called "research papers" are actually stance or position papers, although some are informative reports, as explained below. A writer rarely does research, whether in the library or in the field or laboratory, simply for the sake of doing research. Rather, a writer does research in order to ascertain what previous scholars have learned about a topic, to examine this prior knowledge critically, and to determine how to interact with the previous research in order to support or qualify his or her own position. Thus, the writer of a research paper is actually writing a position paper in which the research plays a formative and supportive role.

A stance or position paper is a thesis-driven text. For such a paper, a thesis statement should be a clear, succinct sentence, placed near the beginning of the paper (ideally in the first two paragraphs), that identifies the stance or position the writer intends to develop about the topic. Only in the rare (and usually long) stance or position paper would the writer provide more than two paragraphs of background, interest-generating material before stating his or her thesis to the reader. Remember that a thesis statement has two parts, the *topic* and the *comment*. The topic, usually the grammatical subject, is what the thesis statement is about, while the comment, usually the grammatical predicate, provides a perspective (or *predicates* something) about the topic. The best thesis statements are those that guide the reader through the development of the stance or position and achieve an ideal level of specificity in both parts. Consider, for example, the urban sociology paper suggested above, the stance or position paper on the effect of storefront churches on neighborhood economic development. Here is an **ineffective thesis statement** for that paper:

Topic	Comment
Religious organizations	are good for a neighborhood's economy.

Such a thesis statement does not specify what kinds of religious organizations the paper will consider, nor does it provide enough specific guidance about what it intends to say about how these religious organizations help the economy. Here is a better thesis statement for such a paper:

Topic	Comment
Storefront churches in large cities	benefit their neighborhoods by providing sites for employment training, by operating child care services for workers entering the job market, and by distributing information about tax-relief programs offered by the city government.

Of course, the most important thing about a thesis statement is neither its placement nor its composition (though both of these are important) but its *function*. A good thesis statement guides the development of the writer's stance or position, a development accomplished by following any and all of the appropriate guidelines for developing academic prose explained in Chapter 1: Consulting testimony; investigating the relationships of comparison, contrast, cause and effect, consequence, and chronology; developing and applying definitions; and exploring the circumstances of capability, possibility, and impossibility.

For most stance or position papers, your audience will be people who meet three criteria: They are generally curious about challenging, intellectual issues; they have some, but perhaps not exhaustive, subject-matter knowledge in the particular field or discipline you are examining; and they expect papers to be written in clear, correct Standard English. A stance or position paper offers you the opportunity to enter metaphorically into a conversation with these readers. Your primary purpose is not to inform them of what you have learned in doing your reading or research, though informing them can be an important secondary purpose in your paper. Instead, your primary purpose is to convince them to consider and at least provisionally accept your thesis, your distinct stance or position on the subject.

Depending on the particular assignment or project, a stance or position paper has three, four, or five sections. The three basic sections are the introduction, body, and conclusion.

Introduction. In the first section, contextualize your subject matter for your readers. Tell them just enough about the subject matter and the issues—the important, central questions you will be addressing—so that they can reasonably predict the directions you will take with your thesis. State your thesis directly and explicitly. If you think it necessary, provide a mapping statement that lets your reader know what points you intend to make as you support your thesis.

Body. In the body of a stance or position paper, support your thesis statement using as many of the methods of constructing supporting arguments explained in Chapter 1 as are appropriate. If you have written a mapping statement in the introduction, follow the order suggested by this statement exactly in the body of the paper.

Conclusion. The conclusion of a stance or position paper should raise a "so what?" question for the paper's audience. In other words, a conclusion should lead the readers to ask themselves, "So what? How is my understanding of the issue being addressed different now from how it was before I read this paper? What do I think, feel, believe, or know now that I did not before I read this paper?" A conclusion should *lead* the reader to ask and answer these questions, rather than state the answers to them directly. Rarely is it a good idea in a conclusion to restate your thesis directly. If your thesis is not memorable by the end, you have not supported it well in the body of the paper, and simply restating it is not going to be effective. In a conclusion, however, you can reconsider your thesis in light of the support you have offered for it, and you can use this reconsideration to guide your reader's thinking about the "so what?" questions.

In addition to an introduction, body, and conclusion, some stance or position papers call for one or two additional sections: a literature review and a works cited or references list. A literature review is a systematic summary of part or all of what has been written about the subject of the paper, in particular about the issues you are addressing. If a separate literature review is required, include it in a section between the introduction and the body of the paper. For many subjects, of course, it would be impossible to review everything. When that is the case, review the major published works that represent the most important and widely accepted views on the subject. In a literature review, for each book, chapter, or article you mention, follow the guidelines explained in Chapter 4 for introducing material acquired through research. In general, for each piece you cite, refer to the author and title in an introductory phrase or clause, and then provide one or two sentences summarizing the work's thesis or principal contribution to the thinking about the subject. Writers typically use one of two methods to structure a literature review: They review the literature in order of publication date; or they review the literature in order of importance, beginning with the most widely accepted view of the subject matter.

Depending on the course or the specific assignment, if you have summarized, paraphrased, quoted, or alluded to published works in any part of the paper, you will be required to list these works at the end of the paper. Chapter 4 explains in detail how to compose and format these lists—sometimes called "Works Cited" and other times called "References"—in the humanities, social sciences, and natural and life sciences.

One final note about the format of a stance or position paper: In some fields, writers are encouraged to label the sections of their papers with headings. Sometimes these headings can be generic—for example, "Introduction" and "Conclusion" (but rarely "Body"). More often, however, when writers use subheadings they write descriptive phrases that cue the reader to the content, not the function, of the section that follows. Check with your instructor to see if he or she prefers that you include such headings and, if so, how descriptive they should be.

Now let's examine the features of the two student sample position papers below. The first position paper was written for a philosophy class entitled "Women: Alternate Philosophical Perspectives." In it, the writer examines why women remain underrepresented and essentially ignored in American politics. She ultimately argues that women need to maximize their potential as a voting bloc to increase female representation, because that will both begin the process of eradicating the inequalities of our society and allow us to address societal issues with the collective perspectives of the entire population of our nation. Note that this paper explores an open-ended question regarding the reasons for women's underrepresentation in the political system and moves to create the hypothesis that women must gain parity if significant societal change is to occur. In other words, in a sense there are two theses (one initial thesis, one hypothesis) for this essay: 1) women are underrepresented within the political structure for various reasons and 2) women must mobilize to change that for the good of the *entire* nation.

The second essay addresses a very specific question, the issue of the illegality of hemp production. The writer first provides readers with some background of the situation; he then moves to his primary purpose, namely, to convince his audience of his view that "hemp cultivation should be legalized immediately." Some position papers explore questions that emerge from a hypothesis or explore open-ended questions that result in a hypothesis, as in the women in politics example. The second essay explores a question—Should the U.S. government once again allow or not allow hemp production?—to which an answer clearly exists. Following the conventions of this genre, this stance or position paper includes the three mandatory sections of introduction, body, and conclusion. The introduction identifies the subject, contextualizes the issue, and states the thesis. The body presents and develops the arguments to support the thesis, progressively attempting to convince the reader to accept the thesis. The conclusion reconsiders the thesis and guides the reader to realize that a new perspective has been gained on the issue at hand. Both papers include a bibliography, which is presented here in MLA format, typical of the humanities. Note that, in keeping with MLA format, it is labeled "Works Cited."

One further note on bibliographies: Sometimes there is a distinction made between a bibliography and a list of works cited. Strictly speaking, a bibliography is a list of *all* of the works consulted, whether for general background information or preliminary or more in-depth research. A list of cited works, as the phrase implies, is a list of *only* those works specifically cited—quoted or paraphrased—within the text. Check with your instructor to determine if he or she wants you to make this distinction.

POSITION PAPER 1

Philosophy

Women in Politics: Finding a Voice for the Future

René Rimelspach
University of Notre Dame

Women in Politics: Finding a Voice for the Future

The introduction establishes the historical context of women's underrepresentation in politics, thus providing a focus for the paper.

The author establishes the thesis, which represents the position that she will defend throughout the paper.

In 1776, when the illustrious Founding Fathers were drawing up what was to become the Constitution of the United States of America, Abigail Adams sent a letter to her husband John. It stated, "In the new code of laws . . . I desire you would remember the ladies, and be more generous and favorable to them than your ancestors. Do not put such unlimited power in the hands of husbands. Remember all men would be tyrants if they could. Your loving wife, Abigail" (Schneir 394-95). Her husband's somewhat disappointing reply stated, "Depend on it, my dear wife. We know better than to repeal our masculine systems" (Schneir 395). And repeal masculine systems they certainly did not, for nearly 220 years later, women in American politics by and large remain underrepresented or ignored.

Since its inception, politics in the United States has been and remains a stereotypically "masculine" pursuit. It is fair to say that politics is neither thought of as feminine nor even gender neutral in America; it is as traditionally "masculine" as watching Monday night football. American society has divided its members into two separate spheres: the private sector, which is primarily the domain of the female, juxtaposed by the public sector, including politics, which falls within the realm of males. As Sharon Brehm states in Seeing Female, "Historically in this country, politics is what men do and political behavior is how they do it" (159). We are left to presume that women do nothing of a political nature, or at least that which they do is unimportant. Just how accurate of an account is this?

The presumption of the masculine nature of politics in America can be argued to have a strong basis in gender socialization. As researchers Renzetti and Curran state, ". . . dispositions toward politics are formed in early childhood when boys are told they can grow up to be president some day; the best girls can hope for is to grow up to marry a man who may one day be a president. Consequently, children learn that politics is a masculine activity . . . " (Renzetti and Curran 243). It seems that women are outwardly discouraged from forming an interest in politics at an early age. Little girls who later grow up to become interested or involved in politics, assuming such women actually exist, must overcome a socialization process that tells them politics and a political life are not suitable for their temperament.

When examining politics as a subculture in America, it becomes apparent that it is predominantly Anglo-Saxon, financially well-off males who control and have the most power in the system. Politics in America epitomizes the "Old Boys' Club," whereby generation upon

The body of the paper delineates the arguments that support the thesis. The first major argument here is underrepresentation is due to gender socialization.

Notice how the writer interweaves her source material within her arguments for greater support.

A second argument is presented: A male network perpetuates the system.

generation of white men network in order to pass on the torch of political authority. In an age of increasing demand to create equal opportunities for women, there are a variety of strategies that men employ to maintain political control. For instance, the majority of political party leaders are men who hold very traditional gender role

Here an example is offered to further illuminate the argument.

stereotypes. According to researchers, under pressure to recruit more female candidates, party leaders have responded by casting women as " 'sacrificial lambs'—that is, as candidates in districts where the party's nominee has little chance of winning the general election" (Renzetti and Curran 247). In addition, because fewer women are in politics than men are, they more often run for election as challengers rather than incumbents. It has often been shown that the most important factor in winning a political election is incumbency, creating another disadvantage for women in politics. Finally, because women have established a much less intricate system of networking than their male counterparts, they have a harder time procuring the money necessary to run effective campaigns. As elections get increasingly expensive, female candidates more often than their male counterparts will feel the financial strain.

However, sexual discrimination does not only affect female politicians within the party structure; they also face resistance on the part of the electorate to put women in positions of political power. In a study done by U.S. News and World Report, 60% of those surveyed said they favored a female presidential or vice presidential candidate, and 55% said they would like to see more women run for congressional or

A third argument purports that the general electorate limits female representation.

gubernatorial positions (qtd. in Renzetti and Curran 245). However, this does not appear to be substantiated when voters actually go to the polls to cast their secret ballots. A study done by the Los Angeles Times illustrates that all other factors being equal, the public remains reluctant to vote for a woman on the basis of gender. As the study reports:

One candidate was described as a business executive who was
married, had two kids, and was a native New Yorker. The other
candidate was presented as a lawyer who was married, had
three children, and was a native Midwesterner. For half the
sample, the New York native was described as "she." "She" lost
to her opponent, the native Midwesterner, 54% to 27%. For the
other half of the sample, "she" was the native Midwestern
lawyer. "She" lost again, this time by a margin of 43% to 38%.
(qtd. in Renzetti and Curran 245)

Obviously, sex is not the only deciding factor in any political race;
however, as these studies seem to indicate, gender does play a role in
establishing voting patterns. Not only do female candidates face
opposition from entrenched members within the party system; they also
face barriers erected by the voting public.

Part of the reason party elites, as well as the voting public, are
against women in politics is because the aims, norms, and expected
behavior of politicians as established by the system favors traditionally
masculine characteristics. For instance, constituencies expect their
politicians to be "tough" on local crime, "tough" on rival politicians, and
"tough" on foreign countries. It is a fine line that female politicians must
walk in order to promote this macho image, yet still remain feminine.
Women in politics must present a much more carefully balanced image
than their male counterparts. As one political observer states, "A woman
candidate must be assertive rather than aggressive, attractive without
being a sexpot, self-confident but not domineering . . . voters may be
more ready to see negative traits in a woman candidate. They may
perceive determined women as shrill, strident or emotional" (Renzetti
and Curran 246). The result is that female politicians may almost have to
reject their gender in order to be successful. It is rumored that former
French prime minister François Mitterand once said he liked working

The writer sub-
stantiates this
argument with a
news report on
voter behavior.

Note how the
writer continues to
build her case by
layering the argu-
ments one by one.

The fourth argu-
ment insists that
the system favors
masculine charac-
teristics and offers
specific examples.

with former British prime minister Margaret Thatcher, because he could "almost forget she was a woman."

The writer presents a fifth argument maintaining that the political reward system inhibits women.

Politics in the United States is largely based on an intricate reward system, by which women are often penalized. As Representative Marcy Kaptur states, "Despite the increase in numbers, it is still unusual for women in Congress to achieve leadership positions" (7). It is by these very positions that are denied to women that politicians are rewarded for their service. In another example, researchers state, "Women also have difficulty securing funds and other resources from the more than 3,700 Political Action Committees operating in the United States" (Renzetti and Curran 247). PAC money towards re-election campaigns is another reward that women are often denied. Finally, it is sad to say that a glitzy social life is often a reward for serving a life in politics. Female politicians, especially those who are based in Washington, D.C., are often excluded from social functions and men-only clubs that their male counterparts are privileged to attend and belong to. Denying female politicians some of the perks of the job is another method that is used to exclude them from the institution.

Note the synthesis of sources within this paragraph to support the main topic (the fifth argument) of this paragraph.

This is not to say that women are not involved in politics at all; on the contrary, women are indeed intricately involved in politics. However, it appears that the status accorded them and the roles they play are highly clustered around the lower end of the political scene. As Bella Abzug once stated, "We are allowed to do most of the drudgery and the dirty work and the detail work of politics. I would venture to say that there is no political party in the United States that could survive were it not for the fact that women are holding up those structures on their backs" (Schneir 395). As another researcher observes, "Women have long served as political 'footsoldiers': canvassing for votes door-to-door or by phone, stuffing envelopes, distributing campaign literature, and so on" (Renzetti and Curran 242). In fact, women run most of the day-to-day operation of the

Here the writer concedes at least one counterargument to her stance, but she immediately minimizes it and counters with her sixth argument, that women are involved but only allowed to participate at low levels.

political machine; they are merely excluded from the top positions. This is not to say that women have not been making gains; according to The New York Times, ten new women were elected to the House of Representatives in this past election. In addition, Jean Shaheen was elected as governor of New Hampshire, making her the second female governor now serving. However, because of the fact that many prominent female politicians retired this year, this past election resulted in a net gain of only two women in the House and one in the Senate ("In Women's Election Victories" A14). At this rate of increase of women in Congress, it will take over 400 years to reach political parity along gender lines in the United States (Renzetti and Curran 249). This again illustrates the fact that women are far from equally represented on the political scene. In addition, where women do serve in politics, they tend to be clustered around lesser-powered positions.

Once again the writer draws upon multiple sources, synthesizing the information within this paragraph to support her sixth argument.

There are more complicated reasons besides outright gender bias why women are less often found in the power positions in politics. For instance, women tend to not enter a political life until after their families are grown, giving them a much later start than men in their careers. As Congressperson Marcy Kaptur states, "Most women are elected too late in life to establish the seniority that is so important in this conservative institution, marked by its respect for tradition and tenure" (8). In addition, Kaptur claims that "lack of education and political experience compared with the education and experience of male members" is also a significant factor in analyzing why more women are not in the power positions (8). This shows that women's exclusion from high positions goes beyond mere gender bias in politics. The entire social system that sets women up first and foremost as mothers and wives also serves to penalize them in the political world as well.

A seventh argument is advanced regarding women's social responsibilities, which often hamper political gain.

The crux is the fact that unequal representation of women in politics negatively affects both men and women. Women compose roughly half of the population, and as women, have life experiences

The eighth argument presented here is moving the reader toward her hypothesis, namely, that underrepresentation affects all citizens.

distinct from those of men. When asked, women often see societal problems in a different light than their male counterparts. Because of their traditional roles as wives and mothers, women may have a unique perspective on issues such as health care, child care, the environment, even war and peace. This is not to say that women would necessarily make different policy decisions in every case than men; it simply means that as a historically marginalized population, they may have insights that are unavailable from other sources. As Bella Abzug states, "But perhaps just because they have been excluded from the governmental process, they have, on the whole, a clearer view of what our nation's priorities should be and a more direct, less encumbered approach to solving human problems" (Schneir 397). By continuing to impede 50% of the population from joining the political sphere, society potentially loses valuable insight in tackling major as well as minor difficulties.

There is, however, a danger in labeling issues such as the environment as "women's issues." As Congressperson Marcy Kaptur states, "A greater percentage of the legislation women introduced fell into 'traditionally feminine' areas of interest, compared with the legislation introduced by men—but not a majority" (12). By dividing important issues into male or female territory, one runs the risk of merely perpetuating harmful gender stereotypes. Men should be as equally concerned with preserving the environment for future generations as women. While it is permissible to allow that women may have different priorities because of their experiences as females, it would be harmful to exempt male legislators from confronting issues like health care. The national legislature, as well as local politics, should strive to be as diverse as its populace in order to fairly represent each individual's issues. As Abzug again states, "I submit that what is good for women will turn out to be good for the entire country" (Schneir 398).

The writer qualifies the eighth argument, cautioning against identifying certain topics as "women's issues."

As Renzetti and Curran proffer, political power is tantamount to social power (237). The political system in the United States is structured in such a way as to allow those who most benefit from the system to maintain it. This makes it difficult for historically marginalized groups such as women, ethnic minorities, and those who are economically disadvantaged to break into the system. In addition, the American political process was designed in such a way as to make political change exceedingly slow, in an effort to maintain stability. Likewise, though many people realize that gender roles are highly socialized, fewer individuals recognize the fact that political values are also indoctrinated at an early age. What can women do in order to change such a firmly entrenched system?

Ultimately, the reason women are underrepresented in politics is the same reason that women are underrepresented or ignored in every other aspect of our culture, because there is a bias against females in our society. It is true that one cannot legislate a change in attitude, or at least not very easily. But gaining equal representation of women in politics can have the effect of institutionalizing change. Granted, it is not enough to merely pass laws against discriminatory policies; we must change the underlying attitudes that cause the bias in the first place. On the other hand, if we are able to set up gender blind institutions by getting more women involved in politics, then we have taken a necessary step towards implementing a new belief system. Unlike gaining equal opportunity for women in other aspects of our culture, such as the arts or the sciences, politics provides its own mechanisms for making change. Women merely have to learn to use the power that is there waiting for them in order to alter their situations for the better. This is not to say that all women need to run for the Senate in order to make a difference; as more than half of the population, women have immense power as a voting bloc should they choose to use it. Gaining parity for

The ninth and final argument that political power equals social power concludes the writer's string of "ammunition" used to clearly establish her stance.

Note her rhetorical technique of posing a question to engage the audience prior to suggesting an answer.

Here the writer leads into her hypothesis-style conclusion in which she will propose a possible "what if" to solve the problem she has established.

The writer posits that, ironically, equality can only come through political change. She poses a potential solution for the problem she has clearly delineated and supported through numerous arguments.

This position paper assumes a philosophical stance, justifies its beliefs, and proposes an alternative plan.

women in the political process will not be easy. However, it can be strongly maintained that the power to define issues, set agendas, and ultimately pass laws is crucial to every other aspect of furthering equality for women.

References are cited in MLA format, typically used in the humanities.

Works Cited

Brehm, Sharon S., ed. Seeing Female: Social Roles and Personal Lives
New York: Greenwood Press, 1988.

"In Women's Election Victories, the Significance Is in the Details." New
York Times 11 Nov. 1996, late ed.: A14.

Kaptur, Marcy. Women of Congress: A Twentieth Century Odyssey
Washington, D.C.: Congressional Quarterly Inc., 1996.

Renzetti, Claire M., and Daniel J. Curran, eds. Women, Men and Society:
The Sociology of Gender. Boston: Allyn and Bacon, 1989.

Schneir, Miriam, ed. Feminism in Our Time: The Essential Writings,
World War II to the Present. New York: Vintage Books, 1994.

INVESTIGATING THE GENRE SAMPLE

1. One distinguishing feature of the stance or position paper as a genre is that its thesis should emerge from its contextualizing introduction, not simply be tacked onto the end of the first paragraph. How well do you think René Rimelspach accomplishes this seamless transition from introduction to thesis in her paper?
2. Notice the number of separate arguments Rimelspach develops in support of her thesis. When you think about the stance or position paper as a genre, what is the *fewest* number of arguments a writer ought to develop in support of a thesis? How do you come up with this number?
3. Based on your reading of Rimelspach's paper, how would you define the writing act of "qualifying" an argument? Why is that an important "move" for writers of stance and position papers to know how to accomplish?

POSITION PAPER 2

Composition

The Ban on Hemp Production

John Mulvaney
Marquette University

The Ban on Hemp Production

"You would have to smoke at least a field of this stuff to get even a smile" (Scott 1). Industrial hemp contains less than one percent tetrahydrocannabinol (THC)—the psychoactive chemical in marijuana (which contains as much as twenty percent) (Wilke 49). Hemp has traditionally been one of the most respected plants. Its uses are widespread and beneficial. The U.S. Department of Agriculture recognized it as "the oldest cultivated fiber plant [and] one of the strongest and most durable fibers of commerce" (Ballanco). At one point in time the U.S. government was begging farmers to grow it. Yet, when Colorado proposed growing it in 1995, the DEA said no. Somehow hemp production became illegal.

Hemp oil was used as a holy oil and even mentioned in the Bible, Exodus 30.23 (etymologists at Hebrew University in Jerusalem said kineboisin does mean and refer to cannabis oil) (Scott 2). Ten thousand years ago the Chinese were making hemp fiber paper (Wilke 48). Aside from the bits of ancient history facts, it was not long ago hemp was the most widely used plant. In the 1800's three quarters of the world's paper was made from it, and in Elizabethan times farmers were fined for not growing hemp (Scott 2). Henry Ford even had dreams of making a car body out of hemp and running it on hemp fuel (2). The plant's uses are no secret and there is a reason why it is grown all over the world. China, England, France, Holland, Hungary, and Russia are major producers of

In the introductory paragraph the writer contextualizes the issue.

Notice how he focuses the issue on a specific event. This will act as impetus for the thesis in the next paragraph.

The author provides some historical background that helps the reader predict the direction of the thesis. In other words, the writer is cultivating a sympathetic audience. He does so, in this case, by reminding the audience of the positive uses of hemp long before the recent ban.

Here the thesis, the author's un-equivocal position or stance, is clearly stated. (Note that the reader has been skillfully pre-pared to "hear" this position.)

The body of the essay begins by employing defini-tion and explana-tion to advance the argument. The writer indicates that this informa-tion is being pro-vided to further il-luminate the issue for the reader—to enable under-standing of a com-mon confusion.

The writer further builds his argu-ment by providing important histori-cal background in-formation.

The writer re-emphasizes the common confu-sion between hemp and mari-juana. Essentially, he is anticipating a counterargument here.

hemp—the U.S. should be on that list. Hemp cultivation should be legalized immediately.

To fully understand the argument for the legalization of industrial hemp it is necessary to know what it is and why it is useful. Yes, hemp and marijuana both come from the plant species Cannabis Sativa L. However, marijuana is the leaves and flowers from the plant, which only grow on low-fiber high-THC-content strains. Hemp strains, on the other hand, are high in fiber and contain almost no THC. The fear that industrial hemp would be used for smoking as a drug is simply ridiculous. However, industrial hemp's uses are so numerous and beneficial that the ban on it is also ridiculous.

Unfortunately, in 1937 the U.S. government passed the Marijuana Tax Act of 1937, making the use of marijuana illegal. The initial intent was anti-drug and not to stop the cultivation of hemp for industrial purposes. "In 1937 and again in 1945 Congress made clear that it was not delegating to the Federal Bureau of Narcotics (FBN) the authority to destroy the legitimate commercial hemp industry (Ballanco)." During World War II, the Navy's need for hemp rope and canvas called for a "Hemp for Victory" campaign. In which time 400,000 acres were cultivated—clearly hemp was legal. Unfortunately, the anti-drug law created so much red tape that hemp production in the U.S. gradually declined to non-existent in 1958. Twelve years later the 1937 Act was repealed and replaced with the 1970 Act. The purpose of the act was to comply with the United Nation's 1961 policy on marijuana. This policy does differentiate between hemp for industrial purposes and marijuana but the U.S. left that distinction ambiguous. Clearly, it was not their intention to outlaw such a useful plant. Yet, since the 1970 Act was passed, the DEA went ahead and defined marijuana in a way that does include industrial hemp. Hemp became illegal by the DEA's definition, not by any legislative law passed.

The DEA's definition should be changed, or clarified, to once again allow the cultivation of hemp for commercial purposes. Any educated person knows that industrial hemp cannot be smoked as a drug; the way in which hemp is planted and grown is not ideal for marijuana cultivation. However, it obviously would be easier to conceal marijuana in a hemp field than a cornfield. To prevent this, hemp farmers would simply have to register with the government, which would then send an official to test the crop. Someone trained for such a task could easily identify if the plants could or were producing many leaves and buds. Also, as a precautionary measure, a simple test would show the THC content of the plant. If the hemp plant contained more than a designated THC percentage, the crop would be destroyed at the farmer's cost. No farmer would become an innocent victim of such a penalty because hemp and marijuana contain such a vastly different amount of THC. Therefore, a fair number could be set and agreed upon to where drug cultivation would have to be the farmer's intent. In 1995 a group in Colorado outlined a specific proposal that if passed would allow farmers to grow hemp.

On January 25, 1995, Colorado State Senator Lloyd Casey introduced the Colorado Hemp Production Act. The Act's intent was to reestablish the hemp industry without legalizing marijuana. The proposal was quite specific, offering reasonable solutions to any and all loopholes an individual could find to warrant the cultivation of marijuana. The Colorado Act is based on defining hemp as "all parts of the cannabis sativa plant containing less than one percent THC" (qtd. in Ballanco). This definition differs from the DEA's definition, which outlaws all parts of the cannabis plant. As an extra measure the plants must contain an equal (to the THC) or greater amount of cannabidol that counteracts the psychoactive effects of THC. To ensure the cultivation of industrial hemp, only certified farmers who purchased seeds from

The writer's "stance" is reiterated here, but now with additional clarifying information.

He continues to build his case by offering additional arguments.

The writer now offers a reasonable alternative to the status quo. Note that he has worked hard to prepare his audience to be sympathetic to this proposal by this point.

registered distributors (who obviously would only deal in seeds that would produce low THC content plants) would be allowed to grow. Also, hemp crops would be tested at least once during their growth. If the THC content were greater than one percent (with a .4 percent buffer), the crop would be immediately destroyed. The Act seemed to be the perfect solution to the problem. Unfortunately, hours before the bill was to be voted on, the DEA faxed a letter to the voting committee telling them to throw out the bill. Despite all the emphasis placed on differentiating hemp and marijuana, the DEA was afraid the bill "would add the force of a Colorado statute to the perception that marijuana is OK" (qtd. in Ballanco). Maybe the DEA was not familiar with all the safety measures that would be taken or maybe they thought that having to send an official out to test the crop was too much hassle to help save the environment.

Many specifics are provided to make the author's position more convincing.

If all of hemp's benefits are considered, it becomes clear that the outlaw of the plant is foolish. Hemp fiber is considered by many to be the strongest fiber in the world. It can be used to make thousands of products, from paper to cosmetics to fuel to food. An acre of hemp after four months of growth produces the same amount of pulp and fiber as an acre of trees after twenty years of growth. It's no wonder why hemp is thought of by many as the solution to deforestation (trees are being cut down three times faster than they can grow). Due to the fast maturation of the hemp plant, it needs no pesticides or herbicides—a farmer's dream. Hemp makes a very durable paper. The U.S. government knows this and even prints many of its banknotes and documents on hemp paper. The rope made from hemp fiber is the strongest in the world and resists salt damage that makes it great for sailing. The hemp seeds are fully edible and high in protein—a hemp seed cheese substitute is available in many health food stores. The oil made from hemp seeds burns brighter than any other lamp oil and

Now the writer recaps several strong arguments. Repetition of key points is a common persuasive strategy used in position papers.

The writer summarizes the main argument and states the thesis as a simple conclusion.

can also be used as a diesel fuel. Hemp's benefits are clearly overwhelming.

The world we live in is fast paced and devoted to "advance" the human race. Unfortunately, our effort to make life a little easier often comes at the cost of the most precious and essential thing—the natural world. Chemicals are depleting the ozone layer; oil is being exploited; and trees are being cut down at an unbelievable rate. Hemp would by no means restore the ozone layer or put oil back in the ground but its cultivation would be a step in slowing down the destruction of forests. George Washington once said, "Make the most of the hemp seed, sow it everywhere" (qtd. in Ballanco). Currently, Colorado, Wisconsin, Kentucky, Oregon, California, Hawaii, Minnesota, and Georgia are all negotiating with the U.S. government to be able to take our founding father's advice (Ballanco). Yet, our government still holds to the non-valid fear that marijuana will be cultivated and refuses to take one simple step to give back to the earth we take so much from. We should heed the words of Chief Seattle, "Whatever befalls the Earth, befalls the sons of the Earth. Man did not weave The Web of Life; he is merely a strand in it. Whatever he does to the Web, he does to himself. Even the White Man cannot be exempt from this common destiny." ("Environmental Quotes.")

> A formal conclusion is signaled by the shift to a broader perspective and a big-picture attitude.

> The writer concludes by emphasizing the environmental benefit of relegalizing hemp production, further strengthening his position.

Works Cited

Ballanco, Thomas. "The Colorado Hemp Production Act of 1995: Farms and Forests Without Marijuana." <http://www.hempfood.com/IHA/iha02215.html>.

"Environmental Quotes." <http://gep.iatp.org.ua/env_quot.htm>.

Scott, Chris. "Some Basic Hemp Facts." <http://www.hemp.co.uk/hempfact.html>.

Wilke, Anne. "Rethinking Hemp." E July 1996: 48-52.

> References are cited in MLA (Modern Language Association) format, the preferred format in the humanities.

1. This paper takes two paragraphs to establish the context and state a thesis. Do you think this is acceptable? Why or why not?
2. In the middle of the paper, John Mulvaney restates his thesis, but he does so for a purpose. What is this purpose? What might be some other reasons a writer of a stance or position paper would feel compelled to restate the thesis?
3. Both of the stance or position papers in this chapter incorporate sources from research and cite those sources using the Modern Language Association format. Does the genre of the stance or position paper always require documentation of sources? What other ways of supporting points are open to the writer of a stance or position paper besides research?

REVIEWS

The term **review** is used extensively in academic writing. While all texts called "reviews" share some common features, they are not all the same genre. One genre is the *book review*; this genre takes slightly different forms depending on the audience for which it is written. Closely related to the book review is the *review of a performance*, an inclusive term for a genre that comprises reviews of dramatic performances, films, musical events, and art exhibits. Another genre is the *review paper*, a type of article found in the scholarly literature of the social sciences and the physical and natural sciences. This genre is considerably different from the other one just mentioned.

For many papers in college and university courses, you might be expected to write what your instructor calls a **literature review**. In a literature review, you summarize and synthesize the published literature that you have read on the subject matter about which you are writing. However, a literature review is more than simply a summary; rather, it offers an argument about theories or data that currently exist on a given topic to which the new research makes a contribution—agreeing, disagreeing, extending, and so forth. Considered in this light, a literature review may be considered a genre in its own right. Frequently, however, it does not stand alone, but rather is an element found within several other genres, especially in critical papers involving extensive research and in some informative reports.

A common misconception about reviews is that their primary purpose is to say whether some subject was good or bad, enjoyable or humdrum. This perception of reviews confuses them with critiques, which are brief evaluations of books and performances that one finds in newspapers and magazines. A review in academic writing—be it a book review, a review of a performance, or a review paper—has three important functions. A review:

- summarizes the central idea or theme of the subject being reviewed;
- evaluates how successfully the subject being reviewed conveys, demonstrates, or performs this central idea or theme; and

- explains the significance of the central idea or theme *and* its demonstration in the subject being reviewed.

The structure of a book review or a review of a performance is usually straightforward and uncomplicated. In the first part, you introduce an important idea that the people who will read the review are interested in, state that the book or performance under review deals with this idea, give the details of the book's publication or the performance's times and location, and—in a sentence or brief passage resembling a thesis—suggest the degree to which the book or performance adds significantly to the readers' understanding or appreciation of the important idea. In the second part, you summarize the central idea of the book or performance and explain how the book or performance manifests, develops, or plays out this central idea. In the third part, you evaluate the degree to which you found the development of the book or the accomplishment of the performance to be engaging, successful, and effective. In the fourth part you explain the degree to which the central idea's development or manifestation in the particular book or performance being reviewed contributes to the readers' intellectual or aesthetic growth.

In the first student sample included below, which reviews a concert piano performance for a journalism class assignment, you can observe the presence of these four parts. This review of a recording of a pianist's performance of some extremely challenging musical compositions contributes to our appreciation of one particular performer and, at the same time, expands our understanding of the attempt to achieve concert-level excellence.

Unlike a review of a single book or performance, a genre commonly found in fields of academia, a review paper in the natural, physical, life, and social sciences is actually a review of many books, chapters, and articles. A review paper in the sciences summarizes the central ideas and most important points found in several published works about a single subject and draws conclusions about common threads or ideas in those works. For example, in a recent issue of the *Journal of Applied Physics*, two scientists at Northwestern University reviewed developments in ultraviolet detector technology. They developed a method for classifying ultraviolet detectors, outlined a general theory of photodetectors, used their classification system to describe all the types of ultraviolet photodetectors, and drew conclusions about uses and future developments of ultraviolet detectors (M. Razeghi and A. Rogalski, "Semiconductor Ultraviolet Detectors," *Journal of Applied Physics* 79 [1996]: 7433–70).

A review paper is usually organized into five parts. In the introduction, you explain generally the subject matter covered in the works you are reviewing and briefly preview the conclusions you will offer at the end of the paper about the field. In addition, it is appropriate in the introduction to state explicitly the criteria you will use to review and evaluate the published works. In the second part, you proceed to review each published work. In this part, you should feel free to group the published works into related categories and use subheadings to show the readers your groupings. The third part, usually labeled "Discussion," explains similarities, differences, and other relationships discovered in the works you reviewed. Here you are making an argument, defending the key points that have emerged from the reviews and often defending a position that serves as the next step for your research or the research of some other scholar. In other words, you bring the reader to a point where you've proven, "X is known or has happened; now we need to proceed to Y to continue the scholarly debate." In the fourth part, usually labeled "Conclusions," you summarize the most important ideas about the subject matter, generalizing about the main ideas that have emerged in your review. The final part of the paper is the listing of the works cited in your review. Most review papers require you to write this listing using a scientific documentation style such as the Council of Scientific Editors style or the American Psychological Association style (see Chapter 4).

The second student paper, written for a psychology class at the University of Illinois at Chicago, nicely demonstrates the inclusion of these five parts in a literature review of two studies on language acquisition. As you read the paper, your understanding of the topic of language acquisition will expand, but your understanding of the nature of academic research, conducted as a "conversation" through its literature and its literature reviews, will expand as well.

REVIEW 1
Journalism

Review of: Liszt—The 19 Hungarian Rhapsodies
Roberto Szidon—piano Deutsche-Grammophon 1988

Arnaud Gerspacher
University of Illinois at Chicago

The performance is clearly identified. (Note that this is a review of a recording, so no specific performance date is given.)

The background contributes to this review; it establishes the credibility of the reviewer by indicating his knowledge of the field.

Review of: Liszt—The 19 Hungarian Rhapsodies

Roberto Szidon—piano Deutsche-Grammophon 1988

Franz Liszt was to the piano as James Joyce was to the novel: Groundbreaking, virtuosic, frightening, beautiful, and full of bravura. Through Liszt, the possibilities of piano music had expanded to orchestral proportions. Not since Beethoven had the piano undertaken such remarkable innovations. Liszt's artistic and technical brilliance may never be equaled. His breadth of work for the piano is massive, spanning a life of seventy-four years, including works for piano and orchestra, and songs for solo piano. Yet, if one wanted to uncover Liszt's

Ulysses, one should look no further than his *Hungarian Rhapsodies*. Through absolute genius of structure, skill and conveyance of emotion, it becomes obvious why many of the nineteen rhapsodies have attained popular appeal, and why they all have secured positions in the repertoires of every serious pianist. They are some of the most technically and emotionally demanding of all piano cycles—a true test of the pianist as a performer and interpreter.

The thesis that this reviewer will explain and support is stated.

Roberto Szidon was up to the task on his comprehensive *Deutsche-Grammophon* recording of the *Rhapsodies*. His skill on the keyboard is quite remarkable, especially in the long and rapid flurry of runs and passages that are prevalent in many of the *Rhapsodies*. Szidon's Spanish origin suits the heavy gypsy influence; after all, Liszt was inspired to write this music upon his return to Hungary. The exotic scales of augmented intervals and the "lassu-friss" (alternations of fast and slow) rhythms are fingerprints of gypsy violins. Szidon has a certain ethnic flair that permeates his playing, giving it an authentic feel. Even so, the piano at times seems distant and Szidon's playing lends itself a dry quality. This may be due to the warm, yet "lacking in clarity" analog source of the 1973 recording, but the deficiency of sound can't rest solely on the recording. His playing at moments is a little coarse and somewhat cold and abrupt, but what he loses at times in sound, he makes up with wonderfully expressive rubato, and with warranted velocity—a rapidness of playing that is far from pompous, rather a cohesive and artistically ornamental effect.

A personal comment is "tacked on" to the thesis; this is appropriate since a review is a kind of personal response/critique.

This summary of the technical challenges of this performance and of the performer's response to the challenges enables the reader to "participate" in the performance.

The reviewer moves beyond summary to critique mode, evaluating the performer's attempt to meet the challenge.

If an attempt were made to sufficiently analyze each *Rhapsody*, a book for musicologists would take form. On the other hand, if each were insufficiently represented for the sake of brevity, there would be blood on the floor. So it seems that the only option left is to find a representative of the whole, one that lends itself as a proper introduction and a doorway to the rest. The one that holds the key is the second. With its typified

The writer defends his approach to reviewing the work holistically, considering the compromises in light of audience concerns and time constraints.

"lassu-friss" construction and with its exotic, sometimes sweet, sometimes devilish melodies, the second has become the most popular.

The piece begins with a "Lento a capriccio" (i.e. Slow and capricious) segueing into the main theme in "Andante mesto" (i.e. Very moderate and mournful), both in C# minor. Szidon's playing of the beginning is a tinge too fast but otherwise very nicely interpreted. His expressiveness captures the mood perfectly. Even his abrupt style suits this opening theme, especially the opening measures of ferocity. One gets the image of animals in the forest cocking their heads in the air at the realization of an approaching storm. What follows the theme is one of the softest and sweetest passages ever written.

Due to its contrast, it is surprising how well Szidon plays this E major transition with such care and delicacy. The "dolce con grazia" (i.e. Sweetly, softly and dreamy) melody is so beautiful it's almost quixotic. But the angels are quickly banished by little demonic entities that scamper in the ensuing "capriccioso," which reverts back to C# minor. Variations of this soft, yet demonic, theme build upon itself until it finally climaxes back into the original and main theme, all of which is handled quite smoothly by the pianist. Then the key changes to F# minor, commencing the "frisk a vivace" (Very lively). In essence, this section is another variation of the "capriccioso" movement, but in another key, and with heightened devilish fervor. This is one area where the remoteness of Szidon's piano lends a sort of mysteriousness and anxiety, which greatly add to the frenzy that follows. The "friska vivace" has a flurry of successive C#'s that are mind-boggling to the listener. His fluidity creates great tension that ultimately finds an outlet in the "tempo giusto-vivace" (i.e. Fittingly quick and lively). Incredibly, the key seamlessly changes yet again in this carnival inspired and euphoric madness (F# major). This section is much faster than the preceding sections, and its complete change of mood is striking. Szidon's playing is

---

Note the specific detail provided with technical terms, demonstrating the reviewer's competence to describe and evaluate the performance. Also note that, in sensitivity to audience variation, the reviewer defines technical terms. That, of course, would not be necessary if this text were appearing in a scholarly music journal.

Notice the personal comments, laced with colorful language and engaging comparisons, interwoven among the technical descriptions. This greatly contributes to the overall tone and appeal of the review. A performance review such as this one typically presents a strong personal voice.

very commendable because, rhythmically, it is extremely demanding on the interpreter. It would be easy for a less qualified player to sound disjointed and to wreak havoc on the rhythm. In fact, Szidon's skill becomes apparent throughout the rest of the *Rhapsody*, not only rhythmically, but also through tremendous runs of "forte" (i.e. Loud) chords and octaves and tremendous reaches of adjacent notes. This all culminates in the "prestissimo" (i.e. As fast as possible) flurry of octaves, which ascends, and then descends into the forceful finale of chords.

Roberto Szidon has achieved something with these recordings that undoubtedly many pianists and music lovers can envy and strive for. Each *Rhapsody* has its own distinctive personality, which he acknowledges with his playing. Yet even though they each have their own story to tell, they are still well represented by Szidon as originally intended, as a whole cycle. In an era where music has become more visual than audible—more suited for soundtracks and promotions—it is wonderful to hear a musician with such craftsmanship and love. It's wonderful to hear such musical purity.

> Again the summary of the performance's challenge is blended with evaluative remarks, typical of this review genre.

> The conclusion explicates the significance of Szidon's piano performance of Liszt's music for today's listeners. In other words, the reviewer moves beyond summary or even critique and presents an argument that this very old, classic piece is still relevant today. That is not uncommon in the review genre.

INVESTIGATING THE GENRE SAMPLE

1. In the genre of the performance review (a review of music, theater, dance, or art), the writer has to frame an introduction that leads his or her audience to care enough about the topic to read further. How effectively do you think Arnaud Gerspacher accomplishes this goal?
2. In any review, the level of specialized vocabulary indicates the degree of experience and education the writer assumes his or her audience has with the topic at hand. What kinds of experience and education in music does Gerspacher apparently assume his audience has?
3. What do you think Gerspacher wants his audience to *do* as a result of having read his review, and why do you think that?

REVIEW 2

Psychology

Language Acquisition and the Critical Period

Grace Lee
University of Illinois at Chicago

Language Acquisition and the Critical Period

Introduction

The introduction to this review paper contextualizes the text by briefly discussing the general subject of language acquisition.

Language acquisition is a complex and somewhat abstract subject. Most people cannot remember a time when they did not know a language, so therefore it is difficult to study the steps in the language learning process. One important aspect of the language acquisition process that has been frequently studied is the age at which a person best acquires either his first or second language. Generally it is believed that the younger a person is when exposed to a language, the more quickly the person will acquire it.

The writer introduces one of the key points of the review—the central concept of the "critical period hypothesis."

Many psychologists do believe that there is a limited span of time in which a person is able to acquire language (Bernstein, Stewart, & Wickens, 1997). This span of time is referred to as the critical period for language learning. The critical period spans from early childhood to puberty. It is believed that after the span of the critical period, language acquisition is more slow and incomplete (Bernstein et al., 1997). The concept of the critical period has led to the formation of the critical period hypothesis, which states that there is a critical period in which language is best acquired.

The writer points out the debate regarding the validity of the "critical period" in relation to second-language acquisition.

The critical period hypothesis can be tested on both first and second language acquisitions (Ramsey & Wright, 1974). There have been many studies done on this hypothesis and not all the results have been in favor of the existence of a critical period (Snow & Hoefnagel-Hohle, 1978). These studies have shown that second language acquisition is the same regardless of the age of a person. However, many other studies have supported the critical period hypothesis and the general assumption that there is an optimum age period to acquire a second language (Ramsey & Wright, 1974). The contrasting results from the testing of the same hypothesis are intriguing. The opposing results can be due to many things. The cause could be experimental errors, differences in the participant pools of each study, or the methods of experimentation in each study. A more important conclusion of this contrast is that the critical period hypothesis itself is false.

Review 1

The study described in the article "The Critical Period for Language Acquisition: Evidence from Second Language Learning" was conducted at the University of Amsterdam. This study was conducted in order to compare the rates of leaning a first and second language among a wide range of ages. The hypothesis of this study was that if a second language is learned before the age of puberty, or in a critical time span, it will be learned at a rate similar to that when learning a first language (Snow & Hoefnagel-Hohle, 1978).

This study was conducted on English-speaking subjects who had moved to the Netherlands. The subjects were separated into two groups. There was a beginners group, which consisted of subjects who were just starting to learn Dutch. The other group was the advanced group, which consisted of subjects who had been speaking Dutch for several months. As a control, two groups of native Dutch speakers were also used. Each group was distributed over a range of ages. The beginning group consisted of 3–5-year-olds, 6–7-year-olds, 8–10-year-olds, 12–15-year-olds, and 16+ year-olds. The advanced group consisted of 6–7-year-olds, 8–10-year-olds, 12–15-year-olds, and 16+ year-olds. The native speakers consisted of 6–7-year-olds and 12–15-year-olds. Most of the subjects were part of middle-class families. The men were exposed to Dutch in

This background information is provided to frame the summary, and more importantly, the "argument" that is the core of this review.

Here the writer speculates about possible explanations for the variant results on the testing of the same hypothesis.

The first article to be summarized is introduced.

The hypothesis of this article is clearly stated. Note that in a scientific review paper, comparisons of hypotheses are frequent; in fact, they are often the essence of the review.

A detailed summary of the study is provided for the reader.

the work environment, the women were exposed to Dutch in the shopping centers and social gatherings, and the children were exposed to Dutch at school (Snow & Hoefnagel-Hohle, 1978).

The researchers conducted nine different language tests on each of the subjects. The beginners group was tested three times every 4–5 months, and the advanced group and the native speakers were only tested once. The researchers ran tests on pronunciation, auditory discrimination, morphology, sentence repetition, sentence translation, sentence judgment, the Peabody Picture Vocabulary Test, story comprehension, and storytelling (Snow & Hoefnagel-Hohle, 1978).

In the pronunciation test, each subject was told to pronounce 80 words. They were told to pronounce them after hearing another person say them and also without a model to follow. The researchers scored the subjects on the basis of how strong an English accent was prevalent. In the auditory discrimination test, similar sounding Dutch words were presented to each subject. The subject was then asked to distinguish the meanings of each word. This test was scored in regards to the ratio of correct responses to auditory confusions (Snow & Hoefnagel-Hohle, 1978).

The morphology test examined the ability of each subject to understand and manipulate the Dutch morphological rules. The subjects were given words and told to change the plurality and/or verb tense. The researchers scored the subjects based on the number of correct responses (Snow & Hoefnagel-Hohle, 1978).

In the sentence repetition test, each subject was read 37 Dutch sentences and was told to repeat them. The scores were based on the number of correct words repeated. The sentence translation test consisted of 60 English sentences. The subjects were told to translate each of these sentences into Dutch. The researchers scored each subject based on the correct grammatical structure and word order. In the sentence judgment test, each subject listened to pairs of sentences and

Details of the test results are offered throughout this section, enlightening the reader. This type of summary groundwork is a key component of the review paper because readers are using this type of paper to gain exposure to and understanding of multiple studies simultaneously.

was told to distinguish which one was correct and which one was incorrect (Snow & Hoefnagel-Hohle, 1978).

Subjects were also given the Peabody Picture Vocabulary Test that tested the amount of Dutch vocabulary that each person knew. The scores on this test were based on the number of correct matches between words and pictures (Snow & Hoefnagel-Hohle, 1978).

In the story comprehension test, each subject listened to a story in Dutch and was told to translate the story into English. The scores were based upon how many important points were recalled. For the storytelling test, each subject was shown pictures and was told to tell a story in Dutch about the pictures. The researchers scored each subject on the fluency of the storytelling (Snow & Hoefnagel-Hohle, 1978).

The results of these tests were surprising to the researchers because they did not support the critical period hypothesis. For the pronunciation test, the scores of all the age groups were very similar. In the auditory discrimination test, there was an inverse relationship between the number of errors made and the age of the subjects. In the morphology test, the scores increased as the age of the subject increased. The same pattern was found in the sentence repetition test and in the sentence translation test. In the sentence judgment test, the relationship between the age of the subject and the number of errors made was once again inversed. The Peabody Picture Vocabulary Test showed the same pattern of results. In the story comprehension test and the storytelling test, the scores from the first two sessions of the beginners group followed the general trend of an increase in scores with increasing age. However, in the third session of testing, the scores of the 6–7-year-olds increased significantly (Snow & Hoefnagel-Hohle, 1978).

The writer indicates that test results were surprising—contradicting the expectations of the hypothesis.

Therefore, the results of this study did not support its hypothesis that the rate that a person learns a second language is inversely related to the age of the person. On the contrary, the results of this study

The reviewer clarifies the conclusions of this study relative to the prevailing hypothesis.

The review is developing an argument for defending an alternate hypothesis.

showed that there is a direct relationship between the age of a person and the rate that he acquires a second language. Overall, this study does not support the widely accepted critical period hypothesis.

Review 2

The second article is introduced, again identifying the study and location.

The study described in the article "Age and Second Language Learning" was performed in the city of Toronto in Canada. This study was conducted in order to test the general concordance that a second language is acquired more quickly and efficiently at a younger age. The

Again the hypothesis is clearly stated.

hypothesis of this paper was that there is a critical period in which a person should be exposed to a second language (Ramsey & Wright, 1974).

Details of the study are provided for the reader.

The subjects in this experiment consisted of immigrants who had come to Toronto. The subjects in this study did not all come from a common background and language. The subjects came from a myriad of languages and the second language that they were all attempting to acquire was English. The population sample for this study was taken from the classrooms in grades 5, 7, and 9 in Toronto (Ramsey & Wright, 1974).

The researchers conducted this study by giving five tests. These tests were picture vocabulary, computational skill, progressive matrices, teacher ratings, and English language skills. The tests that were directly pertaining to language were the picture vocabulary and the English language skills tests. In the picture vocabulary test, the subjects were told to identify the vocabulary word orally. The English language skills test consisted of auditory perception, sound discrimination, sound recognition, intonation, and vocabulary (Ramsey & Wright, 1974).

The test results are provided for the reader as well.

The results of this study supported its hypothesis that there is a critical period in learning a second language. When the mean test scores from each grade level were reviewed, it was apparent that there was an inverse relationship between the scores and the age of arrival of each subject (Ramsey & Wright, 1974).

Therefore, this study supports the critical period hypothesis in second language learning. It supports the idea that the younger a person is when he is exposed to a second language, the faster and more efficiently he is able to acquire it.

Discussion

For the same exact hypothesis, the studies "The Critical Period for Language Acquisition: Evidence from Second Language Learning" and "Age and Second Language Learning" produced contrasting results. Generally, the critical period hypothesis, which states that there is an optimum language acquisition period, is widely accepted. Studies such as "Age and Second Language Learning" conduct tests and obtain results that support the critical period hypothesis (Ramsey & Wright, 1974). However, in studies such as "The Critical Period for Language Acquisition: Evidence from Second Language Learning," the results obtained do not support the critical period hypothesis (Snow & Hoefnagel-Hohle, 1978).

The language tests used in both of these studies were similar. Therefore, it is difficult to blame the differences in results upon the methods of experimentation. However, some possible confounding variables may have been the descriptions of the subjects. The Canadian study consisted of subjects from a variety of different languages (Ramsey & Wright, 1974). However, in the Dutch study, all of the subjects came from an English-speaking background (Snow & Hoefnagel-Hohle, 1978). This homogenous sample may have caused this study to reject the critical period hypothesis and decrease its generalizability. Another possible factor that may have accounted for the contrasting results is the amount of tests that each subject group took. In the Dutch group, the subjects were given the test three times (Snow & Hoefnagel-Hohle, 1978). The study done in Toronto only tested the subjects once (Ramsey & Wright, 1974). This increases the probability of

The reviewer points out that a result contrary to the first study occurred in this second study.

This discussion section is the key component of the review paper. Here the reviewer defends an interpretative position of the significance of the conflicting study results.

Details of similarities and differences between the two studies are provided.

The writer speculates about possible explanations for the variant results.

statistical regression in which a subject's score may have been uncharacteristically extreme and therefore not a clear representation of the subject's true ability.

Conclusions

In this conclusion, the reviewer offers an interesting personal perspective on the critical period hypothesis. While she has entertained counterarguments throughout this review paper, in essence she concludes her argument defending the prevalent hypothesis.

Through my own experience, I support the critical period hypothesis. I agree with the results of the Canadian study that there is an optimum arrival age in learning a second language (Ramsey & Wright, 1974). Observing the rate at which my relatives from Korea acquire English strengthens my support of the critical period hypothesis. The difference in learning between my young cousins of ages between 5 and 12 and their middle-age parents is immense. The children grow up and learn their second language to the point where an accent is no longer evident. However, the adults who continue to live in the United States for 15 to 20 years still speak with a thick accent and limited vocabulary. This may not be the case at all times, as seen in the Dutch experiment, but by my own personal experience, the critical period hypothesis seems to be accurate.

Full documentation for the works cited in the review is provided. Note that the writer follows the APA format that is always used in the field of psychology and is frequently used within the other social sciences as well.

References

Bernstein, D. A., Clarke-Stewart, A., Roy, E. J. & Wickens, C. D. (1997). *Psychology.* (4th ed.) New York: Houghton Mifflin Company.

Ramsey, C. A., & Wright, E. N. (1974). Age and second language learning. *The Journal of Social Psychology, 94,* 115–121.

Snow, C. E., & Hoefnagel-Hohle, M. (1978). The critical period for language acquisition: Evidence from second language learning. *Child Development, 49,* 1114–1128.

INVESTIGATING THE GENRE SAMPLE

1. One of the hallmarks of the literature review as a genre is its ability to reduce and synthesize very large articles, which probably have several sections themselves, into one or two paragraphs. What strategy does Grace Lee use to accomplish this reduction of content in her review?
2. How would you characterize the quantity and quality of transitions from one section of this paper to the next? What does the nature of the transitions tell you about a literature review as a genre?
3. Lee brings a bit of her personal experience into the conclusion of this paper. Do you think such a move would be acceptable in literature reviews in many academic disciplines? Why or why not?

LITERARY ANALYSIS ESSAYS

Many college students will elect or be required to study literature as part of their curriculum. Some will take a topic-based course like "Images of American Women in Contemporary Literature" or a genre or period-based course such as "Renaissance Drama" or a course based on a compilation of literary texts, studied under a generic title such as "Introduction to Fiction," and so forth. Some will study certain literary texts within their required composition courses or as part of a university seminar program aimed at teaching critical thinking and analytical skills. Regardless of course structure, literature in its widely varied forms and content continues to be a frequent area of study.

Indeed, literature has been a valued part of humankind's experience for thousands of years. Why? Perhaps because whatever the differences, essentially *all* literature looks to "story" as an entertaining and thought-provoking lens to better understand the nature of the human condition and experience. In short, literature helps us "see" and "know" who we are as human beings. Not surprisingly, then, people find value and enjoyment in paying close attention to those storied texts—to analyzing them carefully to gain even greater insights than were provided at first reading. Writing a **literary analysis essay** provides you with an opportunity to do just that.

A literary analysis essay is, as the name states, a text that analyzes a work of literature. The two significant terms here are "literature" and "analyzes." Thus, this genre of writing looks intently at a specific work (or works) of literature—such as a short story by Amy Tan, a tragedy by William Shakespeare, a sonnet by Elizabeth Barrett Browning, a novel by Toni Morrison, or a descriptive essay by Joan Didion—and then scrutinizes it closely for insights, judgments, strategies, ideas, and on and on. Remember that this type of writing is not a *summary* of a literary text, though it certainly may be necessary to include summary remarks within your analysis to ensure that your reader knows or recalls the details of the text and, thus, can follow your discussion. However, the focus must always be upon *analysis*.

Let's examine that difference between summary and analysis for a moment. Read the following passage from a student-written literary analysis essay on John Milton's seventeenth-century epic, *Samson Agonistes*:

> Samson is imprisoned in his own body by his blindness and is literally held in captivity by the Philistines. At the beginning of the poem, he exists also in a mental prison of depression and hopelessness. Samson, as a captive of the Philistines, is reduced physically to little more than a workhorse. His body and form are debased by servitude.

This passage, basically a summary of key details of the text, is provided to remind the reader of Samson's literal circumstances. The details of his blindness and his captivity are literally present in the epic. Now read another passage that occurs later within the same paper:

> Each of the visitors presents Samson with a test or challenge. He passes them all, learning more about himself and his past, and arriving at a point that is stronger and clearer in purpose than before. Both his physical blindness and his confrontation with the mental blindness of the characters around him make inward clarity and illumination possible. Samson is able to evaluate, or re-see, his history. This reframing of history has enabled him to see a future in which he can fulfill God's prophecy.

In this passage, the writer is analyzing the character of Samson, offering an interpretation of his behavior, and drawing conclusions about the value of his experiences. Those details are not stated literally within Milton's text. Rather, the writer creates that reading of the poem in her essay by scrutinizing passages, drawing connections between them, inferring certain changes, and so forth. The comments in the second passage are the work of literary analysis.

Though always focused upon analysis, this genre of essays can vary widely in its intended audiences, explicit purposes, and selected methods or approaches. Your audience will most often be a combination of your college peers and your professor. However, it may also consist of literary scholars if you are planning to present your text at a literary conference or submit your text to a journal for consideration for publication. Literary analyses can also serve varied purposes for both the writer and the reader. You may write or read primarily to explore the text itself for further insights, to demonstrate your detailed knowledge of the text to your audience, to form or understand an argument about a particular way to read the text, or to make connections to other works of literature or theories of literary study and so forth.

Let's examine some of the possible approaches to writing a literary analysis essay. All of these essays basically fall into one of two categories: You can write a completely self-created analysis, which uses only *one* source to write the essay—the primary source of the work of literature itself; or you can write an analysis that draws upon secondary sources, most commonly works of literary criticism, to aid you in your analysis. If you are directed to use outside sources such as critical essays found in literary journals that are written by professional scholars of literature, remember that you must credit the ideas you borrow from those scholars by properly citing them, both within the paper and in a fully documented list of sources in a reference list at the end of the paper. In this genre, you will nearly always be directed to use the conventions of MLA (Modern Language Association) style to format your essay and document your sources. In MLA format your sources will appear in "works cited" list. (See Chapter 4 for further discussion of those details.)

Aside from those two broad divisions of using only the primary source for your analysis or augmenting it with secondary sources, there are several approaches you might take to structure your essay. One common approach is to do a "close reading" of textual features. With this method, you select one or more of the common literary elements such as plot, character, setting, theme, style, imagery, tone, etc.; trace their occurrence throughout the text; and then examine them closely to speculate on their meaning. For example, you might read the text for its use of figurative language, concentrate on character development, or focus on aspects of the setting (details of time and place) and examine their relevance to the overall message that seems to emerge from the text. Another method is commonly called a "reader-response" approach. Here you would concentrate on the text's effect on you as a reader, noting emotions it aroused and determining how that was accomplished, articulating connections that you made between the text and other experiences you have had outside of the text, or specifying what ideas you agree or disagree with within the text and so forth. Sometimes literary analysis essays demand an even more sophisticated approach. If you are involved in more advanced literary study, you may be asked to write an essay that assumes a particular "critical perspective" to analyze the text. For example, you might construct an interpretation of the text relative to feminist critical theory, viewing gender roles and stereotypes closely; examine the social-class issues of a text through a lens of cultural studies theory; draw on autobiographical criticism that provides crucial details about the author to help you analyze his/her text; and so forth. If your professor is expecting a specific critical frame such as one of these, you will surely be alerted to this. Such an analysis demands an understanding of that specific theoretical approach and ordinarily draws upon an array of scholarly secondary sources.

All of the approaches share something in common. A literary analysis forms an argument for a particular reading or interpretation of a work of literature. Consequently, in *any* literary analysis essay, you typically would be expected to formulate a thesis, which represents your major conclusion or interpretative statement about the text, and then to defend that thesis or controlling idea with details, examples, and formal arguments throughout the course of your essay. The thesis should be clearly stated early in the essay, most probably in the opening paragraph. It provides a road map for your reader in following your argument. In other words, this genre will, in many respects, look like the papers described in the section on stance or position papers above. Consider following the same organizational pattern as suggested there.

In this genre, however, the supports will be somewhat different. As discussed earlier in this section, they may come exclusively from the text itself and your own thoughts and previous experiences, or they may be supplemented by the thoughts and writings of others, usually literary scholars who write professional literary criticism. However, you may occasionally draw upon a journalist's comments in a book review or critique appearing in a general-interest source rather than a scholarly journal. (Differences between such sources will be discussed in Chapter 4.) One other crucial detail: Be sure that you clearly establish the title, author, edition, and genre of the specific work of literature you are exploring. Most likely you will include this information in your opening paragraph although some specific publication details, such as the precise edition, can simply be included in the Works Cited list.

The two student essays that follow provide examples of close textual analyses of literary works. The first essay, written by an English major at Boston College for her senior seminar on Milton, explores Milton's use of the imagery in his famous epic poem *Samson Agonistes*. While it is clear that this writer is familiar with other Miltonic works, the analysis does not draw on any secondary sources. Rather, the writer relies heavily upon the lines of the poem itself to trace the changes that occur in the main character, which are largely exemplified through the ironic play on the true nature of the words "vision" and "blindness." The second essay, written by an English major at Elmhurst College for a course on American fiction, examines the use of setting as an influential element in two different novels. This essay supports its thesis not only through the use of detailed examples from the text and original interpretation by the writer but also by integrating ideas of literary critics.

LITERARY ESSAY 1
Literary Studies (Milton Seminar)

Samson's Inner Vision

Mary Weicher
Boston College

Samson's Inner Vision

Notice that the writer opens her essay with a general statement about a feature of Milton's writing, thereby establishing a context for this analysis.

The notion of a trial by experience is one that recurs frequently in Milton's literature. Frequently his protagonists can only prove their abilities and virtues by passing a test or overcoming a serious obstacle. The Lady in *Comus*, for example, must resist the temptations of drink and debauchery to prove her chastity. The hero of *Samson Agonistes* must struggle with a very Miltonic obstacle—blindness, an affliction that had personal meaning for Milton himself. Samson's physical blindness serves not only to lock him away from a vision of his surroundings. It is juxtaposed with reason and understanding to serve as a metaphor for mortal, limited vision. The tropes of vision, blindness, and captivity are intertwined in the work to ultimately represent the way in which Samson is able to view himself and his history with a distance and accuracy that is given by God. This theme is not new to Milton; the Bard in *Paradise Lost* also contrasts mortal blindness and inner illumination in his attempt to "justifye the ways of God to men" (Book 1, line 26).

Samson is imprisoned in his own body by his blindness and is literally held in captivity by the Philistines. At the beginning of the poem, he exists also in a mental prison of depression and hopelessness. Samson, as a captive of the Philistines, is reduced physically to little more than a workhorse. His body and form are debased by servitude. His physical change is related through the reactions of the Chorus, Manoa, and Harapha. The Chorus exclaims "O change beyond report, thought, or belief! / See how he lies at random, carelesly diffus'd, / With languished head unpropt, / As one past hope, abandon'd, / And by himself given over; / In slavish habit, ill-fitted weeds, / O're worn and soild" (117–123). Samson's own father has a similar reaction of surprise and disgust: "O miserable change!" (340), he exclaims rather unfeelingly.

Samson inwardly views himself at the beginning of the poem in similarly depressing, negative terms. His inner thoughts (the only means through which he can view himself) are disturbed.

"I seek / This unfrequented place to find some ease, / Ease to the body some, none to the mind / From restless thoughts, that like a deadly swarm / Of hornets arm'd, no sooner found alone, / But rush upon me thronging, and present / Times past, what once I was, and what am now" (16–23).

The hellish, nagging image of hornets buzzing and the emphasis on Samson's change from a heroic past reflect the same type of limited vision with which Samson's visitors regard him—as a man afflicted and pathetic. In a moving and passionate passage, Samson laments

---

The thesis is clearly stated. Now the entire analysis will be focused upon the three tropes and their relation to Samson's revelation. This claim will then be tied to an additional work of Milton's.

The body of the essay provides some brief background detail in order to move into the analysis of Samson.

Notice how skillfully the writer intertwines lines from the poem to summarize the poem here.

The writer continues to establish the troubled state in which the reader first finds Samson.

Notice the analytical comments provided. The writer is arguing for a specific interpretation of the text.

bitterly the physical blindness that has struck him. In these lines, Samson mourns this dual captivity and even goes so far as to question God. Although he first states, "I must not quarrel with the will / Of highest dispensation" (60–61), he immediately contradicts these lines with a long speech of self-pity and complaining. He states, "O first created Beam, and thou great Word, / Let there be light, and light was over all; / Why am I thus bereav'd thy prime decree?" (83–85). This religious suggestion is implicitly a questioning of God's will. Samson pities himself and regrets his failure, but does not view his past with an eye to analyze his faults and learn from them. Contrasting images of light, dark, and death reflect the tumult of Samson's self image as well as his present state of depression. "As in the land of darkness yet in light, / To live a life half dead, a living death" (98–99). Samson refers to his body as a "Sepulcher, a moving Grave" (101). The former hero at this point is utterly without hope; he lives in darkness both literally and mentally.

The writer continually returns to her thesis's focus on the concept of vision, which Milton explores throughout the poem.

These various "visions" of Samson's physical appearance and debasement are limiting and unproductive. In fact, although Samson is dirty, debased, and blind physically, his mental clarity and freedom of thought are proven to be greater than before. Through Samson's interactions with the Chorus and his four visitors, the difference between physical darkness and inner illumination becomes apparent. "Blindness" in the poem paradoxically works to reveal Samson to himself. At the same time, the "seeing" characters in the poem are frequently blind to the truth. Samson's mental clarity is tested and improves with each successive visitor; in a sense, Manoa, Dalilah, Harapha, and the messenger are tests of faith and vision that Samson overcomes and from which he learns valuable lessons about himself and his past. As a result, his tragic and heroic decision to sacrifice himself in the theatre is made possible for the right reasons.

Textual clues are provided for the reader. The writer indicates that her argument will be based upon a close look at the interactions between Samson and his visitors.

Samson's first visitor is Manoa, his father, who does not recognize him by sight. In a speech with truly epic overtones, Manoa wails about the former greatness of Samson in unequivocal terms. "Can this be hee? / That Heroic, that Renown'd, / Irresistible *Samson*?" (123–125). Manoa aptly recognizes Samson's state of abjection, but remembers him historically without a fault: "O mirror of our fickle state, / Since man on earth unparallel'd!" (164–165). Flattering as this vision of Samson may be, Manoa is blind to the reality of Samson's failings, even at the height of his strength and prowess. Although blind, Samson's mental clarity surpasses his father's; this exchange provides Samson with the opportunity to evaluate himself justly at a historical distance. At this point he rightly assesses some of his mistakes. Although willful enough to resist certain temptations, he had a weakness for women—the prime cause of his downfall. Regarding his troublesome affection for Dalilah, he admits, "These rags, this grinding, is not yet so base / As was my former servitude, ignoble, / Unmanly, ignominious, infamous, / True slavery, and that blindness worse than this, That saw not how degenerately I serv'd" (415–419). In response to Manoa's desire to elevate him from servitude to the Philistines, Samson replies, "Spare that proposal, Father, spare the trouble / Of that sollicitation; let me here, / As I deserve, pay on my punishment; / And expiate, if possible, my crime, / Shameful garrulity" (488–492). As painful as it may be to admit the gravity of his sin towards God, this revelation is a sign of Samson's increasing mental vision and clarity.

In this way Samson passes the test represented by Manoa, and is more prepared by these revelations than he otherwise would have been to receive Dalilah, see through her misleading explanations, and recognize her for what she truly is. Dalilah waltzes onto the stage bedecked in all the riches her betrayal has awarded her. She professes her love for him and tries to justify her actions with slippery arguments.

Each visit, however painful, brings a new sense of "vision" for the blind Samson.

Above all else, she tempts Samson with the sexual physicality that he previously found so irresistible: "Though sight be lost, / life yet hath many solaces, enjoy'd / Where other senses want not their delights / At home in leisure and domestic ease, / Exempt from many a care and chance to which / Eye-sight exposes daily men abroad" (14–19). Dalilah wants Samson to use his blindness as an excuse to become idle and indulgent. Instead, blindness enables Samson to see the weakness of her argument; he is armed against her physicality. Ultimately he evaluates each of her lousy excuses, sees how they are false, and rejects her: "No, no, of my condition take no care; / It fits not; thou and I long since are twain; / Nor think me so unwary or accurst / To bring my feet again into the snare / Where once I have been caught" (928–933). Not only does Samson recognize where he formerly failed—he also has the strength to resist a similar misstep.

Both Manoa and Dalilah have given Samson the opportunity to see his failings through their eyes, and evaluate them justly where they cannot. The visit of Harapha has a different effect; it allows Samson the opportunity to display confidence and bravado. In a sense, Samson is using what he has learned about his formerly excessive pride to express courage and strength when it is appropriate. Harapha compares the legend of Samson's greatness to his blind servitude, and regrets having missed the opportunity to test Samson's prowess on the battlefield (1080–1090). Perhaps the most ironic threat Samson levies against Harapha is this short and sweet phrase: "The way to know were not to see but taste" (1092). It is difficult to imagine the depressed, hopeless Samson at the beginning of the poem expressing confidence in his abilities in a way that hints so strongly at his former bravado. Moreover, the statement is accurate—the way to discover the truth, as Samson has discovered in his own life, has nothing to do with observation, but rather with experience. In addition to abandoning vocal laments about

Notice the repeated use of direct quotes from the poem (the slash indicates a line division in the poem) to justify the writer's assertions—i.e., her analytical comments.

his present physical state, Samson begins to express faith in God. "My trust is in the living God who gave me / At my Nativity this strength, diffus'd / No less through all my sinews, joints and bones" (1140–1142). It is significant that Samson is now able to recognize God's central role in his strength and success. Harapha also represents a different kind of challenge—one in the present. Although Harapha repeatedly refers to the past, to the great legend that *was* Samson, the former hero himself for the first time does not speak of the past as over. It seems that Samson feels his strength as a palpable, present gift. He refers to his ability to meet Harapha's challenge: "Go baffl'd coward, lest I run upon thee, / Though in these chains, bulk without spirit vast, / And with one buffet lay thy structure low, / Or swing thee in the Air, then dash thee down / To the hazard of thy brains and shatter'd sides" (1236–1240). Again, the Samson of the first passages of the poem would never have believed himself capable of such a display of strength.

The final visitor is the messenger who arrives with orders to bring Samson to the theatre to make a spectacle of himself. Repeatedly, Samson rebuffs him, refusing to submit to further humiliation. "Can they think me so broken, so debas'd / With corporal servitude, that my mind ever / Will condescend to such absurd commands?" (1335–1338). Actually, it is not unbelievable that the Philistines would have assumed Samson to be so far debased; he believed it himself at the beginning of the poem. Interestingly, Samson makes a clear distinction in these lines between corporal and mental servitude. The theme of Samson's mental clarity and inner illumination is becoming a central support for his decisions. When he decides finally to accompany the messenger, it is not because he is forced, but because he feels "Some rouzing motions in me which dispose / To something extraordinary my thoughts" (1381–1382). Samson has relied increasingly on his own mental powers since the beginning of the poem, up until the pivotal point of this decision to

The writer begins placing greater emphasis on the second part of her initial thesis, namely, that Samson's new vision brings him a greater under-standing of God's role in his life.

accompany the messenger and appear before the Philistines. It seems apparent from this passage that Samson has an idea of the deed he is about to perform.

Here the writer summarizes her major arguments.

Each of the visitors presents Samson with a test or challenge. He passes them all, learning more about himself and his past, and arriving at a point that is stronger and clearer in purpose than before. Both his physical blindness and his confrontation with the mental blindness of the characters around him make inward clarity and illumination possible. Samson is able to evaluate, or re-see, his history. This reframing of history has enabled him to see a future in which he can fulfill God's prophecy.

Now the writer transitions into the second aspect of her discussion, which links her analysis of Samson to a pattern found in other Miltonic works. Recall that she signaled the reader of this inclusion at the end of the first paragraph.

The notion of physical blindness versus mental illumination is not a new one in Milton's poetry. The Bard in *Paradise Lost* provides an excellent example of this theme. The Bard calls for divine inspiration in Book 3: "So much the rather thou Celestial light / Shine inward, and the mind through all her powers / Irradiate, there plant eyes, all mist from thence / Purge and disperse, that I may see and tell / Of things invisible to mortal sight" (51–55). The notion that there are truths unavailable to "mortal sight" is central to Milton's concept of writing poetry and of discerning the truth. Until one abandons the struggle to see in this limited way and relies on a less material, more divine illumination, the kind of clarity that the Bard and Samson achieve is inaccessible.

INVESTIGATING THE GENRE SAMPLE

1. Discuss the ways that this literary analysis essay is similar to the papers in the section on stance or position papers. In what ways is it a slightly different kind of genre?
2. Obviously, an audience who is very familiar with the literary text under analysis is a more informed and critical reader. Assuming you are *not* familiar with Milton's epic, are you still able to understand this analysis? If so, why? Point to specific features of this essay that enable your understanding. If not, what might Weicher have done differently?

3. The most important aspect of this genre is moving away from summary to genuine analysis. Evaluate how well Mary Weicher succeeds in doing this. Find specific passages where the analysis is particularly strong. Discuss how that works.

LITERARY ESSAY 2

Literary Studies (American Fiction)

A Place of Importance:

The Influence of Setting in *My Ántonia* and *Absalom, Absalom!*

Aaron Sandberg
Elmhurst College

A Place of Importance:

The Influence of Setting in My Ántonia and Absalom, Absalom!

Within Willa Cather's My Ántonia and William Faulkner's Absalom, Absalom!, setting, background, landscape, and location are primary factors in defining America in American fiction. Setting within these texts determines what is American and establishes the American experience perhaps even more so than the characters. In My Ántonia, it is the new freedom of the frontier; within Faulkner's piece, it is the influence of the settled and dying landscape of the post-civil war South. Within both texts, the location directly plays into the lives of the characters—molding them as opposed to the characters molding the land, and consequently, controlling their lives.

Looking first at My Ántonia, we see clear influences of land on the motivations of characters. As literary critic Reginald Dyck notes about the book, "social and economic problems receive little attention" (26). However, issues of the surrounding environment are crucial to the understanding of characters. Jim, for instance, arrives in the Midwest and notes, "I had the feeling that the world was left behind, that we had got over the edge of it, and were outside man's jurisdiction" (Cather 12).

The writer immediately identifies the literary works to be examined, and points to the feature of "setting" as the focus.

The opening paragraph ends with the thesis statement, a common practice in this genre; the argument is clearly outlined.

Launching the discussion of the first novel, the writer skillfully interweaves a quote from a literary critic. This is commonly used as "evidence" or support for the argument.

Notice the combination of primary- and secondary-source material used to develop the analysis.

Jim even feels "erased, blotted out" (13). From this description, the plains are characterized as otherworldly, unbound by man, a place where the grasp of society does not reach. Coming from an established town in the east, Jim now experiences a changing mindset as he enters this new world—a world that seems to rob his notions of "identity." Here, it is only the individual alone with nature, and in this world, nature dominates, becoming much more important in the relationship with the individual. For it is now the only factor one must come to terms with, and therefore, its influence on the characters is strong, its role in shaping identity is amplified.

The writer continues his analysis of the narrator character, Jim.

We must note that it is the land itself that is the trigger for Jim's reactions and motivations--not the other way around. His initial response is shaped by the landscape itself and is the cause for his projections onto it. His ideas about the land are not isolated in a neutral vacuum. The land defines itself, and Jim merely interprets this definition. Jim does not define the land. And if he does, then he is simply naming what is already there and active. It is the land itself that begins to influence not only Jim, as we have seen, but virtually all the other characters as well. Regarding the relationship and interaction with the land, critic Saposnik-Noire maintains, "Human characteristics given the land do not act as mere projections by characters onto the land. Although there are projections and introjections made by characters in the book, these are made as if the landscape were a breathing living thing, capable of response" (173).

Note the use of the "tag," where an authority is introduced; here the word "critic" in front of the name justifies the use of this quote. Developing this type of credibility for sources is common in the humanities especially.

To further that view, the landscape seems more of a controlling force than Jim leads us to believe. Jim naively discloses, "The new country lay open before me: there were no fences in those days, and I could choose my own way over the grass uplands, trusting the pony to get me home again" (Cather 28). This "trust" is misleading. Although Jim feels he has a newfound freedom (which to a certain degree, is true, since he is loose from the influence and control of city society), he softens the power of this new and foreign land by using such words. In fact, Jim has no choice but to "trust" nature and the setting to which he belongs. Yes, the country "lay[s] open before [him]," but that does not mean Jim holds power over that land. He "trusts" the pony, when in fact he has no other choice. A similar conflict in the reliability of Jim comes in such passages as: "The great land had never looked to me so big and free. If the red grass was full of rattlers, I was equal to them all" (Cather 43). I would argue that Jim is not so equal as he claims to be. In this scene, the death of one snake, he assumes, gives him power over (or at least equates him to) the land. Yet, Jim fails to realize and admit the land is much more than one, old snake. However, it is understandable for Jim to swim in such illusion--a way to cope when he inherently knows that he is powerless in this land. Therefore, any small triumph over his surroundings is seen as a great wielding of power over the country itself.

Frequently personified, this "breathing living" land gives us further understanding of the relationship the characters have with it. We read that "[t]here was so much motion in it; the whole country seemed, somehow, to be running" (Cather 18). The land is personified so intensely that, in fact, one critic mentions that "plot and character are subservient to setting" (Saposnik-Noire 171). Through this personification, the landscape can then come alive, and the characters can in turn have an "interactive, interdependent, and at times symbiotic relationship to nature" (171). Often, if not always, within this novel, the power and dominance reside in the environment as opposed to the characters who occupy and attempt to control it. For example, it is not Mr. Shimerda, Ántonia's father, who holds the power over the family, for even they must bow to the oppression of the prairie winter. They must only work on nature's terms, and therefore, the land they inhabit ultimately shapes them. Saposnik-Noire points out that "in nature's

Here the writer clearly states his argumentative position, using first person. Within this genre, third person was the common practice for many decades. That is shifting more recently as scholars increasingly admit to the subjectivity of all knowledge claims.

The writer continues his analysis, now applying the thesis to additional characters.

triumph over the will of Peter and Pavel, Jim learns that nature is not simply the source of life and nurture he knows his prairie land to be" (173). Clearly, Jim realizes that nature is an active force, not only in positive terms of growth and fertility, but as a destructive force as well. That force is the characteristic of the environment that enables it to shape the lives of the characters. It is at once a source of strength, and also a source of weakness. Through this tension, the characters rely on it, but then are also forced to submit to its terms. Therefore, no matter what the experience at the moment, nature always has the hand in power.

Note the use of terms of literary analysis, common to this genre. The terms are not defined as the audience for this essay would surely understand this vocabulary.

Indeed, the environment, including the weather, is clearly personified and holds a large degree of power over the characters. "Winter came down savagely over a little town on the prairie" (Cather 139). Jim "was convinced that man's strongest antagonist is the cold" (Cather 57). In this passage, the weather is literally an "antagonist," a character within the story, and therefore, responsible for how the characters act and respond. And in their actions and responses, they are ultimately shaped according to the circumstances of environment. Winter is even called the "reality" and "truth" (Cather 139–140).

This reality and truth of not only the weather, but of the landscape as well, has deep psychological influences on many of the characters. For example, "Cutter often threatened to chop down the cedar trees which half-buried the house. His wife declared she would leave him if she were stripped of the 'privacy' which she felt these trees afforded her" (Cather 170). This passage seems to suggest that life on the plains offers freedom, yet a certain amount of "openness" and lack of privacy. It's ironic, but this seems to suggest the crowded city offers more opportunity to remain hidden among the masses than the wide-open, empty space of the prairie. Therefore, Mrs. Cutter values the few trees, which shade the house and offer some sense of protection from the world. Again, the landscape here is highly influential in regards to what certain individuals value--in this case, it's a need for privacy, which seems counterintuitive to the freedom the plains offers.

Since nature holds such power--psychologically and physically-- it's expected that the main character be virtually fused with the idea and power of the landscape itself, since they have no choice but to be shaped and molded by it. Ántonia, especially, is virtually forced to shape herself in accordance to the land. In fact, "Through Ántonia, Cather celebrates the pioneer values: determination, love of the land, and human rather than materialistic concerns" (Dyck 28). Cather does this, by merging Ántonia with the land itself, so that they are one in the same. Saposnik-Noire notes "she becomes merged with the land, identified with it in such a way that in Jim's mind she is the land" (177). Also, "Ántonia's selfhood is carved out of the prairie" (Saposnik-Noire 178). Clearly, Ántonia becomes the land. But while she argues that "Ántonia gives herself to the land and merges with it" (178), I think Saposnik-Noire's word choice fails to convey the true essence of the power residing within the landscape. The idea of "giving one's self over" is a false notion in this case. Rather, I would argue, it resembles more of a submission of will. The author's word, "gives," connotates ideas of choice, when clearly, Ántonia has little, if any. She is a slave to the land and she "gives herself" not because she chooses to, but because she must to survive. The land is too powerful for choice. If the land gave the characters choice, then the land would not wield the influence that it possesses within the prose of Cather.

Cather continues to further develop the relationship between Ántonia and the land she inhabits. "Tony was barefooted, and she shivered in her cotton dress and was comfortable only when we were tucked down on the baked earth, in the full blaze of the sun" (Cather 36). It seems her true place is the land. In fact, the land seems to

The writer now moves to a discussion of the title character. Note how the thesis in this essay is justified through the layering of examples from the primary source and the interweaving of testimony of professional scholars in secondary sources.

design her destiny. "I ain't got time to learn. I can work like mans now . . . School is all right for little boys. I help make this land one good farm" (Cather 100). She works the land, mostly, because she has no choice. So by this fate, Ántonia becomes "the land" because the land has made it so.

The analysis continues to invoke supportive statements from the criticism of professionals to help develop the claim.

However powerful the land truly is, it is this power that attracts the admiration of Jim. Such romanticism is seen most explicitly when he witnesses the plow against the sun. It is important to realize that "the plow is the symbol of the pioneer on the plains" (Saposnik-Noire 175). Although a simple image in reality and symbol, Jim is taken by this image. Suddenly, and yet all along, he finds this moment to be beyond beauty and wonder. In this scene, we see Jim's romanticized view of the mundane and harsh life on the prairie; clearly, he idealizes the life of the pioneer. If we follow this, then Jim most likely loves Ántonia because she is identified and inseparable from his idea of the prairie. Ántonia is a true prairie woman, works with her hands in the land, and in turn, becomes the land. He only loves Ántonia because he first loves the prairie. Clearly, setting and nature are the root of Jim's projections and behaviors, especially towards Ántonia. His reaction towards her is merely an extension of his reaction to the prairie. Jim ultimately leaves the prairie, as Dyck points out, "because he has no place there" (28). Note, however, it is not Jim who decides where he belongs and where he does not. It is the land that defines us. The land is unwavering, and if Jim finds he doesn't belong, then Jim can do little to change that. The land has spoken, and has ultimately left Jim behind. He must move out of the land not merely because he wishes to (since he loves it), but because the land has caused him to wish for this, and therefore, the land directs the lives and motivations of the characters. As we have noted before, Ántonia is inseparable from the idea of the land she inhabits. Therefore, if "Ántonia's life judges Jims" (28), which Dyck points out, then clearly the land is responsible for judging and defining Jim and not the other way around. While we would tend to believe that man defines his surroundings, it seems quite clear that in truth, it is the surroundings that define man.

The writer frequently reminds the reader of the central focus—the influence of setting.

When Jim moves back to town, "his love of country keeps him from belonging to that life" (Dyck 28) as well. Saposnik-Noire similarly points out "Jim is forever split between two worlds, the prairie and the city" (178). While "Ántonia can embrace and find harmony with the plains" (Dyck 35), Jim, on the other hand, cannot. Although one might say he defines himself by two worlds, it would be more accurate to say two worlds define Jim, and this conflicting definition is fundamental to the identity of Jim.

Landscape influence on character seems to affect others outside the main characters, which ultimately makes the influence of the environment that much stronger. In regards to the cornfields, "They would enlarge and multiply until they would be, not the Shimerdas' cornfields, or Mr. Bushy's, but the world's cornfields; that their yield would be one of the great economic facts, like the wheat crop of Russia, which underlie all the activities of men, in peace or war" (Cather 111). It's clear from this passage the influence of the land, not only on the characters in the novel, but on the rest of the world. In fact, the land before them "underlie[s] all the activities of men," regardless of time and circumstance. And if the land has impact on the lives of others outside the town, then for the inhabitants of the town, this land is everything, and influences every aspect of their lives. They work in the shadow of the land because the land holds true sway. Without the land, the characters would cease to be the characters they believe themselves to be now.

Finally, the writer includes examples of the impact of setting on minor characters in the novel as well. This provides further evidence of the validity of the thesis.

And this is exactly what the characters in Faulkner's Absalom, Absalom! are faced with--defining themselves without the land they

Here the writer clearly transitions into the second part of the essay, analyzing the second novel selected for comparison.

Features of comparison and contrast between the two works are noted.

once knew. Within this novel, similar themes are uncovered as were uncovered in <u>My Ántonia</u>, yet the setting has changed. No longer do we find ourselves on a new and untouched prairie, but now we enter an established, old, and now-dying South. Yet, whether it be on the new Plains or in the old South, influence of place and setting are equal in degree. However, the effects of the altered landscape differ between characters identifying with a land being born, and those identifying with a land submitting to death. Nowhere in the novel is this idea of identity/land more clear than in the land known as Sutpen's Hundred. Thomas Sutpen seems determined to remake the land that made him. So inseparable are the ideas of Sutpen as a man, and Sutpen's land, that one can even refer to Sutpen's Hundred as Sutpen himself.

Transitioning to a background topic, the writer continues building a case to accept the thesis.

To examine this, we must first understand that within the old South, land and values are closely tied. So with the loss of the Civil War, to an extent, both of these were lost. The war marked the end, not only to the power of land guarded by great plantations, but also the ideas and values associated with such plantations. Plantations only existed because of the ideals from where they were built. So with the death of those ideals, so follows the death of the plantations and the land they ruled.

The writer must explain the historical conditions to contextualize his thesis for the contemporary reader. This is commonly done in discussing literary works from earlier time periods.

Before the war, no black individual could own land (just as no black had any individual rights or recognized identity). Land, virtually, was entirely defined by the white landowners who also defined the values of "Southern Culture." "Blacks were often denied access to material possessions on the basis of their lack of ideological possessions" (Saunders 753). So in order to keep white privilege, whites kept the practice and ideology that the black man is inferior, and therefore, has no right to land because he has no dominion over his own mind. This subjection of the black mind resulted in physical differences in work

status defined by whites that owned the land. Therefore, "Black farmers
. . . 'not only worked the white man's land but,' according to
Woodward, 'worked it with a white man's plow drawn by a white man's
mule' " (Saunders 753). So with the death of the Southern ideal via the
Civil War, so came the death of the power of land, and with it, the idea
of a strong identity. Southern culture (established on Southern land) had
defined itself by what it was not (the black slaves). So with the death of
slavery, came the death of Southern-white identity. Clearly, land,
environment, and setting have enormous influence on character and
how the South was defined.

The historical realities are related to the thesis of this essay.

In Saunders' essay, this changing identity and value are seen
through "transfer of property, the redistribution of possessions, and the
remapping of territorial boundaries. These transfers and redistributions
include the redistribution of value, knowledge, and identity" (732). The
land, and what becomes of it, is an integral part of what becomes of the
individual since it is clear that the land defines the individual. So when
Sutpen's Hundred is transferred to the state by the end of the novel, the
idea of Thomas Sutpen as a character is forever altered--now the identity
and the estate are one in the same.

"Material and ideological property are not, of course, unrelated; on
the contrary, they are inevitably collusive because possessions function
as signs. Material property, that is to say, is often the procurer, and
guardian, of ideological property" (Saunders 733). Clearly then, Sutpen's
material property is merely an extension and representation of his
ideological property. The actual Sutpen's Hundred is a physical
extension of the idea of what Sutpen's Hundred really is. Consider, for a
moment, the loss of the material property. With the loss of such property,
the ideological property would be quick to follow, since the ideological
cannot stand without the realized and materialized entity. Therefore,

without the land to realize the idea, the idea ceases to exist (or if not ceases to exist, at least becomes powerless and unrealized). Thus, the physical location of land is the determining and base factor in ideology, especially the ideology we see in the South and even more so, the ideology of Sutpen himself.

Establishing this idea of land/identity, critic Rebecca Saunders points out:

Note that the convention of including an occasional long quote (more than four lines) requires a different format in MLA style.

> In Absalom, the catastrophe of the Civil War effects transfers of real property that are simultaneous redistributions of identity: landowner becomes merchant, slave-holding heiress becomes land-lord employer, slave becomes freedperson, and (in the reverberations of that catastrophe a generation later) a college boy becomes inadvertent plenipotentiary of the South. (734)

In the novel, a passage reads regarding returning soldiers, "returned now to a ruined land, not the same men who had marched away but transformed" (Faulkner 126). The loss of ideals inseparable from the ownership of land (and slaves) results in the detrimental effects regarding the notion of identity. Saunders states that:

Once again the analysis of setting in this novel unfolds as a combination of specific textual examples from the primary source and authoritative, critical support from secondary sources.

> As a man's land has become other, or become the property of another, so has the man become other to his former self. Likewise, when Sutpen returns from war, he, like the ruined fields, fallen fences, and crumbling walls of his property, has become other, indeed has become alien to his own physical being. (736)

And just as Sutpen is forced to rebuild his land, so is he forced to rebuild himself--the part in him that has fallen along with the fences of his Hundred.

As we can see, it's clear that setting, landscape, nature, and environment play fundamental roles in shaping the lives of the characters in My Ántonia and Absalom, Absalom! Not only are our characters physically connected to the environment in which they live, but they are also psychologically connected to the settings they inhabit. It's clear that the environment is by no means a neutral backdrop. In fact, setting and nature become literal characters--interacting with and shaping the lives of the human characters on levels to which we have only begun to discover. In Dyck's comment about the closing lines of My Ántonia, he states that Jim and Ántonia share the belief that "early life has shaped all they have done" (34). If this is indeed true, then we can say that the land in turn shaped this early life. If we once thought that we were isolated to the individuals that make up a society, then what happens to that idea of society when we begin to understand the influence nature and place has on such society? We must realize that "where we are" is just as important as our notion of "who we are," often because there is little difference between the two.

The writer signals the conclusion by drawing our attention back to both novels and by essentially restating the thesis. This is the common pattern in a literary essay.

A final critical quote is offered to help solidify the credibility of the thesis.

A virtual restatement of the thesis occurs here in an even more personal voice.

Works Cited

Cather, Willa. My Ántonia. 1918. New York: Signet Classics, 1994.

Dyck, Reginald. "Revisiting and Revising The West: Willa Cather's My Ántonia and Wright Morris' Plains Song." Modern Fiction Studies 36.1 (Spring 1990): 25–37.

Faulkner, William. Absalom, Absalom! 1936. New York: Random House, 1986.

Saposnik-Noire, Shelley. "The Silent Protagonist: The Unifying Presence of Landscape in Willa Cather's My Ántonia." The Midwest Quarterly 31.2 (Winter 1990): 171–79.

Saunders, Rebecca. "On Lamentation and Redistribution of Possessions: Faulkner's Absalom, Absalom! and The New South." Modern Fiction Studies 42.4 (Winter 1996): 730–62.

Full reference information is provided in MLA format, the preferred documentation style in the field of literary studies. This list of sources is referred to as "Works Cited," since only the sources specifically mentioned in the essay are included here.

INVESTIGATING THE GENRE SAMPLE

1. Compare and contrast this literary analysis to the first one. Discuss the strengths and weaknesses of each argument. Where do you feel Sandberg is most convincing? Where was Weicher most convincing?
2. Consider the contribution of the secondary sources to this literary analysis. What are the advantages and disadvantages of supporting your argument this way?
3. Note the multiple ways that Sandberg integrates the literary criticism within his text. Locate three or four different instances and discuss *how* he interweaves the material. Which seems to be most effective? Is it valuable to use multiple strategies? If so, why?

ABSTRACTS AND ANNOTATIONS

Very frequently academic writing demands that you summarize and/or narrow down extensive amounts of reading for specific purposes. Sometimes you need to know only the main points of a given text, and, therefore, a summary is sufficient. Sometimes for a larger project you need to attempt to reduce the sheer amount of reading material on a given topic by creating shorter texts to review later, and in that case, summaries will serve as very useful memory refreshers. Sometimes creating shorter texts enables you to provide other readers with a sampling of a text (yours or another author's), so that they can know the usefulness of it (or not) to their research or decision-making process.

A common type of academic summary is called an **abstract**. It literally "abstracts" or siphons off the key points. You may have noticed as a reader that abstracts frequently introduce an academic journal article or a comprehensive research report. They act as overviews or previews for a reader to determine if the entire text merits reading at that particular time for further detail. Thus, although the purpose for shrinking an original text can vary, the action of doing so is a common academic and even workplace endeavor.

This section will explore the general characteristics, audience expectations, and format features of two very common activities of text reduction—summaries of a sort—in academic writing: the *abstract* and the *annotated bibliography*. Following a general explanation of these genres, this section includes two student samples: an abstract of a reference book in the field of marketing and an annotated bibliography for a research project on the relationship between Shakespeare's *Hamlet* and popular culture. Explanatory notes will highlight features exhibited and strategies used within the texts.

An abstract is a brief document, anywhere from a paragraph to a page in length, usually about 100–250 words. It is a carefully crafted summary of a text—

most often a book, a section of a book, or a journal article. Some summaries may merely make descriptive statements like, "This book is about the current status of American-Iraqi relations following the war." Notice that this sentence tells what the article is about, but *not* what the author actually states *about what the article is about.* For instance, it does not tell if the relations between the two nations are improving or deteriorating or if the relations have been aided by the assistance of other mediating countries, etc. Therefore, this is not a useful statement for an abstract.

An academic abstract must do more than offer a simple description; it should provide, as the name implies, an "abstraction" of the key arguments or the central ideas of the text. Consequently, when you write an abstract, you need to work hard to avoid statements that merely indicate "what something is about" and instead provide statements of content that give the idea or arguments in a shortened format. For example, in contrast to the general descriptive statement above, an abstract might say, "This article argues for more aggressive American intervention by way of rebuilding the infrastructure of Iraqi cities." In other words, an effective abstract works hard to re-create the arguments of the text and to make every sentence count.

In addition to offering a comprehensive, short summary of the arguments or essence of a text, an abstract often includes a broad statement contextualizing the text and/or relating the text to a broader issue, and the abstract identifies the thesis or overall focus of the original text. Sometimes an abstract offers an indication of a particular text's contribution to the field of study or at least to the issue at hand. Depending on the context and circumstances of the abstract, it may specify the method(s) used by the author to come to his/her particular conclusion. And it should summarize any conclusions and/or recommendations offered in the original text. The first abstract that follows includes all of these features. You'll see them noted in the margin comments.

The second sample in this section is an annotated bibliography. An annotated bibliography is a slightly different type of "mini-version" of a text that is frequently seen in academia. It is used widely by different disciplines as a means of simultaneously providing a compilation of sources on a given topic *and* detailed summary information about the content of those source materials. Consequently, an annotated bibliography can be much more useful than an ordinary bibliography, which lists sources but offers no summary of their content.

Annotated bibliographies can vary greatly in length. They may consist of a few pages with five or six entries, serving as a resource for a short research paper, or they may be book-length documents, offering comprehensive information on a broad topic. But despite the variance in length, all annotated bibliographies essentially do the same thing: itemize a group of sources, provide complete reference information on a single topic, *and* supply a brief abstract for each source entry. Sometimes an annotated bibliography relates the contents to other sources being considered for the research. It may even include significant short quotes from the original text to help establish the author's main points, attitude, opinion, and/or style. Sometimes, as is the case below, a formal annotated bibliography begins with an introduction that contextualizes the research question and offers brief background information about the topic being researched.

Most often, annotated bibliographies consist of three distinct features: 1) a list of entries introduced with the full citation in a given documentation format (such as MLA or APA) to enable retrieval of the source in its entirety, 2) a brief abstract of the content of that source, and 3) an evaluative statement on the usefulness and/or quality of the given source for a particular audience or research project. Because of the inclusion of this third component, the annotated bibliography has an obvious bias. It is not intending to be totally neutral in the way many abstracts are; rather, it is offering a perspective on the content and value of a group of related resources.

Keep in mind that to write an annotated bibliography, as opposed to a simple bibliography, a writer must read (or at least carefully skim) the sources in order to compose effective abstracts. They are much more demanding to create than ordinary bibliographies, which simply list resources according to the format rules of some particular system of documentation. Not surprisingly, annotated bibliographies are also much more useful to a reader and/or potential researcher seeking information on a given topic.

The first sample, written by a student in a professional communications class, is a traditional abstract of a journal article. It offers a reduced version of the text by identifying the focus, the target audience, the primary arguments, and the recommendations. The second is an example of an annotated bibliography, which characteristically provides abstracts within each reference entry. Notice that this formal, annotated bibliography also includes a contextualizing introduction described above.

ABSTRACT 1

Business Communication

Abstract of "Ethics and Compliance in the Business of Life Insurance"

Dan MacDonald
Elmhurst College

The abstract opens by identifying in MLA format the text to be summarized.

The writer immediately summarizes the main focus of the article and clearly indicates the primary target audience.

Abstract of "Ethics and Compliance in the Business of Life Insurance"

Duska, Ronald. "Ethics and Compliance in the Business of Life Insurance." Journal of Insurance Regulation 18.2 (Winter 99): 246–57.

Abstract: The article highlights the drastic changes in the insurance field that are prompting field leaders to encourage a stronger focus on ethics in communication with clients, agents, and other members of the insurance community. Traditionally, compliance has been recognized as a ruling agent that ensures that the work of the representatives follows the law. Duska argues that compliance officers need to start focusing on ethics, as well as law. The ethics of compliance include: fulfilling one's responsibilities, being fair, and doing no unnecessary harm. Conventional phrases such as, "If it's legal, it's moral" and, "You can't legislate morality" are forces that work against compliance officers' new initiative. However, phrases such as, "Good ethics is good business" will improve and expand the ethics of compliance. Compliance officers are advised to use reward systems and external behavioral controls, as well as to demonstrate ethical attitudes personally, in order to inspire ethically sound behavior throughout the insurance community.

The author's main argument is indicated here.

Some detail is provided giving the reader a sense of both the content and tone of the article.

The abstract concludes by summarizing the primary recommendation offered in the article.

INVESTIGATING THE GENRE SAMPLE

1. What specific kinds of information does MacDonald succeed in providing?
2. An abstract should cover all key arguments of the journal article. Retrieve this particular article (note that you are provided with all the bibliographic information to do so) online. Read the article and evaluate the thoroughness of this abstract.
3. An abstract can serve a variety of purposes. Discuss what purposes are accomplished here.

ABSTRACT 2

Advanced Composition

Annotated Bibliography on Shakespeare's *Hamlet* and Popular Culture

Anne Kraley
Elmhurst College

Annotated Bibliography on Shakespeare's Hamlet and Popular Culture

A brief introduction offers a context for this annotated bibliography, which introduces the question of whether or not Shakespearean plays should be taught along with film versions from popular culture.

Although Shakespeare made his debut five centuries ago, the impact of his plays and poetry is still felt today in cultures across the globe. Shakespeare has grown, in many societies, to be the epitome of literature and poetry, with teachers introducing him to students at a young age and continually teaching his works through the college years. But Shakespeare is not only a part of the classroom setting; his works have heavily been transposed into modern, popular culture over the past hundreds of years through film. His plays have progressed in the film industry from the silent adaptations at the turn of the seventeenth century to complete modernization of them by bringing his texts into complete present settings. It has often been a dilemma for educators to find new ways to teach their students Shakespeare, and one question continues to be: "Should multimedia and popular culture be brought into the classroom?" as well as "How is this done and what are the benefits of doing this?"

With particular emphasis on Shakespeare's Hamlet, these sources offer insight into these questions with which educators struggle.

Each entry begins with a full reference citation; here it is in MLA format, appropriate for the discipline of English studies.

Beehler, Sharon A. "Making Media Matter in the Classroom." Ed. Ronald E. Salmone and James E. Davis. Teaching Shakespeare Into the Twenty-First Century. Athens: Ohio University Press, 1997. 247–54. Sharon Beehler, an educator, writes her piece as a guideline as well as a source for secondary teachers to gain tips on teaching Shakespeare. By her development and description of three plans—one, the artistic use of filmic devices; two, questions for students on filmed Shakespeare; and three, the recommended procedures for incorporating Shakespearean films and videos in the classroom—teachers can see the "how's and why's" of bringing multimedia into a classroom. As there are many critics of this method, Beehler makes this statement, "Whereas most English teachers are well versed in the complexities of literary text composition, they fail to realize that film composition is equally complex" (248). Through the study of the productions of Shakespeare on film, students and teachers not only have means of a deeper understanding of Shakespeare, they also learn what elements make up a film and what techniques are used by producers to get the desired effect. While Sharon Beehler is an advocate for this teaching method, she ends her piece admitting that "The strategies of film are indeed magical, but Shakespeare was able to create enchantment of another sort, through words uttered by actors on stage. Students who can appreciate this skill will have learned more about the powers of language and communication than all the computers in the world will ever convey" (254).

Coursen, H. R. "Uses of Media in Teaching Shakespeare." Ed. Ronald E.
    Salmone and James E. Davis. Teaching Shakespeare Into the Twenty-
    First Century. Athens: Ohio University Press, 1997. 193–200.
Contrary to the title of H. R. Coursen's piece, the majority of it consists of the comparison of film and television as well as a look into the roles of Shakespeare in popular culture. With the majority of Coursen's arguments not properly supported by specific examples, with few elements of "how media aids teaching," he does not offer a solid base of where to start and build curriculum. This source, not on the same par with Beehler, Kranz, or Felter, poorly states that media can be used to teach Shakespeare. Educators will find many other sources more informative and helpful.

The writer identifies an appropriate audience for this resource—this is commonly done in this genre.

A summary of the article is provided for the reader. This is the primary function of the genre of the annotated bibliography, enabling the reader to get an overview of related sources on the same topic without locating and reading/ skimming each one individually.

Notice that the writer includes a significant quote to provide further insight into the attitude of the author featured in this entry.

Another entry with complete reference information in MLA format is indicated.

Typical of this genre of the annotated bibliography, the author offers a judgment about the limited value of this resource relative to others considered.

Again the entry is provided in full MLA format. This, of course, enables the reader to locate the source for a complete reading.

A summary of the key points introduces the entry, which clearly focuses upon Felter's method of teaching Shakespeare through film.

The writer indicates the usefulness of this text for a very specific audience.

A third reference entry is provided in MLA format.

This summary emphasizes the intent of this author's approach.

Felter, Douglas P. "Exploring Shakespeare through the Cinematic Image: Seeing Hamlet." English Journal 82.4 (Apr. 1993): 61–64.

In this article, high school English teacher Douglas Felter shares his experiences and methods of using film to enhance his students' understanding and appreciation of Shakespeare, particularly in their study of Hamlet. He explains these methods for educators, in hopes to alleviate the intimidation they may find in teaching Shakespeare. Felter reformed his teaching process for the students so that they could finally "discover the mysteries of Hamlet," and by these discoveries "they would also know the pleasure of Hamlet" (61). By using film in the classroom, Felter adapts a medium adolescents today easily relate to into an effective teaching tool. Through this method, Felter states: "[1] I wanted students to experience Shakespeare's classic on a more personal level than they had previously; [2] I wanted them to employ higher-order thinking skills in the pursuit of that goal; [3] I wanted the cinematic image to be the conduit for their exploration" (61). Through bringing in multiple versions of Hamlet, analyzing the same scenes from each, Felter found great results in his students' comprehension and appreciation of Shakespeare. This article is great for educators who are looking for new and interesting teaching techniques to elicit students' better understanding of the "world of Shakespeare."

Kranz, David. "Cinematic Elements in Shakespearean Film: A Glossary." Teaching Shakespeare Through Performance. Ed. Milla Cozart Riggio. New York: The Modern Language Association of America, 1999. 341–60.

Dedicated towards teachers of both high school and college levels, the purpose of David Kranz's entry is to have teachers become aware that they can and should utilize students' natural familiarity with film to aid in the class coverage of Shakespeare. While Kranz gives pointers and instructions on how to do this effectively, he emphasizes the necessity of assuring the text's importance. He does not intend this teaching method to replace the study of the text, but to enhance it. Kranz's methods include having the students critically analyze the make-up of particular scenes by looking at the possible camera angles, the types of shot (long, deep-focus, medium, close-up, etc.), the lenses used, speed distortion (fast motion, slow motion, reverse motion, and freeze frame), and finally camera movement (344–50). By doing this, students are able to grasp a deeper understanding of the text by the connotation these effects bring to the scene.

Lake, James H. "The Effects of Primacy and Recency upon Audience
    Response to Five Film Versions of Shakespeare's Hamlet."
    Literature and Film Quarterly 28.2 (2002): 112–17.

James Lake uses a recent study as a basis for his article, which was conducted at the University of Auckland, that shows how the strength of primacy and recency (audience response to first and last impressions) affects the score of student papers, and how this artistic device applies to film. In other words, he wants to show how these effects can be used in film to "convey a sense of artistic coherence" (112). Intended for general educated readers, Lake proves, through comparing five film adaptations of Hamlet, that Shakespeare incorporates the effect of primacy and recency, the "ancient rhetorical strategy" of synthesis, in his works originally for his timeless audiences (115). Furthermore, Lake also proves that the same "unconscious" responses from the audience can easily be elicited by the use of this concept by producers and directors by using reoccurring, symbolic images throughout their film, thus giving it "artistic coherence" (113,112).

Li Lan, Yong. "Returning to Naples: Seeing the End in Shakespeare Film
    Adaptation." Literature Film Quarterly 29.2: 128–34.

This source is a great explanation, full of detailed, accurate examples, of how cinema is able to enhance the text of Shakespeare. This one source

---

Here the annotator offers a summary of the primary methods involved and then provides an evaluation of the usefulness of the methods.

A fourth reference entry in MLA format is provided.

Once again, the writer summarizes the primary method and intent of this article. Notice how this entry is further enhanced by the use of a few direct quotes. This gives the reader a sense of the voice and flavor of the entry, not merely the content, which the summary provides.

An additional reference entry is presented appropriately in MLA format.

This entry particularly emphasizes the value of this resource.

A useful component here is the writer's indication of the relationship between this source and others on the topic.

Of course, the entry, as is demanded by this genre, summarizes key points of the article.

Note the emphasis on the intended audience. Many resources are very useful, but only for a specific audience. Therefore, this is important information for a reader.

Another reference entry is indicated in the appropriate format.

This entry is a Web resource. Providing a reader with a variety of types of resources in an annotated bibliography is valuable.

affirms all the arguments made by the diverse educators who promote the integration of film into their Shakespeare lessons. Yong Li Lan's article expands the concept of the effect of recency that was mentioned in James H. Lake's article by showing how "the medium of cinematic space and visuality [can be used] as a medium of revising [Shakespeare plays] through re-visioning" (128). A few major points that Li Lan states are: the camera serves the audience in two ways as it presents the scene to "our eyes" as well as "pretends to be our eyes," specific editing techniques build up "cliffhangers" beyond the text, and the conclusion of a production, theatrical or cinematic, "is central and defining to how it is remembered" (129). The latter is easily captured by film's ability to have "mobile framing and editing between simultaneous spaces [that] combine to re-tell and re-sell Shakespeare in terms of the performance of image" (129). Li Lan also states how the director and producer use strategies such as the long camera take, "the long runway" perspective, the "slow track-and-crane" out of the scene by the camera, and the soundtrack to "promote a self-consciousness about the desire for ritual re-watching," meaning the audience repeatedly reinforces the images that are reoccurring in their mind with the real scene in hope that the same initial emotions are triggered. This article is great for any individual who doubts how film can make a difference in the education of students.

Murphy, Debra. 1990 Hamlet Directed by Franco Zeffirelli Starring Mel Gibson. 2002. <http://www.bardolatry.com/gibhani.htm 1-3>. This source is one of the many commentaries found on the web page bardolatry.com. This particular commentary reviews Franco Zeffirelli's adaptation of Hamlet. From the first paragraph, where she states that this version is a "mutilation of Shakespeare's text," one would assume that Debra Murphy's opinion of this film is negative but as the commentary continues, Murphy shows readers what aspects make

Zeffirelli's film a work of true art. She comments on the great use of the sets by the actors, Zeffirelli's gift of capturing past time periods and cultures, as well as the deep and emotional performances of the characters, especially that of Mel Gibson as Hamlet. Murphy credits Gibson as "one of the few Hamlets I've seen who actually thinks his words as he speaks them" (2). Not only does Murphy comment on the film itself, she compares and contrasts it to other filmed versions of this famous Shakespeare tragedy, such as Kenneth Branagh and Michael Almereyda's. This source is useful for any student studying Hamlet, as it displays both the negative and positive attributes of the film.

> The summary of the main points is again followed by a comment on the appropriate audience for this entry.

Walton, W. G., Jr. "Bringing Performances into Classrooms Through Multiple Media." Teaching Shakespeare Through Performance. Ed. Milla Cozart Riggio. New York: The Modern Language Association of America, 1999. 321–40.

> A final reference entry is given in appropriate MLA format.

Once again, this entry is an educator trying to educate other educators of the endless world of Shakespeare and how to better elicit appreciation from students. Similar to the beliefs of many previous educators such as Felter and Kranz, W. G. Walton states from the start the importance of the original productions of Shakespeare's works, and secondly how those are transposed into the modern versions audiences view on television and film. Different from Felter's article, however, is the fact that a portion of Walton's entry deals with having students recognize the difference between forms of multimedia, particularly of film and television, by contrasting the "conditions of production" (322). These include lighting, sound, and composition and camera placement and movement, very similar to the glossary David Kranz provides in his entry (323, 324). Within his article, Walton also expresses his views on the practicality of bringing videocassettes into the classroom.

> The entry extends the summary and offers comparisons and contrasts to other entries. This is frequently done within the genre of the annotated bibliography, allowing the reader to make connections and to obtain a broader sense of the scholarly discussion of a particular topic.

INVESTIGATING THE GENRE SAMPLE

1. An annotated bibliography as a genre can present more than a collection of abstracts of published articles and chapters; it can also offer an evaluation of the literature for a particular audience. What audience does Anne Kraley seem to be writing to? How do you know?
2. In a good annotated bibliography, the writer will make some reference to the main idea and the audience in each entry. Can you notice Kraley accomplishing this goal in each of her sections? Are there specific sections where this reference should be clearer?
3. Why do you think Kraley begins to compare and contrast the usefulness of the sources once she has offered abstracts of a few of them?

INFORMATIVE REPORTS

Some writing assignments and projects require you not to review, summarize, or respond to readings, nor to generate an argument and write a critical paper supporting it, but instead simply to read widely about a subject and to write an **informative report** sharing with your readers what you have learned. An informative report may resemble a position paper in scope and audience, but it differs in purpose and often in format. A position paper generates and supports an argumentative thesis, while a report teaches readers about a body of information that they did not know prior to reading the paper. In an informative report, as the name implies, you will share information, but you will often not take a particular stance or position.

Three important concepts underlie the writing of an informative report, all of them related to accommodating an audience of curious generalists, of careful users of English, and of relatively well-informed specialists. The first is surprise value. No one really enjoys reading about information that he or she already knows, so an informative report should not dwell on what amounts to "old news" for its readers. When you read widely about a subject in order to write an informative report, you should constantly look for facts, ideas, data, and perspectives of which you think your readers are probably unaware. As you read, play a game with yourself: Imagine that you are one of your readers, and for every bit of material you learn, ask yourself if you could truthfully say, "Gee, I didn't know that." Facts, ideas, data, and perspectives that truly elicit this response can be said to have surprise value for your readers. They will constitute the most important parts of your informative report.

The second underlying principle in an informative report is comprehensiveness. When you write informatively about any subject, there may be certain angles and perspectives that your readers expect you to address, depending on how familiar they are with your subject. Addressing these angles and perspectives gives your paper a sense of comprehensiveness, a sense that you have covered the territory that your readers expected you to cover. For example, if you were writing an informative report about political movements that either threatened or led to the dissolution of Communist governments, your readers would expect you to pay at least some attention to the Tiananmen Square riot in the People's Republic of China in 1989, the collapse of Communist governments in Eastern Europe in 1989 and 1990, and the dismantling of the Union of Soviet Socialist Republics in 1991. Accounts of the political movements behind these events would probably not hold much surprise value for your readers, but they would consider incomplete any report that failed to mention them.

Finally, an informative report depends on supportability. When you report information, you cannot simply assert data, ideas, and perspectives to be true. You need to support your assertions. The most informative material in a report is that which you can back up with examples and illustrations that verify it. Only then will it be judged as credible by interested readers.

You can use the principles of surprise value, comprehensiveness, and supportability to organize an effective informative report in three sections: an introduction, a body, and a conclusion.

In the introduction, you should contextualize the subject of your report by letting the reader know what question or questions you addressed in preparing to write it. Then you should explain the one fact, idea, perspective, or piece of data that you think has the most surprise value for your reader. In other words, start with something that is really news. Explain this element in detail, supporting your explanation with examples and illustrations.

The body of an informative report can have two subsections. In the first, explain what other items, beyond the one developed in the introduction, have surprise value, and support your explanations with examples and illustrations. In the second, consider the concept of comprehensiveness and ask yourself, "What else do my readers expect me to explain about this subject?" Then offer explanations of this material, supporting them with examples and illustrations.

The conclusion of an informative report will briefly summarize key points. Furthermore, you can conclude an informative report by addressing the "so what?" questions for your readers. What would you propose that your readers do with the information you have just reported to them? What are the implications of your report for future investigations of this subject? What new perspectives have you provided? Brainstorming about these questions will help you generate an interesting conclusion.

Informative reports can vary somewhat widely in format, according to the conventions of different academic disciplines. You may be assigned a report without any designations regarding specific subsections. In that case, the format is probably entirely your choice. However, some fields have prescribed formats for informative reports. In business classes, for example, if asked to write an informative report on the proceedings of the volatile stock market in the first two years of the twenty-first century, you would be expected to include a section commonly used in the workplace known as the "Executive Summary." As the name implies, it offers a shortened version for executives (or any other interested, but busy, readers), enabling a quick scan of the highlights of the report. Chances are that an informative report for your history class would never include an Executive Summary, but it may require a sort of academic version of it called an "abstract." (See the earlier section on abstracts for more details.) When assigned an informative report in any class, it is wise to inquire about format specifics.

You will notice several differences in the two student sample informative reports that follow. The first one, written by a geography major, reports on the gray wolf in Yellowstone National Park. The second report, written by an Elmhurst College student for a professional writing class, examines the history, activities, and trends within her chosen career field of communication studies. While the content and format clearly vary, both reports extend valuable information to their readers, incorporating the principles of surprise value (even if not in an especially dramatic fashion), comprehensiveness, and supportability discussed above.

INFORMATIVE REPORT 1

Geography

A History and Evaluation of the Reintroduction of the Gray Wolf to Yellowstone National Park

Jill Damato
University of Illinois at Chicago

A very descriptive, informative title is provided. Often titles such as this also serve as a "mini-abstract" for readers.

An abstract includes a brief summary of the purpose and results of the research, enabling a reader to know immediately if this is a useful report for his or her research.

The surprise value of these statistics may encourage further reading.

The introduction explains the background of this research issue.

A History and Evaluation of the Reintroduction of the Gray Wolf to

Yellowstone National Park

Abstract. The progress of the reintroduction of the experimental gray wolf populations into Yellowstone National Park was evaluated in order to determine if the program was a success, as measured by original program goal standards. The 1995 starter population consisted of fourteen individuals. Successful breeding, few deaths, and additional wolves released in 1996 brought the total population to close to 100 within a three-year period. The majority of the packs have stayed within park boundaries. Some conflict has occurred between wolves and coyotes, as well as between wolf packs. There were few problems with wolves attacking local livestock, a major concern of the public and park officials. These findings support the hypothesis that the wolves have stayed within program expectations and are thus far a success.

Introduction

In March 1995, fourteen gray wolves were released into Yellowstone National Park. The reintroduction of the gray wolf to Yellowstone National

Park and central Idaho is an attempt to establish an ecosystem that has not existed for close to half a century. Gray wolves had a functioning role in the northern Rockies ecosystem but were purposely exterminated by government order from the northern Rockies by the 1930s because they were seen as a threat to livestock. Today, for the most part, people want the gray wolf returned to that region of the United States. The essential question is this: "Is their return possible in *today's* Yellowstone?"

The purpose of this paper is to evaluate the events that have happened with the wolf packs of Yellowstone since the beginning of the program and to determine if the packs have been a success so far. The actions of the packs—their activity, reproduction, mobility patterns, interactions among themselves as well as other park inhabitants—play a key role in whether this experimental program becomes a success or a nuisance. From this, possible predictions about the future of the program can be made.

Literature Review

The reintroduction of the gray wolf to Yellowstone National Park (YNP) and central Idaho is being done with a "nonessential experimental population" (Bangs and Fritts, 1996). This classification means that ". . . in areas without resident wolf packs, liberal management would be allowed to address local concerns about livestock, land use restrictions and ungulate populations" (U.S. Fish and Wildlife Service, 1993, p 1). This design allows for more flexibility and provides more options to government agencies depending on the situation (Yellowstone National Park Wolf Restoration Fund, 1996). In an experimental population, information is only known once the packs have done something, biologists have observed, recorded and analyzed it, and it is then made public.

The effort to reintroduce wolves into YNP and central Idaho began in 1971 with an interagency meeting (Bangs and Fritts, 1996), although

Note that the purpose of this report is clearly delineated. This kind of direct statement of thesis is preferred in many science and social science reports because of the clarity and efficiency it provides. (In the humanities, however, often such a direct indication of thesis, i.e., "This paper is about X," is generally frowned upon for being less than creative or engaging. In other words, different definitions of "good style" are at work in different genres.)

Introductory material continues with this review of relevant literature on the issue of the gray wolves.

wolves were not actually in either of the two areas until 1995. The state that the wolves reside in is the one that manages the packs. Management was initially under the guidance of the U.S. Fish and Wildlife Service but has since been taken over by the National Park System.

Events have been carefully documented since the program began. Location sites and release methods as well as pack formation, numbers, and movement have been recorded. Initially fourteen wolves were brought in from Canada and released into YNP. They formed three packs and produced nine pups (between two litters) in the first year (Yellowstone National Park, 1995). By the end of 1996, eleven wolves had died and ten additional wolves were brought in from Montana (Yellowstone National Park, 1997). As of September 1997, there were a total of eleven packs within and around the park. Over ninety individuals make up the entire population and eight females are producing pups (Wolfstock Foundation, 1997). The original plan of this reintroduction effort was to establish ten breeding pairs of wolves for three consecutive years (U.S. Fish and Wildlife Service, 1993). This plan was terminated in 1996 because of reduced funding and the fact that the wolves had early breeding success, an unexpected result (Yellowstone National Park, 1997).

Methodology

Data on the wolf reintroduction effort in Yellowstone National Park is limited because the project is only a few years old. A majority of the data available is from narrative books and from short articles in journals or park newsletters. The biggest limitation in finding wolf restoration data is that current information is hard to obtain. Since the program studies animals in a relatively remote area, updates must be passed down through various channels, which takes time, before reaching the public. Human resources, such as park employees, and computer resources such as the Internet, were of great help in finding out about the most recent events. For more historical facts, government documents, science journals, and government publications, such as

This extensive literature review adds to the "comprehensiveness" of this report, and it also serves as an argument for justifying the value and necessity of the current report/research. (Think of a literature review as a rationale for a new project.)

Methods of research on the reintroduction of the gray wolf are explained in detail. Methodology is very important to the credibility of an informative report, especially in the sciences.

Environmental Impact statements, were key resources. Very few books have more recent information with the exception of one by Thomas McNamee; the author has been on the project since its beginning and published his observations in May of 1997.

Findings

Gray wolves (*Canis lupus*) were original inhabitants of the northern Rockies, including the area that Yellowstone National Park now occupies. Yellowstone was established in 1872 and the last wild wolves in the park, two pups in the Soda Butte Creek area, were poisoned in 1924. All wolves in the area were being exterminated at this time under government order because they were seen as a threat to livestock of the people migrating into the region. Since the extermination, a few lone wolves have traveled into northwest Wyoming, including Yellowstone, from northern states and Canada. However, none of these wild wolves stayed or formed any packs. Therefore, from an ecological standpoint, no wolves had influence on the functioning of the greater Yellowstone ecosystem (Maughan 1997, p 1).

Since 1971, various groups have advocated the return of the gray wolf to Yellowstone. The general feeling is that wolves should be returned to Yellowstone because they were original inhabitants and would most likely have remained in the area if not for a policy of extermination. In January 1995, after an enormous amount of red tape and debating, fourteen wolves were captured in Alberta, Canada, and brought into Yellowstone.

These wolves are designated as "non-essential-experimental" under section 10(1) of the Federal Endangered Species Act. This designation allows for restoration while at the same time allowing for flexible management to deal with local public concerns. For example, there are no land restrictions for the wolves, but if a wolf were to be severely affecting wild ungulate populations or attacking domestic animals, other than livestock, on private land three times in a calendar

Acknowledging key sources of information and support also adds ethical and intellectual credibility to a report.

This lengthy section summarizes all of the major findings/results of the reintroduction project; in other words, it is truly the "information" of this informative report.

Valuable background information is provided.

year, the wolves would be removed. Furthermore, landowners or public grazing permittees could legally harass wolves in a noninjurious manner when the wolves are near or harassing their livestock. If wolves were actually killing livestock, they could be killed, legally, by the livestock owners. Any livestock owner that has an animal killed and has proof that it was done by a wolf is reimbursed for the dead animal's value by a private fund.

Details about each group of wolves are examined.

The fourteen wolves brought into Yellowstone were divided among three acclimation enclosures—the Rose Creek, Crystal Creek, and the Soda Butte enclosures. Each enclosure was named after a part of the Lamar Valley, which is in the northeast portion of Yellowstone, where they were located. Subsequently, each of the packs that lived in their respective enclosure was given that enclosure's name. These wolves were part of a "soft-release" program. The wolves were kept together for three months in an enclosure. This gave them time to become familiar with the local sounds, smells, and diet as well as time to either establish or restructure their pack hierarchies and possibly mate. Food was provided for them, but human interaction was kept to a minimum. This method is the opposite of a "hard-release," which was the release method used with the Idaho wolves. Here, the wolves are simply released from their traveling crates as soon as they reach the release site.

The fourteen wolves released in 1995 formed four packs. Two litters were produced, totaling nine pups. All packs tended to stay near their release sites, with some actually refusing to leave the enclosures for weeks after openings were made. Biologists first thought that the wolves were not leaving because the only available opening was where food was dropped off and the wolves may have been associating humans with it. Two holes were then cut into the fencing towards the back of the enclosures and motion sensors were placed on them. Even then the wolves would venture out of the enclosure but would then return. It took almost five weeks for them to wholly leave. There was the exception of the Rose Creek pack though. This pack consisted of a male and female, originally of different packs, that had been paired by biologists and the yearling daughter of the female. The yearling was left behind and the adult pair almost immediately moved northward out of park boundaries upon release. The male was illegally killed and the female, along with the pups that she had given birth to, was captured and brought back into the park. She has since paired up with another male and has produced more pups.

In 1996, seventeen additional wolves were captured in Canada and released into Yellowstone. Three packs formed out of this population. By the end of the year, eleven wolves, including the 1995 population, had died of various causes—accidental, shootings, and natural. Despite that mortality level, forty still roamed the park. Since the 1996 release, twenty-three pups have been born—this from just four packs. For 1997 there are six existing groups that could produce pups. As of May 1997, the number of wolves in Yellowstone was close to 100 (Maughan, 1997).

The relationship of wolves and livestock was one of the most controversial aspects of the reintroduction program. The local economy is largely based on cattle and sheep ranching. Ranchers who opposed the program feared their livestock would serve as easy prey. Biologists predicted an average yearly loss of 19 cattle and 68 sheep per year with a population of 100 individuals. To date, there have been 102 sheep killed and 10 calves, as well as one domestic dog. It should be noted that 12 of the 102 sheep and 5 of the 10 calves were all killed by an individual wolf during fall 1997. This means that wolf 27F alone is responsible for 12% of all sheep mortalities and 50% of calf mortalities.

Wolf interaction with other park inhabitants was another concern. Elk became the primary prey of wolves, as predicted. Elk are abundant in and around the park and their populations could withstand the numbers

Note the numerous reasons and details given to support the rationale for reintroducing the gray wolf into the park. Keep in mind that though this is primarily a report to provide information, an argument of a sort is always present in any discourse. Here the use of detail supports her underlying argument that this is a crucial issue needing attention.

This indicates a particularly controversial aspect of the program, providing further insight into the author's perspective.

being killed. A few bison were also killed, but not as many as anticipated.

Comments on the relationships between various animal groups and the wolves add significant information for the reader by expanding the context of this issue.

Interaction between wolf packs and coyote packs has been of interest. Coyotes and wolves have not adjusted well to sharing territories. In 1995 and early 1996 researchers documented twelve coyote mortalities, eleven of which were at or near elk that had been killed by wolves. An additional six coyote carcasses were found near other wolf-killed elk, but attacks on these coyotes were not actually witnessed. Preliminary studies show that at least five out of the ten coyote packs in the Lamar Valley have been socially and spatially disrupted since the wolf release. Three of the ten coyote packs have disintegrated; no such disruption of coyote packs has been recorded in the past twelve years. Biologists believe that the wolves view the coyotes as competition and not prey. (Crabtree and Sheldon, 1996). At least three wolves have been killed by other wolves in the park due to territorial disputes.

When the 1995 wolves were first released, there was concern because at one point or another each pack headed northward out of park boundaries. One pack went as far as 150 miles out and back, but with the exception of one pack, all returned to Yellowstone of their own accord. The exception was a mated pair that left the park and denned on private ranching land. The male was illegally shot after they arrived, and the female would not leave because of her pups. Park biologists retrieved her and the litter. She has since established a pack with another male and has not left the park. Some of the 1996 release wolves also traveled out of park boundaries, usually northeastward. However, these wolves were brought back into the park by officials. Very recently, in October/November 1997 one of the last packs to establish themselves, the Washakie pack, became notorious for their excursions out of the park and their escapes out of the enclosures when brought back in. Yellowstone is debating what action to take next with this pack.

All wolf groups primarily use Yellowstone resources, but this is because of management actions that return wolves to the park (Bangs and Fritts, 1996). Wolf groups released in Yellowstone tended to stay together and restrict their movements more than the Idaho wolves (Bangs and Fritts, 1996). Yellowstone wolves traveled an average of 22 km from their initial release sites and quickly formed home ranges.

The goal of this restoration program was to establish ten breeding pairs for a period of three consecutive years. With ten breeding pairs the population should reach and remain at 100 individuals. When this has been attained, the gray wolf may be taken off the endangered species list and their management relinquished to the states. In May 1997, there were close to 100 wolves in the park, a number that will presumably be reduced by mortality. When pups are born in 1998, a stable population is expected to be established. Obviously, the project is well ahead of schedule as far as breeding success. However, due to political difficulties it is unclear what status the wolves will be given when the goal population is reached. The project is also under budget and without as much conflict as anticipated. Thus far, program funding has been reduced and planned releases into the park have been suspended, since the wolves seem to be sustaining their own numbers.

Discussion/Conclusion

From the available material, it can be concluded that the reintroduction of the gray wolf to Yellowstone National Park has been a success by the standards originally set. The wolves have exceeded expectations as far as breeding success; they are years ahead of schedule. They have also been able to keep negative interaction with local livestock, an issue of enormous debate and concern, to a minimum, with the exception of one individual wolf. In regards to pack travel, the wolves have kept their mobility within reason; expecting to maintain complete control over wild animal movement is not realistic. When the

An informative report almost always addresses issues of goals for a particular issue/topic. Readers need this to make a meaningful decision about the information presented in the report.

Information on the current status of the program is provided for the reader.

A very brief conclusion section in this report provides only minimal interpretation of the results, indicating the success of the project and the status of future plans.

Contrast this to the discussion/conclusion section of many scientific research reports.

wolves have left the park, a phenomenon anticipated by program officials, they were simply brought back. The project met and surpassed the original goals sooner than expected.

References

Bangs E, Fritts S. 1996. Reintroducing the gray wolf to Idaho and Yellowstone National Park. Wildlife Soc Bull 24(3): 402–413.

Crabtree R, Sheldon J. 1996. Researchers observe wolf-coyote interactions. The Buffalo Chip Newsletter, Yellowstone National Park. 5–6.

Maughan R. Wolf page. Hp. 18 Nov 1997 [last update] Online. Snake River Valley Net. Available: http://www.poky.srv.net/~jjmrm/maughan.html

McNamee T. 1997. The return of the wolf to Yellowstone. New York: Henry Holt and Company.

U.S. Fish and Wildlife Service. 1993. The reintroduction of gray wolves to Yellowstone National Park and central Idaho. Environmental Impact Statement Summary. Helena, Montana: U.S. Fish and Wildlife Service.

Yellowstone National Park. 1995. Natural Resources Programs, wolf restoration. Yellowstone Center for resources annual report: (5) 9–67.

Yellowstone National Park. 1997. Chronology of wolf recovery related to Yellowstone National Park. Unpublished report: 1–9.

Yellowstone National Park Wolf Restoration Fund. 1996. How are they doing? A status report. Unpublished report: 3.

Wolfstock Foundation (author unknown). 1997. The Yellowstone wolves. The Yellowstone Wolf Tracker. 1: n.p.

Sources are documented in CSE (Council of Scientific Editors) style, which is common to some sciences; note the limited use of punctuation compared to MLA or APA style. (This may reflect scientists' fascination with formulas and numeric shortcut notations, rather than a concentration on details of narrative style.)

INVESTIGATING THE GENRE SAMPLE

1. As a genre, the informative report can sometimes accomplish other purposes besides informing the audience, and Jill Damato acknowledges that her paper is not only informative but also evaluative. What features of the paper, however, make it *primarily* an informative report?
2. When producing an informative report, a writer often uses headings to organize the information for the reader. What do you think of the headings Damato uses? What might she do to make the headings even more descriptive?
3. When informative reports are written for an audience of readers in a particular discipline, they frequently use specialized terminology that those readers expect to see in papers in their field. Notice, for example, Damato's use of the term *acclimation enclosures* in the "Findings" section. Where else do you see her employing specialized disciplinary terminology?

This business report begins with a transmittal memorandum. This type of memo is frequently used to introduce professional reports, especially in the corporate world. It serves to officially "deliver" the report to the appropriate party, most often someone in authority who has requested specific information. It briefly indicates the purpose and contents of the report to follow.

Note: In reports for an external party, a letter format is used, and then this document is referred to as the "letter of transmittal." In either case, it literally "transmits" the informative report.

Note that this document also includes an indication of the author's willingness to further assist and adopts a very conciliatory tone.

INFORMATIVE REPORT 2

Communication Studies

Interdisciplinary Communication

Agata Trzaska
Elmhurst College

Interdisciplinary Communication Memo

To: Dr. XXX

From: Agata Trzaska

Date: November 7, 2002

Subject: Interdisciplinary Communication

Enclosed is the completed report on the Interdisciplinary Communication major. To provide assistance to all new students, this report examines Elmhurst College requirements and possible career choices for the future. All the findings and recommendations found in this report are based on extensive library and Internet research, interviews with professionals, and my personal experience as an interdisciplinary communication student.

After a general overview of courses that students need to complete in order to receive a bachelor degree, I present in-depth analyses of skills, responsibilities and employment of three communication-related careers: public relations specialists, editors, and technical communicators. In addition, to help students focus on the career path that most suits their needs and interest, I indicate some of the differences between corporate and non-profit organizations. Finally, I emphasize benefits of joining professional associations and provide contact information for four organizations relevant to communication students.

I hope this report provides answers to most of the questions that students grapple with prior to selecting Interdisciplinary Communication as their major. If any of them needs further assistance I can be reached by email address.

INTERDISCIPLINARY COMMUNICATION

Prepared by Agata Trzaska

November 7, 2002

Elmhurst College
Professor X

A formal title page follows the memo (or letter) of transmittal.

Companies and institutions frequently expect a very formal document for reports. Sometimes it is bound for sturdy filing for future reference.

The table of contents, which always appears on a separate page, itemizes all main sections and subsections of the report. Notice the differences in fonts. Fonts are varied within the document, but consistent by the "level" of the subheading. This then serves as a way of indicating the relationship of the parts to each other and to the whole document.

TABLE OF CONTENTS

*(Page numbers match only original student paper.)

ABSTRACT

This report scrutinizes the nature of Interdisciplinary Communication for prospective students. Because this major integrates departments of humanities and business, students have an opportunity to choose among several careers. This report looks closer at three communication-related career options: public relations, editing, and technical communication. I examined qualifications, duties, and working conditions, so that students can easily match their skills and interest against the requirements for each of these occupations. Additionally, to help students get focused on the most suitable career, I highlighted differences between corporate and non-profit organizations. In this report students will also find contact information for four professional organizations related to Interdisciplinary Communication. Recommendations for students pursuing this major are provided.

The abstract provides a *very* brief summary of the purpose and scope of the report. It allows a reader to gain a quick glimpse of the report to determine if it merits a detailed read or not, depending on the responsibilities and/or interests of a given audience.

Some formal reports exclude the abstract in lieu of the more detailed "Executive Summary," which follows on the next page. Some, as seen here, include both to meet different audience needs.

An executive summary is standard in most formal reports for professional environments. As the name implies, this document affords a short narration for busy, upper-level executives, some of whom are only marginally involved in projects and merely want an overview and recommendations.

Notice that this document includes the purpose of the report, the intended audience, and a fairly detailed overview of the content subsections.

EXECUTIVE SUMMARY

This report examines the nature of Interdisciplinary Communication. Because selecting a major is one of the most important and difficult decisions that students face, this report addresses some of the uncertainties and confusions in regards to the field of Interdisciplinary Communication.

This report provides an overview of Elmhurst College requirements that students need to meet to earn a bachelor degree in Interdisciplinary Communication. Because Interdisciplinary Communication is a major that integrates departments of humanities and business, communication students are able to pursue their careers in public relations, journalism, editing, publishing, marketing, consulting, or technical communication. This report offers in-depth analyses of three communication-related career options: public relations specialists, editors, and technical communicators.

Analyses of skills, duties, and employment of public relations professionals, editors and technical communicators indicate some overarching similarities, as well as subtle differences between each profession. Among must-have skills, strong communication skills and good judgment are crucial for all three careers. Although communication products slightly differ from profession to profession, they all involve a great deal of writing. As estimated in *Occupational Outlook Handbook*, the employment of public relations specialists, editors and technical communicators should increase through 2010.

In addition, this report indicates that in order to become well-prepared for the first entry-level position, students need to enrich their academic experience through hands-on experience. Employers expect that students complete one or two internships prior to finishing their study. Ideally, internships should introduce communication students to writing and/or editing external and internal publications, such as news releases, newsletters, brochures, and planning special events, for instance fundraisers and promotions.

This report also reveals benefits of joining professional organizations. Through participation in numerous national programs and conventions organized by professional associations, students have an opportunity to stay up-to-date with current issues and trends in the industry, and make professional contacts.

Moreover, this report distinguishes between corporate and non-profit organizations. While non-profit organizations have lower salaries than corporate companies, jobs in non-profit institutions offer higher personal rewards. While it usually takes longer to be promoted in large corporate companies, they often finance employees' trainings and seminars.

Finally, this report offers several recommendations to communication students. Membership in professional organizations, participation in the EC Shadowing Program, careful selection of electives, as well as frequent visits to Career Services help students to make the most of their Interdisciplinary Communication major.

Typically, this document also includes the recommendations being made based upon the research findings.

You may notice a fair amount of repetition within the so-called front matter of this business report. This is typical since different sections are often being read by different individuals. Key points need to be included in all sections of the report.

The first section of the actual report is always the introduction. Most often it is simply labeled as "Introduction."

The audience and purpose of the report are emphasized again.

INTRODUCTION

Singling out one major out of forty-eight choices that Elmhurst College offers might be a difficult and confusing process for many undergraduate students. This report explores the essence of Interdisciplinary Communication, a major that bridges more than one academic department. Approaching the day of my graduation, I would like to use the experience I gained as an Interdisciplinary Communication student, as well as extensive library research, and guide new students through the ins and outs of this major.

First, this report spells out Elmhurst College requirements that students need to meet in order to receive a bachelor degree in Interdisciplinary Communication. Although students need to pay close attention to the core of seven courses that are mandatory, there are three areas of concentration to choose from: Track one-Mass Communications, Track Two-Advertising/Public Relations, and Track Three-Organizational/Human Resources. Because I centered my education on Track Two, this report focuses on Track Two-Advertising/Public Relations in a greater detail.

Indications of the focus areas within the major are provided.

In addition, this report explores a wide range of occupations for which Interdisciplinary Communication prepares students. Although all these careers are bridged by similar skills, analysis of subtle differences in responsibilities and working conditions can help students to make the right choice.

An explanation of the choice of subsections is given here, providing the reader with both a "sneak peek" and a rationale.

Apart from must-have skills, duties, and employment information for each career, another factor that students need to consider is the type and nature of an organization at which they will look for employment. That's why this report offers an overview of differences between non-profit and corporate organizations.

ANALYSIS OF INTERDISCIPLINARY COMMUNICATION

ELMHURST COLLEGE REQUIREMENTS/OFFERINGS

Core

As pointed out in the Elmhurst College Catalog, each student majoring in Interdisciplinary Communication is required to take a core of seven courses (193):

- Design Studio
- Composition III
- Visual Communication
- The Nature of Language
- Interpersonal Communication
- Communication Theory
- Writing in Professional Fields OR Theory and Research

These seven courses are the same for all three tracks because they give communication students the opportunity to polish their speaking and writing skills, develop a strong sense of visual and aesthetic appeal, and stimulate analytical thinking.

Areas of Concentration

Depending on the area of concentration, students are required to select five courses, which represent a minimum of two departments. Courses in Track Two--Advertising/Public Relations range from Graphic Design through Marketing, Advertising, Mass Communication, and Digital Imaging.

Internships

However, apart from the solid liberal arts and business background received in college, employers expect communication students to have some hands-on experience. This is why the Elmhurst College faculty highly recommends that all students pursue at least one internship during the course of their study. Since internships are often the first job experiences that students acquire, they help them in getting the first job after graduation. Moreover, internships provide students with the opportunity to "try out" the career they selected before it is too late to make any changes in their majors. During their internships students meet and interact with individuals whose careers are somewhat related

---

Title of the first major section of the body of the report—it is given a content-specific name.

Note that the first subheading of this section is indicated by an underlined, capitalized, centered title. Other such subheadings will follow.

Still another level is established with the use of nonunderlined, left-justified italics titles (i.e., "*Core*").

Note: Numerous patterns of headings and subheadings and sub-subheadings are possible in this type of report. The important thing is to label sections of comparable weight in the same manner and to be consistent throughout the report.

This first section indicates three subareas of the college requirements and offerings: core course requirements, available areas of concentration, and internships.

to their own interests. This allows for networking, as well as exploring other career choices available to communication students. For instance, a public relations intern working closely with an editor may realize that the nature of an editorial career suits his or her personality better than public relations does. Students can learn more about internships at the office of Career Services.

While students may have different expectations of an internship, the Public Relations Society of America suggests that the most beneficial internship should expose communication students to the following:

- Writing news releases
- Assisting with layout of newsletters, brochures, announcements
- Editing for external and internal publications
- News gathering
- Helping to arrange or take part in special events
- Assisting in fundraising programs
- Designing audiovisual presentations

COMMUNICATION-RELATED CAREERS

Since choosing the right career is often a trial-and-error process, following are analyses of three careers that communication students can pursue: public relations specialists, editors, and technical communicators.

Public Relations Specialists

The primary goal of public relations professionals is to maintain a good relationship with the public, stockholders, and consumers, on which opinions the company's profitability often depends. In order to be able to project goodwill to all these groups, it is crucial that public relations specialists are persuasive communicators at all times. Here are some of the elements of public relations, as pointed out by the Public Relations Society of America:

- Community relations
- Government affairs
- Public affairs
- Financial relations
- Media relations
- Development/Fundraising
- Employee/Member relations
- Multicultural affairs

Notice the return to the higher level of subheading to shift the focus to three career options. Each one of the three sections is divided in the same manner: goals, responsibilities, skills required, employment outlook, and salary information. This type of consistency is highly typical of this genre because it allows for easy readability and ready comparisons of information.

Responsibilities of Public Relations Professionals

Informing--serving as advocates for an organization; providing the general public, stockholders, or special interest groups with the information on the company's accomplishments, policies, and future goals (U.S. Department of Labor).

Writing and editing--trying to reach and persuade large communities through the written word; preparing press releases, annual reports, proposals, brochures, articles for professional publications, and drafting speeches for company officials.

Speaking--preparing visual presentations, and speaking on the behalf of the company at conventions, public assemblies, and community meetings; cooperating with the media.

Fact-gathering--conducting surveys, evaluating opinions of the public, or stockholders, through interviews, informal conversations or library research (Public Relations Society of America).

Generally, a great deal of stress accompanies a career as a public relations specialist. It is not unusual for them to have various deadlines all pending at the same time. In addition, as many crises and unexpected scenarios develop, public relations professionals have to work overtime. A large portion of public relations is often carried on outside of the office. Community functions, business lunches, travel assignments, and various special speaking commitments are activities that often extend beyond a nine-to-five schedule. Therefore, working in public relations may often require much more than a standard 35- to 40-hour week (U.S. Dept. of Labor). Here are some of the activities and assignments with which a public relations professional might be involved during one day (Public Relations Society of America):

- Answering calls for information from the press and public
- Working on invitation lists for some special event
- Gathering facts for a press conference
- Escorting visitors and clients
- Helping with writing a brochure
- Delivering press releases to editorial offices

Must-have Skills for Public Relations

Good Judgment--Public relations professionals often serve as "counselors" during a company crisis. When the company's reputation

This informative report, typical of professional reports, makes ample use of white space and of graphic highlighting (things like subheadings, font variations, bulleted lists, etc.) to allow for maximum readability. Keep in mind that readers of such a report are seeking quick access to usable information and little else. In other words, efficiency is a primary goal of this genre.

is put to a test, they need to be able to think analytically, draw quick conclusions, and practical solutions (Public Relations Society of America).

Notice that various sources are indicated in parentheses throughout the report to satisfy ethical requirements of avoiding plagiarism, to lend credibility to the report, and to afford readers further avenues to pursue.

Communication Skills--Whether it is an annual report or press conference, public relations practitioners need to be able to convey their messages clearly and simply. Frequent face-to-face encounters with the public call for a confident and outgoing personality.

Empathy--Public relations professionals need to have the capacity to place themselves in the shoes of their audience. The more empathic communicators they are, the more they anticipate, and respond to, people's needs and concerns about a company's policies or activities.

Imagination--Original and creative ideas are essential to motivate the company's supporters, and sustain the public's interest in the company. Public relations specialists need to be inventive, so that they are able to anticipate, and prevent future problems for the company (Public Relations Society of America).

Employment

Organizations hiring for an entry-level position in public relations generally look for a candidate with a college degree that combines communication, journalism, advertising, creative and technical writing, and business administration (Monster Career Center). In addition, employers expect that a college graduate acquired some work-related experience in public relations while attending school. That's why a public relations internship is one of the best preparatory steps that students should take before they look for their first job.

Notice the frequent citing of the Occupational Outlook Handbook, a major government-sponsored resource for career research.

- According to Occupational Outlook Handbook, public relations professionals held about 137,000 jobs in 2000.
- According to the Bureau of Labor Statistics, more than half of the people employed in public relations are women.
- As pointed out in Occupational Outlook Handbook, it has been estimated that six out of ten public relations practitioners were pursuing their careers in services industries: membership organizations, social service agencies, healthcare organizations, educational institutions, and non-profit associations.
- The remaining number of public relations specialists found employment in communications firms, financial institutions, and government agencies.
- Approximately 8,600 public relations professionals were self-employed.

Employment in public relations is expected to grow because companies, rather than having their own PR departments, turn for services to large, specialized public relations firms on project-to-project bases. In addition, the significance of public relations professionals will increase because high competition demands on-going efforts to attract, and sustain, consumers' interest in the company (U.S. Dept. of Labor).

Salary

According to Salary.com Salary Wizard, the median expected salary for a public relations specialist with 0-2 years of experience in the Chicago area is $40,198.

Editors

Writing, revising, and proofreading are at the core of an editorial career. However, what editors write, how they write, and where it appears strictly depend on the audience they try to reach. Therefore, studying and analyzing the intended audience is the groundwork of an editorial process (Garson).

The second of the three career choices is indicated with a style of subheading consistent with the first career path considered.

Editors respond to the needs of very specific audiences, for instance: less or more affluent neighborhoods, bilingual communities, senior citizens, and households with or without children. The following distinction between two groups of readers illustrates the importance and consideration with which editors analyze and approach the audience (Tobler):

- Low-income neighborhood--articles have short and simple sentences, more graphics and larger font.
- Well-to-do suburb--articles are longer and have in-depth analysis with some technical or scientific terminology.

Responsibilities of Editors

- **Revising the content--**today's editors take advantage of computerized tools like: grammar and spelling checkers, advanced marking and comment systems, redlining and overstrike features.
- **Evaluating system-oriented tools--**editors of online information pay close attention to system-oriented tools like: menus, windows, prompts; they scrutinize the logic of labeling and design consistency (Porter and Coggin).
- **Organizing information--**editors need to be able to divide complex text into manageable and easy-to-follow chunks of

information. To draw and sustain readers' attention, editors employ bullet points, white spaces, and different fonts.

Must-have Editorial Skills

Strong Writing Skills--editors' ability to communicate clearly and logically cannot be overstressed. Checking any type of writing piece for accuracy, grammar and style calls for detail-oriented and organized individuals (Tobler).

Good Judgment--whether it is a small in-house newsletter, an article for a trade magazine or an online journal, editors need to exercise their best judgment to decide what makes the content most appealing, and which layout encourages most action, for example: True or False quizzes, check-in boxes.

Strong Sense of Ethics--editors need to make objective and unbiased choices when selecting materials for publishing (Monster Career Center). In addition they should be continuously examining if the changes they incorporate into someone else's writing take away the original meaning (Tobler).

Knowledge of Desktop Publishing--many editorial projects require some familiarity with desktop publishing software. Microsoft Publisher, Adobe and Quark XPress are the most popular applications that allow editors to produce high-quality, professional documents (Garson).

Employment

According to Occupational Outlook Handbook the employment of editors should increase through 2010. Following are factors that drive the demand for editors:

- The number of magazines geared to audiences with special interests is continuously growing.
- Online publications and editorial services are in high demand.
- Both corporate and non-profit organizations develop a variety of their own publications in order to reach their clients.

Employers look for candidates with college degrees in communications, journalism or English (Monster Career Center). In order to be considered for an editorial position, often a portfolio of sample writings is required even from college graduates. Editorial careers usually start with the entry-level position of editorial assistant. Depending on the advancement opportunities of a particular organization, an editorial assistant can be promoted to associate editor, then to editor, and subsequently to senior editor.

Salary

According to Salary.com Salary Wizard, the median expected salary for editors with 2-4 years of experience in the Chicago area is $54,543.

Technical Communicators

Technical communication is one of the newer, rapidly expanding career choices for communication students. Technical communicators design and develop communication products that present information from experts in a clear and user-friendly format (Society for Technical Communication). Table 1 shows the wide range of communication products that fall under technical communication.

Table 1. Technical Communication Products.

Purpose of Information	Examples of Communication Products
Explain usage of products,services, and policies	User's guides, help, references, policies and procedures guides, online wizards, and online cue cards
Exchange "basic" scientific information	Technical reports, articles, and books
Market products and services	Proposals, catalogs, brochures, videotapes, audiotapes, and demonstrations
Train users	Workbooks, tutorials, quick references, videotapes, audiotapes, online cue cards, and online coaches
Combination of purposes	Newsletters, magazines, and e-zines

(*Source:* "Industry Report: Overview of the Technical Communication Industry.")

Responsibilities of Technical Communicators

- **Writing--**the main challenge that technical communicators face is finding a language for specialized and scientific information that will match the levels of readers' comprehendibility.
- **Editing--**technical communicators break down specialized information, so that it is user-friendly (Society for Technical Communication).
- **Producing graphic images--**very often they need to employ visual images in screen design.

The third career choice is introduced.

Tables, requiring specific formats, are frequently used within formal professional reports.

Notice that the table is first signaled within the narrative with a reference to "Table 1."

Tables are descriptively titled.

This table has been imported from an outside source. This is common, acceptable practice as long as the source is properly referenced, as it is here in the separate source credit line below the table.

- **Evaluating usability--**a large portion of technical communicators' tasks involve assessing and testing communication products, anticipating troubles, and correcting them.

Since technical communication reiterates some of the skills and duties embedded in public relations and editing, this field attracts many communication students. Having strong communication skills, they can subsequently build their technical expertise either while on the job, or from various seminars and professional publications. Since about 180 colleges and universities have already established undergraduate, graduate and doctoral programs in technical communication, some students may choose to pursue a degree strictly in this field ("Industry Report").

Employment

It is not uncommon that technical communicators work for a variety of departments, working as a part of groups for Publications, Documentation, and Technical Communication departments. Following are industries, in which technical communicators find employment, as pointed out in the "Overview of the Technical Communication Industry":

Note the appropriate use of parallel phrasing. Parallelism is commonly insisted upon within such formal reports, once again to aid readability and provide easy comparisons.

- **Software industry--**developing products for programmers, end users, technical support staffs, and potential customers.
- **Environmental engineering--**writing proposals for large contracts, designing safety instructions.
- **Pharmaceuticals--**preparing reports needed for approval to test and introduce new drugs to the market, communicating the results from development labs to the scientific and medical communities.
- **Defense--**developing instructions for using and maintaining equipment; writing proposals for large government defense projects.

Salary

According to Salary.com Salary Wizard, the median expected salary for technical communicators with 0-2 years of experience in the Chicago area is $46,423.

The third major subsection of the body of the report is indicated here.

NON-PROFIT OR CORPORATE WORLD

Interdisciplinary Communication majors can choose between the non-profit and corporate sectors to practice their professions. The following points indicate basic comparisons/contrasts between the two environments.

- Entry-level jobs in corporate organizations are paid approximately $5,000 to $10,000 more than in non-profit (Public Relations Society of America).
- Generally, corporate companies offer better benefits (profit sharing, a 401(k) sharing plan, medical coverage).
- Large corporate companies have resources to send their employers to conventions and seminars (Jaye).
- In a non-profit, small organization, one can take on full-scale responsibilities, and gain experience faster because there are fewer people to do the work (U.S. Dept. of Labor).
- Generally, personal rewards are much higher in non-profit organizations than in corporate companies ("So You Want To Work").

PROFESSIONAL ASSOCIATIONS

Joining a professional association is highly advisable to communication students. Following are some of the benefits of membership:

- Professional organizations give access to information directly related to students' field of interest. They issue professional publications, which apart from being credible sources for school assignments help students to stay up-to-date with current issues and trends in the industry.
- Professional associations offer one of the best arenas for networking. This is where one can make professional contacts while still attending school. Students can receive career assistance from seasoned professionals.
- By exploring several professional associations related to the communication field, students can compare their skills and interests against the requirements for a particular career. This is especially significant in a major as broad and complex as interdisciplinary communication. Table 2 shows some of the associations relevant to communication students.

Table 2 Professional Associations for Communication-related Careers.

Public Relations Society of America (PRSA) 33 Irving Place New York, NY 10003 212-995-2230 <www.prsa.org>	• The largest professional organization for public relations specialists • Two award wining publications: The Strategists, Public Relations Tactics • Accreditation programs • PRSA Mentoring Program

The fourth section, titled with consistent font style, is indicated here.

The table is signaled to avoid any confusion.

A descriptive table title is provided for easy readability.

A useful table of appropriate professional organization information is provided. Note the consistency of the format and type of information for each organization profiled.

Public Relations Student Society of America (PRSSA) 33 Irving Place New York, NY 10003 212-460-1474 www.prssa.org	• Founded by PRSA; more than 7,000 members and 227 chapters on college campuses across the country • Students can become members by joining an established PRSAA chapter in college if it exists, or can establish new chapter • The closest chapters are in Columbia College, DePaul University, and Illinois State University
The Society for Technical Communication (STC) 901 N. Stuart Suite 904 Arlington, VA 22203 703-522-4114 www.stc.org	• The largest professional organization for technical writers, editors, web designers, teachers of technical communication; 20,000 members and 153 chapters worldwide • Scholarship opportunities for students • STC's Annual Salary Survey—statistics on pay and benefits • STC's Jobs Database • Special Interest Groups—members with similar backgrounds exchange ideas
National Communication Association 1765 N Street Washington, D.C. 20036 202-464-4600	• Represents 7,100 communication scholars and students • Organizes an annual convention that promotes research and exchange of information between professionals • Publishes seven scholarly journals • Honor Societies for students: Lambda Pi Eta and Sigma Chi Eta

(Source: Internet).

Tables and figures are frequently used within informative reports for the professions. This report does not include a separate table of contents for figures and graphs, which is sometimes done.

CONCLUSIONS

Interdisciplinary Communication is one of the most complex majors. It offers a solid liberal arts education that combines many different fields, from humanities to business. Interdisciplinary Communication students have a chance to develop and polish their speaking and writing skills, strong sense of visual and aesthetic appeal, and ability to think analytically.

Because Interdisciplinary Communication bridges humanities and business, it often draws the interest of those students who start college without a clear and specific career in their minds. During the course of study, students have the opportunity to excel in logical and persuasive writing, explore different theories of human communication, and learn the principles of visual communication. It is no wonder that some of them turn to graphic design; some lay their eyes on consulting; and yet some fall in love with editing. That's why it is strongly recommended that students try to apply their academic preparation by pursuing an internship. During internships students learn the responsibilities that a particular career entails, explore related professions, and network with other employees. It is not uncommon for Interdisciplinary Communication students to modify their original career objectives after realizing that their skills and interest match the needs of a different profession.

For all those students who still hesitate whether or not they are good candidates for an Interdisciplinary Communication major, answering the following questions might help:

- Do you enjoy communicating with people through the written word?
- Do you like meeting and interacting with new people?
- Do you feel comfortable speaking to a large group of people?
- Would you mind being challenged by hostile speakers?
- Are you good at influencing people?

RECOMMENDATIONS

- **Join professional organizations--**get to know the industry, current issues and trends, take advantage of their job search, start networking with professionals.
- **Take advantage of the EC Shadowing Program** offered by the Center for Professional Excellence—spend one day with someone who does the "real" job.

Notice the return to the original heading font size given only to the most major sections.

This section summarizes the main findings of the research and the overall impressions of the researcher.

Note that there are separate Conclusions and Recommendations sections. These are not to be confused, nor do they usually follow the same format.

The recommendations are based upon the conclusions drawn after the completion of the research. They appear in a separate section of the report with a subheading consistent with the most important sections.

Notice that recommendations are action steps nearly always introduced by present-tense verbs. This format enables them to be easily read by some audience members who might only be interested in the recommendations.

References are listed as "Works Cited" because this sample is documented in MLA format.

- **Choose your electives wisely**--by taking courses in desktop publishing, Web design, and programming, you can make yourself more marketable.
- **Pay frequent visits to Career Services**--read about current internships, check job postings, and always leave with the most recent copy of Job Choices magazine.

WORKS CITED

Elmhurst College Catalog. 2002–2003. 193.

Garson, Tina. Personal interview. 28 Oct. 2002.

"Industry Report: Overview of the Technical Communication Industry."
    The Commerce of Content. 20 Oct. 2002 <http://saulcarliner.
    home.att.net/idbusiness/workoftcshtm>.

Jaye, James R. "Non-profit or Corporate PR: Where Do You Fit In?" 20
    Oct. 2002 <http://www.prsa.org/Resources/profession/
    6c099616.html>.

Monster Career Center. 22 Oct. 2002 <http://iobprofiles.monster.com>.

Porter, Lynnette R., and William O. Coggin. "Technical Editing and
    Online Information: Features, Formatting, and Friendliness."
    <Academic Search Elite>. 13 Sept. 2002.

Public Relations Society of America. "PRSA Member Code of Ethics."
    Oct. 2000. 20 Oct. 2002 <httn://www.prsa.org>.

Salary.com Salary Survey. 28 Nov. 2003 <http://www.salary.com>.

"So You Want To Work For A Nonprofit?" Nonprofit Charitable Orgs. 23
    Oct. 2002 <http://www.about.com>.

Society for Technical Communication. 2002. 20 Oct. 2002
    <http://www.stc.org>.

Tobler, Ellen. Personal interview. 29 Sept. 2002.

U.S. Department of Labor. Occupational Outlook Handbook. 20 Oct.
    2002 <http://www.bls.gov/oco>.

Notice that extensive resources were consulted in creating this report. This lends credibility to the report and provides future references for the reader.

1. The title of an informative report is an important indicator to the reader of the scope of coverage in the paper. Compare and contrast the title of Agata Trzaska's report to that of Jill Damato's. What, if anything, would you recommend to Trzaska about revising her title?
2. Of course, the primary purpose of an informative report is to provide information for the targeted audience. How well does Trzaska succeed in fulfilling that purpose? What areas of the report are the *most* informative? Are there areas about which you'd like more information?
3. Informative reports frequently incorporate tables and figures. Locate Trzaska's use of these features and identify the use of other visual features as well. Discuss their purpose and contribution to the report.

LABORATORY REPORTS

Almost all college students, regardless of their majors, take at least one laboratory science as part of their general education or core curriculum or as part of the courses for their major. Whether that course is biology, chemistry, physics, astronomy, or another science, chances are you will have a mandatory laboratory component requiring **laboratory reports**. Lab reports as they are commonly referred to, are the "write-up" of lab results from specific experiments conducted to gain further insights into the topics and issues covered in your course. It is clearly a writing assignment that is based upon empirical work—i.e., upon very specific activities that the lab reporter performs.

The purpose of the lab report is actually threefold. First, it enables the laboratory experimenter to systematically record his/her observations and data and take time to reflect on the meaning of that data. It also enables a reader who has *not* conducted the experiment personally to acquire a capsule view of the experiment and gain some of the same knowledge and insights that the original experimenter did. And finally, it allows for continuing conversations about the research issue. Indeed, often readers/scientists disagree with the interpretations of the data, but the mere presence of the report enables continued debate.

A good lab report satisfies very specific audience expectations. Essentially, it must re-create the essence of the laboratory experience in a very concise manner. It is basically always structured around some hypothesis (or question) that is proposed and tested under laboratory conditions. The procedure and the results of the tests must be carefully reported and analyzed by the lab report writer. It may often be one of the briefest formal writing assignments that you create in your college career, yet it can potentially offer a great deal of information and insights into some scientific concept.

Ordinarily, a lab report follows a very structured format. Most typically, it would contain six parts that in essence mirror the scientific method. These six parts include:

1. the formal title—a scientific title is frequently rather long and very descriptive
2. the Introduction—this section contextualizes the issue or problem to be considered; ordinarily it will include a formal statement of the hypothesis; some professors will insist that the hypothesis be stated as an "if-then" statement
3. the Materials and Methods/Procedure section—this section gives a detailed list of specific items used in the lab and discusses specific steps of the procedure followed for the experiment; note that sometimes these sections are divided. In that case, a separate list of materials is itemized and followed by the Methods section.
4. the Observations/Data Collected—specific results collected from the observation/experiment are conveyed; oftentimes these are reported in a combination of figures, graphs, and tables; sometimes these are summarized in the lab report and complete detailed figures are included in separate appendices
5. the Discussion or Interpretation section—this section allows the experimenter/writer to explain the observations and data and to analyze those results relative to previous knowledge; this is usually the most challenging section of the lab report, as it allows the most latitude of interpretation
6. the Conclusion—this section considers all results of the analysis and then states a specific conclusion of the most salient factors; this may also include unanswered questions, attempt to explain contradictions, or propose further hypotheses for future experimentation.

Two student laboratory reports are included below. The first report is typical of most introductory science class lab reports. It was prepared by a chemistry student at Virginia Tech. It is concise and relatively simple in format. The second is a sample report from an advanced biology class at Elmhurst College. Note that is it an extremely comprehensive lab report, including a references list of sources consulted for the interpretation section and very detailed data collections reported in a separate appendix.

LABORATORY REPORT 1

Chemistry

Measurement of Water Temperatures Under Variable Conditions

Courtney Callahan
Virginia Polytechnic Institute and State University

Measurement of Water Temperatures Under Variable Conditions

Objective

- To measure temperature changes in water under different experimental conditions.
- To become familiar with common laboratory equipment, with measuring, and with the concept of significant figures.
- To make a good laboratory notebook record of my work.
- To write a report of my laboratory results including written description, tabulation of results, and the presentation of graphs.

Experimental Data

Part A data chart: Temperature (in °C)

	0 min.	5 min	10 min.	15 min	20 min.	25 min.	30 min.	35 min.	40 min.	45 min.	50 min.	55 min.	60 min.
100 mL beaker	60.0	37.1	35.0	32.0	30.0	29.0	28.0	27.3	26.6	26.0	25.0	25.0	24.0
Poly-styrene cup	75.2	56.0	49.5	44.0	41.7	38.0	35.2	34.0	32.0	29.0	27.3	26.0	25.1

Part B data chart

step	volume in cup (mL)	volume added (mL)	Initial T (in °C)	Final T (in °C)
1	50.0	10.00	75.1	58.1
2	60.0	10.00	57.2	48.9
3	70.0	10.00	48.8	42.4
4	80.0	10.00	42.3	40.6
5	90.0	10.00	38.9	36.5

Sample Calculations

$\Delta T_{hot} = T_h - T_f$
75.1 °C − 58.1 °C = **17.0°C** °C

$\Delta T_{cold} = T_f - T_c$
58.1°C − 24.1 °C = **34.0**

A fairly lengthy, very descriptive title is expected for laboratory reports, enabling other readers to immediately know the focus of the experiment.

Specific experiment objectives are distinctly stated. This allows all users of the report to share a common ground regarding the intent of the laboratory work.

Raw data of the experimental steps are provided in numerical format.

Note in this lab report that these data charts function as a "Methods" section.

These calculations also function as part of the "Methods" or "Procedures" section. Note that in this genre a condensed numerical representation of hours of actual work is usually the preferred reporting style. This is contrary to the extensive narrative reports that often accompany social science or humanities research.

Results of the procedures indicated above are discussed and analyzed here. This being a relatively simple and brief experiment, the "Results" discussion is brief, but nonetheless important, to laboratory research and to this reporting genre.

$$g_H \, \Delta T_h = (H_2O \; _hg)(\Delta \; T_{hot})$$
$$(73.1 \text{ g})(17.0 \text{ °C}) = \mathbf{1240}$$

$$g_C \, \Delta T_c = (H_2O \; _cg)(\Delta \; T_{cold})$$
$$(9.96 \text{ g})(34.0°C) = \mathbf{339.0}$$

Density of H_2O at 24.1 °C = 0.9971 = $\dfrac{(.0011)(4.1)}{5}$

$$= 0.9962 \text{ g/ml}$$

Mass of $H_2O \rightarrow m = d^* \, V$
$$= (.9962 \text{ g/ml})(10.0 \text{ mL})$$
$$= 9.962 \rightarrow 10.0 \text{ g}$$

Results and Conclusions

Part A:

After plotting the points of the Temperature-Time Data on a graph, I found the lines did not follow the same pathway, but they did both have a negative slope. They did not follow the same pathway due to the containers in which the water was held. A 100 mL beaker allows heat to escape at a faster rate than a polystyrene cup, thus causing the slope of the 100 mL beaker data to be greater. I believe if there were to be very few uncertainties, the lines would be parallel to each other on the graph.

Part B:

Step	Mass of Hot H_2O (g)	Mass of Cold H_2O (g)	T_{hot} °C	T_{cold} °C	T_{final} °C	Δ T_{hot}	Δ T_{cold}	g_H ΔT_h	g_C ΔT_c
1	73.1	10.0	75.1	24.1	58.1	17.0	34.0	1240	339
2	83.7	10.0	57.2	24.1	48.2	9.0	24.1	750	240
3	93.9	10.0	48.7	24.1	42.5	6.2	18.4	580	183
4	104.1	10.0	42.5	24.1	40.9	1.6	16.8	160	167
5	114.1	10.0	38.5	24.1	36.1	2.4	12.0	270	120

Consistent with this genre, the writer offers conclusions upon consideration of the data.

I found that the numbers seem to decrease as the temperature decreases. Also the $g_C \, \Delta \, T_c$ column contains a lot smaller numbers than the $g_H \, \Delta \, T_h$ column. The numbers seem to be in a 4 to 1 ratio until the 4th and 5th step, and then it is unclear if there is any relationship between them at all.

Uncertainties

This lab had many inconsistencies that led to uncertainties I have about the accuracy of my data. One very clear problem we had was the loss of heat to the atmosphere. With no way of accounting for this lost heat, every bit of data we took was off by an unknown amount of degrees. Also, the H_2O might not have been exactly room temperature; that could have made the hot H_2O colder than should be or not cold enough (if the "cold water" was too warm, it could not adequately cool down the hot water). A final reason as to the nature of uncertainties is that we had more than one person checking the temperature as well as checking the time. Every person perceives things differently, so the data taken was not consistent with one person. Rather it was two people making judgments on what the readings were.

Discussion of inconsistencies is common in scientific reports.

INVESTIGATING THE GENRE SAMPLE

1. Notice that this laboratory report begins with a list of objectives for the laboratory experience and a given set of data. Do you think this is standard in all laboratory reports or just those done for class exercises?
2. Courtney Callahan uses "I" and active-voice verbs in her "Results and Conclusions" section. How does that cause her paper to differ from the Methods section of Dimova's "The Effects of GA3" laboratory report that follows? Which paper do you think sounds more scientific and why?
3. Callahan includes a section called "Uncertainties" in her laboratory report, probably at the direction of her instructor. Many people would contend that conjectures about uncertainty are not part of the genre of the laboratory report. What do you think about its inclusion in Callahan's paper?

LABORATORY REPORT 2
Biology

The Effects of GA3

Kristina Dimova
Elmhurst College

This much more complex and lengthy lab report is introduced by a research question that serves as the focus of the research and the report.

The writer includes an abstract (mainly because of the length of this report). This abstract briefly summarizes the experiment procedure, the hypothesis, and the results for the reader.

The introduction provides a scientific context for this study, explaining the focus on plant growth regulators. Note that the writer assumes a scientific audience who is knowledgeable of the technical terms employed.

The Effects of GA3

Does GA3 increase the rate of germination and the length of the radicle and stem in certain monocot seeds?

Abstract

Ten seeds of each—wheat, oat and barley—were obtained. Five seeds of each ten were treated with GA3 and the other five were treated with H2O. All of the seeds were placed in dishes and put in a dark drawer, to control their light deprived environment. All radicles and stems were periodically measured and recorded. Our null hypothesis is that GA3 has no effect on the length of the radicles and stems in wheat, oat, and barley and the rate of the germination process. Our hypothesis is that treated by GA3, wheat, oat, and barley seeds will germinate faster and their radicles and stems will be longer than the untreated/H2O wheat, oat and barley seeds. A t-test was used to validate our hypothesis. However, the data was not significant enough to reject our null hypothesis.

Introduction

At the most basic level, the developmental paths of plants and animals share many key elements. Some of these elements are chemical substances called hormones. In plants these hormones are called plant growth regulators, or PGRs, because they lack the specificity of the animal hormones. PGRs are involved in many internal, signaling pathways as well as in responses to the environment and internally regulated development (Johnson and Raven 2002). The activity of PGRs results from their capacity to stimulate certain physiological processes and to inhibit others. Usually how they act in particular moments is influenced both by the PGR and the tissue that receives it. There are seven major kinds of PGRs, but the one that is involved in this experiment is gibberellins. Gibberellins, or gibberellic acids, are found in virtually all plants. More than sixty gibberellins have been found in various fungi and plants. Gibberellins are synthesized in many parts of the plant, especially in actively growing areas such as developing embryos, and meristematic or developing tissues. Gibberellins have the unique ability among PGRs to promote extensive growth in plants. They also promote germination of dormant seeds. Research has shown that wheat seed dormancy is most likely a result of an interaction between PGRs. GA3 has been found to influence growth activities in dormant embryos (Grilli, Pollone, and Meletti 1999). Researchers Foley, Nichols and Myers discovered in an experiment that oat seeds could be induced to germinate with GA3 (Foley, Nichols, and Myers 1993). Research has also shown barley seeds as well as wheat, and oat seeds can be induced to germinate faster with GA3 (Shuurink 1995). In this experiment, we are going to focus on the effects of GA3 in seed germination of wheat, oat, and barley. The purpose of the experiment is to stimulate seed germination of wheat, oat and barley seeds with GA3 in a light-deprived environment, and after measuring the length of the radicle and stem, to compare them to wheat, oat and barely seeds that germinated during the same period of time, in the same environment without GA3, with water. Our null hypothesis is that GA3 has no effect on the length of the radicles and stems in wheat, oat, and barley and the rate of the germination process. Our hypothesis is that treated by GA3, wheat, oat, and barley seeds will germinate faster and their radicles and stems will

Discussion of previous research is included; this offers justification for pursuing this related research as the potential key to a next step.

A specific experimental focus is stated, allowing writer and reader to share a common focus.

Here the purpose of the experiment is clearly outlined in even clearer detail. Note that this type of specific delineation of intent and procedure is expected within this scientific genre.

The hypothesis to be tested is clearly stated. This limit the scope of experime both be longer than the untreated/H2O wheat, oat and barley seeds. To validate our hypothesis we will use a t-test.

Materials and Methods

This Materials and Methods section provides a detailed description of exactly what was used and how it was used in the experiment. This detail serves two purposes: It demands accountability from the researcher and it allows the reader to closely follow the actions of the researcher. This enables both groups to begin interpreting and/or questioning the activity.

The Results section offers a narrative description of occurrences during the experiment; it references tables and graphs for the precise mathematical results.

0.5 mg of GA3 were mixed in 1 L of water to prepare a GA3 solution. Ten seeds of each—wheat, oat, and barely—were obtained. Five out of each set of ten were placed in small dishes on top of a water-soaked napkin. The other five of each set were placed in small dishes on top of a GA3 solution-soaked napkin. All dishes were labeled properly with the name of the plant, and either GA3 or H2O. After that they were placed in a drawer in the botany lab, which provided their light deprived environment. The initial lengths of the radicle and the stem were 0. After that, data was collected 5 to 6 days per week for approximately 3 weeks. The lengths of the radicles and the stems were measured with a ruler and recorded in organized and labeled tables. If the napkins of any of the plants were drying out, they were wet with the appropriate GA3 solution or water.

Results

The basic measurement included total length of the radicle and the stem from the seed coat. Table 1.1 shows the growth of the stem and radicle of all GA3 treated and untreated/H2O seeds during the first 4 days. The radicles of the GA3 treated wheat and untreated/H2O barley seeds began to emerge during the first day. Nothing happened in the treated and untreated/H2O oat dishes. During the second day some of the stems of the treated wheat seeds emerged as well. Radicles and stems emerged from some of the untreated/H2O wheat seeds. Radicles emerged also from some of the treated barley seeds. Nothing happened to the oat seeds. During the third day, most of the treated and untreated/H2O stems and radicles emerged from the wheat and barley seeds. Nothing happened to the oat seeds once again.

Table 1.2 shows the growth of the stem and radicle of the treated and untreated/H2O seeds between days 5 and 10 when the measurements were taken. The stems and radicles of the treated and untreated wheat and barley continued to elongate gradually. However, a radicle emerged only from one of the treated oat seeds. The rest—treated and untreated/H2O—remained unchanged.

Table 1.3 shows the changes that occurred during the last 7 days of the experiment. The stems and radicles of most treated and untreated/H2O wheat and barley seeds continued to elongate. A stem emerged only from one of the treated oat seeds, the same one that had a radicle emerging several days ago. All the rest of the treated and untreated/H2O oat seeds remained dormant. The average length of the radicle of treated wheat seeds was 85.75 mm, and the length of the stem was 134.25 mm. The untreated/H2O wheat seeds had a significantly lower radicle length average of 60.75 mm. However, there was almost no difference in the length of the stem, which was 139 mm, slightly longer than the average stem length of the treated seeds. The average lengths of the radicle and stem of treated barley were 80 mm and 167 mm. The average length of the radicles and stems of the untreated/H2O barley seeds were 96.2 and 186 mm, surprisingly somewhat longer than those of the treated seeds. Table 2 is a summary of the averages of all treated and untreated/H2O seeds during the experiment.

Lastly, the graphs attached are a nice visual representation of the change in lengths of the treated and untreated/H2O radicles and stems. Graph 1.1 is a comparison between the length of the treated and untreated/H2O wheat radicle. It shows the faster elongation of the radicle of the treated seeds. It also demonstrates that even though the treated and untreated/H2O seeds elongated almost parallel to one another, the treated seeds seem to run out of nutrients faster. This may be due to their head start. Graph 1.2 shows the elongation of the stem of

Notice the narrative style in lab reports; they are nearly always written in third person even when one person performed the action and is clearly sharing his/her actions. This reflects a genre concern for apparent objectivity and authority.

The writer mentions that a visual representation of the growth of the seeds tested is provided in graphs below. Inclusion of visual representations that greatly condense narrative descriptions is the norm in this genre, where efficiency is greatly valued.

treated and untreated/H2O wheat seeds. The treated ones seem to elongate faster than the untreated/H2O.

Graphs 2.1 and 2.2 are representations of the elongation of the radicle and stem of treated and untreated/H2O oat seeds. In both cases, the stem does not appear to emerge at all and the treated stem and radicles seem to grow longer and faster. The next two graphs, 3.1 and 3.2, demonstrate the elongation of stem and radicle of treated and untreated/H2O barley seeds. The radicles and the stems of the untreated seeds seem to grow faster and longer than those of the treated seeds. The last chart, graph 4, is a summary of the elongation size and period of all treated and untreated/H2O wheat, oat, and barley seeds. It shows that the treated wheat radicle had the largest length.

A t-test was performed on most of the data to find whether the variances were significant. According to the t-test on the treated and untreated/H2O wheat seeds, there is not a statistically significant difference between the treated and untreated/H2O groups. The P value is 0.1764. The t-test on the treated and untreated/H2O barley seeds, however, shows a statistically significant difference, with a P value of 0.0175. The t-test on the treated and untreated/H2O oats demonstrates a statistically significant difference, with a P value of 0.0193. Overall the differences in the t-test were controversial and probably were not significant enough to reject our null hypothesis. The Pearson Product Moment Correlation and the Spearman Rank Order Correlation for the treated and untreated/H2O wheat, oat, and barley seeds show no significant relationship between the variables—treated and untreated/H2O.

Discussion

We were unable to reject our null hypothesis. Even though there were some differences between the length of the treated radicles and stems of

---

Note that all of the tables and graphs referenced in this section appear in an appendix at the end of the report. This saves space and also allows a reader to turn quickly to a separate section of graphed results. Some readers of laboratory reports will do that almost immediately depending upon their purpose and relationship to the writer and to the research issue.

This is an explanation of the specific test performed to determine if the variances found were significant. This term holds a particular meaning to scientists. Lab reports will frequently highlight "significant" results.

The Discussion session offers an analysis of the results presented above. Note the return to the initial hypothesis, the focus of the report.

wheat, oat and barley and the untreated/H2O, they were not significant enough. The differences in the rate of germination seem to be also statistically not significant. There are several factors that might have led to these statistical results.

Some of the speculations as to why there weren't significant differences between the treated and untreated/H2O seeds are the environment, the germination stimuli and the concentration of GA3. The light-deprived environment might have been the reason for the similar lengths of radicles and stems of treated and untreated/H2O seeds. The majority of the oat seeds might have been dead since the beginning of the experiment or they might have not received enough stimuli to trigger their germination. The concentration of GA3 might have not been high enough in order to change the germination rate and the lengths of radicles and stems significantly. Some of the stems grew larger than the dish, and had to swirl around it in order not to break, and others broke. This also might have slowed down the elongation of the stems.

Not only the conditions under which the experiment took place might have led to insignificant results, but also the possibility of experimental error might have done so. Some stems were broken into two, three or four pieces and were all measured separately and then the length of each was added to the rest. However, there is room for a measurement or calculation error.

Literature Cited

Foley M, Nichols M, Myers S. 1993. Carbohydrate concentrations and interactions in after ripening responsive dormant Avena fatua caryopses induced to germinate by gibberellic acid. Seed Science Res 3: 271–278.

Results were not statistically significant to verify the hypothesis. In other words, the experiment does not fully resolve the question.

Potential reasons for the inconclusive, non-statistically significant results are discussed in this section. In this genre, a Discussion section of inclusive results is often very important since it can clarify issues and/or raise additional questions about the topic.

Note that the title of this section is in CSE format.

All references are provided in CSE, Council of Scientific Editors (formerly CBE, Council of Biological Editors), format.

Grilli I, Pollone E, Meletti P. 1999. Poly (A) polymerase in dormant embryos of triticum durum. Annals of Botany 84 (1): 71–78.

Johnson R, Raven P. 2002. Biology. The McGraw. New York. 1238 p.

Schuurink R C. 1995. Dormant barley aleurone shows heterogeneity and a specific cytodifferentiation. J of Cereal Sci 25: 27–36.

Appendix 1. Graphs of Experiment Data

Data results are reported in these detailed graphs in a separate appendix.

Graph 1.1

Comparison between WHEAT Radicles treated with GA3 and H_2O

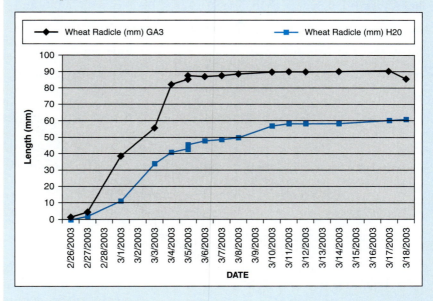

Graph 1.2

Comparison between WHEAT Stem treated with GA3 and H$_2$O

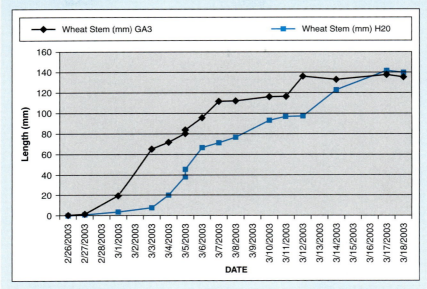

Graph 2.1

Comparison between OAT Radicles treated with GA3 and H$_2$O

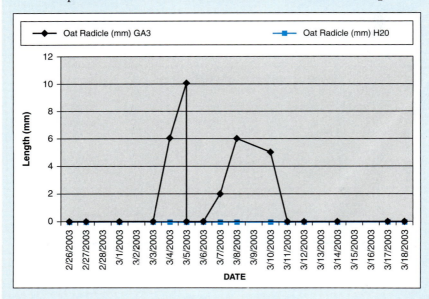

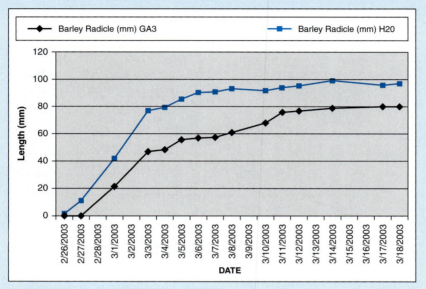

Graph 2.2

Comparison between OAT Stem treated with GA3 and H_2O

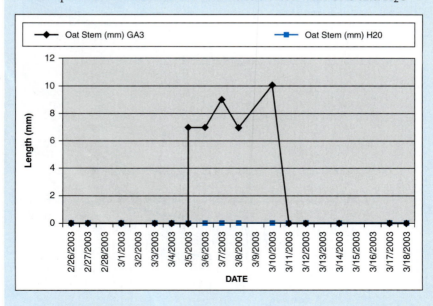

Graph 3.1

Comparison between BARLEY Radicles treated with GA3 and H_2O

Graph 3.2

Comparison between BARLEY Stems treated with GA3 and H₂O

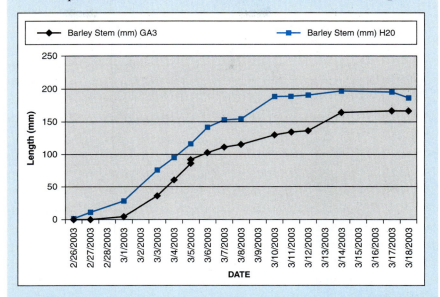

Graph 4

Comparison between WHEAT, OAT and BARLEY Radicles and Stems treated with GA3 and H₂O

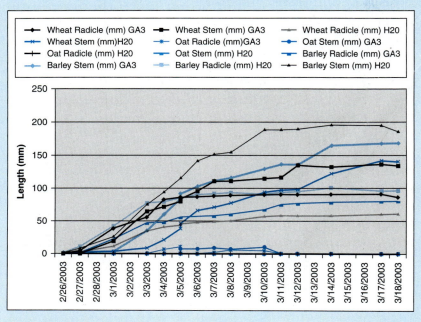

Table 1.1

DATE:	Time:	Name:	WHEAT				OAT				BARLEY			
			Wheat Radicle [mm]	GA3 Stem [mm]	Wheat Radicle [mm]	H2O Stem [mm]	Oat Radicle [mm]	GA3 Stem [mm]	Oat Radicle [mm]	H2O Stem [mm]	Barley Radicle [mm]	GA3 Stem [mm]	Barley Radicle [mm]	H2O Stem [mm]
2/25/2003	16:15	Started	0	0	0	0	0	0	0	0	0	0	0	0
2/26/2003	9:00am	Val	0	0	0	0	0	0	0	0	0	0	0	0
			0	0	0	0	0	0	0	0	0	0	0	0
			0	0	0	0	0	0	0	0	0	0	0	0
			0	0	0	0	0	0	0	0	0	0	0	0
2/26/2003	9:00am	Val	0	0	0	0	0	0	0	0	0	0	0	0
2/26/2003	2:15pm	Val	1.5	0	0	0	0	0	0	0	0	0	2	0
			2	0	0	0	0	0	0	0	0	0	1	0
			1	0	0	0	0	0	0	0	0	0	2	0
			1	0	0	0	0	0	0	0	0	0	0	0
2/26/2003	2:15pm	Val	0	0	0	0	0	0	0	0	0	0	0	0
2/27/2003	11:15am	Kristina	1.375	0	0	0	0	0	0	0	0	0	1	0
			5	2	6	2	0	0	0	0	1	0	17	14
			6	2	2	0	0	0	0	0	1	0	15	12
			4	1	0	0	0	0	0	0	0	0	15	13
			3	0	0	0	0	0	0	0	0	0	5	2
			0	0	0	0	0	0	0	0	0	0	1	0

Table 1.1 (*continued*)

DATE:	Time:	Name:	WHEAT				OAT				BARLEY			
			Wheat	GA3	Wheat	H2O	Oat	GA3	Oat	H2O	Barley	GA3	Barley	H2O
2/27/2003	11:15am	Kristina	4.5	1.25	2	0.5	0	0	0	0	0.4	0	10.6	8.2
3/1/2003	11:55am	Kristina	53	30	4	1	0	0	0	0	35	0	55	50
			34	18	5	3	0	0	0	0	35	5	60	45
			34	18	1	0	0	0	0	0	20	0	4	3
			35	9	6	4	0	0	0	0	15	6	35	2
			0	0	30	5	0	0	0	0	0	0	53	30
3/1/2003	11:55am	Kristina	39	18.75	11.5	3.25	0	0	0	0	21	2.75	41.4	26
3/3/2003	1:00pm	Sebastian	11.5	120	53	18	0	0	0	0	66	30	42	30
5 alive			70	56	1	0	0	0	0	0	59	50	73	52
4 alive			69	26	13	2	0	0	0	0	0	0	73	117
3 alive			73	54	40	4	0	0	0	0	62	48	97	100
2 alive			0	0	29	6	0	0	0	0	45	46	98	74
3/3/2003	1:00pm	Sebastian	55.875	64	34	7.5	0	0	0	0	46.4	34.8	76.6	74.6
ALL dead			4 - alive & 1 dead				ALL-dead				5- alive & 0 dead		5-alive & 0 dead	

181

Table 1.2

			WHEAT				OAT				BARLEY			
DATE:	Time:	Name:	Wheat Radicle [mm]	GA3 Stem [mm]	Wheat Radicle [mm]	H2O Stem [mm]	Oat Radicle [mm]	GA3 Stem [mm]	Oat Radicle [mm]	H2O Stem [mm]	Barley Radicle [mm]	GA3 Stem [mm]	Barley Radicle [mm]	H2O Stem [mm]
3/4/2003	2:20 pm	Kristina	82	65	43	20	6	0	0	0	70	97	95	85
		Valerie	59	25	30	16	0	0	0	0	84	50	40	40
		Sebastian	84	59	0	0	0	0	0	0	30	78	69	134
			105	133	30	11	0	0	0	0	53	70	100	85
			0	0	60	33	0	0	0	0	0	0	90	125
3/4/2003	2:20pm	KVS	82.5	70.5	40.75	20	6	0	0	0	47.4	59	78.8	93.8
3/5/2003	9:25am	Valerie	65	25	36	36	10	0	0	0	40	114	93	140
			107	145	48	32	0	0	0	0	93	75	103	90
			90	75	60	63	0	0	0	0	61	110	45	65
			80	70	28	20	0	0	0	0	82	124	110	115
			0	0	0	0	0	0	0	0	0	0	70	165
3/5/2003	9:25am	Valerie	85.5	78.75	43	37.75	10	0	0	0	55.2	84.6	84.2	115
3/5/2003	3:52pm	Sebastian	86	77	46	39	0	7	0	0	61	127	111	120
			88	68	38	43	0	0	0	0	42	111	70	157
			67	32	63	74	0	0	0	0	93	86	101	87
			107	155	35	24	0	0	0	0	79	127	90	142
			0	0	0	0	0	0	0	0	0	0	50	70
3/5/2003	3:52pm	Sebastian	87	83	45.5	45	0	7	0	0	55	90.2	84.4	115.2

Table 1.2 (continued)

DATE: Radicle / Stem	Time: Stem	Name: Radicle	WHEAT				OAT				BARLEY			
			Wheat Stem [mm]	GA3 Radicle [mm]	Wheat Stem [mm]	H2O Radicle [mm]	Oat Stem [mm]	GA3 Radicle [mm]	Oat Stem [mm]	H2O Radicle [mm]	Barley Stem [mm]	GA3 [mm]	Barley [mm]	H2O [mm]
3/6/2003	9:12pm	Sebastian	86	95	0	0	0	7	0	0	93	105	106	95
			70	36	40	37	0	0	0	0	82	130	77	130
			84	85	58	105	0	0	0	0	43	135	83	145
			107	165	50	61	0	0	0	0	65	138	70	185
			0	0	43	57	0	0	0	0	0	0	111	152
3/6/2003	9:12pm	Sebastian	86.75	95.25	47.75	65	0	7	0	0	56.6	101.6	89.4	141.4
3/7/2003	1:00pm	Kristina	108	200	0	0	2	9	0	0	0	140	106	158
			85	95	50	67	0	0	0	0	43	180	70	189
			70	50	45	61	0	0	0	0	68	125	92	177
			87	97	42	43	0	0	0	0	82	106	84	140
			0	0	58	112	0	0	0	0	92	0	100	95
	1:00pm	Kristina	87.5	110.5	48.75	70.75	2	9	0	0	57	110.2	90.4	151.8
3/8/2003	4:00pm	Sebastian	86	97	46	61	0	7	0	0	115	106	112	160
			70	30	43	63	0	0	0	0	79	125	87	177
			90	112	0	0	0	0	0	0	64	195	90	145
			108	205	51	60	6	0	0	0	42	145	71	190
			0	0	59	123	0	0	0	0	0	0	101	100
3/8/2003	4:00pm	Sebastian	88.5	111	49.75	76.75	6	7	0	0	60	114.2	92.2	154.4

Table 1.3

DATE:	Time:	Name:	WHEAT				OAT				BARLEY			
			Wheat Radicle [mm]	GA3 Stem [mm]	Wheat Radicle [mm]	H2O Stem [mm]	Oat Radicle [mm]	GA3 Stem [mm]	Oat Radicle [mm]	H2O Stem [mm]	Barley Radicle [mm]	GA3 Stem [mm]	Barley Radicle [mm]	H2O Stem [mm]
3/10/2003	9:35am	Valerie	110	210	65	155	5	10	0	0	91	159	100	200
			88	125	48	75	0	0	0	0	65	230	70	219
			71	30	30	70	0	0	0	0	85	130	89	210
			90	95	85	70	0	0	0	0	95	122	85	211
			0	0	0	0	0	0	0	0	0	0	110	103
3/10/2003	9:35am	Valerie	89.75	115	57	92.5	5	10	0	0	67.2	128.2	90.8	188.6
3/11/2003	2:10pm	Valerie	90	210	80	145	0	0	0	0	94	125	104	103
			90	30	42	80	0	0	0	0	81	14	86	230
			110	95	45	78	0	0	0	0	65	235	90	193
			71	130	0	0	0	0	0	0	95	159	114	199
			0		65	82	0	0	0	0	40	140	73	220
3/11/2003	2:10pm	Valerie	90.25	116.25	58	96.25	0	0	0	0	75	134.6	93.4	189
3/12/2003	6:00pm	Sebastian	87	210	65	83	0	0	0	0	82	15	86	231
			90	105	81	147	0	0	0	0	94	126	106	105
			112	95	45	79	0	0	0	0	67	236	92	194
			71	131	42	80	0	0	0	0	97	159	116	200
			0	0	0	0	0	0	0	0	41	140	74	220

Table 1.3 (*continued*)

DATE:	Time:	Name:	WHEAT				OAT				BARLEY			
			Wheat	GA3	Wheat	H2O	Oat	GA3	Oat	H2O	Barley	GA3	Barley	H2O
3/12/2003	6:00pm	Sebastian	90	135.25	58.25	97.25	0	0	0	0	76.2	135.2	94.8	190
3/14/2003	9:15am	Valerie	90	150	55	90	0	0	0	0	43	158	80	220
			111	215	43	100	0	0	0	0	70	255	100	210
			70	35	48	130	0	0	0	0	97	130	110	110
			90	130	87	165	0	0	0	0	100	117	93	235
			0	0	0	0	0	0	0	0	82	159	111	208
3/14/2003	9:15am	Valerie	90.25	132.5	58.25	121.25	0	0	0	0	78.4	163.8	98.8	196.6
3/17/2003	9:15am	Valerie	90	132	90	200	0	0	0	0	100	123	85	230
			70	35	45	105	0	0	0	0	97	132	111	208
			112	230	50	138	0	0	0	0	75	255	110	120
			90	150	55	120	0	0	0	0	43	165	95	205
			0	0	0	0	0	0	0	0	82	159	75	215
3/17/2003	9:15am	Valerie	90.5	136.75	60	140.75	0	0	0	0	79.4	166.8	95.2	195.6
3/18/2003	3:00pm	Kristina	75	140	54	126	0	0	0	0	82	159	71	215
			111	230	0	0	0	0	0	0	44	180	90	200
			70	32	59	105	0	0	0	0	76	250	125	100
			87	135	40	135	0	0	0	0	100	123	110	195
			0	0	90	190	0	0	0	0	98	123	85	220
3/18/2003	3:00pm	Kristina	85.75	134.25	60.75	139	0	0	0	0	80	167	96.2	186

Table 2

DATE:	Time:	Name:	WHEAT				OAT				BARLEY			
			Wheat Radicle [mm]	GA3 Stem [mm]	Wheat Radicle [mm]	H2O Stem [mm]	Oat Radicle [mm]	GA3 Stem [mm]	Oat Radicle [mm]	H2O Stem [mm]	Barley Radicle [mm]	GA3 Stem [mm]	Barley Radicle [mm]	H2O Stem [mm]
2/26/2003	9:00am	Val	0	0	0	0	0	0	0	0	0	0	0	0
2/26/2003	2:15pm	Val	1.375	0	0	0	0	0	0	0	0	0	1	0
2/27/2003	11:15am	Kristina	4.5	1.25	2	0.5	0	0	0	0	0.4	0	10.6	8.2
3/1/2003	11:55am	Kristina	39	18.75	11.5	3.25	0	0	0	0	21	2.75	41.4	26
3/3/2003	1:00pm	Sebastian	55.875	64	34	7.5	6	0	0	0	46.4	34.8	76.6	74.6
3/4/2003	2:20pm	KVS	82.5	70.5	40.75	20	10	0	0	0	47.4	59	78.8	93.8
3/5/2003	9:25am	Valerie	85.5	78.75	43	37.75	0	7	0	0	55.2	84.6	84.2	115
3/5/2003	3:52pm	Sebastian	87	83	45.5	45	0	7	0	0	55	90.2	84.4	115.2
3/6/2003	9:12pm	Sebastian	86.75	95.25	47.75	65	2	9	0	0	56.6	101.6	89.4	141.4
3/7/2003	1:00pm	Kristina	87.5	110.5	48.75	70.75	6	7	0	0	57	110.2	90.4	151.8
3/8/2003	4:00pm	Sebastian	88.5	111	49.75	76.75	5	10	0	0	60	114.2	92.2	154.4
3/10/2003	9:35am	Valerie	89.75	115	57	92.5	0	0	0	0	67.2	128.2	90.8	188.6
3/11/2003	2:10pm	Valerie	90.25	116.25	58	96.25	0	0	0	0	75	134.6	93.4	189
3/12/2003	6:00pm	Sebastian	90	135.25	58.25	97.25	0	0	0	0	76.2	135.2	94.8	190
3/14/2003	9:15am	Valerie	90.25	132.5	58.25	121.25	0	0	0	0	78.4	163.8	98.8	196.6
3/17/2003	9:15am	Valerie	90.5	136.75	60	140.75	0	0	0	0	79.4	166.8	95.2	195.6
3/18/2003	3:00pm	Kristina	85.75	134.25	60.75	139	0	0	0	0	80	167	96.2	186

1. When producing laboratory reports, writers frequently need to use specific terminology related to the process of scientific research. Notice, for example, Kristina Dimova's use of the term *null hypothesis*. Where else do you see Dimova employing the language of scientific experimentation?
2. In teaching the laboratory report as a genre, some instructors insist that writers use passive-voice verbs in the Methods and Materials section, while other instructors are beginning to urge the use of the active voice. What do you think of the choices Dimova makes with verbs in her Methods section?
3. Notice the extensive use Dimova makes of tables and graphs in this report. Do you think the report comments on these tables and graphs sufficiently? Why or why not?

SCIENTIFIC RESEARCH REPORTS

Much of the work of scientists occurs in the form of experimentation. Experiments are conducted by all types of scientists—natural scientists, such as biologists, chemists, physicists, or microbiologists; and social scientists, such as psychologists, anthropologists, or sociologists. In all of these fields, the nature of the experiments may differ greatly in terms of goals, materials, methods, location (some inside a sterile laboratory, some in a conference room, some out "in the field"), and so forth. However, the results of all of the experiments are shared in an amazingly similar way, in form of a **scientific research report**.

This section will explain details of this genre by focusing upon the general characteristics, the purpose(s), the expectations of the audience, the overall organization, and the format. It will include two sample student scientific research papers with explanatory comments. The first one, written for a chemistry class at Elmhurst College, reports on an experimental attempt to detect DDT in water samples. The second example is from the social science of psychology. Its author, a student from Augustana College, reports on the influence of violent film clips on cognitive tasks.

Scientific research reports are formal written documents that can vary a great deal in length. Typically, an undergraduate report of this kind will be 10–15 pages, though professional ones can be much longer. Even relatively brief ones, however, often represent hours and hours, sometimes weeks or months, of experimentation and observation. In other words, the actual written report often condenses extensive amounts of raw data into a compact, readable format.

The report serves both the scientist and his/her audience in multiple ways. The report provides a summation of the actual results of the experiment, enabling the scientist and his/her audience to see a collective version of the experiment data. But it also provides a medium for the discussion and/or potential interpretation of those results, a platform for conclusions drawn from the results, and a means of disseminating those results to a potentially much wider audience. The audience for these reports, most often scientists themselves, bring certain expectations. They expect that the experiment was ethically and carefully conducted and that the results are honestly presented, in as objective manner as possible. They also expect that the report will follow a very prescribed manner.

Overall, these reports are organized to explain the exact means by which the experiment was conducted and the specific results were obtained, and to offer conjecture as to the larger meaning of those results. To accomplish this, these reports have a very structured format, in essence reflecting the preciseness that is a characteristic goal of the science they report.

These reports are formatted into specific subsections that are given rather generic titles. These subsections include the title, an abstract, introduction, materials/methods, summary of results, discussion/interpretation, conclusion, and list of references. Let's consider these one at a time, since they are not always as simple as they seem.

Right from the start you'll notice that the title of a scientific research report is generally *not* simple. The sciences are especially noted for providing lengthy, detailed titles for their research reports that offer a very focused description of the exact nature of the experiment. This enables easy tracking of the texts for comparisons to other works. In fact, the titles are sometimes so detailed that they serve as "mini-abstracts" for other researchers. Note the eight-word title of the student chemistry paper seen below: "Detection of DDT Using Quartz Crystal Microbalance Technology." This formal title appears on the separate title page (not included below) and at the top of the first page of the actual report. Because of the lengthy, complex nature of scientific report titles, a common practice is to provide another title, referred to as the "running head." The running head is an abbreviated version of the actual title and is most often designated on the bottom of the title page and then repeated in the upper-right corner of each page of the report. Notice, for example, that in the psychology sample included here, the actual title is "The Influence of Viewing a Violent Film on a Word Generation Task," whereas the running head is "Influence of a Violent Film."

The title page is followed by the abstract. An abstract briefly summarizes the basic procedure(s) of the experiment, offers a skeletal version of the results, and indicates the primary conclusion. For more details regarding the nature of an abstract, consult the abstract section earlier in this chapter. Essentially, the abstract here provides a sufficient glimpse of the report to enable the reader to determine if it will be useful to read the report in its entirety and/or to jar the reader's and/or writer's memory of contents previously examined.

The introduction follows the abstract. As the name implies, this section introduces the research project. It offers relevant background information and explains the rationale or goals of the experiment. In most reports, this section also provides an overview of related experiments and previously issued reports. Sometimes it is specifically labeled a "Literature Review." In the case of the chemistry report reprinted here, there is a brief introduction followed by a review section titled "Theoretical Analysis." Regardless of the title, this section essentially summarizes and evaluates the important documents/reports giving data results of other scientists in order to provide a context for the current research. Keep in mind that most research is conducted in response to previous research, to either further confirm or challenge previous findings or to determine the next step. Consequently, scientists need to know—and need to convince their audience that they know—what previous research has been done on a given question or issue. This previous research is reviewed in these introductory sections.

Following the introduction and/or theory review sections, the researcher reports the specifics of his/her *own* experiment. This section of the research report begins with the materials and methods section(s). Sometimes these are separated; sometimes they are combined. Slightly different subtitles may occur. For example, notice that in the psychology report, the "Method" section includes subsections of "Participants," "Materials," "Design," and "Procedure," whereas in the chemistry report, this information is provided in the "Experimental" section, which includes subparts labeled "Regents," "Instrumentation," and "Procedures." Though the specific labels may vary (you may need to consult your professor for details regarding your specific discipline), keep in mind that this section is basically reporting *exactly how* the experiment was conducted.

After this detailed procedural explanation is presented, the scientist shares the results obtained. Occasionally, there is a separate section of raw data provided within the body of the report. Sometimes only key points of this are stated in the results section, with the minute details given in separate appendices at the end of the research report. The results are most often reported in figures that provide graphs depicting the results, or in tables that itemize raw data figures. You will see examples of these result visuals in both of the reports below.

Following the formal presentation of the results is the discussion section. In many respects, this is the most important section of the report. This section offers the scientist's interpretation of the results. He/she explains what the results potentially *mean* to the scientific community and to the general reader. It often relates the results of this experiment to previous ones mentioned in the theory (review) section to help further explain some accepted theory, begin to refute it, or propose a new theory.

Often there is a separate conclusion section that follows, although in some reports, as in the psychology one here, the conclusion is part of the discussion section. At any rate, the scientist somehow must complete the report by drawing broader conclusions than the immediate results dictate. Usually there is mention of the implications for future research and/or conjecture about the relation of this research to significant issues in the field.

The report ends with a list of references consulted for background information. The references section always lists the sources according to the dictates of a specific documentation system, which vary quite a bit among scientific disciplines. For instance, psychologists use the fairly commonly used format known as the APA (American Psychological Association) system. The student psychology paper reprinted here is documented in APA format. Sociologists, on the other hand, although also "social" scientists, follow the ASA (American Sociological Association) system. The "hard" or "natural" sciences follow still different systems of documentation. Biologists generally follow the CSE (Council of Scientific Editors) format, whereas chemists follow the

ACS (American Chemical Society) format, as shown in the sample below. (More details regarding documentation are discussed in Chapter 4.) Be sure to ask your professor which system of documentation he/she wishes you to follow.

SCIENTIFIC RESEARCH REPORT 1

Chemistry

Detection of DDT Using Quartz Crystal Microbalance Technology

Mark Nelson
Elmhurst College

Detection of DDT Using Quartz Crystal Microbalance Technology

Descriptive, informative titles are typical in scientific reports.

Abstract:

In this experiment, solid phase microextraction (SPME) coupled with quartz crystal microbalance (QCM) technology was used to detect 1,1 -bis(p-chlorophenyl)-2,2,2-trichloroethane (DDT) in water samples. The data that was obtained showed that the DDT could be detected in the part per billion range. It was also shown that the frequency response was Sauerbrey, and an increase in mass on the QCM resulted in a decrease in the frequency. There were also several techniques that were found to be extremely useful in preparation of the crystals and the DDT samples. Experimental results show that SPME/QCM may be an excellent method to detect DDT and other pesticides in water samples.

The abstract includes a brief summary of the results of this research and an indication of the primary conclusion to enable a reader to know if it worth his or her time to read the report in its entirety.

Introduction:

The compound 1,1 -bis(p-chlorophenyl)-2,2,2-trichloroethane, or DDT as it is commonly called, is a very toxic compound used as a pesticide. Outlawed in the United States, DDT is commonly used in less developed nations to protect crops from pests. It has been proven that ingestion or contact with DDT can cause cancer and genetic damage. The compound itself targets the liver and pancreas and is a very toxic poison.

The introduction explains the background of this research issue.

Currently, DDT can be detected in water with GC to a low concentration of 40 parts per trillion. This is an excellent detection range; however, a GC instrument can cost up to a hundred thousand dollars. Total, the quartz crystal microbalance (QCM) system costs approximately a thousand dollars. The purpose of this experiment is to develop a low cost system to determine DDT in water with a detection limit similar to that of the GC.

Theoretical Analysis:

Solid Phase Microextraction: To determine the concentration of DDT in natural waters, solid phase microextraction was combined with quartz crystal microbalance technology. In 1989, Belardi and Pawliszyn developed a technique that allowed an analyte to be extracted without use of a solvent known as solid phase microextraction (SPME) (*1*). The ability of the solid to extract the analyte is determined by the level of attraction between the analyte and the water as compared to the attraction of the analyte to the solid material. If the attractions are stronger between the analyte and the solid material, then an extraction can be carried out. At equilibrium, the concentration of analyte extracted into the solid phase is defined as

$$Cs K_d ji Ca \qquad \text{(Eq. 1)}$$

where Ca is the molar concentration of the analyte in the aqueous phase, and K_d is the partition constant of the analyte for the interface between the solid and water phases. The value of K_d is dependent on the level to which the analyte is attracted to the solid phase over the aqueous phase. By rearranging this equation, it can be shown that the number of moles of analyte absorbed into the solid phase, n_s, is directly related to the concentration of the analyte in the aqueous sample prior to its extraction, C_0.

$$n_s = \frac{K_d V_s C_0 V_a}{K_d V_s + V_a} \qquad \text{(Eq. 2)}$$

The purpose of the report is succinctly explained. Note that the topic is "signaled" by an obvious indicator— "the purpose of this experiment." That type of direct statement is common in the social sciences and the sciences. It is less common, even frowned upon, within the humanities.

Introductory material continues with this review of relevant background information on this research.

Note that there are references to previous research studies, indicated by italicized numbers in parentheses. These numbers correspond to the numbered items in the reference list at the end of the report.

Note the inclusion of numerous chemical equations. These are a significant part of the "argument" presented or reviewed in scientific research.

V_s and V_a are the volumes of the solid phase and the aqueous sample. SPME is best used when the amount of analyte extracted is small when compared to the amount in the bulk solution ($V_a >> K_d V_s$). Under such conditions, Eq. 2 can be simplified to state $n_s = K_d V_s C_0$, which makes the volume of the introduced sample irrelevant. However, if $V_a << K_d V_s$, then the number of moles of extracted analyte is equal to $C_0 V_a$. If this were the case, then almost all of the analyte would need to be extracted from the solution in order to reach an equilibrium state.

This lengthy section summarizes all of the major findings/results of the detection project.

Applications: SPME can be used for a variety of compounds. Such compounds include volatile and semi-volatile compounds (2), pesticides (3), and drugs (4) in combination with various instrumentation such as GC, IR, and UV-Vis. Volatile and semi-volatile compounds have been studied using light-based methods. Detection by interference spectrometry has been utilized by Gauglitz and coworkers, IR, UV, and Raman spectroscopy by Tilotta's group and GC/MS by Langenfeld et al. for BTEX compounds. These separate analyses were worked with aqueous samples with direct contact to solution. Yang has used headspace SPME to detect semi-volatile aromatic compounds from soil by attenuated total reflectance (ATR) IR (5). Soil samples were first heated to vaporize the analyte, then a stream of nitrogen carried the analyte to the polyisobutylene film where the analyte was then trapped. The solid phase was lined on an ATR crystal and was used for direct detection. Detection limits on the order of 150 ppb were established with a working range of 0.5-10 ppb depending on the analyte.

Pesticides have also been analyzed through a system that integrates SPME to GC. Most of these analyses were performed using polydimethylsiloxane fibers, OV-1. Fibers of different materials such as polydimethylsiloxane, polyacrylate, carbowax-divinylbenzene and polydimethylsiloxane-divinylbenzene have been examined with respect to ability to extract two organophosphorous pesticides (6). Polyacrylate was determined to have the highest K_d value and still retain a linear response with a 30-minute equilibration time.

SPME has many other applications, only a few of which have been mentioned. These examples show how SPME can reduce the amount of time required to analyze samples as compared to older methods.

Acoustic Wave Sensors: Acoustic wave sensors include thickness shear mode, surface acoustic wave, acoustic plate mode, and thin-membrane flexural-plate wave devices. Out of these four devices, the first three are prepared from quartz-based materials. The reason quartz is selected is due to the strong piezoelectric effects produced by its crystalline structure. This property allows quartz to be used as a transducer between electrical energy and mechanical energy. When applied in oscillator circuits that determine the resonance frequency, the low cost, ruggedness, small size, high resonance stability and inertness to chemical reactions makes quartz a practical way to control and monitor frequencies.

In this experiment, quartz crystals are used in the thickness shear mode (TSM). The earliest use of TSM resonators was mass sensing to determine the thickness of a material deposited in vacuum deposition systems *(7)*. This type of system was given the name quartz crystal microbalance (QCM) due to its ability to measure extremely small mass changes on the order of 0.1 ng. It must be noted that QCM is a specific term assigned to TSM resonators, which work under a limited regime. The TSM resonator is affected by numerous properties other than mass, where QCM responds only to a mass applied to its surface. In 1959, Sauerbrey described the relationship between the change in resonance frequency and the mass of material deposited on a quartz crystal surface.

$$f - f_0 = \frac{f_0^2 m}{A(c_q p_q)^{1/2}} \qquad \text{(Eq. 3)}$$

In the Sauerbrey equation, f is the frequency after the addition of a mass, f_0 is the baseline frequency of the crystal (Hz), m is the mass deposited (kg), A is the piezoelectrically active area (m^2), c_q is the piezoelectric quartz elastic constant (2.957×10^{10} N/m^2), and p_q is the density of quartz (2650 kg/m^3) *(8)*.

The Sauerbrey equation assumes that the material deposited on the crystal has a uniform thickness over the entire area and that the material has the same density and viscoelastic properties as the quartz. These assumptions work well for very thin and rigid deposits, but do not work for thick and elastic substances. Due to this, films that do not follow the Sauerbrey equation cannot be referred to as a QCM system, and must be called their more appropriate name of TSM resonator.

<u>Sensing Applications of TSM Resonators</u>: Since the discovery of the Sauerbrey equation, many applications have been found to work well with TSM sensors. In 1980, Nomura and Minemura showed that TSM resonators could be used with one electrode in contact with a solution *(9)*. Prior to this discovery, it was thought that applying a liquid to the sensor would wet the crystal enough to cease its resonating. This discovery opened the door to many TSM resonator applications for liquid sensing.

In 1964, King developed the first hydrocarbon vapor sensitive TSM resonator based circuit *(10)*. This resonator was coupled to a GC to use as a gas-phase absorption detector. Recently, TSM resonators have been coated with polyeurethane type compounds to determine hydrocarbons and aromatic substances. Hauptmann used a TSM sensor coated in polyvinylpyrrolidone to detect for impurities in solvents, and had detection limits of up to 10 ppm of impurity *(11)*.

Zhou et al. have used polymer-coated TSM resonators for the determination of organic solvents in water. The polymers included poly(etheracetate), poly(epichlorohydrin), poly(octadecylmethylacrylate) and trimethyloxypropylsilane/octadecyltrimethoxysilane *(12)*. The group tested for chlorinated hydrocarbons and toluene. The detection limits were found to be on the order of 100 ppb. The individual analytes were

Note that the highly technical scientific language is clearly aimed at a specific, knowledgeable audience.

studied individually in water/methanol solutions. All of the polymers used worked in the QCM regime, and showed no dampening on the quartz crystal. This allowed for application of the films greater than 1 urn, and thus better sensitivities were possible. In addition, the polymer gives a good level of selectivity when analyzing for compounds in solution. Experimental:

Regents: Silicone OV-1 was purchased from Alltech (Deerfield, IL). Methanol, THE, 1,1 -bis(p-chlorophenyl)-2,2,2-trichloroethane (DDT) was purchased from Sigma-Aldrich (St. Louis). DDT samples were made up from high standard 500 ppb in methanol, dissolved in Millipore water (18 u/cm), and diluted to 25 mL.

Instrumentation: Polished, AT-cut quartz crystals were purchased from International Crystal Manufacturing (Oklahoma City, OK). The quartz disk was 15 mm in diameter and had a resonance frequency of 10 +/− 0.03 MHz. The quartz disk was set between two electrodes that were the piezoelectric active area. These electrodes were composed of an underlayer of 30 nm of chromium and a top layer of 100 nm of gold leaf. The diameter of both electrodes was 0.511 cm. This figured into a total sensing area of 0.205 cm^2. The crystals were attached to HC-48/U holders by silver conductive paint (SPI Supplies, West Chester, PA) at the flags of the electrodes.

An acrylic flow through cell (International Crystal Manufacturing, Oklahoma City, OK) was used to contain the sample solutions during the analysis. This cell was comprised of two blocks that were drilled for separate solution chambers. One block was drilled for a static well to hold 1 mL of solution. The second block was machined for a 70 uL flow through compartment. The flow through configuration was used for this work. Solutions were flowed through the input and output tubing (1/16" Teflon) that was connected to the 70 uL chamber with flangeless fittings (Upchurch Scientific, Inc., Oak Harbor, WA). A crystal was then placed between the

This section is the equivalent of the methods section of many scientific papers.

Note that this section, explaining the actual experiment, is divided into appropriate subsections: regents, instrumentation, and procedures.

two blocks and two o-rings. Two 6-32 inch screws were used to compress the two blocks until each solution chamber was watertight. Nylon washers of 0.60" thickness were placed on the screws to ensure that the apparatus was not overtightened, which would result in a shattered crystal.

Frequency measurements were taken using a BK International Crystal Manufacturing, Inc. lever oscillator circuit connected (model #35366) to a BK Precision frequency counter (model #18030). Frequency data were recorded manually in a notebook. The oscillator circuit and frequency counter were powered from a 12 V AC/DC converter.

Procedures:

Film preparation: OV-1 films were prepared by dissolving a small amount (ca. 0.1 g) of the polymer in tetrahydrofuran. Once dissolved, a small drop was applied to the gold leaf section of the crystal. The crystal was then placed in a 105°C oven for 20 minutes. Once the THF had evaporated off of the OV-1, the crystals were allowed to cool to room temperature. Once the crystals had cooled, they were plugged into the oscillator circuit. The crystals were wiped with a Kimwipe® once with the cloth held between the thumb and index finger. The crystals were then rewiped with the cloth, except this time the cloth was pressed and run across the crystal in a circular pattern to smear the OV-1 and OV-73 across the crystal. The OV-25 was a bit harder to properly smear across the crystal, due to the stickiness of the polymer. To aid in this process, a Kimwipe® was moistened with THF, and then the THF was allowed to almost completely evaporate. With this slightly moistened Kimwipe®, the polymer was then smeared over the crystal surface. At this point, if the change in frequency from the original crystal without film was equal to 2500–2800 Hz, or up to 3000 Hz for OV-25, then the crystals were placed aside for future use. If the frequency was too high, the crystals were rewiped in a similar fashion. If the frequency was too low, the crystal was given another drop of the appropriate polymer mixture and the process was repeated.

This procedures section is further subdivided into film preparation and trial runs. Notice the frequent use of subheadings and graphic highlighting to assist the reader in understanding the segments of the entire report, specifically the relationship of the parts to the whole.

The crystal was then placed in the flow through cell. The cell was filled with a concentration of 1 ppb DDT and allowed to stand overnight. This provided adequate time for the crystal and film to become hydrated and acclimated to the DDT before the sample was run through the system.

Trial runs: Before the DDT was introduced into the flow through cell, a blank consisting of methanol and water was injected every five minutes until three consecutive readings were within 2 to 3 hertz of one another. The amount of methanol in the blank was equal to the amount of concentrated DDT in the methanol used to make the highest concentration standard. Once a baseline reading was reached, the DDT samples were introduced into the flow through cell. Each successive concentration was injected with a syringe, then five minutes were allowed to elapse before the frequency was recorded. This was done successive times until three successive frequencies within 3 Hz were obtained. After the final three injections, an average was taken, and the resulting data was used in combination with Microsoft Excel© to produce a graph of concentration versus frequency for DDT.

Discussion:

Results of standard curve analyses of DDT on OV-1 coated crystals are shown in the table. The crystals did respond in a linear manner to the concentration of pesticide present.

Concentration (ppb)	I (Hz)	II (Hz)	III (Hz)	Average (Hz)
0	0	0	0	0
63	−33.67	−32.00	−30.00	−31.89
126	−40.00	−43.33	−54.67	−46.00
315	−66.67	−76.60	−65.67	−69.68
631	−99.00	−100.00	−86.00	−95.00

Specifics of the procedures are explained in explicit detail. Attention to detail and accuracy are high priorities to scientific researchers.

This discussion section offers an interpretation of the results.

Note that the inclusion of the table summarizing key results is the main aspect of this discussion section. This is a much briefer section than the highly elaborated methodology section above. Notably, a great deal of research, time, preparation, and performance are represented in this one table of results.

Notice the somewhat qualified conclusion that the results indicate detection "may be possible." This study is not purporting to have definitive results.

The lower detection limit (LDL) test was performed on a crystal coated with OV-1. Low concentrations of DDT were injected into the flow through cell until seven consecutive readings obtained were nearly identical. During the test, it was determined that OV-1 had a lower detection limit of 100 ppb.

From what was gathered, it was determined that QCMI/SPME detection of DDT in water may be possible. It was also found that the detection followed a Sauerbrey relationship, with the frequency decreasing with the addition of mass. Future experimentation will be needed to perform an adequate number of trials and to negate any sources of error from this determination. Also, tests comparing this method to standard methods accepted for the analysis of pesticides would need to be checked for validity of the new method. Real sample analysis would also have to be studied for correction of complex matrices.

Conclusions:

A separate conclusion section is included, offering broader statements of interpretation and generalization than the discussion section.

As is typical of much academic research, the report ends with suggestions for future research, inviting further scholarly participation.

In conclusion, further experimentation will be needed to determine if SPME/QCM can be used to detect DDT in water samples. Due to the nature of the experimentation, there are many obstacles that must be overcome before this method can be proved to be an accurate way to measure DDT concentrations. If it is later found that SPME/QCM can be used to detect DDT, it could be a significant tool for the EPA. This low cost and compact system can be taken into the field to test for possible pesticide contaminants in the groundwater and soil. Future studies will also be done to determine if SPME/QCM can be used to detect other types of pesticides, which may be harmful to humans and animals.

References are documented in ACS (American Chemical Society) style in a citation-year system. The references match the order of the internal notes.

References:

1. Belardi, R.P.; Pawliszyn, J. *J. Water Pollution Res. J. Can.* **1989**, *24*, 179.

2. Kraus, G. et al. *J. Anal. Chem.* **1994**, *348*, 598.

3. Choudhury, T.K. et al. *Environ. Sci. Technol.* **1996**, *30*, 3259.

4. Kataoka, H. et al. *Anal. Chem.* **1999**, *71*, 4237.

5. Yang, J.; Her, J-W. *Anal. Chem.* **1999**, *71*, 4690.

6. Sng, M.T. et al. *J. Chromatogr. A.* **1997**, *759*, 217.

7. Oberg, P.; Lingensjo, J. *Rev. Sci. Inst.* **1959**, *30*, 1053.

8. Sauerbrey, G.Z. *Physik.* **1959**, *155*, 206.

9. Nomura, T. *Anal. Chem. Acta.* **1981**, *124*, 81.

10. King, Jr., W.H. *Anal. Chem.* **1964**, *36*, 1735.

11. Auge, J. et al. *Sens. and Actuators B.* **1994**, *101*, 518.

12. Zhou, R. et al. *Sens. and Actuators B.* **1996**, *35–36*, 176.

Note one distinction here is the boldfacing of dates because the timeliness of the experiments is crucial.

INVESTIGATING THE GENRE SAMPLE

1. One feature of the scientific research report as a genre is its progressive narrowing of focus in the introduction, so that by the end of the introduction, the reader will know precisely what the report is about. How effectively do you think Mark Nelson accomplishes this goal in his introduction?

2. Nelson makes extensive use of abbreviations throughout his report. How does he make sure that his readers always know what an abbreviation stands for?

3. Notice the extensive use of subheadings in the instrumentation section of Nelson's paper. What kinds of assistance do these subheadings offer to the reader of the report?

SCIENTIFIC RESEARCH REPORT 2

Psychology

The complete title, which is both descriptive and informative, appears on the title page.

The Influence of Viewing a Violent Film on a Word Generation Task

Kathleen R. Beety Diviak
Augustana College

An abbreviated form of the title, called a "running head," appears at the top right of each page of the actual report. This shorter title enables easier reference to the study.

The abstract includes a brief explanation of the nature of the study, a summary of the major results, and an indication of a primary conclusion.

Note that in APA style, the abstract appears with no indentation, in a single paragraph, and on a separate page of the report.

The title is repeated on the first page of the report.

The introduction explains the background of this research issue.

Influence of a Violent Film

Abstract

A study was designed to assess whether the arousal induced by observing a violent film would affect task performance. A word generation task was used to measure performance. Ten undergraduates at a Midwestern college were shown a violent film and a neutral film, each 10 minutes in length. After observing the first film, 5 randomly assigned participants were asked to generate words about a category congruent with the theme of the film. The other 5 participants generated words for a category that was not congruent with the theme of the film. This procedure was then repeated for the second film. Participants generated more exemplars after observing the neutral film and less exemplars after the violent film. Congruent or noncongruent categories did not have a significant main effect. These results suggest that arousal caused by observing a violent film will hamper task performance.

The Influence of Viewing a Violent Film on a Word Generation Task

It is a common belief that arousal affects one's cognitive abilities and performance. For example, students often attribute a low exam score to their depression or exhilaration. Research has supported the theory that arousal, in general, plays an important role in cognition; however, there has been no research examining arousal elicited by violence. This is the first study to explore the effect of the arousal that violence evokes.

Psychologists Yerkes and Dodson (1908) examined the effect of arousal on task performances. Their study proposes a normal curve (a mesokurtic distribution) with extremely low or high arousal leading to poor task performance. The median level of arousal yielded the highest performance scores. Kebeck and Lohaus's (1986) participants were asked to recall the plot of a film immediately following the film and 14 days later. They found that high emotional involvement does not lead to higher recall scores. Goss, Nueliep, and O'Hair (1985) assigned university students to either a negatively induced group or a control group with no induction. The participants were shown a videotape and later asked to recall the conversation they observed. The control group had significantly higher scores on the recall test. In addition, a negative correlation was found between recall scores and negative arousal. These studies support the hypothesis that extreme arousal, either positive or negative, will lead to poor performance.

It is conceivable that observing violence will alter one's current state of arousal in some manner. The purpose of this study is to determine the effect that the arousal induced by watching a violent film has on a word generation task. Perhaps the violent film arouses and distracts the participants from their assigned task, leading to a poor performance. Overall the participants will be less attentive to the task at hand, the word generation in this study. Consequently, the number of words generated should be higher for the neutral film, because this film will not arouse the participants. In addition, the category that the participants generated words about was either congruent or noncongruent with the theme of the film. Perhaps generation for a congruent category would be easier due to priming effects of the film. Bowles and Poon (1988) studied the priming effects that context had on a word generation task. Their prime was the category name, which should limit the exemplars the participants generated. They found that

This introduction offers a "mini" literature review to justify the undertaking of this experiment.

Note that the references to previous research studies are indicated by authors' last names and date.

Dates are emphasized more frequently in scientific reports because of the sequential nature of much empirical research.

The purpose of this study is clearly explained.

The "Method" section explains details of the method used in this research. Methodology is extremely important in the sciences and social sciences because empirical results are strongly influenced by the accuracy and integrity of the methods used.

This methods section is subdivided into four categories: participants, materials, design, and procedure.

Note that in some older reports, "participants" are referred to as "subjects." This has been changed within the field of psychology to avoid a possible derogatory implication.

their participants made use of the context when generating words, thus exhibiting a priming effect.

Method

Participants

Ten Augustana College undergraduates from an advanced statistics class participated as a part of a course requirement.

Materials

Two 10-minute film clips were used to represent the two types of film, violent or neutral. The violent film clip was taken from the movie *Platoon*. The scenes contained abusive and offensive language, showed American soldiers *acting* viciously towards Vietnamese civilians, and numerous acts of beating and killing. The neutral film was a clip from *News Hour* and showed the U.S. Attorney being interviewed about the case of Marion Berry, the Washington, D.C., mayor arrested for drug possession.

Design

There are two independent variables in this experiment. The first is type of film. The two levels are violent or neutral. The neutral film is used as the baseline measure. The second independent variable is the type of category. The category that was chosen for the participants to generate exemplars for was either congruent or noncongruent. The congruent word is descriptive of the type of film. The dependent measure is the number of words generated about the given category. The experiment is a mixed design. All 10 participants observe both types of films (within participants' design). Following the film, 5 of the participants are randomly selected to generate exemplars for the congruent category and the other 5 are given the noncongruent category (between participants' design).

Procedure

Weeks before the experiment was conducted, the participants were to generate words that exemplified violence or neutrality. The words were then rated on a scale of 1–7 in terms of how strongly they characterized violence or neutrality. A rating of 1 was not at all characteristic of the category and a 7 was highly characteristic. The two words with the highest rating and equal means were chosen for the type of category. These words were "war," congruent with the violent film, and "mineral," congruent with the neutral film. Students enrolled in another statistics course generated words for "war" and "mineral" to ensure that an equal amount of exemplars could be generated for both word categories. The participants were then tested in a group and asked to watch a 10-minute film clip. The film order of the violent and neutral films was randomly selected. When the film clip was over, the participants were randomly assigned to the congruent or noncongruent condition. The students were given a piece of paper with the category "war" or "mineral" and told to generate as many words as possible that related to their category. The participants were given 3 minutes to do so. This procedure was repeated for the second film. Following the second word generation task, students were instructed to count the number of words they generated for each category. Then participants were debriefed as to the purpose of the study and the expected results. The session lasted approximately an hour.

Results

Means for the two independent variables, type of film (violent or neutral) and type of category (congruent or noncongruent), were computed. These data are shown in Figure 1.

As can be seen in Figure 1, more words were generated after viewing the neutral film than after viewing the violent film. These data were subjected to a two-factor mixed design ANOVA, one within factor (type of film) and one between factor (type of category). The main effect for the type of film was significant, $F(1,8) = 9.56$, MSE = 65.6, indicating

Specifics of the procedure are explained in detail to ensure that the reader understands exactly how the experiment was conducted.

The specific results of the experiment are relayed here.

The results are discussed in narrative form and are also depicted in a visual and numerical format in an appendix.

Note the reference to a figure, which is included at the end of the report.

that violence had a detrimental effect on performance. The type of category was not significant, $F(1,3) = 1.78$, MSE = 44.9. As illustrated in Figure 1, there was no interaction, $F(1,8) = .076$, MSE = 65.6. The significant results for the type of file indicate that the violent film hindered task performance.

Discussion

The discussion section offers an interpretation of the results. This is frequently considered the most important section of the report. Here the researcher offers his/her interpretation of the happenings and the significance of those happenings.

The results obtained reveal that after viewing a violent film, the number of words the participants generated was significantly lower than after viewing the neutral film. The type of word category (congruent or noncongruent) was not significant. The results support the hypothesis that the arousal caused by the violent film will impede performance because the participants will devote less of their ability to the task.

The results are important and they add to our study of this phenomenon because it demonstrates the relation between the arousal evoked by violence and task performance. Other researchers have supported the theory that extreme high or low arousal in general will negatively affect task performance (Yerkes and Dodson, 1908). Goss, Nueliep, and O'Hair (1985) found a significant negative correlation between the participants' recall scores and negative arousal. Our research supports the principle that any type of extreme arousal will hinder task performance. There are broad implications for the results of this study. Task performance is significantly substandard when participants are aroused after watching a violent film; hence, the arousal from actually witnessing an act of violence would probably lower task performance as well. Many people find themselves in occupations, such as soldiers in combat or police officers, where observing violent acts is an everyday occurrence. Their ability to perform cognitive tasks at the highest and most accurate level is a necessity. Soldiers, police officers, and others in comparable professions must possess the ability to think

This section also includes conclusions. Sometimes conclusions are reported within a separate section in scientific reports. Frequently in the social sciences they are combined.

accurately and quickly; a mistake or misjudgment could cost human lives. Perhaps future research could manipulate acts of violence to determine the long-term effects of daily exposure to acts of violence. The conclusions could be put to use immediately in many real-life settings.

Perhaps the type of category (congruent or noncongruent) was not significant because of the ages of the participants used in this study, 19–21. Bowles and Poon (1988) found that older adults, ages 65–78, showed significantly greater priming effects than did younger participants, ages 18–28. The experimenters suggest that older adults make greater use of the context and the primes than younger adults do. In the future, a similar study using a violent and neutral film clip could be run with older and younger adults as participants. Conceivably, the results of this future study would indicate whether the ages of the participants or the theme of the film, violent or neutral, had an effect on word generation for congruent and noncongruent categories. Each of the variables in this study has broad implications, which need to be researched further.

Notice the comments and suggestions for future research. This is a common closing to all types of academic research. It points to the ongoing nature of academic research. Indeed, research can be viewed as a kind of unending "conversation" among researchers and scholars.

References

Bowles, N. L., & Poon, L. W. (1988). Age and context effects in lexical decision: An age by context interaction. *Experimental Aging Research, 14*, 201–205.

Goss, B., Nueliep, L. W., & O'Hair, D. (1985). Reduced conversational memory as a function of negative arousal: A preliminary analysis. *Communication Research Reports, 2*, 202–205.

Kebeck, G., & Lohaus, A. (1986). Effect of emotional arousal on free recall of complex material. *Perceptual & Motor Skills, 63*, 461–462.

Yerkes, R. M., & Dodson, J. D. (1908). The relation of the strength of stimulus to rapidity of habit formation. *Journal of Comparative and Neurological Psychology, 19*, 459–482.

A list of references is provided to lend credibility to the experiment.

Sources are documented in APA (American Psychological Association) style.

Figure Caption   Mean Number of Words Generated as a Function of the Type of Film and Type of Category.

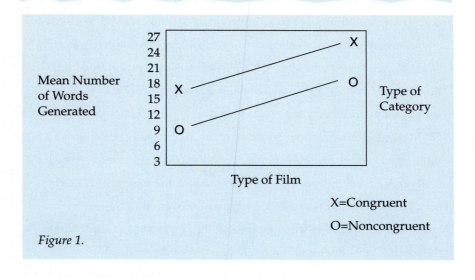

Figure 1.

INVESTIGATING THE GENRE SAMPLE

1. What differences do you detect between the literature review section of this paper and the corresponding section of Mark Nelson's paper on DDT? What are the similarities and differences in the ways sources are referred to?
2. A person writing a scientific research report often has to display his or her knowledge of the terminology of experimental research design. Notice, for example, Kathleen R. Beety Diviak's use of the term *independent variables*. What other evidence do you find in the paper that the author was well trained in social science experimental research?
3. In the genre of the social science research report, a writer may sometimes speculate in the discussion section about implications of the research for practitioners in applied social science fields. Where do you see Diviak accomplishing this goal?

FIELD OBSERVATION REPORTS

Some academic disciplines such as archeology have required **field observation reports** for decades. Recently, these reports have become increasingly popular in many other fields, especially such areas as education, nursing, speech pathology, and so forth. The more educators advocate that students make crucial connections between purely academic work (which often focuses upon theory or basic content) and practical applications of that work within future professions, the more appropriate field observations and their reportings become. The growing emphasis on internships across all fields is certainly testament to this position. Consequently, it is not unlikely that you may now be required to conduct and report on field observations in any class—engineering, business, psychology, and even history.

The purpose of a field observation or site inspection is fairly straightforward. Things tend to come alive for all of us if we see them in action, in their "natural" context. Understanding a theory as explained in a textbook or treatise and seeing it applied in operation can be two very different, though complementary, types of learning experiences, both quite valuable.

The purpose of the observation itself is to experience firsthand some activity pertinent to your academic study, and the purposes of the observation report are multiple:

1. to encourage you to critically reflect upon your observations, rather than to observe passively;
2. to allow you a forum to report on your observations and your opinions on those findings, weighing advantages and disadvantages;
3. to demonstrate to your professors your observational and analytical skills;

4. to forge critical connections between theory and practice as you attempt to frame your observations relative to background knowledge acquired through course readings and discussions as well as through previous life experiences; and

5. to practice effective communication skills, sharing details with an audience who has not often witnessed the same activity you have.

When preparing to conduct a field observation and then to report it, you should consider the variety of audiences you will encounter. During the actual observation, your subject will often simultaneously be your audience; be conscious of the fact that most often while you watch, you will be watched. Observe reactions to your presence and to your reactions to what/whom you are observing. Of course, you must always be respectful of any procedures, restrictions, and/or sensitivities that need to be attended to while observing a particular site. Remember, too, whatever audience(s) with whom you'll need to share your findings. Be conscious of what details you will need to relate, especially with anyone who may be unfamiliar with such a site or activity.

In preparing your report, you may have to consider multiple audiences as well. No doubt for an academic assignment, you will be preparing your report for your professor. However, you may also be preparing it for fellow students or perhaps for the site members whom you observed. Sometimes you may be preparing your observation report for larger, nonpresent stakeholders, such as teacher accreditation boards or internship review panels. Be sure to consider the various audiences for whom you are preparing the report and include appropriately focused information with sufficient examples to allow your audience members to experience at least some of the things that you did at the site.

In order to write an effective field observation report, you must, of course, take careful notes. Record as many details as possible about the actual appearance of the site, the people involved, the "feel" or tone of the site, the interactions that you notice, the activity or activities that take place, and so forth. The more detailed notes you have, the easier it will be to write up your observation. In some cases you may wish to tape-record or even videotape a field site. If you do, be certain to receive any necessary written permissions. Keep in mind that tape recording usually requires very time-consuming transcription. Sometimes it is more labor-intensive than fruitful. No matter what method of recording you choose, allow yourself some time for an immediate "debriefing," if at all possible. That is, while the observation is still clearly in your mind, take time to fill in any holes in your notes, to jot down things that occurred to you once you left the site, and to log any critical, theoretical, or previously acquired empirical connections you noted. Finally, be sure to confirm all necessary names, with proper spellings, and contact information should you need it for your report or for follow-up clarification questions.

The procedure for the actual report and its exact format will vary by discipline. In some cases, you may be given a specific set of guidelines to follow or even a questionnaire to complete. In other cases, you may be required to follow an informal investigation report form with specified subheadings. No doubt your professor will inform you of these specifics. Sometimes the requirements will be almost entirely open-ended, the only instruction being to "write up your observation." Keep in mind that the most successful reports will not only record the details you saw but also include an *analysis* of what you saw. Chances are your observation will be assigned to provide you with an opportunity to scrutinize, in context, an activity that reflects some theory, principle, or procedure that you are studying in your class. While observing, concentrate on analyzing what you observe in relation to that theory or mindset, in order to offer a more insightful, critical reflection in your follow-up report.

Essentially, your observation report will include:

- recorded details of what you observe;
- a critical analysis of these details, often in relation to certain principles or theories;
- an evaluation or assessment of the value and/or effectiveness of the location or activity observed;
- a conclusion reflecting your overall experience;
- and, sometimes, recommendations for improvements or changes at the site.

Looking closely at the two sample field observation reports below, you'll see evidence of all of the above features. The first example is written by a College of DuPage student who is preparing to be a library science assistant through a community college paraprofessional program. The report details an observation of an actual community library to determine its compliance with the American Disabilities Act. The second sample, written by an education student from Elmhurst College for an education psychology course, presents observations and analyses of activities within a middle school classroom that are considered from specific theoretical perspectives.

FIELD OBSERVATION REPORT 1

Library Science

A.D.A. Library Visit

Mildred Sabath
College of DuPage

A.D.A. Library Visit

The library I chose to visit for the American Disabilities Act library visit was the LaGrange Park Public Library. The library at 555 N. LaGrange Rd. is a new, modern, and rather imposing structure that I had never visited before. With the building being modern and built more

The writer establishes the purpose of the observation.

The specific observation site is clearly identified.

Note that this brief conclusion statement functions as a kind of "thesis" for the observation provided.

The writer not only offers observational data, but in keeping with this genre's expectation, relates the observation to the overall intent or focus—i.e., here the writer indicates the discrepancy regarding the ADA code mandates and offers a possible explanation for the deviation.

Additional features are analyzed for compliance; variances are always noted.

The writer continues to report observations and analyze them in relation to her overall focus—namely, code compliance. Remember that the analytical component is a significant aspect of this genre.

recently than other local libraries, I hoped to see an ideally designed library. Most of my findings were favorable to the A.D.A. guidelines.

My initial measurement of the curb cut was very disappointing. It was only 39 1/2" wide. I knew visually it was way off the 96" wide directive. One reason for it being less than prescribed might be the location's angle. The entrance is to the right of the curb cut, and to the left, the property slopes down very noticeably and at a rather difficult angle to maneuver a wheelchair safely.

Fortunately, the doors were automatically opened with a large, low, square sign with a wheelchair graphic button. The width of the double doors measured 34 1/2" and, happily, there was not a post between them. Indeed, my entry was accomplished with relative ease. The second set of doors was identical in size and operation.

The bathrooms were not on the main entry level, so the elevator transported me to the lower level. Happily, I found the bathroom adjacent to the elevator. The elevator controls were placed low enough to access easily from a wheelchair. The physically challenged stall was generously sized with grab bars at 34" from the floor. The south wall had the wall mounted grab bars that measured 42", and the north side of the toilet area had a triangular shaped grab bar assembly that I had not encountered before. I found this to be very sturdy and solidly attached. The only mirror was 40" from the floor and had a small metal shelf. The bathroom had one regular sink and a lower dished-out, larger, easily accessible sink with a single control faucet.

The long circulation desk was higher at 40' than the ideal, but the eastern quadrant, a 30" section, was desk-like and available with a staff computer. The computer stations were all at 30" high tables and counters. The study tables were all 30" high also. All of the aisles in reference, fiction and non-fiction averaged 41 1/2 to 42 inches, and the turnarounds ranged from 56" in reference to 48" in fiction.

The signage looked large enough to my view, but upon measuring, the capital letters were only $2^1/_4$" and the lowercase letters were $1^5/_8$". The signs were 7' above the floor. That would come in 2" over the minimum.

I consulted the library online catalog with the keywords "mentally challenged," and many volumes were listed. However, what surprised me was that the first selection was fiction, *A Face in Every Window* by Nolan Han. It definitely peaked my interest. When I queried "physically challenged" in the online catalog, the first selection was more what I expected. It returned *The Physically Challenged* by Don Nardo (962.4).

The circulation desk clerk was very busy, but pleasant, when I arrived with my notes and yardstick. Later, near the end of my visit, when I inquired if their collection included Braille editions, he was not able to answer fully, and he sent me to the reference librarian. When he realized that there was no one at the reference desk, he walked over and pointed out the reference librarian, who was returning to his desk. He exhibited a most helpful and caring attitude.

The reference librarian checked his computer and informed me of the single Braille volume—a western, *Mata Gorda* by Louis Lamour—but quickly offered to check Inter Library Loan for additional selections. I explained that this was a question for class and that I wasn't in need of Braille editions. He very pleasantly asked how the library fared on my measurements. I said that they did well, at which point he told me that future plans are to expand to the upper level, which will afford more spacious placement.

The LaGrange Park Library does not provide any deaf interpreters for any of their programs, according to a youth services clerk. However, the LaGrange Public Library, about a mile farther south on LaGrange Road, does have a TDD-only phone number listed in the local phone book.

The writer offers a personal observation and a more "scientific" discussion as well. Keep in mind that parameters of a field observation will vary.

The writer indicates a brief analysis of catalog offerings pertinent to A.D.A. issues. Note the use of first person, an acceptable, even expected, dimension of most field observations.

Analytical comments on the helpfulness of the personnel in relation to code issues are provided.

The writer includes a discussion of the facilities for blind patrons, noting the limited facilities at this site. However, services are possible through the larger networked system.

Here the writer analyzes the facilities for deaf patrons. Note that special-interest groups are considered within the "general" population of the disabled, providing a more specific observational analysis.

The writer observes additional items of assistance for disabled patrons.

> As I perused the back (east) end of the library, where the majority of their computers are located, I found two assistive devices. There is a Kurzwiel reader and a Freedom machine with a sign next to these devices that reads, in part, "Those with visual needs can read again. . . ," which I thought was quite helpful. The collection includes the whole spectrum of audiotapes, CD books and large print volumes.

Personal comments of the observer are appropriately included within this genre.

> I now have a new appreciation of the difficulties encountered by the physically impaired.

INVESTIGATING THE GENRE SAMPLE

1. As was the case with informative reports, field observations can have important secondary purposes besides simply describing what the author observed. What other purposes do you see Mildred Sabath's paper accomplishing?
2. Field observations as a genre allow the writer to refer to himself or herself as "I" and use strong, active verbs. What is the effect of these strategies on the reader?
3. Sabath uses a spatial organization to structure her paper. What kinds of transitional words and phrases does she use to enable the reader to move through the library with her as she reports on her visit?

FIELD OBSERVATION REPORT 2
Education

Middle School Field Experience

Mindi Johnson Colón
Elmhurst College

Middle School Field Experience

The writer begins with an indication of the perspective adopted for the observation: adolescent development.

> While in the middle school, I observed several characteristics of adolescent development in the students. Based on the peer interaction, clothing, and behaviors of the students, I would classify their developmental stage to be *identity versus role confusion* in Erikson's stages

of development. The classroom was adorned with collage posters the students in the seventh grade homeroom had made; these projects were eclectic collages of things that expressed each student's personality, likes, and dislikes. Studying these collages gave me some insight into the different roles these adolescents are trying on.

The classroom was set up to foster peer social interaction. Desks were grouped in fours and students would collaborate on tasks and share their written work with the other students in their group. The make-up of the groups was long-term; they are extrinsically motivated by a point system in which each group can collect or lose points based on cooperation and group interaction. As discussed in class, taking away points in a behaviorist system like this one could create a negative situation where a group could be in debt and then give up trying to gain points. However, the arrangement of groupings in the classroom is developmentally appropriate for this age and a great way to promote prosocial behaviors.

In the realm of moral development, I saw evidence of some students being at the good boy/good girl stage on the conventional morality level of Kohlberg's theory of moral development. Mary and Joe, both seventh graders, displayed some show-off/goof-off behaviors, including sarcastic comments just quiet enough that Miss Anderson could not hear. In both cases, Mary and Joe looked to the students around them with facial expressions that clearly were seeking approval and awaiting laughter. What they were seeking from their peers was the confirmation that their behavior was good or right. Their peers were the authority figures they were looking to for a judgment of the behavior.

One of the most obvious traits of adolescent physical development is the varying degrees of physical development. This characteristic of development was something that I noticed immediately. Most of the girls were taller than the boys. It was amazing to see the difference

(Keep in mind that the same site could be observed from varied perspectives for multiple intents, so the indication of the "lens" is significant.) The writer immediately applies knowledge of a key educational psychology theorist to the observation, giving the report a further focus and a certain authority and credibility as well.

The writer observes the classroom arrangement, analyzing it relative to a major focal point of the report: peer interaction.

The writer again theorizes about her observation. She analyzes peer interaction in relation to another theory prevalent in educational psychology. This type of informed analysis is significant in the genre of field observations.

Notice the continued relaying of observational detail followed by analysis and, specifically, analysis of variances.

between the students in terms of physical development; between the smallest and the biggest in both sexes was great variance.

The writer offers analytical comments on positive features of this observational site.

I saw many things about this junior high school that I found to be positive aspects. There were many new, young and enthusiastic teachers. Language arts and reading were taught in a block schedule. I observed Miss Anderson, a language arts and reading teacher. So she has three classes for two periods each. I had never seen this type of scheduling before and found it to have many positive aspects. For example, reading and writing greatly overlap; it is good for transfer and teaching across the curriculum to have them taught in a block schedule.

Here she offers analysis of the positives and potential negatives of another site feature she observed. Keeping the observation as balanced and objective as possible is usually very important in field observation reports.

Another new thing I saw at this school was a school-wide reward system for positive character traits and behaviors. All of the teachers have forms and when they observe students being helpful, kind, or otherwise going above and beyond, they fill out a form and give it to the student. Every week all of the forms are turned in and a drawing is held for a prize. I had mixed feelings about this behavior modification system. On one hand, it is a good thing to recognize and acknowledge positive character building behaviors and attitudes in students at this age; it promotes self-esteem and helps develop a positive self-concept. However, this system also rewards behaviors that should be displayed for the intrinsic reward of being a good person. Adolescents are in the transition period between elementary school, where many teachers reward all work and behaviors extrinsically, to high school, where students are individuals and often behaviors are not noticed and more often not acknowledged. I had mixed feelings, too, because there is such a range among adolescents in terms of their moral development. Some students may still need extrinsic rewards; some students may satiate with the rewards and only display those positive behaviors when they will be rewarded.

The only thing I saw that I felt was developmentally inappropriate was the teacher's use of sarcasm. It was Miss Anderson's second year teaching, and it was my impression that she wants the students to like her and think she is cool (as I am sure all teachers want to a degree). However, I felt that the way she used sarcasm was demeaning and humiliating to the students at which it was directed. For example, Joe had done his assignment on spiral paper in pink pen. Miss Anderson scolded him for the paper and made him tear off the spiral edge. Then as Joe was going to the front of the classroom to read his paper, Miss Anderson made fun of the fact he had used pink ink on the paper. I felt this would be wrong at any age, but especially inappropriate at this stage of development. So much in adolescence revolves around acceptance by peers and teachers. The self-concept and self-esteem are so fragile and easily damaged at this stage that sarcasm, especially as Miss Anderson implemented it, is too dangerous.

> The writer discusses a negative feature that emerged during the observation. She analyzes potential harm by offering a specific example and justifying her conclusion. (Note that though there is a clear effort to provide a balanced observation, personal opinion is most often highly relevant and valued within this genre.)

INVESTIGATING THE GENRE SAMPLE

1. A field observation paper is often geared toward a specific, disciplinary audience. What terminology does Mindi Johnson Colón use that shows she is writing to an audience of professional educators?
2. How would you describe the organizational structure of Colón's paper? How does it differ from the organization of the other field observation paper?
3. What do you notice about the nature of the conclusion of a field observation paper, based on your reading of these two samples?

CASE STUDIES

A **case study** is a common genre in academic writing that requires you to rely primarily on your experiences and powers of observation as data sources, without extensively analyzing other sources or gathering controlled, experimental data. This type of study is characterized by the report of an extensive empirical observation followed by theoretical or conceptual conclusions.

A case study, also known as a *case report*, is a genre usually written by students and scholars in the social and behavioral sciences, business, and education to describe and analyze a single subject: a person, object, group, event, state, condition, or process. At the heart of a case study is empirical observation. To prepare a case study, the writer examines the subject in the context of a relatively brief, self-contained situation that is important to the subject in some way. It may be a particularly formative situation where the subject is displaying evidence of some important growth or development. It may be an especially critical moment when the future of the subject is uncertain and could move in a number of different directions. It could be an instance of culmination in which the subject is concluding some process. Or it could simply be a "representative," "traditional," or "normal" episode in which the subject is behaving as it does most of the time.

A wide range of writing projects may employ case studies. In a course on early childhood psychology, you might write a case study after observing one preschool-age child playing with other children his age for an hour. In a course on management ethics, you might write a case study after observing a company's upper-management officers deliberate for a week about whether to pay insurance benefits for part-time workers. In a course on assessment and evaluation in education, you might write a case study after observing a group of experienced and inexperienced teachers evaluate student performance portfolios for an entire afternoon.

Case studies serve two valuable functions. First of all, case studies are valuable in their own right because they provide writers with actual, observable data, which they can then draw upon to generate theoretical conclusions. For example, the writer of the educational case study described above might suggest some ideas about how mixed groups of teachers tend to operate when they are reading student portfolios. However, because a case study is usually built on the observation of a single "case"—that is, just one person, object, event, condition, process, or state—the conventions of writing in an academic field may not allow the writer to generalize his or her conclusions beyond the boundaries of the single case at hand so that they apply to other cases—similar people, objects, events, and so on—in the field. In other words, some audience members will rightly question the validity of the small sample. Therefore, the second function of case studies comes into play.

Conducting a case study is considered an appropriate method of generating hypotheses that could be tested in a study involving a group of research subjects larger than the single subject being studied. So, to continue our example, the educational case study described above might generate a hypothesis about the relative amount of time an experienced teacher spends reading a portfolio in contrast to the amount of time a beginning teacher spends; this hypothesis could he tested in an experiment, and the results could be written up in a more detailed, formal scientific research report (see the section on laboratory reports).

The genre of the case study requires writers to abide by six basic ground rules:

1. Writers must report what they observe as truthfully as possible, without allowing their mind to fabricate what they had hoped to see in the case.
2. Writers must be able to state the aims of the case study clearly so that their observations can be as efficient and effective as possible.
3. Writers must recognize the inherent limitations of the case study—only one case is being studied—and assess the effectiveness of the case study within those boundaries.
4. Writers must acknowledge the degree to which they are qualified to draw conclusions based on the data they observe.

5. Writers must do their best to describe the richness of the context in which the case is situated.
6. Writers must strive to describe what they observe in the case as clearly and simply as possible.

The written report of a case study has at least three sections. The first section provides a background statement of the central problem under investigation in the case study. Sometimes this section contains a review of scholarship, often called a "Literature Review," which summarizes and connects relevant research to the problem being studied. An actual literature review section functions not only as a summary or recap of previous research but also as an argument. Essentially, by placing the current research study in relation to previous works, a literature review helps justify a position or clarify the need for additional research. The second section provides a detailed account of the observations made in the case study. The final section offers generalizations and conclusions that the writer draws on the basis of whatever he or she has observed. Some case studies are preceded by an abstract. Case studies that cite scholarship about the problem being studied should provide a list of references or works cited; most case studies use the American Psychological Association (APA) style for citing sources, as explained in the third section of Chapter 4.

The first of the two student samples is a case study written by an Elmhurst College student for an upper-level sociology course on complex organizations. You'll note that this study does begin with the optional abstract mentioned above. It also includes a literature review and, of course, an introductory statement to contextualize the purpose of the study, details of the observations, and a rather lengthy discussion section. The second sample, written by a psychology major at the University of Notre Dame, examines a specific after-school tutoring program for underprivileged children. It, too, includes the appropriate sections of a case study.

CASE STUDY 1
Sociology

Case Study: Jennifer's Dance School

Teresa Stock
Elmhurst College

Case Study: Jennifer's Dance School

Abstract

This case study focuses on entrepreneurship as well as growth and change within an organization. A dance school located in a suburb of Chicago that offers dance classes to children and adults of all ages was

This case study begins with a useful abstract, which briefly outlines the topic, the methods, and the conclusions relative to specific sociological theories.

studied. Interviews and observations were used to collect data, and the history of the organization was obtained. Data was used to see if various existing theories having to do with entrepreneurship, change, and development within organizations were supported by this case. Support was found for Granovetter and Romanelli's theories, and some support was found for Aldrich's ideas. At this point in the organization, Greiner's life cycle does not apply, but it may apply in the future.

In the introduction, the writer establishes the intent of the case study and the nature of the specific site to be observed.

Introduction

In order to understand why people start their own businesses, it is important to consider the conditions under which people are able to create their own organizations. There is a great deal of existing literature that examines entrepreneurship, or how new organizations are created. There are also different ideas that try to explain how organizations change and develop. Knowing the conditions under which organizations are created, as well as having an idea of how organizations deal with change and growth, can help potential entrepreneurs prepare for their own businesses in the future. Here, the natural history of an organization known as Jennifer's Dance School was obtained to determine whether or not current ideas and theories apply to the start and growth of this organization.

Note that consistently formatted subheadings are used for sections of equivalent weight throughout the report. This provides for easy readability and clearly signals the writer's organizational pattern.

Literature Review

When studying a young and growing organization such as Jennifer's Dance School, it is only natural to look at how the organization got started in the first place. A great deal of literature out there examines entrepreneurship, or how new organizations are created. Although earlier research has focused on the traits and characteristics of entrepreneurs, modern research focuses more on the *context* in which organizations were created (Scott, 2003). Even though many different theories have been created to explain how new organizations arise, there is no agreement on any one theory that can explain every situation (Romanelli, 1991).

In her article on new organizational forms, Romanelli (1991) starts out by defining the concept of an organizational form as "those characteristics of an organization that identify it as a distinct entity and, at the same time, classify it as a member of a group of similar organizations." For example, Jennifer's Dance School is classified as a dance studio, and it is easy to distinguish it from a restaurant. After defining the concept of an organizational form, a number of theories and approaches that explain how new organizations are created are described.

Aldrich (1999) notes the importance of networks in establishing new organizations. Networks have to do with strong and weak ties. In his work "The Strength of Weak Ties," Granovetter (1973) focuses on how weak ties provide us with more opportunities than strong ties. In his research, he asked a random sample of people who found a new job through another person how often they *saw* this person around the time they were told about the job. "Often" was considered seeing the person at least twice a week, "occasionally" was defined as seeing the person more than once a year, but less than twice a week, and "rarely" was defined as seeing the person once a year or less. He found that 16.7% saw the person often, 55.6% saw the person occasionally, and 27.8% rarely saw the person. This demonstrates that overall, people's weaker ties helped them find a new job more often than their stronger ties did. The findings show support for Granovetter's idea that people who we are weakly tied to have access to information that is different from the information we would receive from our strong ties (Granovetter, 1973). Granovetter's research and ideas were important to consider when looking at how Jennifer got her dance studio started and how she was able to build her clientele. For example, did she build her clientele through her weaker ties or through her stronger ones?

Where Granovetter focused mainly on the importance of weak ties, Aldrich (1999) sees strong ties as being crucial to entrepreneurship as

This literature review focuses on previous studies of entrepreneurship and organizational models.
Remember that a literature review is essentially an argument; it justifies a focus or position by reviewing other work already performed and then places the current work in relation to the earlier research.

The writer establishes the particular organizational form that is focused upon here.

Reviewing theories of organizational structures and development enables the reader to understand the potential importance of the coming case study and enables the writer to build her case for her eventual interpretation of her observations.

Notice how the writer specifically interweaves previous research theories and findings with particulars of her case example.

The writer considers counterpositions prevalent in the research.

well. Aldrich notes that strong ties provide people with emotional support in all areas of their life, and that they are more reliable than weaker ties. People go to their strong ties for advice and assistance, and there is a strong sense of trust between the two parties. Interestingly, Aldrich notes that strong ties with family members supply emotional support, but not financial support. He even cites research saying that the more family members there are in an entrepreneur's business discussion network, the less of a chance there is of that entrepreneur actually starting his own organization (Renault, Aldrich, & Moody, 1998 in Aldrich, 1999). This was an interesting finding to consider while researching Jennifer's Dance School, since the studio actually started out in the basement of Jennifer's parents' house.

Here the writer notes that her case offers an exception to one theory. Essentially, she is posing a counterargument in this section of the literature review.

Continuing the review of sociological theories and research creates the basis for the position the writer will assume in her case.

Aldrich also focuses on the importance of knowledge in forming new organizations. Entrepreneurial knowledge can come from previous work experience, from experts, and from imitation and copying. Entrepreneurs can use their contacts from previous jobs as well as what they have learned in their previous jobs to help them build their own organization. Some research shows that entrepreneurs purposely create their own organizations to be similar to ones in which they have previously worked, and that they aim to serve some of the same customers (Aldrich, 1999). This was important to focus on in Jennifer's case, since she had taught dance somewhere else prior to opening her

The writer demonstrates that she is clearly making connections between theories and her specific case site. This is usually crucial to the credibility of this genre.

own studio. It was also important to see if her previous work experience at non-dance-related places influenced how she formed her own organization. There was the possibility that Jennifer may have copied or imitated other dance schools that she had either taught at and/or was a student at herself, and it was also necessary to see if she had consulted with any experts before opening her own studio.

One approach Romanelli focuses on is the environmental imprinting approach. This approach has roots in Selznick and

Stinchcombe, who believe that organizations tend to take on the characteristics of the people and surroundings that make up the environment of the organization when it is created. The approach therefore focuses on both the individual characteristics of the entrepreneur as well as environmental characteristics. It realizes that the characteristics of the founders of the organization are important, but also realizes that the founders are limited by the environmental conditions. The creation of the new organization is dependent on the environmental conditions at the time, and "because the forms tend to become institutionalized, the basic structure of the organization tends to remain relatively stable" (Stinchcombe, 1965 in Romanelli, 1991). For example, research has shown how a shortage of doctors in the U.S. along with trends toward specialization resulted in a new medical school specifically created to train general practitioners (Kimberly, 1979 in Romanelli, 1991). While researching the dance studio, it was important to examine under what conditions Jennifer was able to establish her studio to see if the original structure of her organization had carried over to the present.

　　To examine how organizations have changed and developed, some researchers have used the life cycle approach. Life cycle theories try to recognize stages that an organization goes through from the time it is established to the time it comes to an end. It states that every organization goes through a general set of phases throughout its existence and that as it grows, certain changes should occur (Scott, 2003, Barnett & Carroll, 1995). Greiner came up with some general stages or "crises" that an organization goes through and must successfully complete in order to survive—each solution to one crisis becomes a problem in the next stage. The first crisis that occurs has to do with a shift in leadership from the entrepreneur to management. The next crisis that occurs has to do with the control being too concentrated; therefore, it is necessary for other

Nearing the end of the literature review, the writer reiterates her focus on the organizational history of this site and its relation to the sociological theories. This justifies the writer's choice of site and helps provide a critical lens for the observations.

people to contribute to decision making (Scott, 2003). This was an interesting facet to look at in the research on Jennifer's Dance School because Jennifer is both the entrepreneur *and* the manager. I needed to see if any of these crises somehow still applied to her organization, or if they would in the future. This case study sought to discover which ideas and theories previously described here were supported or rejected by the organizational history of Jennifer's Dance School.

Methods

Jennifer's Dance School is a dance studio located in a suburb of Chicago, offering ballet, pointe, tap, jazz, hip-hop, and lyrical classes to children, as well as adults, of all ages. The majority of the students, however, are either in elementary or high school. All classes meet once a week, the session starting in September. There are usually a couple of smaller performances throughout the year, but the main show is held in June. Much of the class time is used learning and preparing dances for this performance. Although participating in the show is not mandatory, the vast majority of students do perform in it. Most classes perform one dance per discipline they are learning in this show.

I have been a student at Jennifer's Dance School since it opened in 1996, and I also started teaching a class of my own this past fall of 2002. Since I have been there right from the start, I have seen Jennifer's business grow over the years. When she first opened her dance school, she held classes in her parents' basement, and only had eleven students. Year by year, she started to expand more and more, and she was finally able to move classes out of her parents' basement and into a studio of her own. This year, she has about seventy-five students, and now has three other teachers (myself included) and one assistant helping her as well. Currently, all of the teachers as well as the assistant are also students at the studio, although Jennifer is thinking about hiring a professional teacher from outside of the studio. Besides conducting

This methods section first details the nature of the dance classes in order to provide the reader with background knowledge for following the case study events.

The researcher relates her own experiences with the studio. Such a disclosure is important as an ethical statement; it provides the reader with knowledge that the writer will have significant firsthand knowledge of this case site but may also have certain biases in reporting her observations or drawing her conclusions. The genre of the case study usually demands that the writer reveal the rationale for the site choice and reveal any personal relationships to it.

class, teachers are also responsible for choreographing dances that will be in the recital in June, as well as picking out costumes.

To obtain the history of Jennifer's Dance School, Jennifer was interviewed and I also observed two classes taught by teachers other than Jennifer (Teacher A and Teacher B). Interviewing Jennifer allowed me to discover how she decided to start her dance school in the first place. (See Appendix for a list of interview questions.) She was asked questions that specifically targeted the number of theories I had found that explain how new organizations are created. For example, I needed to ask questions to find out the conditions under which Jennifer was able to create her studio in order to find out if the original structure of her dance school had carried over to the present. Interviewing Jennifer not only allowed me to discover how her dance school got started, but also how it has grown and developed, as well as how it has and has not changed.

One of the classes observed (Teacher A's class) was a ballet and tap class for children ages four to seven. The other class observed (Teacher B's class) was a jazz and hip-hop class for children ages twelve to seventeen. I observed the classes because I wanted to examine the differences and similarities of teaching styles between Jennifer and the other teachers. Observation allowed me to look for how the organization has changed as well as how it has not changed. I take a class with Jennifer myself—a jazz, hip-hop, and tap class with girls ages eighteen to twenty-three—so I already knew what her teaching style was like. While I was observing, I looked for two specific aspects of the teacher's class: the overall attitude and presentation of the teacher, as well as the format of how the class was run.

Results

The overall history of Jennifer's Dance School was learned by interviewing Jennifer herself. Jennifer said that she decided to open her own dance school after teaching at other places—she wanted to be able to

The writer explains her methods procedures: an interview of the director and observations of two different classes in the school.

Already familiar with the owner's teaching style, the researcher is able to compare the other two teachers to her.

In this results section, the researcher shares details of the observations and interview.

"do her own thing" and not be under someone else's rule. She feels that her studio changes every year as she learns what works and does not work. She also feels that she has become more professional since she first started out in her parents' basement, and said that she now branches out to more age groups and does more performances within the community than she did originally. One aspect that Jennifer feels has not changed is her teaching philosophy—she is not overly strict; she wants people to learn as well as enjoy themselves and have fun. She places an emphasis not only on the dance steps, but showmanship as well.

The writer explains the procedures for the owner's building of the organization.

To build her original clientele, Jennifer said that she kept some of her class rosters from her previous places of employment and sent out flyers to these people. She also drew in students from another local dance school that had recently closed. She also walked around the neighborhood with flyers to advertise. Now she says that she puts anyone who calls the studio on her mailing list and continues to walk around passing out flyers. However, she feels that she now gets most of her clientele by word of mouth.

When I asked her how her family has impacted her establishing the dance school, she said that her parents encouraged her and were entirely supportive of her idea—they let her turn their basement into a dance studio! Her parents and other family members still help her out—for example, they assist at the dress rehearsals that take place right before the recital. She said that her husband, on the other hand, was more concerned with the risk of her having her own business, and was worried that it was not feasible. However, since she had already established the school before they were married, she decided to keep going with it. She said that her parents helped her "reach for the stars," and her husband "brought her back down to earth."

Jennifer was asked how her previous jobs (dance and non-dance related) as well as her student experiences influenced how she formed her own school. She said that she learned about business politics through other jobs that she has had, and she also learned how to communicate with people on more of a professional level. She feels that her teaching style and philosophy were molded by her teaching for other people at other places, as well as by the people who had previously taught her.

Jennifer did not consult with any experts before opening her dance school, and said that she just "jumped right in." When asked if she thought that she would eventually get to the point where she felt like she could no longer be the entrepreneur *and* the manager over other people, she said that she could see someone else handling the business aspects of the school, but that she would definitely want to work together with him or her. She said that she would turn the school over to someone else if for some reason she could not do it anymore, but that she would have to turn it over to the "right person." She could see having a joint management with someone else in the future, but she still intends to be the main person "calling the shots."

To interpret the results of the two observations, the overall teaching style and attitude as well as the format of the classes were compared with Jennifer's teaching style and format. I found that both of the other teachers had classes that were similar to Jennifer's across the board in many ways. (Of course, some aspects needed to be modified according to the age group and/or level being taught.) Like Jennifer, Teacher A's attitude toward her students was one in which she emphasized having fun, yet staying focused on what they needed to get done. She asked her students many questions about what they had learned and did not give away the answers all of the time—for example, "What do you do if you are dancing on stage and your shoe falls off?" Teacher A even went to Jennifer for input a couple of time throughout the class to discuss ending poses for the girls' dances.

Noting earlier influences on the current organization, the writer is providing significant detail for the reader prior to analyzing it in her discussion section.

The writer notes that this site was founded with a strong entrepreneurial spirit. Details such as this will be important in her later analysis.

The writer indicates that her interpretation of the class observations is based largely upon a comparison among the three classes.

Significantly, the comparisons come from firsthand experience on the part of the writer/observer.

The format of Teacher A's class was the same as Jennifer's classes as well. Teacher A started with stretching, did some exercises at the barre, practiced some steps across the floor, and finally worked on their dances for the upcoming recital. She also used the same "baseball" game that Jennifer uses with her younger students, an activity where each student has to do a particular dance step until she reaches the next base.

Teacher B's style and class format were also much like those of Jennifer. Jennifer sometimes asks her older students what music they want to listen to while warming up, and since this was a class of mostly high schoolers, Teacher B did the same. Teacher B also wanted her students to learn and have fun at the same time. When she pointed out some parts of their recital dances that needed improvement, she would also point out the parts of the dances that they did especially well. Like Teacher A, Teacher B also asked for Jennifer's input at one point during the class.

Note the detail of the observational comments. This attention to detail is crucial for this genre.

The writer discusses potential changes of the organizational form with the owner; recall that organizational form was discussed in the literature review above. As expected in this genre, interview questions are related to the literature review, which provides the theoretical basis of the study.

The overall format of Teacher B's class was extremely similar to Jennifer's as well. She started the class with stretching exercises to get the students warmed up, and even used many of the same stretches that Jennifer uses. After that, she went right into their recital dances, which is also typical of Jennifer to do with her older students at this time of year. The class would do the dance once all together, review any parts they needed to, and then Teacher B would have the girls do the dance in groups—another technique that Jennifer uses with her students as well. When asked what she would like to see change about her dance school in the future, Jennifer said that while she wants to keep teaching the majority of the classes, she would like to hire some professional teachers. She feels that having new teachers would give the school more variety, and would bring in instructors who have different strengths than she does. While she would want the new teachers to have similar teaching philosophies, she thinks getting some "new blood" in the school would benefit both her and the students. Jennifer would also like to keep expanding and keep growing, but does not want to get too big too soon. Ideally, she would eventually like to have about one hundred to two hundred students enrolled at her school, but this would be contingent on space and whether or not she hires more help. Overall, she wants to keep a friendly family atmosphere and said that she is willing to "go with the flow."

Jennifer said that she cannot picture not having the dance school in her life right now, and that she has no intentions of closing the school any time soon. She said that she did not expect her school to become so big so fast, and as a result, her business responsibilities have grown, too. As the school got bigger, she needed to become more of a legitimate business, and this was harder to do that she originally thought. However, she does not feel that this constrained any of her decisions—she feels that her long term goals and plan of action have never drastically changed.

Discussion

The results of this case study show support for both Granovetter and Romanelli' s ideas, while showing limited support for Aldrich's theory. Granovetter's work focuses on how people's weak ties provide them with opportunities. To build her original clientele, Jennifer did in fact rely on her weak ties. Contacting former students, advertising to students who used to attend a studio that had closed, and passing out flyers around town are all examples of how she used her weak ties to establish her initial clientele. She basically still uses her weaker ties to build her clientele today. However, since she now mainly gets new students by word of mouth, the ties she presently uses to build her clientele are somewhat stronger than they were originally.

Some aspects of Aldrich's theory were supported by this research. Although Jennifer did not consult with any experts before opening her

In this discussion section, the researcher now analyzes her interview and observations in light of the sociological theories reviewed earlier.

Here the writer indicates aspects of agreement with the theories.

own dance school, she used what she had learned from her previous work experiences to establish her own school. Her previous teaching experiences helped her form her own style of teaching, and even her non-dance-related work experiences helped her learn more about the professional and business aspects of starting her own business. Jennifer did stress that she opened her own dance school so she could have the freedom to do what she wanted, but overall, her previous experiences did affect how she began a dance school of her own.

The writer highlights an obvious contradiction to one of the theories. A good discussion section of a case study will explore both agreements and contradictions to prevalent theories reviewed above. Recall that one major purpose of a case study is to suggest possibilities for future research by providing new insights on existing literature.

Here the writer indicates another point of agreement with a theory of successful organizations.

The one major contradiction between Aldrich's ideas and the results of this case study has to do with the role of the entrepreneur's family. According to Aldrich, strong ties are important to the entrepreneur, but he also believes that the more family members that are involved in the entrepreneur's business discussion network, the less of a chance there is of the entrepreneur actually starting his or her own organization. This was the total opposite in Jennifer's case, as her family members were the main ones supporting her and pushing her to help her start the dance school. Her parents not only supplied her with emotional support but with financial support as well by letting her start the school down in the basement of their house. Perhaps these results would have been different if she had already been married and had a child at the time she wanted to establish her own studio.

Romanelli focuses on how the basic overall structure of an organization remains stable over time, and this in fact is true of Jennifer's Dance School. Although the school's enrollment has grown approximately seven times its original size, Jennifer has managed to keep the same teaching philosophy of incorporating fun with learning, and she has also managed to keep more of a friendly family tone to her business. Perhaps she is able to do this because her family had such a big impact on her starting the dance school—if her parents had not let her use their basement, she may not have been able to open the studio when she did.

Although Jennifer's responsibilities have changed with the growth of her school, she is still the one who is teaching the vast majority of classes, and she is still the one who handles all of the business aspects that go along with the school. Even though she does not teach all of the classes herself, the people who are teaching for her are all students at her school as well. This is yet another reason as to why the initial structure of the school has carried on to the present.

While the results of this research do not specifically show support for Greiner's life cycle model, there is the possibility that it may apply to Jennifer's Dance School in the future. Jennifer did express that she can see having someone take over the business aspects of her school, but that she still wanted to be the main one in charge. While she has not had to deal with the first crisis of the model yet—a shift in leadership from entrepreneur to management—this crisis may in fact occur if and when she decides to have a co-manager. Right now, it is impossible to determine whether or not this crisis will eventually occur within Jennifer's Dance School, but if she does decide to have a co-manager someday, perhaps there is more of a chance that the crisis will occur in the future.

The writer speculates on future compliance with another theory not currently reflected in this case site. This genre invites this type of speculation.

Even though this case study of Jennifer's Dance School shows and does not show support for various existing ideas, it is clear that more research needs to be done on entrepreneurship as well as change and growth within organizations. Because only one organization was examined here, there is the possibility that there are conditions within the organization that are unusual, and this could affect the results. For example, perhaps there is a certain aspect about how a dance school is run that is unique; therefore, the results could not be generalized to other organizations. Future research should examine a larger number of organizations so that we can be more confident in the results. Learning about the conditions under which people decide to start their own business, as well as learning about how their businesses grow and change, can help potential entrepreneurs succeed in the future.

The writer admits to the limitations of a single case site in relation to making generalizations about organizational form. However, as is typical of this genre, she invites future research on a larger plan, based upon some of the findings of her study.

References

Aldrich, Howard. 1999. *Organizations Evolving*. Thousand Oaks, CA:
    SAGE Publications Inc.

Barnett, William P. and Glenn R. Carroll. 1995. "Modeling Internal
    Organizational Change." *Annual Review of Sociology* 21: 217–236.

Granovetter, Mark S. May, 1973. "The Strength of Weak Ties." *American
    Journal of Sociology* 78(6): 1360–1380.

Romanelli, Elaine. 1991. "The Evolution of New Organizational Forms."
    Annual Review of Sociology 17: 79–103.

Scott, W. Richard. 2003. *Organizations: Rational, Natural, and Open Systems*
    (5th Ed.) Upper Saddle River, NJ: Prentice Hall.

References are cited in ASA (American Sociological Association) format, commonly used by sociologists.

Appendix

Questions for Interviewing Jennifer, owner of Jennifer's Dance School

- How did you decide to open the studio? What made you decide to open it? Under what conditions were you able to establish the studio?
- In what ways do you feel the studio has changed since you first opened it?
- In what ways do you feel the studio has not changed since you first opened it?
- What would you like to see change about your studio in the future?
- What would you like to see stay the same within your studio in the future?
- How have your relationships with students, teachers, and parents changed as the studio has grown?
- What has motivated you to keep running the studio?
- What do you think has motivated teachers and/or students to stay or leave the studio?

This appendix lists the interview questions used; this is a common practice. Indeed, in many fields it is ethically required that researchers include the specific questions asked of participants.

- Would you like for your studio to keep growing in size, or are you satisfied with its current size?

- Why are you now thinking about hiring a teacher from outside of the studio? How do you think this will change the studio?

- How has the studio changed in ways that you did not anticipate? Were there any surprises along the way? Did some of these changes constrain other decisions?

- How did you build your clientele?

- How has your family impacted your establishing the studio?

- How have your previous jobs influenced how you formed your own studio? Previous student experiences?

- Did you consult with any experts before opening the studio?

- Do you think you will get to the point where you feel like you can no longer be the entrepreneur and the manager?

INVESTIGATING THE GENRE SAMPLE

1. In the genre of the case study, a writer never simply describes the details of the case at hand but instead examines these details through the lens of some theoretical or conceptual positions explained in the introductory section. What kinds of lens for examining the case does Teresa Stock describe in her introduction?

2. Stock plays the role of a *participant observer* in this case study. In other words, she draws on her experience as a student at Jennifer's Dance School as well as on her study of it as a case. What particular features of the methods section provide evidence of Stock's participant observer status?

3. Notice the prevalence of speculation and conjecture in the discussion section of this case study. Would you advise Stock to sound more certain of the points she discusses in this section? Why or why not?

CASE STUDY 2

Psychology

Teamwork for Tomorrow:

A Model Tutoring Program or Room for Improvement?

Sarah Novak
University of Notre Dame

Teamwork for Tomorrow:

A Model Tutoring Program or Room for Improvement?

Introduction

a.) Background and Overview

A brief personal narrative introduces and contextualizes this case study.

In the spring of my freshman year, I applied to join Teamwork for Tomorrow, a tutoring and mentoring program that I had heard about from girls in my dorm. It sounded like a great program, but I had no idea how my involvement with Teamwork would influence my life. Since September 2001, I have tutored a girl named Elizabeth, who is now in the fourth grade. This fall I also began tutoring a boy named Furquan, who is in the first grade. Occasionally, both of them have great days, working really hard and showing enthusiasm for Teamwork. But, more often, they are tired, do not want to read, and misbehave while we are working together. I often leave Teamwork feeling tired and frustrated. Yet, by the next day of Teamwork, I'm ready to go back and see them again. Teamwork has become a huge part of my life, and I am currently in the process of applying to be the program director for next year. To prepare for this possible role, I was interested in what an after-school tutoring and mentoring program should do to make a difference for at-risk children. In light of that, I found that Teamwork is a model after-school program, but that we have room to improve if we want to maximize the benefits for the children that we serve.

The writer openly admits to her personal interest in conducting this case study.

b. Literature Review

Recent studies have estimated that 25% of American adolescents are at serious risk and another 25% are at moderate risk for not developing into productive and competent adults (Shann, 2001). Clearly, our society is not doing an adequate job of protecting our children if 50% of them will be considered "at-risk" by the time that they reach adolescence. While the causes of such a frightening statistic are vast and include drugs, single-parent homes, unemployment and the cycle of poverty, steps must be taken in every community to prevent children from being at-risk before even reaching high school. Currently, it is estimated that 7.5 million children between the ages of 5 years old and 14 years old are unsupervised after-school (Weisman & Gottfredson, 2001). Children in this age range are often being left unsupervised because of welfare reform that forces their parents into the work force in low-paying jobs where they cannot afford child care. Instead, the children are spending their time in unsafe settings and are more likely to participate in risky behaviors or be the perpetrators or victims of crime or abuse. Specifically, juvenile crime rates consistently jump at 3 p.m. when minors find themselves unsupervised (Shann, 2001). Unsupervised youth has been found to have lasting negative outcomes beyond delinquency, specifically academic and emotional problems and drug use. Once youths are delinquent, it is harder to prevent future delinquency because they are resistant to interventions as a result of their antisocial activity (Conduct Problems Prevention Research Group, 2002). Clearly, there are children who need a structured and well-monitored place to go during these after-school "at-risk" hours and would benefit from participation in programs during that time of day (Weisman & Gottfredson, 2001). Consistently, studies have found that the most important features of these programs are that they are structured with

This introductory section includes an extensive formal literature review. This literature review provides author credibility indicating her knowledge of this aspect of the field and argues for the justification of her chosen study and future results.

Discussion is focused on the increased need for after-school care programs and supervised tutoring sites, establishing a rationale for the program to be examined.

routines where expectations are set and there is minimal free time (O'Donnell & Michalak, 1997).

Children who are already at-risk face challenges besides being unsupervised after school. They are more likely to drop out of school, to have peer drug models, to miss more school and to have more social disorganization in their lives (Weisman & Gottfredson, 2001). High-risk children also tend to enter school unprepared for the work and subsequently fail (Conduct Problems Prevention Research Group, 2002), often because they have difficulty paying attention, following directions, and controlling negative emotions of anger and distress. As a result of children's disruptive behavior, teachers do not provide these students with as much positive feedback as their peers. Children who act in antisocial ways are also less likely to be accepted by their peers and participate less in school (Raver, 2002). The resulting peer rejection and academic difficulties in elementary school are correlated with an increase in serious delinquency in adolescence. The good news is that these problem behaviors can be reduced if addressed early enough. One study was able to reduce classroom aggression and these results were sustained in a 2-year follow up. Another study was able to reduce school misbehavior, frequency of violent acts and use of alcohol for 6 years after the intervention began (Conduct Problems Prevention Research Group, 2002).

While there is no clear answer as to what works best, programs that target at-risk children before adolescence clearly can make a difference in the lives of these children (Shann, 2001). However, one study found that children who receive intervention programs in school tend to receive fewer special education programs in school (Conduct Problems Prevention Research Group, 2002). Because of this and the previously described problem of unsupervised time after-school, it is important that students be offered help outside of school, regardless of

Notice the considerable number of sources interwoven into the discussion of topics. Remember that a literature review should not proceed like an annotated bibliography that reviews works one at a time, but should rather synthesize the ideas of multiple and varied sources to develop a credible argument for justifying this case study.

Here the writer presents research substantiating the value of the specific type of site under examination. In other words, she is building her case.

the services being received during the school day. Additionally, children who have nurturing relationships with mentors who care about their well-being fare better than children who have not had such relationships (Westhues, Clarke, Watton, & St. Claire-Smith, 2001).

Because child, family and community factors all contribute to the risks facing many children from a lower socioeconomic group, a successful program must take into account all three types of risk factors (Conduct Problems Prevention Research Group, 2002). Specifically, community risk factors include low levels of neighborhood attachment, community disorganization, and extreme economic deprivation; school risk factors include antisocial behavior, failure, and a lack of commitment; individual and peer risk factors include friends who act out and have favorable attitudes towards problem behaviors (O'Donnell & Michalak, 1997). Another important aspect of a successful program is having a clearly defined core purpose for the program (Hock, Pulvers, Deshler, & Schumaker, 2001). Specifically, goals that "promote the development of social and emotional competence by teaching social problem solving, anger management, empathy and emotional regulation skills" are important in successfully helping at-risk children (Conduct Problems Prevention Research Group, 2002). Programs must provide opportunities for status, peer group approval, independence and tests of physical, personal and social endurance (Weisman & Gottfredson, 2001). Children who have had such opportunities and are able to handle their emotions and behavior when facing multiple stressors tend to do better academically (Raver, 2002).

Programs that aim to tutor in specific subject areas face additional challenges to being successful. They must start by determining what type of tutoring they wish to offer—instructional, assignment assistance or strategic. Several studies have found that one-on-one instruction in

Sharing research that describes attributes of a successful after-school care program is another means of developing her argument.

The writer continues the discussion of research, documenting successful program designs.

Admitting to significant challenges with this type of program, the writer establishes credibility by providing a balanced perspective in this literature review.

skills, strategies and content is largely effective, as measured by increases in grades and test scores (Hock et al., 2001).

Another challenge for programs that are geared towards at-risk children is effectively recruiting and retaining children from this population. When children do drop out, 34% do so because they find the program boring, 19% do so because the child moves, and 14% do so because of lack of transportation. While little can be done about the second cause, children can be encouraged to stay in the program by offering attendance incentives to children who are likely to drop out and providing transportation. Additionally, it is important to provide a hook to gain a child's initial interest in the program (Weisman & Gottfredson, 2001).

Emotional development is another area where at-risk children frequently need extra help and a quality program can address this deficiency. Many at-risk children have not been taught to recognize and label their emotions or to respond to situations without aggression. Additionally, they may not know how to manage and regulate their negative emotions that influence whether they respond in a prosocial or antisocial manner. Programs can target such knowledge of emotions and emotional and behavioral self-control through games that reward cooperation and discipline. Such activities have been found to lower rates of conduct disorder, suspensions and the later need for mental health services (Raver, 2002). Social skills training is also important for the success of at-risk children. One program focused on emotional awareness and understanding, peer-related social skills and social problem solving to increase social competence (Conduct Problems Prevention Research Group, 2002). Such social skills training, especially if it occurs in mixed groups of children demonstrating prosocial and antisocial behavior, is vital to preventing a child from ending up one of the 50% of adolescents who are at-risk to not become successful adults (O'Donnell & Michalak, 2001).

The writer discusses another specific need in this review section—social skills training. These topics foreshadow the type of observational comments that will follow in the case study description below.

This type of training also occurs indirectly in the responses to problem behaviors that occur in the program. It is important to set clear behavioral guidelines from the beginning so that children know what is acceptable. It is also crucial that tutors or mentors reward positive behaviors and model appropriate problem solving and conflict resolution skills. Children can benefit from an opportunity to verbalize what the norms are to be against involvement in problem behaviors (O'Donnell & Michalak, 1997). Finally, when problems do arise, tutors or mentors should provide guidance to prosocial solutions and help the children generalize such situations to typical social problems (Raver, 2002).

Clearly, no after-school program can be successful without quality people to be the tutors and mentors for the children. After-school tutoring programs are more successful if they have enough adults to provide one-on-one support for the children. Specifically, one study found success using university students who tutored in a one-on-one situation for 45 minutes, two to three times a week (Hock et al., 2001). Another study found that it is especially effective to use mentors who are from the same community and culture as the children. However, one mentor felt diversity among the staff was more important saying, "having different ethnic group leaders is important because, when kids see different ethnic group leaders getting along, this helps them in turn to get along." Either way, another factor that is important to the success of the program is that there is a bond among the staff, as this helps to identify the group as working towards the common goal of helping the children. Such a bond can be established through retreats, weekly staff meetings, and frequent group social activities (O'Donnell & Michalak, 1997). In addition, practice, guidance and feedback for tutors are necessary for the children to truly benefit (Hock et al., 2001). Initial tutor training should cover assertive, preventive and proactive discipline, effective communication, anger de-escalation, child development, child

The writer introduces another topic: the attributes of tutors in successful programs. Note that this section functions as a gradual development of all of the key points to be considered within the observational section.

abuse reporting, prejudice awareness, cultural sensitivity, gang involvement, and site rules. Weekly training should include anger management, leadership styles, responsibility, CPR and first aid, conflict resolution, group dynamics, higher education, career choices, multicultural tolerance, assertiveness, and computer literacy. Additionally, weekly training sessions provide opportunities to identify and solve challenges as well as share positive experiences (O'Donnell & Michalak, 1997). These types of intense training programs have been found to increase the positive interactions between the tutor and the student as well as having overall positive effects (Hock et al., 2001).

The writer examines still another important aspect of this study by examining research on necessary psychological bonding between program participants and between tutors and tutees.

Not only it is important for the staff of a tutoring program to be bonded to one another, but it is important for them to bond to the children in the program. Bonding provides the children with a consistent socialization process, which is important in developing social skills. To bond, children need active involvement and experiences that promote skills for successful participation with consistent reinforcement from their mentors. By providing opportunities for bonding, the skills to do so, and rewards for doing so successfully, mentors are preventing later problem behaviors. Specifically, children who are bonded to the group are less likely to show problem behaviors because they do not want to threaten valued relationships (O'Donnell & Michalak, 1997).

The writer concludes with research that substantiates the potential contribution of such sites/programs to at-risk children. In this extensive review she has clearly created interest and justified the value the case study to follow.

Studies have also found that one-time interventions do not maintain the improvements in children over time without regular "boosters" of intervention (Raver, 2002). After-school programs can provide just enough intervention on a regular basis to maintain improvements already gained through other programs. It is also important that programs bring children, families and mentors together socially (O'Donnell & Michalak,) as well as communicate with parents, especially about missed sessions (Weisman & Gottfredson, 2001).

Observations

a. Background: Teamwork's History and Mission

Several Notre Dame and St. Mary's students had been involved with various tutoring programs in the South Bend community and had grown frustrated with the lack of structure, inconsistency of tutors and children, and overall lack of purpose in these programs. In July, 1998, these students got together and decided to start a tutoring program that would be different. Teamwork for Tomorrow was born as a program that would "improve literacy and social and recreational development through structured tutoring and concerted mentoring" (www.nd.edu/~teamwork, 2002). Teamwork joined efforts with the South Bend Housing Authority, which agreed to provide the children for the program from their housing areas as well as transportation for the children and insurance while the children were on site. Teamwork aimed to provide their program for 35 children between 8 and 12 years old living in South Bend Subsidized Housing, a predominately African-American neighborhood that faces the usual problems that accompany poverty, such as single mother families, violence and drugs. The founders recruited about 50 tutors from Notre Dame and St. Mary's to run the program at St. Patrick's Church every Tuesday and Thursday from 4 to 6 p.m.

The goals of Teamwork were identified early and are reviewed frequently by the children and tutors. These goals are to improve reading skills, to foster positive mentoring relationships and to embrace recreational and social development. Teamwork is also founded on five core values: purpose, commitment, mutual trust and respect, affirmation and accountability. These beliefs were expanded in 2002 with the writing of the Teamwork for Tomorrow Creed: "Working **T**ogether we strive for **E**xcellence through **A**ccountability, **M**utual respect, and commitment. **W**e appreciate Teamwork as an **O**pportunity and **R**ealize that

The second major section presents the history of the program under examination and a detailed description of the daily operations.

A history of the program provides a context for the nature of the current operations to follow.

Note this Web site is cited to allow the reader to access valuable information about this organization. However, in keeping with APA style, it is not listed in the References Section at the end of the paper.

The writer explains the specific goals of this case program, allowing the reader to assess the coming program description in relation to the goals.

Knowledge empowers us to make a difference in our lives." Everyone in Teamwork discusses the creed at the beginning of the semester, focusing on how the creed should influence actions while on site. When children are facing disciplinary actions, they are asked to review the creed and helped to understand how their actions went against the creed.

In addition to the creed, Teamwork has grown remarkably over 4 years. Today, Teamwork is also partnered with the Institute for Educational Initiatives at Notre Dame, which provides structured training for tutors, leadership training for the program's student-based executive staff and an experienced teacher from the South Bend community who is in-residence at the IEI. We are also in the process of replicating the program at a new site for the first time, with the goal of future replications at other colleges and universities. Starting in January, 2003, Teamwork will expand to a second site, St. Casimir's Church. The second site will serve the surrounding neighborhoods that are composed of predominately Hispanic families that face many of the same problems as the families in the original Teamwork program. Tutors for both sites complete an application process and an interview before being invited to join the program. Fluency in Spanish is recommended for St. Casimir, but not required. In the fall semester, all tutors enroll in Tutoring in the Community, a one-credit course offered in the Education, Schooling and Society minor and taught by the teacher in-residence with the IEI.

b. Current Operation: Description of a Typical Session

The "blue bus," which is actually a 15-passenger van driven by a representative from the South Bend Housing Authority, pulls into the parking lot at St. Patrick's Church. The 10 or so children on the bus hop out and rush past Mary, the Teamwork president, to get in the doors of St. Pat's and out of the cold. In the hall, some rush to get their nametags, as others greet tutors who are also arriving. A few of the children go to the correct

The second part of this observations section details specifics of the site and the program operation. Recall that the essence of the genre of the case study is critically observed and carefully reported detail.

room immediately—either the Reading Room if they are 10 to 12 years old or the Snack Room if they are younger than 10 or older than 12. Tutors help the children hang their coats and chase a few children back into the correct rooms after they take off for the gym at the end of the hall. Meanwhile, the "red bus," another housing authority van, arrives with about 10 more kids and several tutors arrive with backseats full of the children who have moved out of the housing authority during the semester.

By 4:10, most of the children have nametags on and are in the proper rooms. In the Reading Room, each tutor has already found his or her child, picked out a book, retrieved the child's journal and found a desk or corner to work in. Each tutor and child pair will spend the next 50 minutes in reading and writing activities, often a combination of the child reading to the tutor, the tutor reading to the child, word games, journal writing, creative writing and art projects. At 4:50, the Reading Coordinator, a tutor with extra training in elementary reading, reminds tutors and children to begin writing in their journals if they haven't already done so.

While this group, referred to as the "older kids," has been in the Reading Room, their younger siblings and friends have moved from the Snack Room down to the gym. In the gym, coaches, many of whom are tutors during the other hour, are each assigned two or three children to supervise. The gym hour starts with a group of one tutor and his or her child coming to the front of the gym where each child is given an exercise card, such as "do 10 jumping jacks" or "do 5 leg lunges," to read aloud and act as the leader for that exercise. After the warm-up exercises, the Recreation Coordinators introduce that day's activity within the current unit, such as soccer or basketball. Most days, the tutors and children do drills within their small group, practicing the necessary skills for the current sport. After the drills, the groups combine to play a scrimmage of the game. At 4:50 the children line up and return

As is appropriate for this genre, considerable attention to minute detail is obvious. The writer is attempting to provide a snapshot of a typical day for the reader.

to the Snack Room where they receive a nutritious snack, such as applesauce, goldfish or graham crackers, and 100% juice. At 5:00 the older and younger kids switch rooms and the process starts over. Most tutors/coaches switch rooms with their child, although a few spend both hours in either the Reading Room or the gym or are only on-site for 1 hour due to schedule conflicts.

The writer continues the description of the very structured program the center offers. Note that in this lengthy section, analysis is largely withheld. That will occur in the discussion section that follows.

While all this has been going on, a third group of students, the Junior Counselors, met in the Snack Room. The JCs are former Teamwork children who are technically too old to participate in the reading and recreation program. There are seven students between the ages of 13 and 16 currently enrolled in the program, although only four or five are present on an average day. They spend the first hour doing enrichment activities with their tutor. These activities can range from reading *Sports Illustrated* to writing poetry, depending on the students' interests. From 4:45–5:15, as the other children eat their snack, the JCs and their tutors play basketball in the gym. For the rest of the session, JCs are permitted to do their homework with help from the tutors.

At 6:00, chaos erupts as tutors clean up, say good-bye to the children, and try to make sure everyone gets on the correct bus or in the car with the correct tutor. The only variation to this routine is on Enrichment Days when the time in the gym is devoted to a different type of activity. Some Enrichment sessions this year have included making pillows and a visit from Notre Dame ROTC students. There are occasionally off-site days, such as the field trips to the College Football Hall of Fame or Trick-or-Treating and a Halloween party on Notre Dame's campus.

Teamwork is run on a daily basis by the Executive Staff, comprised entirely of undergraduate students at Notre Dame. The president is responsible for both sites and coordination of staffs at the two sites. She serves as the liaison with the Housing Authority, other community partners, and the Board of Advisors. She also supervises the Business Manager, who is responsible for the Teamwork budget, and the Recruitment and Outreach Coordinator, who organizes and runs the recruitment drive for new tutors each semester. The program director for each site is responsible for daily operations, discipline, risk management, and supervision of the remaining coordinators. The Recreation Coordinators plan and lead the gym and provide guidance for the coaches. The Reading Coordinators are responsible for the reading room; specifically, they provide outside knowledge of reading theory, level and organize the books, update supplies, administer reading tests to each child twice in the semester and provide guidance for the tutors. The Junior Counselor Coordinators are responsible for leading the JC program on a daily basis and providing guidance for the tutors in the JC program.

Note the detailed description of the session's activities.

At the start of each semester, all participants in the program, tutors and children, are required to sign contracts that specify their responsibilities throughout the semester. The tutor's contract specifies all expectations for conduct, responsibility and commitment so that there are not any questions later. Children's parents also sign the contract that each tutor brings to his or her child's house early in the semester. The most important point on the children's contract is their commitment to attendance. Specifically, children are allowed three unexcused absences each semester. If a student exceeds these absences, the president and program director will evaluate the child's continued participation in the program.

A final description explains the contractual aspect of the program.

There are four basic rules in Teamwork: do not swear, keep hands and feet to yourself, do not wander or run from tutors, and participate. These rules are presented to the children on the first day and as a group, we discuss why it is important to follow these rules at Teamwork. Specifically, we talk about how the rules come from the creed and are necessary for Teamwork to live up to the creed.

This third major section analyzes the extensive observations provided above and then offers generalizations and/or conclusions.

Admitting to shortcomings of the program adds to the credibility of the writer as an open-minded observer. (That attitude lends integrity to this genre.)

The writer acknowledges successful aspects of the program.

The writer admits to attendance problems at the site.

Notice that in this section, discussion of specifics is usually related to the research cited above. This adds authority to the analysis.

Discussion/Analysis

Overall, Teamwork is a model tutoring and after-school program for at-risk children. Teamwork serves a basic need of this population by providing the children with a safe place to go after school 2 days a week. While these children would ideally have such an after-school program 5 days a week, Teamwork is not equipped, at this point in time, to offer such a program. At least 2 days a week are better than none, for the time being. Two common problems that tutoring programs face are attendance and retention rates. Thus far, we have not had a problem getting initial interest in Teamwork as most children in the neighborhoods that we serve are familiar with the program and have seen their friends go on outings with their tutors. Thus, the Housing Authority often has a waiting list of children who would like to join the program. However, once we have the 35 or so children for the semester, we have faced problems with attendance and retention. While the attendance policy is intended to prevent some of these challenges, it is not very effective. Some days there are as few as 20 students on-site, a situation that detracts from the students' experiences while frustrating tutors who find themselves without a child. Research has found that the most common reason for withdrawing from after-school programs is boredom. Thus, it becomes the responsibility of the tutor to ensure that his or her student remains interested and stimulated for the entire hour of tutoring. Throughout the tutoring hour, Reading Coordinators should look for signs of boredom in the children, such as a child looking around the room, putting his or her head down, or not being able to focus or pay attention. If they see signs of boredom, it would be beneficial for the coordinators to meet with the tutors and provide specific guidance for how to better stimulate the child for the hour. Perhaps the child needs hands-on activities such as an art project that complements the story they are reading or different types of reading materials that better reflect the child's interest, such as *Sports Illustrated for Kids* or comic books.

Additionally, the research suggests that incentives for attendance can be helpful in motivating children to come on a regular basis. Currently, we have a negative focus on this issue, with the policy that children who miss too many sessions will be asked to leave the program. A better policy, or additional one, should be to reward students who have regular attendance. A good system for recording attendance would be to have a chart hanging in the entrance with each child's name and Teamwork session listed. As children arrive on-site, they would receive a sticker to place by their name and the current date. Thus, they could always see how many stickers they have, especially in comparison to children with perfect attendance. At the end of the month, children who had not missed more than one session would receive a reward, such as a special treat at snack time. Seeing other children receive rewards would hopefully motivate those with poor attendance to make an effort to improve.

During the tutoring hour, Teamwork focuses on instructional and strategic tutoring in reading, two types of tutoring that have been found to be especially effective in raising grades and test scores. As children read aloud, tutors have the opportunity to correct mistakes as well as teach specific reading and decoding strategies such as looking for context clues. This has been found to be more effective than assignment assistance tutoring and is reflected in Teamwork's policy that homework may not be done in the Reading Room.

Discipline and problem behaviors from the children are other issues that come up frequently at Teamwork. Studies have pointed to the importance of establishing clear rules and guidelines for behavior from the beginning of the program and explaining the logic behind such expectations. Through the creed and written rules, Teamwork does an excellent job of this from the first day. There is also a "no tolerance" policy

Here the writer further analyzes the attendance problem and offers suggestions to counter the problem.

The writer introduces another major topic, discipline. Recall that it was discussed in the literature review above.

when children break the rules and they are immediately removed from the situation and taken to the president or program director, who discusses with the child why his or her behavior hurts the goals of Teamwork, reviews the creed with the child, and suggests better responses in the future before the child can return to the group. This is the first year that the creed has been in existence and that there is such a set procedure for when rules are not obeyed. So far, it appears to be a successful system. We still deal with problem behavior on a regular basis, but children tend to respond faster to discipline and show more respect for the leaders of the program in such situations. The discipline would be more beneficial to the children if the program director or president also related their inappropriate actions to common social problems to help the children generalize appropriate behavior to other situations.

The researcher proposes a shift in policy from a focus on negative motivation to positive motivation.

Here she discusses the operation of the discipline policy.

However, we only focus on punishment for negative behaviors. Instead, there should be a greater emphasis on positive reinforcement for positive behaviors, specifically for appropriate problem solving or conflict resolution and other prosocial behaviors. This could be achieved through a simple reward system, enforced by all tutors, coaches and coordinators. Each child would have a card with his or her name on it. When a staff member witnessed positive behavior, he or she would notify the appropriate coordinator or program director, who would identify the positive behavior to the child and provide him or her with a sticker to be placed on his or her card. When a child reaches a preset number of stickers, such as 15, he or she would be allowed to select a prize, such as a sheet of stickers, a dollar-store toy, or a $1 gift certificate to a fast food restaurant. Such rewards for positive behavior would hopefully encourage such responses as opposed to the negative responses commonly seen.

The writer reiterates her argument for a more positive approach to discipline problems.

Research consistently emphasizes the importance of emotional development for at-risk children, specifically targeting their limited abilities to recognize and label negative emotions and respond in a non-aggressive manner. Teamwork provides opportunities for such development when team sports are played in the gym. However, it is important to maintain close control over the situation so that when a child responds to teammates in an inappropriate manner, the coaches are aware that the behavior occurred and can immediately take the child aside to explain why it is an inappropriate response and discuss a better way to handle the situation. While this currently occurs to a certain extent, it would be better if the coaches had a one-on-one ratio with the children, as in the Reading Room. Thus, if each coach was only responsible for supervising one child, no inappropriate behavior could occur without a coach noticing it. Additionally, inappropriate behavior in the Snack Room or during the reading hour must be addressed in a similar matter, with tutors helping children to label their emotions and suggesting appropriate and prosocial ways to respond to a given situation. However, neither tutors nor coaches are necessarily prepared to use such strategies when providing discipline. If this method is to be beneficial to the children, tutors and coaches must be trained in such an area to ensure that consistency is maintained among the staff. An experienced teacher could provide such training with frequent reminders and guidance from the program director.

In addition to emotional development, it is important to work on social skills training. Currently, this is not an area that is addressed at Teamwork, although experts on programs with at-risk children emphasize the importance of including social skills training. An easy way to incorporate activities that emphasize problem solving and conflict resolution should be introduced as part of the reading hour. One or two reading hours a month would be set aside for group projects. This would work best if the groups were preassigned to include a mix of children who primarily demonstrate prosocial and antisocial behaviors.

Emphasizing the application of research on antisocial behavior to situations at the center lends further credibility to the argument the writer is developing within this case study.

Note that the writer highlights the importance of social skills training, an area that received significant attention in the literature review above.

Groups would be given a specific and age-appropriate project or activity for each group session or older children could be given a project to work on as a group throughout the semester, such as performing a play of a story they read as a group. Tutors would provide guidance as needed as well as intervene to encourage positive group interaction and conflict resolution.

Returning to another main point in the literature review section, the researcher emphasizes the importance of staff training in a successful program.

The staff clearly plays a crucial role in both the execution and the success of the program. Thus, it is vital that an after-school program be comprised of motivated and committed individuals. Because of Teamwork's application process, we consistently have an outstanding staff. Through the Tutoring in the Community class, Teamwork provides the training necessary for the tutors to assist the children and help them gain the most benefits possible. However, it is also important that the staff be bonded a group. While many tutors are friends, either from experiences in Teamwork or from joining because their friends were already in the program, the group is not very bonded as a whole. Small efforts such as staff dinners and parties work to address this issue and it usually gets better over the course of the semester, but there is room for improvement. Typically, on the first day of Teamwork, the staff has only come together as a group once or

Suggestions of the value of more intensive bonding and more comprehensive training opportunities for the staff echo findings of previous research (as discussed above) regarding factors of a successful program.

twice. Some research suggests that a retreat is beneficial in helping tutors get to know one another and emphasize the common mission and goals for all those involved with the program. Such an experience could easily be incorporated into Teamwork by taking an afternoon retreat on a Sunday prior to the first day on-site. This would replace the current 2-hour orientation program, since this material would be covered on the retreat. It would also provide an opportunity to address larger issues that the children face as well as larger issues related to tutoring such as motivation and discipline. Finally, such a retreat would provide time to simply allow the tutors to get to know one another and to learn such basic information as everyone's names. This would help the staff appear to the children as a unified group from the first day of Teamwork.

Another recommendation for tutoring programs is that the tutors be from the same community as the children or represent diverse racial backgrounds. Because Teamwork tutors are from Notre Dame, it is unlikely that any of them will be from the same community as our children. However, we should make an effort to expand the diversity on our staff. Currently, the staff's racial diversity is limited to one African-American tutor and one Hispanic tutor. This lack of diversity should be a serious concern for the leadership of Teamwork and must be addressed. While tutors should not be selected based on race, perhaps extra recruitment efforts should be focused on minority students at the university. The office of Multicultural Student Programs and Services may be able to provide suggestions for specific recruitment of minority students. The Teamwork staff should, at the very least, be representative of the racial diversity at Notre Dame, although this should be a minimum, not a goal.

Studies have also emphasized the importance of the children forming a bond to the staff of the tutoring program. Teamwork has excelled in this area by providing each child with one tutor who works with him or her at every session for the semester. This consistency allows the children to bond to a staff member, who they can see as being committed to them, their well-being and their improvement. For some, forming this bond can take longer than for others. I started tutoring my current child in the fall of 2001. It was this past October before she began to show signs of being bonded to me, such as affection, disappointment when I had to miss a session and knowledge that I am proud of her when she does well. Yet, regardless of how long it may take to form this bond, the benefits to the children are numerous and Teamwork is an excellent way for the children to experience stable bonds with people who are devoted to them and care about them.

The writer continues to offer recommendations for an even more successful program.

Note that this analysis section is blending in conclusions and recommendations as well. This is often done within the case study genre because of the singular focus of the study.

Finally, it is important that programs with at-risk children bring the families, children, and mentors together and emphasize communication between parents and mentors. Teamwork encourages communication between parents and tutors and requires tutors to take the children's contracts to the parents early in the semester to be signed. However, there is much room for improvement in this area as well. Regular communication with parents should be a requirement. An easy way to improve communication would be to provide each child-tutor pair with a "What We Did Today" sheet during their reading hour. Depending on the child's writing level, the child and tutor could work together to summarize what they did in Teamwork that day for the child's parent to see. Such a daily summary may spark conversation between the parent and child at Teamwork or provide evidence to the parent of the importance of Teamwork for their child's academic progress, which may facilitate better attendance. Also, when children do not show up at Teamwork, their tutor should immediately go to the child's house to find out why they are absent and remind the parents of the attendance policy. Such immediate responses would demonstrate to the parents how much the tutors care about their children. Finally, it would be helpful to have a few events for the children and their families so that parents have a chance to see the tutors interact with their children. Some events could include a kick-off picnic in the children's neighborhoods at the beginning of the year, an open house mid-semester, and invitations to the Christmas party and end of year party. Such events would facilitate communication between parents and tutors as well as develop a bond between the tutors and the children's communities. In the end, such progress would benefit the children, which is the primary purpose of Teamwork.

Conclusion

As Teamwork prepares for our first replication, it is important to consider to what extent we fulfill our mission as tutors and mentors. In

Again the writer interweaves suggestions with her analysis.

Note that since the conclusion and recommendations were included above in the discussion section, only a very brief summary statement is provided in this section, labeled "Conclusion."

light of current research, Teamwork appears to be doing an excellent job, but with room for improvement. To truly benefit the children we serve, it is important that we constantly be looking for ways to improve and never become satisfied with simply maintaining the status quo.

References

Conduct Problems Prevention Research Group. (2002). Evaluation of the first three years of the fast track prevention program with children at high risk for adolescent conduct problems. *Journal of Abnormal Child Psychology, 30,* 19–26.

Hock, M. F., Pulvers, K. A., Deshler, D. D., & Schumaker, J. B. (2001). The effects of an after school tutoring program on the academic performance of at-risk students and students with LD. *Remedial and Special Education, 22,* 172–187.

O'Donnell, J., & Michalak, E. A. (1997). Inner-city youths helping children: After-school programs to promote bonding and reduce risk. *Social Work in Education, 19,* 284–294.

Raver, C. C. (2002). Emotions matter: Making the case for the role of young children's emotional development for early school readiness. *Social Policy Report, 16,* 1–3.

Shann, M. H. (2001). Students' use of time outside of school: A case for after school programs for urban middle school youth. *The Urban Review, 35,* 339–356.

Weisman, S. A., & Gottfredson, D. C. (2001). Attrition from after school programs: Characteristics of students who drop out. *Prevention Science, 2,* 201–205.

Westhues, A., Clarke, L., Watton, J., & St. Claire-Smith, S. (2001). Building positive relationships: An evaluation of process and outcomes in a big sister program. *The Journal of Primary Prevention, 21,* 477–493.

The reference list is formatted in APA style, the preferred style for the discipline of psychology.

INVESTIGATING THE GENRE SAMPLE

1. Notice how substantial the review of literature is in this case study. Do you think that all case studies need to cite published scholarship as extensively as this one does? Why or why not?
2. The observations section of this case study has two parts. Which part do you think is actually more "observational"?
3. The discussion section of this case study is also quite substantial. Would you say that the discussion section could stand on its own as a stance or position paper? Why or why not?

PROPOSALS OR PROSPECTUSES

Proposals are frequently created in both academic and workplace settings. Sometimes within academia, a proposal is referred to as a "prospectus." Though a **proposal** or **prospectus** can be created for a wide variety of reasons for countless audiences, each one is essentially doing two things: First, it is suggesting or "proposing," as the name implies, a particular action, project, or plan; secondly, it is attempting to convince someone (or a group of individuals) that it is a good plan that merits acceptance and support.

Proposals can be classified according to two basic types: solicited or unsolicited. If they are solicited, then some other individual, institution, or association has issued a "call for proposals" or an RFP (request for proposals), as it is frequently referred to in the businessworld. As a student, you may be requested by your professor to submit a proposal directed to him/her outlining the particulars of a specific group or individual project or explaining the details of an extensive paper or report. Or you may be requested to create a proposal for a real-world audience, fictitious or actual, describing the details of some service that you will provide or some plan that needs an outsider's support. Unsolicited proposals are created in response to a need that the person doing the proposing assumes exists. Sometimes such "blind" proposals are less successful than solicited ones, but not always.

Remember that proposals are always *persuasive* documents and, therefore, you must work hard to construct a convincing argument with your proposal. One of the most important preliminary steps to creating a successful proposal is carefully analyzing the audience for your proposal. You need to carefully assess the interests, agendas, resources, and concerns of a particular audience and then construct your proposal in a manner that will appeal to that particular audience. If a solicitation has been issued, multiple individuals or groups will be responding to it, and, therefore, you must do a strong "selling" job to get your proposal accepted. When writing a solicited proposal, at least you know something of the nature of your audience and their specific needs, because they have outlined them in their request. When creating an unsolicited proposal, you often need to do even more research on the nature of your audience in order to successfully convince them. Whether the proposal is solicited or unsolicited, the audience has a right to assume that the proposer is submitting an ethical request that fairly, honestly, and comprehensively represents the details of the plan proposed.

Solicited proposals will usually include specific instructions of what information or data needs to be provided. In general, they require a brief statement of the problem or need with some background information regarding it, an explanation of the steps of the plan to meet the need, specific mention of the resources to be used or required, a discussion of the personnel and their qualifications necessary to implement the proposal, and a summary of the costs involved, if appropriate. Sometimes they may require detailed lists of resources to be consulted or appendices that provide technical information or samples of proposed materials and so forth. The specific sections of a proposal can vary considerably from one discipline to another.

The first example provided below is a prospectus from the field of history. It is a solicited proposal responding to a professorial request that students propose a specific plan for a senior-thesis project. The specific requirements of the prospectus designated the inclusion of: 1) a statement of the "precise" historical problem to be explored, 2) a historiographical essay that tells the reader which historians have dealt with the problem and what they have written about it, and 3) a catalogue of the primary source collections to be used for the exploration of the problem. In this case, the author of the prospectus is trying to persuade her audience—i.e., her professor—that this project is comprehensive and meaningful enough for a senior thesis. Furthermore, she is attempting to convince him that she has adequately assessed the scholarly coverage of the problem to date and will be exploring sufficient and appropriate primary historical sources in order to substantially contribute to the discussion of this topic.

The second example, from a business communications course, mimics an unsolicited proposal for a "real" corporate audience, Mattel, Inc. This proposal is seeking support funds from a large toy manufacturer's charitable foundation for a not-for-profit organization's family-centered activity. This proposal is attempting to persuade its audience (the Mattel Foundation) that the provider (CoACH Care Center) is offering a service worthy of Mattel's financial support. It follows the highly structured format of typical business proposals including: a letter of transmittal; a title page; a table of contents; an executive summary; the body of the report comprised of an introduction, a detailed rationale, and a plan section with a services description, a timeline, and cost analysis sections; a description of the organization; and a conclusion. Notice that this discipline makes extensive use of subheadings and graphic clues for easy reader response.

Though the format of each of these proposals varies tremendously, in each situation the intent is to persuade an audience of the value of a plan. In both cases, the proposers are attempting to convince the respective audiences of their ability to meet a specific need by providing specific details of the plan and by establishing the credibility of their research and preparation.

PROPOSAL 1

History

Prospectus for the Senior Thesis "The Suffrage Movement in South Carolina"

Joye Shields
Columbia College, South Carolina

The writer establishes a context for the problem to be studied, in essence, justifying the existence of the proposal.

A clear indication of the project's focus is given: to explore the South's participation in the women's suffrage movement.

The writer suggests reasons the South lagged behind the North in supporting this cause, which provides further justification for proposing this study.

Note that the writer continues the analysis of reasons for Southern reticence to become involved, thereby further arguing for the validity of her study and strengthening the persuasive component of the proposal.

Prospectus for the Senior Thesis "The Suffrage

Movement in South Carolina"

In writing about the national women's suffrage movement, historians usually focus on the movement in the North and on leaders such as Sarah and Angela Grimke and Lucretia Mott. The South is often overlooked, since the movement started much later in the South than it did in the North. Some historians, however, have attempted to determine why this was the case. Some have come to the conclusion that Southerners resisted the women's movement because they associated it with the North. Others believe that the South was still recuperating from the consequences of the Civil War. Still others argue that Southerners, particularly after Reconstruction, opposed any widening of the electorate as opening the door for African-Americans to vote.

Another consideration is whether the slow progress resulted from the kinds of people who were recruited into the movement. Some believe that the women who were involved shared the same attributes in terms of class and race, and that that helped the movement. Because women shared the same background, it was easy to form associations, which sought out particular goals to advance the status of women; women from different classes had different aims. Others claim that the exclusion of any class or race of women from the movement hampered its success.

The suffrage movement of the South stemmed from the work of the suffragists of the North. The influence of the North reached the

South with the most success in the last decades of the nineteenth century. The National American Woman Suffrage Association decided to campaign in the South when the group made the decision to focus on gaining the right to vote from the federal government. Some women of the South opposed this strategy, believing that the federal government had no place in the individual states' political affairs.[1]

Others, including the Southern political and industrial elite, opposed the idea of women's suffrage because they still believed in the "ideal" Southern women. They thought women needed to stay in the home and deal with the problems of maintaining a stable home. The Southern woman was to be obedient to her husband and not worry about the financial and political affairs. This ideal was slowly being changed due to the opportunities becoming available to women.

One factor that helped pique interest in the Southern women's suffrage movement was the availability of work outside of the home, an opportunity that came with the industrialization of the South. Many men had been killed in the Civil War, so the work force of the South had been depleted. Women were also left without husbands, fathers, or brothers to support them, so they had to work to earn income for their families. As women were earning wages, some of them began to feel that they should have a voice in the way their states were run. Women from the upper classes also gained independence; for them, they did this by attending institutions of higher education or working at jobs that demanded more respect, for example as doctors or lawyers.[2]

Based on letters, diaries, public speeches and writings, and transcribed oral interviews of leaders of South Carolina's women's

[1]Marjorie Sprull Wheeler, "The History of the Suffrage Movement," n.d., http://www.pbs.org/onewoman/suffrage.html (November 15, 2002).

[2]Wheeler, "Suffrage Movement."

Note the use of superscript numerals to indicate footnotes, where all bibliographical information is provided; this follows the Turabian format of documentation commonly used by historians.

The writer indicates the types of primary sources that will be used for this exploration; in essence, she provides her methodology.

The thesis or main focus of the proposal is clearly stated. It will explore four areas of the women's suffrage movement in the South.

As directed by the requirements for this proposal, a review of the historical research conducted to date begins here.

Notice that the writer is not merely listing sources or potential references. Rather, the writer of this prospectus discusses the content of the work of other historians in order to argue for the position that these sources are crucial to the development of her research.

suffrage movement, I hope to understand all these issues better. In particular I will examine the reasons these women joined the movement, the ideas they believed in, their attempts to recruit others, and the strategies they employed to win the right to vote for women.

Other historians have done valuable work on the women's suffrage movement in the South. Eliza Herndon, for example, argues that the women's suffrage movement did not begin in the mid-nineteenth century. She believes that there was activity during the Revolutionary era and during the early nineteenth century; however, at this time the movement was complementary to the women's temperance movement, labor welfare, and the movement for education of females; no one organization existed specifically for the task of pursuing suffrage rights for women.[3]

Herndon explains that the early leaders of the national suffrage movement, such as Lucretia Mott, Frances Wright, and Elizabeth Cady Stanton, decided to take action after they realized that they could not be an asset to society until they could have a voice in who led it. As time progressed and states began to grant women more rights, women started to form organizations that pushed for women's suffrage.[4] Herndon states that the South did not keep up with the movement that was going on in the North because the states of the South gave women fewer rights. The state of South Carolina in particular viewed feminism negatively, and Herndon argues that officials of that state did not want women to be involved in politics at all. Before the Civil War, South Carolina lagged behind even other Southern states in terms of women's rights.[5]

The Republican government of South Carolina during the Reconstruction era, known best for extending voting rights and other

[3]Eliza Herndon, *Woman Suffrage in South Carolina: 1872–1920* (Columbia, South Carolina: University of South Carolina Press, 1953), iv.

[4]Herndon, v.

[5]Herndon, xii.

rights to African-Americans, also reformed the position of women in the state. However, it was overthrown after only eight years and the traditional political leaders returned to power in 1876. These leaders were divided about how the race issue related to women's suffrage. Many of the first suffragists had also been abolitionists, and many leading white South Carolinians saw women's rights as a "Yankee" idea that had been forced on them—like the abolition of slavery. On the other hand, some political leaders understood that the white upper- and middle-class women who led the women's suffrage movement did not want black women to have the right to vote. Therefore some of the state's male leaders were anxious to allow women to vote, so the women could possibly help defend white supremacy.[6]

Martha M. Solomon's book *A Voice of Their Own: The Women Suffrage Press, 1840–1910* looks at the role of journalism during the suffrage movement. Her book compares the rhetoric of suffragists in different states and evaluates the quality of their campaigns to draw women into the movement and to influence male politicians. She concludes that in general Southern suffragists used many of the same tactics as their northern colleagues to stir up interest and involvement in the movement. The publications she studies were usually run by and for upper- and middle-class white women who had free time and needed something to occupy their minds and time. They stressed the promise of occupational and educational achievements in order to entice women to join the cause. The women who had education and worked outside of the home realized they should have a voice in the political organizations of the state. The book includes examples from the different methods that were used to reach each class of women, including the African-American community. Solomon also discusses

The writer continues her argument by presenting the research contribution of a second historian, Solomon.

[6]Herndon, xii.

the anti-women's suffrage press and discusses how women combated this opposition.[7]

Virginia Bernhard's *Southern Women: Histories and Identities* is a compilation of speeches and essays by Southern women in the movement. These documents illustrate the different strategies used by Southern women to help their political movement. In her analysis of these documents, Bernhard finds the exploitation of the feminine identity to be a key component of their strategy. Southern women used the commonly accepted idea that women are morally superior to men in order to bolster their campaign for voting rights.

According to Bernhard, upper-class women of the South not only led the movement in their states; they also helped finance advertisements and rallies. These women could also win cooperation of men by influencing their wealthy husbands to recruit other men. She also considers the issue of race, concluding that subordination of African-American women hindered the progress of the African-American movement.[8]

In her book *Southern Strategies: Southern Women and the Women Suffrage Question*, Elna C. Green seeks to understand why some Southern women actively sought to gain power in the government, and why others were indifferent or even hostile to women's suffrage. Green sees many different suffrage organizations, some elite and exclusive, others more middle-class and inclusive. Green observes that the different organizations were independent of each other but often built on and

[7]Martha M. Solomon, ed., *A Voice of Their Own: The Women Suffrage Press, 1840–1910* (Tuscaloosa: University of Alabama Press, 1991), 27–29.

[8]Virginia Bernhard, ed., *Southern Women: Histories and Identities* (Columbia, Missouri: University of Missouri Press, 1992), 7.

Similarly, the author reviews Bernhard's research. Notice how she is slowly building her case for the value of her research relative to what has already been presented.

Here the writer discusses Green's scholarly contribution to the question. The inclusion of a broad range of source discussions not only develops the writer's argument but also establishes her scholarly credibility, indicating that she "knows the field."

responded to each other's initiatives.[9] Like Herndon, Green contends that women in the South increased their demands for voting rights as a result of increased opportunities for work outside the home.[10] Also, Green contends that the important issue of race is too often overlooked in the Southern suffrage movement. She agrees with Bernhard that white women were not interested in working with African-Americans and that they lessened their impact as a result.[11]

Green also considers the impact of the issue of states' rights on women's suffrage in the South. She believes that the women who supported women's suffrage and states' rights are a separate entity from the other suffragists. These women urged their states to grant women access to political power instead of allowing the federal government to exert control over state affairs by doing so.[12] Green believes that the division among all these groups is the key to understanding the slow progress of women's suffrage in the South.

Barbara Bellows Ulmer examines the life of South Carolina suffragist Virginia Durant Young as a case study of the backgrounds and ideas that drew participants into the movement and the actions they took to further the suffrage movement. Ulmer believes that women were empowered after the Civil War because of their participation in the war effort. They felt a sense of betrayal because when the state was in crisis, they could help, but when they wanted to be represented, they were not considered equal citizens.[13] Durant, like many Southern suffragists, was

Notice that this discussion is somewhat similar to an annotated bibliography; however, the author's intent is far different. These references are summarized and briefly analyzed in order to support an argument for adopting a particular course of research outlined in this prospectus.

[9]Elna C. Green, *Southern Strategies: Southern Women and the Women Suffrage Question* (Chapel Hill: University of North Carolina Press, 1997), xv.

[10]Green, xv.

[11]Green, xv.

[12]Green, xiii.

[13]Barbara Bellows Ulmer, *Virginia Durant Young: New South Suffragist* (Columbia: University of South Carolina, 1972), 1.

not a feminist, whom she defined as someone who wanted women to be equal with men; she was simply a woman who felt that women had a right to vote because they were citizens of their state. Women of the South felt the actions of the northern movement were too radical.[14]

The writer indicates the potential contribution of this proposed research to the question at hand.

Ulmer points out that many Southern suffragists came from well-to-do families. Many of the women were also religious and had experience in women's temperance organizations and other movements that grew out of their religious beliefs. The women also tended to be married to men who were intelligent and wealthy and gave the women almost anything they wanted or needed. Young and other suffragists were given a great deal of freedom by their husbands, who were usually supporters of the progressive women's movement.[15]

Ulmer also stresses that while some of the women had formal education, others had attended in-state "seminaries" where they learned how to be better housewives or took other subjects that men believed did not strain a woman's mind too much. A key point about the South Carolina suffragist movement was that the women still wanted to be thought of as domestic and capable housewives. They did not like the idea of being stereotyped as unfeminine, as many northern suffragists were.[16]

Here the writer indicates her proposed plan to build upon the research of previous historians. She notes her focus on primary sources such as letters and speeches as a significant part of her research plan. Specifically, the writer names the key women of the South's suffrage movement whose papers will be examined.

I hope to build on the work of previous historians by focusing on the South Carolina women's suffrage movement in order to understand the motivations, strategies, and ideology of the women who led the movement. I will rely largely on the writings of leaders such as Anita Politzer, Ida Salley Reamer, Laura Bragg, Wil Lou Gray, and Eulalie Salley.

The Anita Politzer papers include correspondence, photographs, and speeches that document Politzer's role in the suffrage movement,

[14]Ulmer, 2.

[15]Ulmer, 11.

[16]Ulmer, 12.

including her leadership of the National Women's Party. They also include Politzer's literary works on artist Georgia O'Keeffe and research files on Politzer's life.[17]

The Ida Salley Reamer papers include documentation of Reamer's involvement in the South Carolina Equal Suffrage League. They include correspondence, meeting minutes, and resolutions of the League and also document some of the activities of the League in Columbia, Spartanburg, and Charleston. The papers also include details of the formation of units of the League in the state.[18]

The Constance Ashton Myers collection includes oral histories of many of the suffragists from South Carolina. These oral histories were compiled by Myers in the years immediately following the success of the suffrage movement. Interviewees such as Laura Bragg, Wil Lou Gray, and Eulalie Salley give details about the political climate during the movement and about other reform movements that accompanied the suffrage movement, as well as their own experiences in the suffrage campaign.[19]

In the Laura Bragg interview, Bragg discusses her move from Massachusetts to Charleston, South Carolina, to run the Charleston Museum. She discusses the activities of the suffragists, specifically about the trip Anita Politzer and Sue Frost made to Washington, D.C., to burn speeches made by Woodrow Wilson.[20] Wil Lou Gray was an educator and advocate for adult education who founded the South Carolina

> The writer carefully details each of the three main women's papers that will be examined.

[17]Anita Politzer Papers 1894–1975, South Caroliniana Library, USC, Columbia, South Carolina.

[18]Ida Salley Reamer Paper, South Caroliniana Library, USC, Columbia, South Carolina.

[19]Constance Ashton Myers Collection, South Caroliniana Library, USC, Columbia, South Carolina.

[20]Laura M. Bragg Oral Interview, South Caroliniana Library, USC, Columbia, South Carolina.

Opportunity School. Eulalie Salley was one of the organizers of the Women's Suffrage League in her hometown of Aiken.

Finally, the writer identifies other valuable resources to be consulted to support her research.

Other collections will also help to fill out my understanding of the movement and the times in which it occurred. The William Apollos James papers include a letter from a South Carolina suffragist, Lottie C. Hammond, from Columbia, South Carolina. Hammond thanks James for his speech supporting women's suffrage, commending his bravery and the bravery of all the men who supported the movement.[21] The David Benjamin Busby papers include articles and editorials concerning the efforts of the women's suffrage movement.[22] The Floride Cunningham collection includes newspaper clippings covering a speech that Cunningham gave at the Atlanta World's Fair. Cunningham was not a South Carolinian, but she specifically addresses the situation in South Carolina, referring to the efforts of politicians to hinder the movement.[23] Finally, the Christensen family papers document the lives of Abbie and Niels Christensen and their descendants, including details of the activities of Abbie and her daughters in the women's suffrage movement. The papers also shed light on the political world of the community of Beaufort, in which they were prominent.[24]

[21]William Apollos James Papers, South Caroliniana Library, USC, Columbia, South Carolina.

[22]David Benjamin Busby Papers 1846-1925, South Caroliniana Library, USC, Columbia, South Carolina.

[23]Floride Cunningham Manuscript, South Caroliniana Library, USC, Columbia, South Carolina.

[24]Christensen Family Papers 1817-1999, South Caroliniana Library, USC, Columbia, South Carolina.

1. In this prospectus, how does the literature review ultimately focus the reader's attention on the brief statement of Joye Shields' actual research project?
2. How would you characterize the function of the literature review that follows Shields' brief statement of what she proposes to do?
3. Notice that this prospectus contains very little description of Shields' *method*. Why is this so? In a history course, should a student be required to explain and justify his or her method of examining a question or issue?

PROPOSAL 2

Business Communications

CoACH Care Center Proposal

Mindi Colón, Jill Shaw, & LaShieka Williams
Elmhurst College

A formal business proposal begins with a "letter of transmittal," which basically presents the proposal to the specific audience, briefly outlines the intent of the proposal, and thanks the audience for considering the plan and/or request.

CoACH
Care Center
859 Rock Road   Naper, IL 60999

December 3, 2002

Mattel Children's Foundation
333 Continental Boulevard
Mail Stop: M1-1418
El Segundo, CA 90245

Dear Foundation Executive:

CoACH Care Center appreciates the opportunity to present the Family Fall Festival 2003 proposal to the Mattel Financial Executives. The outstanding reputation of working for the good of children with special needs that Mattel has cultivated led CoACH Care Center to approach Mattel with this event.

The sponsorship of this family-oriented event would build the goodwill CoACH families have towards Mattel. It would in turn allow us to provide a unique and rare opportunity to families whose children have special medical needs; enjoying recreational activities together is something these families do not often experience.

The enclosed proposal outlines the details of the event, as well as the timeline and budget specifics. If more information is required regarding the costs or plans, please contact the Family Activity Advisory Board at CoACH Care Center at (630) 27X–XXXX.

Thank you for allowing us the opportunity to present this proposal to Mattel. We look forward to partnering with you to support these families in need.

Sincerely,

LaShieka Williams
Family Activity Advisory Board Member

CoACH Care Center Fall Festival Proposal
December 3, 2002

Mattel Children's Foundation

CoACH Care Center
Family Activity Advisory Board
Mindi Colón, Jill Shaw, & LaShieka Williams

CoACH
Care Center
859 Rock Road Naper, IL 60999

A formal title page follows the letter of transmittal, indicating the name of the proposal, the audience of the proposal, the names of the proposers, and their organization contact information. Note the prescribed format and definite formality of this proposal. This is typical for a business or professional audience.

A table of contents indicates all of the parts of the proposal, enabling a reader to easily locate the various sections of the proposal.

Note that a proposal for a business environment focuses on being reader-friendly and efficient. These features, appreciated by a busy business professional, can contribute to the persuasiveness of the proposal.

Table of Contents

EXECUTIVE SUMMARY

The charitable events that CoACH Care Center funds seek to improve the lives of children in need so they may grow happy and healthy. These events are especially designed to support medically disabled children. CoACH Care Center works attentively with Mattel, Inc. to plan these activities so that the children do not feel they have limited opportunities in society. A future event intended to benefit these children is the Fall Festival 2003. This event will take place on Saturday, October 11, 2003. It will give medically fragile children and their families the opportunity to explore the various recreational opportunities available to them.

Since Mattel, Inc. is well known for their concern with children and the community, CoACH proposes that Mattel sponsor this event. The proposal expresses the details and significance of this event. Such details include the financials, timeline, and entertainment. The following summarizes the highlights of the proposed event:

- The total cost to sponsor the Fall Festival 2003 is $11,269.
- The timeline will be continuously evaluated at monthly Family Activity Advisory Board meetings for reassurance of a successful and cost-effective event.
- There will be a variety of entertainment and activities for children and their families to engage in. Such entertainment will include rides, games, clowns, magicians, ponies, petting zoo animals, and a live band.

In sponsoring this event, Mattel can expect to benefit from the partnership formed with CoACH Care Center. Because Mattel continues to be one of the world's leading toy manufacturers, the donation of toys will provide further great exposure to children. Families will gain respect for Mattel and the support they provided. Mattel's sponsorship of the festival will create a lasting impact on the children and families.

INTRODUCTION

CoACH Care is a non-profit organization that influences the lives of children and families in the Chicagoland area. They care for children who are medically fragile as they provide services and recreation to these families. The organization has been serving the local communities since 1992. We are supportive of families and proactive in assisting them.

An executive summary is an abbreviated version of the proposal that enables busy executives to skim the contents quickly; it is often a crucial section for acquiring audience attention.

Notice that most of the business proposal is single spaced; this is characteristic of business reports.

The writers provide a summary of all of the main points of the proposal.

Notice the important inclusion of benefits for the audience (Mattel, in this case). Keep in mind that a proposal is always a persuasive endeavor.

The introduction provides a brief background and explanation of the situation.

Notice how this section solicits sympathy for the cause.

The authors indicate other corporate supporters to encourage Mattel. Inclusion of other well-known supporters can promote a healthy, competitive spirit and provide credibility to the cause.

The writers include an acknowledgement of Mattel's history of supporting similar causes. This is a valuable persuasive strategy.

The specific request is provided in highly abbreviated form.

A clear statement of the purpose of the proposed event is crucial to the readability of the proposal.

A comprehensive description of the facilities and event begins here. This detail is crucial to the success of any proposal.

Families that have children with medical problems are limited in activities and events in which they can participate. With the increasing amounts of children with these problems, CoACH Care Center proposes that Mattel sponsor a Fall Festival to help these children and their families relax and recreate together in a safe environment. This would be held October 11, 2003 and would be a great way to allow the families of medically fragile children to enjoy a festival where their children would be safe.

For the festival, McDonald's Corporation has offered to supply all of the food at no cost. The Family Activity Advisory Board is proposing to Mattel to supply prizes for the children at the festival. This would be a great contribution to the children and their families. Mattel Corporation faithfully contributes $25 million to the University of California-Los Angeles Medical Children's Hospital. The donations of toys will continue Mattel's generous reputation towards children.

In addition to the donation of toys, CoACH Care Center is proposing that Mattel fund the remaining costs of the festival.

RATIONALE AND PLAN

The purpose of the CoACH Care Fall Festival is to strengthen relationships among families with medically fragile children. Family activities, such as this one, provide families that face medical challenges with their children an opportunity to relax, have fun, and be with their children in an environment that is equipped and able to care for their children.

DESCRIPTION OF SERVICES AND EQUIPMENT

Facilities

The DuPage County Fairgrounds in Wheaton, Illinois, was selected as the location for the Fall Festival. The facilities are designed for events such as this one, and the location is central to most of the CoACH Care Center families.

Parking will be supervised by the staff at the fairgrounds and is included in the facility rental package price.

Rides and Games

Carnival rides will be provided by Awesome Amusement. Game booths will be rented from Zebra Entertainment. Charges are based on four-hour increments. Zebra Entertainment and Awesome Amusement deliver the equipment and provide qualified operators for the rides. Operators handle all of the moving and setting up of the equipment.

The number of rides and game booths rented will be proportionate to the anticipated number of people in attendance, which is five hundred.

Entertainers

A band has been selected to provide family-oriented music throughout the festival. They will be playing from 11:00 a.m. to 5:00 p.m. Sound equipment will be supplied by the band.

Clown Images will provide clown entertainers and magicians throughout the festival from 9:00 a.m. to 5:00 p.m. It is recommended to have one entertainer per fifty guests; the anticipated number of needed entertainers is ten. Clowns and magicians will mingle with the guests, make balloon animals, perform their basic routines, and provide comic entertainment.

Food Arrangements

McDonald's Corporation has agreed to provide food and beverages at no cost for the five hundred guests in attendance at the festival. Additionally, they will donate the paper products and condiments necessary.

Our trained volunteers will coordinate the serving of the food. Allergies and medical conditions have been factored into the menu, and alternatives will be provided for those guests that need them.

Ponies and Petting Zoo

Ponies and a petting zoo will be rented from Party Time Ponies. They charge in four-hour increments and will be set up at the festival from 9:00 a.m. to 5:00 p.m. There will be no additional charge to families for pony rides or entrance to the petting zoo. Again, our goal is to provide this event for families at no cost.

Notice the varying types of subheadings; each type indicates a different level of importance. Consistency of subheadings is very important within a business proposal such as this. Attention to this type of detail reflects the level of professionalism of the proposal—a quality highly valued by this genre's audience.

Print Materials and Services

Printing services will be provided by Kinko's. The committee will typeset and design the invitations, volunteer-recruitment flyers, and training manuals, which will then be printed by Kinko's. CoACH Care Center has an existing and amicable relationship with Kinko's.

Volunteer Staff for Festival

Indication of the "in-kind contributions," such as the help of the Care Center's staff mentioned here, usually helps persuade the proposal's audience to participate.

To staff the festival from the game booths to the food services, volunteers will be recruited from CoACH Care Center (our staff and interns), local hospitals, and the Naperville Park District.

Volunteers will attend a training session with our CoACH Care staff coordinators. They will learn about our philosophy and goals, as well as how to run the festival. A schedule of shifts and stations will be coordinated at the training meeting.

Within the budget, an allowance has been made for small thank-you gifts to be purchased and given to the volunteers. They are a vital part of our organization and all of our events.

Prizes and Toys

In addition to the financial donation we are proposing that Mattel makes, we are also soliciting toys and games from Mattel and its affiliates to be used as prizes and giveaways to the children and winners of the games.

Indicates the rationale for the choice of Mattel as the audience for this proposal.

Note that background research on the audience was required. That research and the complimentary tone assumed are very appropriate to this proposal genre.

We chose to approach Mattel with this proposal based on your financial history of generosity that has been shown to children's organizations and hospitals in the past. We are confident that a partnership in this event would be beneficial to Mattel as it will create goodwill towards families in difficult situations, who will in turn respect the corporation that is responsible for entertaining and educating children.

TIMELINE

The proposed timeline for the planning of the CoACH Care Fall Festival follows. Dates are tentative and will be evaluated at Family Activity Advisory Board meetings monthly.

Task	Date
Establish a budget	December 6, 2002
Make arrangements for rental services/equipment	January 6, 2003

- Clowns
- Magicians
- DuPage Country Fairgrounds
- Carnival Games
- Carnival Rides
- Ponies and Petting Zoo
- Band

Meet with DuPage County Fairground representative	January 21, 2003
Coordinate food arrangements with McDonald's	May 5, 2003
Review budget and timeline	May 27, 2003
CoACH Care Fall Festival 2003 Committee Meeting	June 16, 2003
Create invitation	June 16, 2003
Collect prizes	July 2003
Send invitation to printers	July 16, 2003
Recruit volunteers for festival	July 27, 2003
Mail invitations to families	August 25, 2003
Second volunteer recruitment	August 27, 2003
Order harvest decorations	September 22, 2003
Training for festival volunteers	September 27, 2003
Set-up for festival (evening)	October 10, 2003
Clean-up and teardown	October 11, 2003

The audience of a proposal often wants a specific timeline in order to understand a project's timing in relation to its other obligations and activities.

COST ANALYSIS

This section of our proposal examines the financial budget that CoACH Care Center advocates must pursue to initiate a successful event. The following figures provide a detailed summary of the cost information that is required to be followed by the Family Activity Advisory Board.

A detailed budget of all proposed costs for the event is provided. This is a crucial component of a business proposal because cost is always a concern.

Category	Total Cost
Rentals	
•Band	$ 500
•Clowns	750
•Magicians	850
•Games s (from Zebra Entertainment	1800
•Rides (from Awesome Amusement)	3000
•Petting Zoo Animals/Pony Rides	844
•DuPage County Fairgrounds	2500
Food Arrangements	
•McDonald's	Donated
Print Materials	
•Kinko's	200
*Carry out print orders including invitations, training manuals, and flyers	
•U.S. Mailing Services	75
*Process mailing requests including invitations and flyers	
Committee Meetings (Family Activity Advisory Board)	
•Facilities to conduct meeting	Onsite
•Catering expenses for lunch	150
Training Sessions (For Volunteers)	
•Facilities to conduct meeting	Onsite
•Create small thank-you packages	600
Total Expenses:	**$11,269**

Notice the visual clarity of the layout of the budget figures, typical of this genre.

The Family Activity Advisory Board has diligently sought other supporters, such as McDonald's Corporation, to fund this event, with the intention that CoACH Care Center families would not have to pay for admission, food, and other costs of attending the festival.

Here the writers emphasize efforts to acquire underwriters for this event and indicate their rationale for doing so.

DESCRIPTION OF ORGANIZATION

Offering an additional, more comprehensive description of the Center provides credibility to the proposal.

At the CoACH Care Center, a non-profit organization founded in 1992, medically fragile children and their families are cared for and educated. Children may stay at the respite house while families work, vacation, or reenergize. Volunteer medical staff provide quality care for the children while they stay.

Additionally, workshops are provided for health education, a child's visit is coordinated and planned, family gatherings are held, and funds are raised for the organization and the families. Training, resources, and consulting services are available to families.

Why help us?

CoACH Care Center works to support children and families with medical challenges. We volunteer our services and facilities to provide a foundation to families and help them cope with their challenges. Incoming funds and donations are used to maintain the facilities and supply families with the physical needs they may have.

We strive to provide recreation and family oriented activities, like the Fall Festival, to strengthen family relationships and build emotional support. Bringing families with medically fragile children together allows them to make connections and create additional support networks in their lives. Supporting our event will allow us to accomplish these goals.

Mattel has a history of supporting and funding events for children. Particularly notable are the donations that have been made to children's hospitals.

Mattel's donation to the CoACH Care Center's Fall Festival will continue the generous and concerned reputation that has been established by the children's foundation over the last twenty-four years. Families in crisis and need at CoACH Care Center will remember the support of Mattel.

The writers of this proposal frame a final plea for Mattel's support with a very direct question. This is often a successful persuasive strategy employed within this genre.

Again the writers compliment Mattel for their history of generous contributions to such causes.

The writers restate the main purpose of the proposal.

CONCLUSION

CoACH Care Center welcomes the opportunity to submit this proposal to Mattel Corporation. Our proposal benefits the medically fragile children in the Chicagoland area. Our center has provided many opportunities that offer a positive environment for the families that deserve an enjoyable event like the Fall Festival.

CoACH Care Center is a reliable and understanding place. Our company takes on many tasks that involve the community and we believe that this proposed plan would benefit the Mattel Corporation as well. Our partnership will strengthen throughout the event and will be beneficial to each of us.

The writers close with an invitation for further inquiry on the part of the audience.

If any other information regarding the proposal is needed, please contact the Family Activity Advisory Board at the CoACH Care Center. The board is willing to meet with you and discuss the proposed idea at your convenience.

INVESTIGATING THE GENRE SAMPLE

1. In this proposal, notice how the writers pay close attention to the thoroughly persuasive nature of the genre. Is there any place in the proposal where they do not seem to emphasize their goal of seeking funding for their center?
2. Why do you think the writers needed to point out to the Mattel Children's Foundation that several other organizations were contributing to this project as well?
3. Throughout this proposal, the authors use formatting and organizational features that make the document accessible and easy to read. What are some of these features?

PROFESSIONAL ACTION PLANS

Some academic majors are very specifically and directly tied to particular professional careers; nursing, education, and architecture are obvious examples. Within these majors, course assignments often involve field work in which students observe and sometimes practice *actual activities* that they will soon be obligated to perform in their given professions. One increasingly popular type of assignment, as more and more educators recognize the value of "experiential education," is the creation of an "action plan." A **professional action plan**, as the name implies, outlines a course of action—a series of steps to be taken—in order to address a specific problem or concern. This section will discuss the specific purpose(s), audience, overall organization, and/or format of a professional action plan as a highly specialized genre of academic writing. It will be followed by two annotated student samples of action plans, one for the education profession and one for the nursing profession.

Generally speaking, the purpose of any professional action plan is to outline a specific, detailed strategy that addresses a particular need, hopefully solving or preventing a problem. To do so, the creator of the plan must first assess the need, research and carefully consider possible courses of action, and then detail the specifics of the plan. That plan, of course, is created for a specific individual or group of individuals. So there is a very real audience for a professional action plan, in a different sense from the audience for some other academic writing assignments.

The audience for an action plan may appear simple but in fact is often rather complex. The immediate audience is, of course, the individual or group with the need.

For example, in the second paper presented here, the immediate audience is the nurse caring for the patient who needs physical care. However, often there are other audiences to consider. In this case, there is potentially the patient, the family and the caregiver of the patient, as well as other nursing and/or premed students who may access this plan. As an academic project, the professor or evaluator is always a significant part of the audience even though he/she is probably not the focus of the action steps at all. Beyond that, there are often peripheral audiences who may need to be considered within your planning. In the case of the first paper, this includes the parents, who have a vested interest in their student's behavior and learning within a given classroom, and the administrators in the school where the plan is to be implemented. As you read the samples below, notice the various audiences that need to be taken into account.

To formulate an action plan, the author must do several things:

- Identify a specific problem or concern within his/her field—sometimes the problem is assigned and, thus, already identified;
- Carefully describe the circumstances of the "problem";
- Discuss the probable causes of the problem or other significant contributing circumstances;
- Identify the goals or objectives of the plan;
- Provide a detailed course of action with very prescribed steps;
- Include a method of assessment or evaluation to determine the effectiveness of the plan;
- Present some type of follow-up for future action or reflection on the validity and/or results of the plan; and
- Provide references—a list of the sources consulted for the creation of the plan and/or the sources consulted for background information to understand the scope and potential ramifications of the problem. These references also offer your audience avenues for obtaining more information about the topic under consideration.

Within the samples below, some aspects of the format vary considerably because of differences between the disciplines. For example, a detailed clinical evaluation of the patient is included in the second action plan. Obviously, this is appropriate information for this nursing student to obtain; but it would be totally inappropriate for the student teacher to obtain some of this information about his students. Nonetheless, despite the different categories included in each plan, essentially both provide:

- An overview or introduction to the problem/need
- A detailed plan of action
- An assessment component
- A list of references/resources

Now let's look closely at the two samples of professional action plans. The first is from the field of education. This plan, created by a senior from Sam Houston State University during his student-teaching semester, presents a "Classroom Management Plan" for adolescents within a special education environment. The second sample, written by a nursing student from Elmhurst College, presents a formal, multilevel nursing plan for the treatment of an elderly patient suffering serious side effects from his decades of cigarette smoking. The second annotated student sample appears quite different from the first, as it assumes an appropriate format and vocabulary for the nursing profession. Nonetheless, though the topics and details are significantly different, certain commonalities of professional action plans do emerge from these samples.

PROFESSIONAL ACTION PLAN 1
Education

Classroom Management Plan

Frank Schiappa
Sam Houston State University

Classroom Management Plan

Introduction

Background information on the overall intent of this action plan and an acknowledgment of sources is provided within the introduction.

My plan is derived from multiple sources ranging from my own ideas acquired from classroom experiences to classroom management models that have proven effective in reaching students so they are learning to the best of their abilities. I want my students to be active participants in "our" classroom. Being active includes being a part of the classroom. This includes my having materials ready for them daily and an organized lesson plan so that students remain engaged and successful in the learning environment. For the students to be successful in group related activities, the students and I will formalize rules to be used in a group setting, and name cards will be used until the students and I know each other's names. Those individuals who provided suggestions to complete my classroom management plan include Wong, Glasser, Kounin, Sloss, Prosise, Williams, and Jones. Along with ideas from these theorists, I will use behavior modification plans because a great deal of my time will be spent in the realm of a special education setting.

A brief explanation of the scope of the plan and the sources are provided for the reader.

On the first day of school, the students and I will formulate rules (expectations) along with the necessary consequences to ensure that the management plan runs smoothly. This procedure will show students that I am ready to teach and that I care about their safety and an effective learning environment. Having consequences does not mean that I will not trust the students; they should be trusted from the moment they enter the classroom. However, this process is to establish a routine and let students know what will occur if they choose not to follow the rules.

To serve as a role model, I will conduct myself in a professional manner. I will always show the students respect even when they have chosen to break a rule as noted by Wong in "How You Can Be a Super Successful Teacher" (1987). When I have to "discipline" a student, it will be with a calm voice without exhibiting emotion, and without other peers present as shown during most of my field experiences.

Objectives (Rules)

1. I want the students to treat peers, all school personnel, and property with respect. Respect comes in many forms; however, for the purposes of my plan it means when an individual is given the floor, everyone else should refrain from talking, making fun of, or in any way physically harming anyone. In regards to property, students should keep books covered and abstain from defacing school property.

2. I want students to be comfortable in the learning process, so our class will be conducted in a collaborative learning manner. Students may interject their thoughts whenever someone has ceased talking during classroom discussion as incorporated in the management plans of many Sam Houston State University instructors.

3. I want students to feel safe and secure in our "positive learning environment" so that they can come to me for their needs regarding learning and/or unforeseen events. I will conference with each student every 6 weeks regarding their progress, and at this time we will discuss my observations. Also, if I see any

The author provides insights into his basic educational philosophy, which inform the overall nature of the plan.

The outline of the plan begins here with the itemization of four basic rules for classroom behavior. Notice that the numbered format contributes to the readability, and presumably, the adaptability of the plan.

Recall that this genre often includes multiple audiences with different needs—here potential adapters of the plan are one significant audience.

situation that needs immediate attention regarding the safety and security of the students, I will visit with those individuals. If I see an object that violates the security of students, it will be removed. If I see signs of neglect, students will be offered support. Any suspicions will also be reported to the proper authorities, as it is my duty to report neglect and abuse in a 48-hour period according to Texas law.

Notice that there are references to different sources throughout this section; these provide credibility and support for the steps proposed.

Specific activities are suggested throughout this section. The writer is sketching the particulars of the action plan.

4. Students will turn in assignments on their due dates. However, if unforeseen events arise, the students will inform me and vice versa. On the second class day, the students will receive a written schedule and calendar as suggested by Harry Wong in "How You Can Be a Super Successful Teacher" (1987).

Activities

The best plan is a plan hidden within the normal academic routine. If I have a thorough strategic plan, the students can begin preparing for class when they walk in the door. A clear lesson includes an engaging warm-up designed to motivate students about the day's lesson. Also, by my being prompt in beginning the day's lesson, there will be less of a chance of non-compliance. I will be proactive and look for avenues of pre-correction as I scan the room, and use with-it-ness as described by Kounin (2002). Also, I intend to offer presentations and simulations that are engaging, stimulating, and whenever possible use media and guests to charge the atmosphere. By promoting group work and encouraging discovery in a manner that is fun, students will be intrigued and follow the plan. While promoting good work habits, I will praise the students' input, prompt them by providing the answers with clues, and then leave to empower them to find the answers as suggested in Jones' PPL plan (1987). In addition, I intend to give feedback whenever possible and encourage students both academically and behaviorally through constructive feedback. To be effective, I will be fair, consistent, humorous, share my feelings, listen, and above all, not be negative.

Further, the source "Giving and Getting Respect" (2002) will aid me in facilitating a positive classroom environment where the child is treated as a special, cared-for human being. When assisting students who become non-compliant, I will talk to them, not at them, find the root of the problem if possible, use "expressive and receptive language" when conferencing, and then "set them up for success" (2). This can be done as follows:

- Establish routines that exhibit the desired behavior.
- Use proactive cooperation by suggesting an action that they would want to do, like—"draw a capital I in the air."
- Give hints and clues so the student is successful in front of others.
- "Catch 'em being good."
- Recognize effort.
- Point out progress.
- State my belief in their potential.

The students and I will role play simulations to ensure that they exhibit the proper classroom behaviors. To facilitate the role play, students will pick a possible rule out of a box. Then, a group of students will role play the correct and incorrect way to follow the rule, such as talking when someone has the floor and vice versa. The students will also help decide on five appropriate rules to encompass all desired actions to be exhibited by the class, and role play those behaviors as well. The students will take the rules and write a contract agreeing to the rules selected. Lastly, the students will bring the rules home to the parents, at which time they too will sign the sheet to show that they support the plan. Further, the next day the rules created by the students will be written on a poster and reviewed via a transparency to ensure once again there is no question as to the behavior to be exhibited. Several days later, the class will play a jeopardy game to review the rules and take a test on them.

A sample test of the rules is as follows:

Continually inter-weaving source material both strengthens the authority of the plan and ethically acknowledges borrowed ideas.

An activity contained within the plan is clearly outlined. Remember that this genre is focused on providing practical details of specific actions that can be implemented in the appropriate environment.

The author provides a sample of a specific handout to be completed as one of the action steps.

Note that it is acceptable to include this sample within the body of the action plan. However, sometimes materials such as these are merely referred to within the body of a plan like this and then appear in their entirety only within an appendix at the end of the report.

Name _____   Date _____

Grade _____

School/Classroom Compliance

1. Describe respect and how it applies to class discussion.

   _____

2. What time does class start? (explain how you should be ready and when)

   _____

3. Describe your actions during group discussion.

   _____

4. Describe how you should act during the discussion time with the teacher.

   _____

5. What are the acceptable actions during announcements?

   _____

6. What are the consequences for not following the rules outlined by the class for respect?

   _____

7. What are the consequences for being late and unprepared for class discussion?

   _____

8. Describe the consequences for improper actions during group discussion.

   _____

9. List at least one unacceptable action along with one consequence.

   _____

10. What are the consequences for not following the proper behavior for announcements?

    _____

    _____

To further involve the students in the academic process, they will fill out an interest inventory. A few questions to be used are "What kind of books or articles would you choose to read above all others?" and "What do you and your friends like to read?" By using the interest inventory, I can gear lessons to further interest the students. Both the interest inventories and student attitudinal surveys, developed by Dr. Leonard Breen (2002), will help me understand my students.

Parents will be involved from the start of the academic school year as encouraged by Harry Wong (1987). The first week, all parents will be called and asked such questions as "What are your child's special needs and interests?" Then, the parents will be called every 2 weeks with an update and positive comments regarding each student's progress. According to Harry Wong in "How You Can Be a Super Successful Teacher" (1987), students should be given many chances for success. His plan suggests that students be tested often, at least once every week and sometimes twice. When the parents are called, Wong states in jest that teachers should mention the students' successes, and then tell them that the students did something fantastic today and simply hang up the phone. That way the students can tell their parents about their many successes. Although I will not hang up the telephone on parents, I will make sure we celebrate many achievements. This promotes self-esteem and students will become more active and energetic in regards to learning.

Further, rewards and consequences will be used in my classroom. The students and I will decide on the rewards. Tangible rewards will include stickers, books, magazines, and much more. Other rewards will include free time at the end of the week, and an occasional edible item. Each Monday, the students will begin with a 30-minute reward for the week. If there are disruptions, 5 minutes will be deducted each time. Harry Wong's "How You Can Be a Super Successful Teacher" (1987) proves the program is successful as he mentioned that within a few weeks the class will typically have 30-minutes of free, structured time to

---

Another significant step of the action plan is described in detail.

Notice the attention to the parents here. They are a significant secondary audience for this professional action plan.

Further explanation of the action plan for maintaining appropriate classroom behavior is provided. Here the discussion refers to a reward system to be established.

finish projects, homework, or read selected materials. As stated there will be consequences; however, first there must be a plan of action. "The 10-R Technique," introduced by Sloss (2001), can be useful to control and change behavior. This process is most effective when used for preschool through fourth grade and developmentally through the ages of 8 or 9. However, I feel it can be effective for all levels. "The 10-R Technique" is as follows:

- Response cost—include student, have student discuss behavior to make the expectations clear, and state what the individual will lose
- Relaxation—have a predetermined location; make sure student is calm when you are ready to talk
- Rectify—have the student provide restitution, such as an apology, or replacement
- Recognize—help student see cause of the behavior
- Rehearsal—rehearse desired behavior, role play
- Reinforce—reinforce good behavior, and remember to praise when applicable
- Reflect—have student identify consequences of behavior
- Re-enter—expect the student to make up missed assignments
- Record—make anecdotal notes for further evaluation
- Repeat—repeat to encode process

An extensive discussion of consequences for violating the expectations is included in this section. Typically, this genre must not only describe an ideal course of action, but must also account for appropriate actions in light of deviations.

This program will be used anytime students need to follow a behavior modification plan. If a student breaks a rule for the first time, the individual will receive a warning and retraining. After the second offense, the student will receive a written warning and a warning that the parents will be called on the next offense. If the student happens to break the same rule a third time, the parents will be called. Most of the time this should curtail the behavior; however, if the student persists in the behavior, the individual will be sent to the office with a signed agreement to follow the rules, documentation of warnings, and a copy of "The l0-R Technique" (Sloss, 2001).

To ensure that there are few negative parent contacts, the student will either communicate feelings or write them. Once the student has calmed down and written the response, the behavior will be discussed. Then the proper behavior will be acted out and rehearsed with the student. The above methods to teach "The 10-R Technique" (Sloss, 2001) will be instructed on a one-on-one basis so that I do not humiliate the student. However, I will prompt and cue the desired behavior as often as needed.

Further specifics of the action plan are detailed here.

Lastly, students will use self-evaluation techniques. In this process the students will set goals based on the class curriculum. The students and I will evaluate once every 6 weeks to ensure follow through. In addition, the students and I will review grades; tests; anecdotal notes regarding observations, projects; and homework.

A basic lesson plan is as follows:

Lesson Plan

Unit: Class rules and school rules

Lesson topic: Empower students by having them help create the class rules, and review school rules.

Objective: The student will explain specific knowledge of school and class rules and consequences via a teacher-made test, with 100% accuracy after reading the school rules, formulating class rules, participating in a class discussion, and role playing. (Role plays include desired and undesired behaviors regarding rules.) For students who do not receive a test score of 100, a role play of the rule(s) missed will be conducted to prove mastery.

Here the writer provides a "lesson plan," a common genre in the field of education, which details ways to implement an aspect of the over-all action plan.

Materials: Pencil and paper, student handbook, and a poster to post class rules.

Content: School rules and five to seven class rules will be discussed by the class to facilitate a smooth management process.

Methods/key questions: As the students arrive, they will be asked to pick up their handbooks and begin reading the table of contents. Once the class is settled, I will ask them to number off starting with one and ending with five. Students will then separate by number and that will be their group. Each group will be given a section to read with a time limit of 10 to 15 minutes. After reading, the groups will be requested to give an outline of what they will discuss and then present the information in detail to the class. Each group will be given 7 minutes to present and/or role play their portion of the handbook to the entire class. This activity should take 50 minutes to complete.

The remaining time will be devoted to agreeing on five to seven class rules. Again, each group will be given 10 to 15 minutes to design two rules each and discuss and/or role play them. The last 13 minutes of class will be devoted to reaching a consensus on the rules and consequences to be followed. I will facilitate the process by asking questions like, "Do you like people talking while you are talking?", "Do you like anyone out of their desk while you are talking?", and "Why is it important for everyone to be on time?".

Evaluation/Closure: The students will be given a written test worth 100 points. The test will include the five to seven rules decided on by the class and three to five school rules. Students will then create a written contract regarding the class and school rules, and they will all agree to follow the rules and the consequences discussed in the activity portion of this plan.

An example contract is as follows:

Behavior Contract

Date of contract _____

I _____, will follow the outline of the classroom and overall school rules 100% of the time. The outline is as follows:

A specific example of this aspect of the plan is provided for the reader. Again, this would be very useful for the potential adopter of the classroom plan.

I will show respect as defined by our class.

I will be on time and prepared for class each day.

I will exhibit proper behaviors during announcements, class discussions, and school assemblies.

I will follow the above rules or the consequences will include a verbal warning and a reiteration of the rules. After the second offense, I will receive a written warning and a warning that my parents will be called on the next offense, and reiteration of the rules. If I break a rule a third time, my parents will be called. If I continue to break any rules, I will be sent to the office with my signed commitment to the rules, documentation of the warnings, and a copy of the written contract.

If I follow the above rules, I will be able to go to lunch 30 seconds early every day and have free, structured time with the class every Friday for 30 minutes. Review of the plan will only happen when there is an infraction. Students will receive constructive feedback daily, and the parents will be called for updates. In addition, they will be called for an overall progress report once every 2 weeks, and a behavior discussion will be included if needed.

Parent's signature _____

Teacher's signature _____

Evaluation

     I will evaluate my plan each day, and then twice a month by tape recording the entire class and analyzing what appears to be effective and ineffective. I will also use the "class talk," introduced in the classroom management text by Williams, Alley, and Henson (1999). Plus, I will have a suggestion box for student input regarding their concerns with specific questions like, "Were the expectations clear?", "What did you like best about the activity?", and "What would you change?" I will also ask a fellow instructor to use the Professional Development Appraisal System form (Texas evaluation instrument) to evaluate me once every 2

Assessment of any action plan is a very important step within this genre. Note how the author describes his method for assessing the effectiveness of his action plan.

months. However, if I feel I need additional evaluations, I will request more. The student evaluations include role plays, simulations, participation, and objective tests to assess comprehension of the management plan.

The student's evaluation will be broken into the following segments:

Test will be 40%

Group work and projects will be 30%

Homework will be 20%

Participation will be 10%

Grading:

90–100 = A

80–89 = B

70–79 = C

60–69 = D

0–59 = F

References

Breen, L. (2002). *Interest and study skills inventories*. Houston: Sam Houston State University.

The interest and skills inventories are used to gain an insight into the students' likes and dislikes.

Giving and getting respect. (2002). http://maxweber.hunter.cuny.edu/pub/eres/edspc715_mcintyre/respect_web_page_.htm

This source was used as an outline to model respect.

Glasser, W. (2001). *The ten step approach*. http://maxweber.hunter.cuny.edu/pub/eres/edspc715_mcintyre/glasser

This source was used as part of the plan to help combat poor behavior in the classroom.

Fulfilling his ethical obligation, the writer lists references that provided ideas and justification for his action plan. Drawing on authorities is common practice in this genre because it lends credibility to an action plan.

Sources are documented in APA style, commonly used in the field of education.

Jones, F. H. (1987). *Positive classroom instruction.* New York: McGraw Hill.

From this source, chapter 5 was used to show how to facilitate learning.

Kounin, J. (2002). *Managing behavior via teaching style.*

http://maxweber.hunter.cuny.edu/pub/eres/edspc715_mcintyre /teachingtips.html

This source was used in order to incorporate a teaching style that engaged students in positive behaviors and helped my classroom management plan work more smoothly.

Prosise, R. (1996). *Beyond rules and consequences for classroom management.* Bloomington: Phi Delta Kappa Education Foundation.

This source was used as a foundation for learning about interpersonal skills necessary for the teacher.

Sloss, P. (2001). The 10-R technique.

http://maxweber.hunter.cuny.edUlpub/eres/ed5PC[7] 1 Smcintyre/ 1 Orplan.html

This source was used as a guide to modify behaviors especially in one-on-one instruction.

Williams, P. A., Alley, R. D., & Henson, K. T. (1999). *Managing secondary classrooms.* Needham Heights: Allyn & Bacon.

This source was used as the primary source for the outline and ideas for various strategies to form my classroom management plan.

Wong, H. K. (Speaker). (1987). *How you can be a super successful teacher.* [Cassette Recording]. Sunnyvale, CA: H. Wong.

This source was used as a resource for constructing my basic classroom philosophy and approach regarding teacher-student relationships and classroom procedures.

Strictly speaking, according to APA style, Web site references should be included only as parenthetical citations and not in the reference list. Apparently, the student was instructed to list all works consulted here.

Notice this is an annotated bibliography. Each entry is accompanied by a very brief explanation of how the source was used as a reference for the report, in compliance with the instructor's directions.

INVESTIGATING THE GENRE SAMPLE

1. How would you characterize the tone of this professional action plan? How does the tone contrast, for example, to the tone of the prospectus for a senior project in history presented in the first sample in the section on proposals/prospectuses?
2. What types of specialized language used frequently by teachers does Frank Schiappa use in this classroom management plan? How does this language affect the readers' perception of Schiappa as a budding professional teacher?
3. Notice that this professional action plan does not have a section specifically devoted to a review of the professional literature. How and where does it cite published scholarship?

PROFESSIONAL ACTION PLAN 2

Nursing

Nursing Care Plan:

"Client #2"

Kristin Poschke
Elmhurst College

Nursing Care Plan:

"Client #2"

Nursing Assessment

Name: N.L.

Age: 71 yrs old

Gender: Male

Admitting Diagnosis: Shortness of Breath

Significant Medical History: History of emphysema, dyslipidemia, CAD, COPD, anxiety, a-tach. Client also has history of lung cancer (diagnosed in 1989), and had a right lobectomy in 1995. Client is a heavy smoker. History of smoking 2 packs a day for the last 50 years. History of heavy alcohol use for 50 years. Bilateral cataract surgery last year.

This section offers a detailed clinical description of the patient involved. It is obtained primarily by interviewing the patient. As it is self-reported, it is considered "subjective information" within the discipline of medicine.

Nature of Illness: Client was admitted from Dr. office on 4/15/02 with complaints of increased shortness of breath, weakness, and poor appetite for the past week. In addition, client noticed increased anxiety levels the last 3–5 days before admission, with the increase in cough making it very difficult to eat or breathe.

Synthesis of Pathophysiology: Client's medical history and current diagnosis can be related back to client's smoking habits. Smoking leads to emphysema and COPD because it destroys the connective tissue and elastin in the lungs resulting in lungs becoming overdistended, increased airway resistance, and altered oxygen-carbon dioxide exchange (Phipps, Sands, & Marek, 1999). Carcinogens within the cigarette smoke also played their role in the client's previous lung cancer. Client's CAD and dyslipidemia can also be associated with the client's smoking history. Nicotine decreases high-density lipoproteins, displaces oxygen from the hemoglobin so the heart must work harder, which leads to high blood pressure and increased heart rate, and leads to plaque formation (Phipps, Sands, & Marek, 1999).

Holistic/Comprehensive Assessment

Airway

Client's main complaint upon admission was shortness of breath with extreme dyspnea during coughing episodes. Client was currently on 3 liters of 02 at 97% with pulse oximetry. Breath sounds were diminished with scattered rhonchi upon auscultation. Respiratory rate was normal, slightly labored, at 24 breaths/mm. No signs of respiratory distress during hours of care. Client receiving Nebulizer treatments with Albuterol QID and PRN. Client receiving chest physical therapy and postural drainage QID. Productive cough noted with yellow-tinged sputum. Heart rate and rhythm was normal, auscultation of S1 and S2 heart sounds. ECG noted sinus tachycardia, no complaints of chest pain.

Note the use of very technical terms, appropriate for the primary audience of this genre, namely, CAD (coronary artery disease) and COPD (chronic obstructive pulmonary disease) appear throughout this report. Clearly, the audience of this genre is health care professionals.

An indication of the main problem necessitating the action plan is provided.

This section identifies more details of the "problem"—i.e., the patient is a heavy smoker with severe medical conditions directly tied to that habit. Note the inclusion of a medical reference to support the nurse's conclusions.

This long section continues a description of the patient. It offers more objective information that can be clinically observed and measured, such as blood pressure and heart rate.

Client had pulse rate of 79. Radial pulses +2 right and left, pedal pulses +1 right and left. Capillary refill was <3 seconds. Blood pressure was 118/60. No pitting edema noted.

Food and Water

Client was saline locked and it was flushed with sodium chloride 0.9% every 8 hours per hospital protocol. Client was on no dietary or fluid restriction. Client was on L's and 0's every shift. Client's oral intake during AM shift was 350 cc's. Client ate 50% of his breakfast, claimed it was difficult to eat due to dyspnea.

Elimination

Client's abdomen was soft, round, and non-tender with bowel sounds present in all four quadrants. Client's last bowel movement was the day of admission, 4/15/02. Client urinated 320 cc's for AM shift, urine was yellow and clear.

Prevention of Hazards

Client was alert and oriented x 3, he was pleasant, cooperative, and compliant with treatment regime. Client moved very little due to dyspnea upon exertion, but could move all extremities independently. Client required 2 assists to walk due to an unsteady gate related to current weakness. Client was on fall precautions and was monitored hourly. Prior to hospitalization, client performed own ADL's by self with minimal assistance from daughter and with assistance of 02 nasal cannula. Client did not complain of pain but did complain of dyspnea, which he resolved by sitting up with 02 NC at 3 liters. Client's skin was dry with moist mucous membranes and was warm to touch. Client's temperature was 99.2 Fahrenheit.

Normalcy/Development

Client was 71 years old and presented in Erickson's integrity versus despair stage. Client presented with positive resolution of this stage (integrity) because he showed acceptance of worth of his life and accepts his own death when the time is his (Erickson, 2000). Client is pleasant

---

Note that "dysp-nea" is referred to repeatedly. It means "shortness of breath."

and cooperative but not willing to change his current lifestyle habits. He lives with his daughter and her son and is really close with his grandson. He is not extremely religious and although he is Catholic, he does not practice the religion. Client's educational level is 10~ grade and claimed, "school was never really for me, I was the troublemaker." He worked as a mechanic and electrician for 45 years and is currently retired.

Activity and Rest

Client was capable of performing most of his ADL's prior to hospitalization with the assistance of 02. Currently, client needs more assistance to perform ADL's and two assists to transfer from bed to chair due to exacerbation of COPD. However, client can still turn and readjust position in bed. Client normally sleeps 9 hours a night, but has only slept in 2-hour intervals while hospitalized.

Solitude and Social Interaction

Client had no problems socializing before hospitalization. No hearing devices used, client does wear glasses. Client stopped drinking 8 years ago but still meets with his buddies for poker games. Client currently experiencing difficulties carrying on long conversations due to dyspnea.

List of Medications

1. Ceftriaxone (Rocephin)—used as an antibiotic
   Given 1 gm IVPBQD
2. Levofloxacin (Levaquin)—used as an antibiotic
   Given 500 mg P0QD
3. Pantoprazole (Protonix)—used as an anti-ulcer agent
   Given 40 mg P0QD
4. Albuterol/Ipratropium (combivent inhaler)—used as a
   Bronchodilator
   Given 2 puffs inhaler QID
5. Fluticasone (Flovent inhaler)—inhalation corticosteroid, works
   as anti-inflammatory
   Given 2 puffs inhaler BID

All of the patient's medications are indicated. They must be taken into consideration in formulating the plan.

6. Alprazolam (Xanax)—used for anxiety

    Given 0.25 mg PO Q6 hours PRN

7. Tramadol (Ultram)—used as an analgesic

    Given 50 mg PO Q6 hours PRN

(Deglin and Vallerand, 2001)

List of Diagnostic and Therapeutic Measurements

CBC—showed elevated WBC (16.3), which is the result from the virus, and/or other organisms that caused the acute exacerbation of COPD.

- Neutrophil count was high, which may be the result of the physical and emotional stress related to the exacerbation and hospitalization and/or the acute infection/inflammatory disorder.

- Lymphocyte count was low (15), which may be directly related to the increase in neutrophils (when one goes up the other must come down to maintain WBC count), OR could be result of the corticosteroids the client is taking.

- MCHC was minimally decreased (31.9) and RDW was increased (17.1), both test for anemia. Both test results point in the direction of slight anemia, possibly related to client's decreased appetite.

BMP—results were all normal

(Pagana & Pagana, 1998)

Toxicology—Client complained of fever and chills the week prior to admission. Theophylline is a weak bronchodilator that the client was currently taking at home, 200mg BID. Fever and chills are a couple signs and symptoms of theophylline toxicity. Client's blood levels were tested and found to be low (2.1), so client was not at risk of toxicity.

(Deglin & Vallerand, 2001)

Further detailed description of objective measurements of the patient's condition are provided. Note that this genre is highly structured in certain technical fields like nursing to ensure common understanding among the appropriate health care providers.

Note sources continue to be referenced to reinforce the credibility of the plan.

Nursing Diagnoses: Prioritized

1. Impaired gas exchange R/T excessive or thick secretions due to smoking AEB dyspnea and decreased 02 saturation.
   - Airway is always the nurse's #1 priority

2. Activity Intolerance R/T acute exacerbation of COPD AEB dyspnea, weakness, fatigue.

3. Impaired Physical Mobility R/T dyspnea and fatigue AEB compromised ability to transfer from bed to chair or ambulate by self
   - Both 2 and 3 result in decreased ability for client to perform ADL's and function independently as was prior to hospitalization.

4. Risk for injury R/T unsteady gait.

5. Altered Nutrition: Less than body requirements BIT decreased desire to eat secondary to dyspnea and cough AEB weight 20% below ideal for height and frame.
   - Decrease in proper nutrition results in increased weakness and increases risk for injury and activity intolerance.

6. Ineffective management of therapeutic regime BIT client's doubts of benefits to treatment and lack of motivation to quit smoking AEB client verbalizes he did not quit smoking in order to reduce the risk for exacerbation.
   - Client has no desire to quit smoking

7. Sleep Pattern Disturbance BIT hospitalization AEB difficulty staying asleep.

(Carpentio, 2000)

Nursing System Design

Nursing Diagnosis:

Impaired gas exchange BIT excessive or thick secretions due to smoking AEB dyspnea and decreased 02 saturation.

More nursing-specific language is used : R/T means "related to," and AEB means "as evidenced by." Many professional fields use discipline-specific language, including technical terms and agreed upon abbreviations such as these.

This section itemizes and prioritizes the multiple dimensions of this patient's problem.

The goals of the plan, both short and long term, are clearly stated as is appropriate for this genre that must provide for a specific plan of action, both immediately and over the long term.

Goals:

Short term:

    1. Client will exhibit less severe dyspnea.

Long term:

    1. Client will describe smoking cessation and its benefits to the nurse.

Now that all of the background information has been provided, the actual action plan is presented.

Interventions:

1. Nurse will give client 02 nasal cannula to maintain proper 02 saturation levels per physician orders.

2. Nurse will maintain adequate hydration to loosen secretions.

3. Nurse will give client bronchodilators to facilitate relaxed airway and decreased dyspnea.

Details of the action plan are provided here, stating exactly what the nurse will do to attempt to meet the goals of the plan. The writer lists eleven specific action steps.

4. Client will receive respiratory therapy with chest percussion and postural drainage.

5. Nurse will encourage client to take slow, deep breaths to help overcome dyspnea.

6. Nurse will provide a pleasant, relaxed atmosphere to minimize anxiety.

7. Nurse will relieve mucous membrane irritation through humidity (sitting client over basin of steaming water with towel draped over head).

(Carpenito, 2000)

8. Nurse will teach client about effects of smoking in simplistic manner.

9. Nurse will use a variety of teaching methods to explain pathophysiology of smoking to client (i.e. Simple flow chart of damages to body from smoking, examples of client's previous hospitalizations as evidence that smoking causes his exacerbations).

Some of the steps are supported by medical references to reinforce the validity of the plan.

10. Nurse will provide resources to help client quit smoking (i.e.: 12-step programs, counseling, nicotine patches, and drug therapy).

11. Nurse will educate family on importance of supporting client in smoking cessation.

(Petty, 2000)

Evaluation:

Client responded well to the medical treatment, however still needed nebulizer treatments every 4 hours and maintained 02 level at 3 liters. Client did not respond well to the information taught about smoking and its negative effects on the body. It appeared as if the client did not believe that smoking is what caused his illness. The only thing different the nurse thought she could try with this particular client would be to ask him what evidence he needs to believe that cigarette smoking has caused his illnesses. What evidence he needs to believe cessation of smoking will help improve the quality of his life. And what motivational factors does the client use in order for him to do things he normally wouldn't want to do. Once the nurse understands what motivates her client and what her client holds as truth she can then better educate her client of his current health and ways he can improve it.

Discharge Planning and Referrals:

Client will be discharged to his daughter's home where he lives with her and her son. Home health care may be needed to provide assistance and respite for the family 2–3 times a week. Upon discharge client will be able to resume ADL's consistent with those prior to hospitalization with a few minor changes. Client will go home on 02 and inhalation bronchodilators. Client will be referred to counselor to assist client with smoking cessation. Client will be set up with follow-up appointments with primary physician to assess progress of health status.

Teaching Plan:

Objective: Importance of smoking cessation

Justification: According to Petty (2000), in a 20-year observational study by Peto et al., "the rate of decline in ventilatory function decreased when

Assessment of the action plan is another important component of this genre. Assessment helps establish the feasibility and the ultimate usefulness (or not) of the plan.

The remaining sections provide follow-up to further support the goals of the plan.

Here the writer provides the outline of the teaching plan. This summarizes the plan as it would be delivered to the patient audience, in hopes of accomplishing the action plan's goals.

patients stopped smoking in their mid-40's. Even those patients who stopped smoking at age 65 experienced a survival benefit." This basically states that smoking cessation may be beneficial at any time in a person's life.

Content:

- Educational materials handed out on lung function, nature and history of COPD, importance of smoking cessation.
- Review the educational material with the client in a simplistic manner until client can voice information back to nurse.
- Discuss methods that may work best for client to quit smoking
  - Set quit date
  - Cut cold turkey on that date, may choose to taper down beforehand or not
  - Nicotine replacement (gum, patches)
  - Drug therapy (Zyban)
  - Counseling to gain support from others going through same experiences

(Petty, 2000)

Method:

Nurse would give client educational material on smoking cessation, lung function, and effects and causes of COPD. Nurse would then sit down and break the material up into smaller, simplistic details to facilitate client understanding. Nurse would then give client some time alone, then go back and ask client if he has any questions. If client has none, the nurse would ask client what his plans are after he is discharged (evaluation). If client does not include smoking cessation as plan of care upon discharge, nurse would go over materials with client again with attempt to explain a little differently. Nurse would continue to evaluate and educate until client is discharged or can repeat the information back to the nurse.

References

Carpenito, L. J. (2000). *Nursing diagnosis: Application to clinical practice* (6th ed.). Philadelphia: J. B. Lippincott.

Deglin, J. H., & Vallerand, A. H. (2001). *Davis's drug guide for nurses* (7th ed.). Philadelphia: F. A. Davis.

Erickson, P. (2000). *Qualitative Health Research, 10*(6), 829–841.

Pagana, K. D., & Pagana, T. J. (1998). *Mosby's diagnostic & laboratory reference.* St. Louis: C. V. Mosby.

Petty, T. L. (2000). COPD: Interventions for smoking cessation and improved ventilatory function. *Geriatrics, 55*, 3–39.

Phipps, W. J., Sands, J. K., & Marek, J. F. (1999). *Medical-surgical nursing* (6th ed.). St. Louis: C. V. Mosby.

References are provided in APA format, as is common in the field of nursing.

INVESTIGATING THE GENRE SAMPLE

1. How are the introductory elements of this care plan designed for easy, quick reference? Who might be reading a care plan? Why might this reader need to peruse such a document efficiently?
2. Notice the extensive use of subheadings in this care plan. How would you describe the functions of the subheadings?
3. References to scholarship are interspersed throughout this care plan. How explicitly do these references establish a connection between the published articles and the points being made in the care plan?

WEB-BASED PROJECTS

Increasingly students are using the Internet to assist in completing college writing assignments. However, some assignments are more intricately involved with online materials than simply using them as resources; sometimes assignments are entirely Web-based. In other words, they could not possibly be completed *without* the use of the World Wide Web. First, we'll explore the purposes, audience expectations, and formats of such assignments. Following that, two student-created Web-based assignments with detailed annotations are presented.

Web-based projects can be a very broad academic genre. Essentially, these assignments fall into four categories:

- retrieval;
- interaction;
- critique;
- creation/original design.

In each case, while overlap is certainly possible, a different assignment purpose will be emphasized.

Some Web-based projects or assignments will be almost exclusively concerned with retrieving information from the Internet, such as finding useful professional, personal, or educational Web sites through search engines; accessing appropriate online academic databases for reference materials; or locating answers to specific questions from online service providers. In these situations, you may be asked to retrieve the information and then simply to summarize your findings, or you may be using the information retrieved for a larger project.

Some Web-based assignments will involve online interaction by requiring participation in synchronous or asynchronous online discussion groups, listservs, or chat rooms. With the aid of modern technology, you are increasingly able to expand contact with individuals with whom you share common interests or concerns and who may live halfway across town, the country, or even the world. You can interact in a live or synchronous session or during a discrete time session of your own choosing, defined as an asynchronous session.

Many Web-based projects will require that you go beyond mere retrieval or interaction, instead demanding "critique" or analysis of the information acquired. Careful analysis of Web-based materials is essential, requiring different considerations from the evaluation of print resources. Many Web-based materials are subject to little or no review or evaluation for credibility or authenticity. As an Internet user, you must carefully determine the reliability of resources; always check the credibility of the source, the dates of the original posting and any updatings, the indication of the site's references or sources, and so forth. (More detailed discussion of evaluation considerations can be found in the electronic sources section of Chapter 4.)

Still other Web-based assignments may demand that you create the Web-based materials. In other words, you may be asked to create your own Web site and/or publish materials at an online location. This will require you to closely scrutinize not only the content of your materials but also the visual presentation, the navigability of the materials, and so forth. It may require you to learn specialized computer language such as HTML. However, it is becoming increasingly easier to develop Web sites and online materials through very user-friendly programs that do the program language conversion for you.

Audience expectations for Web-based projects are somewhat unique. Of course, as a school assignment, your immediate audience is always your professor and often your fellow classmates. However, with Web-based assignments, especially the type that requires you to design your own Web site, your audience may literally be "the world"—or at least the world of millions of Internet users. Depending on the type of Web-based assignment, you may want to conceive of a very diverse audience or a very small special-interest group of Internet users.

Formats for Web-based assignments will vary widely. If the assignment involves a written report, these may be simple, loosely structured written summaries, while others will be lengthy, formal reports with subheadings. Many may have specific links to additional online materials, necessitating very accurate Web addresses. Some, of course, will be Web sites themselves, in which case elements of the format will be entirely different from those used to create standard academic prose.

The two samples that follow reflect the range of Web-based assignments. The first one is a critique in the form of a formal rhetorical analysis of three specific, but extremely different, Web sites pertaining to the widely popular *Harry Potter* books. This assignment, written by an upper-level English writing major at Elmhurst College, was produced for an advanced composition class that focused on rhetorical theory and application of the principles of classical rhetoric to contemporary texts. The completed assignment is formatted largely as a traditional term paper, but it clearly could not have been produced without using the Internet.

The second student sample comes from a chemistry course at Elmhurst College. For this Web-based assignment, students needed to retrieve and critique Web materials that provided information on a chemistry-based topic of contemporary concern and then to contribute to an original class Web site as a Web resource for the entire college community in celebration of Earth Day. In fact, it is a Web site available to all Internet users. The completed assignment, a Web site itself, offers accessible hyperlinks and an analysis of various features of the sites mentioned. The Web designer, of course, had very different format concerns than did the first student, who was writing a traditional term paper-style review.

WEB-BASED PROJECT 1
Advanced Composition

Harry Potter:
Wicked Wizard or Sensational Sorcerer?

Carrie May
Elmhurst College

Harry Potter:

Wicked Wizard or Sensational Sorcerer?

Hearing the words "Harry Potter" can provoke different responses from different people. For some people, the Harry Potter series provides enjoyable books to read and also acts as a source of entertainment. Other people, however, view the Harry Potter series as dark, dangerous books that should not be read by children. The web sites <www.spiritwatch. org> [then link to Harry Potter], <harry-potter-movies.net> and

The writer establishes the focus of this text as the *Harry Potter* books.

Notice that the writer provides a context for this rhetorical analysis, indicating that a wide range of Web sites created in response to the books exists.

Some specifics of the three Web sites critiqued are provided.

<scholastic.com/harrypotter/home.asp> all effectively present information about Harry Potter, although they do it in different ways. Each web site is structured differently and has a different focus, thus attracting different audiences. The Scholastic Inc. site structures its focus on marketing the series for reading purposes and attracts an audience consisting mostly of teachers and fans of the series. The Harry Potter movie site, on the other hand, focuses more on the entertainment aspect of the series and targets a somewhat older audience. The Spiritwatch site differs from both Scholastic Inc. and the movie site in that it structures its site around the controversy surrounding the series, thus targeting parents as the audience.

The writer appropriately provides background details on the Harry Potter series to further contextualize this Web site analysis.

To understand the web sites, it is also important to understand what the Harry Potter series is about and what the controversy surrounding the series is. The series consists of four books: *Harry Potter and the Sorcerer's Stone, Harry Potter and the Chamber of Secrets, Harry Potter and the Prisoner of Azkaban*, and *Harry Potter and the Goblet of Fire*. Written by British author J. K. Rowling, the books are about a young boy named Harry Potter who lives with his aunt and uncle. They treat Harry very poorly, and one day Harry discovers that he is a wizard and has magical powers. He then goes to Hogwarts School of Witchcraft and Wizardry, where he learns how to use his magical powers. The concepts of witchcraft and wizardry that are presented in the books remain a controversial issue. Some people, such as the Spiritwatch group, think that the ideas presented in the book are too dark and intense for children. People who believe this position argue that the books promote evil and practices of the occult. The official publisher web site for the series, however, does not construct its site around this argument.

Indication of the primary controversy of the series—the witchcraft elements—is crucial.

The writer introduces the first site to be analyzed, indicating the site's source, which is significant information in this comparison.

The web site <scholastic.com/harrypotter/home.asp> is the official publisher site for the Harry Potter series. Authored by Scholastic Incorporated, this site is created for fans of the series, devoting certain aspects of the site specifically to teachers. With the site last modified in

2001, this remains a reliable source for readers. The site is visually attractive, with the homepage decorated with a black background and the same illustration that appears on the cover of the fourth book in the series, *Harry Potter and the Goblet of Fire.* Scholastic Inc. does use entertainment to promote the series, although the focus is not as much on merchandise as it is on the books themselves. To promote the reading of the series, the site includes a link that summarizes each book, as well as a link with a pronunciation guide and a discussion guide for teachers. People can write in their comments about the books in a discussion chamber provided on the site. Considering that this is a site from the publishers of the series, its structure is effective. To reach its audience, Scholastic also includes items for people to purchase on the site. By doing this, Scholastic Inc. is able to market its selling power to readers. Thus, not only does the site provide educational entertainment for readers; it also promotes its selling power. Considering that part of the audience for the site includes teachers, this is effective.

    With the movie *Harry Potter and the Sorcerer's Stone* coming out soon, the web site *harry-potter-movies.net* is devoted to trivia regarding the movie and the book series. However, the site is not from the official studio creating the movie. The authors name the site "The Harry Potter Connection" and are named simply as Andy, Matt, and Danny. Those three are named as the webmasters of the site; a woman named simply as Elaine maintains the mailbag. With no credentials listed and a statement saying that the site is unofficial, one may question the trustworthiness of the site. However, trust may not be as important of an issue, considering that the site is concerned entirely with providing entertainment. It does this by providing a list of cast members, facts about the movie, games for readers to play, and activities for readers to explore on the site. It does not appear to be trying to educate readers about the books or the controversy surrounding the series. It tries to attract readers with all the news and entertainment bits that it provides.

The writer also comments on the reliability of the site.

The rhetorical analysis continues with a detailed description of the site's features and links.

The writer emphasizes the possibility for interaction on the site, comments on the audience range, and notes the skillful use of audience-appropriate features.

The second site being critiqued is introduced.

Note that this site is no longer accessible. Nonetheless, the rhetorical evaluation is interesting. It may be useful to contrast this to the official Warner Bros. site at <harrypotter.warnerbros.com>

The writer comments on a potential lack of credibility. This type of evaluative remark is highly appropriate to this assignment.

However, readers may not be persuaded by the information on the site because of the fact that the site is not the official site from the film studio.

The writer assesses the purpose as purely entertainment, not education or marketing, unlike the site critiqued above.

This is an entertaining site to explore; readers can find many pieces of intriguing news. Using mostly dark colors such as black and dark blue, the site includes a picture from the movie and numerous links for readers to explore. People who are fans of the books will probably enjoy reading the facts and entertainment briefs listed about the movie. Despite this, the site has negative aspects as well. The Harry Potter series is widely popular among children of all ages. However, the site does not seem to target an audience of younger children who are fans of the series. The site does not have many pictures; it consists almost entirely of text. While the reading level is not especially difficult, it is not at a level easy for young children to understand. While the web site cannot be judged for attracting the audience it does, it may be to the author's advantage to include younger children in its audience. It would reach a larger fan base that way.

A discussion of the negative aspects of this site, citing limited audience appropriateness, is an important component of the analysis.

With a target audience of mostly older children and adults, the site constructs a consumer relationship with readers. Its focus is to promote the movie and provide entertainment for fans of the series. By including mostly movie facts, trivia, and games, it is clear that the site is not trying to educate readers about the series, promote the reading of the series, or discuss the controversy surrounding the series. The site assumes that readers want to be entertained, not educated. At the same time, the site tries to promote the movie, treating the readers as consumers. While this site is enjoyable for people who are fans of the series and want to know something about the movie, it is not an entirely trustworthy site. With the credentials of the authors not listed, the fact that the site is unofficial and not affiliated with the studio making the movie, the site may not be entirely reliable.

The writer reemphasizes the limited credibility of this site.

The writer effectively transitions into the third, very differently focused, *Harry Potter* Web site.

While the Scholastic Inc. web site and The Harry Potter Connection web site were attempting to promote the Harry Potter series in some form, the web site <www.spiritwatch.org>, which is an organizational site, discusses the controversy surrounding the series. The author of the site is a group called Spiritwatch, which is part of the Tennessee Valley Bible Students Association. This web site is structured for warning and educating parents about the potential dangers of the series. The site explores the issues of the book from a Christian perspective, using detailed references from the Bible.

Extensive background discussion of this Web site sponsor is essential to support the writer's opinions here.

This site is very thorough and presents quite a bit of detailed information in it. It provides detailed articles about recurrent themes in the Harry Potter series, such as witchcraft, wizardry, violence, and the occult. These issues are considered evil by many religious groups, and this site attempts to educate and warn people about this. It does this by including articles such as "What Shall We Do With Harry?" The author of the article, Lindy Beam, includes a list of issues that the book deals with and offers advice on how parents should handle them. An excerpt from *Family Life* magazine is included, which provides reviews on the books. The author, John Younts, compares the books with the Bible to make his case. This helps readers to be able to understand the books from a Christian perspective.

The writer emphasizes the focus of this Web site on the controversy surrounding the content of the *Harry Potter* books.

Audience is a key factor in this site. This site obviously caters to members of the Christian religion and specifically targets parents. This is evident by the articles presented that give parents advice on how to handle the issues that arise in the Harry Potter series. By offering advice to its readers, the site treats the readers as parents and attempts to educate them. In order to be educated, readers have to be aware of the issues that are presented in the Harry Potter series and also understand the Christian religion and its viewpoints. The site does not in any way try to provide entertainment or promote reading; it is a site devoted strictly to how Christian parents should handle the issues.

Note that the writer gives significant attention to audience analysis here. The very distinct focus and target audience of this Web site merit in-depth analysis.

While Spiritwatch's site does effectively use links and articles to prove its point, the use of pictures and graphics on the site negatively impacts the structure of the site. Three pictures are included on the

The writer critiques the use of dreary photographs on the site.

homepage. One is a drawing of Harry Potter standing in front of a fireplace. He is wearing clothes that appear to be too big for him and has a very unhappy look on his face. It is unclear exactly why this picture is included; it may be up to the reader to decide. Another picture on the homepage shows two news anchors; again, it is unclear why this picture is included. The third picture simply shows the cover of the book *Harry Potter and the Goblet of Fire*. These pictures really do not seem to be serving much of a purpose. No explanation is given for them; therefore, they do not seem to belong on the site. An explanation for why they may have been included could be to enhance the dark and dreary appearance of the site. This dark look may serve as a warning for readers of the series' connection with the occult.

The writer clearly signals the conclusion of this rhetorical analysis, briefly reviewing the primary focus of each of the three Web sites.

By examining these three web sites, one can see how each site is structured differently and how each targets its audience. Scholastic Inc. chooses to focus on the educational entertainment aspect of the series while also using its selling power to promote the reading of the series. By doing this, Scholastic Inc. is able to effectively reach its targeted audience of teachers and fans of the series. The Harry Potter movie site, on the other hand, is structured more toward the entertainment aspect of the series and movie, thus targeting an older fan base audience. Differing from both of these sites, the Spiritwatch site chooses to examine the controversy surrounding the series, offering solutions on how to deal with the issues to its audience of Christian parents.

Note that the conclusion ends with an attempt to establish a somewhat-unbiased analysis of the value of each Web site.

Although each of the sites is structured differently and targets a different audience, each site effectively provides information on the Harry Potter series. By providing these different viewpoints, people are able to explore the series from different angles and determine which one they identify with the most.

1. The critique of Web sites is a relatively new genre in academic writing. What more traditional genres does it seem related to? How, for example, does the critique of Web sites differ from the second sample in the section on reviews?
2. What do we learn from this paper about the changeable nature of Web sites?
3. Some instructors ask students to write critiques of Web sites because the sites are often unrefereed—that is, no independent organization reviews Web sites to ascertain their legitimacy before they are posted. What specifically do we learn from this paper about the unrefereed nature of the World Wide Web?

WEB-BASED PROJECT 2

Chemistry

Solar Powered Cars

Joey Feldman
Elmhurst College

Alternatives to Gasoline Powered Vehicles

Welcome to the Chemistry 110 Earth Day Site!

The Chemistry 110 (Spring 2003) class has created this World Wide Web site in recognition of Earth Day 2003. Our objective is to provide a web resource for members of the Elmhurst College Community to explore issues related to Chemistry and the environment. As a class, we chose to explore the issue of alternative power for automobiles. Each student chose a specific issue to explore within this topic.

Issues addressed: (Attractive images are provided with each link.)

- Solar Powered Automobiles
- Hydrogen Powered Vehicles
- Hybrid Automobiles
- Biodiesel Vehicles

This teacher-created introduction to the class Web site provides a context for student postings.

Note: This Web site can be viewed at www.elmhurst. edu/~ksagarin/ chem110/cars. html.

This Web site provides direct links to five distinct Web sites providing information on a student-selected topic—solar powered cars.

Web address is provided.

Web site sponsor is indicated.

Primary audience is identified.

A brief summary of the contents of the site is given.

All sites are rated on a 10-point quality scale.

Unique features are indicated.

Note that the primary intent of this entire Web site review is to provide information. Thus, the writer strives for a consistent, readable format, a relatively unbiased voice, and a somewhat nonemotional tone.

Resources

Solar Powered Cars

by: Joey Feldmann

http://www.eere.energy.gov/RE/solar.html

Run by: The U.S. Department of Energy

Intended Audience: Amateur in the field, but with a science background

What's on it: This site has information on how solar plates work. It also includes information on how different solar technologies work. Perhaps the most useful parts of the site are an alphabetical index of energy links and an ask-the-expert section, where visitors can e-mail questions that they have about energy.

Rating: 6/10—It is very informative, but does not include much information on solar powered cars.

Notable Feature: It includes a section of solar power news updates

http://www.wsc.org.au

Sponsored by: The World Solar Challenge Organization

Intended Audience: Anyone with an interest in the competition

What's on it: This site explains what the World Solar Car Competition is. It also includes information about car regulations, the official route, and frequently asked questions about the competition.

Rating: 7/10—Very interesting and informative, but not very useful for those of us who are not interested in entering the competition

http://www.sunpowercorp.com/

Sponsored by: Sunpower Corporation

Intended Audience: Those who would be interested in purchasing products from this company

What's on it: This site contains information on the company and the products that they produce, including solar powered cars and solar powered airplanes. It also includes technical papers that explain the science behind their products.

Rating: 8/10—Informative, easy to use, good balance of information that is easy to understand and information that is more scientific in nature.

Notable Feature: List of jobs that Sunpower is currently hiring for, as well as the benefits that each job comes with.

http://www.ases.org/

Run by: The American Solar Energy Society

Intended Audience: Members of the organization and those who are interested in the organization

What's on it: This site contains information about the organization and upcoming events that they are sponsoring. It also contains a catalog of solar energy publications of all types. Its most useful segment is a Solar Guide Factbase, which contains introductory information on solar power.

Rating: 7/10—It seems like a fairly informational site and is easy to use. Furthermore, its link to the organization's magazine would be useful for anyone who is doing research on solar power.

Notable Feature: a link to the organization's magazine, *Solar Today*

http://www.users.bigpond.net.au/dollsandtoys/tribridindex.html

Run by: California Tribrid

Intended Audience: Those interested in how to use alternative fuels, especially those who might be interested in tribrid cars

What's on it: This site contains information on what tribrids are, how they work, and an update on the closeness of their availability. It also has a small list of links to hybrid and tribrid car sites.

Rating: 7/10—This is an interesting idea, is somewhat informational, and the site is easy to use. However, I would have liked links that gave more depth to the information presented.

This site receives a higher rating, apparently linked to the scientific quality of the material. This is no doubt a reflection of the particular academic audience of this Web site critique—a chemistry class.

Note that the site sponsor sounds very official.

The writer provides comments on the usability of the site—an appropriate category in this informative review.

Web address and sponsor are provided.

Notice that the straightforward tone and consistent layout of this information are appropriate for this genre—a quick reference guide for comparing Web sites on a given topic.

INVESTIGATING THE GENRE SAMPLE

1. What do you think Joey Feldman was trying to accomplish with the graphic design of this text? How effectively do you think he accomplishes this goal?
2. What do you think of the quantity and quality of the evaluations offered in this project? Would you like more or less evaluation, and why?
3. What do you think Feldman hopes his readers will do after they examine his project? How do you know?

Developing Research Skills

As Chapter 3 made clear, one hallmark of academic writing is its dependence on research, defined in the broadest sense as reading, searching the Internet, observing, and experimenting. While such genres as personal essays, some response and reaction papers, and some stance and position papers can be written using only your own experiences, observations, and ideas, most of the other genres discussed in Chapter 3 require you, as a college-level writer, to find articles, books, press releases, Web site materials, and so forth, and to use those sources appropriately, according to the expectations of the particular genre. This chapter, therefore, is devoted to explaining the research skills involved in locating and retrieving sources, evaluating sources, and then incorporating source materials and citing them properly and ethically in all of your academic papers.

Conducting research is one of the most exciting and challenging aspects of your academic career. You will have the opportunity to search for and uncover information from the work of numerous experts, in a wide variety of fields. But you will also have the opportunity to make those materials your own and, more importantly, to create something original when you write a paper or report. You will draw upon the work of others to expand your own understanding, and then by making important intertextual connections, you will contribute to the academic "conversation" each time you create a new text. That task can be both exhilarating and daunting. Understanding some basic research strategies and resources can ease your task considerably. This chapter will provide extremely useful information on many aspects of research and research writing, specifically: **information literacy skills, basic research writing strategies,** and **cross-disciplinary documentation formats.**

Even though these topics are covered in separate sections, do not interpret the activities as a set of linear processes. In reality, researching and writing are recursive processes, as we have discussed. For instance, of course you must have some information before you can write, but sometimes it will be information you already possess, in which case you can begin prewriting activities; other times you will have no information and will need to do preliminary research before you begin any aspect of drafting; most frequently, you will do some research, do some drafting, realize you need more research and thus return to that process, then eventually return to your writing, and so forth.

The first section of this chapter examines the increasingly complex area of **information literacy skills.** The section is broadly divided into a discussion of print and electronic sources, but you'll notice some overlap between these two categories. In addition to explaining some features of the many types of resources available, valuable information on the retrieval and the evaluation of these resources is presented. We all know that we are living in an explosive "Information Age." Now, more than ever, you as a reader, writer, and researcher must be alert not only to the mind-boggling range of the available materials but also to the range in the quality of those materials.

The second section covers four basic strategies: **summarizing, quoting and paraphrasing, analyzing,** and **synthesizing.** All of these skills build upon each other, as your work becomes increasingly complex. Keep in mind that although these are discussed individually here, you will most often interweave them simultaneously as you proceed with your research writing.

The final section presents information on the extremely complex topic of **documentation of source materials.** Documentation is crucial for two main reasons: One, it enables your readers to evaluate your use of other researchers' work, and two, it fulfills your ethical obligation to give credit to the authors of that borrowed material. You must, of course, formally document all borrowed material to avoid plagiarizing. Documentation styles vary considerably across disciplines, and even within each style system, there is an amazing degree of variation.

ACQUIRING INFORMATION LITERACY SKILLS

Print and Miscellaneous Nonprint Sources

Academic writing is occasionally written by drawing exclusively upon your own personal resources, as evidenced in the sample student papers in the first section of Chapter 3. Things such as journal entries or personal response papers do not generally call for outside research. But clearly, as you can see from the numerous other genres discussed in Chapter 3, the majority of academic writing assignments do require you to retrieve credible sources and then to closely read and analyze them. The type of assignment you are given, the intended audience, and the guidelines of your professor will all dictate which type(s) of sources you should acquire for your research. This chapter will closely examine your most common source options, considering types, means of retrieval and evaluation, and documentation procedures. The complex skills needed for this examination is now referred to as **information literacy.** Acquiring strong information literacy skills is crucial to your success as an effective academic writer.

Understanding source features is a major information literacy skill. Keep in mind that your sources will vary widely in content. However, most academic sources will be nonfiction materials unless, of course, you are writing a paper for a literary studies class using a novel or book of short stories as a primary source for your work. One frequently used means to categorize materials for academic research is to separate them into either scholarly or popular sources. Understanding and appropriately responding to this distinction is crucial to being a successful academic writer.

The characteristics of scholarly and popular sources listed below should help you distinguish them. Keep in mind that these generalizations are not applicable unilaterally. Furthermore, some sources clearly fall in between these two categories. Nonetheless, being alert to these potential differences usually eases your research and enhances the quality of your end product.

Scholarly Sources

- Written by experts in the field to which they contribute

- Often more challenging to read
- More serious and more in-depth coverage of the topic, indicating extensive research
- Often focuses on narrow subtopics within a field
- Often has little visual appeal; emphasis is on the content

- Material is heavily referenced and cross-referenced, indicating a knowledge of the work of other experts in the field—i.e., an extensive bibliography is included at the end of the article or book
- Frequently includes supplemental information or guides in the form of appendices, indexes, bibliographies, detailed graphs, and so forth
- Geared to specialized audiences of other experts in the field or of novices preparing to enter the field
- Frequently published by academic presses that often have the word "university" in the title

Popular Sources

- Written by professional writers but not historians, chemists, psychologists, rhetoricians, etc.
- Usually easier to read
- Less in-depth coverage; more generalized; research is often relatively superficial
- Generally provides broad overviews of topics
- Frequently has great visual appeal, allowing for a quick determination of the "gist"
- Few, if any, references are provided other than brief quotes from practitioners or participants; content is generally assumed to be from the realm of "common knowledge" or from personal experience
- Frequently includes photographs and simplistic graphs or charts; rarely offers indexes or appendices

- Geared to the general public interested in gaining an overview of a particular topic
- Most often published by popular presses

Frequently, college writing assignments will require "scholarly sources only." Keep in mind that for fields such as pop culture or cultural studies, popular sources may be not only appropriate but essential to conducting your research and will indeed be considered "scholarly" for the insights they yield. Similarly, for historical research some primary sources such as letters or diaries may in fact be popular sources (i.e., not written by scholars) and yet they will be considered "scholarly" materials in that they are essential primary sources for the historian's research. In other words, once again remember that there are fine lines between categories of anything and that the demands of academic writing are indeed complex.

Besides the broad distinctions between scholarly and popular sources, which admittedly blur at times, you'll find that sources also vary widely in format, since dozens of different genres exist. Typically, the sources will fall into two broad categories: **print** and **electronic** (with some miscellaneous exceptions of multimedia-type materials). This first section of Chapter 4 will specifically examine print sources, as well as a few types of nonprint sources that are generally not available online. Online sources are discussed in the next section, "Electronic Sources."

Major Categories of Print Sources

The two most common types of academic sources are **books** and **periodicals,** their basic distinction being that the former is published only once (except for occasional reprints or updated editions) while the latter is published repeatedly at designated intervals of time. However, within these two groups are numerous subgroups. Materials are categorized by genres, all requiring different strategic approaches from you as a reader and different methods of documentation from you as a writer.

Books   **Books**, useful for academic research and writing, may be popular texts, but more frequently will be scholarly. Some books, such as novels or plays, are fiction. Most of your book sources will probably be nonfiction, however. These books offer extensive studies of specific topics; they may be largely informational or heavily analytical, and often will explicitly argue for a particular view of an event, individual, or phenomenon. These studies may be written by a single author or coauthored by two or more scholars who are jointly conducting the research and collaborating to write the text. Some short but scholarly book-length studies of a specific, often very specialized topic are referred to as **monographs.** Monographs cover a single topic and most often are not divided into chapters. They appear almost like very lengthy essays.

Very frequently, you'll find that scholarly books are compilations of the work of numerous scholars in a field. These texts are edited by an individual who combines chapter-length studies by various authors into one **edited book.** Such books are frequently invaluable sources, providing a range of information and viewpoints on a given topic. In essence, they often give a snapshot of a professional conversation, the give-and-take means by which knowledge and meaning are created in a given field. Edited books that are compilations of literary or artistic selections by the same or varied authors are referred to as **anthologies.** You have probably encountered anthologies—collections of poems or short stories representing a given time period, exploring a specific theme, or collecting the lifetime works of a single author—in your English classes.

Reference Books   Clearly, many of the books referred to in the above section may be read and consulted for academic writing; however, they are generally not categorized with the largest group of resources commonly called **reference books.**

Their label probably springs from the fact that these books, while extremely useful, are rarely read cover-to-cover but rather are "referred to" on an as-needed basis.

Within the category of reference books, are numerous distinctions. No doubt you are familiar with one of the most commonly used multivolume reference works, **encyclopedias.** Encyclopedias present valuable information on a vast array of topics and are generally considered good sources for an overview of a field—for "getting started" on a topic with which you are quite unfamiliar, or to retrieve specific facts such as dates of key events, names of significant leaders, locations of resources, and so forth. Encyclopedia entries are frequently nonauthored, since they are often written by a team of researchers or writers for the encyclopedia press. Some instructors may not consider encyclopedias significant sources for your research because they frequently provide a rather generic and generalized discussion, with little detailed analysis and no apparent individualized, argumentative voice. Nonetheless, in some circumstances they can be extremely valuable. Remember that encyclopedias, like all of these categories, are a complex genre. There is a wide range of encyclopedias, some of which are highly reputable and offer a broad range of information, such as *Encyclopaedia Britannica* or *World Book*; numerous encyclopedias that are subject specific and offer extremely detailed entries focused on specific disciplines, such as *Routledge's Encyclopedia of Philosophy*; and some even narrower in scope that focus on specific subfields, such as the *Encyclopedia of Women in Religious Art* or the *Encyclopedia of Nautical Knowledge*.

Dictionaries are another invaluable, sometimes underestimated resource. Dictionaries can be used for much more than retrieving the definition or accurate pronunciation of an unfamiliar word. There are, for example, etymological dictionaries that offer extensive commentary on the derivation of a word, tracing its changes in meaning or explaining varied nuances or connotations in different contexts over centuries. Foreign language dictionaries offer cross-translations between languages. For example, you might use a Spanish-English dictionary, but a foreign-exchange student in your Spanish class might use an Arabic-Spanish dictionary. The most comprehensive dictionary of the English language is the *Oxford English Dictionary,* commonly called the *OED*. It includes every English word ever appearing in print. The *OED* lists the known definitions of a word and cites contextual examples of its usage, identified by date. There are also numerous subject-specific dictionaries offering explanations of technical terms in a given field, such as the *New Grove Dictionary of Music and Musicians* or the recent *Whatis.com* dictionary of computer terms.

Handbooks are another common category of print sources of information. Handbooks generally offer practical details such as "how-to" information, definitions of terms, lists of resources, etc. They, too, cover a wide variety of topics and are published in a broad range of fields. Academic handbooks are frequently published by professional associations, such as the *AAAS Handbook* published by the American Association for the Advancement of Science, or the *Activities Handbook for the Teaching of Psychology* published by the American Psychological Association. Many are published by governmental offices, such as the *Environmental Assessment Guide for Housing Projects,* one of a series of handbooks issued by the U.S. Department of Housing and Urban Development, or the *Occupational Outlook Handbook,* offering invaluable information on various career choices. Still others are published by scholarly presses, such as the *Handbook of Literary Terms* published by the Citadel Press.

Another broad category of reference books, often somewhat similar to hand-books, is **directories.** Directories generally consist of numerous short entries that direct you to other places for more detailed information. Probably the most commonly used directory is the telephone book, where, of course, you can retrieve phone numbers and addresses in order to contact individuals or institutions for more detailed information. Some directories are very subject specific such as, *The Corporate Directory of U.S. Public Companies by Walker's, 2001: Company Profiles and Indexes,* which lists, as the name implies, hundreds of publicly held corporations in America and provides details regarding size and scope and as well as addresses, phone numbers, Web site addresses, etc, of these corporations. Many associations publish directories that are available only to fellow members of the association for internal networking purposes, while others intentionally publish directories for a public audience for assistance with growing client business.

A commonly overlooked but extremely useful reference source is the book-length **bibliography.** No doubt you are familiar with the concept of a bibliography as a list of resources or works cited (like the ones you include at the end of your research papers). A book-length bibliography is a compilation of sources on a single topic, which can be invaluable. For example, Anna Hanneman wrote *Ernest Hemingway: A Comprehensive Bibliography,* which details in 586 pages nothing but specific sources on Hemingway. Obviously, such a resource could be extremely useful if you were doing research on Hemingway. Much of the time-consuming "digging for sources" may already done for you if you are fortunate enough to locate a book-length bibliography on your topic. Bibliographies typically provide both book and periodical sources with full documentation information for retrieval purposes, and most frequently they are annotated bibliographies that provide a mini-summary of each source and some sort of evaluative comment. (See Chapter 3, the section on abstracts and annotations, for more details on annotated bibliographies.) Of course, if you are using a book-length bibliography for your research, it is very important that you note the date of compilation. You will need to search for current resources from that date onward to ensure that your research is up-to-date. For example, the Hanneman book referred to above was published in 1967. That date is significant because the book will include references for a lot of valuable early research on Hemingway (he was a popular subject in the 1960s) but will include none of the research of the past three decades. Critical interpretation of Hemingway is significantly different in recent years, especially in light of recent feminist and postcolonial criticism. On the other hand, James L. Harner's *Literary Research Guide: An Annotated Bibliography of Reference Sources in English Literary Studies,* published in 2002, is very current and should be extremely useful for tracking down resources for your literary research projects.

Still another helpful type of reference book is the **index.** Similar to the index appearing in the back of your course textbook, these book-length indexes sort information for readers and provide an easier means of accessing that information. There are literally hundreds of book-length indexes that sort all kinds of information on a wide variety of topics. For example, you might want to consult the *Consumer Price Index* for an economics project, the *Book Review Index* for a literary studies paper, the *PDR Guide to Drug Interactions, Side Effects, and Indications* for your nursing report, or biographical indexes for useful facts on individuals, living or deceased, for any number of projects. Indexes exist for nearly any topic imaginable. You can search by topic and then include "index" as a subtopic and/or consult your reference librarian.

One final category of valuable reference books is **abstracts.** You may be familiar with abstracts as brief summaries that appear at the beginning of a journal article or are required as part of your scientific research report (see Chapter 3, the section on abstracts and annotations, for more information on abstracts); but don't overlook that such summaries exist for various topics in book-length collections. Some abstracts are discipline specific, such as *Sociological Abstracts* or *Psychological Abstracts.* Some are very broad based such as the extremely useful *Statistical Abstracts of the United States,* published by the U.S. government. This text offers a wide range of statistics on various topics recorded by the government census. These abstracts are generally updated annually and can provide useful specific details for a report or point you to valuable additional resources for more in-depth information.

Periodicals   Besides reference books, the most common reference source used for academic research is surely **periodicals.** In fact, depending upon your topic, you may use periodicals almost exclusively for your research because, of course, they generally provide the most current information. Be aware that anything that is published over time in increments is referred to as a periodical (as opposed to a book that is ordinarily published only once). However, this is a very broad category that ranges significantly not only in terms of subject matter but also in terms of quality. Periodicals include everything from major **scholarly journals** such as the *Harvard Business Review* to well-respected **popular magazines** such as *U.S. News & World Report* to **daily newspapers** such as the *New York Times* to so-called **rag sheets** such as the *National Enquirer.* When conducting your research using periodicals, you should pay particular attention to the distinctions between scholarly and popular sources (as indicated in the lists above) and always note your professor's criteria for the research; some insist on scholarly sources only for certain research projects. Many popular periodicals can be obtained in print versions for purchase at newsstands and for checkout at your library, if the library purchases a subscription to the particular periodical. Scholarly periodicals are exclusively available in print through individual or library subscription. Increasingly, periodicals are available online, some for free but most by subscription (see the section entitled "Electronic Sources" later in this chapter for details). Note that each type of periodical requires a different type of documentation format. (See later in this chapter for further information on citing sources.)

You may occasionally want to access parts of periodicals rather than whole articles. For example, political cartoons, reviews of books or theatrical performances, or letters to the editor are sometimes valuable resources for research. These parts of periodicals frequently have specific documentation formats that differ from the format used for citing the periodical itself. Also, they are occasionally indexed separately, either in print collections such as *Dr. Seuss Goes to War* or in online databases for particular newspapers.

Miscellaneous Print Categories   In addition to books and periodicals, the most common resources for academic research, there are a number of additional print resources available. Though more obscure, these are often very valuable. This category includes things like **brochures** and **pamphlets,** many printed by the U.S. government and some by professional associations. These are available from the issuing agencies themselves, such as the many pamphlets that PETA (People for the Ethical Treatment of Animals) publishes on animal rights. They are also available in many libraries in so-called vertical files, and increasingly these materials are available online as well.

Similarly, informally published **conference proceedings** or **papers** presented at conferences are sometimes available as print resources (or online). They generally appear in a kind of brief, white report format, not nearly as sophisticated as a magazine. At times, you might want to access the **transcripts** of a particular TV or radio show such as *Meet the Press,* the *Oprah Winfrey Show,* or the *Rush Limbaugh Show,* especially for information on contemporary popular culture. Sometimes **newsletters, agendas,** or **minutes** of specific organizations can provide helpful insights for your research. While these must often be obtained from the issuing agencies themselves, some are available in libraries. **Letters** and **diaries,** important primary sources, frequently offer important insights into the minds of individuals, the nature of specific relationships, the customs of a time period, etc. Historians and literary critics, for example, make frequent use of such print sources. Some of these materials are catalogued as noncirculating items in the reference or archival collections of specific holding libraries. However, some are published in book-length collections, and some are indexed as part of archival collections now available online in photographed versions.

Some of the most cutting-edge research might be available in **dissertations** or theses being published by graduate students required to produce original research in their field in order to obtain their degree. Dissertations are always available in the library of the degree-granting institution, but they are frequently not available for circulation. However, sometimes enough of a useful insight is available in *Dissertation Abstracts,* and if the research seems invaluable to your project, dissertations are available for purchase through the Dissertations Microfilm Service operated out of the University of Michigan.

Be conscious of the fact that all of the above miscellaneous print sources require their own unique documentation format, according to the dictates of a particular style guide such as MLA or APA. For these more obscure types of references, it is frequently best to consult the style guide directly for the format. Style guides are always available in print format at the reference desk of your college or university library.

Miscellaneous Nonprint Categories

In addition to all of the above-mentioned print resources and the electronic sources to be discussed in the next section, there is another broad category of reference materials. This group can be loosely labeled **multimedia sources.** This group of materials falls between traditional print sources, conceived of as written words appearing on paper to be held, and online sources to be viewed on a computer screen. These multimedia resources include such items as **photographs** or other forms of artwork, magazine or television **advertisements, maps, performances** (viewed live or on tape), **taped interviews, television** or **radio shows, movies,** and **audio** or **audiovisual recordings.** Note that in keeping with the complicated world of formal academic documentation systems, all of the above types of resources usually have their own designated citation format within a given system. Check the unabridged print version of the style guide of the system you are using and/or with your reference librarian for details.

Accessing Print, Nonprint, and Multimedia Sources

Nearly all of the materials referred to above are catalogued in the traditional library sense. That is, they are assigned a classification number that enables a patron to access them. Most often these numbers are within one of the two major library cataloguing systems: the Library of Congress system (the classification numbers of which always begin with two letters followed by numbers) or the Dewey Decimal System (the classification numbers of which always begin with three numerals). Of course, the boxed-card systems known as "card catalogues" that itemized all of these access numbers are long gone. Now the materials are accessed through a much easier and more extensive "online catalogue." However, within that system, you will still see LC (Library of Congress) or Dewey Decimal System accession numbers assigned to items for retrieval purposes from the shelves of a given library. Materials issued by publishing houses are also assigned an ISBN (international standard book number) that can be useful in searching for or purchasing a book but not for physically retrieving it from a library shelf. Many periodical materials are now available in full text online that can be read on the computer screen or printed out to read as a paper version. Government documents have their own complex cataloguing system that is adhered to from library to library. However, special collections within libraries such as archival collections are organized in any number of different ways. The reference librarian at your given institution is always the best resource for information on these collections.

Evaluating Print, Nonprint, and Multimedia Sources

While it is generally safe to assume that the materials in your college or university library are authentic and credible, a good researcher must always evaluate his or her sources according to a number of criteria. In order to determine the appropriateness of a given resource for your particular writing project, you should consider specific features of the source including the author, the date, and the publisher; the intended audience; and the nature of the content itself.

In analyzing the source, be certain to assess the author. Is it a name you recognize from your course texts or class discussions? Is it a name you've notice referenced in other sources? Can you verify through earlier citations or by checking his/her background in an index like *Book Review Digest* or *Who's Who in America* that this person has written other things about this topic? Are there credentials such as an advanced degree in a specific field provided within the text or in a biographical blurb on the inside cover or at the back of the text? Are there acknowledgments given to previous publications of earlier materials by this author? If you are unsure of anything about the credibility of the author, check with your professor and/or reference librarian.

The date of a given source is another critical piece of information. For some writing projects, older materials are exactly what you need. For example, if you are studying public reaction to U.S. Constitutional amendments at the time they were ratified, then reading newspapers and/or scholarly essays from many decades past might be extremely appropriate. However, if you are writing about the burgeoning popularity of personal computers, an article from 1960 will not be very useful. Of course, you might want to study older materials to formulate a comparison-contrast paper, tracing changes over time. In that case, you'll need to consult old and current texts for your information.

It is also valuable to consider the publisher of the work (or the producer, in the case of a film or musical production). What is the reputation of that publisher? Is it a familiar name to you or to your professor? Many publishing houses tend to specialize in particular types of materials. Knowing that you are selecting materials from a publisher of many works in a particular field can be very useful because such a publisher will tend to have very highly skilled and highly critical reviewers who carefully screen materials prior to publication.

Knowing something about the publisher and the type of works they have previously produced gives you an idea of the intended audience of those works. Some presses are known for publishing the writing of scholars in a very specific field. Southern Illinois University Press, for example, has published a number of texts on the history of rhetoric. Similarly, certain journals and periodicals are directed to a very specific audience. Sometimes this is identified in a statement in the beginning of the publication or on the Web site of the publisher. Sometimes a reader can determine the audience from the title; for instance, *The Journal of Accountancy* or the *Geographical Review* have fairly specific audiences. However, even from these titles you may not know the level of the research or whether the audience is primarily scholars or practitioners in the field. You will need to examine the periodical itself to determine that. Two very helpful resources for assessing the appropriateness and credibility of specific periodicals are *Magazines for Libraries* and *Ulrich's Periodicals Directory*. Of course, your reference librarian can also guide you to certain databases that index materials for specific audiences.

You must also examine the nature of the content itself. Before reading in depth, you can glean a lot of useful information with a pre-read. Check to see if the text has a preface or introduction that provides a useful overview of the text and that states the intent, philosophy, or perspective of the text. Is it a scholarly work? If so, you should expect numerous references and cross-references substantiating the sources of the material shared or interrogated in the text. Is it in a peer-reviewed journal, a text where other experts in the field assess the contributions? Check, too, for the inclusion of graphs, charts, photographs, and so forth. In certain fields, these things are extremely important. For example, no scientific research would be considered very credible without supportive data in appropriate figure format, and no discussion of art history would be complete without reproductions of some of the works being scrutinized. Considering the length and apparent depth of the coverage is also crucial. A one-page article in a popular magazine with no cited references is certainly not going to give the same type of information that a 15-page article with two pages of citations in a peer-reviewed journal can offer. Of course, to fully assess the content, you will need to read the text more in depth, but an initial reading can certainly give you insights into the credibility of the source and its appropriateness for your use. Careful assessment of all the aspects of a given resource will enable you to judge its usefulness for your specific writing project. (See the section on

"Electronic Sources" for further discussion of evaluating sources.) Many tips for evaluating online sources are also applicable to print and other media.

Documenting Print, Nonprint, and Multimedia Sources

Appropriate documentation of all your sources, regardless of medium—print, non-print, multimedia, or online—is a serious academic obligation. All "borrowed" information, outside of the realm of so-called common knowledge, needs to be properly credited and documented when used as a resource for any new text you are writing. When in doubt about whether something is common knowledge, ask your professor or reference librarian. If those individuals are unavailable, always err on the side of too much citing rather than not enough.

Documentation procedures are complex. Properly identifying your sources within the body of your text as well as at the end of it can be tedious and confusing. Citation rules vary depending upon the type of genre you are documenting and the documentation system your discipline/professor dictates. For example, the citation rules for multiple-author books are different from those for an edited collection, those for a government document, and so forth—even within the same style guide. And there are significant differences between format systems. Consult the documentation section in this textbook for more details on citing resources.

Electronic Sources

Increasingly, students are turning to online or electronic resources to conduct research of all kinds across many different disciplines. The Internet has offered a veritable explosion of information over the past decade or so, and it is growing daily, both in offerings and in popularity. Clearly, it provides access to untold amounts of resources across the globe almost instantly with the mere click of a mouse. The challenge now is twofold: to understand exactly what types of sources are available and to learn to critically and efficiently evaluate those sources. Let's explore these two challenges in some detail.

Understanding the types of electronic sources available is crucial for your success as an academic writer. In a broad sense, there are two categories of electronic sources. First, there are those available on the World Wide Web (WWW), which we'll refer to as "open-access resources." These are primarily free of charge, widely varied in subject, and created for the general public via any number of access paths to the Internet. The second group of electronic sources is available through specified private "proxy servers," such as at your college or university library. These are very costly services (for the host, not for you directly) and are limited to specific patrons who have earned access rights by virtue of their membership in a particular organization—i.e., most often by paying tuition at a given educational institution. Within both types of sources, a wide variety of material exists. You may frequently access the general WWW for useful information from a popular site such as mapquest.com and even for technical research such as statistical information available to the public on government-sponsored sites. However, most resources for your academic writing will come from the "limited-access" sites on the Internet, such as the numerous ones your college library subscribes to on your behalf.

Let's examine several of the popular types of open-access resources; then we will look at resources available to you through limited-access servers, namely, your college or university library system. Note that each of these types of sources is slightly different in its intent and format; consequently, each is documented in a slightly different way within your written projects. For specifics regarding how to cite these different types of sources, see the section in this chapter on documenting sources and consult the style guides of the documentation system that you are following.

Open-Access Resources on the World Wide Web

The first very broad category of electronic sources are those that are available free of charge to the general public on the World Wide Web. Within the past decade or so, the Web has grown almost beyond imagination, allowing instantaneous access to vast amounts of information on virtually any topic conceivable. Keep in mind that the WWW has absolutely no quality controls: Anyone, with *any* or *no* credentials, at *any* time, with *any* agenda, can publish materials on Web sites, which are then immediately accessible everywhere to everyone who has an Internet connection. Consequently, there is an extremely broad range of materials available on the Web in terms of credibility and usefulness—some are excellent in every regard; some are trivial; some are completely inaccurate; some are dated; some are primarily factual; some are highly opinionated; and some are offensive and even potentially dangerous. Let's examine some types of Web sites available on the World Wide Web.

Web sites

Web sites vary tremendously. Some are personal Web sites of individuals who simply choose to share their interests, viewpoints, and/or resources online; some display extensive research by experts. One clue for sorting them in some way is the "domain" of the Web site address. Domains sometimes provide a first step at sorting out Web sites by focus and even by reliability. The broadest domain, .com, which stands for "commercial," offers the widest variety of for-profit resources. Slightly smaller, though still a for-profit domain, is .net of "networked" sites. These two domains host Web sites of individuals, small businesses, special-interest groups, large corporations, or broad based public services. For example, at a .com address you can find anything from special offers for John Lindo's swing dance instruction to instructions for providing reptile care to detailed corporate information about General Motors to national weather information for virtually any location imaginable.

The other three major domains, .edu, .gov, and .org, representing "education," "government," and "organization," respectively, all host not-for-profit Web sites for somewhat more focused sources than .net and .com. (These are the five most common domains; however, there are additional domains, especially for international sites, that will not be discussed here.) These three domains, .edu, .gov, and .org, can also represent a broad range of information and even credibility. For example, included in .edu sites are informational Web sites of colleges, universities, or school districts as well as Web sites of instructors and personal Web sites of students that may or may not provide valuable or even credible information.

While gov. Web sites are all government sponsored, they, too, offer a wide range of materials. Some of the government-sponsored sites offer general information for citizens such as requirements for obtaining a driver's license or the latest income tax changes; some of these Web sites offer highly technical information and specific agency reports of current research findings; all of them, of course, will present information from a government point of view, which may need to be considered when evaluating them for certain research projects.

The domain of organization Web sites, .org, can similarly run the gamut. Hundreds of organizations and professional associations sponsor highly useful Web sites with valuable research information that are open to the general public. Web sites of long-established, highly reputable organizations such as the American Medical Association provide credible, yet often self-interested, information. Nonetheless, some .org sites are extremely trivial or even bogus. It is possible for a small group of individuals to present itself as a legitimate organization when, in fact, it may not even exist and/or may not provide reliable information on a given topic.

Besides those Web sites that you may access for specifically focused information, such as www.harvard.edu or www.ablongman.com, there are numerous other types of online materials available on the WWW. For example, you can read some whole journals and magazines online, free of charge, on the WWW. You can even access entire books that are available for downloading and printing. These books are largely ones whose copyright has expired. Some classic texts are bundled on CDs and made available unabridged at www.projectguttenberg.com at greatly reduced prices. In contrast to more traditional publications, there is a new category on the Web called "zines." Hundreds of self-published zines are available on a wide range of topics. They tend to be unconventional and are sometimes experimental and very controversial; some zines are quite credible, whereas others might be considered highly suspect as reference sources.

Additional Web-based materials   Other Web-based materials include "bulletin boards" and "blogs." Bulletin boards are essentially the Web equivalent of the Listservs discussed earlier in this book. Individuals with common interests post and share information for any other interested individuals to read on the World Wide Web. Some bulletin boards allow open posting; some have membership restrictions. There are hundreds of bulletin boards on almost any topic imaginable, and the range in quality is extreme. Another more recent Web genre is the blog, the abbreviation for "Web log." Blogs are essentially personal journals available online for public viewing, and they are extremely varied in topic and format. Many appear in personal diary format; some include pictures; some invite responses; some exist as running threads of conversation; and some prohibit interaction and allow posts solely by the "blogger." While it may be rare to include information from a blog within a research project, it is conceivable. Imagine, for instance, that you were conducting sociological research on dating rituals or pop culture research on video games; in those cases, it may be quite useful to consult a popular blog.

Limited-Access Resources

Database articles   Literally thousands and thousands of journal/magazine articles can currently be accessed electronically through online databases. Databases are indexed collections of journals that are usually published in print versions but are now available online as well. Your institution pays substantial amounts to subscribe to these databases. Many are grouped by subject matter. Some are very broad based, such as Academic Search Elite, which catalogues hundreds of journals in the fields of social sciences, humanities, general science, multicultural studies, and others. Some are much more subject specific, such as PsyARTICLES or the Music Index. The journal articles in any of these databases are sometimes available only as abstracts but more often are available in full text. You'll notice that in many of the databases, you have a choice of viewing the full-text article in two formats, HTML or PDF. The first, HTML, is the official language of computers. It provides a text-only version of the article. Often this is sufficient and provides a quicker download and shorter print job. The second option is a scanned photocopy of the original and thus includes all photographs, graphics, etc., as they originally appeared in print. Sometimes you will need or want to see the article *exactly* as it originally appeared. Still other databases might be referred to as "image databases." These resources, such as AMICO, provide access, by subscription, to digitized images that may be of art collections or even of photographs for use in advertising and elsewhere.

Electronic books Some whole books, referred to as "e-books," are available electronically. Sometimes these are books that were previously produced in print, and sometimes they are books published exclusively online. Some are available exclusively through subscription databases, similar to the journal databases discussed above. These books are generally still under copyright and, thus, the publishers and authors are entitled to obtain profits and/or royalties from their works' consumption. These books, accessed through a book database such as NetLibrary, provide instant access to many books. However, usually these databases limit the time allotted for viewing and /or restrict the print function in order to prevent patrons from simply downloading an entire book without paying for it, even though the subscribing library also pays hefty prices to participate in the database. There are some entire books, however, that are available free of charge electronically.

Electronic reference books Electronic reference books by and large are well-known general or subject-specific reference texts that exist in print but are now also available in an electronic version. These are often broad based and provide the same excellent quality as their print counterparts because they are controlled by expert review boards. The *Encyclopaedia Britannica*, the *Oxford English Dictionary*, and *Clinical Pharmacology* are examples of reference books that are now available online as well as in print. Electronic reference books such as these are generally available only through subscription; in other words, they are limited-access resources not available in their entirety on the WWW.

Online archival collections Another interesting type of electronic resource is on-line archival collections. These collections function like online "mini-museums." Generally, they consist of scanned images of personal photographs; original documents such as handwritten letters, diaries, and early court records; pictures of physical artifacts; and so forth. Many of these highly specialized collections are available only by subscription, generally through large research universities. Some of these special archival collections are available through government-sponsored open-access sites, however. To view an example, go to the Library of Congress Web site at www.loc.gov, link to "Exhibitions," and then click on "African-American Mosaic."

Listserv postings   There are hundreds of specialized "lists" where individuals with common interests share information and exchange ideas. Each list, commonly referred to as a "Listserv," is generally accessible only to individuals who subscribe to the list or are subscribed by some group monitor. Some of your courses may have a Listserv that's limited to members of the class, which provides for electronic postings from members of the group. A posting to a Listserv, which may occasionally be a resource for your research, requires a specific type of citation as indicated in online citation guides for different documentation systems. You may find it very useful to join a specific Listserv as a reference source, since they are essentially "electronic, asynchronous conversations" that often allow you cutting edge-information on hot topics in a given field. These Listservs can be highly specialized, covering such topics as writing consulting, dessert du jour, reef aquarists, or advanced Web design. For a directory of Listservs, including subscription information, see www.liszt.com.

E-mail messages   E-mail messages are limited-access resources because they are password protected, available only to designated individuals. Most college students are *extremely* familiar with e-mail messages and may never consider them "reference sources." In fact, they can sometimes be very valuable reference sources, allowing you to get extremely current firsthand information from an individual directly connected to a topic you are researching. For academic purposes, an e-mail message can sometimes function as an "electronic interview." As such, it must be cited within your research, giving proper credit to the knowledgeable individual who shared information with you.

Online journals   There are more and more full-text journals, covering an almost unlimited range of topics, available electronically. Some of these "e-journals" are published exclusively electronically, and some are merely an electronic version of a journal that also exists in print, such as *Time* magazine. Just as with print journals, some are intended for a wide audience of the general public; other online journals are intended for a very specific academic audience, such as *Kairos*, an online journal about rhetoric, technology, pedagogy, and language issues. Some of these journals are limited-access resources in that they require a subscription, paid either by the individual reader or by the library provider, in order to read them; others are available for free on the Web. Note that online journals are documented in a slightly different manner than print journals. And in fact, articles from online journals—that is, articles from journals available electronically in their entirety, accessed at their own site—are documented differently from articles in journals that were accessed through library-held databases as discussed above. Documentation is complicated indeed!

Accessing Electronic Sources   Clearly, there is an untold wealth of information available electronically. How does a researcher begin to access all of these different sources? Most of the limited-access, non-WWW resources must be accessed through a proxy server, such as at your college, university, or local public library, which has paid for the access rights. Only through these servers can you link to article databases for full-text academic journal articles or to specialized subject-specific reference sources such as the Twayne Author Series, which provides detailed information for advanced literary study. On-site reference librarians can provide you with more details regarding accessing electronic sources at a given library.

Accessing information on the World Wide Web is a different matter. Just as the materials are widely available to the general public with virtually no screening or limitations, so, too, is most of the searching capacity. Essentially, there are three different types of Web searches: search engines, metacrawlers, and subject directories.

Search engines, or search services, conduct computerized searches of literally millions of Web sites almost instantaneously. They retrieve very high numbers of hits, which can be helpful but can also be very confusing. Even more significantly, search engines do not sort by reliability or quality. However, they can be very useful if you have a specific topic to submit and/or if you want very generic information. They will generally *not* access many scholarly or academic resources, as these are generally limited-access sources as discussed above. There are several different search engines; currently, some of the most popular ones are www.google.com, www.altavista.com, and www.yahoo.com. Keep in mind that search engines don't search all of the same Web sites, so it can be useful to consult more than one for a given project.

A multiengine search can be conducted through so-called meta-search engines or metacrawlers, which search many sites simultaneously and then deliver the information in collective bundles from the various search engine sites. These search mechanisms result in more "hits" for a given submission, sometimes in the millions. Popular metacrawlers include www.dogpile.com and www.search.com. These metacrawlers will access vast amounts of material indiscriminately, rank them by relevance (according to *its* criteria), and sometimes offer a very limited amount of material. For example, a Dogpile search on "college students" produced 114 hits, sorted by relevance, and 125 hits, sorted by search engine. Viewing the 10 Google results retrieved by Dogpile leads a searcher back to Google for more; at the Google site, "college students" retrieved about 35 million hits.

The most "academic" Web-based search mechanisms are **subject directories.** These directories, unlike search engines, provide lists of Web sites that are recommended and annotated by experts in various fields. Specific criteria are applied by human screeners, not random computer programs, which generally results in more accurate and more high-quality hits. Examples of subject directories include the Librarians' Index to the Internet, accessed at www.lii.org, and About, available at www.about.com. The first one, funded by the libraries of California as a public service for state and national library users, clearly states its selection criteria for site recommendations by its staff of numerous librarians; the second, while a for-profit site, also provides links to quality information that is hand-selected by subject specialists. Accessing Web sites through subject directories, rather than through search engines, certainly provides more "quality control."

Evaluating Electronic Sources   All resource material, either print or electronic, should be carefully and critically evaluated by the researcher or academic writer. When using online materials, the challenge can be even greater because the researcher may not have the benefit of filters like publishing house teams of reviewers who prescreen materials for accuracy and credibility.

Certain quality controls are clearly in place when using limited-access materials usually acquired through proxy servers like the college library. Teams of experts screen the journal and magazine articles that appear in databases accessible only through such servers. Many databases provide additional helpful category limitations, such as "peer-reviewed journals," which restrict the citations retrieved to academic journals that have subjected all submissions to the close scrutiny of specialists within a given discipline. In other words, resources accessed through library servers are assumed credible and generally of relatively high quality. Nonetheless, these resources still need critical screening on the part of the researcher, depending upon the scope and nature of his/her project. Always check the source, date, and author's credentials. Also, be aware of a one major distinction when retrieving articles from a database—whether the article is from a popular magazine or a scholarly journal.

Useful and reliable information is available in both popular magazines and scholarly journals, but the nature of the information and, thus, of its credibility for particular types of research projects can vary tremendously. Generally speaking, popular magazines are written by journalists who glean information from a variety of sources, including experts in the field. Scholarly journals, on the other hand, present the research of subject specialists firsthand. In other words, scholarly journals are written by field experts and published in a source aimed at other field experts, usually a highly critical audience. Information in popular magazines is usually more readable, since it appeals to a broad-based audience with much less technical knowledge. For some research projects, your professors may limit you to using only scholarly resources. These resources include scholarly books, most often published by university presses; scholarly articles, published in subject-specific, peer-reviewed journals; and items on scholarly Web sites from technical associations.

When using open-access Web-based materials as resources, you have an even greater evaluation challenge. Since literally *anything* can be placed on the Web, it is up to you to be diligent about evaluating the Web site in order to ensure that your project will be acceptable. Web sites can vary widely. Some market a product or service; some share news or information on a particular topic; some promote or advocate a specific special-interest and/or political agenda; some are simply personal statements, including everything from résumés seeking employment to lonely heart announcements seeking companionship.

No matter the intent or content, all Web sites need careful evaluation. There are certain Web page review sites that can offer some useful information, but you, as the researcher, must also scrutinize sites closely. Certain basic criteria can be very useful in evaluating Web sites. These most often include evaluating authority, accuracy, objectivity, currency and permanence, coverage or scope, and means of presentation. Let's briefly examine some aspects of these criteria.

Authority   It is important to check that the organization, group, or individual responsible for the contents of the Web site is clearly indicated. There should be current contact information including address and phone number. You should be able to verify the legitimacy of the source; for example, is it connected to a larger national organization? To a university? To a well-known company? Look for an about-us–type statement providing some background and context for the site. Pay attention to the domain of the site and assess its appropriateness for the topic and for your research needs.

Accuracy   Carefully consider the accuracy of the content by checking to see if sources and dates of specific information are identified and to see if pertinent, useful links are provided for additional information or verification. Are the sources credible and appropriate for the topic of the Web site? Screen the content for logic, reliable evidence, and a sufficient number of supporting examples or details to help comprehend the topic.

Objectivity   Determine the point of view or perspective of the Web site's proprietor. Examine it closely to see if the site clearly identifies any special-interest links or biases. Are there advertisements or philosophy statements linked to the page that suggest a certain position or affiliation? You may or may not want to support these, but you definitely need to be aware of them.

Currency and permanence   Always confirm the dates of when the material was first placed on the Web and when it was last updated. Note how frequently it is revised. Also pay attention to how frequently the Web site changes location. Is it simply a matter of organizational logistics because site management rotates with administrative positions, or is it an indication of instability?

Coverage or scope   Determine if topics are clearly identified, and scrutinize the range of those topics relative to your research needs. Consider whether the topics adequately cover the overall intent of the site or if things seem to be missing or are very sketchily covered. Identify the audience targeted by considering the depth of the coverage, the reading level, the amount of text versus graphics, the interactive nature of the site, and so forth. Determine if this is a site "under construction" that will be adding more information soon or if it is ostensibly complete.

Means of presentation   Evaluate the user-friendly nature of the site. Does its methods of presentation and organization seem appropriate for its audience and purpose? Is it easy to navigate throughout the site to appropriate links and back to the home page, for instance? Is it visually attractive? Is it easy to locate the information you are seeking? Look for useful features such as alphabetized lists of "hot topics," a broadly defined search index, a frequently asked questions section, a help link, and an easy means of contacting the site sponsor.

For further help on evaluating specific Web sites, always turn to your reference librarian and/or to guides posted on your college or university library home page. Many academic libraries provide links to such information, and, in fact, many of them have posted this information on the WWW for use by the general public.

Documenting Electronic Sources Keep in mind that regardless of the content, domain, or format, all electronically accessed information, whether through library servers or via the WWW, needs to be properly credited and documented if used for a research project. For example, there are citation rules for individual Web sites and for full-text articles that appear on a given Web site. Similarly, there are citation formats for Listservs and bulletin boards, e-mail messages, articles from online databases and government reports published on Web sites, and so forth. Consult the documentation section in this textbook for further information on citing electronic resources.

PRESENTING AND ORGANIZING INFORMATION

Summarizing

Most often your academic writing tasks will involve consulting other texts for background information, for current opinions, for data on research that's been conducted, and so forth. As you can tell from the preceding section, the amount and type of information is essentially infinite. In order to make use of these resources, you will need to call into play a very important research skill: your ability to effectively *summarize* vast amounts of information.

When you summarize, you are basically doing two things: extracting and reducing. That is, you are looking carefully at the original source and extracting the main points, leaving behind points of lesser importance and many of the minor details or extraneous examples. Indeed, determining what to extract is often the hardest part of preparing an effective summary! In the process of extraction, you are attempting to reduce the size of the original in order to create a new version of the text that is only a fraction of the original. Most of your summary will be a paraphrase of the original—i.e., written in your own words. However, you may decide to use a few brief quotations from the original simply because the wording of the text seems the very best option for conveying the point or in order to help you establish the tone or "feel" of the original text. Remember that if you do use direct quotations, you must follow all of the rules for doing so. (Study the conventions of paraphrasing and quoting in the following section.)

Keep in mind the word *original* as it is used here. A summary is supposed to merely "re-present" the original in every sense. It must preserve the main points of the content including the opinion and the tone of the original work, even if you do not agree with them at all. A summary does not include any commentary, analytical remarks, or evaluations that were not present in the original version of the text.

In other words, when you summarize, you attempt to be as objective as possible though, of course, some subjectivity is inevitable merely by virtue of what you decide to include or exclude. You must be careful to fairly represent the ideas of the original text (even if that "text" is an event, though we are primarily referring to written works here) and *not* to add your own opinions about those ideas.

In other words, the characteristics of a good summary are as follows:

- It shrinks the length of the original text.
- It retains the main content points, clearly reflecting the stance of the original author, and includes a limited amount of detail or examples.
- It strives for objectivity.
- It does not offer opinion, evaluation, or *any* additional information not contained in the original piece; rather, it simply "re-presents" the original in reduced format.

Let's look for a moment at the various purposes a summary can serve. A summary can be of value to both readers and writers. Sometimes readers benefit from a shortened version of a text for the purpose of time efficiency. If more details are needed or desired, the reader can always retrieve the text in its entirety. Sometimes a reader may want to use a summary of a text previously read in full to jar his/her memory regarding the main points.

Similarly, a writer can benefit in a variety of ways from creating a summary. In order to create a summary, you as a writer must read the original text carefully, determine the main points, and re-create the text in your own words. That cognitive process will soon reveal if you indeed understand the material in the original. So writing a summary can be a great study tool. You might also write a summary of a text because you are attempting to use numerous texts as sources for a research project. It is impossible, and unnecessary, to retain all of the details of all of your materials. If you create summaries, you will have workable-size versions of your source materials for beginning to formulate your analysis or the production of your full-length report.

Now let's consider the procedure for writing a summary. Before you begin writing your summary, conduct a quick overview of the text as a whole. Note the type of source, the title of the text, the date, and the author; and determine the amount and type of references. This will help you understand the general context. For example, is this a scholarly article in a discipline-specific journal with lots of references, or is it a broad overview typical of a popular-interest magazine with no references and perhaps no author identified? You will, of course, encounter very different types of information in both of the above.

To actually write the summary, try the following procedure:

- Carefully read the entire text and immediately write a two-to-three-sentence summary of the overall content and purpose of the article. Identify the thesis of the text.
- Go back and carefully reread the text. While reading, annotate the text by marking off the main subsections.
- Read one subsection at a time and try to rephrase that chunk in your own words in a few sentences; repeat this procedure for each subsection.

- Tie these small sections of text together, working on transitions and overall readability. This will be the body of your summary.
- Draft an introduction that:
  - Provides an overall idea of the content of the report. In other words, contextualize the text by relating it to a specific discipline as a whole.
  - States the thesis of the text clearly.
- Includes the bibliographic information in your introduction so that a reader could retrieve the original in its entirety, if desired.
- Reread carefully to be sure you've included all main points and a few supporting details. Check for flow and readability.
- Proofread your summary carefully for adherence to all conventions of Standard Written English.

Now read the following article on college students' use of ecstasy, written by Scott Walters, Betsy Foy, and Ralph Castro (all experts on behavioral science and/or drug addiction), reprinted from the *Journal of American College Health*. Then study the sample summary that follows to enhance your understanding of what constitutes a strong summary. Notice that the student summary is documented in APA format, common to social science research.

The Agony of Ecstasy:

Responding to Growing MDMA Use Among College Students

The recent increase in ecstasy use among college students has left prevention workers feeling anything but euphoric. Although the use of alcohol and most other drugs has remained steady over the last 5 years, ecstasy use has more than doubled. (*n1*) This dramatic increase, coupled with the unique characteristics of this substance, warrants a concerted prevention effort specific to this drug. In the present article, we outline the history and current epidemiology of MDMA, more commonly known as ecstasy, X, E, or XTC, and provide directions to equip readers to respond to this growing problem.

- Ecstasy is unlike any other drug in terms of its effects and the myths surrounding its use.
- Students who use ecstasy fit a very different profile from students who use other drugs.
- Recent scientific studies reflect growing concern about the possibility of long-term neurological damage as a result of recreational use of MDMA.
- Current drug prevention efforts seem to have failed with ecstasy users. Although rates of other illegal drug use by young adults have remained stable, the use of ecstasy has risen in nearly every age group.

History and Myths

2 Ecstasy is a drug like no other. This simple statement is borne out in the somewhat unusual history of ecstasy and in the myths surrounding its use and effects. "Pure" ecstasy is MDMA (3,4-methylenedioxymethamphetamine)—not a difficult substance to make. However, most ecstasy purchased on the street or in clubs is nothing close to pure. Other chemicals, such as ephedrine, codeine, caffeine, and ketamine (a general anesthetic) are frequently added or passed off as ecstasy. ("Herbal" ecstasy, which can be purchased legally, is mostly ephedrine and caffeine, and contains no MDMA.)

3 The pharmaceutical company E. Merck in Germany first developed MDMA in the early 1900s. It is chemically related to both hallucinogens and stimulants in the way it induces euphoria and enhanced self-awareness, but it does not seem to produce psychotic effects or visual distortions. As a serotonin agonist, it works on the same system as antidepressants such as fluoxetine (Prozac[TM]), paroxetine (Paxil[TM]), and sertraline (Zoloft[TM]), with which it is sometimes taken in combination. Whereas these substances influence mood through inhibiting the reuptake of serotonin, MDMA substantially boosts serotonin release, producing many times the effect.

4 Before MDMA was scheduled as a Class I illicit substance in 1985, ecstasy was prescribed by some psychiatrists and psychotherapists as an adjunct to therapy because of its reported ability to facilitate communication, acceptance, and fear reduction. After the Food and Drug Administration criminalized the use of the drug, MDMA "went underground" and began to be used in the same settings as other hallucinogenic drugs, such as LSD and, more recently, "club drugs," including date rape drugs GHB (gammahydroxybuterate) and Rohypnol (flunitrazepam) known on the street as "roofies." (*n2*)

5 What makes ecstasy unique? First, no drug has ever been characterized in quite the same way as ecstasy. Individuals almost universally describe its effects as "euphoric," "blissful," and "love inducing." The drug experience appears to be greater for women, (*n3*) and the ecstasy experience can be amplified by such factors as room temperature, overcrowding, and dancing. (*n2*) These qualities make ecstasy distinct from other substances sold on either licit or illicit markets. The positive effects, coupled with its wide availability, seem to ensure ecstasy's continued use by young people. It is also readily taken in combination with other medications, such as fluoxetine (Prozac[TM]), sildenafil (Viagra[TM]), herbal and caffeinated "energy" beverages (Red Bull[TM]), and alcohol, which may further enhance or change its effect.

6 In addition to the euphoric and carefree feeling ecstasy produces, belief in the "cleanness" of the substance appears to be another reason for its continued use. The myths surrounding ecstasy use—especially those promulgated on Internet Websites and chat rooms—are that it can make an individual more social and energetic without the intoxication, side effects, and risk of overdose that accompany other drugs. Users admit some drawbacks of ecstasy, including increased sweating, jaw clenching, and reduced sexual functioning. In addition, some side effects, such as deteriorated mood and energy, (*n2*) are apparent in the first few days following use. However, these immediate consequences seem to be relatively minor compared with those related to most other drugs. Furthermore, the scare factor of overdose that is present with other illegal drugs does not appear to be an issue for ecstasy users. In fact,

among those few persons admitted to an emergency room following ecstasy use, the vast majority are treated for dehydration, hyperthermia, or toxicity of other drugs that have been passed off as ecstasy, all of which are unattributable to MDMA per se.

As of this writing, ecstasy also has not been proved to be addictive. Patterns of use do not appear to follow the stereotypic addictive patterns of physical dependence, drug-seeking behavior, and withdrawal after one stops using it. However, some evidence of tolerance has been noted. It appears that as the positive effects of ecstasy diminish, the negative effects increase when the drug is taken more frequently. "The majority of people who have taken more than 5 individual doses of MDMA state that the good effects of the drug change with successive doses." As stated by one college student, "Freshmen love it; sophomores like it; juniors are ambivalent; and seniors are afraid of it." (n4(p191))

These factors have led many students to believe that ecstasy can be used with relative impunity. However, despite this common belief, new evidence suggests the possibility of deleterious effects from recreational or even a single use. Recent studies have indicated that regular use of ecstasy can produce small but detectable deficits in attention, memory, reasoning, impulse control, and sleep (n5) and that the effects may persist long after the individual has stopped using the drug. (n6) For example, memory deficits have been seen in moderate users with an average lifetime ecstasy use on 10 to 20 occasions. (n7) A recent article about studies of memory in MDMA users concluded, "While the neurotoxic effects of MDMA on [serotonin] neurons in the human cortex may be reversible, the effects of MDMA on memory function may be long lasting." (n8 (191)) This study is the first to examine MDMA users who have abstained from using the drug for at least 1 year.

In addition, several animal studies have shown brain damage after a single dose or after repeated moderate doses. In one such study, rats that were given a single large dose of MDMA had more difficulty than untreated rats in learning to complete a maze, even after 80 days. (n9) Although these animal findings may not be directly applicable to humans, they offer some early evidence that MDMA may have subtle long-term consequences even for one-time users. Such results must also be viewed in light of surveys (discussed below) that show that ecstasy users do not differ from other students in grade point averages (GPA5). Nonetheless, what does seem certain is that many of the positive myths about the safety of this drug will be proved to be inaccurate over the next decade.

Current Ecstasy Use

National surveys show that rates of ecstasy use have risen sharply in recent years. The Monitoring the Future 2000 study first suggested that use of the drug appears in younger age groups each year. For instance, among eighth-grade students, the data show an increase from 1.7% of those who had used ecstasy in the last 30 days during 1999 to 3.1% in 2000. Similarly, 30-day prevalence over this period increased from 4.4% to 5.4% among tenth graders, and from 5.6% to 8.2% among twelfth graders. (n10) Data from the Harvard College Alcohol Study (CAS) revealed an increase in annual ecstasy use in college students from 2.8% in 1997 to 4.7% in 1999, an increase of 69%. (n1) The CAS, the first study to examine epidemiologic information specific to ecstasy use among college students, also provided important information about behavioral and lifestyle factors associated with using this substance. The investigators found that ecstasy users were not the academic underachievers one might associate with other illicit drug use. In fact, ecstasy users did not differ from other students in terms of GPA and the importance they placed on community service. Of 8 demographic factors associated with MDMA, marijuana use was the variable that far outweighed all others (92.1%). Other factors that were more common in ecstasy users than among other students were (1) binge drinking, (2) more time spent socializing and less time studying, (3) having more sexual partners, (4) smoking cigarettes, (5) rating arts and parties as more important than academic pursuits, and (6) viewing religion as less important. Because ecstasy is primarily used in group settings, it is not surprising that users were more likely to attend a residential college, hold memberships in fraternities or sororities, and spend larger quantities of time engaging in social activities than were non-using students.

Prevention

11   College students' increased use of ecstasy and scientific evidence suggesting that occasional MDMA use may have long-term consequences present a challenge to college health providers. Because prevention programs are still in their infancy, one of us (BF) conducted an informal telephone survey of staff involved with alcohol and drug services at 9 public and private institutions across the US and 1 institution in Canada in July 2001. Among this group, only 2 schools were currently developing prevention materials for ecstasy, and none had any programs or materials in use at the time. One campus was using a harm-reduction model and the other used a social-norms model, both popular strategies adapted from existing high-risk drinking prevention programs.

12   In what direction is prevention of ecstasy use heading? We know that educational campaigns sometimes disseminate the latest research to parents and administrators. Many universities already relay information about high-risk drinking to parents through admissions material and orientation programs, and ecstasy may also warrant this approach. In terms of reaching students directly, offering safer social alternatives to all-night "raves" may be one way to limit exposure to the substance. Because the effects of regular use are more subtle and long lasting than the effects of using other drugs, the myths about the safety of ecstasy have persisted. Thus, creative media campaigns and peer education programs might be ways to raise awareness of the potential consequences.

13   Finally, if it can be confirmed that even a single use of MDMA has long-term repercussions in humans, this will undoubtedly influence the programs that are offered. If ecstasy is indeed in a class by itself, prevention programs must weigh the benefits of creating a safe environment for ecstasy use against the risks that may be inherent in any use at all.

14   Although increasing numbers of students are using ecstasy in high school, the number of students who use ecstasy for the first time while attending college is still very high. Thus, peer and media influences may well have an effect on students before they try ecstasy for the first time. As college health providers, our challenge to correct beliefs that ecstasy won't hurt you is enormous, and it will require creative

thoughts on prevention and intervention. In our opinion, this is a challenge that must not go unnoticed or unattended.

REFERENCES

(*n1.*) Strote J, Lee JE, Wechsler H. Increasing MDMA use among college students: Results of a national survey. J Adolesc Health. 2002;30:64–72.

(*n2.*) Pan-ott AC. Human psychopharmacology of ecstasy (MDMA): A review of 15 years of empirical research. Human Psychopharmacology: Clinical and Experimental. 2001;16:557–577.

(*n3.*) Liechti ME, Gamma A, Vollenweider FX. Gender differences in the subjective effects of MDMA. Psychopharmacology. 2001;154:161–168.

(*n4.*) Peroutka SJ. "Ecstasy": A human neurotoxin? [Letters to the Editor] Arch Gen Psychiatry. 1989;46:191.

(*n5.*) Morgan MJ. Ecstasy (MDMA): A review of its possible persistent psychological effects. Psychopharmacology. 2000:152:230–248.

(*n6.*) Morgan MJ, McFie L, Fleetwood H, Robinson JA. Ecstasy (MDMA): Are the psychological problems associated with its use reversed by prolonged abstinence? Psychopharmacology. 2002;159:294–303.

(*n7.*) Pan-ott AC, Lees A, Gammas NJ, Jones M, Wesnes K. Cognitive performance in recreational users of MDMA or "ecstasy": Evidence for memory deficits. J Psychopharmacol. 1998;12:79–83.

(*n8.*) Reneman L, Lavalaye J, Schmand B, et al. Cortical serotonin transporter density and verbal memory in individuals who stopped using 3,4-methylenedioxymethamphetamine (MDMA or "ecstasy"). Arch Gen Psychiatry. 2001;58:901–906.

(*n9.*) Mechan AO, Moran PM, Elliott M, Young AJ, Joseph MI-I, Green R. A study of the effect of a single neuotoxic dose of 3,4-methylenedioxymethamphetamine (MDMA; "ecstasy") on the subsequent long-term behaviour of rats in the plus maze and open field. Psychopharmacology. 2002;159:167–175.

(*n10.*) Johnston LB, O'Malley PM, Bachman JG. Monitoring the Future: National Survey Results on Drug Use, 1975–2000. Vol 2: College Students and Young Adults Ages 19–40. (NIH Publication 01-4925).Bethesda, MD: National Institute on Drug Abuse; 2001.

Summary of "The Agony of Ecstasy"

Shelly Rozicka

Elmhurst College

"The Agony of Ecstasy: Responding to Growing MDMA Use Among College Students," an article appearing in the November, 2002 issue of the *Journal of American College Health*, is a combined effort of

Introductory paragraph includes mention of the article title, source, authors, and their background.

three college health providers. Dr. Scott T. Walters is a professor of behavioral sciences at the University of Texas. Betsy D. Foy, MHS, CHES and Ralph J. Castro, MS are administrators of substance abuse services at Washington University, St. Louis and Stanford University respectively. The article discusses the increased use of the drug ecstasy on American college campuses. The authors focus on the history and myths of the drug, its current use, and means of prevention.

Ecstasy's technical name is 3,4-methylenedioxymethamphetamine, or MDMA. Originally made by a pharmaceutical company, the once prescription drug was later criminalized by the FDA. It is related to hallucinogens and stimulants, and produces the effects of a strong antidepressant. Walters, Foy, and Castro (2002) report that MDMA, as described by users, produces a "euphoric," "blissful" feeling unique to the drug (p. 140). The authors assert that MDMA's continued use by young people is due to its positive effects, availability, and supposed safeness. While the immediate negative side effects such as increased perspiration, and decreased mood or energy seem minor, new evidence indicates possible brain damage and long-term effects in memory function from using the drug one time. The authors predict that any current assumptions about MDMA's safety "will be proved . . . inaccurate over the next decade" (p. 140).

Current use of ecstasy among college students, however, is on the rise. According to the Harvard College Alcohol Study, college ecstasy users are not stereotypical underachievers. They do not differ from their peers in GPA or view of community service. They do tend to share certain commonalities such as being more likely to attend residential colleges, and partaking in more social activities than nonusers.

Due to the current rising use of MDMA, and new evidence of negative long-term effects, the authors believe that college health providers are responsible for providing ecstasy prevention. Although

---

Introduction also includes a brief summary statement offering an overview of the entire article.

The first of the three main sections is briefly summarized, emphasizing the authors' primary contentions.

Note the appropriate and effective use of a brief direct quotation, tying the summary directly to the source.

Section 2 is briefly summarized.

Following the order of the article, section 3 is aptly summarized here.

few ecstasy-specific programs exist on US campuses, the authors provide suggestions, including offering alternative activities to raves (parties where the drug is often used), along with "creative media campaigns and peer education programs" discussing newly discovered dangers (p. 141). Walters, Foy and Castro end the article stating that the challenge of ecstasy prevention must not be overlooked.

Walters, S. T., Foy, B. D., Castro, R. J., (2002). The agony of ecstasy: Responding to growing MDMA use among college students. *Journal of American College Health, 51*, 139–141.

Note that there is no separate conclusion. Frequently, summaries merely end with the ending point of the original source.

Complete reference is provided in APA format.

MEETING THE CHALLENGE

Practice your summary skills with this reading.

- Select one of the subheaded sections of the ecstasy article. Read it closely, take notes if necessary, and then write a strong one-paragraph summary of it without looking at the text.
- Return to the article itself and compare your summary with the original. Did you leave out any major points? What did you feel was acceptable to leave out? Explain how that decision could vary by audience.
- Compare your paragraph to a peer's paragraph. Discuss any different choices in what you included or excluded.
- Compare your summary to the corresponding section in Rozicka's above. Discuss similarities and differences.

Practice your summary skills with a different reading.

- Select any one of the readings from Chapter 5 and write a 300–500-word summary of it.
- Remember to begin by providing an overview of the text and giving complete source documentation information.
- Compare your summary with a writing partner's. Discuss differences, especially in terms of which points you included.
- Redraft your summary following your discussion.

Quoting and Paraphrasing

When you conduct research and write papers that incorporate what you discovered, you may regularly need to quote particular words, phrases, sentences, and perhaps even multisentence passages. In addition, you may need to paraphrase material you find in your research—that is, put it in your own words but keep it about the same length as the original. Writers need to learn to quote and paraphrase not only correctly but also wisely. They need not only to know the formal conventions involved with quoting and paraphrasing but also to develop the sense that lets them know when a quote or a paraphrase would be effective in their paper.

Many inexperienced writers are tempted to quote too much—to use more of the source's actual language than they really need to. In general, a rule of thumb is this: If the specific language of the source is striking, distinctive, and unique—if the author's original words say something better than you could possibly say it, or if the original words would cause your reader to perk up and pay attention to your text—then it's a good idea to quote the original source directly. If the language of the original source is quite straightforward, even commonplace, you may quote it directly if the material fits into the flow of your paragraphs and sentences, but you may also simply paraphrase it. It's important to note that in either case—whether you quote or paraphrase—you *must* acknowledge and cite your sources following MLA, APA, CSE, or Turabian format.

If you choose to quote material directly from a source, you need to decide further whether you want to quote part of a sentence, an entire sentence, or several sentences. To illustrate how to do these things, let's work with two chunks of the article reprinted earlier, "The Agony of Ecstasy: Responding to Growing MDMA Use Among College Students," written by Scott Walters, Betsy Foy, and Ralph Castro and published in the *Journal of American College Health*. The explanation that follows deals with quoting directly in MLA and APA formats. See the section in this chapter on documenting sources for more information on using the CSE and Turabian formats.

Here again is the opening paragraph of the Walters, Foy, and Castro article:

> The recent increase in ecstasy use among college students has left prevention workers feeling anything but euphoric. Although the use of alcohol and most other drugs has remained steady over the last 5 years, ecstasy use has more than doubled. (*n1*) This dramatic increase, coupled with the unique characteristics of this substance, warrants a concerted prevention effort specific to this drug. In the present article, we outline the history and current epidemiology of MDMA, more commonly known as ecstasy, X, E, or XTC, and provide directions to equip readers to respond to this growing problem.

And here again is the third-to-last paragraph in the article:

> In what direction is prevention of ecstasy use heading? We know that educational campaigns sometimes disseminate the latest research to parents and administrators. Many universities already relay information about high-risk drinking to parents through admissions material and orientation programs, and ecstasy may also warrant this approach. In terms of reaching students directly, offering safer social alternatives to all-night "raves" may be one way to limit exposure to the substance. Because the effects of regular use are more subtle and long lasting than the effects of using other drugs, the myths about the safety of ecstasy have persisted. Thus, creative media campaigns and peer education programs might be ways to raise awareness of the potential consequences.

Suppose you are writing a stance or position paper for a first-year composition course about recreational drug use among college students, and since you like the catchy sound of the first sentence of the article, you decide to quote it in its entirety. In doing so, you should introduce the quoted sentence with a phrase that both introduces the source and embeds the quoted sentence in your own paper. Here is one way such a direct quotation could look in MLA format:

> According to three experts on college students' drug habits, "The recent increase in ecstasy use among college students has left prevention workers feeling anything but euphoric" (Walters, Foy, and Castro 139).

The same direct quotation would look like this in APA format:

> According to three experts on college students' drug habits, "The recent increase in ecstasy use among college students has left prevention workers feeling anything but euphoric" (Walters, Foy, & Castro, 2002, p. 139).

Notice, though, that you may also choose to mention the three authors' names in the introductory phrase. In MLA format, such a direct quotation would look like this:

> According to Scott Walters, Betsy Foy, and Ralph Castro, three experts on college students' drug habits, "The recent increase in ecstasy use among college students has left prevention workers feeling anything but euphoric" (139).

This type of direct quotation would look like this in APA format:

> According to Walters, Foy, and Castro (2002), "The recent increase in ecstasy use among college students has left prevention workers feeling anything but euphoric" (p. 139).

MLA format recommends that you use the authors' first names and last names the first time you cite them, but then simply use their last names in later citations of the same authors. APA format, on the other hand, recommends that you always refer to authors by their last names only.

If you decide to directly quote only part of a sentence, bear in mind two important points: First, be sure the quoted material fits within the syntax of your own sentence (in other words, be sure that the quoted material flows with your own words); and, second, follow exactly the same format conventions that you would use when quoting complete sentences. For example, suppose you like the phrase "concerted prevention effort specific to this drug" from the opening paragraph of the Walters, Foy, and Castro article. In your paper, you might write a sentence embedding this phrase in your own work. Here is one way this sentence might look in MLA format:

> Three experts on college students' use of ecstasy call for a "concerted prevention effort specific to this drug" (Walters, Foy, and Castro 139).

As above, in MLA format you could also cite the authors' names (first and last the first time you mention them, and last names only after that) in the introductory phrase:

> Scott Walters, Betsy Foy, and Ralph Castro, three experts on college students' use of ecstasy, call for a "concerted prevention effort specific to this drug" (139).

Quoting a part of a sentence in APA format follows the same conventions described above. Here are two versions of the sentence with the phrase embedded, this time in APA format:

> Three experts on college students' use of ecstasy call for a "concerted prevention effort specific to this drug" (Walters, Foy, & Castro, 2002, p. 139).
> Walters, Foy, and Castro (2002), three experts on college students' use of ecstasy, call for a "concerted prevention effort specific to this drug" (p. 139).

In addition to quoting entire sentences or embedding part of a direct quotation in your own prose, you may occasionally want to directly quote longer passages of an original source. In MLA format, any direct quotation that takes longer than four lines to type (or word process) in regular 12-point font should be "blocked"—in other words, set off 10 spaces (or one inch) from the left margin. In APA format, quotations longer than 40 words should be blocked by indenting five spaces (or one-half inch). The conventions for introducing such blocked quotations and citing the bibliographic information are the same as those for complete sentences and embedded sentences.

Suppose, for example, that you want to write a paragraph in your paper about ways people can learn about the dangers of using ecstasy. You might want, therefore, to directly quote a substantial passage from the third-to-last paragraph above. You can do so by writing an introductory phrase and then adding the blocked quotation. Here are two versions of how you could quote this material in MLA format:

> According to three experts on anti-ecstasy informational efforts,
>> We know that educational campaigns sometimes disseminate the latest research to parents and administrators. Many universities already relay information about high-risk drinking to parents through admissions material and orientation programs, and ecstasy may also warrant this approach. In terms of reaching students directly, offering safer social alternatives to all-night "raves" may be one way to limit exposure to the substance. Because the effects of regular use are more subtle and long lasting than the effects of using other drugs, the myths about the safety of ecstasy have persisted. Thus, creative media campaigns and peer education programs might be ways to raise awareness of the potential consequences. (Walters, Foy, and Castro, 141)

OR

> Scott Walters, Betsy Foy, and Ralph Castro, three leaders in higher education counseling, report the following:
>> We know that educational campaigns sometimes disseminate the latest research to parents and administrators. Many universities already relay information about high-risk drinking to parents through admissions material and orientation programs, and ecstasy may also warrant this approach. In terms of reaching students directly, offering safer social alternatives to all-night "raves" may be one way to limit exposure to the substance. Because the effects of regular use are more subtle and long lasting than the effects of using other drugs, the myths about the safety of ecstasy have

> persisted. Thus, creative media campaigns and peer education programs might be ways to raise awareness of the potential consequences. (141)

In APA format, the same two versions would look like this:

According to three experts on anti-ecstasy informational efforts,

> We know that educational campaigns sometimes disseminate the latest research to parents and administrators. Many universities already relay information about high-risk drinking to parents through admissions material and orientation programs, and ecstasy may also warrant this approach. In terms of reaching students directly, offering safer social alternatives to all-night "raves" may be one way to limit exposure to the substance. Because the effects of regular use are more subtle and long lasting than the effects of using other drugs, the myths about the safety of ecstasy have persisted. Thus, creative media campaigns and peer education programs might be ways to raise awareness of the potential consequences. (Walters, Foy, & Castro, 2002, p. 141)

OR

> Walters, Foy, and Castro, three leaders in higher education counseling, report the following:

> We know that educational campaigns sometimes disseminate the latest research to parents and administrators. Many universities already relay information about high-risk drinking to parents through admissions material and orientation programs, and ecstasy may also warrant this approach. In terms of reaching students directly, offering safer social alternatives to all-night "raves" may be one way to limit exposure to the substance. Because the effects of regular use are more subtle and long lasting than the effects of using other drugs, the myths about the safety of ecstasy have persisted. Thus, creative media campaigns and peer education programs might be ways to raise awareness of the potential consequences. (2002, p. 141)

Whether you use MLA or APA format, notice that with blocked quotations, the period goes at the end of the quoted material and before the bibliographic information in parentheses.

Finally, there may be places in your paper where you need to paraphrase material from the original source. When you do so, you follow precisely the same conventions described above for quoting directly, but you simply omit the quotation marks. For example, suppose somewhere in your paper you want to convey the following opinion, as expressed by Walters, Foy, and Castro in the third-to-last paragraph, in your own words:

> In terms of reaching students directly, offering safer social alternatives to all-night "raves" may be one way to limit exposure to the substance.

Your paraphrase in MLA format could look like this:

> Experts on anti-ecstasy informational campaigns call for college administrators to provide social events that would keep students away from ecstasy (Walters, Foy, and Castro 141).

In APA format, the same paraphrase would look like this:

> Experts on anti-ecstasy informational campaigns call for college administrators to provide social events that would keep students away from ecstasy (Walters, Foy, & Castro, 2002, p. 141).

MEETING THE CHALLENGE

Practice your own paraphrasing skills.

- Select one paragraph from an essay in the reading units in Chapter 5 to paraphrase.
- Compare your paraphrase with those of at least two classmates.
- Discuss similarities and differences and determine the most appropriate wording.
- Redraft your paraphrase.

Practice your own quoting skills.

- Now redraft your paraphrased paragraph to include two brief quotations from the original text, documenting your paragraph in MLA format.
- Compare your attempt to those of two classmates and redraft your paragraph.
- Repeat the activity in APA format.

Analyzing

During your academic career, you will sometimes be assigned to write a summary to demonstrate your knowledge of a text's content or an event's highlights or to provide a usable reduced version of a text for yourself or other readers. It is important that you don't underestimate the task of writing a good summary; it is frequently a more demanding task than many students assume. However, more than likely most of your academic writing will challenge you to go beyond pure summary. To take your reading and writing to the next level, you will be required to **analyze** the materials and ideas that you encounter.

To understand the difference between summary and analysis, certain prompt questions are often useful. Essentially, to create a summary you need to ask one primary question: "What?" In other words, your main purpose is to determine the essence of what the author has stated or what has occurred at a particular site, and then report that in a shortened version in your own words. Strictly speaking, a summary prohibits commentary, opinion, and interpretation of the "what" the author presents.

Analysis is quite the opposite. Creating an analysis demands that you move beyond determining "what" and ask several other questions such as "Why?", "How?", "So what?", and "What if?" Now you must take the information given to you and consider carefully what it might really mean, how it relates to other facts or ideas you already possess, what implications it might offer for certain actions or other perspectives, and so forth. And then you must assert certain opinions and interpretations about the information or ideas you have analyzed. When you analyze a text, you move well beyond simply restating the author's language or ideas—you completely repackage them. Analysis requires that you create a claim, stake a position, or offer an interpretation and defend it. Some people will no doubt disagree with your claim or interpretation. In other words, analysis makes you much more vulnerable to criticism. You are presenting a critique of someone else's work or thoughts and, subsequently, your analysis is subject to similar critique.

Surely we encounter this frequently. Think of the last time you heard a clip of a political speech or a presidential press conference. Soon after, commentators from all different perspectives "analyzed" what the words delivered. Even though the literal "what" was the same for all hearers, you could immediately tell from the commentaries or analyses that the "Why?", "So now what?", and "What if?" questions were absolutely not answered in the same way by all listeners. In other words, analyses of the same words or ideas will often vary considerably.

Your critiques may be of a varied phenomenon. For example, you may be asked to analyze raw data from a lab, political editorials, observations in a health care facility, or a scholarly journal article on business ethics. But regardless of the nature of the "information," when asked to analyze it further, you face a serious challenge: Exactly what does it mean to analyze something, and how might you proceed to do it?

One useful approach to analysis is provided by some of the earliest language theorists and philosophers. The ancient rhetoricians Aristotle and Cicero, for example, provided a framework for analyzing discourse that is still very useful. In simplistic terms, that framework consists of three lenses: **ethos, pathos,** and **logos.** Those Greek terms may sound daunting but, in fact, you experience them daily.

Ethos refers to the image of the speaker, which clearly influences the listeners or readers. Whenever you are asked to analyze the language or ideas of another, look closely at the speaker/writer. Is he or she qualified to discuss a given topic? For example, following advice from Tiger Woods on ways to improve your golf swing would no doubt be useful, but his opinions on the appropriateness of standardized testing for college admissions would probably be questionable. Determine how confident you are in the writer's ability—based on reputation, previous works, recommendations of others, level of personal involvement, and so forth—to offer information on this topic. Assess how effectively he or she "delivers" the information. Closely analyzing the attributes of the speaker, especially relative to the particular topic involved, is crucial to conducting a credible analysis.

Pathos refers to the emotional appeals made to influence an audience. Frequently, information is presented to us in a very emotionally charged package that attempts to make us fearful, sympathetic, excited, angry, competitive, etc. These emotional wrappings no doubt affect the way we process the information provided. Therefore, when conducting an analysis, look closely for the emotional appeals present in the argument. They can be highly effective and often are highly appropriate. However, sometimes they might be unethically manipulative. A skillful analyst must always be attentive to emotional appeals and their appropriateness and function in a given text.

Finally, logos refers to the formal arguments, reasons, facts, and logical appeals being presented. In conducting an analysis, first identify the claim(s) asserted and then trace the reasons and evidence provided. Consider the facts offered and the sources of those facts. Remember that even with seemingly hard-and-fast mathematical statistics, the truth can be skewed. Study them carefully. Sometimes there are illogical or fallacious reasons presented to defend a position. Weigh the logic of a given assertion. To do so, ask the hard questions: Is the claim based on a flimsy sample and then projected to apply to a large group? Is it making an assumption that what applies in one set of circumstances automatically applies in all? Is the evidence provided no longer timely and, therefore, no longer valid since newer research has negated the results?

There are other ways to think of the process of analysis without specifically adopting the classical rhetorical lenses just discussed. You may want to use the following guidelines to begin your analysis:

- Scrutinize all raw data; question the use of statistics.
- Itemize the facts and check on their sources and apparent credibility.
- Reiterate the specific reasons provided to support a given position or claim; assess their reasonableness.
- Study the context of the work under analysis; determine if there is an expressed or implied perspective or agenda and assess its appropriateness.
- Consider the audience being addressed.
- Establish the overall purpose of the work. For example, is it largely informative? Personally and/or emotionally expressive? Entertaining? Intentionally persuasive? And then determine how effectively it meets that purpose.
- Question the authenticity of the lab conditions or the publication criteria.
- Uncover faulty reasoning. For example, if you are analyzing a speech or a written document, ask yourself if the author is basing his or her statements on broad generalizations or on illogical connections between ideas and is assuming that one thing causes something else when, in reality, they are unrelated.

While some of these same criteria will be applicable to all situations, clearly some things are discipline specific. Similarly, analysis will appear in different formats depending upon disciplinary context. Sometimes, as in a laboratory or scientific report, your analysis will be specifically labeled "Analysis or Discussion Section." For example, read this section from the student-written psychology research report on the effects of viewing a violent film (presented in its entirety in Chapter 3, the section on scientific research reports). The writer, Kathleen Beety, offers the following interpretation or analysis of the data collected in the "Discussion" section of her report:

> Our research supports this principle that any type of extreme arousal will hinder task performance. There are broad implications for the results of this study. Task performance is significantly substandard when subjects are aroused after watching a violent film; hence, the arousal from actually witnessing an act of violence would probably lower task performance as well. Many people such as soldiers in combat or police officers find themselves in occupa-

tions where observing violent acts is an everyday occurrence. Their ability to perform cognitive tasks at the highest and most accurate level is a necessity. Soldiers, police officers, and others in comparable professions must possess the ability to think accurately and quickly; a mistake or misjudgment could cost human lives. Perhaps future research could manipulate acts of violence to determine the long-term effects of daily exposure to acts of violence. The conclusions could be put to use immediately in many real-life settings.

Note that the writer is now stepping back to consider what her "lab" findings might actually mean, trying to determine if there are generalizations that can be drawn, asking if there are implications for other contexts, and so forth.

At other times the analysis will be interwoven throughout an entire paper as the writer comments on research material and defends his or her thesis or claim. Consider two such samples, one on the future of Iraq and the other on the self-image of college women.

The first sample, a paper analyzing the potential for democratization in Iraq, was written by Holly Jackson, an Elmhurst College student, as a final paper for an honors history symposium. Jackson examined more than 20 credible sources to conduct her analysis of the Iraq situation and then to write her research paper. Note the careful analysis in the section below. Here the writer examines relatively recent attempts to democratize countries recouping from destruction (i.e., Japan and Germany) as touchstones for the potential within Iraq:

> In answering this question of whether or not Iraq has the capability to democratize successfully, it is compulsory to research and observe past models of reconstruction and democratization such as Japan and Germany. After World War II, the Japanese were forced to surrender under the Potsdam Conference. Japan was then forced to demilitarize and had to fulfill certain "expectations" such as forming a peaceful and responsible government and ridding itself of "war-potential" industries as they were forbidden (Encyclopedia: Japan *2002*, 5). This occupation stage began immediately under the control of General Douglas MacArthur and eleven nations were involved in supervising all activities of this occupation. Unfortunately, growing tensions between the Soviet Union and Western Nations left the ultimate control in the hands of the United States. Therefore, the United States used the previous modes of government within Japan to build a more democratic government and in 1946 a new constitution was adopted, which then went into effect in 1947.
>
> Proof of Japan's successful democratization can be seen from its weathering of crises in 1997. However, Japan's parliament "approved legislation to allow the government to nationalize failing banks . . ." in 1998 (Encyclopedia: Japan *2002, 7*). The government took this action in response to the past crises in order to avoid any future turmoil or confusion. Through several crises including scandals, earthquakes, and terrorist attacks, Japan has stood strong. Japan's strong industrial base and homogenous population allowed for Japan to democratize very successfully as it had the beginning of the prerequisites needed for this form of government. This industrialization provided Japan with a strong military, a high literacy rate, and a rational economy (Encyclopedia: Japan *2002, 3*).

After World War II Germany provides a second model of democratization as the Allies agreed that it was necessary for them to consider the future of Germany. Two sessions occurred in the spring of 1948 called the Six Power Conference located in London, which "called for convening a national convention to draft a constitution for a German state. . . ." (The Birth of the Federal Republic of Germany *2003, 1*). This convention then led to the Federal Republic of Germany, which had incredible similarities to the United States. The Federal Republic of Germany respected all basic rights and the dignity of the individual. Their constitution, called the Basic Law, promoted principles such as a free market and the implementation of a social security system. Thus, Germany developed a democracy within only a few years and within the devastating conditions that followed World War I and World War II (The Birth of the German Democratic Republic *2002, 1–2*). Through this example, maybe there is hope for Iraq as Germany was in such a horrible economic, social, and political state when democratization was forced upon them. The split between West and East Germany, showing internal separation, also proves that there may be some possibility for Iraq to democratize successfully.

Unfortunately, these are not viable models in comparison to Iraq for several reasons. Both of these countries were culturally and religiously homogeneous unlike the Iraqi people today. Japan and Germany were also somewhat industrialized before their reconstruction and democratization. These exceptions among others prove that these models cannot provide any hope for the future of Iraq, as they are incredibly dissimilar. Furthermore, both were done during the Cold War, when bipolar struggle forced allies to go along with the United States.

In order for Iraq to enter the process of democratization and reconstruction with success, it must begin by meeting several criteria. First, it is necessary to implement culturally-appropriate democratic political institutions, as these will provide some stability and unity. Secondly, a key factor of great importance is meeting the basic humanitarian needs along with infrastructure needs as well. A third necessity requires economic growth as a result of actually industrializing within the country. Along with the third requirement, these economic gains must be equally distributed among the Iraqi people to create order and equality. Another reason for this final necessity is that if the money and power are invested in the hands of so few, it is likely to cause problems not only economically, but politically as well. Given the political fragmentation within Iraq, the political fragmentation between the United States and its allies, and the current economic climate in the United States, the prospects seem dim.

MEETING THE CHALLENGE

Conduct your *own* analysis of Jackson's analysis.

- Summarize the specific details that the writer provides regarding the success of the Japanese and German democratizations.
- Determine the conclusions she draws regarding the potential of Iraq to democratize. Indicate the bases for these conclusions. Be specific about her examples and arguments.
- Formulate your own position on her claim.
- Assess the credibility and effectiveness of this analysis.

Now let's examine another sample of an analytical discussion. This example is a "microethnography" analyzing the confidence levels in academic and social arenas of female college students at Georgetown University. The author, Mary Lenahan, first recounts her extensive field notes, interviewing several female students, and then offers an analysis of her field notes in this section of the paper for her anthropology course. Note how Lenahan provides a succinct analysis in this summary section, which in her paper is preceded by 17 pages of detailed field notes:

For my microethnography studying the culture of Georgetown I set out to discuss how females of my generation perceive the constraints to one's self-confidence in different settings. I found that there was a significant difference between females' self-confidence in academia compared to social situations. I interviewed four girls and included my analysis of their comments. I found that all four of the girls I interviewed were self-assertive in the classroom. But, the same four girls still relied on media images, rather than internal conviction, to provide essential guidelines for their physical bodies. Therefore, female confidence in social settings was volatile and frequently contradictory, unlike in the classroom where it appeared stable.

After asking the four females to define self-confidence I basically came to the understanding that the informants' definitions fit their view of themselves in an academic setting. Anna and Jackie saw it as a belief in one's "capabilities and abilities." Mary said that confidence was the "factual" abilities one is given. In general from these definitions, I found that Georgetown girls were very confident in terms of their intellectual competence. They received positive marks in high school and therefore used and built on that foundation when they entered college. I did not see constraints for females in day-to-day academia. Their academic performance, therefore, is something females consider themselves to be in control of. They have agency, or room to maneuver, to determine their level of success.

Unfortunately, socially girls have not yet come close to breaking through old constraints of society's views. All the girls I spoke with felt it necessary to conform to specific images of the media's TV commercials and magazine covers. They felt that these media images of how women are supposed to look permeated their everyday lives. To all females these images were either inescapable or extremely difficult to overcome. Their body image and looks cannot easily be controlled. Therefore, girls turn to eating and workout disorders, according to Mary, in order to "manipulate and control things that are God's gifts." Perhaps this also answers the question as to why Georgetown females judge each other so critically on their dress, makeup and clothes. Lilly stated it best when she spoke of Georgetown girls, "I think that it's just too hard not to compete with other girls and therefore [I] give into the stereotypes we face every day." Girls are constantly concerned with keeping this playing field level. The females with whom I spoke thought there was a definite, basically unavoidable, standard physical image that authenticated who they were as individuals. According to Lilly, "I think that confidence is based on the fact that if I know somebody has accepted my physical image, I feel more confident allowing them to accept the rest of my personality." They felt that this pressure was uniquely a female pressure. Therefore, I see it as a serious, continuous constraint to females' self-confidence levels. I found males are not the source of the constraint, only an additive to the volatile levels of females' social self-confidence. All of the girls I interviewed judged a large part of their self-confidence on looks and not on actual "abilities" that they claimed to possess. These contradictions lead me to believe that the female ideology of their definition of self-confidence is not reflected in their own personal practices in a social setting

In the end, I was surprised that the females I interviewed did not believe that their self-confidence was restricted or constrained in academia. Despite that good news, it is troubling that media's standard body images are still so important for females' self-confidence levels. But, each day that another female is educated and brought up with supportive family members, peers and advisors, the more stable bases their level of self-confidence will become. In turn, females will have to continue to use their agency in the classroom and link it with determination to escape society's narrow views on female appearance in social settings. It is not necessarily that females don't have agency socially; rather, to me it seems like we fear the lack of control over our rejection or affirmation. Basically, we must realize that to succeed, we may have to accept setbacks.

MEETING THE CHALLENGE

Conduct your *own* analysis of Lenahan's analysis.

- Summarize the specific conclusions that the writer provides regarding college women's self-images.
- Determine the bases of her conclusions. Be specific about her methods and examples.
- Formulate your own position on her claim. Compare/contrast her analytical comments to what you know of the college women in your institution.
- Assess the credibility and effectiveness of this analysis.
- Locate a newspaper or journal article that discusses the self-image of college women and compare its analysis to this one.

Synthesizing

Occasionally in doing academic writing, you will simply be asked to summarize and/or to analyze a single text in conducting research. However, more often than not, you will be expected to analyze numerous texts simultaneously. To do so, you will be utilizing one of the most challenging research skills—**synthesizing.**

When you synthesize, you create something new by combining or blending other entities. The word *synthesis* may call to mind other words. For example, you have probably listened to music on a "synthesizer." That is, you've listened to music created by combining the sounds of other instruments through an instrument that is able to fuse the features of multiple other sources of music. Or perhaps you have created such music yourself. Have you worn clothing made of "synthetic" fabrics, such as nylon or rayon? These fabrics, unlike natural fabrics such as cotton or wool, are produced through a chemical combination and/or procedure that mixes elements of several substances. Perhaps you have created a compound in chemistry lab. If so, you conducted a kind of synthesis, intermingling two distinct substances to create a new substance.

When you combine information from various sources, including your own original ideas, in order to write an academic report of some kind, you will again be creating something new through a process of synthesis. This time you will be merging your own language and ideas with the ideas of others, borrowing their language either as paraphrased content or as direct quotations in order to create an original text of your own. Of course, you must be very careful not to plagiarize by unfairly presenting borrowed terms and ideas as if they were your own. You must cite everything that you borrow according to the rules of an accepted style formats such as MLA, APA, or CSE. In doing so, you will be giving proper credit to the original source and, therefore, legitimately borrowing material from experts— something scholars do all the time.

But a synthesis must not simply gather different source material into one new place. Rather, when you synthesize you should be thinking critically to analyze the sources individually and then to weigh them against each other and against what you already know in order to create something new: a new argument to defend, a new approach to a dilemma, a new explanation of some phenomenon, and so forth, based on your own ideas *and* on your analysis of each source. In other words, a good synthesis will always:

- consider multiple sources, including your own thoughts and opinions;
- reflect thoughtful, critical analysis of each source;
- smoothly integrate the varied sources;
- create an end result that's distinct from any one of the sources evaluated singly; and
- carefully avoid plagiarism by fairly crediting all borrowed material.

Let's look for a moment at when and why you might use a synthesis. A synthesis can be challenging to write, but it really enables you to make a significant contribution as a writer. Your critical reading skills will be tapped and your personal judgments and analysis skills will be challenged in order to produce a worthwhile original text. A synthesis enables you to use different ideas and segments of appropriate texts very creatively. It will be up to you to evaluate the worth of each of your sources in relation to the purpose of your entire project. Every major research project is essentially a synthesis project. It always draws on previous research and attempts to offer something new to the knowledge base of some specific discipline. Sometimes you will be provided with sources and required to synthesize their content in relation to some thesis you are defending in your own paper; sometimes you will need to locate the sources yourself and then synthesize them. The skills necessary for this type of assignment were discussed in the section on information literacy.

There are two basic types of synthesis approaches: One is strictly informational, and the other is argumentative. In an *informative* synthesis, you are interweaving sources' ideas and your own ideas with the intent of providing background information for yourself and your reader(s). You are not seeking to establish sides or persuade an audience to take a particular viewpoint, but rather simply trying to broaden the knowledge base of your audience. In an *argumentative* synthesis, you are fusing sources with the distinct purpose of defending a position in order to argue for a particular stance on an issue. While the intents and end results of these syntheses will vary, a somewhat similar procedure can be adopted for each.

Recognizing its importance to a successful academic career, we need to look closely at how you might proceed to create a synthesis essay or to use synthesis skills within a larger project. In essence, you must begin by drawing on the summary and analysis skills discussed earlier in this chapter. In order to synthesize material, you must first "get the gist" of your resources (i.e., be able to summarize the main points) and then analyze them critically to determine the nature of their arguments, their contribution(s) to your larger project, and their relationships to each other. For example, are the sources presenting similar contentions, or are they presenting conflicting information that draws on different theories or data but still offers reliable and sufficient evidence for their arguments?

Here's what a sample synthesis procedure for interweaving four sources might look like:

- Carefully reread the four texts involved, taking notes on their main points. Be sure that you clearly understand the material you are synthesizing.
- Reflect upon and record any personal connections triggered by the readings. In other words, do the readings remind you of anything you've read previously for this or any other class? Do the readings relate to current events or discussions in the news, in spirit if not in content?
- Look for some pattern that emerges after reviewing all of the above. For example, do the authors repeat any of the major points? Do they use similar types of arguments for support? Do they offer comparable examples? Was their research done at different time periods or in different locations? If so, how have those factors seemed to affect their conclusions, and do you need to point that out in your discussion?
- Formulate a central "organizing idea" that emerges from your notes. (This will become the thesis for your report or at least for the section of a larger report in which you are using details from these resources. Remember that a thesis is

essentially the conclusion that you have arrived at and are now defending through the development of your paper.)

- Return to your sources and take notes on specific details that you can use to support and explain your organizing idea.
- Sketch a tentative outline for yourself that may well change as you proceed since writing always triggers new ideas. Don't be afraid to alter it as you go.
- Include additional information from personal experiences and previous readings, if appropriate to your project.
- Draft the body of your paper. Be sure to cite your references (using quotation marks and page numbers where appropriate) within the body of the paper, following designated documentation format.
- Read over the draft of the body and create a strong introduction that will engage the reader's attention, explain the kind of research you are drawing upon, and indicate the organizing idea (the thesis) that you will be developing.
- Develop a concluding paragraph that ties together your main points, but feel free to suggest an unanswered question for further consideration.

In an argument synthesis, you will pay greater attention to persuasive strategies such as using repetition effectively, arousing emotions within your audience, emphasizing your credibility as the speaker, etc. You will then highlight specific reasons for your beliefs, developing strong arguments for your position and usually considering and refuting counterarguments to your position. In doing so, you can organize your synthesis argument in one of two patterns: 1) the traditional argument-counterargument-argument pattern or 2) the comparison-contrast pattern (organized by sources or criteria).

Let's take a close look at a brief section of a position paper (included in its entirety in the section on stance or position papers in Chapter 3 of this textbook) to see how the author, René Rimelspach, effectively synthesizes materials from multiple texts.

Politics in the United States is largely based on an intricate reward system, by which women are often penalized. As Representative Marcy Kaptur states, "Despite the increase in numbers, it is still unusual for women in Congress to achieve leadership positions" (7). It is by these very positions that are denied to women that politicians are rewarded for their service. In another example, researchers state, "Women also have difficulty securing funds and other resources from the more than 3,700 Political Action Committees operating in the United States" (Renzetti 247). PAC money towards re-election campaigns is another reward that women are often denied. Finally, it is sad to say that a glitzy social life is often a reward for serving a life in politics. Female politicians, especially those who are based in Washington, D.C., are often excluded from social functions and men-only clubs that their male counterparts are privileged to attend and belong to. Denying female politicians some of the perks of the job is another method that is used to exclude them from the institution.

This is not to say that women are not involved in politics at all; on the contrary, women are indeed intricately involved in politics. However, it appears that the status accorded them and the roles they play are highly clustered around the lower end of the political scene. As Bella Abzug once stated, "We are allowed to do most of the drudgery and the dirty work and the detail work of politics. I would venture to say that there is no political party in the United States that could survive were it not for the fact that women are holding up those structures on their backs" (Schneir 395). As another researcher observes, "Women have long served as political 'footsoldiers': canvassing for votes door-to-door or by phone, stuffing envelopes, distributing campaign literature, and so on" (Renzetti 242). In fact, women run most of the day-to-day operation of the political machine; they are merely excluded from the top positions. This is not to say that women have not been making gains; according to *The New York Times,* ten new women were elected to the House of Representatives in this past election. In addition, Jean Shaheen was elected as governor of New Hampshire, making her the second female governor now serving. However, because of the fact that many prominent female politicians retired this year, this past election resulted in a net gain of only two women in the House and one in the Senate (*N.Y. Times* A-b). At this rate of increase of women in Congress, it will take over 400 years to reach political parity along gender lines in the United States (Renzetti 249). This again illustrates the fact that women are far from equally represented on the political scene. In addition, where women do serve in politics, they tend to be clustered around lesser-powered positions.

Note in the student-written passage above that the author interweaves ideas from four distinct sources to help support her contention that women do not have equal access to the reward system of the world of politics, and, in fact, that their involvement is often confined to subordinate, less powerful positions. Drawing upon the ideas of four experts (Kaptur, *The New York Times,* Schneir, and Renzetti), she presents examples and details to support her position and further strengthens her case with each additional resource. Notice that the direct quotations are all cited in MLA format, giving appropriate credit to the sources and, thus, avoiding plagiarism.

MEETING THE CHALLENGE

Practice synthesizing skills.

• Select any *three* readings from Chapter 5.
• Read them carefully and prepare brief summaries for yourself to ensure that you understand the basic content and position of each author.
• Consider your own views on the topic and make notes on your ideas.
• Formulate a strong thesis that will be the controlling point in your essay.
• Then write a three-to-four-page paper in which you synthesize your ideas with some of the ideas of the three readings.
• Receive feedback from a writing partner and provide feedback to him/her.
• Revise your paper following your discussion.

DOCUMENTING SOURCES IN MLA, APA, CSE, AND TURABIAN FORMATS

While the majority of your academic writing will be your own, it will often be necessary to incorporate into your papers the language and ideas of other writers for several different reasons: Sometimes you will need to consult the texts of experts in various fields in order to expand your understanding of a particular topic; sometimes you will want to survey the opinions of other writers on your topic to determine compliance or variance of your opinion; sometimes you will be writing entirely in response to another text, which you will need to quote sporadically in order to authenticate your response; and so forth.

Professional writers and scholars always interact with each other's texts. They borrow ideas; they agree and disagree; they expand upon or reject previously published works. This is the process of making knowledge and making meaning of that knowledge. That exchange is not only perfectly legitimate; it is also crucial to your work as an academic writer. However, you must remember to give credit to those with whom you are interacting. In other words, whenever you borrow the language or ideas of another individual, you must credit him or her by documenting the work as one of your sources. If you fail to do so, you will be committing plagiarism—a serious ethical violation.

There are two basic types of documentation that you as an academic writer need to recognize: internal and external. Internal documentation is an indication of outside sources given within the body of your text. It occurs in one of three forms:

1. Parenthetical expressions—references to the sources are presented in an abbreviated form within parentheses directly after the point of usage in your text;
2. Footnotes—references are initially indicated at the point of usage, most often with a superscript numeral, and then abbreviated source information is provided at the bottom (foot) of the page;
3. Endnotes—references are initially indicated at the point of usage, with a superscript numeral or some equivalent indicator, and then source information is provided in a list of numbered statements at the very end of the text.

External documentation refers to the bibliography, the formal list of references presented at the end of your text.

Documentation formats (for both internal and external citations) are numerous. They are extremely structured guidelines for formatting and documenting information within a text that vary considerably from one system to another. Different disciplines generally agree upon one specific documentation style for all publications within their field although some allow more variance than others.

Though there are approximately two dozen style manuals recognized by different disciplines, only a few are used widely. This section will present features of *four* of the most widely used documentation styles: MLA, APA, CSE, and Turabian. MLA, an acronym for the Modern Language Association, is widely used in the fine arts and humanities fields such as literature, rhetoric, English and foreign languages, art history, and philosophy. APA, an acronym for the American Psychological Association, is most often used by the social sciences, including psychology and sometimes anthropology (though that is a field with wide variance), and by education and business. CSE, an acronym for the Council of Scientific Editors (formerly the Council of Biological Editors), is used by biologists as well as some other scientists, though chemistry, for example, has its own system referred to as ACS, an acronym for the American Chemical Society. Turabian is a shorthand reference to the author of the system, Kate L. Turabian, and is a method commonly used by historians and advocated by some secondary schools as the system to be used across all fields. Turabian is closely tied to another popular system that's found in the *Chicago Manual of Style.*

Be aware that all of these systems have many complex variations for citing specific types of sources. There are also detailed instructions for formatting your overall paper and for presenting different types of technical material such as graphs and charts. For information that's more specific than what is available here: 1) Consult the reference librarian at your college or university; 2) consult the printed reference guide of each of these style systems, available at your library reference desk; and/or 3) consult some of the useful, though limited as well, reference guides placed online by numerous university libraries such as: http://www.lib.duke.edu/libguide/citing.htm or http://writing.colostate.edu/references/ or www.wisc.edu/writing/Handbook or http://www.pace.edu/library/pages/instruct/guides.

Internal Documentation by Style System

MLA   The Modern Language Association uses a system of parenthetical citation to reference sources used within a text. These parenthetical expressions are used at the point of any direct quotation as well as to indicate the paraphrasing of an author's ideas and theories. The author and the page number are generally indicated within parentheses in the following format: (Smith 10). (Notice that there is no "p." before the number or a comma between the name and page number.) If the author is already referenced within the sentence, then only a page number is necessary. For example:

> According to Smith's interpretation, author Edith Wharton writes in a deceptively simple style "to weave a complex tapestry of character motivation" (10).

If more than one work by the same author is cited within a given text, indicate which work is being quoted or paraphrased by including an abbreviated version of the title following the author's last name. For example, the parenthetical expression would state: (Smith, "Understanding Wharton's" 10).

APA   The American Psychological Association also uses a system of parenthetical citation to reference sources used within a text. These parenthetical expressions are used at the point of any direct quotation as well as to indicate the paraphrasing of an author's ideas and theories. The author, the year of publication, and the page number (indicated by "p.") generally appear within parentheses in the following format: (Smith, 2003, p. 10). If the author is already referenced within the sentence, then only the year is necessary. For example:

> According to Smith's interpretation, author Edith Wharton writes in a deceptively simple style "to weave a complex tapestry of character motivation" (2003, p. 10).

If the work is being paraphrased rather than specifically quoted, no page number reference is necessary (only the year). If more than one work by the same author is cited within a given text, ordinarily the date will indicate which work is being referenced. However, in the event that you have two different works by the same author that are both published in the same year, add a letter suffix to the date to distinguish them. For example, the parenthetical expression would be: (Smith, 2003a, p. 10).

CSE (formerly CBE)

CSE style recognizes *two* different ways to fulfill internal documentation: the citation-sequence method and the name-year system. With the citation-sequence method of documentation, a superscript numeral is assigned to every reference at the point of the first mention of it in your text. Those numbers then correspond to a numerically sequenced list of references that appears at the end of the text. Thus, the internal citation will simply be a footnote number. For example:

> The data suggest that additional experimentation needs to be conducted before any definitive conclusion can be reached.[1]

The name-date documentation system, also recognized by CSE, is somewhat similar to APA style. In general, you state the author's last name and the date of publication in parentheses with no comma between them. Thus, the sentence might read:

> The study (Smith 2003) concludes that global warming is an increasing threat.

If the name of the author appears elsewhere in the sentence, simply provide the year of publication. If an exact quotation is cited, a page number is also needed. Then the parenthetical reference will look like this: (Smith 2003, p 25). Notice that there is a comma only between the publication year and the page number, not between the author and the date, and that the page number is signaled by a "p" without a period after it.

Turabian

Turabian style similarly recognizes *two* different ways to provide internal documentation: the humanities style (or note system) and the author-date system. The humanities style is signaled by the use of superscript numerals for either footnotes or endnotes where complete bibliographic material is provided. (Sometimes additional substantive information is also provided within these footnotes or endnotes.) At any rate, within the text with this system, only a footnote appears, as in the citation-sequence sample of CSE above. The author-date system, also recognized by Turabian, is again somewhat similar to APA style. In general, you state the author's last name and the date of publication in parentheses with no comma between them. Thus, the sentence might read:

> The study (Smith 2003) concludes that global warming is an increasing threat.

If the name of the author is clearly evident, simply provide the year of publication. If multiple works by the same author published in the same year are used as resources for your project, add a letter suffix to the date to distinguish them. For example, the parenthetical expression would state: (Smith 2003a). For exact quotations, page numbers are also provided, with no "p" preceding it. For example, your sentence might read:

> "Readings of the slave narratives provide invaluable insights into a tragic chapter of American history" (Smith 2003, 16).

External Documentation by Style System

The tables below provide samples of reference entries as they would appear in the formal bibliography, the list of sources at the end of a text. Ordinarily, the list is assembled alphabetically according to the first word appearing in the entry, usually the author's last name. However, in some scientific systems, the entries are arranged numerically according to the order in which the sources are cited within the text. Note that in MLA format, this list is called "Works Cited"; in APA it is titled "References"; in CSE it is titled "References"; and in Turabian it may be titled "Works Cited," "References," or "Literature Cited." However, some disciplines, most notably history, use the Turabian note system only, and, therefore, references appear as footnotes (with complete bibliographic information) at the bottom of each page rather than in an assembled list at the end of the text.

Book with a Single Author	Sample Entry
MLA	Gaines, Ernest J. The Autobiography of Miss Jane Pittman. New York: Bantam Books, 1971.
APA	Gaines, E. J. (1971). *The Autobiography of Miss Jane Pittman*. New York: Bantam Books.
CSE	Gaines E. 1971. The autobiography of Miss Jane Pittman. New York: Bantam Books. 259 p.
Turabian	Gaines, Ernest J. *The Autobiography of Miss Jane Pittman*. New York: Bantam Books, 1971.

Book with Two Authors	Sample Entry
MLA	Fishman, Stephen, and Lucille McCarthy. John Dewey and the Challenge of Classroom Practice. New York: Teachers College Press, 1998.
APA	Fishman, S., & McCarthy, L. (1998). *John Dewey and the challenge of classroom practice*. New York: Teachers College Press.
CSE	Fishman S, McCarthy L. 1998. John Dewey and the challenge of classroom practice. New York: Teachers College Press. 259 p.
Turabian	Fishman, Stephen, and Lucille McCarthy. *John Dewey and the Challenge of Classroom Practice*. New York: Teachers College Press, 1998.

Section of a Book/Entry Within an Anthology	**Sample Entry**
MLA	Addams, Jane. "Twenty Years at Hull House." <u>Written By Herself: Autobiographies of American Women: An Anthology</u>. Ed. Jill Ker Conway. New York: Vintage Books, 1992. 506–25.
APA	Addams, J. (1992). Twenty years at Hull House. In J. K. Conway (Ed.), *Written by herself: Autobiographies of American women: An anthology* (pp. 506–525). New York: Vintage Books.
CSE	Addams, J. 1992. Twenty years at Hull House. In: Conway JK, editor. Written by herself: Autobiographies of American women: An anthology. New York: Vintage Books. p. 506–525.
Turabian	Addams, Jane. "Twenty Years at Hull House." In *Written By Herself: Autobiographies of American Women: An Anthology*, ed. Jill Ker Conway, 506–25. New York: Vintage Books, 1992.

Print Magazine	**Sample Entry**
MLA	Newman, Christine. "A Modern Maverick." <u>Chicago</u> August 2003: 113–19.
APA	Newman, C. (2003, August). A modern maverick. *Chicago, 52*(8), 113–119.
CSE	Newman, C. A modern maverick. Chicago 2003 Aug: 113–119.
Turabian	Newman, Christine. "A Modern Maverick." *Chicago*, August 2003, 113–19.

Print Academic Journal	**Sample Entry**
MLA	Sheridan-Rabideau, Mary. "The Stuff That Myths Are Made Of: Myth Building as Social Action." <u>Written Communication</u> 18.4 (Oct. 2001): 440–69.
APA	Sheridan-Rabideau, M. (2001). The stuff that myths are made of: Myth building as social action. *Written Communication, 18*(4), 440–469.
CSE	Sheridan-Rabideau M. 2001. The stuff that myths are made of: Myth building as social action. Wr Comm 18(4): 440–469.
Turabian	Sheridan-Rabideau, Mary. "The Stuff That Myths Are Made Of: Myth Building as Social Action." *Written Communication* 18, no. 4 (October 2001): 440–69.

Web Site	Sample Entry
MLA	<u>Biographical Information About Edith Wharton</u>. 20 Sept. 2002. The Edith Wharton Society. 18 Oct. 2003 <http:guweb2.gonzaga.edu/faculty/campbell/wharton>.
APA	The Edith Wharton Society. (2002, September 20). *Biographical information about Edith Wharton*. Retrieved October 18, 2003, from http:guweb2.gonzaga.edu/faculty/campbell/wharton
CSE	Biographical Information About Edith Wharton. [Internet]. Spokane (WA): The Edith Wharton Society; [updated 2002 September 20, cited 2003 October 18]. Available from: <http:guweb2.gonzaga.edu/faculty/campbell/wharton>.
Turabian	(No sample is provided in the most recent edition of the Turabian *Manual for Writers*: The system often uses the form recommended by the *Chicago Manual of Style*, to which it is closely related.)

Responding to Texts

This section of the textbook provides you with an opportunity to practice the reading, writing, and researching skills discussed previously. Four different thematic units, each addressing a different topic of interest to today's college students, are included. Topics are varied: 1) Music and the College Experience, 2) Work in America, 3) Perceptions of America, and 4) The Internet: Responsibilities, Rights, Results. These units consist primarily of multiple readings on the same topic, each representing a different genre of writing and/or a different academic discipline. The units also include visuals for your response. You'll quickly notice the variety of treatments of the same topic across those genres and disciplines.

To assist you in understanding and extending the ideas explored within the readings, two types of questions are included at the end of each text. Some invite you to succinctly reiterate the essence of the information provided, while others encourage you to interpret the information and then to extend it by connecting it with previous experiences. Following each visual, there is a prompt inviting further exploration as well. At the end of each unit, an extensive list of writing activities is suggested to enable you to practice writing some of the various genres examined earlier in the textbook. Study the samples carefully before you attempt to draft the particular genre involved, since the purposes, priorities, features, and formats vary considerably, as you've seen.

MUSIC AND THE COLLEGE EXPERIENCE

Music plays a central role in the lives of most college students. Researchers estimate that students spend four to five hours each day listening to music and/or watching music videos. That estimate might be conservative for those who tend to do nearly everything with music in the background.

Music is important as a source of entertainment or relaxation, but it is actually much more than that for most college students. It frequently defines their interests, their pastimes, their outlet for spending money, even their choice of friends. Many young people gravitate to particular groups of friends based upon favorite music group preferences, for instance.

The readings in this chapter explore from a variety of perspectives the role of music in the lives of college students. Scholars have studied this phenomenon as a sociological and cultural issue, as an economic issue, and even as a moral issue. The readings included here provide a range of perspectives as to the significance and influence of music in the lives of young people today. They also represent a variety of academic disciplines including sociology, philosophy, journalism, and communications. Note that there is also a range of different academic genres of writing including a scholarly research study, a newspaper editorial, and a book review. You will see how the length, language, tone, and even visual presentation of the content vary throughout these genres. Notice also the differences in documentation styles and the inclusion or exclusion of reference. In each case the audience and the purpose of the text dictate a variety of genre choices.

Reading 1

This reading appeared in New York Times Upfront, *a well-written contemporary magazine for teens. This article is largely an opinion piece on the relationship between youth culture and rock music that also offers an interesting and entertaining "brief" history of the rock scene. Since this text is geared to a general audience and is not intended as a scholarly publication, you will notice the absence of many conventions of strictly academic genres such as cross-references, footnotes, and a reference list at the end. Conversely, note the inclusion of a less technical vocabulary, numerous short paragraphs, and attention-getting devices such as the abbreviated all-cap headlines within the article.*

"Those Crazy Rockin' Teenagers"

Sean McCollum

1   In the 1950s, a new creature appeared on the American cultural scene: the teen.

2   The police decided they had to act. Connecticut adolescents were going wild at dance parties with a new kind of music. So Bridgeport's police superintendent banned such events. The New York Times reported his explanation:

3   "Recently there was real trouble and the authorities outlawed this 'rock 'n' roll' business. I think the musicians start it with their capers. The kids take it up and pretty soon the whole thing is out of hand."

4   The year was 1955. No crime was reported, but to adults something indeed was out of hand: For the first time, America's teenagers were claiming a new culture all their own.

Today, the nation's 32 million teens—the biggest group of teens ever—are recog- [5]
nized as a giant market that spends more than $100 billion a year on hip-hop music,
gross-out movies, instant messaging, and the like. But while there have always been
people aged 13–19, they haven't always been a cultural, social, and economic world
unto themselves. That world came into full flower in the 1950s, the decade that gave
us the wild, moody, rebellious, soulful, and idealistic creature we know as the
American teenager.

For most of U.S. history, young people were either treated as children or set to [6]
work as apprentices learning adult jobs or domestic skills. As late as 1890, only 6 percent of children went to high school. But during the Great Depression in the 1930s,
Congress passed laws limiting most jobs to adults. By 1940, two-thirds of Americans
ages 14 to 16 attended school.

With the prevalence of high school came the increasing recognition of adoles- [7]
cence as a distinct phase of existence. In the 1940s, the press began using the word
"teen-ager," and these teens began to adopt their own styles of dress. So many girls
wore white rolled anklets called bobby socks that they became known as "bobby-soxers." Teens also began to choose their own music. Many bobby-soxers were among
the 10,000 people who blocked traffic in New York City on October 12, 1944, trying
to get into the Paramount Theater to hear a skinny young crooner named Frank
Sinatra. Sinatra didn't belong to teens alone, but the frenzy he created was a taste of
things to come.

In the 1950s, America was prosperous, at peace, and rapidly growing. The new [8]
medium of television was linking the nation's households, and housing developments
were sprouting like weeds, in the nation's suburbs. But it was a New York City kid in
the pages of a book who became one of the decade's first teen icons. Holden Caulfield,
hero of J. D. Salinger's 1951 novel The Catcher in the Rye, was a literary embodiment
of teenage angst and alienation that teens took to heart. He was a sensitive, 16-year-
old screwup, and his first-person story told of a world full of "phonies"—like the old
history teacher he visits as he flunks out of another in a series of prep schools:

BE REALLY REFRESHED. . . . DRIVE-IN FOR COKE! [9]

"Do you feel absolutely no concern for your future, bay?" [10]

"Oh, I feel some concern for my future, all rot. Sure. Sure I do." I thought about it [11]
for a minute. "But not too much, not too much, I guess."

"You will," old Spencer said. "You will, bay. You will when it's too late." [12]

I didn't like hearing him say that. It made me sound dead or something. It was [13]
very depressing.

"They think he's a cool guy, so they imitate his casual talk and nonchalant atti- [14]
tude," wrote one young critic about the teen attraction to Holden. But another young
antihero soon captivated millions of teens. In 1955, actor James Dean lit up movie
screens in East of Eden playing a tormented youth vying with his brother for his father's affections.

Dean's virile but vulnerable screen image sent girls into a swoon—and boys to the [15]
bathroom mirror to work on their slicked-back hair and soulful looks. When he
screamed "You're tearing me apart!" to his doting but bickering parents in the film
Rebel Without a Cause, a whole generation knew just what he meant.

16   By then, Dean's screen presence had extra poignancy. Rebel included a drag-racing scene, and in a promotional trailer made for the film, Dean, an off-screen race-car enthusiast, had warned America's teens that fast driving was for the racetrack, not the highway. "Take it easy driving," he had joked. "The life you might save might be mine."

17   But on September 30, 1955, less than a month before the release of Rebel, James Dean was killed when he crashed his Porsche on a California highway. He was 24. He would forever be remembered for the teens he played in his three starring roles; no one would ever see him grow old. One teenage boy mourned: "Something in us that is being sat on by convention and held down was, in Dean, free for all the world to see."

18   LOVING HIM TENDER: The bedroom walls of teenager Ruby Hoff in Atlantic City, N.J., in 1957 are a shrine to her king: Elvis.

19   ROCK ON: The fans became the stars as teens boogied around the dance floor on the afternoon TV hit American Bandstand, broadcast from Philadelphia. In the eye of the storm: ageless host Dick Clark.

20   IMAGE OF COOL: Teens envied actor James Dean's glamour—but not his fate. By the time his film Giant hit theaters, Dean was dead at 24.

21   Dean's popularity helped awaken Hollywood to the huge potential of the teen movie-going market. Ever since, whole genres of films have been aimed at teens. But it was in music that the new teenage cultural revolution really shook the rafters.

22   It started with rhythm and blues (R&B), music with a heavy beat that was popular in the African-American community. In 1951, Alan Freed, a Cleveland disc jockey, heard that a friend's black-oriented record store was full of white teens dancing to R&B records. Freed started playing those tunes on his radio show and emceeing live concerts. Then a white group with a country-music background, Bill Haley and the Comets, began to record R&B songs. "Rock Around the Clock" had modest sales when it was released in 1954, but a follow-up, "Shake, Rattle, and Roll," hit the Top 10. And in 1955, when "Clock" was re-released and featured in the film Blackboard Jungle, it hit No. 1 and set teens around the world dancing in movie-theater aisles.

23   Rock 'n' roll, as Freed dubbed the new music, spread like wildfire—and made record sales soar. By 1958, teens were buying 70 percent of the records sold in the U.S. Rock 'n' roll transformed song lyrics overnight from the tame sentimentality of "How much is that doggie in the window?" (Patti Page, 1953) to the anarchic zaniness of "A wop-bop-a-loo-bop-a-wop-bam—boom!" (Little Richard, 1955).

24   Then came the King. When the golden-voiced, pompadoured Elvis Presley sang "Hound Dog" on The Ed Sullivan Show in September 1956, the cameras stayed above the waist so viewers wouldn't see the scandalous way he swiveled his hips.

25   Rock was loud, rhythmic, and full of energy. And best of all, adults didn't get it. FBI Director J. Edgar Hoover called the new music "a corrupting influence," and the Times quoted Joost A. M. Meerlo, a Columbia University psychiatrist, who compared rock-inspired dancing to the nervous malady known as Saint Vitus' dance. Meerlo went on:

> Rock 'n' roll is a sign of depersonalization of the individual, of ecstatic veneration of mental decline and passivity. If we cannot stem the tide with its waves of rhythmic narcosis [stupor] and of future waves of vicarious craze, we are preparing our own downfall in the midst of pandemic [widespread] funeral dances.

Across the country, defenders of virtue tried to ban rock and held public record-   26
burnings, only cementing its place as the soundtrack of teen rebellion.

The rockin'-and-rollin' 16-year-olds paving the way to hell in 1957 are now 60. Their   27
heroes have been supplanted again and again by those of new waves of adolescents—
including the baby boomers of the 1960s, who embraced "flower power" and crusaded
against a war in Vietnam. But the teen subculture born in the 1950s lives on, and is
constantly renewed. Teens still rebel, still cling to ideals, and still savor the power of
their icons to baffle the unhip. What, for instance, would Meerlo say about Eminem?

Things are out of hand, all right, and they seem likely to stay that way.   28

UNDERSTANDING THE AUTHOR'S IDEAS

1. When, why, and how was the American teen created?
2. What major events does McCollum select to mark the development of the current popular music culture?
3. Explain the importance of James Dean to the rock music culture.
4. Discuss the initial reactions of civic leaders and scholars to rock music.

EXPLORING YOUR OWN IDEAS

1. Explore the "subtext" of McCollum's article. Besides recounting various landmarks of rock music history, what do you think he is really saying about teens and popular music?
2. Do you think that rock music poses a threat to intergenerational relations? To cultural development? Why or why not?
3. Discuss the irony of James Dean's untimely death. How is he simultaneously a symbol of freedom and constraints?
4. Look closely at the genre features of this piece. Describe them and discuss their relationship to the intended audience and the author's apparent purpose.

Reading 2

This somewhat challenging reading is an excerpt from the book-length scholarly study entitled Popular Music and Youth Culture: Music, Identity, and Place *by British scholar Andy Bennett. This study draws upon and contributes to research in the academic fields of sociology, anthropology, music history, cultural studies, and media studies. In his introduction to the book, Bennett explains that his primary methodologies included conducting field research as a "participant observer," involving himself in the youth music scene, and conducting numerous interviews and focus groups. Of course, he also read and analyzed countless written texts of previous researchers.*

In this text, the author is primarily addressing other researchers. In fact, his study would be considered a contribution to the "scholarly conversation" taking place among social scientists who are pursuing similar research. Consequently, that primary audience dictates his genre choices. You will notice the extensive use of footnotes, cross-references, in depth discussion of theoretical concerns, and so forth. Bennett provides some important insights into the relationships between popular music and youth culture for fellow scholars as well as for less serious readers like ourselves.

(Note that the British spelling of several terms throughout this text is slightly different from the American spelling.)

"Youth Culture and Popular Music"

Andy Bennett

Chapter 2

1   In many different parts of the world popular music is a primary, if not *the* primary, leisure resource for young people. Popular music features in young people's lives in a variety of different ways and in a diverse range of contexts. From nightclubs, live concerts, cinema films and TV commercials to what Japanese music theorist Hosokawa refers to as the 'autonomous and mobile' form of listening facilitated through the invention of the personal stereo, for a great many young people, popular music is an omnipresent aspect of their day to day existence (1984, p. 166). The significance of popular music as an aspect of youth culture can be traced back to the advent of rock 'n' roll in the early 1950s. Prior to rock 'n' roll popular music comprised, to use Middleton's description, 'a relatively narrow stylistic spread, hounded by theatre song on the one side, novelty items deriving from music hall and vaudeville on the other, with Tin Pan Alley songs, Hollywood hits and crooners in between' (1990, p. 14). With the arrival of rock 'n' roll, however, not only did the stylistic direction of popular music radically alter but it also acquired a distinctly youth-orientated and oppositional stance. This manifested itself during 1956 with the release of *Rock Around the Clock,* a feature film scripted around live performances by artists of the day such as Bill Haley and the Comets, the Platters and Tony Martinez (Denisoff and Romanowski: 1991). Early screenings of the film in the US and Britain resulted in unruly behaviour in cinemas as young audiences danced in the aisles and ripped out seats (Street: 1992, p. 304). Across Europe *Rock Around the Clock* sparked off reactions that were, in some cases, even more extreme than those witnessed in Britain and the US. In the West German city of Hamburg cars were overturned and shop fronts and street signs were vandalised by young people as police used water cannons in an attempt to quell the unrest (Krüger: 1983). In Holland, where *Rock Around the Clock* was banned in several major cities, 'young people took to the streets to demonstrate for their right to see the film' (Mutsaers: 1990, p. 307).

2   If rock 'n' roll music and the sensibilities that it had apparently inspired were incomprehensible to the parent culture, then the development of subsequent genres, such as psychedelia, punk and, more recently, acid house, has continued to drive a wedge between the generations and to mark off youth from the parent culture ever

more dramatically. The cultural impact of post-war popular music on young people has also posed a series of questions for popular music theorists. Indeed, the continuing centrality of popular music in youth culture since the 1950s has underlain much of the theoretical debate about how to approach the study of popular music and the various stylistic sensibilities to which it has given rise. In this chapter, I want to both examine and critically assess some of the theoretical approaches that have been put forward in an attempt to explain popular music's socio-cultural significance for youth. I will begin by considering the contrasting views of Adorno and Benjamin, whose work on mass culture during the first part of the twentieth century continues to inform much of the research on popular music in the related fields of sociology, cultural and media studies. This will be followed by a review of some of the most important contemporary popular music studies with particular reference to the ways in which these studies have attempted to deal with what continues to be a highly problematic issue, that is, how to reconcile popular music's position in the marketplace with its function as a potentially counter-hegemonic cultural resource. In addition to drawing upon examples from Britain and the US, I will also consider aspects of music production and consumption in Holland, Germany, Japan and Australia. Similarly, the chapter will also look at how popular music has featured in key moments of social change in countries such as Russia, China and the former East Germany.

Popular music and the work of Adorno and Benjamin

Much of the current debate concerning the socio-cultural significance of popular music derives directly from a polemical discussion on the nature of mass culture between Adorno and Benjamin during the 1920s and early 1930s. In order to properly understand the ideas of Adorno and Benjamin it is necessary to briefly relate their work back to the theoretical tradition with which it is most strongly associated, the mass cultural critique of the Frankfurt School. Founded during the 1920s, the Frankfurt School, whose leading theorists also included Horkheimer, Marcuse and Habermas, was chiefly concerned to study the negative social effects that, they argued, were produced as a consequence of modern society's increasing reliance upon mass cultural commodities. According to the Frankfurt School, the mass cultural profile of modern society signalled the fate of individual autonomy, this being steadily replaced by a 'scientific-technological rationality' (Bottomore: 1984, p. 41). The implication here is that with the rise of mass culture the individual is denied any possibility of creative participation in leisure activities and becomes simply a cultural 'dupe'. Thus, as MacDonald argues, expounding a view clearly inspired by the Frankfurt School's approach: 'Mass Culture [sic] is imposed from above. It is fabricated by technicians hired by businessmen; its audiences are passive consumers, their participation limited to the choice between buying and not buying' (1953, p. 60).

3

Each of the Frankfurt School theorists varied in their account of the way in which mass culture served to suppress individual autonomy. Adorno was particularly concerned with the fetishising effects of mass culture upon art. In the case of music, argued Adorno, because it 'had been invaded by the capitalist ethos, its fetishisation was almost total' (Jay: 1973, p. 190). At the centre of Adorno's argument lies a distinction between serious 'art' music and commercial 'pop' music. The social reception of music, he suggests, is essentially pre-programmed, musical composition and

4

production following precise guidelines which are calculated to produce a specific and uniform response among listeners. However, according to Adorno, in the case of art music, meaning becomes apparent to the listener only after a considerable degree of listening skill has been applied, this being essential if the essence of a given musical piece, its 'concrete totality', is to be properly understood (Adorno: 1941, p. 303). In the case of popular music, however, no such listening skill is necessary as, according to Adorno:

> The composition hears for the listener . . . Not only does it not require effort to follow its concrete stream; it actually gives him models under which anything concrete still remaining may be subsumed. The schematic build up dictates the way in which he must listen while, at the same time, it makes any effort in listening unnecessary. Popular music is 'pre-digested' in a way strongly resembling the fad of 'digests' of printed material (ibid., p. 306).

5   Adorno goes further in his critique of popular music, suggesting that it also plays a role in maintaining the social relations of capitalist production. According to Adorno, popular music does this in two main ways. First, it acts as a form of distraction, in unison with other forms of mass-produced leisure, ensuring that working-class consumers remain oblivious to the mechanisms of oppression that underpin the capitalist mode of production. Second, the 'patterned and pre-digested' nature of the music offers relief 'from both boredom and effort simultaneously' with the result that periods of leisure can be tailored to provide maximum relaxation and refreshment for the workforce (ibid.).

6   Adorno's work poses a number of problems for contemporary theorists seeking to explain the cultural impact of popular music since the post-Second World War period. In particular, by concentrating on the alleged regulating and standardising effects of popular music, Adorno closes off any possibility of social actors themselves playing a part in determining the meaning and significance of popular music genres and texts. Consequently, the work of Adorno has been taken to task on a number of occasions. Middleton, for example, argues that 'the reception of cultural products cannot, as Adorno contends, be taken to represent a direct appropriation of the consumer into a pre-given framework but is *mediated* by other, varied interpretative assumptions associated with other social institutions and values' (1990, p. 60). Similarly, Frith argues that Adorno's theory of consumption reduces 'a complex social process to a simple psychological effect' (1983, p. 57). In attempting to rethink Adorno's interpretation of the effects of mass culture upon the individual, some theorists have turned to the work of Benjamin. In contrast to Adorno, Benjamin argues that 'technological reproduction gives back to humanity that capacity for experience which technological *production* threatens to take away' (Buck-Morss: 1989, p. 268). Although none of Benjamin's work focused upon music as such, his ideas can be easily applied to the study of music, especially mechanically reproduced music. A particularly effective demonstration of this is offered by Middleton, who compares Benjamin's thesis on the film audience to the listener's reception of a piece of recorded music. Thus, observes Middleton:

> Benjamin sees the film audience, detached from the moment of production, as being in the position of a *critic,* identifying with the analytical work of the camera rather than with the experience of the characters. The transparency of

technique and the ubiquity of the reproductions turns everyone into an *expert,* hence a potential *participant* . . . This approach has enormously suggestive potential for analysis of listening, for it fully accepts the significance of new perceptual attitudes and situations while by-passing or at least putting into question the usual, too easy Adornian assumptions of passivity (1990, pp. 65–6).

To some extent the ideas of Benjamin, as interpreted by Middleton, enable popular music theorists to overcome the more restricting aspects of Adorno's work by awarding the music listener a degree of participation in the construction of musical meanings. The problem remains, however, to determine the degree of freedom that individuals have in constructing meanings around a form that '[subsists] within the nexus of capitalist production processes' (ibid., p. 66).

The contested nature of popular music

In tackling this issue, the starting point for many popular music theorists has been the music industry itself, or rather the opposing interests around which the modern music industry is constructed. Again, the cultural impact of rock 'n' roll on young people in the 1950s serves as a useful introduction to this issue. Thus, while music 'was a commercial product long before rock 'n' roll', the arrival of the latter together with its pronounced cultural effect upon young people created a number of problems for the music industry (Frith: 1983, p. 32). Of these, the crucial problem was how to market a music that was clearly viable as a commercial product but at the same time highly controversial. In particular, the nature of its partly African-American roots made rock 'n' roll vulnerable to a range of accusations, particularly in the USA, its place of origin. The Reverend Albert Carter of the Pentecostal Church, Nottingham, for example, expressed the view that: 'Rock 'n' roll [was] a revival of devil dancing . . . the same sort of thing that is done in a black magic ritual' (Street: 1992, p. 305). Likewise, rock 'n' roll was criticised by the parent culture because of the damage it was perceived to be causing to the moral fabric of white US society, allegedly inciting teenagers to unruly behaviour (Hill: 1992, pp. 52–3). Indeed, such antagonisms were shared by the industry itself. Thus, the initial reaction of record companies was to attempt to clean up rock 'n' roll for white teenage consumption. However, this move on the part of the music industry proved contrary to the wishes of white teenage audiences themselves. Thus, as Gillett explains:

> The implication was that people didn't want their music to be as brash, blatantly sexual, and spontaneous as the pure rock 'n' roll records were. But although the position was maintained through to 1963, the success in the United States around this time of British groups with similar qualities suggested that the audience still did prefer this kind of music, if it knew about its availability (1983, p. 41).

A parallel example of this music industry response to rock 'n' roll is illustrated in a study by Mutsaers on the Dutch rock 'n' roll scene of the late 1950s and early 1960s. As Mutsaers points out, rock 'n' roll music in Holland was performed largely by Indonesian immigrants (Indos) whose 'apparently natural musical abilities' and affinity with the guitar—which was used in traditional Indonesian music—enabled them to monopolise rock 'n' roll music in Holland (1990, p. 308). Indobands were, however, very hard to work with in the recording studio; their inability to read music meant that they could not follow music scores and, consequently, were unable to produce the clean, predictable three minute *takes* that studio producers were looking for. Similarly, there were concerns over reactions of audiences to the live shows of Indobands. At dance halls where the groups played there were often violent clashes between white Dutch boys and 'Indo' boys, who, it was alleged, were 'stealing' the girlfriends of the white boys (ibid., p. 310). The point remained, however, that Indobands were ex-tremely popular and thus highly lucrative, both in Holland and in neighbouring Germany, with the result that they continued to play a central role in the Dutch music industry up until the 1960s when their appeal was eclipsed by Merseybeat.

10   The way that rock 'n' roll music crucially differed from earlier forms of popular music was in the reflexivity of the discourse that was established between rock 'n' roll and its newly emerging youth audience. Indeed, despite the apprehension of the cul-ture industries regarding the potential threat of rock 'n' roll, the visual representation of rock 'n' roll stars in film and on TV also did much to tie the cultural bond between artists and audience. Moreover, it wasn't simply the visual representation of artists themselves that counted in this respect. Thus, as Shumway explains with reference to the early TV appearances of Elvis Presley:

> When Elvis is featured on national TV programmes, the audience becomes part of the show . . . the film cuts between shots of Elvis and shots of the audience, not as a large mass of indistinguishable faces, but of particular faces whose re-sponse tells us of the excitement the performer is generating . . . These pictures showed other fans how to respond appropriately to rock acts (1992, p. 127).

11   Ehrenreich *et al.* (1992) have noted a similar process at work with the arrival of the Beatles in the US where fans already knew how to respond to the group having watched TV footage of the Beatles performing in Europe, such footage being similarly intercut with scenes from the audience. The meaning of rock 'n' roll then could not be separated from the contexts in which it was consumed and this has been a continuing feature of subsequent post-war and contemporary popular music styles. This aspect of popular music's cultural significance is particularly well summed up by Grossberg, who argues that the latter 'involve[s] more than just the relationships between logics of production and logics of consumption [but] define[s] particular ways of navigating the spaces and places, the territorializations of power, of daily life' (1994, p. 48). Like other forms of post-war popular culture then, popular music has become an increas-ingly contested medium. Thus, as Garofalo points out, popular mass culture is:

> one arena where ideological struggle—the struggle over the power to define—takes place. While there is no question that in this arena the forces arrayed in support of the existing hegemony are formidable, there are also numerous in-stances where mass culture—and in particular popular music—issues serious challenges to hegemonic power (1992a, p. 2).

12   The ability of popular music to serve as an effective platform for the delivery of such challenges is, in turn, further enhanced by the uncertainty of the music market itself. If the music industry was relatively unprepared for the arrival of rock 'n' roll,

then this scenario has since been repeated on numerous occasions, for example by punk rock in the mid-1970s and acid house in the late 1980s. In his study *Sound Effects,* Frith suggests that: 'Record companies by nature don't much care what forms music takes as long as they can be controlled to ensure profit—musics and musicians can be packaged and sold, whatever their styles' (1983, p. 32). Another way of stating this argument would be to say that all the recording industry can maintain with certainty is that it is in place to package and market forms of popular music. Beyond this assertion, however, the trajectory of popular music's stylistic development and its impact upon audiences becomes rather less of an exact science. Indeed, as Attali has pointed out, the music industry occupies a particularly precarious position situated 'on the borderline between the most sophisticated marketing and the most unpredictable of cottage industries' (1985, pp. 102–3). Thus, while record companies would like to think that they are able to predict which artists and musical styles will prove to be the most commercially viable this remains largely an erroneous game of intuition.

Herein lies the central contradiction in modern music marketing, for in attempting to work as closely as possible within the 'organisational conventions [and] commercial logic of capitalism' the music industry is at the same time forced to exercise a looser control over the commodities that are marketed, the performing artists themselves (Negus: 1992, p. vii). In the final analysis, it is the stylistic or ideological appeal of performing artists and their music that generates profit for the industry. Harron, for example, has stated that in the wake of the 1960s hippie movement 'record companies . . . , were confused and even alarmed by the strange groups whose music was so profitable [and had to] bring in young outsiders to tell them what would make a hit' (1988, p. 184). This tendency on the part of record companies to hire in 'street wise' youngsters in order to keep up with the rapidly shifting nature of the youth music market has continued. Thus, for example, Negus relates a discussion with an executive from a top record company who had launched a new 'dance label' and brought in 'dance specialists' on the grounds that he didn't 'know that market' (1992, p. 54). **13**

Perhaps more than any other mass-produced commodity then, popular music is a contested form. While successful artists may generate vast amounts of income for the record companies to which they are signed, at the same time they frequently utilise the mass dissemination of their music or the magnitude of their public profile to communicate a variety of socio-political issues 'that have implications beyond their immediate impact on mass media entertainment (Ullestad: 1992, p. 37). This aspect of popular music performance has manifested itself at regular intervals during the last fifty years. I have already discussed the socio-cultural impact of rock 'n' roll upon young people from the mid-1950s to the early 1960s. During the late 1960s, popular music became increasingly controversial as artists aligned themselves with a variety of socio-political issues. In the US this was evidenced for example in James Brown's 'Say It Loud, I'm Black and I'm Proud', a tribute to the Black Power movement, and Country Joe and the Fish's 'Fixin' to Die Rag', a powerful anti-Vietnam War song which contained the line 'You can be the first ones on the block to have your boy come home in a box' (Gleason: 1972, pp. 139–40). As Gleason points out, this song was 'heard and understood by millions' with the effect that there was no 'comparable medium' for the anti-war message (ibid., p. 139). **14**

15   The subversive quality of popular music has also been witnessed in Britain, the possibilities for pop expression having been further enhanced by the art school training of many leading exponents of British pop. Since the 1950s, art schools have produced a succession of musical innovators, such as John Lennon, who, according to Frith and Home, 'inflected pop music with bohemian dreams . . . and laid out the ideology of "rock" ' (1987, p. 73). The artistic training of such musicians prompted them to experiment with different musical styles and to begin using the medium of song as a means to communicate a whole new range of sentiments, feelings and viewpoints. Thus, as Frith and Home suggest, 'pop rhetoric—once concerned solely with sentimentality, the language of love, dancing and having a good time' suddenly acquired a whole new level of significance (ibid., p. 66).

16   In other parts of the world popular music has become a key medium in the articulation of socio-political causes and the fight against forms of political extremism. Wicke, in a study of music's role in the political disintegration of the former East Germany, argues that East German popular music groups and artists 'helped prepare the ground for the heightened popular political consciousness' that resulted in the fall of the Berlin Wall in November 1989 (1992, p. 196). Similarly Easton's study of the Soviet 'rock community' during the mid-1980s suggests that rock groups such as Aquarium played an important role in articulating the disillusionment of Soviet youth with the communist system. Moreover, according to Easton, attempts by the Soviet government to outlaw the performance of rock groups merely 'created a sense of confinement and repression in which underground movements flourish[ed]' (1989, p. 58). Ching-Yun Lee also examines the potential of popular music for political comment in her study of Cantopop, a mainstream style of Cantonese popular music in Hong Kong. As Ching-Yun Lee points out, in the period immediately following the violent military oppression of the Chinese student uprising in Beijing's Tiananmen Square during May 1989, Cantopop lyrics became increasingly supportive of the Chinese student movement, for example, by ridiculing the Chinese government, mourning the students who died in the uprising and pledging support for the democracy movement (1992, p. 129).

17   A further example of popular music's potential for the articulation of socio-political statements is provided in Davies's study of Aboriginal rock music in Australia. According to Davies, much of this music is linked with the Aborigines' attempt to recover their cultural homelands from white landowners. As Davies explains: 'Cultural survival for the Aboriginal Australians is tied to land rights, to origins, to a cultural integrity beyond contemporary industrial arrangements (1993, p. 253). As such, argues Davies, Aboriginal rock music performs two main functions above and beyond its status as a commodity form. First, the music represents a form of empowerment through its 'reversal and decentering of colonial social relations' (ibid., p. 256). Second, when the music of Aboriginal rock bands is distributed through mainstream channels such as national radio and MTV, the usually marginalised Aborigine community is given the opportunity to voice its discontent through a central and highly strategic medium (ibid., p. 257).

18   Between the mid-1980s and early 1990s, the relationship between popular music and socio-political issues took a new turn as pop became the focus for a series of 'mega-events' beginning with Live Aid in July 1985 (Garofalo: 1992b). Live Aid was a

globally televised live music event—in aid of the famine in Ethiopia—that brought together 'stadium acts' of the day, such as Queen, Elton John and David Bowie, with a view towards using the medium of a live music performance as a way of simultaneously increasing public awareness of the famine and raising funds to fight it. The success of Live Aid as a media spectacle led to a series of similar events including Farm Aid, which aimed to raise funds for small independent farmers in the US after the Regan administration withdrew its subsidisation of small farming concerns, and the two Nelson Mandela concerts—the first held in 1988 to mark the imprisoned ANC leader's seventieth birthday and the second in 1990 to celebrate his release from prison. The Mandela concerts were also intended to promote human rights issues on an international scale (Garofalo: 1992c).

BIBLIOGRAPHY

(Note the numerous differences in this British documentation style.)

Adorno, T.W. (1941) 'On Popular Music' in S. Firth and A. Goodwin (eds) (1990) *On Record: Rock, Pop and the Written Word,* Routledge, London.

Attali, J. (1985) *Noise: The Political Economy of Music,* (trans. B. Massumi) Manchester University Press, Manchester.

Bottomore, T. (1984) *The Frankfurt School,* Tavistock, London.

Buck-Morss, S. (1989) *The Dialectics of Seeing: Walter Benjamin and the Arcades Project,* MIT Press, Cambridge, MA.

Ching-Yun Lee, J. (1992) 'All for Freedom: The Rise of Patriotic/Pro-Democratic Popular Music in Hong Kong in Response to the Chinese Student Movement' in R. Garofalo (ed.) *Rockin' the Boat: Mass Music and Mass Movements,* South End Press, Boston, MA.

Davies, C.L. (1993) 'Aboriginal Rock Music: Space and Place' in T. Bennett, S. Frith, L. Grossberg, J. Shepherd and G. Turner (eds) *Rock and Popular Music: Politics, Policies, Institutions,* Routledge, London.

Denisoff, R.S. and Romanowski, W.D. (1991) *Risky Business: Rock in Film,* Transaction, New Jersey.

Easton, P. (1989) 'The Rock Music Community' in J. Riordan (ed.) *Soviet Youth Culture,* Indiana University Press, Bloomington and Indianapolis.

Ehrenreich, B., Hess, E. and Jacobs, G. (1992) 'Beatlemania: Girls Just Want to Have Fun' in L.A. Lewis (ed.) *The Adoring Audience: Fan Culture and Popular Media,* Routledge, London.

Frith, S. (1983) *Sound Effects: Youth, Leisure, and the Politics of Rock,* Constable, London.

Frith, S. and Home, H. (1987). *Art into Pop,* Methuen, London.

Garofalo, R. (ed.) (1992a) *Rockin' the Boat: Mass Music and Mass Movements,* South End Press, Boston, MA.

Garofalo, R. (1992b) 'Understanding Mega-Events: If We Are the World, Then How Do We Change It?' in R. Garofalo (ed.) *Rockin' the Boat: Mass Music and Mass Movements,* South End Press, Boston, MA.

Garofalo, R. (1992c) 'Nelson Mandela, The Concerts: Mass Culture as Contested Terrain' in R. Garofalo (ed.) *Rockin' the Boat: Mass Music and Mass Movements,* South End Press, Boston, MA.

Gillett, C. (1983) *The Sound of the City: The Rise of Rock and Roll,* 2nd edn, Souvenir Press, London.

Gleason, R.J. (1972) 'A Cultural Revolution' in R.S. Denisoff and R.A. Peterson (eds) *The Sounds of Social Change,* Rand McNally and Company, Chicago.

Grossberg, L. (1994) 'Is Anybody Listening? Does Anybody Care?: On Talking About "The State of Rock" ' in A. Ross and T. Rose (eds) *Microphone Fiends: Youth Music and Youth Culture,* Routledge, London.

Harron, M. (1988) 'McRock: Pop as a Commodity' in S. Frith (ed.) (1990) *Facing Music: Essays on Pop, Rock, and Culture,* 2nd edn, Mandarin, London.

Hill, T. (1992) 'The Enemy Within: Censorship in Rock Music in the 1950s' in A. DeCurtis (ed.) *Present Tense: Rock and Roll and Culture,* Duke University Press, Durham, NC.

Hosokawa, S. (1984) 'The Walkman Effect' in *Popular Music,* 4: 165–80

Jay, M. (1973) *The Dialectical Imagination: A History of the Frankfurt School and the Institute of Social Research 1923–1950,* Heinemann Educational Books, London.

Krüger, H.H. (1983) 'Sprachlose Rebellen?: Zur Subkultur der "Halbstarken" in den Fünfziger Jahren' in W. Breyvogel (ed.) *Autonomie and Widerstand: Zur Theorie und Geshichte des Jugendprotestes,* Rigidon, Essen.

MacDonald, D. (1953) 'A Theory of Mass Culture' in B. Rosenberg and D. White (eds) (1957) *Mass Culture: The Popular Arts in America,* Free Press, Glencoe, IL.

Middleton, R. (1990) *Studying Popular Music,* Open University Press, Milton Keynes.

Mutsaers, L. (1990) 'Indorock: An Early Eurorock Style' in *Popular Music,* 9(3): 307–20.

Negus, K. (1992) *Producing Pop: Culture and Conflict in the Popular Music Industry,* Edward Arnold, London.

Shumway, D. (1992) 'Rock and Roll as a Cultural Practice' in A. DeCurtis (ed.) *Present Tense: Rock and Roll and Culture,* Duke University Press, Durham, NC.

Street, J. (1992) "Shock Waves: The Authoritative Response to Popular Music" in D. Strinati and S. Wagg (eds.) *Come on Down?: Popular Music Culture in Post-War Britain,* Routledge, London.

Ullestad, N. (1992) 'Diverse Rock Rebellions Subvert Mass Media Hegemony' in R. Garofalo (ed.) *Rockin' the Boat: Mass Music and Mass Movements,* South End Press, Boston, MA.

Wicke, P. (1992) 'The Role of Rock Music in the Political Disintegration of East Germany' in J. Lull (ed.) *Popular Music and Communication,* 2nd edn, Sage, London.

UNDERSTANDING THE AUTHOR'S IDEAS

1. When and how did rock really arrive?
2. Explain Bennett's statement regarding a continuing problematic issue—"how to reconcile popular music's position in the marketplace with its function as a potentially counter-hegemonic cultural resource." (*Note: Scholarly readings such as this will probably use some terms that are unfamiliar to you. Locate definitions where necessary.*)
3. Explain the distinction between "art" music and "pop" music.
4. Bennett draws on two earlier theorists to begin his discussion. Identify those theorists and briefly summarize their key points.
5. According to Bennett, what was "the crucial problem" of the new phenomenon of rock music?
6. What is the primary difference between rock'n'roll and earlier forms of popular music?
7. Explain the key purposes of rock music. Give examples.

EXPLORING YOUR OWN IDEAS

1. Bennett writes, ". . . for a great many young people, popular music is an omnipresent aspect of their day to day existence." Consider that statement in light of your own experience and respond. Evaluate it and consider its implications.
2. What did you think about as you read about the youth reactions to the first major rock film, *Rock Around the Clock?* Does that situation have any relevance today?
3. Do you agree or disagree that rock music encourages an audience of passive consumers? Explain.
4. Consider the cultural issues (in various societies) that rock music has influenced. Explore examples of cultural blending and/or tensions that have occurred in the United States in response to certain rock music.
5. Imagine you have been given the editorial assignment to update Bennett's study. What significant forms of rock have entered the music scene since the early 1990s (when Bennett first conducted his research)? How are they similar and/or different from the ones he discusses, in style and in impact?
6. Explain similarities and differences in both content and genre conventions between McCollum's article and Bennett's study.

EXPLORING VISUAL IMAGES

Sum41 in Concert

Rock music plays a major role in the lives of many college students. Study this picture of a "pop punk " rock concert. Have you ever attended a concert like this? If so, what were your feelings? What does this image suggest about the music scene for college students today? Write a brief response essay in which you characterize the overall atmosphere, the behavior of the performers, and the mood of the crowd. Relate these impressions to some of the ideas expressed in the readings for this unit.

Reading 3

This article appeared in America, *a contemporary, somewhat liberal, intellectually respected Catholic journal. Nantais, a Jesuit priest and advanced student of philosophy and theology, offers his views shortly after the tragic Columbine shootings in Colorado on the social influence of rock music. Similar to the McCollum article, it is an opinion piece in a nonscholarly source. As such, it shares certain genre conventions. However, note the differences dictated largely by audience differentials.*

"CD's Don't Kill People"

David E. Nantais

Pop music has not yet caused the downfall of Western civilization.   1

Billy Joel once said in an interview on "60 Minutes" that he thinks of his songs as   2
his children. He remarked that some of them go on to become doctors and lawyers
(presumably the Top 40 Hits), while others grow up to be bums. I wonder if Billy believes that any of his "kids" could ever grow up to be mass murderers or terrorists.

Ever since the horrible shootings in Littleton, Col., many groups around the coun-   3
try have been engaged in quasi-psychological ranting about the negative effects pop
music has on teenagers. I believe that much of this fingerpointing is unwarranted, although hardly surprising. Pop music, which is a blanket term referring to rock, alternative, Top 40, metal, hip-hop, rap, goth and industrial music, has not caused the
downfall of Western civilization as predicted by many critics since the mid-1950's;
but Americans like quick-fix answers to tough, murky questions, and pop music is an
easy scapegoat.

I vividly remember my mom warning me as a young and impressionable second   4
grader that I should not listen to the music of KISS and I should likewise stay away
from the kids who carried lunch boxes pasted with this group's frightening clown-like
visages. At the time, I had no idea what or who KISS was, but the urgency of my
mother's voice served as a warning that I was facing something more evil than I could
imagine. KISS went on to achieve immense fame, fortune and misfortune, and recently reunited, with middle-aged paunches and all, as lampoons of their former
selves—hardly the type of aural monster Hercules would have encountered on one
of his mythic journeys.

Why did my mother feel so strongly about warning me against the dangers of pop   5
music? Perhaps her mother and father had given her the same speech about Elvis.
For three generations, parents have felt the impetus to point their critical fingers at
pop music and blame it for every vice St. Paul warned about, with a few more thrown
in for good measure. Parents should be concerned about the well-being of their children, but they are fooling themselves if they believe that little Billy will develop more
normally if he renounces pop music and instead listens to country and western.

America has been involved in a tense relationship with pop music for at least four   6
decades. In the late 1960's Sharon Tate was murdered by Charles Manson and his
group of deranged followers. As this story was being investigated, the press picked up
and ran with a phrase that had been written in blood on a wall in Tate's home:
"Helter Skelter." Taken from a song on the Beatles' highly praised "White Album," it
all at once became the anthem of the Four Horsemen. Similarly, in the mid-80's the
heavy metal artists Ozzy Osbourne and Judas Priest were put on trial for supposedly
influencing teenagers to kill themselves.

In the wake of the recent high school shootings, pop music again has become a   7
culprit. Shock-rockers Marilyn Manson, and especially this band's namesake front
man, were lambasted for inspiring the evil intentions and menacing "goth" lifestyle of

the two gun-wielding teenagers. In addition to the fact that Marilyn Manson and goth have nothing to do with each other (mistakenly connecting them betrays the stereotypical musical illiteracy of the older generation), the juxtaposition of pop music with horrible crimes is sad for other reasons as well.

8   I have been involved in a love affair with pop music ever since I purchased my first album, Def Leppard's "Pyromania," in 1983. This affair has continued into my four years as a Jesuit, during which time I have played drums in a rock band and written numerous rock CD reviews for a student magazine in Chicago. I do not see a dichotomy between religious life and my musical interests. In fact, through my ministerial experiences as a Jesuit, I have witnessed the hand of God at work through the interaction of teenagers and popular music. In response to the negative press pop music has recently received, I would like to highlight three positive ways popular music can affect teenagers.

Community-Building

9   The teen-age years are a time of transition from childhood to adulthood, and teenagers need to find their own identity apart from their parents and family. This is very normal and healthy, and those readers who are parents should take the time to recall just how difficult it was to gain a foothold on independence during their adolescent years. A very popular way for teenagers to establish independence is by identifying with a group of other teenagers who share their musical interests. Very often, this musical interest is combined with fashion and lifestyle changes that allow the teenagers to feel they are forging their own way toward adulthood without assistance from Mom and Dad. Parents may be disturbed by the musical tastes of their teenagers, but this is to be expected. The music most teenagers listen to in the late 90's is not going to be well received by parents any more than it was in the late 60's. But it serves the same purpose, allowing teenagers to form friendships with peers who share a common interest in a particular music artist or group.

Therapeutic Release

10   Many times, while giving retreats to high school students, I have heard them remark that they will listen to different types of music depending upon their mood. When they are depressed, R.E.M. has just the right song that speaks to them; Ani DiFranco and Tori Amos know what to say to the angry teen-age girl whose boyfriend has just dumped her; Lauryn Hill's infectious grooves are just what the doctor ordered to lighten the spirit on a lonely Friday night; listening to Limp Bizkit after a fight with their parents gives teenagers permission to be angry in a nondestructive way. It is very heartening to witness teenagers turning to music to touch their souls and help them deal with strong emotions because they feel that the music speaks to them in a way that parents, priests or teachers cannot at that moment. Teenagers often associate pop music with special events in their lives, as manifested by the numerous compilation "mix" tapes many teenagers make by collecting the music that meant a lot to them during a particularly enjoyable summer or while they were involved in a special relationship, and teenagers can use these musical souvenirs to help them recall these enjoyable experiences.

Spirituality

The first two points touched upon aspects of teenagers' spirituality, but I refer here   11
to the use of pop music in a specifically spiritual context, such as a retreat. My experience conducting retreats for teenagers has helped me to understand what a powerful tool pop music can be for tapping into spiritual themes such as darkness/light, death/resurrection and love in a way teenagers can understand and to which they can relate. Pop music can be used at the beginning and end of a retreat talk to provide the proper punctuation to the spiritual matter being conveyed. I am not referring solely to acoustic guitar, bubble-gum lyric pop music, but all types. Since teenagers do invest a lot of time listening to music, building community around music and associating strong emotions with particular music, it is not difficult to bring God into their experience of music. Communicating the power of God's love and companionship by theoretical means to a group of teenagers is not a simple task, but when they can listen to music in a group setting and feel the deep emotions associated with the music, teenagers can be helped to connect their desires and passions with God; and, I hope, God can become more of a real presence in their lives.

Teenagers who are troubled are going to listen to pop music just as much as   12
teenagers who are not, so attempting to make a direct correlation between teen-age violence and music is problematic at best. Pop music is not predicted as an agent of mass destruction in the Book of Revelation, and Marilyn Manson is no more responsible for the Littleton shootings than Joan Osbourne's sappy oeuvre "(What if God was) One of Us" is responsible for effecting mass conversions to deism. Teenagers are going through difficult transitions and definitely need guidance from their elders, but demonizing the music they listen to is not a constructive way to provide support.

UNDERSTANDING THE AUTHOR'S IDEAS

1. Briefly summarize Nantais's position on popular music.
2. What consequences do some people attribute to rock music?
3. How does this author refute the argument that pop music is morally destructive?
4. Summarize the three positive influences of popular music.

EXPLORING YOUR OWN IDEAS

1. Characterize the audience(s) that Nantais addresses in this article.
2. Were you at all surprised by the connections he makes between rock music and religion? Why or why not?
3. How might other cultural groups of differing perspectives benefit from Nantais's argument?
4. Offer a personal response to the author's overall position on the influence of rock music. Anticipate counterresponses to his and/or your position.

Reading 4

> *This reading is an excerpt from Chapter 3 of a scholarly study entitled* It's Not Only Rock & Roll: Popular Music in the Lives of Adolescents, *which examines the role popular music plays in the lives of young people. It is written by communication studies researchers Peter G. Christenson and Donald F. Roberts. Similar to the Bennett excerpt in this chapter, it also draws upon and contributes to research in the academic fields of sociology, anthropology, music history, cultural studies, and media studies. Ironically, neither study references the other in their extensive lists of resources. Given the closeness of the publication dates and the transatlantic publication locations, the authors may have been unaware that they were conducting similar research, providing important insights into the relationships between popular music and youth culture.*

"Equipment for Living: Adolescent Uses of Popular Music"

Peter G. Christenson and Donald F. Roberts

The Social Uses and Significance of Popular Music

1   We have referred to the social or subcultural meanings of music—its importance as an aid to peer group interactions, its use in establishing group identity, and so on. Some scholars contend that, important as certain personal affective gratifications are, these social aspects of popular music provide the real key to understanding its niche in the lives of youth (Frith, 1981; Lull, 1987; Roe, 1984, 1985). For instance, Roe (1985) refers to popular music as essentially a "group phenomenon" (p. 355). Indeed, even though most listening is solitary, many of music's functions are social in the broad sense that they relate to adolescents' relationships with each other and with the culture at large.

2   Of course, some uses are literally social in that they take place in the company of others. As our partial inventory of music uses indicates (see Table 3.4), music is used to form friendships, to provide atmosphere for parties, to make conversations and interactions flow more smoothly, and to serve as grist for the conversation mill. Even these functions, though, may be served by solitary listening (as, for instance, when one listens alone to acquire music expertise to be trotted out in later conversations) and may deliver affective as well as social gratifications. The distinctions we have introduced, then, are far from airtight. Solitary listening may be partly or mostly social in some sense or degree, and listening with others may be at once a form of personal mood management as well as a mechanism for encouraging social interaction.

3   For this discussion, we suggest three divisions within the broad category of social uses:

- quasi-social uses, by which we mean uses of music listening that usually do not occur in the company of others, but that nevertheless serve goals and needs that surround or influence social relationships
- socializing uses, which occur in dyadic or group contexts such as dates and parties
- cultural uses, which establish and maintain the cultural boundaries between youth and adult culture and between various adolescent crowds and subcultures.

Quasi-social uses. The best evidence of popular music's association with adolescent social relationships is the strong connection between interest in popular music and peer orientation. In a fundamental sense, those who are concerned with "the group" are also more oriented toward popular music. This connection between the self and others may be felt even during solitary listening. Perhaps the key manifestation of the social dimension of solitary listening occurs in the form of replacing or invoking the presence of absent peers. Teens frequently report listening to music in order to relieve feelings of loneliness. For instance, Gantz et al. (1978) reported that two thirds of their college respondents said they listened either "somewhat" or "very frequently" to "make me feel less alone when I'm by myself." This study and others also suggest that the use of music to relieve loneliness—that is, to provide the sense of company when one is alone—is significantly more common for girls than for boys (Larson et al., 1989; Roe, 1984).   4

As we have noted, at the extreme music may provide a basis for what media theorists often refer to as "parasocial" or imaginary personal relationships with music stars. This, too, appears to be more common among females, although it is hardly rare among males. Simon Frith (1981) has linked girls' greater interest in romantic lyrics with their greater tendency to idolize and fantasize about opposite-sex stars. For many of the British girls he interviewed, the phenomenon often assumed the form of a bittersweet, confidential romantic (and sexual) relationship with the "ideal boy next door." Boys are more likely to engage in another form of parasocial fantasy, imagining themselves on stage sharing the glory with their favorite rock groups (Arnett, 1991a). Solitary listening may evoke the presence of peers even when one is not feeling particularly lonely. Although we find no quantitative estimates of its frequency, anecdotal and qualitative references abound as to popular music's singular ability to stimulate reminiscences and evoke vivid memories of past loves, friendships and social occasions (Lull, 1992).   5

Solitary music listening may also perform a number of "delayed" social uses (Lull, 1987) by preparing adolescents for future peer interactions and relationships. Involvement and expertise in music are a crucial basis for relationships with peers. In many instances, those who know nothing about a group's favorite music or about the latest music trends are simply excluded from conversations. Often a shared interest in a certain type of music is both the spark that begins a friendship and the adhesive that binds it over time (Frith, 1981; Lull, 1992). Although most adolescents would find it ludicrous to judge a potential friend on the basis of his or her favorite TV show, agreement about music is widely considered to be a condition for friendship or clique membership. This connection between group membership and pop music orientation extends to seeking information about music. Those with more   6 friends are more likely to report that they listen to [the] radio in order to keep up with the latest music trends (Dominick, 1974), and the amount of time adolescents spend reading pop music magazines is strongly related to the number of friends they have who share their taste in music, suggesting that teens seek information about music as much to impress friends with their expertise as to satisfy their personal curiosity about favorite musicians (Clarke, 1973).

7   One of the earliest and most instructive examinations of the relationship between popular music and the teen social structure is Roger Brown and Michael O'Leary's (1971) study of British secondary school students. Brown and O'Leary found several interesting connections between involvement in popular music and aspects of the school experience. Their primary conclusion—and this should surprise nobody today—was that popular music occupied a central place in the adolescent social system. They found, for instance, that students with higher levels of integration into teen pop culture (defined as a combination of music knowledge, record buying, and radio listening time) had more friends than did those who were less involved in pop culture. In addition, students with reputations as pop music experts were judged by their peers as higher in both popularity and leadership.

8   The importance of music knowledge in peer acceptance was further emphasized by the considerable weight students gave music expertise relative to other sources of prestige. When asked what dimensions they found most crucial in judging their schoolmates' status, over half said music knowledge was an important factor. Only school performance and clothing were ranked higher: Knowledge of TV shows, number of friends, and the kind of house one lived in were all less important than music expertise. In general, then, the choice of popular music over other cultural forms correlated with higher social status in the school . . .

9   However, by a different criterion, pop music involvement seemed to indicate *lower* status. Brown and O'Leary (1971) reported that high levels of involvement in pop music were negatively correlated with standard measures of academic success. In both the middle and lower classes, students with higher reputations for pop music knowledge were lower achievers. Similarly, those who listened to more music and bought more records received lower teacher assessments. Because these patterns held without regard to social class, Brown and O'Leary concluded that involvement in the teen culture is more a function of where youngsters are headed in the social structure than where they have come from in terms of parental status (p. 411). Finally, they argued that pop music involvement and academic achievement seemed, to a certain extent at least, to be conflicting pursuits. Of all groups in the study, middle-class low academic achievers were the most involved with music, suggesting that for them music expertise served as a sort of "Plan B" in the search for social standing in school.

10   *Socializing uses.* When adolescents congregate on their own terms, popular music frequently functions as an integral part of the occasion. Moreover, given their general preference for the company of peers and the fact that music tends to elevate their mood when with peers (Larson et al., 1989), it is reasonable to say that most adolescents are happiest when pop music is part of the scene. Whether in dyads involving romance or sex, small groups gathered for a party, or the larger social gatherings at concerts or clubs, music makes three essential contributions to social occasions: (a) it sets the proper mood for the gathering; (b) it facilitates interpersonal interactions;

and (c) it fills the silence when nobody is talking. Perhaps the best testimony to the importance of music in socializing is the impossibility of envisioning a party, of any size, without a sound system of some kind to provide the appropriate environmental backdrop. When teens or college students organize a party, the appropriate music is as crucial as the appropriate (or inappropriate) beverages.

James Lull (1987) points out that the "socializing" uses of popular music occur at several levels of interaction and in a variety of contexts. In male-female dyads, music is used to accompany dancing, courtship, and sexual behavior. In friendship dyads, music often provides a basis for the initial bond and often helps maintain the friendship. In larger gatherings, such as parties, dances, or clubs, music reduces inhibitions, attracts attention and approval, provides topics for conversation, and of course enables dancing. Popular music is even incorporated into situations in which adolescents gather to work or work out. Whenever teens mount a "free" fundraising car wash, the boombox is there doing its work along with the students. High-energy music propels participants through aerobics classes and weight-lifting sessions. When kids gather together to work on school projects or for "homework parties," music, for better or worse, is there in the background.

Of course, adolescents differ in the extent to which they incorporate popular music into social interactions. Obviously, teens who are not particularly interested in music or who affiliate more with parents and other adult figures rarely build their social occasions around pop music. Females exhibit socializing uses more frequently than males (Carroll et al., 1993; Gantz et al., 1978), and on average females report more interest in dancing, although males are just as likely to be true dance club zealots (Roe, 1985; Wells, 1990). Racial differences also exist. African-American youth, for example, are not only more involved with music generally than Whites, but they are more involved in dancing and more likely to view the ability to dance well as an important personal trait (Kuwahara, 1992; Lull, 1992).

The use of music in social contexts also varies according to music taste and subcultural membership. Two University of Houston researchers conducted an ethnographic study of audience behavior at a Houston area nightclub and found quite different styles of participation depending on the type of crowd drawn on different nights (Kotarba & Wells, 1987). The male-dominated heavy metal crowd tended not to socialize across genders as much as other groups of clientele did. Most of their communicative behavior was directed to other male fans—ritualized handshakes of solidarity, for example—or to nobody in particular, as in their unison salute to the stage with arms outstretched and pinkie and index finger extended from the fist. Very little "traditional" boy-girl dancing occurred. Rather, these "metalheads" tended to crush into a pulsating throng in front of the stage as their comrades engaged in "stage diving" (climbing on stage and then taking running swan dives into the audience) and "head-banging," that is, crashing their foreheads against the stage in time with the music. (Metal and punk crowds also "mosh" or "slam-dance" at clubs and concerts. In slam-dancing a group of individuals near the stage hurl themselves into one another at full running speed—not infrequently with at least minor injury.)

This style of club behavior contrasted sharply with groups that frequented the club on other nights. The crowd referred to as "yuppies" or "preppies" were not only attracted to a different type of music (Top 40) than the metal fans, but they dressed more traditionally (fewer tattoos, more Calvin Klein apparel) and exhibited different patterns of social behavior. They engaged in more verbal interpersonal communication in general and much more male-female communication than the heavy metal crowd. They were also more likely to laugh, hug, kiss, and smile. Dancing in this crowd invariably took the standard one-male-with-one-female form. For the preppies, in other words, socializing was the foreground activity and the music the background or context for it. The music played a much more pivotal role in the club experience of the heavy metal clientele.

15   *Cultural uses.* Music also works at a more diffuse level to define the important subgroups or "crowds" in adolescent culture and to identify who belongs to them. Although it is far from the only cue about group membership—academic achievement, extracurricular interests, social background, clothing, and other elements of personal style figure in too—an adolescent's music affiliation says much about his or her social affiliation. Popular music at once expresses, creates, and perpetuates the essential "us-them" distinctions that develop between groups, and not just symbolically. Whether played by groups in public places or by individual teens in upstairs bedrooms, music stakes a powerful territorial claim. Indeed, it may be the most highly charged "No Trespassing" sign in adolescent society.

16   The most basic us-them distinction is between youth and adults, and we have already remarked on the connection between involvement in popular music and the quest for independence from parental authority. Some scholars have argued that music's essential significance and usefulness to youth rests in its power to express opposition to the authority of parents and the adult mainstream culture. Lull wrote: "Generally, young people use music to resist authority at all levels, assert their personalities and learn about things that their parents and the schools aren't telling them" (p. 153). Lawrence Grossberg (1984, 1987) has made an even stronger assertion of this ideological function. He contends that the basic "work" of popular music is to provide a mechanism for the formation of what he calls "affective alliances," the fundamental one being the alliance of adolescents against the straight, boring, adult world. According to Grossberg, rock music embodies for many youth a deeply felt sense of rebellion against the discipline and expectations of parents, school and work. Music stands for the alternative: freedom from the restraints of authority and the right to seek pleasure in one's own way and in the moment.

17   Writers such as Grossberg and Lull also note music's importance in the formation and perpetuation of subcultures within the broader youth culture. Every U.S. or Canadian high school is divided into subgroups, and many are identified with a specific type of music. For those who are unsuccessful in school or alienated from the mainstream (e.g., racial and ethnic minorities), music allegiance is much more than one cultural marker among many—it is a primary means for expressing solidarity, pride, and defiance. Thus it makes sense to speak of alternative, punk, rap, heavy metal, or reggae subcultures because for these groups music may form the central pillar of group identity. The use of music to express subgroup resistance to the mainstream is not limited to the high school setting. Kuwahara (1992) finds that rap music provides Black students in predominantly White universities an important focus of resistance against the dominant authorities and cultural values of the university. To these students and others who either cannot or choose not to fit into the mainstream, music represents a sense of power and insurgence.

18   Despite these examples, however, there is reason to question the centrality of mu-

sic's role in the teen-versus-parent power struggle and the pervasiveness of its oppositional uses outside certain music-centered subcultures. If, as suggested in Chapter 2,
most kids are in fact not in a state of open warfare against their parents, not separated
from adult culture by yawning generation gaps, and not on the fringe of adolescent
culture—in other words, not rebelling—then it is obvious that popular music cannot
be the crux of their rebellion. In other words, although it is certain that some 14-year-
old boys crank up their favorite death metal album at least in part to infuriate their
parents, we question whether popular music represents for most adolescents
themselves their alienation from parents, teachers, and other adult cultural authorities.
When they are asked directly why they listen to music or why they like a certain musician, song, or genre, relatively few suggest that it is because music cements their affil-
iations with crowds or subcultures or expresses their conflict with authority.

In fact, none of the "uses and gratifications" studies reviewed in this chapter—that   19
is, studies in which a fairly large sample of students have responded to questions on
why they listen to music and what they get from the experience—report explicit evidence of these subcultural or oppositional uses. It is possible, of course, that the
methods used to elicit the information are too blunt to detect such uses. The self-re-
port instruments employed in most uses and gratifications studies have been criticized
for their insensitivity to any latent or unconscious motivations that may lurk below the
surface. Any of us—adults, teens and children alike—may be unaware of certain of
our motivations for music listening or unable to express them in words. Still, we would
argue that if popular music's oppositional uses pervaded and defined adolescents' relationship with music, such uses should make more than just a cameo appearance in
the research, whatever the methodological blind spots. That references to such uses
appear as infrequently as they do suggests that most youth use music more for the affective and social ends described earlier in this section than to express cultural rifts.

Indeed, we believe many teens pursue adult-disapproved personal styles and music   20
preferences less to offend or distance themselves from adults than to cultivate a public
image of rebelliousness and independence. Even if things at home are running smoothly
enough, status is gained by making a show of conflict with parents and the adult world.
Thus, for instance, one finds that adolescents report much "tougher," more rebellious
music tastes in the presence of their peers than they report individually in private
(Finnas, 1989). This tension between respect for parental authority and the need to project an independent public image is nicely illustrated by Kotarba and Wells' (1987) description of young adolescents' arrival at the Houston all-ages club described earlier. Too
young to drive, many of these young patrons depended on their parents for transportation. Thus parents were aware of what their children were doing and had permitted it.
The kids insisted, however, on being dropped off a full city block away and then walking
to the club alone or with their friends. As one said: "It isn't cool to have everyone see
your mother driving you to Roma's" (pp. 402–403).

We do not mean to say that popular music lacks a political dimension or that it   21
never performs a consciously oppositional function. These elements are undeniably
important for certain groups of youth (e.g., African-Americans), certain types of youth
(e.g., those who are in some way "at risk," operating on the social margins, doing
poorly in school), and during certain times. The Depression-era protest folk songs of
Woody Guthrie, the protest rock of the late 1960s and early 1970s and the rap music
of the late 1980s and 1990s represent high water marks in this ebb and flow. Nor do

we deny that music can symbolize, publicize, and exacerbate group and individual differences. From Memorial Day picnics in city parks to college dorm rooms on Friday afternoon, popular music is often broadcast by insiders as an anthem and taken by outsiders as a challenge, often leading to serious conflict (Margolis, 1992). For most adolescents, at most times, however, music use is motivated more by personal and social pleasure than by any purposeful attempt to articulate hostility or difference.

Table 3.4. A Partial Inventory of Popular Music Uses and Gratifications.

Pleasure, fun
Improve or intensify a certain mood
Ruminate on a bad mood
Get energized, "pumped up"
Relieve tension
Relax
Pass the time when there's nothing else to do
Distraction from troubles
Evoke past experiences and memories
Form impressions of others and establish new friendships
Acquire status in the peer culture
Stay current with popular culture
Reduce drudgery of homework, work, chores
Ambiance for parties, social gatherings, ceremonies
Something to talk about with friends
Dancing
Singing (or other participation)
Rhythm for exercises (aerobics, weight lifting, etc.)
Provide company when lonely
Fill gaps in conversation
Social lubricant—make conversations flow more smoothly
Learn how to sing or play a musical instrument
Stimulate interest in sex
Offend or irritate others
Establish private, personal space
Block out or mask unwanted sounds
Relate to the meaning of lyrics
Learn new language, slang
Learn about the world, other cultures, alternative points of view
Identify with one's "crowd" or subculture
Claim public space for one's group
Express resistance to authority
Identify with favorite artists
Articulate social or political attitudes

REFERENCES

Arnett, J. (1991a). Adolescence and heavy metal music: From the mouths of metalheads. *Youth and Society, 23*(1), 76–98.

Brown, R. & O'Leary, M. (1971). Pop music in an English secondary school system. *American Behavioral Scientist, 14,* 401–413.

Carroll, R., Silbergleid, M., Beachum, C., Perry, S., Pluscht, P., & Pescatore, M. (1993). Meanings of radio to teenagers in a niche-programming era. *Journal of Broadcasting and Electronic Media, 37*(2), 159–176.

Clarke, P. (1973). Teenager's co-orientation and information-seeking about pop music. *American Behavioral Scientist, 16,* 551–556.

Dominick, J. (1974). The portable friend: Peer group membership and radio usage. *Journal of Broadcasting, 18*(2), 164–169.

Finnas, L. (1989). A comparison between young people's privately and publicly expressed musical preferences. *Psychology of Music, 17,* 132–145.

Frith, S. (1981). *Sound effects: Youth, leisure and the politics of rock 'n' roll.* New York: Pantheon.

Gantz, W., Gartenberg, H., Pearson, M., & Schiller, S. (1978). Gratifications and expectations associated with popular music among adolescents. *Popular Music and Society, 6*(1), 81–89.

Grossberg, L. (1984). Another boring day in paradise: Rock and roll and the empowerment of everyday life. *Popular Music, 4,* 225–258.

Grossberg, L. (1987). Rock and roll in search of an audience. In J. Lull (Ed.), *Popular music and communication* (pp. 175–197). Beverly Hills: Sage.

Kotarba, J. & Wells, L. (1987). Styles of adolescent participation in all-ages, rock 'n' roll nightclub: An ethnographic analysis. *Youth and Society, 18*(4), 398–417.

Kuwahara, Y. (1992). Power to the people, y'all: Rap music, resistance, and black college students. *Humanity and Society, 16*(1), 13–31.

Larson, R., Kubey, R., & Colletti, J. (1989). Changing channels: Early adolescent media choices and shifting investments in family and friends. *Journal of Youth and Adolescence, 18*(6), 583–599.

Lull, J. (1987). Listeners' communicative uses of popular music. In J. Lull (Ed.), *Popular music and communication* (pp.140–174). Newbury Park, CA: Sage.

Lull, J. (1992). Popular music and communication: An introduction. In J. Lull (Ed.), *Popular music and communication* (2nd ed., pp.1–32). Newbury Park, CA: Sage.

Margolis, D. (1992). Backyard soundings: An exploration of boundaries. *Humboldt Journal of Social Relations, 18*(2), 85–100.

Roe, K. (1984, August). *Youth and music in Sweden: Results from a longitudinal study of teenager's media use.* Paper presented at the meeting of the International Association of Mass Communication Research, Prague.

Roe, K. (1985). Swedish youth and music: Listening patterns and motivations. *Communication Research, 12*(3), 353–362.

Wells, A. (1990). Popular music: Emotional use and management. *Journal of Popular Culture, 24*(1), 105–117.

UNDERSTANDING THE AUTHOR'S IDEAS

1. Identify the three broad categories of "social uses of popular music." Briefly explain their focus.
2. Explain the relationship between pop music and teen peer relationships.
3. What correlation did these scholars find between pop music and academic success?
4. Explain the primary "social[izing] uses" of popular music.
5. Discuss audience variance among types of pop music.
6. What are the major "us-them" distinctions of pop music culture?
7. Explain the dominant reasons young people listen extensively to pop music.

EXPLORING YOUR OWN IDEAS

1. Explore the social aspects of music in your personal life. What role does pop music play in your life? What type of music do you prefer? Consider all of the different reasons you listen to it.
2. Do you agree or disagree with Christenson and Roberts's contention that music serves "social uses" beyond personal and/or affective uses? Explain with examples.
3. Examine the "us-them" distinction within pop music culture. In your experience, where and how do you see it manifested?
4. Discuss your views on the potential of cultural cohesion and/or of cultural rifts stemming from the influence of pop music.

Reading 5

This text is a review of the Christenson and Roberts book It's Not Only Rock & Roll: Popular Music in the Lives of Adolescents, *excerpted as the prior reading of this chapter. Book reviews frequently appear in various magazines and journals to give readers a "sneak preview" of a newly published text. All reviews follow certain genre conventions, which include opinion on the overall merit of the text, a brief summary of the contents, and a critique of its strengths and weaknesses. Notice how this scholarly review, written for the* Journal of Communication, *which has a distinctive scholarly audience (communication studies researchers), discusses the merit of the text in relation to the existing research in the field.*

Review of *It's Not Only Rock & Roll: Popular Music in the Lives of Adolescents*

James Lull

Immediately after two teenage boys marched into Columbine High School in Colorado and murdered more than a dozen of their classmates, many journalists, politicians, and defenders of traditional values resorted to the "Marilyn Manson made 'em do it" explanation for the grisly event. Such a reaction could be expected. Popular music of all types—even those forms that circulated long before the birth of rock and roll—have often been blamed for social problems that involve youth.   1

It's not a completely unreasonable explanation. Young people connect to popular music in extraordinary ways. If music makes people move and groove, sing and shout, then who knows what else it can make them do. Although Peter Christenson and Donald Roberts would not blame Marilyn Manson or any other musician for what happened in Colorado, they would agree that for young people already in trouble, popular music can help push them to the edge and beyond. What all this means in terms of public policy is a main focus of the book, which arrives at a very interesting time in the history of American cultural politics.   2

The power of popular music—and the complex and contradictory influences music has in American society—is the subject of this very comprehensive and sophisticated volume by two West Coast scholars. Christenson and Roberts painstakingly evaluate what has now become an impressive corpus of empirical and theoretical work done on the social significance of popular music. The scope, thoroughness, and balanced treatment of the subject are the book's main contributions. It is a comprehensive, well-organized, and well-written analysis of much of the best published work on popular music that has appeared to date. The book will surely serve for years to come as the basic reference text on popular music studies in the United States.   3

That is very good news for graduate students especially. Despite music's obvious potential as an important domain for research, students in communication studies until 15 years ago had almost nowhere to turn for academic sources on popular music as a social and cultural force. Since that time lots of research on popular music has been carried out across the social sciences and humanities, and the subject has gradually found a niche in the academy.   4

This important book documents the growth of that body of work, particularly as it relates to adolescents. The authors open by trying to define the "nature of adolescence" and "music media." They then discuss how adolescents use popular music, including music video. Drawing from Christenson's path-breaking, early empirical work, the authors then explore the range of music preferences young people have, paying particular attention to heavy metal and rap—the genres most frequently criticized as antisocial. The authors then consider the role of lyrics in relation to other musical elements.   5

6   The last two chapters compare scientific approaches to the study of popular music and provide competing explanations of music's influence that are structured in a way consistent with familiar discussions of direct and limited media effects. The last chapter then raises the question that parents and politicians in particular have been asking since the Colorado shooting, "What should we do about popular music?" The research behind this volume was originally funded in part to help answer just such perplexing questions of popular music policy.

7   The authors claim that the book is "the first written about what social science research has to say about adolescents and popular music," and they stay focused on that theme. The nature of the book—an extensive literature review with a distinct emphasis on quantitative empirical research—does indeed separate this volume from other contemporary treatments of popular music. The careful, systematic, and moderate tone is refreshing in many ways and potentially very useful for students looking for inspiration. Some readers, though, will wonder why cultural studies work on popular music has been largely ignored. In this sense, the book strongly reflects the biases of its institutional origin—the Communication Department at Stanford University where cultural studies still has not made inroads against a hermetic kind of "communication science" rooted in disciplinary developments of the 1960s and 1970s.

8   The authors write in a conversational way that personalizes what could otherwise have been quite a deadly 300-page literature review. Though it has the look and feel of a reference volume, the text moves along nicely. Christenson and Roberts's enthusiasm for and knowledge of popular music combines nicely with the well-reasoned and balanced treatment they give the subject. Their measured analysis of Sut Jhally's reactionary, moralistic diatribe against MTV, Dreamworlds, is one splendid example of the evenhandedness that permeates the text.

9   Unfortunately, the publisher must have been looking to cut a few corners as the production quality of the text leaves much to be desired. The typeface is small and sometimes fades off the page, making the book difficult to read at times. Notwithstanding the limitations, the book makes an excellent contribution to the growing literature on popular music. It is a superb resource for anyone interested in learning why and how popular music has become so terribly important to American adolescents.

Source: Review of Christenson and Roberts' *It's Not Only Rock & Roll: Popular Music in the Lives of Adolescents* by James Lull, *Journal of Communication* 49, no. 4 (Autumn 1999): 212–213 ISSN: 0021-9916 Number 47272032. Used by permission of Oxford University Press.

UNDERSTANDING THE AUTHOR'S IDEAS

1. How does Lull begin his review? For what purpose?
2. Summarize Lull's overall response to this text.
3. Briefly reiterate Lull's summary of the contents of the Christenson and Roberts book.
4. What are the major strengths of this text, according to Lull?
5. What negative comments does Lull offer about the text?

EXPLORING YOUR OWN IDEAS

1. Discuss the differences between this reading as a "review" of the book and the excerpt of the book itself (the previous reading).
2. Comment on the overall usefulness of this review genre to you as a potential reader of the Christenson and Roberts text. To whom else would the review be especially useful? In other words, speculate on the audience(s) for this genre.
3. Locate an additional review of this text, using your library's online and/or print resources. Compare and contrast the reviewers' assessments.
4. Based upon your reading of a brief excerpt of this text, would you agree or disagree with Lull's critique? Explain.

Reading 6

This article, appearing in the scholarly Journal of Popular Culture, *is a revised version of a paper originally presented at a conference for communication studies scholars. This is a common occurrence within the world of scholarly research. Here Professor Burns examines a different aspect of popular music culture than the other readings in this unit. Despite the slightly different focus, and dated nature of "generational examples," interesting similarities to the other readings can be noted. Burns provides interesting insights into the relationships between popular music (and its extensions into television) and generational cultures. Notice that despite the popular subject matter and somewhat casual conversational tone of this text, it adheres to the genre conventions for a scholarly journal article and, thus, includes scholarly vocabulary, endnotes, and a formal Works Cited.*

"Popular Music, Television, and Generational Identity"

Gary Burns

Conventional wisdom has it that popular music is oriented toward the present. It is here today and gone tomorrow. It resonates with other current "lifestyle" trends (fashion, dancing, movies) and news events. It celebrates the new, the young, and offbeat deviations from tradition.

While this view is certainly correct in many ways, it is equally true that there is a growing "cult" of the past in popular music. The principal forces driving this phenomenon are demographics and, curiously, technological advancement. New technologies such as the compact disc make it possible to reclaim and "correct" more and more of the past, while hyperformatted FM radio and satellite cable TV networks such as MTV and VH1 direct this music-of-youth to the Rock Generation, an ever-expanding category that seems to include an age range of about 5–50 (as of 1994). Thus technology and generational narcissism spur the desire for a constantly widening reclamation project.

The Me Generation Goes to Heaven

3   Abbie Hoffman said it shortly before he died: Don't trust anyone under 30. This reversal of the 1960s slogan captures well a certain demographic stereotype that crystallized about the time of the movie The Big Chill (1983). At that moment, it became fashionable for Baby Boomers to wallow self-righteously in middle-age angst, to the tune of 1960s hits. The purpose of the music in this case was not to establish [a] diegetic period as in Shampoo or Coming Home—the action of The Big Chill takes place in the present. Rather, the main function of the music is to engender nostalgia and the aforementioned wallowing.

4   Although previous generations have by no means been disloyal to the popular music of their youth, the tenacious attachment of the Baby Boom to Motown, the Beatles, et al. seems unprecedented. Three main reasons account for this: (1) the Baby Boom has a dearer sense of generational identity than any other generation has had; (2) the Baby Boom generation refuses to let go of childhood and youth; and (3) the mass media, especially in their marketing and advertising functions encourage (1) and (2).

The Generation Thing

5   Not many generations have names, and certainly no generation has as many names as the Baby Boom—Bulge—Me Generation—Age Wave—Yuppies. (nl) While one could argue that these five terms are not exactly synonymous, they are so nearly so that they all apply nicely to the main characters in both The Big Chill and the TV series thirtysomething.

6   Having been named so well and so often, Baby Boomers know who they are and that they are distinct from previous generations. They are incessantly studied, written about, renamed, "targeted," and otherwise reminded of their own supposed uniqueness and importance. They are indelibly associated with The Sixties, that most hallowed/wallowed and intensely scrutinized of all decades. The metaphors that bind the generation together, at least according to popular mythology, include Vietnam, protest, and civil rights. Shoved back "in the closet" in such bowdlerized wallowings as the TV series Family Ties are the more decisive Big 3 metaphors of the 60s: sex, drugs, and . . . rock and roll. These are arguably even more powerful glue, although drugs are increasingly, and have always been, fairly sharp dividers as well as unifiers—separating those who do from those who don't, and those who used to from those who still do and those who never did. In fact, sex (especially as idealized in the hippie credo of free love) and drugs are mainly "honored" as faded, even discredited, ideologies, whereas music fondly evokes both the idea and experience of youth well wasted. Even one whose youth was "deprived" of profligate sex and drugs can, through music, relive the solidarity that ostensibly united the generation that pioneered the sex-drugs-rock combination.

Forever Young

It is not only a sense of generation that causes such interest in 1960s music. The same generation has lived through the 1970s and 1980s, yet there is no consensus of interest in popular music from these periods. Rather, radio stations, for example, play "the music you grew up with," thus directing their format to a specific age group eager to be reminded of a particular stage in their lives.   7

A poetically appropriate authority in this matter is Timothy Leary, (47–58, esp. 51–52), who theorized that adolescence is a time of heightened neural activity, during which music imprints itself with particular vigor on the nervous system. Barring subsequent "reprogramming," the music of adolescence becomes the music of one's life.   8

But there is more than biology at work in the canonization of 1960s music. Equally fundamental to the longevity of these "oldies" is what Harold Schechter called the myth of the eternal child. As Schechter points out, this myth was especially prevalent in the 1960s. In a sense, World War II ended history and established "Year Zero." The assassination of John F. Kennedy may have done something similar, so that a Baby Boomer in 1963 was both an adolescent or young adult and also a "child" in the sense of having been psychosocially "reprogrammed" or "wiped clean" by the Kennedy assassination. Thus the Baby Boomers' childhood is detached from history because of World War II, and his or her adolescence or young adulthood is similarly detached because of 11-22-63 (see Hoffman).   9

Lacking a clear connection to an acceptable history, Baby Boomers tried to create their own substitute through the "counterculture" or "Movement" or "Woodstock Nation." The archaism of these monikers, which were momentarily plausible as synonyms for "Baby Boom," indicates the failure of this generational project and also suggests a societal "wiping clean" of an envisioned page of history.   10

Born three times into worlds without history, the Baby Boom is finally flowing in the mainstream, but some of the ghetto mentality remains from memories of school and other institutional encounters between Them and Us. Childhood having lasted so long, it is a familiar and sometimes comforting frame of mind, transcending, at least temporarily, such barriers as class, occupation, and geography. To the Baby Boom, popular music is history, both personally and generationally. It provides solace from the pains of both the past and present. Old songs are good songs. And as popular culture frequently reminds us, from Casablanca to Elton John's "Sad Songs," even if a song was popular during a period of personal strife, the music provided solace then and it is the solace (qua wallowing) we reexperience when we hear the song today.   11

Radio Plays That Forgotten Song

Those who run the mass media have been acutely sensitive to these trends. A recent example is the 1989 repackaging of the VH-1 video channel into "the first channel for you." (n2) Who is "you"? Of course, it is "my generation," as one of VH1's recurring segments has been titled. Lest there be any doubt which generation this is, the network has specifically engaged history by airing features such as "Woodstock Minutes," which ran during summer 1989 to commemorate the twentieth anniversary of the Woodstock rock festival. A year later, the network began running a sort of "greatest hits" package of "ABC   12

News reports about major events from the past 40 years" (Rosenthal 36). As senior vice-president Juli Davidson explained, "We're constantly looking for a kind of programming that's going to say 'Hey 25-to 49-year-old, this is your channel, this is where things you remember are important'" (qtd. in Rosenthal 36).

13   Thus bite-sized chunks of history cascade along with the rest of the network's "flow," intermingling, in the case of "Woodstock Minutes," a once-transgressive or -transcendent festival with up-to-date videos and commercials. This sort of past-iche is occasionally reinforced via other means such as VH-1 Milestones (old news footage of Martin Luther King, Robert Kennedy, Muhammad Au, the 1972 Republican convention, etc.) and compilation-type videos. The latter, including Marvin Gaye's What's Going On and Michael Jackson's Man in the Mirror, are in a way the ultimate form of historical-regurgitational wallowing, with topical footage decontextualized to serve the soundtrack as almost-abstract imagery. Once-urgent news events become aesthetic spectacle to remind My Generation of pre-couch-potato dialectics.

14   Of course, "my generation" is also the "me generation," as demonstrated both by the aforementioned pronouns and "you," and also by the focus on convenience in the VH-1 slogan "whenever you want it" ("it" casting the tube as metaphor for sex, the breast, and history-as-drug). Some of the promos from 1989 show a couple (and their young child) in bed watching VH-1. In a sense, they are watching themselves (a common theme also in music video), since VH-1 is you/me—narcissism is neatly combined with idealized imagery of the nuclear family.

15   The most puzzling ingredient in the VH1 mixture is the insipid vjs, who, with a few exceptions, have not been suitably hippified to address the older-than-MTV generation. In fact, MTV's too-pretty vjs often seem positively articulate by comparison. VH-1 seems to have adopted, at least in many of its vj segments, a strategy based on what John Hartley called "paedocracy," which in the present situation means addressing the middle-aged "target" audience as if they were children. Not a bad scheme for dealing with viewers who, despite being adults, are still called the baby boom. As VH-l's then-president Ed Bennett put it, "We're targeting adults who are still growing up" (qtd. in Grossman 11).

16   The strategy behind this targeting seems to have changed somewhat in 1994. Whereas in 1993 VH-1 defined itself as "the difference between you and your parents," (n3) by late 1994 the network was targeting "graduates" of MTV. The aim is still to flatter the viewer into feeling young, but now with music video itself (MTV) as an explicit frame of reference (see Mendoza). (n4)

17   Another example of media exploitation of the musical past, but with a different twist, is the ill-fated song "I Heard It Through the Grapevine." Today it is, unfortunately, best known as the theme song for a group of claymated raisins who appeal to children and presumably to the child in us all. Previously the song was, also unfortunately, best known as the opening theme of The Big Chill. The raisin commercial transforms a sinister, on-the-edge love song into a jive sales vehicle, with black-stereotype raisins strutting their good rhythm while ex-counterculture demigod Buddy Miles stands in for the tragically departed Marvin Gaye on the voice track. The Big Chill similarly decontextualizes the Gaye recording (not to mention Gladys Knight and even Creedence Clearwater Revival) and reframes the song as very-meaningful-to-white-people.

18   At a more general level, it is clear that advertising recontextualizes old songs in ways that are disturbing and even shocking. The Nike shoe commercial that cannibalized the

Beatles' "Revolution" was a notorious case in point (see Wiener). Whatever John Lennon may have really meant about revolution, he did not mean to be selling shoes. Even more blatantly, a Nissan automobile commercial that aired in 1989 completely inverts the meaning of the O'Jays song "For the Love of Money." The song condemns avarice. The commercial celebrates it by showing currency erupting from various orifices of a Nissan car, to dramatize how the car supposedly saves the buyer money. The song is changed so that only the refrain "Money money money" is used.

19   Hit songs are by definition enmeshed in the commercial system through which radio plays records and sells shoes, cars, and practically everything else that can be sold. Thus any hit that criticizes this system is born in irony. Still, hearing an anti-money song on AM radio in 1974 was somehow exhilarating, while hearing it much later on TV as a paean to filthy lucre is infuriating.

20   Much of advertising's recycling of old music has this same character. Its purpose does not at all honor what the song originally meant but rather the sales objective of the moment. Objections to music video on grounds that the fixed visuals rob viewers' imaginations are misplaced. The real insidiousness lies in the theft of musical-countercultural ideologies of freedom, dissent, and revolution by TV hucksters who feel free to use any piece of music to sell any product. The violation even extends to religious music such as "Carol of the Bells," which has been used in TV commercials for wine and other products.

21   Similarly, records played unaltered and in their entirety, as on oldies radio, also change meaning as a result of the web of context that develops around them over the years. "Satisfaction" no longer clearly evokes summer 1965, because that evocation is diluted by the dozens of other times one has heard the song—on oldies radio, in concert, in remakes, at the ballpark, in Apocalypse Now. And as the listener becomes older and presumably wiser, it is possible one begins to notice that "Satisfaction" is not a very good song. A good performance and recording, yes, brimming with snarl—but as a piece of songwriting, "Satisfaction" is undistinguished. One could excuse this in a hit from summer 1965, if that were all the song is. But after the 500th hearing, the song's flaws become acutely noticeable. One asks, why did I like that song in 1965? Why is it still ubiquitous more than a quarter-century later? Does this song really deserve to be in the Eternal Top 40?

22   Every time we hear an old song, we hear, and rearrange, its accumulated baggage. Repetition is "dialogic," and when we say a song has or has not "worn well" or "aged well," we are evaluating the original text and all its subsequent "baggage" in light of our present position. Those songs that have "worn well" with the masses, or at least with a demographic subset thereof, are identified by market research and played on radio almost as relentlessly as in their heyday. But the pleasure of oldies radio comes not only from the familiarity of the songs and the predictability of the format. The more interesting moments, actually, are those that violate one's expectation.

"The Music Lasts Forever—This Offer Won't"

23   Film theorist Andre Bazin held that the invention of cinema resulted from human beings' psychological impulse toward a "recreation of the world in its own image" (21). In the case of oldies radio, MTV "Closet Classics," greatest hits albums, and other repackaging ventures, a similar but distinct impulse is at work, namely the desire to

preserve and reexperience the "image" (in this case, an acoustic image) that we have produced. The desire for stereo is often conceptualized as a quest to simulate a concert hall with perfect fidelity. But this is no longer the primary function of stereo sound and multitrack recording. The stereo recording is now usually the "original," and a concert performance is often a "reproduction," faithful or otherwise, of the recording (see Attali; see also Goodwin Dancing).

24   Walter Benjamin notwithstanding, the original recording has aura. This aura is based on time, rather than on place as in Benjamin's discussion of statues in temples. The aura of a record arises from its immutability and repeatability. We hear the exact same text (immutability) numerous times (repeatability). Further, the text of "Satisfaction" I heard on radio in Chicago in 1965 is exactly the same as the one someone else heard on a jukebox in Poughkeepsie in 1970.

25   Oldies radio and similar phenomena depend on our desire to reexperience an exact acoustic image. We want the Rolling Stones' version of "Satisfaction," not Devo's. However, there are cracks in the system that are both interesting and annoying.

26   If you listen to oldies radio, you are quite likely to hear recordings that differ from the texts originally played on AM radio. Examples include "Let's Hang On!", "Tighter, Tighter," "Cherry, Cherry," "Bend Me, Shape Me," "Penny Lane," "War," "I Can't Turn You Loose," and many others. The stereo mixes used on FM today often sound quite different from the mono and dj versions heard on AM years ago. CD rereleases often involve remixing, re-recording, restoring, and otherwise tampering with the "original."

27   These alterations disturb the aura of a recording, in much the same way that colorization changes a monochrome movie. Recording engineers reclaim a past we did not even know was there. Suddenly the text, and in a sense the past, is no longer immutable. The new improved past gains relevance but loses authenticity. The past changes not through inversion or denial, but through enhancement.

28   And so it is that the Columbia CD Club advertised best-of collections by the Who, Doors, and Led Zeppelin on Postmodern MTV in 1990. "The music lasts forever—this offer won't." In lasting forever, the music nonetheless changes, both in actual textual substance and in meaning. The Who and Doors especially were once countercultural but are now, apparently, postmodern. As audio fidelity becomes clearer and dearer, meaning blurs.

29   Similarly, as music becomes more intertwined with visual imagery, especially through music video, we see more but know less. More than a decade after MTV's sign-on, there is general agreement that music video is trivial and vapid, yet somehow important. The semiotic slippage often attributed to video clips themselves has spread to MTV as the vehicle of their presentation. What originally was a carefully contrived package of rec-room set, brother/sister-next-door vjs, and New Wave-heavy metal dips in a rotation-format flow has now become something much different.

30   Gradually and quietly, MTV has taken a turn away from narrowcasting and format programming. Its "targeted age group" of 12–34 (MTV Press Release; Russell "MTV in 2nd" 96) reaches into Baby Boom territory and far beyond the pimply teenage range one would expect. (n5) Significant programming changes include forays into alleged comedy, game shows, and "real"-life soap operas; expanded roles for vjs and other personalities; and increased reliance on titled programs (as distinct from for-

mat). As MTV Networks chairman Tom Freston put it, "We found that the application of proven television-programming techniques—like, you know, shows—gets people to watch longer once they land on the dial" (qtd. in Goldberg 64).

While MTV's publicity as of 1989 maintained that its new programs were on the "cutting edge," many of the changes looked a bit like retreat into tried-and-true formulas. Club MTV merely updated American Bandstand, with Tartar-Control Julie Brown in place of Ipana Dick Clark. Remote Control was the network's best comedy effort to that point, but mainly because it was a parody of worn-out game-show formulas.   31

More recently, MTV has taken a lesson from the Fox network in expanding its "crossover" appeal, not only along racial lines (Yo! MTV Raps), but especially across generations. Like Fox's The Simpsons, MTV's Ren and Stimpy, Beavis and Butt-Head, and Speed Racer are cartoon series that appeal to young people but also "cross over" to an adult audience. Speed Racer reminds the older generation of the program's original run in syndication in 1967. Beavis and Butt-Head combines timeless "male" bad taste with timeless bad videos from throughout MTV's brief history. The viewer can enjoy the videos on their own terms or can revel in Beavis and Butt-Head's voice-over commentary (see Roberts 81–109).   32

In a sense, Beavis and Butt-Head is itself a recycling of MTV's earlier efforts at retrospection. These included Martha's Greatest Hits (1990), an intriguing, quasi-historical presentation that dished up a gumbo of past and present videos. The "classics" in this program were disappointingly few and conservatively chosen. Host Martha Quinn was the main link with the past, since she was "one of MTV's original VJs," as an MTV press release proudly noted. In the short period she had been away from MTV she had grown up and was now a sexy broad rather than a girl-next-door. Originally part of an undistinguished staff of interchangeable, hip-to-be-square presenters, she was in 1990 the major object of promotion in a titled, scheduled slice of format disguised as a program. Ostensibly designed to appeal to people who had watched MTV five years earlier and who perhaps were less inclined to do so in 1990, Martha's Greatest Hits was actually extremely soft as a dose of history or nostalgia. Nonetheless it is significant that MTV repeatedly lays claim to video's past, as it has also done with the past of Baby Boom rock in Closet Classics. Late in 1994, VH1 began its own version of Martha's Greatest Hits, minus Martha and in fact without any host at all. This flow of old videos, known as The Big 80's, is identifiable as a "program" only by virtue of a brief bumper/title sequence and an intrusive logo continuously present in the upper left corner of the screen. Taken together, VH1 and MTV (and possibly their companion network Nickelodeon) seem to be embarked on an ambitious project of engaging the Baby Boom and subsequent generations from "cradle to grave." (n6).   33

Go Ahead—Make a Wish

As a final example of musical/televisual attempts to drag the past into the present (or, alternatively, to reconfigure the present as consistent with one's past ideals), we might look briefly at the Madonna "Like a Prayer" Pepsi commercial. Madonna is in many ways the quintessential music-video star. By bringing together things that are not supposed to be brought together, she proposes new ways of understanding. For the most part, she does this visually, so that her propositions are largely nonverbal,   34 nondiscursive, and intuitive. They are also ambiguous and leave her with plausible deniability that she intended to offend or blaspheme.

35   The 1989 Pepsi commercial was an interesting attempt to have synthesis without any clash (an advertiser's dream) in three of Madonna's customary registers—race, religion, and generation. (n7) The generational domain is stressed, probably because it connects with the ad campaign slogan "Pepsi, a generation ahead." Adult Madonna, in color, sits in her living room watching what is supposed to be home-movie footage. A hand-held sign in the monochrome "home movie" identifies the footage as "Madonna's eighth birthday." Magically, 8-year-old Madonna and 30-year-old Madonna change places and explore each other's worlds.

36   The monochrome world expands into a joyous, interracial, church-and-school environment filled with dancing and singing. Thirty-year-old Madonna immediately becomes something of a Pied Piper in this world. Meanwhile, 8-year-old Madonna roams in awe, and in color, through 30-year-old Madonna's luxurious home. There are no other people in this world, but that does not bother 8-year-old Madonna. "Like a Prayer" wails triumphantly in both worlds. Suddenly the music stops, each Madonna is back in her proper world, and 30-year-old Madonna, sipping a Pepsi and addressing 8-year-old Madonna and the camera, instructs us: "Go ahead—make a wish." A graphic delivers the Pepsi slogan to conclude the commercial.

37   The ad flatters and congratulates the Baby Boom audience. The depicted means of generational articulation is the magic screen, a common device in music video. Thirty-year-old Madonna watches 8-year-old Madonna, and vice versa. The rapport between the two suggests a mother-daughter relationship. Madonna is both adult and child, mother and daughter (as in her video Papa Don't Preach, which also includes supposed home-movie footage of Madonna as a child). She is both the adult star and the child who longs to be a star. She is self-contained—the adult and child, because they are magically in touch and identical, are each other's fulfillment.

38   This commercial, expensively produced and itself promoted in advance by other commercials, was aired only once before being withdrawn by Pepsi in response to pressure from groups offended by the music-video version of "Like a Prayer," released one day after the commercial (see Marsh). The commercial's "world premiere" (and unanticipated swan song) took place during that sitcom oasis of racial and generational harmony, The Cosby Show.

39   Pepsi's textual strategy in the commercial is clear—identify itself with racial harmony, religion, and the timeless unfolding of "new" generations. Just as laxative makers try to "have it both ways" by calling their product "gentle yet effective," Pepsi seeks to present itself as old yet new, black yet white, religious yet sexy. The formula for obtaining this unity in your own life is simple: make a wish.

40   So far so good for Pepsi, but the music-video version of Like a Prayer carries unity a dangerous step further, beyond the bounds of home-movie narcissism and doctor-lawyer, both-black family sitcom. It also suggests the necessity to act, rather than just wish. As innocuous or enlightened or muddle-headed as the video may appear to some viewers, Pepsi could not endorse it, even indirectly by allowing the commercial to be replayed. For one evening, Pepsi was "a generation ahead," but quickly decided it was too far ahead. Unity of opposites is a theme that can be pushed to one limit on MTV and VH1, and quite another in a Pepsi commercial. Interestingly, the only unity that Pepsi explicitly rejected was that of the commercial

and video, which were after all united only by their soundtrack. Paradoxically, the music itself, once confined to the fringes of television, is now mainstream. For better or worse, much of rock's residual potential for transgression is located in video, despite the fact that this potential is only rarely used. (n8) For her transgressions, we should absolve Madonna for making the video, even while lamenting that she made the commercial. Pepsi apparently hoped she was controversial yet safe, but discovered that she is only the former.

Conclusion: Because the Past Is Just a Goodbye

"People try to put us down," as pre-corporate Pete Townshend wrote, but sometimes it is hard to see how the process works. The "generation gap" is a concept as extinct as that of the "counterculture," yet Townshend's generation is still put down by virtue of being so often a "targeted" group.   41

While it may sometimes appear that Baby Boomers have control, directly or indirectly, of much of the television and music industries, the relationship is reciprocal. The control of the Baby Boom depends in large part upon ideological regulation of the contested past, of what are now called "wonder years" and "Woodstock Minutes." Nostalgia is safe. Thinking too seriously about the past and how it led to the present is dangerous.   42

Ultimately, the successful incorporation of the Baby Boom into the System involves redefinition of some basic terms. When Ed Bennett became President of VH-1 in June 1989, he quickly charted a new course for the network: "Now, [Bennett] says, 'the attitude is "having fun with love and work"'.. . . it's relevant and at times irreverent, and it values experience'" (Grossman 11). (n9) Voila—new meanings for "relevant," "irreverent," and "experience." Even more to the point is Bennett's attitude toward "attitude." Woodstock, historical "milestones," and memories of counterculture notwithstanding, present-day love and work are, above all, "fun." Ah—what a relief that our troubles are all behind us!   43

Notes

(n1) Some other names that did not stick: Pepsi Generation, Woodstock Nation, Movement, Counterculture, and, I predict, Destructive Generation.

(n2) Late in 1994, VH-1 dropped its hyphen and rechristened itself/VHI. I will use hyphenation when referring specifically to the period before the name change.

(n3) VH-1 advertisement in Rolling Stone. A 1994 VH-1 promo referred to the network as "the fountain of youth—with a volume control."

(n4) My thanks to Elizabeth Kizer for bringing the Mendoza article to my attention.

(n5) Russell ("MTV in 2nd") also notes that the target demographic of VH-1, as of 1993, was 25–49, and especially "the 25–34 core" (96).

(n6) My thanks to Joe Laposa for this idea. For a discussion of the evolution of MTVs programming through the early 1990s, see Goodwin, "Fatal." For a discussion of the intentionality of MTV, VH-1, and other Viacom-owned networks in promoting the perpetuation and expansion of "youth culture," see Schultze et al., 178–210.

(n7) My discussion of the commercial is built upon Bums and Kizer, 7–9.

(n8) As Paul Attallah argues: "Whereas rock is confronted with the broadening of its audience and the impossibility of maintaining any youth specificity, television is confronted with the fragmentation of its audience and the consequent necessity of maintaining it at all costs. This is most clearly exemplified in the movement from traditional broadcasting to modern narrowcasting, and music video is the outstanding example of this shift" (33). As we have seen, however, the cable-TV impulse toward narrowcasting is periodically blunted by the fear of becoming too narrow and by the hope of being able to "cross over" to a larger audience by means of strategic deviations from the narrowcasting formula. See Hill; Russell, "MTV in 2nd"; and Russell, "MTV Experiments."

(n9) Ed Bennett was fired in 1994. It is his replacement, John Sykes, who has renamed the network (minus hyphen) and implemented the targeting of MTV "graduates."

WORKS CITED

Attali, Jacques. Noise: The Political Economy of Music. 1977. Trans. Brian Massumi. Minneapolis: U of Minnesota P, 1982.

Attallah, Paul. "Music Television." Watching All the Music: Rock Video and Beyond. Ed. Gareth Sansom. Montreal: Working Papers in Communications, McGill U, 1987. 19–40.

Bazin, Andre. "The Myth of Total Cinema." 1946. What Is Cinema? Ed. and trans. Hugh Gray. Berkeley: U of California P, 1967. 17–22.

Bums, Gary and Elizabeth Kizer. "Madonna: Like a Dichotomy." American Culture Association conference, Toronto, 8 March 1990. ERIC ED 371 417.

Goldberg, Michael. "MTV's Sharper Picture." Rolling Stone 8 Feb. 1990: 60–64+.

Goodwin, Andrew. Dancing in the Distraction Factory: Music Television and Popular Culture. Minneapolis: U of Minnesota P, 1992.

_____."Fatal Distractions: MTV Meets Postmodern Theory." Sound and Vision: The Music Video Reader. Ed. Simon Frith, Andrew Goodwin, and Lawrence Grossberg. London: Routledge, 1993. 45–66.

Grossman, Andrew. "VH-l: Born Again." Cable World 20 Nov. 1989: 1+.

Hartley, John. "Invisible Fictions: Television Audiences, Paedocracy, Pleasure." 1987. Television Studies: Textual Analysis. Ed. Gary Burns and Robert J. Thompson. New York: Praeger, 1989. 223–43.

Hill, Doug. "MTV Changes Its Tunes." TV Guide 5 Sept. 1992: 18–19.

Hoffman, Paul Dennis. "Rock and Roll and JFK: A Study of Thematic Changes in Rock and Roll Lyrics Since the Assassination of John F. Kennedy." Popular Music and Society 10.2 (1985): 59–79.

Leary, Timothy, with Robert Anton Wilson and George A. Koopman. Neuropolitics: The Sociobiology of Human Metamorphosis. Los Angeles: Starseed/Peace P, 1977. 47–58.

Marsh, Dave. "Acts of Contrition." Rock & Roll Confidential May 1989:1–2.

Mendoza, Manuel. "VH-l Aims at First MTV Graduates." St. Louis Post-Dispatch 3 Nov. 1994: 6G.

MTV. Press release, undated (ca. Dec. 1989).

Roberts, Robin. Ladies First: Women in Music Videos. Jackson: UP of Mississippi, 1996.

Rosenthal, Herma M. "Cable Outlets Scare Up Viewers." TV Guide, Chicago metropolitan edition, 8 Sept. 1990: 36.

Russell, Deborah. "MTV Experiments to Hold Viewers." Billboard 3 July 1993:1+.

_____. "MTV in 2nd Decade: A True Network." Billboard 26 June 1993: 1+.

Schechter, Harold. "The Myth of the Eternal Child in Sixties America." The Popular Culture Reader. Ed. Jack Nachbar, Deborah Weiser, and John L. Wright. Bowling Green, OH: Bowling Green State University Popular Press, 1978. 64–78.

Schultze, Quentin J., et al. Dancing in the Dark: Youth, Popular Culture, and the Electronic Media. Grand Rapids, MI: Eerdmans, 1991.

VH-1. Advertisement. Rolling Stone 14 Oct. 1993: 84.

Wiener, Jori. "Beatles Buy-Out: How Nike Bought the Beatles' 'Revolution.' " 1987. Professors, Politics and Pop. London: Verso, 1991. 289–93.

UNDERSTANDING THE AUTHOR'S IDEAS

1. Why is the Baby Boom generation particularly loyal to the music of their youth?
2. What is somewhat unique about the "history" of the Baby Boom generation? What impact does this have on their music? In what ways has modern media exploited the music of previous generations? Give examples.
3. Explain Burns' notion that "Repetition [of music] is 'dialogic.' "
4. What changes in music have occurred with the increase in popularity of music videos?
5. Briefly explain the role of MTV in pop music culture.
6. Briefly summarize the Pepsi incident. What is Burns' main point in relating it?
7. Express Burns' position in a sentence or two.

EXPLORING YOUR OWN IDEAS

1. Explore the applicability to your generation of Burns' idea of generational identity with a particular type of music. Will your generation be loyal to a particular type of music 20 years from now? If so, why and to what type? If not, why not?
2. Discuss the appeal of music versus music videos. What do you see as the primary personal and "social" uses of each?
3. Discuss the impact of public pressure on music marketing. Consider current examples.
4. Examine the current relationship between Internet technology and the pop music world. Consider the relationship from the perspective of young people, the music companies, the recording artists, and the general consumer.

SINGING ALONG WITH THE MUSIC...

(*Source:* Anthony DiBerardo, ©diberardo.com.)

Each generation is said to create its own music identity. Discuss the characterization of the 1970s and now portrayed in this cartoon. Briefly characterize your own music identity in a short personal essay, relating it to Diberardo's portrayal of your generation and to Burns' ideas in the essay above. Then draw your own cartoon to help depict your music identity.

UNIT WRITING ASSIGNMENT SUGGESTIONS

1. Think about the role(s) that music plays in your life. Write a **personal essay** about the significance of music in your everyday experience as a college student.
2. Conduct a field observation of the audience at one or more concerts. Write a **field observation report,** making note of specific details of audience reaction and interaction. Consider individual and group behaviors. Attend more than one concert of varying types and then compare and contrast the audiences at each type.
3. Keep a **journal** tracking your own music preferences for at least two weeks. Note when and where you listen to music, what type you listen to, what specific performers you enjoy the most, if and when you listen alone or with others, etc. Reflect upon what your own music choices reveal about your interests, values, and behavior as a college student today. Compare your journal responses to those of fellow classmates.

4. Attend a musical event and write a **review** of the performance. If possible, read some earlier reviews of the group's work. Compare the reviewers' thoughts to your own.

5. Conduct research on some specific type or period of music and then write an **informative report** on your findings. Predetermine the level of your audience's musical knowledge.

6. Locate one or two interesting journal articles on the role of music in the lives of college students. Write a succinct and useful **abstract** of the article(s).

7. Attend a musical event of a type different than you ordinarily attend—perhaps an opera or a chamber music concert. Note your response and write a **reaction paper** about your experience.

8. Write a **proposal** to your campus administration or student activities office soliciting approval and funds to sponsor a music event for next semester.

9. Write a **social science research** paper on some aspect of music and youth culture. You might consider tracing the ethical debate about the downloading of music off the Internet or researching the role of music within some specific ethnic group.

10. Locate five valuable Web sites on a type of music you enjoy. Identify them and then write a **Web site critique** comparing and contrasting their features and credibility.

11. Read additional sections of one of the scholarly texts excerpted in this chapter. Then interview numerous college students about the role of music in their lives. Write a **stance or position paper** synthesizing the scholarly ideas with your personal observations.

WORK IN AMERICA

A great many students in American colleges and universities work while they attend school. At the university where one of the authors of this book teaches, for example, 78 percent of the full-time students have jobs, and the average number of hours they work each week is 22. This means these students are taking four or five classes, working at a job that most people would consider part time, plus trying to have friends, interact with their family, enjoy the culture they live in, and so on. The working student is a very busy student indeed.

There is some evidence that working college students in the United States are not very different in one respect from all adults in the nation. In general, Americans tend to work very hard. Why do they do so? Is there something unique in American culture that drives people to work extremely hard? Is hard work necessary to prosper in America? Are there other factors that lead to success in America besides hard work? Does schooling prepare students to enter the world of work, or is schooling an end unto itself, not directly related to work?

The readings in this unit address these and other questions that face today's students, who must think about the work they do while they are students and the work they will do after they finish their studies. The readings, which vary in content, also vary in genre. They range from an excerpt of a personal field study of today's low-wage workers to a chapter of a scholarly study of the overworked American to a public radio address on the working teenager to an economic treatise on the future of work in our nation.

Reading 1

Schor's 1992 book, which draws on the scholarship of both economics and sociology, is the first major study to explain, or even acknowledge, that the number of hours Americans spend working has been steadily increasing for two decades. Schor's study is not apolitical or free from bias: She clearly believes that Americans should not work as hard as they do and that they should treasure leisure time more than they do.

Excerpt from *The Overworked American: The Unexpected Decline of Leisure*

Juliet B. Schor

Chapter 1—The Overworked American

1   In the last twenty years the amount of time Americans have spent at their jobs has risen steadily. Each year the change is small, amounting to about nine hours, or slightly more than one additional day of work. In any given year, such a small increment has probably been imperceptible. But the accumulated increase over two decades is substantial. When surveyed, Americans report that they have only sixteen and a half hours of leisure a week, after the obligations of job and household are taken care of. Working hours are already longer than they were forty years ago. If present trends continue, by the end of the century Americans will be spending as much time at their jobs as they did back in the nineteen twenties.[1]

2   The rise of worktime was unexpected. For nearly a hundred years, hours had been declining. When this decline abruptly ended in the late 1940s, it marked the beginning of a new era in worktime. But the change was barely noticed. Equally surprising, but also hardly recognized, has been the deviation from Western Europe. After progressing in tandem for nearly a century, the United States veered off into a trajec-

---

[1] In attempting to keep the main text simple, I have relegated detailed discussion of these estimates, discussions of sources and methods, and debates among scholars to the notes and the appendix.

tory of declining leisure, while in Europe work has been disappearing. Forty years later, the differences are large. U.S. manufacturing employees currently work 320 more hours—the equivalent of over two months—than their counterparts in West Germany or France.[2]

The decline in Americans' leisure time is in sharp contrast to the potential provided by the growth of productivity. Productivity measures the goods and services that result from each hour worked.[3] When productivity rises, a worker can either produce the current output in less time, or remain at work the same number of hours and produce more. Every time productivity increases, we are presented with the possibility of either more free time or more money. That's the productivity dividend.   3

Since 1948, productivity has failed to rise in only five years. The level of productivity of the U.S. worker has more than doubled.[4] In other words, we could now produce our 1948 standard of living (measured in terms of marketed goods and services) in less than half the time it took in that year. We actually could have chosen the four-hour day. Or a working year of six months. Or, *every worker in the United States could now be taking every other year off from work—with pay.* Incredible as it may sound, this is just the simple arithmetic of productivity growth in operation.   4

But between 1948 and the present we did not use any of the productivity dividend to reduce hours. In the first two decades after 1948, productivity grew rapidly, at about 3 percent a year. During that period, worktime did not fall appreciably. Annual hours per labor force participant fell only slightly. And on a per-capita (rather than a labor force) basis, they even rose a bit. Since then, productivity growth has been lower, but still positive, averaging just over 1 percent a year. Yet hours have risen steadily for two decades. In 1990, the average American owns and consumes more than twice as much as he or she did in 1948, but also has less free time.[5]   5

How did this happen? Why has leisure been such a conspicuous casualty of prosperity? In part, the answer lies in the difference between the markets for consumer   6

---

[2] Author's estimates, 1988, from Bureau of Labor Statistics, Office of Productivity and Technology, "Underlying Data for Indexes of Output per Hour, Hourly Compensation, and Unit Labor Costs in Manufacturing, Twelve Industrial Countries, 1950–1988," June 1989.

[3] I am using the term *productivity* as a shorthand for "labor productivity," which is, strictly speaking, measured as output per hour of labor input. Official statistics assume that productivity growth for government workers is always zero. Also, productivity figures are calculated only for the "market" economy and exclude unpaid work in the home.

[4] Figures are from *Economic Report of the President (ERP)* (Washington, D.C.: Government Printing Office, 1991), 338–39, tables B–46 and B–47. They are for the business sector.

[5] These are from my calculations of total working hours per capita and per labor force from the National Income and Product Accounts. Between 1948 and 1969, per-capita hours rose from 1,069 to 1,124, or 55 hours. Annual hours per labor force participant fell slightly—from 1,968 to 1,944 hours. See the appendix for the methods used in calculating these figures.

On a per-person basis, gross national product went from $9,060 in 1948 to $19,900 at the end of 1988 (measured in constant 1988 dollars). See *ERP*, 1989 ed., 308, table B–1 and 344, table B–32.

products and free time. Consider the former, the legendary American market. It is a veritable consumer's paradise, offering a dazzling array of products varying in style, design, quality, price, and country of origin. The consumer is treated to GM versus Toyota, Kenmore versus GE, Sony, or Magnavox, the Apple versus the IBM. We've got Calvin Klein, Anne Klein, Liz Claiborne, and Levi-Strauss; McDonald's, Burger King, and Colonel Sanders. Marketing experts and advertisers spend vast sums of money to make these choices appealing—even irresistible. And they have been successful. In cross-country comparisons, Americans have been found to spend more time shopping than anyone else. They also spend a higher fraction of the money they earn.[6] And with the explosion of consumer debt, many are now spending what they haven't earned.

7   After four decades of this shopping spree, the American standard of living embodies a level of material comfort unprecedented in human history. The American home is more spacious and luxurious than the dwellings of any other nation. Food is cheap and abundant. The typical family owns a fantastic array of household and consumer appliances: we have machines to wash our clothes and dishes, mow our lawns, and blow away our snow. On a per-person basis, yearly income is nearly $22,000 a year— or sixty-five times the average income of half the world's population.[7]

8   On the other hand, the "market" for free time hardly even exists in America. With few exceptions, employers (the sellers) don't offer the chance to trade off income gains for a shorter work day or the occasional sabbatical. They just pass on income, in the form of annual pay raises or bonuses, or, if granting increased vacation or personal days, usually do so unilaterally.[8] Employees rarely have the chance to exercise an actual choice about how they will spend their productivity dividend. The closest substitute for a "market in leisure" is the travel and other leisure industries that advertise products to occupy our free time. But this indirect effect has been weak, as consumers crowd increasingly expensive leisure spending into smaller periods of time.

9   Nor has society provided a forum for deliberate choice. The growth of worktime did not occur as a result of public debate. There has been little attention from government, academia, or civic organizations. For the most part, the issue has been off the agenda, a nonchoice, a hidden trade off. It was not always so. As early as 1791, when Philadelphia carpenters went on strike for the ten-hour day, there was public awareness about hours of work. Throughout the nineteenth century, and well into the twentieth, the reduction of worktime was one of the nation's most pressing social issues.

10   Employers and workers fought about the length of the working day, social activists delivered lectures, academics wrote treatises, courts handed down decisions, and government legislated hours of work. Through the Depression, hours remained a ma-

---

[6] Full citations for these claims can be found in note 38, chap. 5, p. 210.

[7] Current GNP per capita is $21,953 per year. Calculated from *ERP,* 286, table B–1 and 321, table B–31. Income figures for other countries can be found in the annual *World Development Report* (Washington, D.C.: World Bank).

[8] The major exception on days off is for the 18 percent of the workforce covered under collective bargaining agreements.

jor social preoccupation. Today these debates and conflicts are long forgotten. Since the 1930s, the choice between work and leisure has hardly been a choice at all, at least in any conscious sense.

Almost as paradoxical as the rise of worktime itself is the fact that it occurred on   11
the heels of widespread predictions that work was disappearing. By the late 1950s, the problem of excessive working hours had been solved—at least in the minds of the experts. The four-day week was thought to "loom on the immediate horizon." It was projected that economic progress would yield steady reductions in working time. By today, it was estimated that we could have either a twenty-two-hour week, a six-month workyear, or a standard retirement age of thirty-eight.[9]

These prospects worried the experts. In 1959 the Harvard Business Review an-   12
nounced that "boredom, which used to bother only aristocrats, had become a common curse." What would ordinary Americans do with all that extra time? How would housewives cope with having their husbands around the house for three- or four-day weekends? The pending crisis of leisure came in for intensive scrutiny. Foundations funded research projects on it. The American Council of Churches met on the issue of spare time. Institutes and Departments of Leisure Studies cropped up as academia prepared for the onslaught of free time. There were many like Harvard sociologist David Riesman who wrote about "play" in the lonely crowd, and the "abyss" and "stultification" of mass leisure.[10]

The leisure scare died out as the abyss of free time failed to appear. Throughout   13
the 1970s leisure was a non-issue. A few lone souls recognized that men's hours had not budged in over two decades. And there were those who argued that we should reduce hours in order to solve the worsening unemployment situation. But virtually no one realized that beginning in the late 1960s the United States had entered an era of rising worktime. Even as the 1980s were ending, the question of time eluded academics. An otherwise excellent and widely read study on the American standard of living by economist Frank Levy failed to broach the subject. Neither leisure nor working hours even appear in the index.[11]

---

[9] Russell Lynes, "Time on Our Hands," in Eric Larrabee and Rolf Meyerson, eds., *Mass Leisure* (Glencoe, Ill.: Free Press, 1958), 346.

  Predictions on current worktime are from 1967 Testimony from a Senate Subcommittee, cited in Nancy Gibbs, "How America Has Run Out of Time," *Time,* 24 April 1989, p. 59.

[10] Reuel Denney, "The Leisure Society," *Harvard Business Review* 37, 3 (May–June 1959): 47, 60, on boredom.

  See Lynes, "Time on Our Hands," for discussion of these efforts.

  See David Riesman, with Reuel Denney and Nathan Glazer, *The Lonely Crowd: A Study of the Changing American Character* (New Haven: Yale University Press, 1950); or "Leisure and Work in Post-Industrial Society," Riesman's contribution to Larrabee and Meyerson, *Mass Leisure*.

[11] The most prominent voice on the stability of postwar hours has been economist John D. Owen, whose books include *Working Lives, Working Hours: An Economic Analysis* (Lexington, Mass.: Lexington Books, 1979), and *Reduced Working Hours: Cure for Unemployment or Economic Burden?* (Baltimore: Johns Hopkins University Press, 1989).

  See, for example, Sar A. Levitan and Richard S. Belous, *Shorter Hours, Shorter Weeks: Spreading the Work to Reduce Unemployment* (Baltimore: Johns Hopkins University Press, 1977).

  Frank Levy, *Dollars and Dreams: The Changing American Income Distribution* (New York: W. W. Norton, 1988).

14   One highly visible aspect of the increase in work finally did draw attention—the growing participation of women in the labor force. Sociologists began writing on "role overload" and the dual responsibilities of home and family. But rising work has been seen as a women's issue. That both women and men are working longer hours has still not been recognized. *Despite the fact that worktime has been increasing for twenty years, this is the first major study to explain or even acknowledge this trend.*[12]

15   In fact, prominent researchers are holding onto the conventional wisdom of declining worktime. In 1990, Brookings economist Gary Burtless wrote that "average time on the job has fallen more than five hours a week—roughly 13%—since 1950." Leading experts on how people use their time draw similar conclusions. According to John P. Robinson of the University of Maryland, Americans "have more free time today than ever before." But we should be skeptical of these claims. As I shall argue in chapter 2, my estimates indicate a major increase in working hours.[13]

16   Contrary to the views of some researchers, the rise of work is not confined to a few, selective groups, but has affected the great majority of working Americans. Hours have risen for men as well as women, for those in the working class as well as professionals. They have grown for all marital statuses and income groups. The increase also spans a

---

[12]This is not to say there has been no attention paid lately to working hours. Historians have recently produced some new and excellent works. These include Benjamin Hunnicutt's *Work Without End: Abandoning Shorter Hours for the Right to Work* (Philadelphia: Temple University Press, 1988); Gary Cross, *A Quest for Time* (Berkeley, Calif.: University of California Press, 1989), *Worktime and Industrialization: An International History* (Philadelphia: Temple University Press, 1988), and his forthcoming *Time and Money: The Making of Consumerist Modernity* (London: Routledge, forthcoming); and David Roediger and Phillip S. Foner, *Our Own Time: A History of American Labor and the Working Day* (London: Verso, 1989). Among sociologists, the work of Carmen Sirianni is exemplary and includes his "Economies of Time in Social Theory: Three Approaches Compared," *Current Perspectives in Social Theory,* vol. 8 (Greenwich, Conn.: JAI Press, 1987), 161–95, and *Working Time in Transition,* jointly edited with Karl Hinrichs and William Roche (Philadelphia: Temple University Press, 1991). Europeans have done far more on this issue, although most of it from the perspective that work is disappearing. A prominent example is André Gorz, whose recent book, *A Critique of Economic Reason* (London: Verso, 1989), is oriented to the issue of working time. See also the work of Claus Offe.

[13]Examples include André Gorz, *Critique of Economic Reason* (London: Verso, 1989); Fred Block, *Post-Industrial Possibilities: A Critique of Economic Discourse* (Berkeley: University of California, 1990), 205–6; Theresa Diss Greis, *The Decline of Annual Hours Worked in the United States Since 1947* (Philadelphia: Industrial Relations Unit, Wharton, University of Pennsylvania, 1984); F. Thomas Juster and Frank P. Stafford, "The Allocation of Time: Empirical Findings, Behavioral Models, and Problems of Measurement," Working Paper Institute for Social Research, University of Michigan, February 1990; and John P. Robinson, "Time's Up," *American Demographics,* 11, 7 (July 1989): 32–35.

Gary Burtless, "Are We All Working Too Hard? It's Better Than Watching Oprah," *Wall Street Journal,* 4 January 1990. Burtless missed the fact that paid time off has fallen substantially in the last decade.

John P. Robinson, "Time's Up," *American Demographics,* 11 (1989): 34. For the same conclusion based on a shorter period of time, but essentially similar data, see Juster and Stafford, "The Allocation of Time," p. 8.

My estimates, which are both more comprehensive and representative of the U.S. population than those of previous researchers, reveal a clear and dramatic trend to more work. For discussion of the differences among estimates, see the appendix. A few economists, particularly those on the left, have alluded to a rise in worktime. See, for example, publications of the Economic Policy Institute.

wide range of industries.'[14] Indeed, the shrinkage of leisure experienced by nearly all types of Americans has created a profound structural crisis of time.

While academics have missed the decline of leisure time, ordinary Americans 17 have not. And the media provide mounting evidence of "time poverty,"[15] overwork, and a squeeze on time. Nationwide, people report their leisure time has declined by as much as one-third since the early 1970s. Predictably, they are spending less time on the basics, like sleeping and eating. Parents are devoting less attention to their children. Stress is on the rise, partly owing to the "balancing act" of reconciling the demands of work and family life."

The experts were unable to predict or even see these trends. I suspect they were 18 blinded by the power of technology—seduced by futurist visions of automated factories effortlessly churning out products. After all, they say, if we can build robots to do humans' work, what sense is there in doing it ourselves? Appealing as this optimism may be, it misses a central point about technology: the context is all important. Machines can just as easily be used to harness human labor as to free it. To understand why forty years of increasing productivity have failed to liberate us from work, I found that I had to abandon a naïve faith in technological potential and analyze the social, economic, and political context in which technology is put to use. Only then was I able to see that the experts vision of our economic system is both analytically mistaken, in ignoring powerful economic incentives to maintain long working hours, and historically inadequate, owing to a selective misreading of the past.

The experts' faith is based on their assumption that capitalism has already proved 19 itself by a hundred years of declining worktime. Before the market system, the majority of people are thought to have toiled from sunup to sundown, three hundred and sixty-five days a year. Today we are blessed with a forty-hour week, annual vacations, and extended years of schooling and retirement. The reigning conventional wisdom is that capitalism has created the world's first truly leisured societies.

Yet the claim that capitalism has delivered us from excessive toil can be sustained 20 only if we take as our point of comparison eighteenth- and nineteenth-century Europe and America—a period that witnessed what were probably the longest and most arduous work schedules in the history of humankind. If we set our sights back a bit farther chronologically, as I do in chapter 3, the comparison underlying the conventional wisdom fails to hold up.

---

[14]Some, although not all, of these conclusions are presented in Laura Leete-Guy and Juliet B. Schor, "Assessing the Time Squeeze Hypothesis: Estimates of Market and Non-Market Hours in the United States, 1969–1987," unpublished mimeo, Harvard University, June 1990, as well as an updated forthcoming version in *Industrial Relations.*

[15]The phrase "time poverty" was used by Clair Vickrey in an important article entitled "The Time-Poor: A New Look at Poverty," *Journal of Human Resources,* 12, 1 (1977): 27–48.

Harris, *Americans and the Arts,* 60, table 1, on the decline of leisure time.

On sleep, see note 22, Chapter 1. Eating figures were calculated from John P. Robinson, "Trends in Americans' Use of Time: Some Preliminary 1965–1975–1985 Comparisons," 1986 mimeo, University of Maryland, Survey Research Center, calculated from table 5, p. 36.

On children see Victor Fuchs, *Women's Quest for Economic Equality* (Cambridge, Mass.: Harvard University Press, 1988); and Sylvia Ann Hewlett, *When the Bough Breaks: The Cost of Neglecting Our Children* (New York: Basic Books, 1991).

21   The first step to a realistic comparison is to reject the idea that the medieval economy entailed continuous toil. It is unlikely that the workday was much above the standards of today. The medieval economy also provided ample opportunities for leisure within the year. And the medieval period appears not to have been exceptional, at least in Western history.[16] Leisure time in Ancient Greece and Rome was also plentiful. Athenians had fifty to sixty holidays annually, while in Tarentum they apparently had half the year. In the old Roman calendar, 109 of 355 days were designated *nefasti* or "unlawful for judicial and political business." By the mid-fourth century, the number of *feriae publicae* (public festival days) reached 175.[17]

22   The lives of ordinary people in the Middle Ages or Ancient Greece and Rome may not have been easy, or even pleasant, but they certainly were leisurely. Initially, the growth of capitalism dramatically raised work effort. In the words of the anthropologist Marshall Sahlins, the market system handed down to human beings a sentence of "life at hard labor."[18]

23   Once we realize that capitalism entailed an expansion of working time, the mid-nineteenth-century turn toward leisure no longer appears as a structural imperative of the market system, as proponents of the conventional wisdom believe. It occurred because workers struggled mightily *against* the normal processes that determined the length of working hours. In this sense, leisure exists *in spite of* rather than as a result of capitalism.

24   In its starkest terms, my argument is this: Key incentive structures of capitalist economies contain biases toward long working hours. As a result of these incentives, the development of capitalism led to the growth of what I call "long hour jobs." The eventual recovery of leisure came about because trade unions and social reformers waged a protracted struggle for shorter hours. Some time between the Depression and the end of the Second World War, that struggle collapsed. As the inevitable pressures toward long hours reasserted themselves, U.S. workers experienced a new decline that now, at the century's end, has created a crisis of leisure time. I am aware that these are strong claims which overturn most of what we have been taught to believe about the way our economy works. To make my case that the market system tends to create work, I compare it with the medieval economy preceding it.

25   Ironically, the tendency of capitalism to expand work is often associated with a growth in joblessness. In recent years, as a majority have taken on the extra month of work, nearly one-fifth of all participants in the labor force are unable to secure as

---

[16]For evidence see chapter 3.

[17]See chapter 3 for a discussion of why Western Europe is a relevant area for comparison.
    On holidays in ancient Greece and Rome, see Hutton Webster, *Rest Days: A Study in Early Law and Morality* (New York: The Macmillan Company, 1926), 394. Gustave Glotz concludes that Greek masons were with certainty "idle for at least one fifth of the year and probably much more." See Glotz, *Ancient Greece at Work: An Economic History of Greece from the Homeric Period to the Roman Conquest* (New York: Knopf, 1927), 283.

[18]Marshall Sahlins, *Stone Age Economics* (New York: Aldine, 1972), 4.

many hours as they want or need to make ends meet. While many employees are subjected to mandatory overtime and are suffering from overwork, their co-workers are put on involuntary part-time. In the context of my story, these irrationalities seem to make sense. The rational, and humane, solution—reducing hours to spread the work—has practically been ruled out of court.

In speaking of "long hour jobs" exclusively in terms of the capitalist marketplace, I do not mean to overlook those women who perform their labor in the privacy of their own homes. Until the late nineteenth century, large numbers of single and married women did participate in the market economy, either in farm labor or through various entrepreneurial activities (taking in boarders, sewing at home, and so on). By the twentieth century, however, a significant percentage of married women, particularly white women, spent all their time outside the market nexus, as full-time "domestic laborers," providing goods and, increasingly, services for their families. And they, too, have worked at "long hour jobs." 26

Studies of household labor beginning in the 1910s and continuing through to the 1970s show that the amount of time a full-time housewife devoted to her work remained virtually unchanged for over fifty years—despite dramatic changes in household technology. As homes, like factories, were "industrialized," refrigerators, laundry machines, vacuum cleaners, and microwaves took up residence in the American domicile. Ready-made clothes and processed food supplanted the home-produced variety. Yet with all these labor-saving innovations, no labor has been saved. Instead, housework expanded to fill the available time. Norms of cleanliness rose. Standards of mothering grew more rigorous. Cooking and baking became more complicated. At the same time, a variety of cheaper and more efficient ways of providing household services failed in the market, and housewives continued to do their own. 27

The stability of housewives' hours was due to a particular bias in the incentives of what we may term the "labor market for housewives." Just as the capitalist labor market contains structural biases toward long hours, so too has the housewife's situation. As I detail in chapter 4, there are strong analogies between the two cases. And in neither case has technology automatically saved labor. It has taken women's exodus from the home itself to reduce their household labor. As women entered paid employment, they cut back their hours of domestic work significantly—but not by enough to keep their total working time unchanged. According to my estimates, when a woman takes a paying job, her schedule expands by at least twenty hours a week. The overwork that plagues many Americans, especially married women, springs from a combination of full-time male jobs, the expansion of housework to fill the available hours, and the growth of employment among married women. 28

The biases of the household and the labor market have been powerful impediments to shorter hours. Yet Western Europe also has both capitalist labor markets and full-time housewives and hours there have fallen substantially. A full explanation for longer hours in the United States involves specifically American factors. For one thing, trade unions are not as powerful here as they are in Europe, where they represent many 29

more workers and have pushed hard for shorter hours. For another, there are the pecu-
liarities of the American consumer.

30   Most economists regard the spending spree that Americans indulged in throughout the postwar decades as an unambiguous blessing, on the assumption that more is
always better. And there is a certain sense in this approach. It's hard to imagine how
having more of a desired good could make one worse off, especially since it is always
possible to ignore the additional quantity. Relying on this little bit of common sense,
economists have championed the closely related ideas that more goods yield more
satisfaction, that desires are infinite, and that people act to satisfy those desires as
fully as they can.

31   Now anyone with just a little bit of psychological sophistication (to go with this little bit of common sense) can spot the flaw in the economist's argument. Once our
basic human needs are taken care of, the effect of consumption on well-being gets
tricky. What if our desires keep pace with our incomes, so that getting richer doesn't
make us more satisfied? Or what if satisfaction depends, not on absolute levels of
consumption, but on one's level *relative* to others (such as the Joneses). Then no matter how much you possess, you won't feel well off if Jones next door possesses more.

32   How many of us thought the first car stereo a great luxury, and then, when it
came time to buy a new car, considered it an absolute necessity? Or life before and
after the microwave? And the fact that many of these commodities are bought on
credit makes the cycle of income-consumption-more income-more consumption
even more ominous. There is no doubt that some purchases permanently enhance
our lives. But how much of what we consume merely keeps us moving on a stationary treadmill? The problem with the treadmill is not only that it is stationary, but
also that we have to work long hours to stay on it. As I shall argue in chapter 5, the
consumerist treadmill and long hour jobs have combined to form an insidious cycle
of "work-and-spend." Employers ask for long hours. The pay creates a high level of
consumption. People buy houses and go into debt; luxuries become necessities;
Smiths keep up with Joneses. Each year, "progress," in the form of annual productivity increases, is doled out by employers as extra income rather than as time off.
Work-and-spend has become a powerful dynamic keeping us from a more relaxed
and leisured way of life.

33   Faith in progress is deep within our culture.[19] We have been taught to believe that
our lives are better than those who came before us. The ideology of modern economics suggests that material progress has yielded enhanced satisfaction and well-being.
But much of our confidence about our own well-being comes from the assumption
that our lives are easier than those of earlier generations or other cultures. I have already disputed the notion that we work less than medieval European peasants, however poor they may have been. The field research of anthropologists gives another
view of the conventional wisdom.

---

[19]For a critique of the idea of progress, see Juliet B. Schor, "Why I Am No Longer a Progressive," *Zeta*,
April 1990.

The lives of so-called primitive peoples are commonly thought to be harsh—their   34
existence dominated by the "incessant quest for food." In fact, primitives do little
work. By contemporary standards, we'd have to judge them extremely lazy. If the
Kapauku of Papua work one day, they do no labor on the next. Kung Bushmen put in
only two and a half days per week and six hours per day. In the Sandwich Islands of
Hawaii, men work only four hours per day. And Australian aborigines have similar
schedules. The key to understanding why these "stone age peoples" fail to act like
us—increasing their work effort to get more things—is that they have limited desires. In the race between wanting and having, they have kept their wanting low—
and, in this way, ensure their own kind of satisfaction. They are materially poor by
contemporary standards, but in at least one dimension—time—we have to count
them richer.[20]

I do not raise these issues to imply that we would be better off as Polynesian na-   35
tives or medieval peasants. Nor am I arguing that "progress" has made us worse off. I
am, instead, making a much simpler point. We have paid a price for prosperity.
Capitalism has brought a dramatically increased standard of living, but at the cost of
a much more demanding worklife. We are eating more, but we are burning up those
calories at work. We have color televisions and compact disc players, but we need
them to unwind after a stressful day at the office. We take vacations, but we work so
hard throughout the year that they become indispensible to our sanity. The conventional wisdom that economic progress has given us more things *as well as* more
leisure is difficult to sustain.

However scarce academic research on the rising workload may be, what we do   36
know suggests it has contributed to a variety of social problems. For example, work
is implicated in the dramatic rise of "stress." Thirty percent of adults say that they
experience high stress nearly every day; even higher numbers report high stress
once or twice a week. A third of the population says that they are rushed to do the
things they have to do—up from a quarter in 1965. Stress-related diseases have ex-
ploded, especially among women, and jobs are a major factor. Workers' compensation claims related to stress tripled during just the first half of the 1980s. Other evidence also suggests a rise in the demands placed on employees on the job.
According to a recent review of existing findings, Americans are literally working
themselves to death—as jobs contribute to heart disease, hypertension, gastric
problems, depression, exhaustion, and a variety of other ailments. Surprisingly, the

---

[20]Sahlins, *Stone Age Economics*, 2.

For these estimates, see Leopold Pospisil, *Kapauku Papuan Economy* (New Haven, Conn.: Yale
University Publication in Anthropology 67, 1963), 144–45 on Kapauku; Richard Lee, "What Hunters
Do for a Living or How to Make Out on Scarce Resources," in Richard B. Lee and Irven DeVore, eds.,
Man the Hunter (Chicago: Aldine Publishing Company, 1968), 30–48 on Kung; C. S. Stewart on the
Sandwich Islands (cited in Sahlins, *Stone Age Economics*, p. 56); Frederick D. McCarthy and Margaret
McArthur, "The Food Quest and the Time Factor in Aboriginal Economic Life," reprinted from *Records
of the American-Australian Scientific Expedition to Arnhem Land,* vol. 2 (Melbourne: Melbourne
University Press, 1960), on Australia.

high-powered jobs are not the most dangerous. The most stressful workplaces are the "electronic sweatshops" and assembly lines where a demanding pace is coupled with virtually no individual discretion.[21]

37   Sleep has become another casualty of modern life. According to sleep researchers, studies point to a "sleep deficit" among Americans, a majority of whom are currently getting between 60 and 90 minutes less a night than they should for optimum health and performance. The number of people showing up at sleep disorder clinics with serious problems has skyrocketed in the last decade. Shiftwork, long working hours, the growth of a global economy (with its attendant continent-hopping and twenty-four-hour business culture), and the accelerating pace of life have all contributed to sleep deprivation. If you need an alarm clock, the experts warn, you're probably sleeping too little.[22]

38   The juggling act between job and family is another problem area. Half the population now says they have too little time for their families. The problem is particularly acute for women: in one study, half of all employed mothers reported it caused either "a lot" or an "extreme" level of stress. The same proportion feel that "when I'm at home I try to make up to my family for being away at work, and as a result I rarely have any time for myself." This stress has placed tremendous burdens on marriages. Two-earner couples have less time together, which researchers have found reduces the happiness and satisfaction of a marriage. These couples often just don't have enough time to talk to each other. And growing numbers of husbands and wives are like ships passing in the night, working sequential schedules to manage their child care. Among young parents, the prevalence of at least one partner working outside regular daytime hours is now close to one half. But this "solution" is hardly a happy one. According to one parent: "I work 11–7 to accommodate my

---

[21]On stress, see Louis Harris, *Inside America* (New York: Vintage, 1987), 8–10. Fifty-nine percent have great stress at least once or twice a week, and 89 percent report experiencing high stress. These polls were taken in 1985–86.

John P. Robinson, "The Time Squeeze," *American Demographics,* 12, 2 (February 1990): 30–33. The question asked was whether respondents "always," "sometimes," or "almost never" feel rushed to do the things they have to do.

Robert Karasek and Töres Theörell, *Healthy Work: Stress, Productivity and the Reconstruction of Working Life* (New York: Basic Books, 1990), 166, on workers' compensation claims and "working to death."

According to the 9 to 5 national stress survey, which was conducted in 1983, just over two-thirds of respondents reported that in the previous year there was an increase in the amount of work required or a speedup. These women also reported increased levels of insomnia, pain, chest pain, tension, anger, depression, and exhaustion. See *The 9to5 National Survey on Women and Stress* (Cleveland, Ohio: 9to5, 1984), 35–38. See also Amanda Bennett, *The Death of the Organization Man* (New York: William Morrow, 1990), which chronicles speed-up in large corporations.

Karasek and Theörell, *Healthy Work,* on stressful workplaces.

[22]Natalie Angier, "Cheating on Sleep: Modern Life Turns America Into the Land of the Drowsy," *New York Times,* 15 May 1990. Recent research by economist Daniel Hamermesh finds a relationship between employment and sleep in "Sleep and the Allocation of Time," *Journal of Political Economy,* 98, 5 (October 1990): 922–43.

family—to eliminate the need for babysitters. However, the stress on myself is tremendous."[23]

A decade of research by Berkeley sociologist Anile Hochschild suggests that many marriages where women are doing the "second shift" are close to the breaking point. When job, children, and marriage have to be attended to, it's often the marriage that is neglected. The failure of many men to do their share at home creates further problems. A twenty-six-year-old legal secretary in California reports that her husband "does no cooking, no washing, no anything else. How do I feel? Furious. If our marriage ends, it will be on this issue. And it just might."[24]   39

Serious as these problems are, the most alarming development may be the effect of the work explosion on the care of children. According to economist Sylvia Hewlett, "Child neglect has become endemic to our society." A major problem is that children are increasingly left alone, to fend for themselves while their parents are at work. Nationwide, estimates of children in "self"—or, more accurately, "no"—care range up to seven million. Local studies have found figures of up to one-third of children caring for themselves. At least half a million preschoolers are thought to be left at home part of each day. One 911 operator reports large numbers of frightened callers: "It's not uncommon to hear from a child of six or seven who has been left in charge of even younger siblings."[25]   40

Even when parents are at home, overwork may leave them with limited time, attention, or energy for their children. One working parent noted, "My child has severe emotional problems because I am too tired to listen to him. It is not quality time; it's bad quantity time that's destroying my family." Economist Victor Fuchs has found   41

---

[23]MassMutual Family Values Study. (Washington, D.C.: Mellman & Lazarus, 1989), 3, on families and time.

Diane S. Burden and Bradley Googins, *Boston University Balancing Job and Homelife Study* (Boston University: mimeo, 1987), 26, on women and stress.

"When I'm at home," from Harris, *Inside America,* 95.

Paul Williams Kingston and Steven L. Nock, "Time Together Among Dual-Earner Couples," *American Sociological Review,* 52 (June 1987): 391–400 See also Arlie Hochschild, *The Second Shift: Working Parents and the Revolution at Home* (New York: Viking Penguin, 1989).

Harriet Presser, "Shift Work and Child Care Among Young Dual-Earner American Parents," *Journal of Marriage and the Family* 50, 1 (February 1988): 133–48. This figure is for couples in which the wife works full time. Among part-timers, the proportion is over one-half.

Quote from Parents United for Child Care (PUCC) survey comments mimeo, Boston, Massachusetts, 1989.

[24]Hochschild, *Second Shift,* 212.

[25]Sylvia A. Hewlett, *When the Bough Breaks: The Cost of Neglecting Our Children* (New York: Basic Books, 1991), 1.

John J. Sweeney and Karen Nussbaum, *Solutions for the New Work Force* (Washington, D.C.: Seven Locks Press, 1989), 209, *n.* 15, for 7 million figure. Burden and Googins, *Balancing Job and Homelife,* 21, table 12, for the local study.

Preschoolers figure cited in Fern Schumer Chapman, "Executive Guilt: Who's Taking Care of the Children?" *Fortune,* 16 February 1987, p. 37.

Quote from PUCC, "Survey comments."

that between 1960 and 1986, the time parents actually had available to be with children fell ten hours a week for whites and twelve for blacks. Hewlett links the "parenting deficit" to a variety of problems plaguing the country's youth: poor performance in school, mental problems, drug and alcohol use, and teen suicide. According to another expert, kids are being "cheated out of childhood. . . . There is a sense that adults don't care about them."[26]

42   Of course, there's more going on here than lack of time. Child neglect, marital distress, sleep deprivation, and stress-related illnesses all have other causes. But the growth of work has exacerbated each of these social ailments. Only by understanding why we work as much as we do, and how the demands of work affect family life, can we hope to solve these problems.

43   Our earlier discussion of primitive peoples raises a thorny issue—what exactly do we mean by work and leisure? Of the hundreds, perhaps thousands of pages that have been written in the attempt to define work and leisure, there are two basic approaches. One emphasizes the subjective. Work is unpleasant—what we have to do. Leisure, by contrast, is what we enjoy. Among "leisure studies" researchers, a variant of this definition is common: leisure comprises discretionary activities; work is mandatory.[27] The problem with this perspective is obvious: work, too, can be pleasurable; and leisure may or may not be. Similarly, "discretion" is not an adequate criterion. Those with plenty of money work by choice. So, too, do many who take second jobs or remain at the office longer than they have to. Upon reflection, the subjective approach turns out to be analytically suspect and operationally flawed.

44   The second approach, which I have chosen, is objective, and concentrates on defining work, rather than leisure. And here I have kept things simple, identifying two kinds of work. The first is hours of paid employment—a reasonably straightforward measure. The second is hours of household labor—a category whose major components are cleaning, cooking, and child care (see the appendix for a precise list). The combination of these two forms of work make "total working hours." Leisure is then defined as a residual. Throughout the book, my quantitative discussions tend to center on work, which I have been able to measure, rather than on leisure.

45   These demarcations are most tenable for the modern period and present relatively little problem for the postwar era. The identification of work with paid employment

[26]Ibid.

    Victor Fuchs, *Women's Quest for Economic Equality* (Cambridge, Mass.: Harvard University Press, 1988), 111.

    Hewlett, *When the Bough Breaks.*

    Expert is Edward Zigler, Yale University, cited in Nancy Gibbs, "How America Has Run Out of Time," *Time,* 24 April 1989, pp. 61–64.

[27]See Chris Rojek, *Capitalism and Leisure Theory* (London: Tavistock Publications, 1985), chap. 1. Other discussions can be found in Michael R. Marrus, ed., *The Emergence of Leisure* (New York: Harper Torchbooks, 1974), and the classic work by Sebastian de Grazia, *Of Time, Work and Leisure* (New York: Twentieth Century Fund, 1962). A feminist discussion can be found in Rosemary Deem, *All Work and No Play? The Sociology of Women and Leisure* (Milton Keynes: Open University Press, 1986).

is standard practice. And for those who are uncomfortable calling household responsibilities "work," I have presented separate estimates throughout. Serious problems arise for comparisons farther back in history—in medieval Europe, for example. A wide body of opinion holds that before capitalism work and leisure were less distinct concepts than they are today. In historian Keith Thomas's words, "The recreational activities of the Middle Ages recall the old primitive confusion as to where work ended and leisure began." Indeed, the terms *leisure* and *free time* were not even in common usage in mid-nineteenth-century England. According to a widely held interpretation, it was the rise of capitalism itself which created today's sharp and identifiable distinction between work and leisure. The imposition of "labor discipline" and the growing instrumentality of work (as a means to a paycheck) combined to create the subjective disjuncture noted by leisure studies researchers. Work is what we dislike but are forced to do; leisure is what we choose. However, while it is plausible that capitalism did clarify what was at times a blurry line between work and leisure, it is important not to overstate the case. Especially among people who worked for others, the notion of labor as a chore was present even in medieval times. As Keith Thomas recognizes, labor services—owed by serfs to their lords—were "deeply unpopular with those who had to discharge them."[28]

In a sense, the historians' characterization of precapitalist societies may teach us most about our own dreams and imaginations. It is hard to avoid at least a touch of nostalgia for a world in which work was more integrated into family and social life, recreation less commercialized, and time more an easy background than a scarce commodity frenetically spent. And from this vision of the past, we are drawn to think about our future. Will the ranks of those who consider themselves "time poor" continue to grow? Or will we find it possible to reclaim the sense of work, time, and leisure we have lost? As I outline in chapter 6, this reclamation will require major, but not infeasible, transformations in attitudes of employers, economic incentive structures, and the culture of consumption.   46

The past forty years should provide a warning. They have brought us nothing in the way of leisure time and a saner pace of life. The bias of the system is strongly toward the status quo. But time poverty is straining the social fabric. Continued growth threatens environmental balance, and gender equality requires new work patterns. Despite these obstacles, I am hopeful. By understanding how we came to be caught up in the cycle of work-and-spend, perhaps we can regain a reasonable balance between work and leisure.   47

---

[28] Keith Thomas, "Work and Leisure in Pre-Industrial Society," *Past and Present,* 29 (December 1964): 53.

On usage of these terms, see de Grazia, *Time, Work and Leisure,* 193.

For a classic article, see E. P. Thompson, "Time, Work-Discipline, and Industrial Capitalism," *Past and Present,* 38 (December 1967). On the instrumentality of work, see Stephen A. Marglin, "Losing Touch: The Cultural Conditions of Worker Accommodation and Resistance," in Frédérique Apffel-Marglin and Stephen A. Marglin, eds., *Dominating Knowledge: Development, Culture, and Resistance* (Oxford: Clarendon Press, 1990)

Thomas, "Work and Leisure," 54.

UNDERSTANDING THE AUTHOR'S IDEAS

1. What does Schor see as the effect on the economy of the *combination* of higher worker productivity and increased work hours?
2. What does Schor argue is the relationship between the allure of market goods and the increase of work hours?
3. What does Schor mean by the "leisure scare"? Why does she believe it disappeared as an important issue to sociologists and other scholars?
4. What are some historical misconceptions that Schor says most people hold about the importance of work in earlier cultures?
5. What does Schor suggest is the relationship between "long hour jobs" and joblessness?
6. What does Schor mean by the "industrialization" of American homes and domestic labor?

EXPLORING YOUR OWN IDEAS

1. Schor suggests that a major impetus for her to write *The Overworked American* is that her principal argument—that Americans work too much and undervalue their leisure—has never been widely debated or seen as an important cultural issue. Do you agree? Why or why not?
2. Schor clearly believes that overwork is more of a problem for women than for men. Why does she believe this? Explain your own views on this issue.
3. Schor hints that many American consumers see "luxury" items as "necessities" that they *must* buy. Do you know of an anecdote that either confirms, refutes, or modifies Schor's belief?
4. Schor hints at the difficulty of balancing the "basic"—food, family, and sleep—with an increased number of work hours. If you hold a full-time or part-time job, explain how you balance these basics. If you don't work, interview one of your classmates who does and find out how he or she balances the basics.

Examine the cartoon above. When the personnel manager says to the applicant, "I must tell you that the position you've applied for is a '24/7' job," what does the applicant think she means? Do you think Jeff Parker, the cartoonist, was trying to imply anything by the very neat, almost empty desk of the personnel manager? What kind of job do you think the applicant might be applying for? How do you know? What kind of jobs would have a starting salary of $24,700? Do you think the person Jeff Parker portrays as the applicant is looking for this kind of job? How do you know? What do you think of the question the applicant asks the personnel manager? Would you ask a similar question? Why or why not? Would this cartoon strike most people as funny? Why or why not? Write a response paper addressing some of these inquiries.

Reading 2

About 10 years after Schor wrote The Overworked American, *Barbara Ehrenreich, an award-winning freelance journalist, accepted a challenge from Lewis Lapham, the editor of* Harper's *magazine, to try to live for one year in the circumstances that many women occupy in today's economy—working in low-paying jobs, living in whatever housing they can find, paying rent, and putting food on the table. Ehrenreich accepted the challenge and "went underground." She moved to Florida and worked as a waitress; she traveled to Maine and worked as a maid and an attendant in a home for elderly people with Alzheimer's disease; she went to Minnesota and worked as an "associate" in a Wal-Mart. She did not reveal until she was about to leave the jobs that she was a journalist working on a book. To her coworkers, Ehrenreich was just one of them. In this excerpt from* Nickel and Dimed, *Ehrenreich describes getting settled into her "home" in Maine—the Blue Haven Motel—and starting her job as a Merry Maid.*

Excerpt from *Nickel and Dimed: On (Not) Getting By in America*

Barbara Ehrenreich

1   Sunday I at last move into the Blue Haven, so pleased to be out of the 6 that the shortcomings of my new home seem minor, even, at first, endearing. It's smaller than I had recalled, for one thing, since a toolshed used by the motel owners takes up part of my cottage space, and this leads to a certain unfortunate blending of the biological functions. With the toilet less than four feet from the tiny kitchen table, I have to close the bathroom door or I feel like I'm eating in a latrine, and the fact that the head of the bed is about seven feet from the stove means that the flounder I fry up for my housewarming dinner lingers all night. Frying is pretty much all I can do, since the kitchen equipment is limited to a frying pan, a plate, a small bowl, a coffeemaker, and one large drinking glass—without even a proverbial pot to pee in. The idea is improvisation: the foil containers that come from salad bars can be reused as dishes; the lone plate becomes a cutting board. The concavity in the center of the bed is rectified by sleeping on a folded-up towel, and so forth. Not to worry—I have an address, two jobs, and a Rent-A-Wreck. The anxiety that gripped me those first few days at the 6 is finally beginning to ebb.

2   As it turns out, the mere fact of having a unit to myself makes me an aristocrat within the Blue Haven community. The other long-term residents, whom I encounter at the communal laundry shed, are blue-collar people with uniforms and overalls to wash, and generally quiet at night. Mostly they are couples with children, much like the white working-class people occasionally glimpsed on sitcoms, only, unlike their TV counterparts, my neighbors are crowded three or four into an efficiency, or at most a one-bedroom, apartment. One young guy asks which unit I'm in and then tells me he used to live in that very same one himself—along with two friends. A middle-aged woman with a three-year-old granddaughter in tow tells me, in a com-

forting tone, that it is always hard at the beginning, living in a motel, especially if you're used to a house, but you adjust after awhile, you put it out of your mind. She, for example, has been at the Blue Haven for eleven years now.

I am rested and ready for anything when I arrive at The Maids' office suite Monday at 7:30 A.M. I know nothing about cleaning services like this one, which, according to the brochure I am given, has over three hundred franchises nationwide, and most of what I know about domestics in general comes from nineteenth-century British novels and *Upstairs, Downstairs.*[4] Prophetically enough, I caught a rerun of that very show on PBS over the weekend and was struck by how terribly correct the servants looked in their black-and-white uniforms and how much wiser they were than their callow, egotistical masters. We too have uniforms, though they are more oafish than dignified—ill-fitting and in an overloud combination of kelly-green pants and a blinding sunflower-yellow polo shirt. And, as is explained in writing and over the next day and a half of training, we too have a special code of decorum. No smoking anywhere, or at least not within fifteen minutes of arrival at a house. No drinking, eating, or gum chewing in a house. No cursing in a house, even if the owner is not present, and—perhaps to keep us in practice—no obscenities even in the office. So this is Downstairs, is my chirpy first thought. But I have no idea, of course, just how far down these stairs will take me.

Forty minutes go by before anyone acknowledges my presence with more than a harried nod. During this time the other employees arrive, about twenty of them, already glowing in their uniforms, and breakfast on the free coffee, bagels, and doughnuts The Maids kindly provides for us. All but one of the others are female, with an average age I would guess in the late twenties, though the range seems to go from prom-fresh to well into the Medicare years. There is a pleasant sort of bustle as people get their breakfasts and fill plastic buckets with rags and bottles of cleaning fluids, but surprisingly little conversation outside of a few references to what people ate (pizza) and drank (Jell-O shots are mentioned) over the weekend. Since the room in which we gather contains only two folding chairs, both of them occupied, the other new girl and I sit cross-legged on the floor, silent and alert, while the regulars get sorted into teams of three or four and dispatched to the day's list of houses. One of the women explains to me that teams do not necessarily return to the same houses week after week, nor do you have any guarantee of being on the same team from one day to the next. This, I suppose, is one of the advantages of a corporate cleaning service to its customers: there are no sticky and

---

[4] Nationwide and even international cleaning services like Merry Maids, Molly Maids, and The Maids International, all of which have arisen since the seventies, now control 20–25 percent of the housecleaning business. In a 1997 article about Merry Maids, *Franchise Times* reported tersely that "category is booming, niche is hot too, as Americans look to outsource work even at home" ("72 Merry Maids," *Franchise Times*, December 1997). Not all cleaning services do well, with a high rate of failure among the informal, mom-and-pop services, like the one I applied to by phone that did not even require a cursory interview—all I had to do was show up at seven the next morning. The "boom" is concentrated among the national and international chains—outfits like Merry Maids, Molly Maids, Mini Maids, Maid Brigade, and The Maids International—all named, curiously enough, to highlight the more antique aspects of the industry, although the "maid" may occasionally be male. Merry Maids claimed to be growing at 15–20 percent a year in 1996, while spokesmen for Molly Maids and The Maids International each told me in interviews conducted after I left Maine that their firms' sales are growing by 25 percent a year.

possibly guilt-ridden relationships involved, because the customers communicate almost entirely with Tammy, the office manager, or with Ted, the franchise owner and our boss.[5] The advantage to the cleaning person is harder to determine, since the pay compares so poorly to what an independent cleaner is likely to earn—up to $15 an hour, I've heard. While I wait in the inner room, where the phone is and Tammy has her desk, to be issued a uniform, I hear her tell a potential customer on the phone that The Maids charges $25 per person-hour. The company gets $25 and we get $6.65 for each hour we work? I think I must have misheard, but a few minutes later I hear her say the same thing to another inquirer. So the only advantage of working here as opposed to freelancing is that you don't need a clientele or even a car. You can arrive straight from welfare or, in my case, the bus station— fresh off the boat.[6] At last, after all the other employees have sped off in the company's eye-catching green-and-yellow cars, I am led into a tiny closet-sized room off the inner office to learn my trade via videotape. The manager at another maid service where I'd applied had told me she didn't like to hire people who had done cleaning before because they were resistant to learning the company's system, so I prepare to empty my mind of all prior housecleaning experience. There are four tapes—dusting, bathrooms, kitchen, and vacuuming—each starring an attractive, possibly Hispanic young woman who moves about serenely in obedience to the male voiceover: For vacuuming, begin in the master bedroom; when dusting, begin with the room directly off the kitchen. When you enter a room, mentally divide it into sections no wider than your reach. Begin in the section to your left and, within each section, move from left to right and top to bottom. This way nothing is ever overlooked.

5   I like *Dusting* best, for its undeniable logic and a certain kind of austere beauty. When you enter a house, you spray a white rag with Windex and place it in the left pocket of your green apron. Another rag, sprayed with disinfectant, goes into the middle pocket, and a yellow rag bearing wood polish in the right-hand pocket. A dry rag, for buffing surfaces, occupies the right-hand pocket of your slacks. Shiny surfaces get Windexed, wood gets wood polish, and everything else is wiped dust-free with disinfectant. Every now and then Ted pops in to watch with me, pausing the video to underscore a particularly dramatic moment: "See how she's working around the vase? That's an accident waiting to happen." If Ted himself were in a video, it would have to be a cartoon, because the only features sketched onto his pudgy face are brown buttonlike eyes and a tiny pug nose; his belly, en-

---

[5] The maids' wages, their Social Security taxes, their green cards, backaches, and child care problems— all these are the sole concern of the company, meaning the local franchise owner. If there are complaints on either side, they are addressed to the franchise owner, the customer and the actual workers need never interact. Since the franchise owner is usually a middle-class white person, cleaning services are the ideal solution for anyone still sensitive enough to find the traditional employer-maid relationship morally vexing.

[6] I don't know what proportion of my fellow workers at The Maids in Portland had been on welfare, but the owner of The Maids' franchise in Andover, Massachusetts, told me in a phone interview that half his employees are former welfare recipients and that they are as reliable as anyone else.

cased in a polo shirt, overhangs the waistline of his shorts. "You know, all this was figured out with a stopwatch," he tells me with something like pride. When the video warns against oversoaking our rags with cleaning fluids, he pauses it to tell me there's a danger in undersoaking too, especially if it's going to slow me down. "Cleaning fluids are less expensive than your time." It's good to know that *something* is cheaper than my time, or that in the hierarchy of the company's values I rank above Windex.

Vacuuming is the most disturbing video, actually a double feature beginning with an introduction to the special backpack vacuum we are to use. Yes, the vacuum cleaner actually straps onto your back, a chubby fellow who introduces himself as its inventor explains. He suits up, pulling the straps tight across and under his chest and then says proudly into the camera: "See, I *am* the vacuum cleaner." It weighs only ten pounds, he claims, although, as I soon find out, with the attachments dangling from the strap around your waist, the total is probably more like fourteen. What about my petulant and much-pampered lower back? The inventor returns to the theme of human-machine merger: when properly strapped in, we too will be vacuum cleaners, constrained only by the cord that attaches us to an electrical outlet, and vacuum cleaners don't have backaches. Somehow all this information exhausts me, and I watch the second video, which explains the actual procedures for vacuuming, with the detached interest of a cineast. Could the model maid be an actual maid and the model home someone's actual dwelling? And who are these people whose idea of decorating is matched pictures of mallard ducks in flight and whose house is perfectly characterless and pristine even before the model maid sets to work?

At first I find the videos on kitchens and bathrooms baffling, and it takes me several minutes to realize why: there is no *water* or almost no water involved. I was taught to clean by my mother, a compulsive housekeeper who employed water so hot you needed rubber gloves to get into it and in such Niagara-like quantities that most microbes were probably crushed by the force of it before the soap suds had a chance to rupture their cell walls. But germs are never mentioned in the videos provided by The Maids. Our antagonists exist entirely in the visible world—soap scum, dust, counter crud, dog hair, stains, and smears—and are to be attacked by damp rag or, in hardcore cases, by Dobie (the brand of plastic scouring pad we use). We scrub only to remove impurities that might be detectable to a customer by hand or by eye; otherwise our only job is to wipe. Nothing is said about the possibility of transporting bacteria, by rag or by hand, from bathroom to kitchen or even from one house to the next. It is the "cosmetic touches" that the videos emphasize and that Ted, when he wanders back into the room, continually directs my eye to. Fluff up all throw pillows and arrange them symmetrically. Brighten up stainless steel sinks with baby oil. Leave all spice jars, shampoos, etc., with their labels facing outward. Comb out the fringes of Persian carpets with a pick. Use the vacuum cleaner to create a special, fernlike pattern in the carpets. The loose ends of toilet paper and paper towel rolls have to be given a special fold (the same one you'll find in hotel bathrooms). "Messes" of loose paper, clothing, or toys are to be stacked into "neat messes." Finally, the house is to be sprayed with the cleaning service's signature floral-scented air freshener, which will signal to the owners, the moment they return home, that, yes, their house has been "cleaned."[7]

8   After a day's training I am judged fit to go out with a team, where I soon discover that life is nothing like the movies, at least not if the movie is *Dusting*. For one thing, compared with our actual pace, the training videos were all in slow motion. We do not walk to the cars with our buckets full of cleaning fluids and utensils in the morning, we run, and when we pull up to a house, we run with our buckets to the door. Liza, a good-natured woman in her thirties who is my first team leader, explains that we are given only so many minutes per house, ranging from under sixty for a 1 1/2-bathroom apartment to two hundred or more for a multibathroom "first timer." I'd like to know why anybody worries about Ted's time limits if we're being paid by the hour but hesitate to display anything that might be interpreted as attitude. As we get to each house, Liza assigns our tasks, and I cross my fingers to ward off bathrooms and vacuuming. Even dusting, though, gets aerobic under pressure, and after about an hour of it—reaching to get door tops, crawling along floors to wipe baseboards, standing on my bucket to attack the higher shelves—I wouldn't mind sitting down with a tall glass of water. But as soon as you complete your assigned task, you report to the team leader to be assigned to help someone else. Once or twice, when the normal process of evaporation is deemed too slow, I am assigned to dry a scrubbed floor by putting rags under my feet and skating around on it. Usually, by the time I get out to the car and am dumping the dirty water used on floors and wringing out rags, the rest of the team is already in the car with the motor running. Liza assures me that they've never left anyone behind at a house, not even, presumably, a very new person whom nobody knows.

9   In my interview, I had been promised a thirty-minute lunch break, but this turns out to be a five-minute pit stop at a convenience store, if that. I bring my own sandwich—the same turkey breast and cheese every day—as do a couple of the others; the rest eat convenience store fare, a bagel or doughnut salvaged from our free breakfast, or nothing at all. The two older married women I'm teamed up with eat best—sandwiches and fruit. Among the younger women, lunch consists of a slice of pizza, a "pizza pocket" (a roll of dough surrounding some pizza sauce), or a small bag of chips.

---

[7] When I described the methods employed by The Maids to housecleaning expert Cheryl Mendelson, author of *Home Comforts,* she was incredulous. A rag moistened with disinfectant will not get a countertop clean, she told me, because most disinfectants are inactivated by contact with organic matter—i.e., dirt—so their effectiveness declines with each swipe of the rag. What you need is a detergent and hot water, followed by a rinse. As for floors, she judged the amount of water we used—one half of a small bucket, which was never any warmer than room temperature—to be grossly inadequate, and, in fact, the water I wiped around on floors was often an unsavory gray. I also ran The Maids' cleaning methods by Don Aslett, author of numerous books on cleaning techniques and self-styled "number one cleaner in America." He was hesitant to criticize The Maids directly, perhaps because he is, or told me he is, a frequent speaker at conventions of cleaning service franchise holders, but he did tell me how he would clean a countertop. First, spray it thoroughly with an all-purpose cleaner, then let it sit for three to four minutes of "kill time," and finally wipe dry with a clean cloth. Merely wiping the surface with a damp cloth, he said, just spreads the dirt around. But the point at The Maids, apparently, is not to clean so much as to create the appearance of *having been cleaned*, not to sanitize but to create a kind of stage setting for family life. And the stage setting Americans seem to prefer is sterile only in the metaphorical sense, like a motel room or the fake interiors in which soap operas and sitcoms take place.

Bear in mind we are not office workers, sitting around idling at the basal metabolic rate. A poster on the wall in the office cheerily displays the number of calories burned per minute at our various tasks, ranging from about 3.5 for dusting to 7 for vacuuming. If you assume an average of 5 calories per minute in a seven-hour day (eight hours minus time for travel between houses), you need to be taking in 2,100 calories in addition to the resting minimum of, say, 900 or so. I get pushy with Rosalie, who is new like me and fresh from high school in a rural northern part of the state, about the meagerness of her lunches, which consist solely of Doritos—a half bag from the day before or a freshly purchased small-sized bag. She just didn't have anything in the house, she says (though she lives with her boyfriend and his mother), and she certainly doesn't have any money to buy lunch, as I find out when I offer to fetch her a soda from a Quik Mart and she has to admit she doesn't have eighty-nine cents. I treat her to the soda, wishing I could force her, mommylike, to take milk instead. So how does she hold up for an eight- or even nine-hour day? "Well," she concedes, "I get dizzy sometimes."

How poor are they, my coworkers? The fact that anyone is working this job at all   10
can be taken as prima facie evidence of some kind of desperation or at least a history of mistakes and disappointments, but it's not for me to ask. In the prison movies that provide me with a mental guide to comportment, the new guy doesn't go around shaking hands and asking, "Hi there, what are you in for?" So I listen, in the cars and when we're assembled in the office, and learn, first, that no one seems to be homeless. Almost everyone is embedded in extended families or families artificially extended with house-mates. People talk about visiting grandparents in the hospital or sending birthday cards to a niece's husband; single mothers live with their own mothers or share apartments with a coworker or boyfriend. Pauline, the oldest of us, owns her own home, but she sleeps on the living room sofa, while her four grown children and three grandchildren fill up the bedrooms.[8]

---

[8] The women I worked with were all white and, with one exception, Anglo, as are the plurality of housecleaners in America, or at least those known to the Bureau of Labor Statistics. Of the "private household cleaners and servants" it managed to locate in 1998, the BLS reports that 36.8 percent were Hispanic, 15.8 percent black, and 2.7 percent "other." However, the association between housecleaning and minority status is well established in the psyches of the white employing class. When my daughter, Rosa, was introduced to the father of a wealthy Harvard classmate, he ventured that she must have been named for a favorite maid. And Audre Lorde reported an experience she had in 1967: "I wheel my two-year-old daughter in a shopping cart through a supermarket. And a little white girl riding past in her mother's cart calls out excitedly, 'Oh look, Mommy, a baby maid' " (quoted in Mary Romero, *Maid in the U.S.A.: Perspectives on Gender* [New York: Routledge, 1992], p. 72). But the composition of the household workforce is hardly fixed and has changed with the life changes of the different ethnic groups. In the late nineteenth century, Irish and German immigrants served the urban upper and middle classes, then left for the factories as soon as they could. Black women replaced them, accounting for 60 percent of all domestics in the 1940s, and dominated the field until other occupations began to open up to them. Similarly, West Coast maids were disproportionately Japanese American until that group too found more congenial options (see Phyllis Palmer, *Domesticity and Dirt: Housewives and Domestic Servants in the United States, 1920–1945* [Temple University Press, 1989], pp. 12–13). Today, the color of the hand that pushes the sponge varies from region to region: Chicanas in the Southwest, Caribbeans in New York, native Hawaiians in Hawaii, native whites, many of recent rural extraction, in the Midwest and, of course, Maine.

11   But although no one, apparently, is sleeping in a car, there are signs, even at the beginning, of real difficulty if not actual misery. Half-smoked cigarettes are returned to the pack. There are discussions about who will come up with fifty cents for a toll and whether Ted can be counted on for prompt reimbursement. One of my teammates gets frantic about a painfully impacted wisdom tooth and keeps making calls from our houses to try to locate a source of free dental care. When my—or, I should say, Liza's—team discovers there is not a single Dobbin in our buckets, I suggest that we stop at a convenience store and buy one rather than drive all the way back to the office. But it turns out I haven't brought any money with me and we cannot put together $2 between the four of us.

12   The Friday of my first week at The Maids is unnaturally hot for Maine in early September—95 degrees, according to the digital time-and-temperature displays offered by banks that we pass. I'm teamed up with the sad-faced Rosalie and our leader, Maddy, whose sullenness, under the circumstances, is almost a relief after Liza's relentless good cheer. Liza, I've learned, is the highest-ranking cleaner, a sort of supervisor really, and said to be something of a snitch, but Maddy, a single mom of maybe twenty-seven or so, has worked for only three months and broods about her child care problems. Her boyfriend's sister, she tells me on the drive to our first house, watches her eighteen-month-old for $50 a week, which is a stretch on The Maids' pay, plus she doesn't entirely trust the sister, but a real day care center could be as much as $90 a week. After polishing off the first house, no problem, we grab "lunch"—Doritos for Rosalie and a bag of Pepperidge Farm Goldfish for Maddy—and head out into the exurbs for what our instruction sheet warns is a five-bedroom spread and a first-timer to boot. Still, the size of the place makes us pause for a moment, buckets in hand, before searching out an appropriately humble entrance.[9] It sits there like a beached ocean liner, the prow cutting through swells of green turf, windows without number. "Well, well," Maddy says, reading the owner's name from our instruction sheet, "Mrs. W and her big-ass house. I hope she's going to give us lunch."

13   Mrs. W is not in fact happy to see us, grimacing with exasperation when the black nanny ushers us into the family room or sunroom or den or whatever kind of specialized space she is sitting in. After all, she already has the nanny, a cooklike person, and a crew of men doing some sort of finishing touches on the construction to supervise. No, she doesn't want to take us around the house, because she already explained everything to the office on the phone, but Maddy stands there, with Rosalie and me behind her, until she relents. We are to move everything on all surfaces, she

---

[9] For the affluent, houses have been swelling with no apparent limit. The square footage of new homes increased by 39 percent between 1971 and 1996, to include "family rooms," home entertainment rooms, home offices, bedrooms, and often a bathroom for each family member ("Détente in the Housework Wars," *Toronto Star,* November 20, 1999). By the second quarter of 1999, 17 percent of new homes were larger than three thousand square feet, which is usually considered the size threshold for household help, or the point at which a house becomes unmanageable to the people who live in it ("Molding Loyal Pamperers for the Newly Rich," *New York Times,* October 24, 1999).

instructs during the tour, and get underneath and be sure to do every bit of the several miles, I calculate, of baseboards. And be mindful of the baby, who's napping and can't have cleaning fluids of any kind near her.

Then I am let loose to dust. In a situation like this, where I don't even know how   14
to name the various kinds of rooms, The Maids' special system turns out to be a lifesaver. All I have to do is keep moving from left to right, within rooms and between rooms, trying to identify landmarks so I don't accidentally do a room or a hallway twice. Dusters get the most complete biographical overview, due to the necessity of lifting each object and tchotchke individually, and I learn that Mrs. W is an alumna of an important women's college, now occupying herself by monitoring her investments and the baby's bowel movements. I find special charts for this latter purpose, with spaces for time of day, most recent fluid intake, consistency, and color. In the master bedroom, I dust a whole shelf of books on pregnancy, breast-feeding, the first six months, the first year, the first two years—and I wonder what the child care-deprived Maddy makes of all this. Maybe there's been some secret division of the world's women into breeders and drones, and those at the maid level are no longer supposed to be reproducing at all. Maybe this is why our office manager, Tammy, who was once a maid herself, wears inch-long fake nails and tarty little outfits—to show she's advanced to the breeder caste and can't be sent out to clean anymore.

It is hotter inside than out, un-air-conditioned for the benefit of the baby, I suppose, but I do all right until I encounter the banks of glass doors that line the side   15
and back of the ground floor. Each one has to be Windexed, wiped, and huffed—inside and out, top to bottom, left to right, until it's as streakless and invisible as a material substance can be. Outside, I can see the construction guys knocking back Gatorade, but the rule is that no fluid or food item can touch a maid's lips when she's inside a house. Now, sweat, even in unseemly quantities, is nothing new to me. I live in a subtropical area where even the inactive can expect to be moist nine months out of the year. I work out, too, in my normal life and take a certain macho pride in the Vs of sweat that form on my T-shirt after ten minutes or more on the StairMaster. But in normal life fluids lost are immediately replaced. Everyone in yuppie-land—airports, for example—looks like a nursing baby these days, inseparable from their plastic bottles of water. Here, however, I sweat without replacement or pause, not in individual drops but in continuous sheets of fluid soaking through my polo shirt, pouring down the backs of my legs. The eyeliner I put on in the morning—vain twit that I am—has long since streaked down onto my cheeks, and I could wring my braid out if I wanted to. Working my way through the living room(s), I wonder if Mrs.W will ever have occasion to realize that every single doodad and *objet* through which she expresses her unique, individual self is, from another vantage point, only an obstacle between some thirsty person and a glass of water.

When I can find no more surfaces to wipe and have finally exhausted the supply   16
of rooms, Maddy assigns me to do the kitchen floor. OK, except that Mrs. W is *in* the kitchen, so I have to go down on my hands and knees practically at her feet. No, we don't have sponge mops like the one I use in my own house; the hands-and-knees approach is a definite selling point for corporate cleaning services like

The Maids. "We clean floors the old-fashioned way—on *our hands and knees*" (emphasis added), the brochure for a competing firm boasts. In fact, whatever advantages there may be to the hands-and-knees approach—you're closer to your work, of course, and less likely to miss a grimy patch—are undermined by the artificial drought imposed by The Maids' cleaning system. We are instructed to use less than half a small bucket of lukewarm water for a kitchen and all adjacent scrubbable floors (breakfast nooks and other dining areas), meaning that within a few minutes we are doing nothing more than redistributing the dirt evenly around the floor. There are occasional customer complaints about the cleanliness of our floors—for example, from a man who wiped up a spill on his freshly "cleaned" floor only to find the paper towel he employed for this purpose had turned gray. A mop and a full bucket of hot soapy water would not only get a floor cleaner but would be a lot more dignified for the person who does the cleaning. But it is this primal posture of submission—and of what is ultimately anal accessibility—that seems to gratify the consumers of maid services.[10]

17   I don't know, but Mrs. W's floor is hard—stone, I think, or at least a stonelike substance—and we have no knee pads with us today. I had thought in my middle-class innocence that knee pads were one of Monica Lewinsky's prurient fantasies, but no, they actually exist, and they're usually a standard part of our equipment. So here I am on my knees, working my way around the room like some fanatical penitent crawling through the stations of the cross, when I realize that Mrs. W is staring at me fixedly—so fixedly that I am gripped for a moment by the wild possibility that I may have once given a lecture at her alma mater and she's trying to figure out where she's seen me before. If I were recognized, would I be fired? Would she at least be inspired to offer me a drink of water? Because I have decided that if water is actually offered, I'm taking it, rules or no rules, and if word of this infraction gets back to Ted, I'll just say I thought it would be rude to refuse. Not to worry, though. She's just watching that I don't leave out some stray square inch, and when I rise painfully to my feet again, blinking through the sweat, she says, "Could you just scrub the floor in the entryway while you're at it?"

---

[10]In *Home Comforts: The Art and Science of Keeping House* (Scribner, 1999), Cheryl Mendelson writes, "Never ask hired housecleaners to clean your floors on their hands and knees; the request is likely to be regarded as degrading" (p. 501).

EXPLORING THE AUTHOR'S IDEAS

1. How would you characterize the Blue Haven Motel?
2. Ehrenreich comments that independent housekeepers earn about $15 an hour, while those who work for Merry Maids get $6.65 an hour. How would you explain this disparity?
3. Merry Maids instructs their workers to use almost no water when they clean a house. Why?
4. What evidence does Ehrenreich cite to suggest the poverty level of her coworkers?
5. How do "dusters" get the best "biographical overview" of the people whose houses are being cleaned?
6. What is the relationship between Merry Maids' announced quitting time and the actual quitting time? How does Ehrenreich explain this disparity?

EXPLORING YOUR OWN IDEAS

1. What kinds of housing are available in your community for low-wage workers who have neither family nor friends with whom they can share lodging?
2. If you have ever held a low-wage job, how does it compare with Ehrenreich's? If you have never held a low-wage job, interview someone who has and compare his or her perceptions of it with Ehrenreich's.
3. Do you think Ehrenreich's training for working at Merry Maids was effective? Why or why not?
4. If you hold a job while you are a student (or have done so in the past), explain how you balance the demands of home, school, and work.
5. Compare and contrast the genre features of this excerpt and the previous one by Schor.

Reading 3

In 1998, Susan Quattrociocchi, director of a program in the state of Washington entitled "A Call to Parents: How to Cut the High Costs and High Risks of Education After High School," recorded the following brief address, which was broadcast on WAMC, a public radio station in Boston.

"Jobs for Teenagers Should be More Than a Paycheck"

Susan M. Quattrociocchi

1   Most parents believe that a teen's first job is temporary, with no long-term consequences. It's just for "while I'm in school," or just to earn a little money. Several years later, stuck doing the same kind of work, 22-year-olds look up and wonder what happened. Four factors conspire to keep kids trapped in boring, poorly paid, dead-end jobs. Remember how much energy it takes to get a job? Young people don't have time or energy to look for new jobs once they're working. They also don't have time to give serious thought to alternate career options.

2   Working teens develop spending habits that require an income. Most of their expenditures ($42 million a year) are for consumer goods, transportation and entertainment. Some expenses are work related. If they land a job and then need a car to get to work, they must then work longer hours to support the car, buy insurance and pay for repairs. Once the merry-go-round of work-spend-work is begun, it's extremely difficult to get off. Teens then find it almost impossible to quit, reduce their hours, or make time for career-building internships or volunteer projects.

3   Studies show that the first jobs students take often determine their field of employment for the next several years. Unfortunately, most entry-level jobs require little or no experience, so few opportunities exist for advancement, or for branching out into related positions with better prospects.

4   Teens today work an average of 15 to 20 hours per week. This means that there are an awful lot of kids out there working more than 20. Kids get tired. The more hours they work, the less time they have for homework, church, sports and their families. They fall asleep in class. Their grades suffer. Then they become discouraged with school, and resist enrolling in challenging courses. These are the courses they need most to prepare for further education or good-paying careers.

5   There are good jobs out there that are beneficial for teens. But finding them requires careful screening. Good jobs connect students—to their interests, to what they learn in school, to mentors within the community. They aid the teen in career exploration and provide opportunities to meet others of all ages and levels of experience.

6   Good jobs contribute to the long-term growth of young workers. They promote the student's short-term and long-term interests. They teach basic jobs skills like punctuality, dependability, responsibility, inner-direction, helpfulness and teamwork. They also help develop decision-making and problem-solving skills that are essential for higher paying jobs in the future.

Heather Ricardi, a senior at Mercer Island High School, has a good job in a field she loves—horticulture. She takes botany and horticulture classes every day at Interlake High School in Bellevue, and then works at Interlake Plant Store three afternoons a week.   7

"I've learned a lot about landscape design, greenhouse management and the retail plant business," says Heather. "Now I know for sure that I want to study botany and horticulture." She has been accepted at a four-year university.   8

Jennifer Bredelhoft and Holly Giovenale combine school and work experience, and earn college credit in high school, while learning about early childhood education. They participate in Newport High School's Careers with Children class, and work in a child care center.   9

Stephanie Pearce of Bellevue High School studies marketing and tourism, and works in the marketing department of a local architecture firm. She plans to use this experience to help her land an internship in travel marketing.   10

Parents can help teens find jobs like these. But it takes a little effort—and resisting their pleas to respond to the first help-wanted sign they see. It requires sitting down with your kids and mapping out a plan. What do they love most to do? How can they best use their high school years to prepare for the future? How can they meet people who can help them attain their dream?   11

The first job is not just a stopgap. Good or bad, it's the door to the future. Make sure it's a positive one that takes teens a long way toward their dreams.   12

UNDERSTANDING THE AUTHOR'S IDEAS

1. What does Quattrociocchi see as the relationship between teenagers' spending habits and their jobs?
2. What, according to Quattrociocchi, is the effect on students' lives of working 15 to 20 hours a week?
3. What does Quattrociocchi suggest that parents do with their teenagers to help them find a good job?
4. Ideally, according to Quattrociocchi, what should teenagers learn in their part-time jobs?

EXPLORING YOUR OWN IDEAS

1. Quattrociocchi reports that "the first jobs students take often determine their field of employment for the next several years." Interview three or four people who held a part-time job while they were in school and determine whether Quattrociocchi's claim is valid.
2. Quattrociocchi asserts that many teenagers are on a "merry-go-round of work-spend-work." Do you agree? Why or why not?
3. What would be an ideal job for you to have as you go to school? Is such a job attainable?

Reading 4

In 1991, the economist Robert B. Reich, who would later serve as Secretary of Labor in the first administration of President Bill Clinton, published The Work of Nations, *in which he described his view of how the American economy and workforce needed to change in the coming century—the one in which we are living now. The title of Reich's book is a deliberate echo of Adam Smith's* The Wealth of Nations, *the seventeenth-century economic treatise that was an important source underlying the first constitution of the United States.*

Excerpt from *The Work of Nations: Preparing for 21st-Century Capitalism*

Robert B. Reich

1   The usual discussion about the future of the American economy focuses on topics like the competitiveness of General Motors, or of the American automobile industry, or, more broadly, of American manufacturing, or, more broadly still, of the American economy. But, as has been observed, these categories are becoming irrelevant. They assume the continued existence of an American economy in which jobs associated with a particular firm, industry, or sector are somehow connected within the borders of the nation, so that American workers face a common fate; and a common enemy as well: The battlefields of world trade pit our corporations and our workers unambiguously against theirs.

2   No longer. In the emerging international economy, few American companies and American industries compete against foreign companies and industries—if by *American* we mean where the work is done and the value is added. Becoming more typical is the global web, perhaps headquartered in and receiving much of its financial capital from the United States, but with research, design. and production facilities spread over Japan, Europe, and North America; additional production facilities in Southeast Asia and Latin America; marketing and distribution centers on every continent; and lenders and investors in Taiwan, Japan, and West Germany as well as the United States. This ecumenical company competes with similarly ecumenical companies headquartered in other nations. Battle lines no longer correspond with national borders.

3   So, when an "American" company like General Motors shows healthy profits, this is good news for its strategic brokers in Detroit and its American investors. It is also good news for other GM executives worldwide and for GM's global employees, subcontractors, and investors. But it is not necessarily good news for a lot of routine assembly-line workers in Detroit, because there are not likely to be many of them left in Detroit, or anywhere else in America. Nor is it necessarily good news for the few

Americans who are still working on the assembly lines in the United States, who increasingly receive their paychecks from corporations based in Tokyo or Bonn.

The point is that Americans are becoming part of an international labor market, encompassing Asia, Africa, Latin America, Western Europe, and, increasingly, Eastern Europe and the Soviet Union. The competitiveness of Americans in this global market is coming to depend, not on the fortunes of any American corporation or on American industry, but on the functions that Americans perform—the value they add—within the global economy. Other nations are undergoing precisely the same transformation, some more slowly than the United States, but all participating in essentially the same transnational trend. Barriers to cross-border flows of knowledge, money, and tangible products are crumbling; groups of people in every nation are joining global webs. In a very few years, there will be virtually no way to distinguish one national economy from another except by the exchange rates of their currencies—and even this distinction may be on the wane.   4

Americans thus confront global competition ever more directly, unmediated by national institutions. As we discard vestigial notions of the competitiveness of American corporations, American industry, and the American economy, and recast them in terms of the competitiveness of the American work force, it becomes apparent that successes or failures will not be shared equally by all our citizens.   5

Some Americans, whose contributions to the global economy are more highly valued in world markets, will succeed, while others, whose contributions are deemed far less valuable, fail. GM's American executives may become less competitive even as GM's American production workers become less so, because the functions performed by the former group are more highly valued in the world market than those of the latter. So, when we speak of the "competitiveness" of Americans in general, we are talking only about how much the world is prepared to spend, *on average,* for services performed by Americans. Some Americans may command higher rewards; others, far lower. No longer are Americans rising or falling together, as if in one large national boat. We are, increasingly, in different, smaller boats.   6

2

In order to see in greater detail what is happening to American jobs and to understand why the economic fates of Americans are beginning to diverge, it is first necessary to view the work that Americans do in terms of categories that reflect their real competitive positions in the global economy.   7

Official data about American jobs are organized by categories that are not very helpful in this regard. The U.S. Bureau of the Census began inquiring about American jobs in 1820, and developed a systematic way of categorizing them in 1870. Beginning in 1943, the Census came up with a way of dividing these categories into different levels of "social-economic status," depending upon, among other things, the prestige and income associated with each job. In order to determine the appropriate groupings, the Census first divided all American jobs into either business class or working class—the same two overarching categories the Lynns had devised for their study of Middletown—and then divided each of these,   8 in turn, into subcategories.[1] In 1950, the Census added the category "service workers" and called the resulting scheme America's "Major Occupational Groups," which it has remained ever since. All subsequent surveys have been based on this same set of categories. Thus, even by 1990, in the eyes of the Census, you were either in a "managerial and professional specialty," in a "technical, sales, and administrative support" role, in a "service occupation," an "operator, fabricator, and laborer," or in a "transportation and material moving" occupation.

9   This set of classifications made sense when the economy was focused on high-volume, and standardized production, in which almost every job fit into, or around, the core American corporation, and when status and income depended on one's ranking in the standard corporate bureaucracy. But these categories have little bearing upon the competitive positions of Americans worldwide, now that America's core corporations are transforming into finely spun global webs. Someone whose job falls officially into a "technical" or "sales" subcategory may, in fact, be among the best-paid and most influential people in such a web. To understand the real competitive positions of Americans in the global economy, it is necessary to devise new categories.[2]

10   Essentially, three broad categories of work are emerging, corresponding to three different positions in which Americans find themselves. The same three categories are taking shape in other nations. Call them *routine production services, in-person services,* and *symbolic-analytic services.*

11   *Routine production services* entail the kinds of repetitive tasks performed by the old foot soldiers of American capitalism in the high-volume enterprise. They are done over and over—one step in a sequence of steps for producing finished products tradeable in world commerce. Although often thought of as traditional blue-collar jobs, they also include routine supervisory jobs performed by low- and mid-level managers—foremen, line managers, clerical supervisors, and section chiefs—involving repetitive checks on subordinates' work and the enforcement of standard operating procedures.

12   Routine production services are found in many places within a modern economy apart from older, heavy industries (which, like elderly citizens, have been given the more delicate, and less terminal, appelation: "mature"). They are found even amid the glitter and glitz of high technology. Few tasks are more tedious and repetitive, for example, than stuffing computer circuit boards or devising routine coding for computer software programs.

13   Indeed, contrary to prophets of the "information age," who buoyantly predicted an abundance of high-paying jobs even for people with the most basic of skills, the sobering truth is that many information-processing jobs fit easily into this category.

---

[1] See Alba Edwards. *U.S. Census of Population, 1940: Comparative Occupation Statistics. 1870–1940* (Washington D.C.: U.S. Government Printing Office, 1943).

[2] Because much of the information about the American work force must be gleaned from the old categories, however, the only way to discover who fits into which new category is to decompose the government's data into the smallest subcategories in which they are collected, then reorder the subcategories according to which new functional group they appear to belong in. For a similar methodology, see Steven A, Sass, "The U.S. Professional Sector: 1950–1968." *New England Economic Review,* January–February 1990, pp. 37–55.

The foot soldiers of the information economy are hordes of data processors stationed in "back offices" at computer terminals linked to worldwide information banks. They routinely enter data into computers or take it out again—records of credit card purchases and payments, credit reports, checks that have cleared, customer accounts, customer correspondence, payroll, hospital billings, patient records, medical claims, court decisions, subscriber lists, personnel, library catalogues, and so forth. The "information revolution" may have rendered some of us more productive, but it has also produced huge piles of raw data which must be processed in much the same monotonous way that assembly-line workers and, before them, textile workers processed piles of other raw materials.

Routine producers routinely work in the company of many other people who do the same thing, usually within large enclosed spaces. They are guided on the job by standard procedures and codified rules, and even their overseers are overseen, in turn, by people who routinely monitor—often with the aid of computers—how much they do and how accurately they do it. Their wages are based either on the amount of time they put in or on the amount of work they do.   14

Routine producers usually must be able to read and to perform simple computations. But their cardinal virtues are reliability, loyalty, and the capacity to take direction. Thus does a standard American education, based on the traditional premises of American Education, normally suffice.   15

By 1990, routine production work comprised about one-quarter of the jobs performed by Americans, and the number was declining. Those who dealt with metal were mostly white and male; those who dealt with fabrics, circuit boards, or information were mostly black or Hispanic, and female; their supervisors, white males.[3]   16

In-person services, the second kind of work that Americans do, also entail simple and repetitive tasks. And like routine production services, the pay of in-person servers is a function of hours worked or amount of work performed; they are closely supervised (as are their supervisors), and they need not have acquired much education (at most, a high school diploma, or its equivalent, and some vocational training).   17

The big difference between in-person servers and routine producers is that *these* services must be provided person-to-person, and thus are not sold worldwide. (In-person servers might, of course, work for global corporations. Two examples: In 1988, Britain's Blue Arrow PLC acquired Manpower Inc., which provides custodial services throughout the United States. Meanwhile, Denmark's ISS-AS already employed over 16,000 Americans to clean office buildings in most major American cities.) In-person servers are in direct contact with the ultimate beneficiaries of their work; their immediate objects are specific customers rather than streams of metal, fabric, or data. In-person servers work alone or in small teams. Included in this category are retail sales workers, waiters and waitresses, hotel workers, janitors, cashiers, hospital attendants and orderlies, nursing-home aides, child-care workers, house cleaners, home health-care aides, taxi drivers, secretaries, hairdressers, auto   18

---

[3] For an illuminating discussion of routine jobs in a high-technology industry, see D. O'Connor, "Women Workers in the Changing International Division of Labor in Microelectronics." In L. Benerici and C. Stimpson (eds.), *Women, Households, and the Economy* (New Brunswick, N.J.: Rutgers University Press, 1987).

mechanics, sellers of residential real estate, flight attendants, physical therapists, and—among the fastest-growing of all—security guards.

19   In-person servers are supposed to be punctual, reliable, and tractable as routine production workers. But many in-person servers share one additional requirement: They must have a pleasant demeanor. They must smile and exude confidence and good cheer, even when they feel morose. They must be courteous and helpful, even to the most obnoxious of patrons. Above all, they must make others feel happy and at ease. It should come as no surprise that, traditionally, most in-person servers have been women. The cultural stereotype of women as nurturers—as mommies—has opened countless in-person service jobs to them.[4]

20   By 1990, in-person services accounted for about 30 percent of the jobs performed by Americans, and their numbers were growing rapidly. For example, Beverly Enterprises, a single nursing-home chain operating throughout the United States, employed about the same number of Americans as the entire Chrysler Corporation (115,174 and 116,250, respectively)—although most Americans were far more knowledgeable about the latter, including the opinions of its chairman. In the United States during the 1980s, well over 3 million *new* in-person service jobs were created in fast-food outlets, bars, and restaurants. This was more than the *total* number of routine production jobs still existing in America by the end of the decade in the automobile, steelmaking, and textile industries combined.[5]

21   *Symbolic-analytic services,* the third job category, include all the problem-solving, problem-identifying, and strategic-brokering activities we have examined in previous chapters. Like routine production services (but *unlike* in-person services), symbolic-analytic services can be traded worldwide and thus must compete with foreign providers even in the American market. But they do not enter world commerce as standardized things. Traded instead are the manipulations of symbols—data, words, oral and visual representations.

22   Included in this category are the problem-solving, -identifying, and -brokering of many people who call themselves research scientists, design engineers, software engineers, civil engineers, biotechnology engineers, sound engineers, public relations executives, investment bankers, lawyers, real estate developers, and even a few creative accountants. Also included is much of the work done by management consultants, financial consultants, tax consultants, energy consultants, agricultural consultants, armaments consultants, architectural consultants, management information specialists, organization development specialists, strategic planners, corporate headhunters, and systems analysts. Also: advertising executives and marketing strategists, art directors, architects, cinematographers, film editors, production designers, publishers, writers and editors, journalists, musicians, television and film producers, and even university professors.

23   Symbolic analysts solve, identify, and broker problems by manipulating symbols. They simplify reality into abstract images that can be rearranged, juggled, experi-

[4] On this point see Arlie Russell Hochschild. *The Managed Heart: The Commercialization of Human Feeling* (Berkeley: University of California Press, 1983).

[5] U.S. Department of Commerce, Bureau of Labor Statistics, various issues.

mented with, communicated to other specialists, and then, eventually, transformed back into reality. The manipulations are done with analytic tools, sharpened by experience. The tools may be mathematical algorithms, legal arguments, financial gimmicks, scientific principles, psychological insights about how to persuade or to amuse, systems of induction or deduction, or any other set of techniques for doing conceptual puzzles.

24   Some of these manipulations reveal how to more efficiently deploy resources or shift financial assets, or otherwise save time and energy. Other manipulations yield new inventions—technological marvels, innovative legal arguments, new advertising ploys for convincing people that certain amusements have become life necessities. Still other manipulations—of sounds, words, pictures—serve to entertain their recipients, or cause them to reflect more deeply on their lives or on the human condition. Others grab money from people too slow or naïve to protect themselves by manipulating in response.

25   Like routine producers, symbolic analysts rarely come into direct contact with the ultimate beneficiaries of their work. But other aspects of their work life are quite different from that experienced by routine producers. Symbolic analysts often have partners or associates rather than bosses or supervisors. Their incomes may vary from time to time, but are not directly related to how much time they put in or the quantity of work they put out. Income depends, rather, on the quality, originality, cleverness, and, occasionally, speed with which they solve, identify, or broker new problems. Their careers are not linear or hierarchical; they rarely proceed along well-defined paths to progressively higher levels of responsibility and income. In fact, symbolic analysts may take on vast responsibilities and command inordinate wealth at rather young ages. Correspondingly, they may lose authority and income if they are no longer able to innovate by building on their cumulative experience, even if they are quite senior.

26   Symbolic analysts often work alone or in small teams, which may be connected to larger organizations, including worldwide webs. Teamwork is often critical. Since neither problems nor solutions can be defined in advance, frequent and informal conversations help ensure that insights and discoveries are put to their best uses and subjected to quick, critical evaluation.[6]

27   When not conversing with their teammates, symbolic analysts sit before computer terminals—examining words and numbers, moving them, altering them, trying out new words and numbers, formulating and testing hypotheses, designing or strategizing. They also spend long hours in meetings or on the telephone, and even longer hours in jet planes and hotels—advising, making presentations, giving briefings, doing deals. Periodically, they issue reports, plans, designs, drafts, memoranda, layouts, renderings, scripts, or projections—which, in turn, precipitate more meetings to clarify what has been proposed and how to get agreement on how it will be implemented, by whom, and for how much money. Final production is often the easiest

---

[6] The physical environments in which symbolic analysts work are substantially different from those in which routine producers or in-person servers work. Symbolic analysts usually labor within spaces that are quiet and tastefully decorated. Soft lights, wall-to-wall carpeting, beige and puce colors are preferred. Such calm surroundings typically are encased within tall steel-and-glass buildings or within long, low, postmodernist structures carved into hillsides and encircled by expanses of well-manicured lawn.

part. The bulk of the time and cost (and, thus, real value) comes in conceptualizing the problem, devising a solution, and planning its execution.

28   Most symbolic analysts have graduated from four-year colleges or universities; many have graduate degrees as well. The vast majority are white males, but the proportion of white females is growing, and there is a small, but slowly increasing, number of blacks and Hispanics among them. All told, symbolic analysis currently accounts for no more than 20 percent of American jobs. The proportion of American workers who fit this category has increased substantially since the 1950s (by my calculation, no more than 8 percent of American workers could be classified as symbolic analysts at midcentury), but the pace slowed considerably in the 1980s—even though certain symbolic-analytic jobs, like law and investment banking, mushroomed. (I will return to this point later.)[7]

3

29   These three functional categories cover more than three out of four American jobs. Among the remainder are farmers, miners, and other extractors of natural resources, who together comprise less than 5 percent of American workers. The rest are mainly government employees (including public school teachers), employees in regulated industries (like utility workers), and government-financed workers (American engineers working on defense weapons systems and physicians working off Medicaid and Medicare), almost all of whom are also sheltered from global competition.

30   Some traditional job categories—managerial, secretarial, sales, and so on—overlap with more than one of these functional categories. The traditional categories, it should be emphasized, date from an era in which most jobs were as standardized as the products they helped create. Such categories are no longer very helpful for determining what a person actually does on the job and how much that person is likely to earn for doing it. Only some of the people who are classified as "secretaries," for example, perform strictly routine production work, such as entering and retrieving data from computers. Other "secretaries" provide in-person services, like making appointments and fetching coffee. A third group of "secretaries" perform symbolic-analytic work closely allied to what their bosses do. To classify them as "secretaries" glosses over their very different functions in the economy. Similarly, "sales" jobs can fall within any one of three functional groups: some salespeople simply fill quotas and orders; others spend much of their time performing in-person services, like maintaining machinery; and some are sophisticated problem-identifiers no different from high-priced management consultants. "Computer programmers" (one of the more recent additions to the standard list of occupations) are as varied: They might be doing routine coding, in-person troubleshooting for particular clients, or translating complex and functional specifications into software.

31   That a job category is officially classified "professional" or "managerial" likewise has little bearing upon the function its occupants actually perform in the world econ-

---

[7] Sass's definition of "professional worker" overlaps significantly with my definition of symbolic analyst (although, as I will explain, not all symbolic analysts are professionals, and not all professionals are symbolic analysts). Sass finds that by 1988 professional workers comprised 20 percent of the American labor force. See Sass, op cit.

omy. Not all professionals, that is, are symbolic analysts. Some lawyers spend their entire working lives doing things that normal people would find unbearably monotonous—cranking out the same old wills, contracts, and divorces, over and over, with only the names changed. Some accountants do routine audits without active involvement of their cerebral cortices. Some managers take no more responsibility than noting who shows up for work in the morning, making sure they stay put, and locking the place up at night. (I have heard tell of university professors who deliver the same lectures for thirty years, long after their brains have atrophied, but I do not believe such stories.) None of these professionals is a symbolic analyst.[8]

Nor are all symbolic analysts professionals. In the older, high-volume economy, a   32
"professional" was one who had mastered a particular domain of knowledge. The knowledge existed in advance, ready to be mastered. It had been recorded in dusty tomes or codified in precise rules and formulae. Once the novitiate had dutifully absorbed the knowledge and had passed an examination attesting to its absorption, professional status was automatically conferred—usually through a ceremony of appropriately medieval pageantry and costume. The professional was then authorized to place a few extra letters after his or her name, mount a diploma on the office wall, join the professional association and attend its yearly tax-deductible meeting in Palm Springs, and pursue clients with a minimum of overt avarice.

But in the new economy—replete with unidentified problems, unknown solutions,   33
and untried means of putting them together—mastery of old domains of knowledge isn't nearly enough to guarantee a good income. Nor, importantly, is it even necessary. Symbolic analysts often can draw upon established bodies of knowledge with the flick of a computer key. Facts, codes, formulae, and rules are easily accessible. What is much more valuable is the capacity to effectively and creatively *use* the knowledge. Possessing a professional credential is no guarantee of such capacity. Indeed, a professional education which has emphasized the rote of acquisition of such knowledge over original thought may retard such capacity in later life.

4

How, then, do symbolic analysts describe what they do? With difficulty. Because a   34
symbolic analyst's status, influence, and income have little to do with formal rank and title, the job may seem mysterious to people working outside the enterprise web, who are unfamiliar with the symbolic analyst's actual function within it. And because symbolic analysis involves processes of thought and communication, rather than tangible production, the content of the job may be difficult to convey simply. In answering the question "What did you do today, Mommy (or Daddy)?" it is not always instructive, or particularly edifying, to say that one spent three hours on the telephone, four hours in meetings, and the remainder of the time gazing at a computer screen trying to work out a puzzle.

---

[8] In the remainder of this [article], when discussing symbolic analysts, I shall, on occasion, illustrate my point by referring to lawyers, management consultants, software engineers, and other professionals, but the reader should understand that this is a shorthand method of describing only the symbolic and analytic work undertaken by such professionals.

35   Some symbolic analysts have taken refuge in job titles that communicate no more clearly than this, but at least sound as if they confer independent authority nonetheless. The old hierarchies are breaking down, but new linguistic idioms have arisen to perpetuate the time-honored custom of title-as-status.

36   Herewith a sample. Add any term from the first column to any from the second, and then add both terms to any from the third column, and you will have a job that is likely (but not necessarily) to be inhabited by a symbolic analyst.

Communications	Management	Engineer
Systems	Planning	Director
Financial	Process	Designer
Creative	Development	Coordinator
Project	Strategy	Consultant
Business	Policy	Manager
Resource	Applications	Adviser
Product	Research	Planner

37   The "flat" organization of high-value enterprise notwithstanding, there are subtle distinctions of symbolic-analytic rank. Real status is inversely related to length of job title. Two terms signify a degree of authority. (The first or second column's appellation is dropped, leaving a simpler and more elegant combination, such as "Project Engineer" or "Creative Director.") Upon the most valued of symbolic analysts, who have moved beyond mere technical proficiency to exert substantial influence on their peers within the web, is bestowed the highest honor—a title comprising a term from the last column preceded by a dignified adjective like Senior, Managing Chief, or Principal. One becomes a "Senior Producer" or a "Principal Designer" not because of time loyally served or routines impeccably followed, but because of special deftness in solving, identifying, or brokering new problems.

38   Years ago, fortunate and ambitious young people ascended career ladders with comfortable predictability. If they entered a core corporation, they began as, say, a second assistant vice president for marketing. After five years or so they rose to the rank of first assistant vice president, and thence onward and upward. Had they joined a law firm, consulting group, or investment bank, they would have started as an associate, after five to eight years ascended to junior partner, and thence to senior partner, managing partner, and finally heaven.

39   None of these predictable steps necessitated original thought. Indeed, a particularly creative imagination might even be hazardous to career development, especially if [it] elicited questions of a subversive sort, like "Aren't we working on the wrong problem?" or "Why are we doing this?" or, most dangerous of all, "Why does this organization exist?" The safest career path was the surest career path, and the surest path was sufficiently well worn by previous travelers so that it could not be missed.

40   Of course, there still exist organizational backwaters in which career advancement is sequential and predictable. But fewer fortunate and ambitious young people dive into them, or even enter upon careers marked by well-worn paths. They dare not. In the emerging global economy, even the most impressive of positions in the most prestigious of organizations is vulnerable to worldwide competition if it entails easily replicated routines. The only true competitive advantage lies in skill solving, identifying, and brokering new problems.

EXPLORING THE AUTHOR'S IDEAS

1. Does Reich believe that such an entity as "the American worker" exists now? Why or why not?
2. Why does Reich suggest that the categories traditionally used to characterize American workers must change?
3. What, according to Reich, do people employed in "routine-production services" typically do?
4. What, according to Reich, do people employed in "in-person services" typically do?
5. What, according to Reich, do people employed in "symbolic-analytic services" typically do?
6. Which of these categories in the future does Reich believe will produce the best jobs? Explain your answer.

EXPLORING YOUR OWN IDEAS

1. Do you think a college education should prepare a student for a specific job? Why or why not?
2. For which of Reich's three categories do you believe a college education currently prepares a student? Explain your answer.
3. Do you agree with Reich that American workers must realize that they hold a place in a global economy? Why or why not?
4. Interview someone who you believe holds a job that Reich would classify as "symbolic-analytic services." In your interview, among other things ask the person to describe how predictable his or her job is on a daily basis.

EXPLORING VISUAL IMAGES

Work comes in a variety of forms. Examine the collage on the next page. How many types of work are referenced here? Now compare this collage to your own personal work history. Find out the jobs that your family members (or the family of close friends) hold or have held, going back at least two or three generations. Consider what job you want to hold in the near future and in 15 years. Write a personal essay on the contributions of your family—past, present, and future—to American work. Or write a short informative report on the changing face of American jobs from your personal perspective.

America at Work

UNIT WRITING ASSIGNMENT SUGGESTIONS

1. Think about your own experiences as a worker in part-time or full-time jobs you have held and write a **personal essay** on some aspect of your life as a worker.
2. Conduct research into some aspect of work (perhaps focusing on the relation between work and education) and write a **stance or position paper** that incorporates your research.
3. Arrange to observe the work and workers at a specific job site that interests you and write a **field report** detailing your observations.
4. Conduct a detailed observation of a particular employee at a job site that interests you and write a **case study** of his or her position.
5. Conduct research on some topic related to work in your community—for example, available housing for low-wage workers or job training for unemployed workers—and write a **proposal** to remedy some negative situation you discover.
6. Find and read two or three journal articles or book chapters on some aspect of work and write an **abstract** of each one.
7. Create an **annotated bibliography** on the topic of work with at least 10 sources.
8. Attend a job fair and write a **response paper** about the experience.
9. Examine carefully two or three Web sites that would help someone find a job in your community and then write a **critique** of these sites.

10. Keep a **journal** for two weeks about your experiences at work, noting the number of hours, the activities, the amount of leisure time you have, etc. Reflect on the balance of things in your own life.

PERCEPTIONS OF AMERICA

In 1831, Alexis de Tocqueville, a French political scientist and diplomat, wrote his now-classic comprehensive review of the strengths and weaknesses of America, *Democracy in America.* In it, de Tocqueville explored the strengths and weaknesses of the government, the culture, and the attitudes of this young nation that mystified much of the world with its daring experiment with democracy. For the nearly 200 years since then, America has continued to both "fascinate and infuriate" (to quote Mark Hertsgaard, one of the authors excerpted in this section) the rest of the world.

Though unquestionably the most powerful political and economic force in the world, the United States of America clearly experiences a mixed reputation among other nations of the world. Our nation is hailed by some as the most innovative, progressive, and democratic nation on earth, while simultaneously scorned by others as the most arrogant, materialistic, and morally and culturally depraved nation on earth. Ironically, as decades have passed, our alliances have shifted, and the views of individual nations have vacillated. But recently, as evidenced in a "Global Attitudes" poll conducted among 16,000 people in more than 20 countries (eight of them Muslim) by the highly respected researchers of the Pew Institute, "foreign approval of America has plummeted."*

Of course, the most blatant evidence of our faltering reputation, at least in some spheres, is the tragedy of September 11, 2001. Even if that intricately designed disaster is judged solely as the work of terrorist extremists, clearly we Americans have been tragically jolted into analyzing our international image. No matter how independent we may claim or desire to be, we must now pay heed to the perceptions of America that others hold.

The readings in this section explore perceptions of America from a variety of viewpoints. Five of the six texts are written by individuals born outside of the United States (though several are *currently* residing in America), coming from countries as diverse as Palestine, China, the Dominican Republic, Germany, and India. Once again, various academic disciplines are tapped, including history, journalism, political science, and literary studies; notably, a wide range of ideologies are prevalent. Numerous genres are represented as well: a personal narrative, a scholarly essay, a magazine photoenhanced historical essay, a social critique, a journalistic essay in letter format, and a short story. Of course, each genre presents information, anticipates and shapes audience response, and promotes particular perspectives differently. Noting those differences as you read will help you develop more meaningful insights into prevalent perceptions of our nation. Indeed, each text encourages you to be a critical reader in order to examine the ambiguous nature of the American image, to better understand the roots of the varied perceptions, and to explore America's strengths and shortcomings.

---

* Details available in "The World Out There." *The Economist* 7 June 2003: 26–27.

Reading 1

The following reading, taken from Mark Hertsgaard's social critique entitled The Eagle's Shadow: Why America Fascinates and Infuriates the World, *is the only selection in this unit written by an American-born author. Hertsgaard, a prolific writer on a wide range of social issues, offers fascinating insights into varied international perceptions of America today. Constructed around a series of vignettes collected during extensive world travel, Hertsgaard explores America's ambivalent reputation (highlighted in his choice of subtitle) among numerous other nations around the world. His firsthand stories hail from countries as wide-flung as South Africa and China, Egypt and Italy, the Czech Republic and Kenya.*

This text provides an interesting genre blend of engaging personal narratives and rich social commentary. Overall, it is heavily documented by the author's primary source research and by his use of credible secondary sources. Notably, Hertsgaard openly characterizes his text as a "dialogue between how foreigners and Americans perceive the United States"; the "dialogue" is aimed at raising questions, not suggesting definitive answers.

(Note: The footnotes are repeated exactly as provided by Hertsgaard in the "Notes" chapter of his text, with the exception of the footnote numbering which is altered to be sensible in this context; his original numbers corresponded to page numbers of his text.)

Excerpt from *The Eagle's Shadow: Why America Fascinates and Infuriates the World*

Mark Hertsgaard

1   For Malcolm Adams, as for most people around the world, America is more a mental image than a real place. He will almost certainly never see the United States with his own eyes—he'll never have enough money to afford the trip—but that diminishes his interest in the place not one bit.

2   I met Malcolm on a bus ride in South Africa in June of 2001. He was a driver for the Baz Bus, a shuttle service known to the backpacker crowd in South Africa as a cheap if not always reliable way to get between major cities and rural tourist areas. The day he picked me up, he was heading east along the coast toward Durban. It was late afternoon, a low winter sun. Along the roadside hundreds of people, bunched in groups of five or six, were walking home. Off to our right, the Indian Ocean frothed and sparkled, crashing against the southern edge of the African landmass.

3   Malcolm was thirty-two, but his smooth-skinned face and ebullient demeanor made him look younger. Like his father, he had worked as a driver all his adult life, though as a teenager he dreamed of becoming a naval officer. "I had the ability," he explained wistfully, "but under the old system your skin color could keep you out of those things." Now he worked fourteen-hour days driving from one end of South

Africa to the other. The scenery was glorious, but he missed his wife and two children, whom he saw only on weekends. Still, he said, this was an improvement over his last job, driving public buses for the city of Cape Town. He quit that job after five fellow drivers were murdered gangland-style while driving their routes. The killer later testified in court that for each murder he was paid 350 rand, about U.S. $50, by bosses of the taxi drivers union, who apparently hoped to frighten passengers into taxis.

"Yeah, I heard about those shootings," I said. "The newspapers back home wrote about them."   4

"And where is back home?" Malcolm asked.   5

I told him, and his eyes lit up with glee as he gushed, "Oh, you are from America! Your country has a very great influence on South Africa."   6

"Really?" I said. "Good or bad?"   7

"Good, good! America is what everyone here wants to be like—American music, American clothes, American lifestyle: nice house, big car, lots of cash. America is the idol for many people in South Africa."   8

His own clothes made the point: a Jack Daniel's baseball cap, black jeans, and a royal blue ski jacket with puffy sleeves. He would have fit right in on the streets of Brooklyn or St. Louis. Malcolm said he and his friends knew about America from songs they heard on the radio, movies they rented at the video shop, TV shows carried on South African channels; *The Bold and the Beautiful* was a particular favorite. I asked whether older people shared his view—did his mother and father idolize the United States? "No, they are more Christian," he replied without irony. "They want to live a South African life."   9

By now, darkness had fallen. Malcolm's face glowed in the reflection of the dashboard lights as he spoke of the Cape Town township where he and his family lived. They had running water, electric light, and paved streets, but many neighbors lacked real jobs and crime was a constant worry: "Gangsters are shooting and robbing people and the police do nothing." We were silent a moment. Then, with the same enthusiasm he showed for anything American, he added, "Did you know that every township in South Africa has two street gangs named for your country?"   10

"No."   11

"Yes! One is called the Young Americans, the other is called the Ugly Americans."   12

"What's the difference?"   13

A wide smile. "The Young Americans dress like Americans. The Ugly Americans shoot like Americans."   14

Good, Bad, But Never Indifferent

America: a place that is very rich and shoots lots of guns. It's not the most sophisticated analysis, but it's a fair shorthand for how the United States is seen by many people around the world. Friend or foe, rich or poor, foreigners tend to fear America for its awesome military power even as they are dazzled by its shimmering wealth.   15

That perspective may sound jarring to some Americans. We see ourselves as decent, hardworking people who wish the rest of the world well and do more than our share to help it. We are proud of our freedom and prosperous way of life, and we understand why others want the same. We would rather not "entangle our peace and prosperity" in foreign toils, as the father of our country, George Washington, advised   16 long ago, but we will use force if necessary to oppose injustice and protect freedom around the world for ourselves and others. We have our shortcomings like anyone else, but we believe we live in the greatest country in the world.

17   Malcolm Adams would, I imagine, agree with that assessment, and he's not alone. In twenty years of living and traveling overseas through thirty countries, I have spoken with many people who think very highly of America and Americans. I have also, of course, met many who find fault with the United States. In fact, the same individual often fits in both categories; some of the most penetrating criticisms of America I've heard came from people who, by and large, admire the place.

18   I began working on this book long before the 2001 terror attacks against America, and I pursued my travels and interviews both before and after September 11. From the start, the book was intended for two separate but related audiences. I hoped to provide my fellow Americans with a sort of traveler's report: "This is how we look to the rest of the world." For non-American readers, I hoped to explain why America and Americans are the way we are. The September 11 attacks gave these goals greater urgency and focus by suddenly illuminating how people everywhere felt about the United States. But the attacks also complicated the project by leaving Americans understandably sensitive to anything approaching candid criticism of their country.

19   A year has now passed since the terrible explosions and fires that killed more than three thousand people in New York, Washington, and Pennsylvania—a year of healing, of taking stock, of fighting back. Are Americans at last ready to hear what people overseas think about us? The message is a lot more complex than the "Why They Hate Us" war cry our media have supplied. And a lot more interesting. Foreigners aren't always right about America, far from it. But neither are they merely embittered fanatics, or jealous of our money, or resentful of our power, or animated by any of the other stock explanations mainstream American pundits and politicians have advanced as substitutes for honest self-examination. Most foreigners are sophisticated enough to see both the good and the bad about the United States, the pluses and the minuses. Which is why Americans can learn from their perceptions, if we choose to.

20   Foreigners can see things about America that natives cannot, and if ever there was a time when Americans needed such perspective, it's now. The horror of what happened on September 11 commands us to look at our homeland with new eyes—in particular, with the eyes of the rest of the world. Osama bin Laden and the Taliban are not representative of international opinion; hatred of America, though intense where it exists, is relatively rare. But Americans should not take false comfort from that, or let the sense of victimhood tragically earned on September 11 blind us to the fact that on September 10 the rest of the world harbored plenty of complaints against us, often with good reason. Indeed, some of the tartest criticisms—of the Bush administration's withdrawal from both the Kyoto protocol on global warming and the Anti-Ballistic Missile Treaty, and of the refusal of the United States to join the international criminal court—were coming from the very leaders who soon stood shoulder to shoulder with America against terrorism, notably British prime minister Tony Blair, German chancellor Gerhard Schröder, and French president Jacques Chirac.[1]

---

[1] Chirac's comments regarding Kyoto were reported by the Associated Press on March 30, 2001; his concern of missile defense was reported in the *Houston Chronicle,* June 13, 2001. Blair's and Schröder's concerns about Kyoto were reported in *The Guardian,* March 20, 2001.

"You Know Nothing About Us"

The first time I traveled around the world, starting in 1991, I was investigating the   21
environmental future for my book *Earth Odyssey.* Most people in the nineteen countries I visited were happy enough to answer my ecological questions, but often their
comments were more dutiful than animated. America, by contrast, is a subject that
never fails to get people talking. Everyone has an opinion about it, and they aren't shy
about expressing it. Compare, for example, the wide-eyed admiration of Malcolm
Adams with the views of three retired terrorists I interviewed a few weeks earlier in a
dusty tea shop in Cairo's Islamic Quarter (even terrorists, it seems, eventually retire).
For these graybeards with ankle-length gowns and bubbling water pipes, America
was a contemptible bully—a protector of Israel and corrupter of Egypt's Arabic soul.
Yet even they had fond memories of Hollywood movies starring Kirk Douglas and
Anthony Quinn.

One way or another, foreigners can hardly avoid forming opinions about the   22
United States. Wherever they look, America is in their face. American movies, television, music, fashion, and food have especially captivated young people throughout
the world even as they spread America's most important export: its consumer lifestyle
and the individualism it promotes. The Internet, computers, and high-tech gadgets
revolutionizing daily life all over the planet either originated in the United States or
find their fullest development there. America's nuclear arsenal has held life-and-
death power over humanity since the bombings of Hiroshima and Nagasaki in 1945.
For even longer, the United States economy has been the world's main engine of
growth and innovation, and it remains today the "buyer of last resort" whose imports
spell the difference between recession and prosperity for rich and poor nations alike.

To top it all off, America receives a disproportionate amount of coverage from   23
news media around the world, reinforcing foreigners' sense of living always in the
Eagle's shadow. "I'm glad I live in South Africa and not in the United States," a young
white restaurant manager in Stellenbosch, the wine-growing region east of Cape
Town, told me. "Any stupid thing that happens in the States is news all over the
world: 0. J. Simpson, the Florida election recount." Did he resent America's ubiquity? "It's not a matter of resentment," he replied. "It's just fact. I have to listen to
what [U.S. Federal Reserve chairman] Alan Greenspan says. It can affect my inventory. Actually, I think we have an advantage over you, because we know everything
about you and you know nothing about us."

Good point. But I would go further: Americans not only don't know much about   24
the rest of the world, we don't care. Or at least we didn't before the terrible events of
September 11, 2001. Until then, many Americans were barely aware the outside
world existed, a fact that both exasperates and amuses foreigners.

"I went to Tennessee a few years ago to attend my sister's wedding to an American   25
guy," Luis, a musician in Seville, Spain, told me. "When people heard my accent,
they asked where I was from. I said Spain. They smiled, Americans are friendly people, and they asked, 'Is that in Mexico?' They were not joking." Even high-powered
Americans sometimes know little about the world beyond. Who can forget former
president Ronald Reagan's imperishable comment after his first visit to South
America? "You'd be surprised," he told reporters, "they're all individual countries
down there." True, Reagan's two immediate successors, George Bush and Bill

Clinton, were worldly men, but George W. Bush had traveled abroad only three times before he became president.[2] Whatever his other qualities as a leader, in this respect the younger Bush was perfectly representative of his fellow citizens, only 14 percent of whom have passports.[3]

26   This is the first of many inequalities that distort America's relationship with the rest of the world: foreigners have to care about America, while Americans have traditionally cared little if at all about them. A corollary is that Americans have no idea how they appear to others; the privileged rarely do. After the September 11 attacks, 52 percent of American opinion leaders surveyed by the Pew Research Center for the People and the Press modestly agreed that "America does a lot of good in the world."[4] Only 21 percent of their overseas counterparts shared that sunny assessment of the United States.

27   There are understandable reasons for Americans' lack of interest in the outside world, starting with geography. Because the United States is so immense and protected on two sides by oceans, the rest of the world seems very far away. Americans lack the sense, so common on other continents, that foreign peoples with different languages, cultures, and beliefs live just over the next ridge or river. (Yes, the United States shares borders with Mexico and Canada, but many U.S. citizens regard their neighbors as honorary junior Americans, welcome as long as they stay in their place.) America's mind-boggling abundance also helps encourage a complacent isolationism. Why bother with the rest of the world when, as a Linda Ronstadt song declares, "everything you want, we got it right here in the U.S.A."?

28   Nevertheless, I have long felt baffled and disappointed by my countrymen and countrywomen's lack of curiosity about the world. Baffled because I myself find the rest of the world so fascinating, disappointed because I think ignorance of our neighbors reflects badly on Americans. Traveling twice around the world has taught me that Americans have no monopoly on parochialism and self-centeredness; the difference is, Americans are parochial and self-centered at the same time that we are the mightiest power in history. What our political, military, economic, cultural, and scientific institutions do has a decisive influence on the lives of people everywhere on earth, shaping the answers to such questions as "Will I have a job next month?" and "Will there be war?" right down to "What's on television tonight?" But with power comes responsibility. Americans' indifference to the world bothers me, I guess, because it seems wrong to have so much power over others and not care more about how it gets exercised.

29   Wrong and, after September 11, also foolish. If Americans rarely paid much attention to the outside world in the past, it's because we thought we didn't have to. As the

---

[2] George W. Bush made three overseas trips on business before he became president – to China, the Middle East, and Gambia, as reported in the *New York Times* of October 29, 2000. Bush's aides later tried to buttress his worldliness by claiming he had made many more overseas trips, but these turned out to be family vacations – to France, Italy, and Bermuda, according to CNN, December 17, 2000.

[3] The percentage of Americans with passports was cited by Rudy Maxa, "The Savvy Traveler," found as http://www.savvytraveler.com, April 13, 2001.

[4] The Pew Center's poll was released on December 19, 2001, and is found on the center's web site, http://www.people-press.org.

richest, most powerful nation in history, the United States could do what it wanted, when it wanted. If foreigners didn't like it, so what?

That invincible image never matched reality, of course. Remember Vietnam? And   30
the gasoline lines after the OPEC oil embargo in the 1970s? And the Iranian hostage crisis? But alas, many Americans don't remember. As a people forever fixated on the promise of a better tomorrow, Americans are barely familiar with our history, much less anyone else's. Besides, any unhappy memories were erased by the reassertion of American power directed during the 1980s by Ronald Reagan, a man who, despite his Alzheimer's disease, remains to this day America's most powerful politician (a theme elaborated later in this book). In the eyes of many Americans, the fall of the Berlin Wall in 1989 was proof that the United States was the chosen nation of God, as Reagan and other Cold Warriors had long proclaimed. And then came the roaring 1990s, when the United States experienced an explosion of economic growth that rewarded the wealthy out of all proportion while—brilliant touch—appearing accessible to anyone with the wit to trade stocks over the Internet. As the Dow and Nasdaq exchanges soared ever higher, creating countless new millionaires every day, who cared what was going on in the rest of the world? Clearly, America was where the action was.

And so America's awakening, when it came, was all the more painful and disori-   31
enting. "All that is solid melts into air," wrote Karl Marx during the turbulence of nineteenth-century industrialization. Many Americans felt the same after the attacks of September 11. One minute, we were enjoying the most privileged way of life in history. The next, terrorists had destroyed totemic symbols of our civilization and inflicted more deaths than the United States had suffered in a single day of combat since the Civil War. Suddenly Americans had learned the hard way: what foreigners think does matter.

The Difference Between America and Americans

What the United States does with this lesson is among the most important ques-   32
tions of our time, for Americans and foreigners alike. The initial response was, perhaps inevitably, military. After all, our country had been attacked in a vivid and horrifying way by sworn enemies whose spectacular assault left approximately three thousand civilians dead and caused countless billions of dollars' worth of economic losses. Any country so attacked would have the right to respond, and the Bush administration left little doubt that it planned to strike back hard. In the words of the Hollywood cowboy adage, "Shoot first, ask questions later." And the shooting went unexpectedly well in Afghanistan (if one leaves aside, as the United States government and media largely did, the deaths of Afghan civilians). The reaction in Europe was less enthusiastic, and the Arab world was downright dismayed; governments, but especially citizens, were distressed by the high civilian casualty figures and the prospect of future U.S. attacks against Iraq. But the fact remained that Afghanistan was liberated, the Taliban were routed, and bin Laden, as Bush boasted in December of 2001, "went from controlling a country three months ago to now maybe controlling a cave."

33   But what about the "ask questions later" part of the cowboy adage? In the immediate aftermath of September 11, many average Americans recognized their ignorance of the outside world and moved to address it, emptying libraries and bookstores of volumes on Islam, the Middle East, and international affairs. The news media, after years of pandering to a lowest-common-denominator audience with stories about sex and celebrities, remembered that news was supposed to be *about* something and began to cover the outside world again. By the turn of the new year, however, as the war against terrorism seemed to be won and domestic scares over anthrax and airports had faded, old habits began to reassert themselves. In one sense a return to normalcy was welcome, but it raised the question of whether the newly inquiring mood after September 11 was a mere blip. Would America aim to understand the frightening new world of the twenty-first century, or be content merely to subdue it?

34   This question begs a distinction that will recur throughout this book. "I contain multitudes," wrote Walt Whitman, America's great poet, and it's true. There is no one American reality, and not merely because of the individualism that is our cardinal national trait; there is also the difference between Americans and America—that is, between the nation's 285 million citizens and the political, military, economic, and media institutions whose policies make up the nation's official posture in the world. While America and Americans can sometimes amount to the same thing, it is a mistake to automatically equate the two. As in most countries, the dominant institutions in the United States are run by elites whose views do not necessarily coincide with those of the general public. In fact, the gap between America's elites and its masses has been growing over the last quarter century as economic inequality intensifies, the wealthy and well-connected increasingly control the political process, and once proud news organizations are gobbled up by giant corporations whose only allegiance is to profits. At the same time, there are many values that most Americans share— President Bush enjoyed a 75 percent approval rating six months after September 11[5]—and national unity is reinforced by the elites' control over the media that provide citizens with much of their information about the world. To oversimplify, the media *reflect* elite opinion but *shape* mass opinion.

35   Foreigners are often baffled that Americans, who are so adept at selling their products overseas, can simultaneously know so little about how they are perceived by others. But then few foreigners appreciate how poorly served Americans are by our media and educational systems—how narrow the range of information and debate is in the land of the free, another theme elaborated later in this book. For now, let a brief comparison of American and European media coverage after September 11 illustrate the point.

36   I was traveling in Europe in the weeks after the attacks. In the leading newspapers in Britain, Germany, France, Italy, and Spain I found plenty of news coverage that both sympathized with the horror inflicted upon my homeland and endorsed the right of the United States to retaliate militarily. But I also found lots of coverage that cautioned against a military response, drew a connection between the attacks and America's foreign policy, especially its perceived favoritism toward Israel, and urged

[5] Bush's 75 percent approval rating was reported in *Time*, March 25, 2002.

attention to the root causes of terrorism, not just to sensational symbols like Osama bin Laden. "Bring the murderers to justice, but tackle the causes of these outrages," the September 14 *London Independent* opined in one typical commentary that urged reconsideration of U.S.-led sanctions against Iraq and America's reflexive support for Israel. In Germany, even the conservative tabloid *Bild* gave space to pacific as well as belligerent viewpoints; one article quoted a German businessman's letter to President Bush urging him to "punish the guilty, not the innocent . . . women and children of Afghanistan."[6]

In the United States, by contrast, the news media's pronouncements were indis-   37
tinguishable from the government's, and neither showed tolerance for anything less than full-throated outrage. At the Fox television network, correspondents wore American flag pins and anchor Brit Hume dismissed civilian deaths in Afghanistan as unworthy of news coverage.[7] CNN chairman Walter Isaacson directed his U.S. staff not to mention civilian casualties in Afghanistan without at the same time re-calling the Americans who died on September 11.[8] (Tellingly, CNN did not impose such restrictions on its overseas broadcasts.) When the American media finally examined the question of how the United States appeared to the rest of the world, that richly complex subject was reduced to simplistic melodrama. The journalistic climate was such that anyone voicing the opinions expressed by the *London Independent* or *Bild* was accused of treasonous nonsense, as writer Susan Sontag discovered when she published an article in *The New Yorker* pointing out that American foreign policy had wreaked terrible damage on other countries in the past, so why all the surprise at being targeted itself now?

The American reaction was bound to be less measured than Europe's, of course; it   38
was we who had been attacked, we who had suffered such grievous losses. But if Americans want to prevent further attacks in the future, we must realize that neither unleashing our fearsome military nor tightening domestic security will alone suffice, and that limiting discussion on supposedly patriotic grounds is positively unhelpful. We need at all costs to understand *why* this happened. Toward that end, we need to consider even those explanations that may not flatter us. We need to recognize, for example, that there is a crucial difference between explaining a given action and ex-cusing that action. One can logically argue, as I would, that the United States in no way deserved the September 11 attacks (there is never any excuse for terrorism, pe-riod) and the perpetrators absolutely should be brought to justice, while adding that the attacks cannot be understood outside the context of American foreign policy and the resentment it has engendered.

There are numerous global hot spots where United States policies are controver-   39
sial enough to feed the kind of rage that found murderous expression on September 11. Would bin Laden have launched his attack if the United States were not financ-ing Israel's occupation of the Palestinian territories and stationing troops in Saudi Arabia? Quite possibly not, though I don't mean to suggest that Washington should

---

[6] The businessman's letter appeared in the September 17 issue of *Bild*.

[7] Brit Hume's comment was reported in the *New York Times*, December 3, 2001.

[8] Walter Issacson's memo was reported in the *Washington Post*, October 31, 2001.

grant terrorists veto power over its foreign policy. The point is, Americans need to have an honest discussion about our conduct overseas: Where is it wise? Where is it not? How often does it correspond to the values of democracy and freedom that we regularly invoke, and how important is it whether we practice what we preach?

America Is the Future

40   If Americans want a healthy relationship with the six billion people we share the planet with, we need to understand who those people are, how they live, what they think and why. This is not charity, it is self-interest. America may be protected by two oceans and the mightiest military in history, but we now know we are not untouchable. The United States sits atop an increasingly unequal world; 45 percent of humanity lives on less than two dollars a day. Peace and prosperity are unlikely under such conditions, as the CIA itself has warned. "Groups feeling left behind [by widening inequality] . . . will foster political, ethnic, ideological, and religious extremism, along with the violence that often accompanies it," an agency report forecast in 2000—as good a prediction of September 11 as one could want.[9]

41   Foreigners have no less a stake in better understanding the United States. Thomas Jefferson wrote over two hundred years ago that "every man has two nations: his own, and France." Today, the second nation of every person on earth is the United States. The world is being made more American by the day, an obvious point to anyone who travels much. What the news media call globalization is in fact largely Americanization, and September 11 has not diminished the trend. But proximity does not equal understanding. At a time when they are increasingly intertwined through economics and technology, the United States and the rest of the world often gaze at each other in mutual incomprehension.

42   How, foreigners ask, can America be so powerful yet so naive? So ignorant of foreign nations, peoples, and languages yet so certain it knows what's best for everyone? How can its citizens be so open and generous but its foreign policy so domineering? And why is it shocked when the objects of its policies grumble or even strike back?

43   What accounts for America's extraordinary optimism, its dynamic "can-do" spirit, its ceaseless pursuit of the "green light" F. Scott Fitzgerald invoked in *The Great Gatsby?* How can it put men on the moon and libraries onto computer chips but still debate the teaching of evolution in public schools and nearly impeach a president over an extramarital affair? How can Americans be so rich in material possessions but so lacking in family and community ties? So inundated with timesaving appliances yet perpetually stressed and hurried? How can the United States have given birth to uplifting cultural glories like jazz and rock and roll and socially resonant ethics like environmentalism yet be a cheerleader for vacuous celebrity, gratuitous violence, and ubiquitous luxury?

---

[9] The CIA's unclassified report, "Global Trends 2015," was released in 2000, was covered by the American news media, and is available at http://www.cia.gov/cia/publications/globaltrends2015.

How can a nation famous as the land of opportunity be spawning a growing underclass for whom the American Dream has become a cruel myth? How could the world's proudest democracy descend to the chaos and corruption that stained the 2000 presidential contest? Was that shameful episode a harbinger of American decline, one now reinforced by the unspeakable tragedy of September 11? Or will the United States become once again the "shining city on a hill" that Ronald Reagan used to so proudly invoke?   44

These are difficult questions, and some Americans have no intention of facing them. The country is at war, in their view, and anyone who doesn't line up behind the commander-in-chief with his mouth shut should be put on the next plane to Baghdad. At times, the understandable surge of patriotism that followed September 11 has evolved into an unseemly superiority complex: a conviction that Americans are inherently more brave, caring, and generous than anyone else. It is "because we are Americans," as one book's title put it,[10] that New York City firemen charged into the burning chaos of the World Trade Center to pull victims to safety—as if rescue workers in other countries were incapable of similar acts of courage and dedication.   45

Personally, I believe our country is strong enough to profit from a searching consideration of both its virtues and its vices. To any who nevertheless insist on accusing me of America-bashing, let me reply clearly, if only to disarm a slander that might otherwise be employed to dismiss this book: I do not hate America. I love America. As a journalist and writer, I feel blessed to live in the land of the First Amendment. I remain awed by the founding ideals of the United States; 225 years later, they survive as an inspiring prescription for, in Jefferson's majestic phrase, life, liberty, and the pursuit of happiness.   46

But America, I fear, has strayed from its founding ideals. September 11 left our people in a frightened, rally-round-the-flag mood. When we are ready to face facts again, we may see that our country was in crisis well before bin Laden's bombers set off on their mission of hate. Politically, we live in a democracy that barely deserves the name. Our government lectures others on how to run elections, yet most of our own citizens don't vote. Abdication of this basic civic responsibility may be rooted partly in the complacency that affluence can breed, but surely another cause is the alienation many Americans feel from a political system they correctly perceive as captive to the rich and powerful. Nor does our economy much resemble our democratic aspirations. In his 1831 classic, *Democracy in America,* Alexis de Tocqueville celebrated us as a nation where "great revolutions will become more rare" because our equality, he believed, was an ingrained tendency. Today, America is more and more divided between an elite that lives in cloistered luxury and a poor and middle class doomed to work hard but not get ahead. Meanwhile, in our foreign policy we say we stand for freedom and often we do, but we can be shamelessly hypocritical, siding with treacherous dictatorships that serve our perceived interests and overthrowing real democracies that do not. The United States has much to be proud of, but it also has things to be sorry for.   47

---

[10]*Because We Are Americans,* edited by Jesse Kornbluth and Jessica Papin, was published as a paperback by Warner Books in November 2001.

Why should Americans find this hard to admit? We will get along better with our neighbors, and vice versa, if we face up to this unsurprising but powerful fact. To insist that we ignore our faults—and label as a traitor anyone who refuses to be silent—is folly. Uncomfortable truths don't go away just because powerful voices want them shouted down. Nor is dissent un-American; quite the opposite. If one lesson of September 11 is that no nation is invulnerable in today's world, surely another is that America can no longer afford to ignore what the rest of the world thinks, even when—perhaps especially when—it is not laudatory. Which brings me to the narrative map of this book. Each of its ten chapters offers a sort of dialogue between how foreigners and Americans perceive the United States. I organize the dialogue around a list of ten things that foreigners think about America that Americans usually don't talk about, as follows:

1. America is parochial and self-centered.
2. America is rich and exciting.
3. America is the land of freedom.
4. America is an empire, hypocritical and domineering.
5. Americans are naive about the world.
6. Americans are philistines.
7. America is the land of opportunity.
8. America is self-righteous about its democracy.
9. America is the future.
10. America is out for itself.

I don't pretend to have all the answers about America. My homeland is too vast, too multifaceted, too full of surprises to be easily summarized. The United States, wrote John Steinbeck, is "complicated, paradoxical, bullheaded, shy, cruel, boisterous, unspeakably dear, and very beautiful."[11] Still a young nation, it remains (one of its greatest strengths) a work in progress.

48   In a book as short as this, it is impossible to explore America in much detail. My purpose, rather, is to raise questions, sometimes awkward ones, about America's behavior and beliefs at the dawn of the twenty-first century. Although this book is based on extensive travel, reporting, and research, it is more an opening argument than a definitive proof. I hope to provoke thought and debate, and if readers don't disagree with at least some of what I write, I probably haven't done my job.

49   I know that parts of this book will be difficult for some Americans to hear. As Tocqueville noted, we tend to "live in a state of perpetual self-adoration. . . . Only strangers or experience may be able to bring certain truths to the Americans' attention."[12] But as the global outpouring of sympathy following September 11 illustrated, the rest of the world harbors great affection for Americans along with other less enthusiastic feelings. And the majority of foreigners differentiate between Americans as

---

[11]Steinbeck's quote, from his 1966 book *America and Americans,* was noted in the *Los Angeles Times Book Review,* March 3, 2002.

[12]Tocqueville's "self-adoration" quote is found in *Democracy in America,* translated by George Lawrence and edited by J. P. Mayer (New York: HarperPerennial, 1988), volume 1, part 2, chapter 7.

people—whom they generally like—and American power and foreign policy, which are far less admired.

Meanwhile, most foreigners recognize that it is in their own interest to understand America as clearly as possible; after all, they all live in the Eagle's shadow. "I have wanted to write an opinion article for the *New York Times* urging that American elections be opened to foreigners, because what the American government decides about economic policy, military action, and cultural mores affects me and all other people around the world," Abdel Monern Said Aly, a journalist who directs the Al-Ahram Center for Political and Strategic Studies in Cairo, told me. "When U.S. economic growth slows, we see the price of oil fall. When the U.S. stock market declines, the grants from the Ford Foundation to my center in Cairo decline." 50

Whatever the realm—economic, military, political, scientific, or cultural—the United States is the world's dominant nation. Its power is by no means absolute, but it is the decisive actor whose behavior, for better or worse, will shape the world that people everywhere will live in during the twenty-first century. Beldrich Moldan, a former environment minister of the Czech Republic, put it best. "As a European," he told me in Prague, "you may like the United States or not like the United States, but you know it's the future." 51

UNDERSTANDING THE AUTHOR'S IDEAS

1. Summarize the "images" of America that emerge from the opening vignette.
2. Explain the "mixed" reputation that America enjoys throughout much of the world.
3. Explain the distinction Hertsgaard makes between America and Americans.
4. Discuss your impressions of the accuracy of Hertsgaard's list of ten things foreigners think about Americans. Can you point to examples to substantiate and/or refute these generalizations?
5. Explain the significance of the title of Hertsgaard's text. What does it suggest about author? What does it imply about the audience?

EXPLORING YOUR OWN IDEAS

1. Hertsgaard states his purpose in writing this extended personal narrative is "to raise questions, sometimes awkward ones, about America's behavior and beliefs at the dawn of the twenty-first century." What questions has he raised for you? Discuss your responses with small groups of classmates.
2. This genre offers a combination of a compilation of personal vignettes acquired through extensive world travel and some social commentary and analysis. Explain your overall reaction to this genre. Compare and contrast it to the scholarly examination of another culture's perception in something like the articles by Berghahn or Chen that follow.

3. Share a personal experience that you have had in traveling abroad and/or in talking with a visitor to America with small groups of your classmates. Reflect on your experience in light of this reading.

4. Discuss any new insights you have gained into your understanding of others' perceptions of America after having read this chapter. How do others' perceptions mesh with *your* perceptions of American culture? Explain.

5. This text was written after the devastating experience of September 11. Explore how your views, as well as those of others you know, have been altered by that tragic event.

6. Discuss in what ways this excerpt becomes a "dialogue," as Hertsgaard purports. Do you find yourself responding to remarks of the foreigners? Where do you agree and disagree?

Reading 2

This scholarly journal article, published in the Journal of Contemporary China, *began as a graduate school seminar paper for a course at the Elliott School of International Affairs at George Washington University in Washington, D.C. In it, the author, herself a native of Taiwan, explores the perceptions of international relations experts on the rapidly changing, yet delicate, U.S.-China relationship. Here Chen discusses the ambiguous nature of the relationship—China clearly rejects certain aspects of American culture while it simultaneously embraces Westernization, especially a capitalist approach to industrialization. The article closely adheres to the genre conventions of a scholarly text with its formal style, a predominantly objective tone (though a certain perspective clearly ensues), and extensive use of footnotes.*

(Note: You'll see that Chen frequently uses the term "Sino" throughout the article. It can be read as a synonym for "China" or "Chinese.")

"China Perceives America: Perspectives of International Relations Experts"

Rosalie Chen

This article seeks to examine Chinese analysts' perceptions of America, particularly their views on US-China policy. It intends to explore how that issue has evolved over time, what progress has been made, what factors have shaped it, what principal impediments have existed, and what the prospects are for future management. Focusing on the period from the mid-1990s to the present, the study finds that there remains a perceptual gap in US-China relations today, though Chinese understanding of America continues to improve. Specifically, there seems to be a lessened diversity of opinions and an emerging consensus on the hegemonic nature of US foreign policy, particularly its intention of containing a rising China—though its dual strategy of containment and engagement continues to exist. More importantly, many Chinese analysts remain highly critical and negative. Thus, American external behavior worldwide would always be viewed with a great deal of suspicion.

The PRC [People's Republic of China] has hundreds of analysts who interpret   1
American policy for a Chinese audience. These 'America Watchers' advise Chinese policy-makers and write internal papers which circulate among the top leadership. It is via China's community of America Watchers that both the leaders and the mass public receive most of their information about the US. By influencing how China's leaders view the US, they indirectly help shape policy. David Shambaugh's book, *Beautiful Imperialist,* examines the conceptual lenses through which America Watchers perceived the US between 1972 and 1990. In his article, *China's America Watchers: Changing Attitudes Towards the United States,* Phillip Saunders updated Shambaugh's research by examining how Chinese analysts have interpreted American policy towards China during the 1990s and reassessing how well they understand the US. In this paper, I wish to update the above studies by surveying Chinese analysts' interpretations of Sino-US relations from the mid-1990s to the present. Have Chinese perceptions of America changed? Has any progress been made? What key factors and events have shaped the change, or lack of change, of views?

History and progress

Sino-US relations have historically suffered from mutual misperceptions, cultural   2
differences and unrealistic expectations. In *Beautiful Imperialist,* David Shambaugh concluded that despite considerable progress, Chinese understanding of America was shallow and seriously distorted. Many Chinese analysts held highly negative, suspicious and stereotyped views of the US. One saw in the America Watchers' interpretations of US foreign policy—particularly Sino-American relations—a strong prejudice toward viewing the US as a hegemonic power driven by the desire for world conquest. Furthermore, fluctuating Sino-American relations reflected the ambivalent images that the US and China held of each other. He predicted that the perceptual gap in both countries would create persistent instability in bilateral relations.[1]

In Saunders' article, he argued that the end of the Cold War exposed underlying   3
weaknesses in Chinese understanding of the US. He found that analysts had a much better understanding of the US but that the quality and the knowledge level of the broader community of America Watchers still varied widely.[2] More importantly, the improvements in Chinese understanding of the US had not translated into more sta-

[1] David Shambaugh, *Beautiful Imperialist* (Princeton: Princeton University Press, 1991), pp. 41–303.

[2] Phillip C. Saunders, 'China's America Watchers: Changing attitudes towards the US'. *The China Quarterly.* (March 2000), pp. 42–43.

ble bilateral relations. Many Chinese analysts interpreted a string of bilateral disputes during the 1990s as evidence of an American strategy to contain China; however, most America Watchers disagreed with the conclusion that the US sought to contain China, though many were reluctant to challenge this view publicly. Instead, they would generally argue that US policy had elements of both containment and engagement, with China being able to influence the mix.

4   Focusing on the period from the mid-1990s to the present, my own exploration of Chinese analysts' views on US-China policy found that the perceptual gap in US-China relations aforementioned remains today, though Chinese understanding of America continues to improve. Specifically, there seems to be a lessened diversity of opinions and an emerging consensus on the hegemonic nature of US foreign policy, particularly its intention of containing a rising China—though its aforementioned dual strategy (of containment and engagement) continues to exist. Perhaps most importantly, many Chinese analysts remain highly critical and negative; indeed, negative views regarding America have become deeper. Thus, as David Shambaugh argued, American external behavior worldwide (and particularly toward China) would always be viewed with a great deal of suspicion.[3] The Chinese simply do not trust American motives given their perception of American hegemony. They fear American manipulation of China in international strategic terms, exploitation in economic terms, and subversion in political and ideological terms.

US global strategy

5   Here, it is important to assess Chinese perspectives on US global strategy. A state's power position in the international system defines its strategic situation and is in itself an integral part of the state's strategic thinking. Chinese analysts believe that US China policy follows and serves US global strategy. Thus interpretations of US global strategy provide the framework through which Chinese analysts interpret Sino-American relations.

6   After the Cold War, assessments by Chinese analysts have shifted from a prediction of imminent US hegemonic decline to a view that US-dominated unipolarity will likely last well into the twenty-first century. They have overall perceived a consistent and malign US strategy of global domination. The views on the enduring and predatory nature of the US hegemony were especially reinforced after the NATO military intervention in Yugoslavia in 1999 (discussed later in this paper). In response, China has tried to balance against US power through developing a strategic partnership with Russia, building new ties with its neighbors and beyond, and increasing its comprehensive national power. Notwithstanding, so far, Beijing's balancing has been overall hesitant, low-key, and inconsistent.[4] Prevailing bandwagoning by other powers, acute domestic insecurity, and perceived high costs of open confrontation with the US combine to explain Beijing's hesitancy.

7   In the first half of the 1990s, views that suggested that the US-dominated 'uni-

---

[3] Shambaugh, *Beautiful Imperialist,* p. 301.

[4] Yong Deng, 'Hegemon on the offensive: Chinese perspectives on US global strategy'. *Political Science Quarterly* 116(3), (2001), p. 344.

polar moment' would be of short duration were widespread in China. It had become clear by the mid-1990s, however, that the world was not marching quickly toward multipolarity as the Chinese analysts had hoped for. Chinese analysts now characterized the world power configuration as one superpower, many great powers (*yi chao, duo qiang*). In 1996–1997, they concluded, 'the superpower is more super, and the many great powers are less great'.[5] Moreover, toward the late 1990s and early 2000s, China witnessed a growing acceptance of the view that US unipolar status could endure; both the description and prognosis about imminent multipolarity became increasingly untenable. But China's official protestations still insist that multipolarization continues, even though they admit that it will be a drawn-out process. Promoting multipolarization now means opposing a single country 'acting unilaterally' and dictating international affairs.[6]

An interesting observation is that while the US gropes for a coherent strategy, Chinese analysts attribute to it a highly cohesive master plan designed to strengthen and expand its global domination. Since the mid-1990s, emerging consensus on the preponderance of US power allows and compels Chinese analysts to pay closer attention to US global strategy than before. Instead of pursuing a globalization based on equality and mutual respect, however, they accuse Washington of 'seeking to turn globalization into Americanization' to fulfill its various national interests.[7] According to Chinese analysts, the US has advocated a view of limited sovereignty and human rights over-riding sovereignty. The ulterior motive is to justify its aggressive interference in other countries' domestic affairs, to demonize certain countries that defy its will, and ultimately to provide a pretext for power politics.

From the Chinese perspective, concentrated power without counterbalancing is both dangerous and unnatural—in an international rather than a domestic sense, of course. Specifically, an unchecked unipolar hegemony is prone to abusive power.[8] US human rights policy toward China and its so-called humanitarian intervention over Kosovo in 1999 proved the danger of dictatorship by the US democracy in the international arena. Thus, a balance of power underpinned by the five principles of peaceful coexistence should represent the basis for a new world order.[9]

Chinese analysts maintain that to pursue absolute supremacy, the US has acted unilaterally and disregarded the ABM Treaty and Missile Technology Control Regimes in an attempt to develop its own national and theater missile defense. Ostensibly the US missile defense is directed against 'rogue countries', but the primary motive is to ensure absolute security against potential adversaries such as Russia and China. In addition, the US revitalized its security alliance with Japan as

---

[5] *Ibid.*, pp. 345–346.

[6] Zhai Xiaomin, 'Lengzhan hou Meiguo Zhudaoshi Baquan Pingxi' ['Analysis of American hegemony after the Cold War'], *Shijie Jingji yu Zhengzhi* [*World Economics and Politics*] 4, (14 April 2000), pp. 72–73.

[7] Zhang Minqian, 'Globalization versus US strategy', *Xiandai Guoji Guanxi* [*Contemporary International Relations*], (June 2000), p. 10.

[8] *Ibid.*, p. 14.

[9] Chu Shulong, 'Mei duei Hua Zhanlui ji Zhong Mel Guanxi Zouxiang' ['US strategy to China and the trend of Sino-US relations'], *Heping yu Fazhan* [*Peace and Development*] 2, (May 2001), p. 64.

well as maintained large forwardly deployed troops in the west Pacific to keep an eye on China.[10] As the US can now act with impunity, it is more tempted to use coercive measures against other states. In fact, it has pursued a comprehensive, offensive neo-interventionism that utilizes all means available, including the use of force to strengthen US global domination.[11]

11   Chinese analysts often use the term *He Ze Yung, flu He Ze Qi* (use when deemed fit, disregard otherwise) to illustrate what they believe is US cynicism toward international institutions.[12] They also accuse America of controlling international organizations to legitimize its aggressive acts against other countries, as well as using its normative power to set the agenda, weaken and isolate its adversaries, and mobilize international support for its policy of hegemonic control. All US hegemonic behavior is now undertaken in the name of achieving some global public good.

12   In sum, Chinese analysts point to American high defense spending, a strong tendency to use coercive double standards in approaching international principles. Chinese writers maintain that the US has leveraged measures in its foreign policy, wanton disregard of international institutions and rules when deemed inconvenient, an aggressive liberal agenda in promoting Western values, unilateral decisions to build a shield and spear through national and theater missile defense, growing control over high-tech information in the age of globalization, arrogant violations of other countries' sovereignty, unprovoked expansion of traditional alliances in Europe and Asia, determined containment of emerging powers, etc. In short, Chinese assessment sees the US as a 'hegemon on the offensive' for power aggrandizement.[13]

Sino-American relations

13   Beijing's predilection to attribute to the US a highly coherent, largely malign global strategy bent on power expansion defines how Beijing perceives American China policy. Such a perception breeds a conspiratorial view, which in turn predisposes China to see ill intentions and sinister motives in every US act. For instance, conspiratorial views explain why Chinese analysts believe the US human rights concerns and humanitarianism in its foreign policy are nothing but camouflage for hegemony and brute power politics.[14] As the US seeks to maintain its superior power position, it

---

[10]Chu Shulong, 'Bilateral and regional strategic and security relationship between China and the US after the Cold War', *Contemporary International Relations*, (May 2000), pp. 3–6.

[11]Huo Jun, 'Meiguo Xin Baquanzhuyi de Genyuan yu Tedian' ['US neo-hegemonism—its origin and features']. *Heping yu Fazhan* 4. (November 1999), pp. 3–9; Chu Shulong. 'Zhong Mei duei Guoji Zhantui Wenti de Kanfa Lichang he Zhuzhang' ['Different views, standpoints and propositions of both China and America on international strategy'], *Shijie Jingji yu Zhengzhi* 7, (14 July 2000), p. 51.

[12]Huo, 'Meiguo Xin Baquanzhuyi de Genyuan yu Tedian', pp. 9–10.

[13]Deng, 'Hegemon on the offensive', p. 352.

[14]Zhu Feng, 'Renquan Wenti he Zhong Mei Guanxi: Bianhua yu Tiaozhan' ['Human rights and the Sino-American relations: changes and challenges'], *Shijie Jingji yu Zhengzhi* 7, (14 July 2000), pp. 20–22; Li Qing and Bi Changhong, 'Qian Tan Meiguo Guojia Anquan Zhanlui zhong de Daode Yensui' ['On the moral factors of America's national security strategy'], *Shijie Jingji yu Zhengzhi* 9, (14 September 2000), p. 50.

logically wants to contain a rising power like China. Seen in this light, the revitalization of the US-Japan security alliance is evidently targeted primarily against China.

Between 1992 and 1995, Chinese policy elites shared a view that their country's   14
security environment was the best since the Opium War (1839–1842).[15] But since 1995, sober assessment of its security environment started to set in. Frustration with a perceived US containment strategy to deny China's entry into the great power club fueled anti-American nationalism. Those anti-American sentiments reflected the public's emotional reactions to events such as rejection of China's membership in the WTO in early 1999, denial of China's right to host the 2000 Olympic Games, and perhaps more generally, growing US arrogance in its treatment of China.

Chinese analysts now emphasize that US China policy has an important element   15
of containment. There is a fear that, despite its avowed engagement policy, the US is maliciously containing China. Indeed, it is argued that 'the US engagement policy towards China has not only intended to coordinate and cooperate with China, but more importantly served as restrictive and preventive measures against China'.[16] Moreover, it is predicted that the US conscientiousness to advocate guarding against and containing China will become increasingly strong as China's economic and military power continues to grow in the twenty-first century.[17]

China's own international strategy is identified as consisting of the following: first,   16
create a peaceful international environment so that China can concentrate on its economic development; second, bring about national reunification with Taiwan; third, strengthen China's comprehensive national power to enhance the Chinese pole in a future multipolar world; finally, build a new international political and economic order with less inequity of power and wealth between the rich and poor and a more rigid adherence to the principle of sovereignty.[18] Clearly, American and Chinese strategic interests do not always coincide; they conflict over Taiwan, over the vision of global order, and over views on the desirability of the existing international structure.

For instance, both China and the US support peace in the Asia-Pacific region, but   17
they differ on what 'peace' means and what a regional order in East Asia should look like. From Beijing's perspective, America's belief that regional security can only be maintained under US unrivaled hegemony over East Asia—as manifested in its balancing against the rising China, forward military presence in the west Pacific, and traditional security bilateral alliances—conflicts with China's vital interests. Since the mid-1990s, China has increasingly seen the US military presence as less of a stabilizer and more as a threat to China's own independence, sovereignty, territorial integrity, and national security, especially over Taiwan.[19]

---

[15]Deng, 'Hegemon on the offensive', p. 354.

[16]Shen Qiang, 'Chong Nai de Yanjing kan Mei duei Hun Jiechu Zhengche de Zhanlui Yitu' ['Strategic intentions of the US engagement policy towards China: What do Joseph Nye's speeches imply?'], *Heping yu Fazhan* 2, (May 1999), p. 62.

[17]Chu, 'Mei duei Hua Zhanlui ji Zhong Mei Guanxi Zouxiang', p. 60.

[18]Chu, 'Zhong Mei duei Guoji Zhanlui Wenti de Kanfa Lichang he Zhuzhang', pp. 48–52; 'Mel duei Hua Zhanlui ji Zhong Mei Guanxi Zouxiang', pp. 63–64.

[19]Chu, 'Bilateral and regional strategic and security relationship', pp. 1–13.

18   In sum, the two countries fundamentally differ over issues concerning the architecture of the post-Cold War global order, the continued relevance of sovereignty, the emerging role of the UN and NATO, the legitimate use of force, and the place of humanitarian interventionism in world politics. More significantly, strategic rivalry is argued to likely increase with the ascension of Chinese power. Indeed, Chinese analysts contend that the US regards China as its potential threat and strategic rival in the twenty-first century. The basic long-term goal of US China strategy has been to try to evolve China. Thus, the US will stick to engaging China to make it change and at the same time take high-handed measures to create changes by pressure.

19   In short, Sino-American conflict is 'structural', as China is on the rise and the US wants to maintain its unipolar dominance. Here, we see an increasingly predominant realist perspective among Chinese analysts on the US. As identified by Saunders, Chinese realism closely resembles Western structural realism.[20] These Chinese perceptions underscore the structural conflict driving the US-China relationship. The two countries may share certain interests in specific issues or in realms such as trade, environmental protection, cracking down on terrorists' activities and international crimes, and preventing the proliferation of weapons of mass destruction, but the vital security interests defined by the two sides are fundamentally at odds with each other at bilateral, regional, and global levels.

20   According to conventional alliance theories, China could opt to join the US side to bandwagon with the predominant power, but Chinese strategists and policy makers have long rejected this option as unrealistic and unpalatable. Apart from the intractable conflict in interest and lack of strategic foundation in Sino-American relations, another explanation has to do with the novel post-Cold War distribution of power. From the Chinese perspective, North America, the European powers, and Japan have coalesced into a grand alliance underpinned by common political values and foreign policy outlook as well as shared interests.[21]

21   The US has led the way to build up a new world order guided by Western values with the alliance formed with the US and other developed nations in the West at the core. There is now a rough congruence of economic, political, military, and normative frameworks shared by a cluster of Western powers.[22] Consequently, aligning with the US does not seem just to entail a shift of alliance policy, but a sea change in China's foreign policy outlook, state character, and national self-identity, which

---

[20]Saunders, 'China's America Watchers', p. 48.

[21]Zhai, 'Lengzhan hou Meiguo Zhudaoshi Baquan Pingxi', pp. 72–74; Huo. 'Meiguo Xin Baquanzhuyi de Genyuan yu Tedian', pp. 8–9; Deng, 'Hegemon on the offensive', pp. 357–358; Chu, 'Zhong Mei duei Guoji Zhanlui Wenti de Kanfa Lichang he Zhuzhang', pp. 49–51; Xin Benjian. 'Anquan Kunjing Juenshi Lilen yu Lengzhan hou Meiguo duei Hua Zhengche' ['Security dilemma, balance theory vs. post-Cold War US policy toward China'], *Xiandai Guoji Guan.xi* 9, (2001), pp. 26–27.

[22]Yuan Jian, 'Idealism and American foreign policy in the post-Cold War era', *Guoji Wenti Yanjiu [International Studies]* 6–8, (1997). pp. 5–12; Huang Yi. 'Lengzhan hou Meiguo duei Hua Zhengche Linian Tan Yuan' ['Conceptual source of post-Cold War US policy toward China'], *Xiandai Guoji Guanxi* 4, (2001), pp. 5–6; Liu Yongtao, 'Lengzhan hou Meiguo duei Wai Wenhua Zhanlui Touxi' ['Analysis of post-Cold War US foreign cultural strategy'], *Xiandai Guoji Guanxi* 5, (2001), pp. 12–15.

China is not ready to embrace. Moreover, from the Chinese perspective, judgment of such in-group identity is as uncertain as it is arbitrary.

Since the mid-1990s, China has publicly identified itself to be a cooperative, peaceful, and responsible power, and Beijing has taken such an image quite seriously in its foreign policy.[23] The main reason for the shift is that the US had insisted that China could be treated as a great power only if and when it acted responsibly. Moreover, the earlier lie-low strategy seemed overly defensive, while a self-identity as a responsible power sounds more assertive and proactive in constructively safeguarding China's national interests.

Here, one should note that Chinese policy elites never specify what 'responsibility' means. Clearly, China and the US differ vastly over the meaning of international responsibility. For example, the US disputes the Chinese belief that it is both its right and responsibility to reunify with Taiwan even with the use of force and to maintain domestic stability even by resorting to a political iron fist if necessary. China no doubt questions the US claim that the war against Yugoslavia and continued coercion against Iraq were for the global public good of humanitarianism and nonproliferation of weapons of mass destruction.[24] In any case, these differences do not matter for Beijing, as rhetorical identification as a responsible power constitutes a scheme to defuse the 'China threat' so that China does not become the target. Like its lie-low strategy, protestations of responsibility represent Beijing's nonconfrontational approach to US hegemony.[25]

Finally, it is also important to note that in Beijing's views, China's external security and international status ultimately rely on a secure domestic base and a more developed economy.[26] China's ability to play its market card to compensate for its political-military vulnerabilities hinges upon a healthy economy. Thus, the Chinese government insists that economic development be taken as the core, while defense work be subordinate to and in the service of the nation's overall economic construction. Through an integrated approach, China's defense industries and technologies strengthen its economy, which in turn enhances national defense. In the post-Cold War era, in order not to lose out on the international competition, China must enhance its comprehensive national power in which economic and technical prowess take the center stage.

Shaping factors

Since the mid-1990s, various events and crises have impacted the way Chinese analysts perceive America and its policy towards China. Here, I intend to focus on three major factors or events and how they have shaped Chinese perceptions of the US as described above.

22

23

24

25

---

[23]Deng, 'Hegemon on the offensive', p. 359; Wang Haihan, 'The current situation and future prospect of Sino-US relations', *International Studies* 12–13, (1998), pp. 17–28.

[24]Li and Bi, 'Qian Tan Meiguo Guojia Anquan Zhanlui zhong de Daode Yensui', pp. 48–53.

[25]Deng, 'Hegemon on the offensive', p. 360.

[26]Chu, 'Mel duei Hua Zhanlui ji Zhong Mei Guanxi Zouxiang', p. 63.

The Taiwan factor

26   The Taiwan issue has long been regarded as the critical core in Sino-US relations. Chinese analysts acknowledge that American attitude and policy towards Taiwan determine its strategic essence on China, and therefore, determine the characteristics and state of Sino-US relations. They indicate that for half a century, the US has always played the 'inglorious' role of an interventionist of China's Taiwan question and obstructer of reunification between the two sides. And the US will continue to play this role in the foreseeable future.[27]

27   *Lee Ten g-hui's 1995 visit to the US.* America's May 1995 decision to allow Taiwanese President Lee to visit the US to accept an honorary degree shocked Chinese analysts. Some argued that the visit hurt American credibility—the US appeared like a country that cannot honor its commitments. Some also accused the US of not fully appreciating the domestic political importance and sensitivity of the Taiwan issue. Perhaps more importantly, Lee's visit discredited the softer Chinese line towards Taiwan and strengthened the position of military hardliners, who viewed Taiwan as an issue of national sovereignty and favored a confrontational policy. Most America Watchers understood at least some of the domestic political motivations that influenced US policy, but many referred to beliefs in military circles that American action reflected official support for Taiwanese independence. Together with the widespread Chinese view that Lee was committed to independence, this pushed China towards a tougher Taiwan policy.[28]

28   *The Taiwan Strait crisis.* Chinese analysts had conflicting interpretations about the goals and effectiveness of the PRC's missile tests during 1995 and 1996. Most Chinese analysts focused on the messages sent to Taiwan and the US. Chinese officials and analysts almost universally identified Lee as the real leader of the Taiwanese independence movement. Many PRC analysts felt time was working against them as democratization and 'Taiwanization' reduced the influence of mainlanders who had dominated Taiwanese politics. Perception of an adverse trend made a soft policy line towards Taiwan difficult. Many felt that the need to check the movement towards independence justified the missile tests.

29   The missile tests also sent signals to the US. Specifically, they sent a clear signal to the US that Taiwan independence was unacceptable. In short, the crisis resulted in two changes in understanding. China realized that the US was willing to use force over Taiwan; the US realized just how serious an issue this was for China. Many felt the missile tests forced the US to take China more seriously and had created a new consensus on China policy (a view shared by American officials). Overall, Chinese

---

[27]Ding Shichuan, 'Duei Meiguo Ganshe Taiwan Wenti Zhanlui Chelui de Hongguan Kaocha' ['Macro observations of US strategy and tactics of interference in the question of Taiwan'], *Guoji Zhanlui Yanjiu [International Strategic Studies]* 4, (October 2000), p. 45.

[28]Wei Hongzhou and Ding Shichuan, 'Lengzhan hou Meiguo Ganshe Taiwan Wenti Zhanlui Chelui Pingxi' ['An analysis of the US' strategy on Taiwan issue in the post-Cold War period'], *Shijie Jingji yu Zhengzhi* 7, (14 July 2000), p. 39; Ding, 'Duei Meiguo Ganshe Taiwan Wenti Zhanlui Chelui de Hongguan Kaocha', p. 19; Saunders, 'China's America Watchers', pp. 54–55.

analysts have concluded that the missile tests were a costly measure that achieved some important goals.[29]

After the Taiwan Strait crisis, China's strategic planners began to have second thoughts about their earlier assessment of the US regional role. They feared that their worst nightmare could come true and that China might become the target of containment through a US-led security alignment in Pacific Asia. Beijing has become increasingly worried about signs that the US now may be abetting rather than checking Japanese remilitarization to limit rising Chinese power. Beijing is particularly wary of TMD's impact on its national security, as such a regional missile defense umbrella would undermine its minimum nuclear deterrent capability and effectively encourage Japanese militarism. Chinese strategists also worry that, even if Taiwan is presently not included in TMD, once the missile defense is in place, it can be easily extended to the island, effectively restoring a political and military alignment between the US, Japan, and Taiwan.[30]

The Taiwan issue feeds the Chinese suspicion that the US is pursuing a strategy of 'divide and rule'. It evokes the collective memory of China's being bullied and dismembered by Japan and the Western powers for more than a century after the Opium War. In 1950, at the outbreak of the Korean War, the Truman Administration dispatched the US Seventh Fleet to the Taiwan Strait. In the Chinese interpretation, that act and the subsequent US support of Taiwan, have kept the island separated from the mainland for more than 50 years.

After the Cold War, America's new strategy towards Taiwan is perceived as aiming at 'maintenance of the status quo, controlling Taiwan and containing China'. Specifically, the US has adopted the following tactics: (1) to pursue the policy of 'restraining independence and obstructing reunification' in handling overall cross-Strait relations; (2) to promote political talks but not peace; (3) to create a 'dynamic balance' in military strength across the Strait; and (4) to enhance the two countries' trilateral 'mutual economic interdependence' among the US, China and Taiwan.[31]

Perpetuating the separation may serve several US interests. First, by keeping China's territory divided and its sovereignty violated, the US may hamper China's drive to achieve the dignity of a great power. Second, Taiwan's ongoing acquisition of US weaponry is good business for US military industries. Third, continued tensions across the Taiwan Strait provide an excuse for Americans to maintain a military presence in the Asian Pacific and to develop their missile projects. Finally, by endorsing Taiwan's democratization, Washington may exert more pressure on Beijing for political change. All these Chinese fears and interpretations of events persist in the face of assurances from the US that its commitment to the security of Taiwan is morally motivated and intended to do nothing more than maintain peace in the area.

30

31

32

33

---

[29]Wei and Ding, 'Lengzhan hou Meiguo Ganshe Taiwan Wenti Zhanlui Chelui Pingxi', p. 40; Ding, 'Duei Meiguo Ganshe Taiwan Wenti Zhanlui Chelui de Hongguan Kaocha', p. 20; Saunders, 'China's America Watchers', pp. 55–57.

[30]Deng, 'Hegemon on the offensive', p. 353; Chu, 'Bilateral and regional strategic and security relationship', pp. 3–8.

[31]Ding, 'Duei Meiguo Ganshe Taiwan Wenti Zhanlui Chelui de Hongguan Kaocha', pp. 20–21.

The Kosovo conflict and embassy bombing incident

34   In the wake of the NATO bombing of China's embassy in Belgrade on 8 May 1999, Chinese policy analysts and scholars heatedly debated the status of China-US relations and how China should respond to America's neo-interventionism. Although pragmatic considerations in favor of stabilizing relations with Washington have thus far prevailed in Beijing, the bombing had a devastating effect. Government officials joined the general public in expressing their indignation—along with their perplexity as to why the bombing had occurred.

35   Indeed, in China, the US-led NATO intervention in Yugoslavia and the bombing of the Chinese embassy led to a further rise in anti-American sentiment. According to one PLA officer, the embassy bombing's negative impact on Chinese perceptions of the US was as great as the Tiananmen massacre's impact on American perceptions of China.[32] PLA concerns about American conventional precision-strike capabilities and the negative precedent set by the Kosovo intervention prompted an unprecedented debate in China challenging the official view that the dominant trend in the international environment was still 'peace and development'. Although hardliners were unsuccessful in overturning the official judgment, the Chinese government's rhetoric took on an increasingly anti-American tone and military spending has reportedly increased significantly.

36   As mentioned above, fear that the US is increasingly leaning toward containing China has been on the rise after the Cold War, particularly since Kosovo. In fact, the Kosovo war heightened Chinese fears of a US threat. After Kosovo, many Chinese analysts conclude that the US has adopted an offensive-oriented, neo-imperialist, neo-interventionist strategy geared toward expanding, perpetuating, and imposing its worldwide hegemony. To them, this means that the US has been highly inclined to interfere in other countries' domestic affairs, to use force if necessary, and to cynically manipulate international rules or institutions—at times flouting them outright, at other times seeking self-interest under the pretext of upholding world order. In short, after the Kosovo crisis, China's analysts have become even more pessimistic about US-China relations.

37   Such a perception breeds a conspiratorial view. That is why it is almost universally believed in China that the NATO bombing of the Chinese embassy in Belgrade in May 1999 was a deliberate, calculated attack to punish China's opposition to the war, to destabilize and humiliate China, and to probe Beijing's external reaction and domestic response to the outburst of nationalism that the bombing was bound to ignite.

The 11 September event

38   From the Chinese perspective, since 11 September, the US has been constantly adjusting the priorities and approaches of its foreign policy in order to meet the needs of fighting terrorism. Indeed, anti-terrorism has provided a turning point for Sino-US

---

[32]Saunders, 'China's America Watchers', p. 63.

relations to pick up the momentum of improvement. As some argued, it provided an opportunity for the two nations to build trust through cooperation.[33]

Due to the need for anti-terrorism, American unilateralism has been refrained somewhat. The efforts to seek the use of a mechanism like the UN, as well as to seek for coordination and cooperation wherever possible, have been stressed more, though here again, American actions are perceived with deep suspicion. Chinese analysts see the US trying hard to garner the long cherished goal of achieving geo-strategic superiority in South and Central Asia by exploiting the opportunity of anti-terrorism. As one put it, 'the US intends to take the advantage of anti-terrorism to control South Asia and to get a foot into the door of Central Asia'.[34]   39

In fact, notwithstanding the adjustments of its foreign policy after 11 September, the basis and essence of the American foreign policy has not been affected. Those adjustments are most likely short-term actions. Specifically, Chinese analysts argue that the American policy of hegemonism and power politics has not been changed fundamentally. The US will go on practicing interventionist diplomacy and seeking for the establishment of a new world order dominated by them. Further still, the American success in its military attacks in Afghanistan might further stimulate the development of American unilateralism and its tendency towards military interventionism. Indeed, the US has apparently increased its effort, in the wake of the incident, in bossing the world' under the flag of anti-terrorism and in intervening in international affairs.[35] With respect to China, the US will maintain the overall framework of engagement plus containment toward China given its own strategic requirements and economic interests.[36] In short, the 11 September event has offered a new opportunity for the US to promote its plan of pushing for a unipolar world.   40

Principal impediments

In his book, David Shambaugh pointed out that cognitive biases and various analytical limitations, including cultural, ideological and historical, encumber Chinese America Watchers' analyses of the US. Furthermore, Saunders pointed out that institutional and political barriers sometimes impede the flow of analysis into the policy-making process. Government policy and the political environment exert a significant influence on America Watchers. Official statements define the limits of permissible debate and create a politically safe framework within which analysts can express their views. Published analysis often explicitly refers to official policy, and analysts frequently restate policy verbatim on sensitive issues such as Taiwan. Absence of an official policy   41

---

[33]Yuan Peng, '911 Shijian yu Zhong Mei Guanxi' ['The September 11 event and China-US relations'], *Xiandai Guoji Guanxi* 11, (2001), pp. 19–23.

[34]Vu Shuman, 'Chuxi 911 Shijian hou Meiguo Waijiao Zhengche de Tiaozheng' ['A tentative analysis of the US foreign policy after the September 11 event'], *Guoji Zhanlui Yanjiu,* (January 2002), p. 25.

[35]Jiang Lingfei, '911 Shijian duei Shijie Zhantui Xingshi he Zhongguo Anquan Huanjing Yingxiang' ['9/11 events' impact on world strategic situation and China's security environment'], *Heping yu Fazhan* 1, (February 2002), pp. 12–14.

[36]Vu, 'Chuxi 911 Shijian hou Meiguo Waijiao Zhengche de Tiaozheng', pp. 19–26.

line does not necessarily result in a freer debate because analysts can become politically vulnerable if they pick the wrong side. This induces caution, particularly among America Watchers who are already suspects of being too close to the US.[37]

42   While surveying the Chinese documents, I found the impediments aforementioned remain in effect. For instance, Saunders identified four main approaches that Chinese analysts use to interpret the US.[38] Chinese analysts have abandoned Marxist jargon, but the intellectual legacy of a Marxist-Leninist education is evident in tendencies to emphasize the primacy of economic factors, to think in dialectical terms, and to see an ideological struggle between socialism and capitalism. More importantly, many Chinese analysts remain heavily burdened by the realist approach in analyzing international relations and the relationship between China and America. Also, there remains a victim consciousness stemming from historical baggage.

43   I also found it interesting how most Chinese analysts repeatedly stressed that Chinese policy is mainly reactive to US policy. As one analyst put it, 'the major factor affecting Sino-US relations is the American China policy'.[39] One might suspect that by stressing 'the nature of Sino-US relations is decided by the nature of the US strategy to China',[40] it enables Chinese analysts, if not China as a whole, to conveniently put the blame on the US whenever there is a fault or upset in the relationship.

Prospects for future management

44   In sum, today, many Chinese continue to hold negative attitudes towards the US. They see that being the sole superpower in the world, the US is well in the position of practicing hegemonism. And because China is now on the rise, America deems it necessary to contain China in order to preserve its own status. As indicated, the premise of studying perception is the belief that behavior is principally a function of perception.[41] As the above analysis shows, despite continued progress, there remains a perceptual gap between the US and China, which contributes to the fluctuating nature of Sino-American relations to a certain extent.

45   What produces stability in US-China relations? To say the least, reduced misperception and improved mutual understanding would certainly help. To be sure, the US should not simply ignore widespread Chinese suspicions about its intentions. Necessary adjustments for mutual accommodation and measures such as enhanced strategic dialogue would help improve relations between the two countries, among other things. The importance of managing Sino-American strategic relations could not be more dramatically demonstrated than by the 1995–1996 Taiwan Strait crisis. Bilateral cooperation in various aspects (as shown after 11 September) is certainly a

---

[37]Saunders, 'China's America Watchers', pp. 44–45.

[38]*Ibid.*, pp. 45–51.

[39]Wang, 'The current situation and future prospect of Sino-US relations', p. 24.

[40]Chu, 'Mei duei Hua Zhanlui ji Zhong Mei Guanxi Zouxiang', p. 60.

[41]Shambaugh, *Beautiful Imperialist,* p. 3.

positive sign. In addition, since personality plays a key role in US-China relations, high level exchanges (like the recent visit by Hu Jintao) could also contribute positively to the relationship. In conclusion, Sino-US relations will continue to be a critical, if not more important, issue for both to manage well into the twenty-first century.

UNDERSTANDING THE AUTHOR'S IDEAS

1. What are the controlling research questions that organize Chen's research?
2. Define "America Watchers."
3. Summarize the history of U.S.-China relations prior to the mid-1990s to explain the skeptical view China holds of the United States.
4. In the section entitled "Sino-American relations," how does Chen characterize the fundamental differences between the United States and China today?
5. Chen focuses on "three major factors . . . [that] have shaped Chinese perceptions of the US" in recent times. Working in small groups or alone, summarize the significant aspects of each of the three factors.
6. Characterize the future of U.S.-China relations, according to Chen's research and perspective.

EXPLORING YOUR OWN IDEAS

1. Explore your perceptions of China in small group discussions. Summarize your views. What are your perceptions based upon?
2. Summarize your reaction to Chen's research on U.S.-China relations. What new insights did you gain from this text?
3. Chen concludes, "Sino-US relations will continue to be a critical, if not more important, issue for both to manage well into the twenty-first century." Do you agree or disagree with her conclusion? Explain.
4. List the genre features of this scholarly article. Compare and contrast these features to those of the Hertsgaard excerpt from *The Eagle's Shadow.* Discuss *why* each genre includes the features that it does.
5. Consult Lexis-Nexis or some other news database for articles concerning U.S.-China interactions within the past six months. Briefly skim the articles and find examples to support or refute Chen's comments.

EXPLORING VISUAL IMAGES

The photo on the next page was taken in Indonesia on September 11, 2003, exactly two years after our national tragedy. The protest signs say, "America go to hell" and "Don't mess with Islam." Study the photo carefully and record impressions of Indonesian culture that emerge. Compare your ideas with classmates. Now consider your emotional reaction to this photo. Discuss your feelings *and* your thoughts in a two-to-three-page reaction paper in light of what you've learned in this unit.

Reading 3

In this short reading, Palestinian writer and editorialist Marwan Bishara shares his views on U.S. foreign policy regarding Israeli-Palestinian relations. Obviously written from a personally informed and invested perspective, this letter to the American people aims to be both instructive and emotionally persuasive. Note in what ways the genre choice of the letter simultaneously establishes and reinforces the author's tone and intent.

This text originally appeared in an issue of Nation, *shortly before the beginning of the Second Gulf War.* Nation *is a respected current-affairs magazine aimed at a general audience while overall maintaining a leftist perspective on the political spectrum.*

"Letter to America"

Marwan Bishara

1   Growing up in Nazareth, an Arab in a Jewish state, a secular Christian in a Muslim society, a leftist in a Baptist school, I learned firsthand how managing ideological, religious and national differences helps us evolve peacefully. Succumbing to them generates fundamentalism and antagonism. Applying brute force to overcome them—as Israel, my country, has done to my people, the Palestinian Arabs—fails utterly.

So it puzzles me as to why America now views the Middle East through Israel's 2
eyes, and why, since 9/11, it has adopted an apocalyptic Israeli vision of an irre-
deemable world that "hates us." Such fatalism on the part of Bush and Sharon is ren-
dering diplomacy a prelude to imminent war in Iraq and Palestine. Their justification—"If it doesn't get worse, it won't get better, and when force doesn't work, more
force will"—threatens to globalize the violent impasse of Israel/Palestine. Judging
from the January Israeli (and last fall's American) elections, more people are buying
into this dangerous paranoia.

In order to confront this logic, I feel it is indispensable to debunk the myths be- 3
hind America's misplaced identification/fascination with Israel, best captured in a
post-9/11 headline: "We Are All Israelis Now." As seen in this light, Israel is a "peace-
seeking" victim of Arab hostility, a "true democracy" that shares "our" values, an "ally"
that serves "our" interests, whose "success" in a "hostile neighborhood" is inspira-
tional in a Hobbesian world. In reality, Israel has consistently expanded its frontiers,
embarked on a number of offensive wars and even contemplated the reconfiguration
of Lebanon and Jordan, while rejecting UN resolutions and American's own initiatives. That hardly qualifies as peace-seeking.

The myth that Israel serves America's interests, while hardly a compliment or 4
honor to any nation, goes against the logic of history. Traditionally, Arabs identified
with an America that stood as a symbol of the right of self-determination against the
British and French colonial powers. Their relations with America turned sour only
when Washington supported Israel's aggression.

America's interests could be secured without imperial support for Israel's hege- 5
mony. A Middle East that is safe for its Arab inhabitants could also be safe for
America (and Israel). America's main interest, oil, is best secured through the market's supply and demand, not another war in Iraq. Needless to say, Arabs—moderates
and radicals alike—seek to sell their oil, not drink it. As far as the "democratic oasis"
fallacy, Israel, by definition, cannot be both a Jewish state and a democracy with one-
fifth of its population Palestinian. Israel has stripped us, its Palestinian citizens, of
two-thirds of our own land, and it has enacted laws that discriminate against us simply because we aren't Jewish. Calls to "transfer" us—that is, to push us out of Israel
altogether—have been gaining momentum among my fellow citizens. Acting with
impunity, thanks to Washington, my country has transformed its conflict into perpetual war by justifying its occupation on security and theological grounds and con-
demning the entirety of my people's struggle for freedom as terrorism.

Hardly a role model. So why, then, does Washington mimic worldwide the worst of 6
Israel's chutzpah and, for lack of a better word, plagiarize Israeli doctrine and policy?
Since its 1967 victory, made possible by Washington's hardware, which transformed its
army posture from defensive to offensive, Israel has functioned as an American laboratory in conventional urban and asymmetric warfare. Instead of being a "safe refuge" for
the Jews, Israel became an American outpost after Washington's defeat in Vietnam. It
was appointed "regional policeman" in the 1960s, a "regional influential" in the 1970s, a
"strategic asset" in the 1980s, and today it is viewed as being at the forefront of the war
on terrorism. Paradoxically, almost every time Israel rejected a State Department draft of
peace initiatives, it was somehow rewarded by a new Pentagon deal!

Washington's militarization of Israel's industries and liberalization of its econ- 7
omy made Israel even more dependent on the United States. Today, although

Israel boasts a high per capita income, the gap between rich and poor is one of the highest among industrial societies, and the military remains the key engine of its economy. And the result of Washington's deformation of Israel's sociopolitical priorities made it natural for Robocop Israel, an ethnic republic at home and a colonial tyranny next door, to slide toward fundamentalism. Religious fundamentalist (one-fourth of the Knesset) and neofascist parties have ruled Israel for more than a quarter-century, with the exception of the two short and ill-fated governments of Generals Rabin and Barak.

8   Naïvely, some of us hoped America would save Israel from itself once Israel's strategic-asset credentials ran out at the end of the cold war. Instead, thanks to Osama bin Laden, a "wag the dog" saga has played out, as fundamentalists dictate policies for all of us. While America internalized Israel's culture of fear, adopted its claustrophobic vision of a world full of evil and charted a pre-emptive doctrine to deal with it, Israel took on America's imperial posturing.

9   For decades now, Washington, and Israel have demanded that we choose between Good and Evil, "with us or against us." In 1958 the devil was Egypt's pan-Arab leader, Gamal Abdel Nasser; in 1968 it became Palestinian guerrilla leader Yasir Arafat; in 1978 Iran's Ayatollah; and when all three were no longer threats, Saddam Hussein emerged as the devil. Predictably, after Saddam was "contained," bin Laden became the devil of all devils, and now, with Saddam again the chief devil, we have been cynically asked once more to choose, as if we had a choice!

10   For those of us who have lived in Israel, it's déjà vu all over again. Spreading a fearmongering political culture and demonizing adversaries while supporting war renders national symbols sacred objects and tolerance unpatriotic—or worse, immoral. Recent polls underline this mounting Israelization of American society: One in three Americans now accepts government-sanctioned torture of suspects, and 60 percent support political assassinations (up from 18 percent in 1981).

11   Israel has tried all such methods but failed to improve security. In fact, annual civilian casualties in Israel today are twenty-five times what they were two or three decades ago. Worse, Sharon's current policy amounts to politicide and econocide, and it is denounced as a series of war crimes and crimes against humanity by the likes of Amnesty International.

12   Watching Al Qaeda's "men" and American/Israeli "gentlemen" cheering for war, I am reminded of what progressive feminism concluded long ago: The problem is not the men per se, but the system of power that grooms them. The Islamists' pseudo-strategy of "die and let die" has failed, as has the American/Israeli strategy of "live and let die." A third way, to "live and let live," must now be given a try, through diplomacy, the art of resolving our differences peacefully.

13   I'm afraid Washington's current hostility to diplomacy stems not only from bad politics but also from the conservatives' commitment to transform America's global power into global domination—Pax Americana, paradoxically, in a time of US decline. As America trails behind an economically growing EU—soon to be twenty-five countries strong—excessive use of force is considered a means of maintaining superpower status. To preserve its supereconomic advantage (30 percent of the world economy) America is augmenting its military expenditures (40 percent of the world's) to stay on top. But the twentieth century has taught us that power is not restricted to

military means. If America continues to increase its military budget to finance offensive wars, it will eventually become, at best, Europe's mercenary. It will also become like those it fights: weak, desperate and isolated.

What better examples exist to illustrate the limits of military force and the growing importance of economic power than Iraq and Turkey? Motivated by membership in the European Union, Turkey's secular military accepted the recent election results, and the Islamists have come to respect the democratic rules of the game as well as Ankara's commitments to the international community. America can hardly point to a similar achievement in Iraq. If you ask Eastern European countries to choose between NATO and EU membership, they would all choose the latter. **14**

Have the United States and Israel changed roles? Though for decades the Middle East has had difficulty struggling with America the superpower and Israel the rogue state, their patron-client relations implied a certain rationale and a limit. Today, however, the empire acts like a rogue state, and the latter acts like an empire. **15**

If America must be a superpower, then it should be superdemocratic in its policy. It could also identify with a tradition other than Israel's. A tolerant heritage of Judaism, combined with traditional American constitutionalism and mature European culture no less ambitious, forged over centuries of war and colonialism, could provide important guidance in an era of uncertainty. **16**

My dear America, allow me to end on a personal note. We need you as much as we all need each other—Palestinians, Israelis, Americans, Europeans, Arabs and others. Our right to security is a universal right. Preserving it in an era of globalization is a multilateral venture. That's why our interdependence is a sign of our maturity, not our weakness. All of us democrats must confront irrational geo-theology and deadly geo-strategy by emphasizing geo-ethics. Putting our values above our interests, our humanity above our nationalism, could help us create coalitions across continents and religions to block the fatalistic and destructive drive to war. In the absence of democracy, Middle East Arabs have not made the choice of their fundamentalists or their leaders. You Americans, on the other hand, are a democracy and have a choice. The fundamentalists and the militarists succeed only when we democrats of the world fail to be what we must. **17**

UNDERSTANDING THE AUTHOR'S IDEAS

1. What is unique about Bishara's perspective?
2. Briefly explain Bishara's main argument regarding ideologies.
3. What, according to Bishara, was once the traditional Arab view of America? What changed it?
4. Summarize Bishara's views of the Palestine-Israel conflict.
5. Summarize Bishara's views of the relationship between Washington and Israel.
6. What does the author suggest as an appropriate role for America in foreign policy?
7. Paraphrase his hope for the future.

EXPLORING YOUR OWN IDEAS

1. What new insights into American policy did you glean from this text? Do you agree or disagree with the picture he presents? Explain. Can you imagine counterarguments to her position?
2. How would you characterize the tone and attitude of the author? Point to specifics in the text to substantiate your position.
3. Explore the significance of the author's genre choice of a letter to explain his views.
4. Discuss your thoughts on Bishara's suggestion that "The Islamists' pseudo-strategy of 'die and let die' has failed, as has the American/Israeli strategy of 'live and let die.' A third way, to 'live and let live,' must now be given a try, through diplomacy, the art of resolving our differences peacefully."
5. This letter was obviously written just before the United States went to war with Iraq. Keeping Bishara's comments in mind and using your hindsight perspective, discuss your view of America's position in the international community today.

Reading 4

Volker Berghahn, author of the article below, is recognized as a prolific scholar of German history and American-German relations. Currently, Berghahn is the distinguished Seth Low Professor of History at Columbia University in New York. Born in Berlin in the 1930s, but educated in the United States, Berghahn possesses an insightful bicultural perspective on German-American relations. In this reading, Berghahn offers a comprehensive discussion of the checkered history of German-American relations over the past century and briefly suggests implications for its future. Employing his keenly honed historical lens, Berghahn concludes that Germany continues to hold an ambivalent perception of America.

Though Berghahn has published numerous books and articles for a distinctly scholarly audience, the article included here was written in 1995 for a general readership. Originally, it appeared as a photoenhanced essay in American Heritage, *a highly respected magazine aimed at an informed, educated audience with an interest in, or even a passion for, American history. Notice how the features of this genre vary from the Chen article, which also addresses topics in international history.*

"Germany's America"

V. R. Berghahn

1   For a century and a half Germans have been deeply ambivalent about the United States, and their contradictory feelings say much about their future in Europe and the world.

In 1989 the Berlin Wall came down. A year later the unimaginable had become a   2
reality: Germany, divided in 1945, was reunified, and it was beginning to raise a major voice not only in Europe but also in world politics. Hopes are high that this time
Germany will assume a role among nations different from the one it played in the
first half of the century. But in East and West there are deep and traumatic memories
of two world wars, of how the Germans saw themselves then and of how they treated
their neighbors.

Nor has the old "German Question" been forgotten in the United States. Many   3
people wonder about the future of a relationship that for more than a century has
experienced repeated ups and downs. The two countries have been bitter enemies
in two world wars and rivals as industrial nations, but they have also had close political, military, and economic ties. However hard they may have tried at various times
to retreat into their shells and ignore each other, neither has ever been able to afford
to do that.

So how have Germans perceived America—that is, America as a society and a cul-   4
ture, not political or economic power? The question opens up intriguing problems
about Germany's and Europe's future. Like many Europeans, Germans have often
been unable to make up their minds about the United States. There have always been
those who felt greatly attracted to the cultural ideas and products that reached them
from across the Atlantic; they have been eager to visit America. Others would flatly
refuse to contemplate such a trip and express nothing but disgust and contempt,
while a third group has remained deeply ambivalent. The latter would probably agree
with the French politician who condemned the Disney theme park near Paris as a
"cultural Chernobyl," and they'd also take their kids to the local McDonald's, of which
Munich, for example, boasts no fewer than eighteen. They would contend proudly
that America has never produced composers like Beethoven or Mozart, while treasur-
ing their collections of classic jazz records. They would deplore the violence and su-
perficiality of Hollywood movies, but never miss an episode of "Dynasty."

Germany today is arguably the most Americanized society of Western Europe, but   5
it is also steeped in native cultural traditions and attitudes; it is inward-looking and
suspicious of strangers and diversity. In short, Germans are confused about what to
make of the United States as a culture and about what to do with its exports, especially Hollywood movies and pop music.

It was no different a hundred and fifty years ago, when during the hungry 1840s   6
and after the failed revolutions of 1848, emigration from Germany rose sharply and
contacts between the two countries intensified. Given the poor communications of
the time, images of the United States were bound to be fuzzy and contradictory, but
Germans had great curiosity about the New World, and people back home implored
those who had made the dangerous journey to report on what it was like. In the
decades before the founding of the German Empire, in 1871, dozens of books appeared offering advice to travelers. These still make illuminating reading, not least
because of the strong ideological messages that they convey. On the one hand, there
are condescending warnings about America as a country without Kultur, as one big
"Wild West"; on the other, we find admiration for the land of liberty and equality.
German novelists who wrote about the New World were similarly divided.

After 1870, as America emerged as a major industrial power, German accounts of   7
the country become more sober and scholarly, designed not only to give practical advice

but to analyze the reality. During the 1890s some four million letters arrived in Germany from across the Atlantic every year. The United States now appeared as a country propelled by a pioneering spirit, mobility, speed, courage, efficiency, modernity, a country with low taxation and no conscription but also a land full of ethnic discrimination, where people worked long hours, instantly lost their jobs, and put up with high medical costs and no social security. For years after 1893 Baedeker's Tourist Guide warned the traveler to prepare for "the absence of deference or servility on the part of those he considers his social inferiors." The greater role of women was frequently remarked on. In 1903 Ludwig Max Goldberger published a book on the American economy titled Land of Unlimited Possibilities, and the phrase quickly caught on in Germany. Three years later the economist Werner Sombart put out a famous essay, "Why Is There No Socialism in the United States?" His answer lay in upward mobility, rising living standards, and the open Western frontier.

8   By the turn of the century, German interest in America, while still inspiring the likes of Karl May's novels about trappers and "Red Indians," increasingly turned to its industries. The United States, for good or ill, was coming to be seen as the embodiment of cultural and technological modernity and progress. At the 1900 Paris World Exhibition the American pavilion, with its demonstrations of new steelmaking techniques, became a magnet for engineers and entrepreneurs. They were particularly fascinated by the standardized production methods and precision-tool machinery on display. Soon scores of experts began to travel across the Atlantic to admire the Brooklyn Bridge and visit the industrial cities of the East Coast, Ohio, and Michigan. By 1903 the journal of the influential Association of German Engineers had opened its pages to reports like Paul Moeller's account of his seven-month journey through industrial America. He urged managers to follow the American example and move toward greater standardization and incentive-based wage systems.

9   Sooner or later visitors from Germany would come across the name of Frederick W. Taylor and the scientific management movement, devoted to the scientific planning and monitoring of the actions of employees. A translation of Taylor's 1906 essay "On the Art of Cutting Metals" appeared quickly, and his famous Principles of Scientific Management, of 1911, published in German within a year, became an instant best-seller and had to be reprinted three times in the spring of 1913 alone.

10   Taylor's 1903 work Shop Management had taken three years to be translated, for it had first raised the large question of whether the attitudes and values that underlay his movement were as easily importable as new steel-cutting technologies. Many Germans harbored serious doubts. As the liberal Frankfurter Zeitung observed in 1906, the adoption of American-style methods in industry would have "cultural consequences" that were still difficult to perceive.

11   German industry resisted cheap mass production for fear that its traditional concern for high quality would be undermined. No less a person than Thomas Edison observed in 1911 that Germans were too responsive to the special wishes of individual customers to fully standardize their products. An executive of the Daimler Company in Stuttgart, makers of Mercedes luxury cars, put it this way: "Here [we do things] meticulously and thoroughly; over there it is skimping and rushing." Indeed, as Henry Ford experimented with assembly-line production, cars all over Europe

continued to be individually built by highly skilled craftsmen in small workshops. In Germany only Opel moved toward cheap volume production, and it was promptly dubbed a "business organized along American lines." Part of the resistance came from craftsmen who were members of trade unions with enough power to disrupt production severely if they disliked new ways.

At the Robert Bosch Electrical Engineering Company in Stuttgart, the directors were very open to technical and organizational ideas developed in America. In 1913 H. Borst, a member of the Bosch board, managed to have a long conversation with Taylor; Borst was won over and subsequently advocated scientific management in Stuttgart. However when Bosch tried to introduce Taylorized production on a large scale, the Metal Workers' Union mounted the barricades. It hated what came to be known as the "Bosch tempo," and suddenly the company had a major strike on its hands. The conservative captains of other German industries could hardly contain their Schadenfreude. They had long been suspicious of the industrial culture emerging on the other side of the Atlantic, and they expected that the innovations of that culture must also mean the loss of social hierarchy and deference, which, as Baedeker had warned, had already disappeared on the other side of the Atlantic. Daimler Cars proclaimed: "Over here we are still a long way away from the American situation where every Mr. Jones owns a car. With us the automobile is for the most part a vehicle for the better-off classes." Finally, might not Germany succumb to "racial chaos," gangsterism, and the spirit of the "Wild West"? Yet the pull of America's relative cultural and technological modernity proved irresistible in peacetime. As the journal Der Motorwagen had observed in 1905, "Americanization" was already under way "at an accelerated pace." 12

War, revolution, and defeat exacerbated many Germans' fears of American culture, while others continued to admire the United States and even see American economic and technological power as the only hope for reviving the ravaged Weimar economy. By the fall of 1923 hyper-inflation had reached such heights that a tourist dollar was worth 4.2 trillion marks; the country faced total collapse. The next year, after a drastic currency reform, things began to look up again. With American diplomatic help an internationally agreed payments schedule, known as the Dawes Plan, was adopted to deal with the thorny issue of German war reparations. The Dawes Plan cleared the way for the flow of American investments into Germany, which was still generally considered the industrial powerhouse of Europe, merely needing its potential to be reactivated. By 1928 U.S. capital exports to Germany had reached $1.4 billion, with another $1.6 billion given in short-term loans. Some seventy-nine American firms established branches in Germany or took major stakes in German companies. Opel Cars, the first German automaker to develop a Model T type of vehicle (the ever cheaper Laubfrosch, or Froggie), was taken over by General Motors. Ford built an assembly plant in Cologne. In Essen, Coca-Cola opened a major bottling plant. Chrysler put up a production facility near Berlin in 1927. IG Farben Chemicals and Zeiss Optics signed cooperative agreements with American trusts. 13

All this hectic activity led to another rush to study the secrets of the New World's industrial success. As P. Rieben-sahm, an engineering professor at Berlin and himself a visitor to America, put it, "At first a few leading personalities came [to the United 14

States] individually; then major firms sent employees in groups of twos and threes. . . . Soon the passenger lists of the beautiful ships of Hamburg-America Line and North German Lloyd looked like a register of the leading industrial firms of Germany." Among the travelers were top entrepreneurs like Carl Koettgen of Siemens, Wilhelm Zangen of United Steel, and Gustav Krupp, who wrote to a colleague afterward: "I have gained valuable impressions in America . . . I can only advise you also to see that country once again."

15   In 1928 IG Farben sent Wichard von Moellendorff on a tour to "examine the transferability of experiences to Germany." He came back particularly impressed by the fact that "both the American and the Russian doctrine of salvation are focusing on the idea that a modem national economy should be more concerned with the 'poor' than with the 'Wealthy' consumers." The liberal economist Moritz Bonn, who knew the United States well, drew a rather more scathing contrast with German ways: "American entrepreneurs like Ford know that the masses will only tolerate the accumulation of great wealth in the hands of a few if they themselves derive a corresponding advantage from it. In a wealthy country like America, one permits the entrepreneur to earn as much as he likes, provided that those through whom he makes his money also benefit from it. The authoritarian German capitalism, and heavy industry in particular, has never allowed others to share in their earnings. Obsessed by technically perfectly correct organizational ideas, it has tried to achieve the removal of all dispensable intermediate links."

16   Meanwhile, in the mid-1920s, not only products and economic theories came from America; so did new ideas about consumption, leisure, and popular culture. Hollywood films, the embodiment of a new mass-consumer culture, became so popular that soon millions of Germans were going to the movies at least once a week. Next came popular live entertainment: the Tiller Girls, the Charleston and the foxtrot, and, above all, jazz. Culture was no longer for a select few to enjoy in concert halls, opera houses, and private theaters; Madison Avenue-style advertising urged ordinary Germans to seek distraction and escape from the drudgery of their daily lives. Department stores put affordable fancy clothes within the reach of "factory girls" and women office workers. It was chic to dress and behave like the emancipated American "modern woman," who wore lipstick and smoked cigarillos.

17   If the United States had shifted in the German imagination from a land of settlers battling Indians to the center of modern urbanism and industrialism, the spread of earlier reactions remained virtually unchanged. There were still those like the famous literary critic Alfred Kerr, who in his 1925 travel account Yankee Land openly declared his love of New York and California and praised the "Yankee" as an unrivaled inventor and daring schemer, and there were those for whom "asphalt jungles" and "Chicago" were the symbols of all the evils America stood for. Jazz and Hollywood were manifestations of decadence, of a sick and doomed urban culture that must be replaced once more by small-scale, harmonious, orderly agrarian communities. These anti-Americans were anti-modern, anti-industrial, anti-urban, and illiberal. Many of them could be found on the extreme right, supporting the rising Nazi movement.

18   In between, as before, there were those Germans who were ambivalent. Surprisingly, perhaps, among them was Adolf Hitler. Historians continue to debate

what, beyond racism and the hatred of Jews, the Nazi leader actually stood for, but it has become increasingly clear that he cannot be identified with the agrarian wing of his party, whose members preached the de-industrialization and de-urbanization of Germany and a return to "blood and soil." Hitler knew the importance of industry and technology, not least for the implementation of his expansionist plans. He realized that in the twentieth century a war of conquest could not be won without a strong industrial and scientific base, with rationalized, standardized production churning out sophisticated weapons. He also learned that satisfying the expectations of a better life among millions of urban consumers was a key to the stability of his regime. That is why he vigorously promoted the growth of production, both for military strength and for popular loyalty. Of course, his war of expansion had to be won, and this would require temporary austerity to finance rapid rearmament. Still, all the while Hitler never stopped talking about a mass-consumption society. In fact, he even began to put it into practice when the first Volkswagen ("people's car") went into production in 1938.

Germany's power and prosperity were to be reflected in the imposing buildings   19
that the architect Albert Speer designed on Hitler's orders. Time and again the Fuhrer wandered among the models for them. The actual buildings were intended to overawe the viewer while symbolizing the might and the durability of the "Thousand Year Reich." Hitler was fascinated by the monuments of ancient Rome, which he thought was the only true world empire that had ever existed, but Rome was not his only or even his primary point of reference. Time and again he looked across the Atlantic as he formulated his mass-production and mass-consumption utopia.

He had a healthy respect for the economic power and military potential of the   20
United States, but a respect modified by skepticism. He believed that American power was threatened from the inside by the country's "inferior races," above all by Jews and blacks. In his warped view of the world, these groups undermined the biological fiber and political hegemony of the white Anglo-Saxon "race." But until this process had run its course, the United States, the Fuhrer feared, would pose a serious threat to his ambition of making Germany a world power.

Given his notion that history was propelled by cutthroat struggles between nations   21
and races, Hitler assumed that a final struggle between Germany and America was inevitable. As he put it in 1928, "The ultimate decision on the outcome of the war for the world market will depend on the use of force rather than on business strategies. . . . Swords must be given priority over plowshares, just as the army takes priority over the economy." To prepare for this global conflict, he would need a territorial base comparable to that of the North American continent. He would also need American technology and industrial organization. He admired Henry Ford not merely as an anti-Semite but also as a brilliant organizer of mass production and herald of the mass-consumption society.

That was the background for Nazi policies and attitudes toward the United States   22
between the late 1920s and President Roosevelt's openly hostile Quarantine Speech of October 1937. Wanting to avoid a premature conflict, Hitler began to woo and appease Washington as soon as he took command of German foreign policy in 1933. In an interview with an American journalist that year, a mere three weeks after his appointment to the Reich chancellorship, he claimed to feel a "sincere friendship"

toward the United States. Until 1936 the Nazi press consistently portrayed Roosevelt and the New Deal in a favorable light.

23   Meanwhile the cooperation that had developed between German and American industry during the 1920s continued. Ford and GM-Opel built cars, trucks, and even military vehicles, and the latter had 50 percent of the market by 1935. ITT took a 28 percent stake in Focke-Wulf's bomber production. Huge posters on city billboards urged Germans to enjoy an ice-cold Coke. In 1936 Ferdinand Porsche, the father of the Volkswagen, studied Ford's plants in Michigan, and in 1937 North German Lloyd advertised more than forty tours of industrial America. Not just steel bosses and engineers went. So did lawyers, marketing specialists, department-store managers, road engineers, and experts of all kinds. Even the German Labor Front organized three trips to study the U.S. economy in the spring of 1939.

24   Hitler's plans for Germany's future socioeconomic organization and culture, especially his architectural ambitions, continued to make frequent reference to the United States. The remodeled main railroad station for Berlin was to be larger than Grand Central Terminal in New York. A bridge to span the Elbe River between Hamburg and Harburg-Wilhelmsburg was to be the "largest bridge in the world," so that Germans could say, in Hitler's words, "What does America mean with its bridges? We can do the same." When it turned out that soil conditions in Hamburg militated against achieving the same long span as San Francisco's Golden Gate Bridge, he ordered that the lanes be broadened to obtain at least the same square footage. Berlin's largest assembly hall, with a seating capacity of 180,000, was going to dwarf Carnegie Hall. "Modesty," Hitler proclaimed in September 1941, "is the enemy of progress. In this respect we resemble the Americans. We are a demanding people." Accordingly the German Stadium in the Party rally grounds outside Nuremberg was to accommodate 405,000 spectators.

25   In this climate of making American technology the yardstick, American cultural imports, like cinema and music, also kept their niche. Propaganda Minister Joseph Goebbels was a movie fan who had long recognized the power of the medium, and Hollywood films were shown widely in the 1930s. Greta Garbo, Joan Crawford, Katharine Hepburn, and Clark Gable were as well known as any German stars. Nazi censors became adept at approving escapist and romantic movies while Goebbels built up a film empire of his own, to counter Hollywood's hegemony and produce films with strong ideological messages.

26   The subversive influence of American jazz and big-band music was harder to control. Jazz, relying on improvisation, free interaction among musicians, and lyrics evoking memories of slavery and repression, became a forbidden fruit, viewed as dangerous by a racist dictatorship that espoused conformity as a virtue. Young, mainly middle-class people who refused to conform listened to jazz in "hot clubs" or bought records with false labels to mislead the authorities. To them this was defiance and dissent. Although the regime harassed and later persecuted so-called Swing-heinis, the Nazi leadership was reluctant to stamp out American music altogether, not wanting to upset those who simply enjoyed big-band dancing. During the war swing was popular with the troops. There is a story of a Goebbels aide who, after a big-band audience had begun to shout " 'Tiger Rag, Bei mir biste

scheen!' [You are wonderful]," declared solemnly that American and Jewish numbers were forbidden, whereupon he was pelted with apples. He told the musicians, "Play what you want!" and scurried off.

Jazz illustrates Nazism's ambiguity toward "Americanism" and American culture particularly well. Hitler's interest in technology and industrial management notwithstanding, the social framework within which America's mass-production and mass-consumption society operated was anathema. Behind the splendid facades of Speer's architecture lurked a regime that had effectively disenfranchised its population; democracy had died in Germany in 1933. Hitler's chauvinism and racism envisioned a homogeneous, closed society that condemned ethnic minorities to helot status and extinction. The specter of Jesse Owens winning gold medals at the 1936 Berlin Olympic Games was intolerable. Nor did the image of the emancipated woman, first imported from across the Atlantic in the 1920s, sit well with the Nazi ideal of a devoted Gretchen bearing future soldiers for the Third Reich's wars of conquest.   27

And so Hitler's respect for, and interest in, America—always ambivalent and never enthusiastic—flip-flopped and then turned into all-out hostility and rage after Roosevelt in 1937 began to block Nazi ambitions. During the war the Fuhrer's anger grew boundless as he slowly realized that American industrial and military superiority was precisely what would destroy him and his dictatorship. World War II was, after all, a struggle over the principles according to which the industrial-technological societies of the twentieth century would be organized.   28

When this gigantic struggle ended in 1945, and Nazism had been wiped out, German images of the United States were confused and twisted not only by the legacy of Goebbels's hate propaganda but also by the total chaos that the Third Reich had left behind. On the one hand, there was bitterness and resentment at the Allied occupation authorities and their initially punitive policies; on the other, there was gratitude for the food parcels and material help extended to millions of destitute people. Whatever American cultural imports reached postwar Germany, they were brought during the occupation by GIs who, when it came to their German girl friends or handing out Hershey bars to children, cheerfully ignored nonfraternization orders. It took until the early 1950s for the economic and political situation to stabilize and for Germans to begin to sort out their feelings toward the United States. By then the Cold War was at its height, and American political and economic predominance in Western Europe was simply irrefutable. Germany's entrepreneurs, many of them back in their prewar roles, were among the first to appreciate this. They knew that the structures and traditions of their businesses would have to be adapted to those of the United States if they were to compete in the new world market being created by Washington and American corporations.   29

For a third time German interest in American technology and industrial organization grew intense, promoted in part by men like the Marshall Plan administrator Paul Hoffman, a former president of Studebaker, and his deputy, Richard M. Bissell, Jr., an economics professor at MIT. As the latter put it, the United States needed to exploit "to the full the example of its own accomplishments and their powerful appeal to Europeans (and others) among all groups." Coca-Cola and the movies, he pointed out, "may be regarded as two products of a shallow and crude civilization. But   30

American machinery, American labor relations, and American management and engineering are everywhere respected." He hoped that "a few European unions and entrepreneurs can be induced to try out the philosophy of higher productivity, higher wages, and higher profits from the lower prices of lower unit costs." He argued that the forces fostering change were so powerful that . . . , it will not require enormous sums of money. . ., to achieve faster increases in production. But it will require a profound shift in social attitudes, attuning them to the mid-twentieth century."

31   Once again a new generation of German engineers, managers, and experts traveled across the Atlantic to study American industry and consumer culture with a view to transferring its practices and ideologies back home. There was enthusiasm, but as before, there was also rejection, with arguments on both sides very reminiscent of the debates on "Americanism" during the 1920s. As before, German attitudes toward Hollywood movies, rock 'n' roll, and American music split along generational lines. By the mid-1950s many young Germans knew more about Louis Armstrong and Gene Krupa than about Beethoven and Mozart. Elvis Presley reduced his German audiences to fits of hysteria. They enjoyed the aura of sexual freedom as they mocked the Prussian stiffness and soldier worship of their fathers.

32   Youth rose in rebellion against the culture of an older generation, anxious, after the moral and cultural catastrophe of Nazism, to provide orientation for a society traumatized by war and Cold War. This "Americanization from below" challenged gender boundaries, deeply worrying conservative politicians and religious leaders. American cultural imports attracted some, including many young women, as vibrant and liberating and offended others as radical and decadent, wild and primitive, and, above all, threatening. This split in perception has persisted to this day.

33   In the end German attitudes toward America tell us less about the United States and its culture than about two Germanys that have been wrestling with each other for more than a century now. One is inward-looking, averse to innovation, provincial, nationalist, and nostalgically tied to its customs. The other has adopted Fordism and all that has grown out of it, blending American ways with German traditions in a new synthesis. The result is the idea of a society open to the outside world, accepting difference and diversity, working toward multiculturalism.

34   The Nazi attempt to combine an inward-looking German culture with American technology and industrialism foundered not merely because of the superior military power of the United States in World War II but also because of the contradiction inherent in Hitler's aims. Ultimately Fordism could not be reconciled with dictatorship or with the destruction of difference and creativity through ruthless state violence. And now we find the old and the new Germany struggling again, with American culture giving both sides the ammunition to support the type of society they cherish and condemn the type they loathe. The outcome of this cultural struggle will determine the future role of a reunified Germany within Europe. What is more, much of this current debate is going on in other European societies with almost identical arguments about homogeneity and diversity. A bitter battle thus is raging over the future place of all of Europe in the post-Cold War world.

UNDERSTANDING THE AUTHOR'S IDEAS

1. Summarize the "ups and downs" of U.S. and German industrial relations, according to Berghahn.
2. Summarize the ambivalent German views of the American entertainment world, as discussed by Berghahn. Be specific with examples.
3. Briefly describe Hitler's views of American society in the 1920s and 1930s.
4. Describe the ambivalent relationship of the United States and Germany after World War II.
5. Explain Berghahn's sense of German-American relations in the post-Cold War period in which Germany is building itself as a reunified nation.

EXPLORING YOUR OWN IDEAS

1. Explain what insights you gained into the history and nature of German-American relations from this article.
2. Berghahn writes, "And now we find the old and the new Germany struggling again, with American culture giving both sides the ammunition to support the type of society they cherish and condemn the type they loathe. The outcome of this cultural struggle will determine the future role of a reunified Germany within Europe. What is more, much of this current debate is going on in other European societies with almost identical arguments about homogeneity and diversity. A bitter battle thus is raging over the future place of all of Europe in the post-Cold War world." Do you agree or disagree with his assessment? Explain with examples.
3. Explore your thoughts on America as an industrial leader and as an entertainment leader in the world. Develop a description of each role as you see it filled today. Be sure to provide specific examples.
4. This text is an example of the genre of a photoenhanced magazine essay written for a well-respected, popular history magazine. Discuss your understanding of its audience, purpose, and features.
5. Berghahn has written widely on German-American relations. Locate one of Berghahn's scholarly articles in a history journal using one of your library's databases. Skim the article and compare and contrast features of that genre to the one you read here.
6. Visit the Web site of *American Heritage* magazine at www.americanheritage. com. Summarize what you discovered and share it in small groups of fellow students.

EXPLORING VISUAL IMAGES

A Nazi Impression of American Culture at Work, 1944

This 1944 poster presents Nazi Germany's impressions of American culture. Study the image closely and identify as many different symbols of American culture as possible. Discuss the overall impressions of both positive and negative aspects of American culture that emerge. Compare and contrast those impressions with foreign perceptions of American culture today (recall the ideas you've encountered in the readings and elsewhere). Now create a thesis regarding some aspect of this topic and write a short position paper defending it.

Reading 5

A native of India who became a U.S. citizen in 1991, Dinesh D'Souza offers another fascinating perspective in this study of the American image. D'Souza, a prolific writer, has studied issues of race and ethnicity for many years and has worked as a White House policy analyst. In the first chapter of this text, he claims to "have a good vantage point to assess how Western civilization has harmed or helped the peoples of the non-Western world" being himself a "person of color" who was "raised in a country that was colonized by the West for several hundred years" but who has now lived in the United States for over 20 years. D'Souza declares that his "identification with America has deepened" and that now he has " 'become an American.' "

The text below is an excerpt of D'Souza's book-length essay of social commentary exploring foreign perceptions of America today. He explores and clearly deconstructs arguments from multiple perspectives, both in support and in rejection of the American way. This text offers an interesting blend of genre features of both popular and scholarly publications. Clearly, it is written with a strong personal voice and an informal enough style to engage its intended general, though well-educated, audience. At the same time, it provides over 100 footnotes, many from scholarly sources, an extensive index, and an obviously highly informed perspective.

Excerpt from *What's So Great About America*

Dinesh D'Souza

But first let us examine the three main currents of foreign opposition to the spread of American influence.   1

First, the European school. Actually this may be more precisely described as the French school, although it has sympathizers in other European countries. The French seem to be outraged by the idea that any single nation, let alone the United States, should enjoy global domination. The French foreign minister, Hubert Vedrine, termed the United States a "hyperpower" and scorned its "arrogance." The French are not against arrogance per se, but in the case of the United States they regard the arrogance as completely unjustified. For the French, the grotesque symbol of Americanization is McDonald's, and many French citizens cheered in 1999 when a sheep farmer named José Bové trashed a McDonald's in France. The French worry that the spread of English threatens the future of the French language and, even more precious, French culture. Their anti-Americanism is based on a strong belief in French cultural superiority combined with a fear that their great culture is being dissolved in the global marketplace.   2

Most Americans find it hard to take the French critique seriously, coming as it does from men who carry handbags. French anti-Americanism is also a political device to legitimate the use of tariffs, thus protecting French products that cannot compete in the global marketplace. But at the same time the French have a point   3 when they object to the obliteration of local cultures and the homogenization of the planet in the name of globalization and Americanization. Probably we can also agree that the world would be a worse place without the French language and French cuisine, although whether we could do without French films and French intellectuals is open to dispute.

4   A second and more troubling critique of America comes from what may be termed the Asian school. This view, which has advocates in Singapore and Malaysia and, most important, China, holds that America and the West have solved the economic problem but they have not solved the cultural problem. As Lee Kuan Yew, the former prime minister of Singapore, has argued, America has generated a lot of material prosperity, but that has been accompanied by social and moral decline. Champions of the Asian school hold that they have figured out a way to combine material well-being with social order. In Singapore, for example, you are encouraged to engage in commerce, but there is no chewing gum in public and if you paint graffiti on cars, as one American visitor did, you will be publicly caned. The result, advocates of the Asian school say, is that people can enjoy a high standard of living but without the crime, illegitimacy, and vulgarity that are believed to debase life in the West.

5   The "Asian values" paradigm is often viewed as an excuse for dictatorship. Admittedly it serves the interest of Asian despots to portray democracy as a debauched system of government, so that they can justify keeping political power in their own hands. But it is hard to deny that there are powerful elements of truth in the way that Lee Kuan Yew and others portray America and the West. That there may be an alternative model better suited to the human desire for prosperity, safety, and public decency cannot be rejected out of hand. Lee Kuan Yew's slogan for this is "modernization without Westernization."[14]

6   Undoubtedly, the most comprehensive and ferocious attack on America comes from what may be termed the Islamic school. From what Americans hear of this group, with its slogans that we are the Great Satan, land of the infidels, and so on, it does not seem that this is a very sophisticated critique of Western society. On television we see protesters in Iraq, Iran, and Pakistan, and they seem like a bunch of jobless fanatics. But behind these demonstrators who chant and burn American flags in the street, there is a considered argument against America that should not be lightly dismissed. Americans should not assume that because they haven't heard much of this argument, it does not exist or has no intellectual merit.

7   On the surface it seems that the Islamic critique is mainly focused on American foreign policy. Certainly many Muslims angrily object to the degree of U.S. political and financial support for Israel. "We consider America and Israel to be one country," one Palestinian man told CNN. "When the Israelis burn our homes and kill our children, we know that it is your weapons, your money and your helicopters that are making this happen." Interestingly the Palestinian problem was not initially a big concern for bin Laden; he seemed more exercised about the effect of American sanctions on the Iraqi people and about the presence of American troops in Saudi Arabia, the "holy soil of Islam." Another issue for bin Laden, which resonates especially with

---

[14]Lee Kuan Yew, "America Is No Longer Asia's Model," *New Perspectives Quarterly,* Winter 1996; Farred Zaharia, "A Conversation with Lee Kuan Yew," *Foreign Affairs,* March–April 1994.

Muslim intellectuals, is the proclaimed hypocrisy of America. In this view, the United States piously invokes principles of democracy and human rights while supporting undemocratic regimes, such as those of Pakistan, Egypt, and Saudi Arabia, that do not hesitate to trample on human rights. Probably bin Laden strikes the biggest chord with the man in the Arab street when he blames the poverty and degradation of the Islamic world on Western and specifically American oppression.

Clearly the foreign policy element is important, but there is much more to the Islamic critique than that. Once we begin to peruse the newspapers and listen to the public discussion in the Muslim world, and once we read the thinkers who are shaping the mind of Islamic fundamentalism, we realize that here is an intelligent and even profound assault on the very basis of America and the West. Indeed, the Islamic critique, at its best, shows a deep understanding of America's fundamental principles—which is more than one can say about the American understanding of Islamic principles. This critique deserves careful attention not only because of its intrinsic power but also because it is the guiding force behind the *jihad* factories—the countless mosques and religious schools throughout the Muslim world that are teaching such violent hatred of America. 8

Islamic critics recognize that other people around the world are trying selectively to import aspects of America and the West while rejecting other aspects that they do not like. Thus the Chinese, the Indians, the Africans, and the Latin Americans all want some of what the West has to offer—especially technology and prosperity—but they want to keep out other things. "Modernization without Westernization" expresses a widespread desire to preserve the treasured elements of one's own culture and identity in the face of Westernization. 9

But the Islamic thinkers argue that selective Westernization is an illusion. In their view modernity is Western, and they regard as naïve the notion that one can import what one likes from America while keeping out what one dislikes. The Islamic argument is that the West is based on principles that are radically different from those of traditional societies. In this view, America is a subversive idea that, if admitted into a society, will produce tremendous and uncontrollable social upheaval. It will eliminate the religious basis for society, it will undermine traditional hierarchies, it will displace cherished values, and it will produce a society unrecognizable from the one it destroyed. As bin Laden himself put it, Islam is facing the greatest threat to its survival since the days of the prophet Muhammad. 10

He's right. And the Islamic thinkers who fear the dissolution of their traditional societies are also correct. America *is* a subversive idea. Indeed, it represents a new way to be human, and in this book we will explore what this means and whether this subversive idea is worthy of our love and allegiance. 11

So what is the Islamic objection to America? In conversations with Muslims from around the world, several common themes emerge. "To you we are a bunch of Ay-rabs, camel jockeys, and sand-niggers." "The only thing that we have that you care about is oil." "Americans have two things on their mind: money and sex." "Your women are whores." "In America mothers prefer to work than to take care of their children." "In our culture the parents take care of the children, and later the children take care of the parents. In America the children abandon their parents." "America used to be a Christian country. Now atheism is the official religion of the West." 12

"Your TV shows are disgusting. You are corrupting the morals of our young people." "We don't object to how you Americans live, but now you are spreading your way of life throughout the universe." "American culture is a kind of syphilis or disease that is destroying the Islamic community. We won't let you do to us what you did to the American Indian people."

13   What stands out about the Islamic critique is its refreshing clarity. The Islamic thinkers cannot be counted in the ranks of the politically correct. Painful though it is to admit, they aren't entirely wrong about America either. They say that many Americans see them as a bunch of uncivilized towel heads, and this is probably true. They charge that America is a society obsessed with material gain, and who will deny this? They condemn the West as an atheistic civilization, and while they may be wrong about the extent of religious belief and practice, they are right that in the West religion has little sway over the public arena, and the West seems to have generated more unbelief than any other civilization in world history. They are disgusted by our culture, and we have to acknowledge that there is a good deal in American culture that is disgusting to normal sensibilities. They say our women are "loose," and in a sense they are right. Even their epithet for the United States, the Great Satan, is appropriate when we reflect that Satan is not a conqueror—he is a tempter. The Islamic militants fear that the idea of America is taking over their young people, breaking down allegiances to parents and religion and traditional community; this concern on their part is also justified.

14   The most important and influential of the Islamic critics of the West is the philosopher Sayyid Qutb.[15] Born in Egypt in 1906, Qutb became disenchanted with Arab nationalism as a weapon against Western imperialism. He became a leader and theoretician of the Muslim Brotherhood, a terrorist organization that is also one of the oldest institutions of radical Islam. Qutb argued that the worst form of colonialism—one that outlasted the formal end of European colonialism—was "intellectual and spiritual colonialism." What the Islamic world must do is destroy the influence of the West within itself, to eradicate its residue "within our feelings."

15   What, for Qutb, was so evil about the West? Qutb argues that from its earliest days Western civilization separated the realm of God from the realm of society. Long before the American doctrine of separation of church and state, the institutions of religion and those of government operated in separate realms and commanded separate allegiances. Consequently, Qutb argues, the realm of God and the realm of society were bound to come into conflict. And this is precisely what has happened in the West. If Athens can be taken to represent reason and science and culture, and Jerusalem can be taken to represent God and religion, then Athens has been in a constant struggle with Jerusalem. Perhaps at one point the tension could be regarded as fruitful, Qutb writes, but now the war is over, and the terrible truth is that Athens has won. Reason

---

[15]John Esposito, ed., "Sayyid Qutb: Ideologue of Islamic Revival" in *Voices of Resurgent Islam* (New York: Oxford University Press, 1983); John Esposito, *The Islamic Threat: Myth or Reality?* (New York: Oxford University Press, 1999), 135–37; Ibrahim Abu-Rabi, *Intellectual Origins of Islamic Resurgence in the Modern Arab World* (Albany: State University of New York Press, 1996), 133, 158, 172; Roxanne Euben, "Pre-modern, Anti-modern or Postmodern: Islamic and Western Critiques of Modernity," *Review of Politics,* Summer 1997, 434–50.

and science have annihilated religion. True, many people continue to profess a belief in God and go to church, but religion has ceased to have any shaping influence in society. It does not direct government or law or scientific research or culture. In short, a once-religious civilization has now been reduced to what Qutb terms *jahiliyya*—the condition of social chaos—moral diversity, sexual promiscuity, polytheism, unbelief, and idolatry that was said to characterize the Arab tribes before the advent of Islam.

Qutb's alternative to this way of life is Islam, which is much more than just a religion. Islam is not merely a set of beliefs; rather, it is a way of life based upon the divine government of the universe. The very term "Islam" means "submission" to the authority of Allah. This worldview requires that religious, economic, political, and civil society be based on the Koran, the teachings of the prophet Muhammad, and on the *sharia* or Islamic law. Islam doesn't just regulate religious belief and practice; it covers such topics as the administration of the state, the conduct of war, the making of treaties, the laws governing divorce and inheritance, as well as property rights and contracts. In short, Islam provides the whole framework for Muslim life, and in this sense it is impossible to "practice" Islam within a secular framework.   16

This is especially so when, as Qutb insists, the institutions of the West are antithetical to Islam. The West is a society based on freedom whereas Islam is a society based on virtue. Moreover in Qutb's view, Western institutions are fundamentally atheistic: they are based on a clear rejection of divine authority. When democrats say that sovereignty and political authority are ultimately derived from the people, this means that the people—not God—are the rulers. So democracy is a form of idol worship. Similarly capitalism is based on the premise that the market, not God, makes final decisions of worth. Capitalism, too, is a form of idolatry or market worship. Qutb contends that since the West and Islam are based on radically different principles, there is no way that Islamic society can compromise or meet the West halfway. Either the West will prevail or Islam will prevail. What is needed, Qutb concludes, is for true-believing Muslims to recognize this and stand up for Islam against the Western infidel and those apostate Muslims who have sold out to the West for money and power. And once the critique is accepted by Muslims, the solution presents itself almost automatically. Kill the apostates. Kill the infidels.   17

Some Americans will find these views frightening and abhorrent, and a few people might even object to giving them so much space and taking them seriously. But I think that they must be taken seriously. Certainly they are taken seriously in the Muslim world. Moreover, Qutb is raising issues of the deepest importance: Is reason or revelation a more reliable source of truth? Does legitimate political authority come from God or from man? Which is the highest political value: freedom or virtue? These issues are central to what the West and America are all about. Qutb's critique reveals most lucidly the argument between Islam and the West at its deepest level. For this reason, it should be welcomed by thoughtful people in America and the West.   18

The foreign critique of America would not be so formidable if Americans were united in resisting and responding to it. Patriotism, then, would be an easy matter of "us" versus "them." But in truth there are large and influential sectors of American life that agree with many of the denunciations that come from abroad. Both on the political Left and the Right, there are people who express a strong hostility to the idea of   19

America and the American way of life. In many quarters in the United States, we find a deep ambivalence about exporting the American system to the rest of the world. Not only do these critiques make patriotism problematic, but they also pose the question of whether an open society, where such criticisms are permitted and even encouraged, has the fortitude and the will to resist external assault. They also raise the issue of whether, if the critics are right, America is worth defending.

20   Conservatism is generally the party of patriotism, but in recent years, since the end of the Reagan administration, patriotism on the Right has not been much in evidence. This is not due just to post–Cold War lassitude. Many conservatives are viscerally unhappy with the current state of American society. Several right-wing leaders have pointed to the magnitude of crime, drugs, divorce, abortion, illegitimacy, and pornography as evidence that America is suffering a moral and cultural breakdown of mammoth proportions. The Reverend Jerry Falwell even suggested that the destruction of the World Trade Center was God's way of punishing America for its sinful ways. Falwell was strongly criticized, and apologized for the remark. But his cultural pessimism is echoed in the speeches of Bill Bennett, former secretary of education, and Gary Bauer, former presidential candidate and head of the Family Research Council, as well as in books such as Robert Bork's *Slouching Towards Gomorrah*, Patrick Buchanan's, *The Death of the West*, and Gertrude Himmelfarb's *The De-Moralization of Society*.

21   How, then, can we love a society where virtue loses all her loveliness, one that has promoted what Pope John Paul II has called a "culture of death"? Some conservatives say we cannot. A few years ago the journal *First Things* argued that America had so fundamentally departed from the principles that once commanded allegiance that it was time to ask "whether conscientious citizens can no longer give moral assent to the existing regime."[16] Pat Buchanan characteristically goes further, asserting that for millions of Americans, "the good country we grew up in" has now been replaced by "a cultural wasteland and a moral sewer that are not worth living in and not worth fighting for."[17]

22   On the political Left, anti-Americanism has been prevalent and even fashionable at least since the Vietnam War. Admittedly a direct attack on the American homeland by Islamic fundamentalists who imprison homosexuals and refuse to educate their women was a bit too much for some, like Christopher Hitchens and David Rieff, who enrolled as supporters of the U.S. war effort. Some on the Left, too embarrassed to rationalize mass murder, and too timid to provoke the public's rage, fell prudently silent. But others could not help muttering that "America had it coming" and that "we must look at our own actions to understand the context for this attack." Columnist Barbara Ehrenreich, for example, said the United States was responsible for "the vast global inequalities in which terrorism is ultimately rooted."[18]

23   This viewpoint was applauded at a Washington, D.C., town meeting sponsored by the Congressional Black Caucus.[19] And on the American campus, several professors

---

[16]"The End of Democracy?" *First Things*, November 1996, 18–42.

[17]Patrick J. Buchanan, *The Death of the West* (New York: St. Martin's Press, 2001), 6.

[18]Cited in "Idiocy Watch," *New Republic*, 15 October 2001, 10.

[19]Ann Gerhart, "Black Caucus Waves the Caution Flag," *Washington Post*, 28 September 2001, C-1, C-8.

went further, blaming the United States itself for the carnage of September 11. University of Massachusetts professor Jennie Traschen suggested that America deserved what it got because throughout the world it was "a symbol of terrorism and death and fear and destruction and oppression."[20] These strong words should not have come as a surprise. For years the left-wing opponents of globalization have carried banners in Seattle and elsewhere saying "America Must Be Stopped" and "The World Is Not For Sale." On campuses across the country, professors have been teaching their students what Columbia University scholar Edward Said recently argued: that America is a genocidal power with a "history of reducing whole peoples, countries and even continents to ruin by nothing short of holocaust."[21] Many intellectuals and activists have devoted a good deal of their adult lives to opposing what one termed "a world laid to waste by America's foreign policy, its gunboat diplomacy, its chilling disregard for non-American lives, its barbarous military interventions, its support for despotic and dictatorial regimes, its marauding multinationals, its merciless economic agenda that has munched through the economies of poor countries like a cloud of locusts."[22] Could bin Laden have put it better? If what these people say is true, then America should be destroyed.

The most serious internal critique of America comes from the political movement called multiculturalism. This group is made up of minority activists as well as of sympathetic whites who agree with their agenda. The multiculturalists are a powerful, perhaps even dominant, force in American high schools and colleges. The pervasiveness of their influence is attested in the title of a recent book by Nathan Glazer, *We Are All Multiculturalists Now.* This group has become the shaper of the minds of American students. The multiculturalists are teaching our young people that Western civilization is defined by oppression. They present American history as an uninterrupted series of crimes visited on blacks, American Indians, Hispanics, women, and natives of the Third World. This is the theme of Howard Zinn's widely used textbook *A People's History of the United States.* Other leading scholars affirm Zinn's basic themes. Cornel West, who teaches African-American studies at Princeton, says that American society is "chronically racist, sexist and homophobic."[23] Political scientist Ali Mazrui goes further, charging that the United States has been, and continues to be, "a breeding ground for racism, exploitation and genocide."[24] 24

The reason America exercises such a baleful influence, multiculturalists argue, is that the American founders were slave owners and racists who established what one scholar terms "a model totalitarian society."[25] No wonder that multiculturalists are 25

---

[20]James Bowman, "Towers of Intellect," *Wall Street Journal,* 5 October 2001.

[21]Stanley Kurtz, "Edward Said, Imperialist," *Weekly Standard,* 8 October 2001, 35.

[22]These words, from the writer Arundhati Roy, were quoted in "Sontagged," *Weekly Standard,* 15 October 2001, 42–43.

[23]Cornel West, *Keeping Faith: Philosophy and Race in America* (New York: Routledge, 1993), 236.

[24]Ali Mazrui, "Islamic and Western Values," *Foreign Affairs,* September–October 1997.

[25]Nathan Irvin Huggins, *Black Odyssey: The African-American Ordeal in Slavery* (New York: Vintage Books, 1990), 113.

not hopeful about the future of the American experiment. In the words of historian John Hope Franklin, "We're a bigoted people and always have been. We think every other country is trying to copy us now, and if they are, God help the world."[26]

26   Multiculturalists insist that immigrants and minorities should not assimilate to the American mainstream, because to do so is to give up one's identity and to succumb to racism. As the influential scholar Stanley Fish puts it, "*Common values. National unity. Assimilation.* These are now the code words and phrases for an agenda that need no longer speak in the accents of the Know-Nothing party of the nineteenth century or the Ku Klux Klan of the twentieth."[27] The multicultural objective is to encourage nonwhites in America to cultivate their separate identities and to teach white Americans to accept and even cherish these differences. For multiculturalists, diversity is the basis for American identity. As a popular slogan has it, "All we have in common is our diversity."

27   Multiculturalists also seek to fill white Americans with an overpowering sense of guilt and blame so that they accept responsibility for the sufferings of minorities in America and poor people in the rest of the world. One favored multicultural solution, taken up by the Reverend Jesse Jackson upon his return from the recent United Nations-sponsored World Conference on Racism in Durban, is for the American government to pay reparations for slavery to African nations and to African-Americans. "The amount we are owed," says black activist Haki Madhubuti, "is in the trillions of dollars."[28]

28   What we have, then, is a vivid portrait of how terrible America is and of the grave harms that it has inflicted on its people and on the world since the nation's founding. These charges of the low origins of America, and its oppressive practices, and its depraved culture, and its pernicious global influence—are they true? If so, is it possible to love our country, or are we compelled to watch her buildings knocked down and her people killed and say, in unison with her enemies, "Praise be to Allah"?

[26]Dennis Farney, "As America Triumphs, Americans Are Awash in Doubt," *Wall Street Journal,* 27 July 1992, A-1; see also John Hope Franklin, "The Moral Legacy of the Founding Fathers," *University of Chicago Magazine,* Summer 1975, 10–13.

[27]Stanley Fish, *There's No Such Thing as Free Speech, and It's a Good Thing Too* (New York: Oxford University Press, 1994), 87.

[28]Haki Madhubuti, *Black Men: Obsolete, Single, Dangerous?* (Chicago: Third World Press, 1990), 28.

UNDERSTANDING THE AUTHOR'S IDEAS

1. Summarize in some detail the "three main currents of foreign opposition to the spread of American influence," according to D'Souza.
2. D'Souza maintains that the Islamic critique is based upon much more than foreign policy decisions. Explain.
3. Explain what D'Souza means when stating, "America *is* a subversive idea."
4. Who was Sayyid Qutb? Briefly summarize his views. Explain his significance, according to D'Souza.
5. D'Souza argues that Americans are not united in their response to the foreign critique he explicates. Summarize the various conflicting factions he identifies in American society today.

EXPLORING YOUR OWN IDEAS

1. Discuss your reactions to the three "critiques" (French, Asian, and Islamic).
2. This short text might be called a monograph of social criticism. Explain its purpose and intended audience(s). Make a list of the similarities and differences between this genre and the genres of the personal essay and the scholarly journal article. Compare your lists with those of fellow classmates.
3. Respond to D'Souza's views of the mixed factions within American culture. Do you agree or disagree with his description? Explain the advantages and disadvantages of varied factions.
4. Create an imaginary conversation between D'Souza, Bishara, and Chen based upon what you know of each one's views from the articles in this section.
5. Why do you think other nations may have mixed views on Westernization? What do you think are the pros and cons of modernization?
6. D'Souza argues, "The most serious internal critique of America comes from the political movement called multiculturalism." Research this movement further and then construct a personal response to D'Souza's description.
7. Consult some of the public discourse that emerged following September 11 on the Web site www.americanrhetoric.com. Discuss some of the views presented in relation to what you've learned from the D'Souza excerpt.

Reading 6

The short story below, the only fiction piece in this unit, offers insights into foreign perceptions of America through a very different genre lens. This story is one of a group of stories that collectively create a novel entitled How the Garcia Girls Lost Their Accents. *Author Julia Alvarez, who was born in the Dominican Republic and later immigrated to the United States, experienced cultural assimilation first-hand. Through her well-crafted stories, primarily based upon her personal experiences, Alvarez provides unique insights into the American culture from an Hispanic perspective.*

True to the genre of quality fiction, this narrative demands that the reader often "read between the lines" to construct a nonarticulated, though clearly present, intriguing perception of American culture. As you enjoy this engaging literary text, try to articulate the description of the values and nuances of American culture that Alvarez subtlety reveals.

"Daughter of Invention"

Julia Alvarez

Mami, Papi, Yoyo

1   For a period after they arrived in this country, Laura Garcia tried to invent something. Her ideas always came after the sightseeing visits she took with her daughters to department stores to see the wonders of this new country. On his free Sundays, Carlos carted the girls off to the Statue of Liberty or the Brooklyn Bridge or Rockefeller Center, but as far as Laura was concerned, these were men's wonders. Down in housewares were the true treasures women were after.

2   Laura and her daughters would take the escalator, marveling at the moving staircase, she teasing them that this might be the ladder Jacob saw with angels moving up and down to heaven. The moment they lingered by a display, a perky saleslady approached, no doubt thinking a young mother with four girls in tow fit the perfect profile for the new refrigerator with automatic defrost or the heavy duty washing machine with the prewash soak cycle. Laura paid close attention during the demonstrations, asking intelligent questions, but at the last minute saying she would talk it over with her husband. On the drive home, try as they might, her daughters could not engage their mother in conversation, for inspired by what she had just [seen] Laura had begun inventing.

3   She never put anything actual on paper until she had settled her house down at night. On his side of the bed her husband would be conked out for an hour already, his Spanish newspapers draped over his chest, his glasses propped up on the bedside table, looking out eerily at the darkened room like a disembodied bodyguard. In her lighted corner, pillows propped behind her, Laura sat up inventing. On her lap lay

one of those innumerable pads of paper her husband brought home from his office, compliments of some pharmaceutical company, advertising tranquilizers or antibiotics or skin cream. She would be working on a sketch of something familiar but drawn at such close range so she could attach a special nozzle or handier handle, the thing looked peculiar. Her daughters would giggle over the odd doodles they found in kitchen drawers or on the back shelf of the downstairs toilet. Once Yoyo was sure her mother had drawn a picture of a man's you-know-what; she showed her sisters her find, and with coy, posed faces they inquired of their mother what she was up to. *Ay,* that was one of her failures, she explained to them, a child's double-compartment drinking glass with an outsized, built-in straw.

Her daughters would seek her out at night when she seemed to have a moment to   4
talk to them: they were having trouble at school or they wanted her to persuade their father to give them permission to go into the city or to a shopping mall or a movie—in broad daylight, Mami! Laura would wave them out of her room. "The problem with you girls . . ." The problem boiled down to the fact that they wanted to become Americans and their father—and their mother, too, at first—would have none of it.

"You girls are going to drive me crazy!" she threatened, if they kept nagging.   5
"When I end up in Bellevue, you'll be safely sorry!"

She spoke in English when she argued with them. And her English was a mish-   6
mash of mixed-up idioms and sayings that showed she was "green behind the ears," as she called it.

If her husband insisted she speak in Spanish to the girls so they wouldn't forget   7
their native tongue, she'd snap, "When in Rome, do unto the Romans."

Yoyo, the Big Mouth, had become the spokesman for her sisters, and she stood   8
her ground in that bedroom. "We're not going to that school anymore, Mami!"

"You have to." Her eyes would widen with worry. "In this country, it is against the   9
law not to go to school. You want us to get thrown out?"

"You want us to get killed? Those kids were throwing stones today!"   10

"Sticks and stones don't break bones," she chanted. Yoyo could tell, though, by the   11
look on her face, it was as if one of those stones the kids had aimed at her daughters had hit her. But she always pretended they were at fault. "What did you do to provoke them? It takes two to tangle, you know."

"Thanks, thanks a lot, Mom!" Yoyo stormed out of that room and into her own.   12
Her daughters never called her *Mom* except when they wanted her to feel how much she had failed them in this country. She was a good enough Mami, fussing and scolding and giving advice, but a terrible girlfriend parent, a real failure of a Mom.

Back she went to her pencil and pad, scribbling and taking and tearing off sheets,   13
finally giving up, and taking up her *New York Times*. Some nights, though, if she got a good idea, she rushed into Yoyo's room, a flushed look on her face, her tablet of paper in her hand, a cursory knock on the door she'd just thrown open. "Do I have something to show you, Cuquita!"

This was Yoyo's time to herself, after she finished her homework, while her sisters   14
were still downstairs watching TV in the basement. Hunched over her small desk, the overhead light turned off, her desk lamp poignantly lighting only her paper, the rest of the room in warm, soft, uncreated darkness, she wrote her secret poems in her new language.

15   "You're going to ruin your eyes!" Laura began, snapping on the overly bright over-head light, scaring off whatever shy passion Yoyo, with the blue thread of her writing, had just begun coaxing out of a labyrinth of feelings.

16   "Oh, Mami!" Yoyo cried out, her eyes blinking up at her mother. "I'm writing."

17   "*Ay*, Cuquita." That was her communal pet name for whoever was in her favor. "Cuquita, when I make a million, I'll buy you your very own typewriter." (Yoyo had been nagging her mother for one just like the one her father had bought to do his or-der forms at home.) "Gravy on the turkey" was what she called it when someone was buttering her up. She buttered and poured. "I'll hire you your very own typist."

18   Down she plopped on the bed and held out her pad. "Take a guess, Cuquita!" Yoyo studied the rough sketch a moment. Soap sprayed from the nozzle head of a shower when you turned the knob a certain way? Instant coffee with creamer already mixed in? Time-released water capsules for your potted plants when you were away? A key-chain with a timer that would go off when your parking meter was about to expire? (The ticking would help you find your keys easily if you mislaid them.) The famous one, famous only in hindsight, was a stick person dragging a square by a rope—a suitcase with wheels? "Oh, of course," Yoyo said, humoring her. "What every house-hold needs: a shower like a car wash, keys ticking like a bomb, luggage on a leash!" By now, it had become something of a family joke, their Thomas Edison Mami, their Benjamin Franklin Mom.

19   Her face fell. "Come on now! Use your head." One more wrong guess, and she'd show Yoyo, pointing with her pencil the different highlights of this incredible new wonder. "Remember that time we took the car to Bear Mountain, and we re-ah-lized that we had forgotten to pack an opener with our pick-a-nick?" (Her daughters kept correcting her, but she insisted this was how it should be said.) "When we were ready to eat we didn't have any way to open the refreshments cans?"(This was before fliptop lids, which she claimed had crossed her.) "You know what this is now?" Yoyo shook her head. "Is a car bumper, but see this part is a removable can opener. So sim-ple and yet so necessary, eh?"

20   "Yeah, Mami. You should patent it." Yoyo shrugged as her mother tore off the scratch paper and folded it, carefully, corner to corner, as if she were going to save it. But then, she tossed it in the wastebasket on her way out of the room and gave a lit-tle laugh like a disclaimer. "It's half of one or two dozen of another."

21   None of her daughters was very encouraging. They resented her spending time on those dumb inventions. Here they were trying to fit in America among Americans; they needed help figuring out who they were, why the Irish kids whose grandparents had been micks were calling them spics. Why had they come to this country in the first place? Important, crucial, final things, and here was their own mother, who did-n't have a second to help them puzzle any of this out, inventing gadgets to make life easier for the American Moms.

22   Sometimes Yoyo challenged her. "Why, Mami? Why do it? You're never going to make money. The Americans have already thought of everything, you know that."

23   "Maybe not. Maybe, just maybe, there's something they've missed that's impor-tant. With patience and calm, even a burro can climb a palm." This last was one of her many Dominican sayings she had imported into her scrambled English.

24   "But what's the point?" Yoyo persisted.

"Point, point, does everything need a point? Why do you write poems?"   25

Yoyo had to admit it was her mother who had the point there. Still, in the hierarchy of things, a poem seemed much more important than a potty that played music when a toilet-training toddler went in its bowl.   26

They talked about it among themselves, the four girls, as they often did now about the many puzzling things in this new country.   27

"Better she reinvents the wheel than be on our cases all the time," the oldest, Carla, observed. In the close quarters of an American nuclear family, their mother's prodigious energy was becoming a real drain on their self-determination. Let her have *a* project. What harm could she do, and besides, she needed that acknowledgement. It had come to her automatically in the old country from being a de la Torre. "Garcia de la Torre," Laura would enunciate carefully, giving her maiden as well as married name when they first arrived. But the blank smiles had never heard of her name. She would show them. She would prove to these Americans what a smart woman could do with pencil and pad.   28

She had a near miss once. Every night, she liked to read *The New York Times* in bed before turning off her light, to see what the Americans were up to. One night, she let out a yelp to wake up her husband beside her. He sat bolt upright, reaching for his glasses which in his haste, he knocked across the room. "*¿Qué pasa? ¿Qué pasa?*" What is wrong? There was terror in his voice, the same fear she'd heard in the Dominican Republic before they left. They had been watched there; he was followed. They could not talk, of course, though they had whispered to each other in fear at night in the dark bed. Now in America, he was safe, a success even; his Centro de Medicina in the Bronx was thronged with the sick and the homesick yearning to go home again. But in dreams, he went back to those awful days and long nights, and his wife's screams confirmed his secret fear: they had not gotten away after all, the SIM had come for them at last.   29

"*Ay,* Cuco! Remember how I showed you that suitcase with little wheels so we should not have to carry those heavy bags when we traveled? Someone stole my idea and made a million!" She shook the paper in his face. "See, see! This man was no *bobo!* He didn't put all his pokers on a back burner. I kept telling you, one of these days my ship would pass me by in the night!" She wagged her finger at her husband and daughters, laughing all the while, one of those eerie laughs crazy people in movies laugh. The four girls had congregated in her room. They eyed their mother and each other. Perhaps they were all thinking the same thing, wouldn't it be weird and sad if Mami did end up in Bellevue?   30

"*¡Ya, ya!*" She waved them out of her room at last. "There is no use trying to drink spilt milk, that's for sure."   31

It was the suitcase rollers that stopped Laura's hand, she had weathervaned a minor brainstorm. And yet, this plagiarist had gotten all the credit, and the money. What use was it trying to compete with the Americans: they would always have the head start. It was their country, after all. Best stick close to home. She cast her sights about—her daughters ducked—and found her husband's office in need. Several days a week, dressed professionally in a white smock with a little name tag pinned on the lapel, a shopping bag full of cleaning materials and rags, she rode with her husband in his car to the Bronx. On the way, she organized the glove compartment or took off   32 the address stickers from the magazines for the waiting room because she had read somewhere how by means of these stickers drug addict patients found out where doctors lived and burglarized their homes looking for syringes. At night, she did the books, filling in columns with how much money they had made that day. Who had time to be inventing silly things!

33   She did take up her pencil and pad one last time. But it was to help one of her daughters out. In ninth grade, Yoyo was chosen by her English teacher, Sister Mary Joseph, to deliver the Teacher's Day address at the school assembly. Back in the Dominican Republic growing up, Yoyo had been a terrible student. No one could ever get her to sit down to read a book. But in New York, she needed to settle somewhere, and since the natives were unfriendly, and the country inhospitable, she took root in the language. By high school, the nuns were reading her stories and compositions out loud in English class.

34   But the spectre of delivering a speech brown-nosing the teachers jammed her imagination. At first she didn't want to and then she couldn't seem to write that speech. She should have thought of it as "a great honor," as her father called it. But she was mortified. She still had a slight accent, and she did not like to speak in public, subjecting herself to her classmates' ridicule. It also took no great figuring to see that to deliver a eulogy for a convent full of crazy, old, overweight nuns was no way to endear herself to her peers.

35   But she didn't know how to get out of it. Night after night, she sat at her desk, hoping to polish off some quick, noncommittal little speech. But she couldn't get anything down.

36   The weekend before the assembly Monday morning Yoyo went into a panic. Her mother would just have to call in tomorrow and say Yoyo was in the hospital, in a coma.

37   Laura tried to calm her down. "Just remember how Mister Lincoln couldn't think of anything to say at the Gettysburg, but then, bang! *Four score and once upon a time ago,*" she began reciting. "Something is going to come if you just relax. You'll see, like the Americans say, *Necessity is the daughter this of invention.* I'll help you."

38   That weekend, her mother turned all her energy towards helping Yoyo write her speech. "Please, Mami, just leave me all alone, please," Yoyo pleaded with her. But Yoyo would get rid of the goose only to have to contend with the gander. Her father kept poking his head in the door just to see if Yoyo had "fulfilled your obligations," a phrase he had used when the girls were younger and he'd check to see whether they had gone to the bathroom before a car trip. Several times that weekend around the supper table, he recited his own high school valedictorian speech. He gave Yoyo pointers on delivery, notes on the great orators and their tricks. (Humbleness and praise and falling silent with great emotion were his favorites.)

39   Laura sat across the table, the only one who seemed to be listening to him. Yoyo and her sisters were forgetting a lot of their Spanish, and their father's formal, florid diction was hard to understand. But Laura smiled softly to herself, and turned the lazy Susan at the center of the table around and around as if it were the prime mover, the first gear of her attention.

40   That Sunday evening, Yoyo was reading some poetry to get herself inspired: Whitman's poems in an old book with an engraved cover her father had picked up in

a thrift shop next to his office. *I celebrate myself and sing myself. . . . He most honors my style who learns under it to destroy the teacher.* The poet's words shocked and thrilled her. She had gotten used to the nuns, a literature of appropriate sentiments, poems with a message, expurgated texts. But here was a flesh and blood man, belching and laughing and sweating in poems. *Who touches this book touches a man.*

That night, at last, she started to write, recklessly, three, five pages, looking up once only to see her father passing by the hall on tiptoe. When Yoyo was done, she read over her words, and her eyes filled. She finally sounded like herself in English! 41

As soon as she had finished that first draft, she called her mother to her room. Laura listened attentively while Yoyo read the speech out loud, and in the end, her eyes were glistening too. Her face was soft and warm and proud. "*Ay,* Yoyo, you are going to be the one to bring our name to the headlights in this country! That is a beautiful, beautiful speech. I want for your father to hear it before he goes to sleep. Then I will type it for you, all right?" 42

Down the hall they went, mother and daughter, faces flushed with accomplishment. Into the master bedroom where Carlos was propped up on his pillows, still awake, reading the Dominican papers, already days old. Now that the dictatorship had been toppled, he had become interested in his country's fate again. The interim government was going to hold the first free elections in thirty years. History was in the making, freedom and hope were in the air again! There was still some question in his mind whether or not he might move his family back. But Laura had gotten used to the life here. She did not want to go back to the old country where, de la Torre or not, she was only a wife and a mother (and a failed one at that, since she had never provided the required son). Better an independent nobody than a high-class house-slave. She did not come straight out and disagree with her husband's plans. Instead, she fussed with him about reading the papers in bed, soiling their sheets with those poorly printed, foreign tabloids. "*The Times* is not that bad!" she'd claim if her husband tried to humor her by saying they shared the same dirty habit. 43

The minute Carlos saw his wife and daughter filing in, he put his paper down, and his face brightened as if at long last his wife had delivered the son, and that was the news she was bringing him. His teeth were already grinning from the glass of water next to his bedside lamp, so he lisped when he said, "Eh-speech, eh-speech!" 44

"It is so beautiful, Cuco," Laura coached him, turning the sound on his TV off. She sat down at the foot of the bed. Yoyo stood before both of them, blocking their view of the soldiers in helicopters landing amid silenced gun reports and explosions. A few weeks ago it had been the shores of the Dominican Republic. Now it was the jungles of Southeast Asia they were saving. Her mother gave her the nod to begin reading. 45

Yoyo didn't need much encouragement. She put her nose to the fire, as her mother would have said, and read from start to finish without looking up. When she concluded, she was a little embarrassed at the pride she took in her own words. She pretended to quibble with a phrase or two, then looked questioningly to her mother. Laura's face was radiant. Yoyo turned to share her pride with her father. 46

The expression on his face shocked both mother and daughter. Carlos's toothless mouth had collapsed into a dark zero. His eyes bored into Yoyo, then shifted to Laura. In barely audible Spanish, as if secret microphones or informers were all about, he whispered to his wife, "You will permit her to read *that?*" 47

48   Laura's eyebrows shot up, her mouth fell open. In the old country, any whisper of a challenge to authority could bring the secret police in their black V.W.'s. But this was America. People could say what they thought. "What is wrong with her speech?" Laura questioned him.

49   "What ees wrrrong with her eh-speech?" Carlos wagged his head at her. His anger was always more frightening in his broken English. As if he had mutilated the language in his fury—and now there was nothing to stand between them and his raw, dumb anger. "What is wrong? I will tell you what is wrong. It show no gratitude. It is boastful. *I celebrate myself? The best student learns to destroy the teacher?*" He mocked Yoyo's plagiarized words. "That is insubordinate. It is improper. It is disrespecting of her teachers—" In his anger he had forgotten his fear of lurking spies: each wrong he voiced was a decibel higher than the last outrage. Finally, he shouted at Yoyo, "As your father, I forbid you to make that eh-speech!"

50   Laura leapt to her feet, a sign that *she* was about to deliver her own speech. She was a small woman, and she spoke all her pronouncements standing up, either for more projection or as a carry-over from her girlhood in convent schools where one asked for, and literally, took the floor in order to speak. She stood by Yoyo's side, shoulder to shoulder. They looked down at Carlos. "That is no tone of voice—" she began.

51   But now, Carlos was truly furious. It was bad enough that his daughter was rebelling, but here was his own wife joining forces with her. Soon he would be surrounded by a houseful of independent American women. He too leapt from the bed, throwing off his covers. The Spanish newspapers flew across the room. He snatched the speech out of Yoyo's hands, held it before the girl's wide eyes, a vengeful, mad look in his own, and then once, twice, three, four, countless times, he tore the speech into shreds.

52   "Are you crazy?" Laura lunged at him. "Have you gone mad? That is her speech for tomorrow you have torn up!"

53   "Have *you* gone mad?" He shook her away. "You were going to let her read that . . . that insult to her teachers?"

54   "Insult to her teachers!" Laura's face had crumpled up like a piece of paper. On it was written a love note to her husband, an unhappy, haunted man. "This is America, Papi, America! You are not in a savage country anymore!"

55   Meanwhile, Yoyo was on her knees, weeping wildly, collecting all the little pieces of her speech, hoping that she could put it back together before the assembly tomorrow morning. But not even a sibyl could have made sense of those tiny scraps of paper. All hope was lost. "He broke it, he broke it," Yoyo moaned as she picked up a handful of pieces.

56   Probably, if she had thought a moment about it, she would not have done what she did next. She would have realized her father had lost brothers and friends to the dictator Trujillo. For the rest of his life, he would be haunted by blood in the streets and late night disappearances. Even after all these years, he cringed if a black Volkswagen passed him on the street. He feared anyone in uniform: the meter maid giving out parking tickets, a museum guard approaching to tell him not to get too close to his favorite Goya.

57   On her knees, Yoyo thought of the worst thing she could say to her father. She gathered a handful of scraps, stood up, and hurled them in his face. In a low, ugly whisper,

she pronounced Trujillo's hated nickname: "Chapita! You're just another Chapita!"

It took Yoyo's father only a moment to register the loathsome nickname before he came after her. Down the halls they raced, but Yoyo was quicker than he and made it into her room just in time to lock the door as her father threw his weight against it. He called down curses on her head, ordered her on his authority as her father to open that door! He throttled that doorknob, but all to no avail. Her mother's love of gadgets saved Yoyo's hide that night. Laura had hired a locksmith to install good locks on all the bedroom doors after the house had been broken into once while they were away. Now if burglars broke in again, and the family were at home, there would be a second round of locks for the thieves to contend with. [58]

"Lolo," she said, trying to calm him down. "Don't you ruin my new locks." [59]

Finally he did calm down, his anger spent. Yoyo heard their footsteps retreating down the hall. Their door clicked shut. Then, muffled voices, her mother's rising in anger, in persuasion, her father's deeper murmurs of explanation and self-defense. The house fell silent a moment, before Yoyo heard, far off, the gun blasts and explosions, the serious, self-important voices of newscasters reporting their TV war. [60]

A little while later, there was a quiet knock at Yoyo's door, followed by a tentative attempt at the door knob. "Cuquita?" her mother whispered. "Open up, Cuquita." [61]

"Go away," Yoyo wailed, but they both knew she was glad her mother was there, and needed only a moment's protest to save face. [62]

Together they concocted a speech: two brief pages of stale compliments and the polite commonplaces on teachers, a speech wrought by necessity and without much invention by mother and daughter late into the night on one of the pads of paper Laura had once used for her own inventions. After it was drafted, Laura typed it up while Yoyo stood by, correcting her mother's misnomers and mis-sayings. [63]

Yoyo came home the next day with the success story of the assembly. The nuns had been flattered, the audience had stood up and given "our devoted teachers a standing ovation," what Laura had suggested they do at the end of the speech. [64]

She clapped her hands together as Yoyo recreated the moment. "I stole that from your father's speech, remember? Remember how he put that in at the end?" She quoted him in Spanish, then translated for Yoyo into English. [65]

That night, Yoyo watched him from the upstairs hall window, where she'd retreated the minute she heard his car pull up in front of the house. Slowly, her father came up the driveway, a grim expression on his face as he grappled with a large, heavy cardboard box. At the front door, he set the package down carefully and patted all his pockets for his house keys. (If only he'd had Laura's ticking key chain!) Yoyo heard the snapping open of locks downstairs. She listened as he struggled to maneuver the box through the narrow doorway. He called her name several times, but she did not answer him. [66]

"My daughter, your father, he love you very much," he explained from the bottom of the stairs. "He just want to protect you." Finally, her mother came up and pleaded with Yoyo to go down and reconcile with him. "Your father did not mean to harm. You must pardon him. Always it is better to let bygones be forgotten, no?" [67]

Downstairs, Yoyo found her father setting up a brand new electric typewriter on the kitchen table. It was even better than her mother's. He had outdone himself with all the extra features: a plastic carrying case with Yoyo's initials decaled below the handle, a brace to lift the paper upright while she typed, an erase cartridge, an [68] automatic margin tab, a plastic hood like a toaster cover to keep the dust away. Not even her mother could have invented such a machine!

69   But Laura's inventing days were over just as Yoyo's were starting up with her school-wide success. Rather than the rolling suitcase everyone else in the family remembers, Yoyo thinks of the speech her mother wrote as her last invention. It was as if, after that, her mother had passed on to Yoyo her pencil and pad and said, "Okay, Cuquita, here's the buck. You give it a shot."

UNDERSTANDING THE AUTHOR'S IDEAS

1. Describe the character of Mami (Laura) as presented by Alvarez in this story. Point to specific passages in the story to defend your conclusions.
2. Explain the feelings of the parents toward their daughters' assimilation into American culture.
3. Why is Yoyo's father so upset with her?
4. What does his effort to reconcile with Yoyo reveal about him?
5. Why does Mami stop inventing? Discuss the significance of the title.
6. Find examples of how Alvarez uses humor in her short story. How does that contribute to this genre?

EXPLORING YOUR OWN IDEAS

1. Read Walt Whitman's famous poem "I Hear America Singing." (You can locate it in numerous anthologies of American literature or online at numerous poetry Web sites such as www.americanpoets.com.) Discuss its implications.
2. Try to imagine more of the text of Yoyo's first speech from the few clues you are provided. Write your version of the speech she wanted to give.
3. The genre of the contemporary short story often makes use of understatement. In other words, much is left unstated. Locate specific passages within this story and articulate some of the thoughts and feelings left unstated. Discuss the effect of this genre feature.
4. Explore the insights this story provides regarding the nature of the American immigrant experience.
5. Identify some of the positive and negative attributes of the two cultures presented here.
6. If you or someone you know has had an interesting experience in trying to assimilate between two cultures, share it with your classmates. Compare it to Alvarez's depiction.

UNIT WRITING ASSIGNMENT SUGGESTIONS

1. Think about the insights you've gained from the readings in this unit about foreign perceptions of America. Write a **personal essay** exploring your understanding of the varied perceptions of America that are prevalent today.

2. Search for political cartoons, available online and in print sources, that provide insights into foreign perceptions of America today. Write a **stance or position paper** that analyzes the arguments underlying some of the cartoons and responds to them.

3. Read the complete text of either the D'Souza or the Hertsgaard books. Write a **stance or position paper** in which you carefully analyze the main arguments projected in either text.

4. Interview students and faculty about their understanding of international perceptions of America. Keep a **journal** of your findings reflecting on your interviewees' responses in light of what you have learned through readings and discussions in this unit.

5. Conduct a search by consulting your library's article databases for at least two book reviews of either the D'Souza or the Hertsgaard text. Summarize the reviews and then write your own **response essay** to the reviews.

6. Locate a different article or book written by one of the authors excerpted in this unit. Write a **review** of that text.

7. Read the Alvarez novel *How the Garcia Girls Lost Their Accents*. Write a **literary essay** analyzing particular literary features of the text and/or responding to the perceptions of both the Dominican Republic and American cultures that are revealed.

8. Conduct some in-depth research on one specific country's past and current relations with the United States. Be sure to acquire resources that lend varied perspectives. Write an **informative report** on your findings that is appropriate for an audience of college students.

9. Research and write a **case study** of some aspect of contemporary U.S. foreign relations with either China, France, Germany, Saudi Arabia, or Iraq. You might consider following for several weeks a few specific newspapers' coverage of our dealings with one of these countries or their responses to us as the basis of a journalistic case study, for example. Or you might develop a case study around the experiences of the international students on your campus.

10. Locate one or two interesting journal articles on some issue of contemporary U.S.-foreign relations regarding a country of your choice. Write a succinct and useful **abstract** of the article(s).

11. Attend a campus or community lecture on U.S. foreign relations and/or aspects of the immigrant experience. Write a **reaction paper** about your experience.

12. Write a **proposal** to your campus administration or student activities office soliciting approval and funds to raise awareness of international perspectives on American culture. Consult your campus office for international students for information and event ideas.

13. Write a **social science research** paper on some aspect of U.S. foreign policy or international perceptions of American culture. Consider tracing the changes in our relationship with Germany since the 1995 publication of the Berghahn article. Or consider pursuing Bishara's remark that the traditional Arab view of America is one of admiration; explore the changes.

14. Locate at least five Web sites providing information on U.S. foreign relations. Identify them and then write a **Web site critique** comparing and contrasting their content, features, and credibility.

15. Interview several international students on your campus to obtain their stories and viewpoints, similar to Hertsgaard's method in *The Eagle's Shadow*. Write a **field observation report** sharing the results of your interviews or a **stance or position paper** synthesizing the ideas of your interviewees with Hertsgaard's findings.

THE INTERNET: RESPONSIBILITIES, RIGHTS, RESULTS

Every now and then, some commentator on our culture writes an essay posing the "How did we ever get along without X?" question to readers. Because people have been asking them for generations, these questions by now are relatively predictable. In earlier times, they were, "How did we ever get along without refrigerators?" or "How did we ever get along without automobiles?" Today, they are, "How did we ever get along without cell phones?" or "How did we ever get along without photocopy machines?" or, most vitally, "How did we ever get along without the Internet?"

In 1945, when a scientist named Vannevar Bush proposed the creation of a device he called the "memex" to store and retrieve data electronically, who would ever have thought that half a century later, people all over the world would be cybernetically connected through something called the Internet that enables them to send and receive messages, images, and information of all sorts at the tap of a key or the click of a mouse? (Indeed, who would even have known in 1945 that a mouse was anything other than a rodent that likes cheese!) Homes, schools, businesses, government agencies, politicians, voters, children, parents—all can now be in touch with one another by Internet communication.

As marvelous an invention as it is, though, the Internet is not problem-free. Like open forums and public squares in earlier eras, the Internet is an arena where people can speak their minds. Any time such a venue is present, questions emerge about thorny issues of rights, responsibilities, and results: Who does or does not have access to the Internet? What can or cannot someone "say," write, or post on it? Who, if anyone, is allowed to keep track of what people say, write, or post on the Internet, and what are these "trackers" permitted to do with that information? How has the Internet as a medium changed communication? Is that change always good?

Since students in the early twenty-first century can look forward to ever-expanding uses of the Internet, the readings in this unit raise these and other questions for serious contemplation.

Reading 1

> *During World War II, Vannevar Bush, an electrical engineer by training, was the director of the U.S. government's Office of Scientific Research and Development. In this capacity, Bush coordinated the efforts of about 6,000 scientists who were looking for ways to apply their expertise to the war effort. Beginning in 1945, Bush turned his attention to issues of scientific advancement during peacetime. In "As We May Think," he considers how science can help humankind gather, store, record, and retrieve the overwhelming amounts of information produced. The following excerpt contains the final three sections of Bush's article. In previous sections, he discussed how conventional libraries at the time were not up to the task of dealing with the burgeoning of information.*

Excerpt from "As We May Think"

Vannevar Bush

6

The real heart of the matter of selection, however, goes deeper than a lag in the adoption of mechanisms by libraries, or a lack of development of devices for their use. Our ineptitude in getting at the record is largely caused by the artificiality of systems of indexing. When data of any sort are placed in storage, they are filed alphabetically or numerically, and information is found (when it is) by tracing it down from subclass to subclass. It can be in only one place, unless duplicates are used; one has to have rules as to which path will locate it, and the rules are cumbersome. Having found one item, moreover, one has to emerge from the system and re-enter on a new path. 1

The human mind does not work that way. It operates by association. With one item in its grasp, it snaps instantly to the next that is suggested by the association of thoughts, in accordance with some intricate web of trails carried by the cells of the brain. It has other characteristics, of course; trails that are not frequently followed are prone to fade, items are not fully permanent, memory is transitory. Yet the speed of action, the intricacy of trails, the detail of mental pictures, is awe-inspiring beyond all else in nature. 2

Man cannot hope fully to duplicate this mental process artificially, but he certainly ought to be able to learn from it. In minor ways he may even improve, for his records have relative permanency. The first idea, however, to be drawn from the analogy concerns selection. Selection by association, rather than indexing, may yet be mechanized. One cannot hope thus to equal the speed and flexibility with which the mind follows an associative trail, but it should be possible to beat the mind decisively in regard to the permanence and clarity of the items resurrected from storage. 3

Consider a future device for individual use, which is a sort of mechanized private file and library. It needs a name, and, to coin one at random, "memex" will do. A memex is a device in which an individual stores all his books, records, and communications, and which is mechanized so that it may be consulted with exceeding speed and flexibility. It is an enlarged intimate supplement to his memory. 4

5   It consists of a desk, and while it can presumably be operated from a distance, it is primarily the piece of furniture at which he works. On the top are slanting translucent screens, on which material can be projected for convenient reading. There is a keyboard, and sets of buttons and levers. Otherwise it looks like an ordinary desk.

6   In one end is the stored material. The matter of bulk is well taken care of by improved microfilm. Only a small part of the interior of the memex is devoted to storage, the rest to mechanism. Yet if the user inserted 5000 pages of material a day it would take him hundreds of years to fill the repository, so he can be profligate and enter material freely.

7   Most of the memex contents are purchased on microfilm ready for insertion. Books of all sorts, pictures, current periodicals, newspapers, are thus obtained and dropped into place. Business correspondence takes the same path. And there is provision for direct entry. On the top of the memex is a transparent platen. On this are placed longhand notes, photographs, memoranda, all sorts of things. When one is in place, the depression of a lever causes it to be photographed onto the next blank space in a section of the memex film, dry photography being employed.

8   There is, of course, provision for consultation of the record by the usual scheme of indexing. If the user wishes to consult a certain book, he taps its code on the keyboard, and the title page of the book promptly appears before him, projected onto one of his viewing positions. Frequently-used codes are mnemonic, so that he seldom consults his code book; but when he does, a single tap of a key projects it for his use. Moreover, he has supplemental levers. On deflecting one of these levers to the right he runs through the book before him, each page in turn being projected at a speed which just allows a recognizing glance at each. If he deflects it further to the right, he steps through the book 10 pages at a time; still further at 100 pages at a time. Deflection to the left gives him the same control backwards.

9   A special button transfers him immediately to the first page of the index. Any given book of his library can thus be called up and consulted with far greater facility than if it were taken from a shelf. As he has several projection positions, he can leave one item in position while he calls up another. He can add marginal notes and comments, taking advantage of one possible type of dry photography, and it could even be arranged so that he can do this by a stylus scheme, such as is now employed in the telautograph seen in railroad waiting rooms, just as though he had the physical page before him.

7

10   All this is conventional, except for the projection forward of present-day mechanisms and gadgetry. It affords an immediate step, however, to associative indexing, the basic idea of which is a provision whereby any item may be caused at will to select immediately and automatically another. This is the essential feature of the memex. The process of tying two items together is the important thing.

11   When the user is building a trail, he names it, inserts the name in his code book, and taps it out on his keyboard. Before him are the two items to be joined, projected onto adjacent viewing positions. At the bottom of each there are a number of blank code spaces, and a pointer is set to indicate one of these on each item. The user taps a single key, and the items are permanently joined. In each code space appears the code word. Out of view, but also in the code space, is inserted a set of dots for pho-

tocell viewing; and on each item these dots by their positions designate the index number of the other item.

Thereafter, at any time, when one of these items is in view, the other can be instantly recalled merely by tapping a button below the corresponding code space. Moreover, when numerous items have been thus joined together to form a trail, they can be reviewed in turn, rapidly or slowly, by deflecting a lever like that used for turning the pages of a book. It is exactly as though the physical items had been gathered together from widely separated sources and bound together to form a new book. It is more than this, for any item can be joined into numerous trails.

12

The owner of the memex, let us say, is interested in the origin and properties of the bow and arrow. Specifically he is studying why the short Turkish bow was apparently superior to the English long bow in the skirmishes of the Crusades. He has dozens of possibly pertinent books and articles in his memex. First he runs through an encyclopedia, finds an interesting but sketchy article, leaves it projected. Next, in a history book, he finds another pertinent item, and ties the two together. Thus he goes, building a trail of many items. Occasionally he inserts a comment of his own, either linking it into the main trail or joining it by a side trail to a particular item. When it becomes evident that the elastic properties of available materials had a great deal to do with the bow, he branches off on a side trail which takes him through textbooks on elasticity and tables of physical constants. He inserts a page of longhand analysis of his own. Thus he builds a trail of his interest through the maze of materials available to him.

13

And his trails do not fade. Several years later, his talk with a friend turns to the queer ways in which a people resist innovations, even of vital interest. He has an example, in the fact that the outraged Europeans still failed to adopt the Turkish bow. In fact he has a trail on it. A touch brings up the code book. Tapping a few keys projects the head of the trail. A lever runs through it at will, stopping at interesting items, going off on side excursions. It is an interesting trail, pertinent to the discussion. So he sets a reproducer in action, photographs the whole trail out, and passes it to his friend for insertion in his own memex, there to be linked into the more general trail.

14

8

Wholly new forms of encyclopedias will appear, ready made with a mesh of associative trails running through them, ready to be dropped into the memex and there amplified. The lawyer has at his touch the associated opinions and decisions of his whole experience, and of the experience of friends and authorities. The patent attorney has on call the millions of issued patents, with familiar trails to every point of his client's interest. The physician, puzzled by a patient's reactions, strikes the trail established in studying an earlier similar case, and runs rapidly through analogous case histories, with side references to the classics for the pertinent anatomy and histology. The chemist, struggling with the synthesis of an organic compound, has all the chemical literature before him in his laboratory, with trails following the analogies of compounds, and side trails to their physical and chemical behavior.

15

The historian, with a vast chronological account of a people, parallels it with a skip trail which stops only on the salient items, and can follow at any time contemporary trails which lead him all over civilization at a particular epoch. There is a new profession of trail blazers, those who find delight in the task of establishing useful

16

trails through the enormous mass of the common record. The inheritance from the master becomes, not only his additions to the world's record, but for his disciples the entire scaffolding by which they were erected.

17   Thus science may implement the ways in which man produces, stores, and consults the record of the race. It might be striking to outline the instrumentalities of the future more spectacularly, rather than to stick closely to methods and elements now known and undergoing rapid development, as has been done here. Technical difficulties of all sorts have been ignored, certainly, but also ignored are means as yet unknown which may come any day to accelerate technical progress as violently as did the advent of the thermionic tube. In order that the picture may not be too commonplace, by reason of sticking to present-day patterns, it may be well to mention one such possibility, not to prophesy but merely to suggest, for prophecy based on extension of the known has substance, while prophecy founded on the unknown is only a doubly involved guess.

18   All our steps in creating or absorbing material of the record proceed through one of the senses—the tactile when we touch keys, the oral when we speak or listen, the visual when we read. Is it not possible that some day the path may be established more directly?

19   We know that when the eye sees, all the consequent information is transmitted to the brain by means of electrical vibrations in the channel of the optic nerve. This is an exact analogy with the electrical vibrations which occur in the cable of a television set: they convey the picture from the photocells which see it to the radio transmitter from which it is broadcast. We know further that if we can approach that cable with the proper instruments, we do not need to touch it; we can pick up those vibrations by electrical induction and thus discover and reproduce the scene which is being transmitted, just as a telephone wire may be tapped for its message.

20   The impulses which flow in the arm nerves of a typist convey to her fingers the translated information which reaches her eye or ear, in order that the fingers may be caused to strike the proper keys. Might not these currents be intercepted, either in the original form in which information is conveyed to the brain, or in the marvelously metamorphosed form in which they then proceed to the hand?

21   By bone conduction we already introduce sounds into the nerve channels of the deaf in order that they may hear. Is it not possible that we may learn to introduce them without the present cumbersomeness of first transforming electrical vibrations to mechanical ones, which the human mechanism promptly transforms back to the electrical form? With a couple of electrodes on the skull the encephalograph now produces pen-and-ink traces which bear some relation to the electrical phenomena going on in the brain itself. True, the record is unintelligible, except as it points out certain gross misfunctioning of the cerebral mechanism; but who would now place bounds on where such a thing may lead?

22   In the outside world, all forms of intelligence, whether of sound or sight, have been reduced to the form of varying currents in an electric circuit in order that they may be transmitted. Inside the human frame exactly the same sort of process occurs. Must we always transform to mechanical movements in order to proceed from one electrical phenomenon to another? It is a suggestive thought, but it hardly warrants prediction without losing touch with reality and immediateness.

23   Presumably man's spirit should be elevated if he can better review his shady past and analyze more completely and objectively his present problems. He has built a

civilization so complex that he needs to mechanize his records more fully if he is to push his experiment to its logical conclusion and not merely become bogged down part way there by overtaxing his limited memory. His excursions may be more enjoyable if he can reacquire the privilege of forgetting the manifold things he does not need to have immediately at hand, with some assurance that he can find them again if they prove important.

The applications of science have built man a well-supplied house, and are teaching him to live healthily therein. They have enabled him to throw masses of people against one another with cruel weapons. They may yet allow him truly to encompass the great record and to grow in the wisdom of race experience. He may perish in conflict before he learns to wield that record for his true good. Yet, in the application of science to the needs and desires of man, it would seem to be a singularly unfortunate stage at which to terminate the process, or to lose hope as to the outcome.

24

UNDERSTANDING THE AUTHOR'S IDEAS

1. What does Bush mean when he refers to the memex as "an enlarged intimate supplement to [a person's] memory"?
2. What do you think of Bush's description of the "piece of furniture" that houses the memex?
3. Bush describes various "codes," "code books," and "levers" that would be involved in the operation of the memex. Do you see in these features the foreshadowing of any of the aspects of today's Internet interfaces?
4. What does Bush mean by "[w]holly new forms of encyclopedias" that might emerge from the development of the memex?

EXPLORING YOUR OWN IDEAS

1. Is it possible that the growth and development of the Internet would someday actually diminish humans' capacity for memory? Why or why not?
2. With the advent of handheld, wireless Internet terminals, we have come a long way from Bush's description of the piece of furniture that could house the memex. What do you see as potential future directions for the development of Internet-access devices?
3. What problems do you see associated with the idea Bush raises with his optimistic prediction that "[w]holly new forms of encyclopedias will appear"? For example, who decides whether the material in these encyclopedias is correct, appropriate, and so on?
4. In the final section, Bush speculates about how the memex could be connected directly to users' brains so that its actions could be guided by their neural impulses. What developments in the computer technology we are living with today do you think Bush was foreshadowing? What potential problems for humankind are inherent in Bush's apparently optimistic prediction?

Reading 2

> *The Internet originated as a communications network operated by the U.S. Department of Defense Advanced Research Projects Administration (ARPA), and went by the name ARPANET from its first transmission in 1969 until 1990. After considerable expansion of the network in the early 1990s, the U.S. government transferred management of the Internet to independent, private organizations in 1995. Soon thereafter, the federal government began to respond to citizens' concerns about the type of material that was accessible on the Internet, and on February 8, 1996, the U.S. Congress passed the Communications Decency Act. Quittner's article, which originally appeared in* Time *magazine in June 1996, shows how quickly the courts were called upon to determine whether the act represented a violation of the First Amendment of the U.S. Constitution, which guarantees freedom of expression.*

"Free Speech for the Net: A Panel of Federal Judges Overturns the Communications Decency Act"

Joshua Quittner

1   It's been a suspenseful spring in cyberspace. Everyone has felt it, from the folks who gather for online chats at Bianca's Smut Shack to the Netizens who post daily dispatches to the "fight censorship" E-mail list. The whole information revolution was jeopardized, the cybernauts believed, by a primly named federal statute called the Communications Decency Act. Signed into law by President Clinton on Feb. 8, after being passed by an admittedly Net-illiterate Congress, the CDA was supposed to squelch online pornography and make the Net safe for children by banning "indecent" content. But the legislation was so vague and broad that uploading Ulysses to the World Wide Web could have been construed as a felony offense punishable by a $250,000 fine and two years in jail. If that's the kind of treatment James Joyce would get, what hope would there be for poor Bianca and her Smut Shack?

2   Relief came last week in a landmark ruling that firmly extends the umbrella of the First Amendment over cyberspace. A panel of three federal judges, specially convened in Philadelphia to review the new law, pronounced the government's attempt to regulate online content more closely than print or broadcast media "unconstitutional on its face" and "profoundly repugnant." The Justice Department was enjoined from not only enforcing the act but even investigating alleged malfeasance, at least for now.

3   The court went further than the most ardent civil libertarians had dreamed. In a striking 175-page memorandum that was published online within minutes of being handed down, the judges declared the Internet a medium of historic importance, a

profoundly democratic channel for communication that should be nurtured, not stifled. Because the Net is still in its infancy, the judges said, it deserved at least as much constitutional safekeeping as books and newspapers, if not more. "As the most participatory form of mass speech yet developed," wrote Judge Stewart Dalzell in an eloquently crafted opinion, "the Internet deserves the highest protection from governmental intrusion."

The unanimous ruling was hailed by civil libertarians as a signal moment in the struggle for free speech. "This is as historic a case as we've had in our history of First Amendment fights," said Ira Glasser, executive director of the American Civil Liberties Union, which led the court challenge on behalf of some 50 plaintiffs ranging from the American Library Association to Microsoft. Marc Rotenberg of the Electronic Privacy Information Center called the decision "the Times v. Sullivan of cyberspace," a reference to the 1964 Supreme Court decision that granted broad protection to journalists.

The legal battle is not over yet. The Department of Justice has 20 days to decide whether to ask the Supreme Court to review the case. While a Justice Department spokesman was noncommittal last week, lawyers for the government said from the outset that they would appeal an adverse decision to the highest court. Which is where proponents of the CDA say the case belongs. "We wrote this law based on previous Supreme Court decisions that have a lot of merit, so it will be looked on very carefully," says Senator J. James Exon, who introduced the original bill and believes, despite last week's rebuke, that it will be sustained.

The proponents of the CDA are fueled by outrage that hard-core pornography can be found on a computer network to which children have access. "We're talking about material going into the hands of young people whose lives can be permanently altered," says Mike Russell, spokesman for the Christian Coalition, which campaigned hard to get Congress to do something about it.

But the Philadelphia jurists (two Bush appointees, one Carter) found no indication that children were at particular risk to exposure to smut online—Time's controversial "cyberporn" cover story last summer notwithstanding. In a kind of Socratic online safari, the judges spent weeks learning their way around the Net. Guided by experts who brought computers and an Internet connection into the courtroom, they searched for online porn and tested software that allows parents to screen out offensive material. They finally concluded that whatever danger was posed for kids by the presence of "indecent" offerings online was best addressed by parents or teachers. Obscenity and child pornography, the judges noted, are already illegal under current statutes.

"There is no evidence that sexually oriented material is the primary type of content on this new medium," they wrote. "Communications over the Internet do not 'invade' an individual's home or appear on one's computer screen unbidden." The judges found that dicey material—whether from Bianca's Smut Shack or Playboy magazine's hugely popular site—was generally preceded by warnings admonishing those under the age of 18 to keep out. Even the government's own expert witness acknowledged that the odds were slim that a user would come across a sexually explicit site by accident.

The contrast between the court's view of the Net and the impression given by the lawmakers who passed the CDA was striking. The difference, says Bruce Ennis, lead attorney for the plaintiffs, was that the judges "did their homework" in a way that

Congress did not. "We made a mistake," admits Republican Congressman Rick White of Washington, who originally supported the CDA, then fought to have the indecency language removed. "The reason we got it wrong this time is that Congress does not understand the Internet."

10   Will there be a next time? That seems likely. Even if the Justice Department decides to forgo a Supreme Court appeal, the Christian Coalition, along with other "family values" groups that don't necessarily agree on other issues, has vowed to keep the heat on politicians. And there are few of those in Washington with the courage to cast a vote for free speech that could later be construed as a vote for pornography. The Administration, for its part, seems to be trying to have it both ways. Two weeks ago, Vice President Al Gore told graduating seniors at M.I.T. that "fear of chaos cannot justify unwarranted censorship of free speech." Yet after the court ruling last week, the President issued a statement reaffirming his conviction that "our Constitution allows us to help parents by enforcing this Act" and promising "to do everything I can in my Administration to give families every available tool to protect their children."

11   In the meantime, local prosecutors will have to grapple with how to apply existing obscenity laws to the new frontier of cyberspace. As spelled out by previous Supreme Court rulings, those laws use a three-pronged standard to test for obscenity: Does the material depict sexual conduct in a patently offensive way? Does it lack artistic merit? And does it violate community standards?

12   That last question puts the globe-spanning Net into direct conflict with local law enforcement. A private computer bulletin-board operator in California has been successfully prosecuted in Tennessee for making obscene material available to a postal inspector in Memphis. The Memphis jury ruled that the material violated local community standards, even though it might have been found acceptable in California or in the "virtual community" of cyberspace. "The question of community standards hasn't been adequately solved in any medium," says Harvard Law School professor Laurence Tribe. Bianca, it seems, is not yet out of the woods.

UNDERSTANDING THE AUTHOR'S IDEAS

1. Quittner uses a newly coined term, *Netizens*. What do you think this term means? Is it an apt term? Why or why not?
2. Quittner suggests that the judges in the specially convened court in Philadelphia apparently believed that the Internet needed even stronger protection from First Amendment violations than other forms of expression. Why?
3. What did the judges mean by their statement that no one's home is "invaded" by the Internet?
4. According to Quittner, how might a congressional representative's vote for freedom of expression be misunderstood or misconstrued by some voters?

1. The Communications Decency Act seemed designed to keep hard-core pornography away from children. How effectively do you think the federal government can achieve this goal?
2. What are the implications of the passage of the Communications Decency Act and its eventual court challenges for the notion of parental responsibility?
3. Do you agree with the U.S. Supreme Court's three-part "standard to test for obscenity"? Why or why not?
4. When the medium of communications is the Internet, how does one define "local community" standards for appropriate and acceptable behavior?

Readings 3 and 4

Shortly after the attack on the World Trade Center in New York City on September 11, 2001, the U.S. Department of Defense intensified its efforts to develop methods to gather information that might provide intelligence about terrorist threats and would ideally prevent such attacks in the future. One such effort, conducted by the Defense Advanced Research Projects Administration (DARPA), went by two names: the Terrorism Information Awareness System and the Total Information Awareness Project. Both were abbreviated TIA.

As news of the development of this project became public, commentators of different political persuasions began to examine the implications of the DARPA system for the rights of U.S. citizens to express themselves freely, as guaranteed by the First Amendment to the Constitution, and to be protected from illegal searches as guaranteed by the Fourth Amendment. The commentators were particularly concerned with how tracking of individual's use of the Internet might be part of the TIA project.

The following two brief pieces represent something of a point-counterpoint debate on the issue of Internet privacy and can be read as companion pieces. Paul Rosenzweig is a senior legal research fellow for the Heritage Foundation. Clyde Wayne Crews, Jr., is director of technology studies at the Cato Institute.

"Proposals for Implementing the Terrorism Information Awareness System"

Paul Rosenzweig

The Terrorism Information Awareness (TIA) program under development by the Defense Advanced Research Projects Administration at the Department of Defense has generated substantial controversy. Much of that controversy is unwarranted, and

1

concerns that the technology will be abused are speculative, at best. A number of analogous oversight and implementation structures already in existence can be borrowed and suitably modified to control the use of the new technology.

2   As six former top-ranking professionals in America's security services recently observed, we face two problems—both a need for better analysis and, more critically, "improved espionage, to provide the essential missing intelligence." In their view, while there was "certainly a lack of dot-connecting before September 11" the more critical failure was that "[t]here were too few useful dots." TIA technology can help to answer both of these needs. Thus, TIA can and should be developed if the technology proves usable.

3   The technology can be developed in a manner that renders it effective, while posing minimal risks to American liberties, if the system is crafted carefully, with built-in safeguards that act to check the possibilities of error or abuse. In summary they are:

- Congressional authorization should be required before data mining technology (also known as Knowledge Discovery (KD) technology) is deployed;
- KD technology should be used to examine individual subjects only in compliance with internal guidelines and only with a system that "builds in" existing legal limitations on access to third-party data;
- KD technology should be used to examine terrorist patterns only if each pattern query is authorized by a Senate-confirmed official using a system that: a) allows only for the initial examination of government databases, and b) disaggregates individual identifying information from the pattern analysis;
- Protection of individual anonymity by ensuring that individual identities are not disclosed without the approval of a federal judge;
- A statutory or regulatory requirement that the only consequence of identification by pattern analysis is additional investigation;
- Provision of a robust legal mechanism for the correction of false positive identifications;
- Heightened accountability and oversight, including internal policy controls and training, executive branch administrative oversight, enhanced congressional oversight, and civil and criminal penalties for abuse; and
- Finally, absolute statutory prohibition on the use of KD technology for nonterrorism investigations.

4   Critics of TIA are wrong to exalt the protection of liberty as an absolute value. That vision rests on an incomplete understanding of why Americans formed a civil society. As John Locke, the seventeenth-century philosopher who greatly influenced the Founding Fathers, wrote: "In all states of created beings, capable of laws, where there is no law there is no freedom. For liberty is to be free from the restraint and violence from others; which cannot be where there is no law; and is not, as we are told, a liberty for every man to do what he lists." Or, as Thomas Powers recently wrote: "*In a liberal republic, liberty presupposes security; the point of security is liberty.*" Thus, the obligation of the government is a dual one: to protect civil safety and security against violence and to preserve civil liberty.

That goal can be achieved. To be sure, it is a difficult task. It is far easier to es- 5
chew the effort. But failure to make the effort—failure to recognize that security
need not be traded off for liberty in equal measure and that the "balance" between
them is not a zero-sum game—is a far greater and more fundamental mistake.
Policymakers must respect and defend the individual civil liberties guaranteed in the
Constitution when they act, but they also cannot fail to act when we face a serious
threat from a foreign enemy.

Indeed, resistance to new technology poses practical dangers. As the 6
Congressional Joint Inquiry into the events of September 11 pointed out in noting
systemic failures that played a role in the inability to prevent the terrorist attacks:

4. Finding: While technology remains one of this nation's greatest advantages, it 7
has not been fully and most effectively applied in support of U.S. counterterrorism
efforts. Persistent problems in this area included a lack of collaboration between
Intelligence Community agencies [and] a reluctance to develop and implement new
technical capabilities aggressively. . . .

It is important not to repeat that mistake. 8

"The Pentagon's Total Information Awareness Project: Americans Under the Microscope"

Clyde Wayne Crews, Jr.

The Pentagon assures us we have nothing to fear from its new Total Information 1
Awareness (TIA) counterterrorism project, a colossal effort to assemble and "mine"
massive databases of our credit-card purchases, car rentals, airline tickets, official
records, and the like. The aim is to monitor the public's whereabouts, movements,
and transactions to glean suspicious patterns that indicate terrorist planning and
other shenanigans. Well, we shouldn't always trust the assurance of the Pentagon.

The Fourth Amendment to the Constitution, which safeguards us against unrea- 2
sonable searches, forbids a total surveillance society if that's where this project's directors intend to go.

It may be appropriate for the government to make use of readily available public 3
information. Yet even here, it's important to remember that such information,
whether driver's license, Social Security, or tax information, is mandated by numerous agencies for specific purposes—not general law enforcement—and should not
be routinely combined for such purposes without a specific court order.

The reason? Government has become too large and pervasive. TIA's commitment 4
not to monitor innocent individuals is not credible. There are so many compulsory cra-
dle-to-grave databases that the mere act of combining, sorting, sifting and interpreting

them may no longer be possible without violating our Fourth Amendment rights.

5   The TIA's logo features an edited version of the Great Seal of the United States: The 13-block pyramid (think 13 original colonies) topped by the Eye of God. The original carries the phrase (translated from Latin) "A New Order of the Ages," reflecting a principled view of individual freedom quite alien to that of the Orwellian TIA office. The TIA's version perverts the proud seal that originally symbolized our freedom. The "eye" is no longer God's, but the federal government's, surveying the entire globe in a single glance. TIA's new slogan? "Knowledge is Power." But whose knowledge? And power to do what?

6   The information economy and electronic commerce increasingly depend on secure and specialized private databases, and TIA could undermine those as well. Corporate America needs to be able to make credible privacy assurances to the public. People need to know that the data they relinquish is confined to an agreed-upon business, transactional or record-keeping purpose, and isn't automatically included in a government database. If the TIA project ends up routinely requiring banks, airlines, hotels, Internet-service providers, and other businesses to hand over such private information, it will undermine evolving commercial-privacy standards, drive transactions underground, and make criminals out of ordinary people who simply want to be left alone.

7   Only two years ago, President Bush entered office promising to protect medical and financial privacy. A number of congressmen still fret over Internet privacy, and people like Rep. Dick Armey (R-Tex.) defiantly protested a national ID card and other surveillance tools.

8   The Pentagon seems willing to ignore that sentiment. While the Homeland Security bill banned a national ID card, the TIA project would seem to accomplish all the data aggregation that would make a national ID both feasible and irresistible to policymakers. Not a road to travel lightly.

9   An aggressive TIA project will threaten privacy and chill healthy civil disobedience. Ironically, the project could also increase security risks. Even the Pentagon's resources are limited: Most people are not terrorists, and it can be a costly diversion to attempt to monitor the torrent of chatter that will be generated by this misguided program. Terrorists already immerse themselves in mainstream society, even using their real names and official government documents. They can learn and anticipate the trigger patterns that will supposedly generate red flags, and then avoid them. You won't see terrorists buying one-way airline tickets, for example. Because terrorists will resemble ordinary people, TIA inevitably means magnifying-glass surveillance of ordinary folks, wasting more time, all in a vicious, misdirected circle.

10   The TIA program contradicts federal cybersecurity goals, too. The government has proven notoriously bad at safeguarding its information databases. Since 9/11, hackers have gained access to secret Department of Defense satellite photos and nuclear missile information. A massive TIA database will be an irresistible target for hackers who, based on the track record so far, will succeed in breaching it.

11   If we're interested in protecting America's security and critical infrastructure, we need to target documented security lapses like lax background checks of airline-security personnel and foreigners in flight-training schools. It's one thing to give up privacy for security if there's no other choice. With TIA we may be sacrificing privacy for no security benefit at all.

UNDERSTANDING THE AUTHORS' IDEAS

1. According to Rosenzweig, what is the need for the TIA project?
2. According to Rosenzweig, how and why are critics of the TIA project wrong?
3. According to Rosenzweig, how and why does "resistance to new technology [pose] practical dangers"?
4. According to Crews, what is the relevance of the TIA project to the Fourth Amendment of the Constitution?
5. How does Crews believe the TIA logo "perverts" the message one finds on the Great Seal of the United States?
6. According to Crews, what kinds of practical (in contrast to ideological) conditions prevent the successful implementation of the TIA project?

EXPLORING YOUR OWN IDEAS

1. What is your reaction to the term *data-mining technology*? What are the connotations of the terms used in that phrase? Do you believe the phrase covers up any of the possible agendas of the TIA project? Why or why not?
2. How can you most clearly explain the Department of Defense's need to balance the people's constitutional rights and the threat of a potential attack by an enemy?
3. Crews claims that the TIA might "chill healthy civil disobedience." What do you think "healthy" civil disobedience consists of? Is Crews right? Why or why not?
4. Early discussions of the TIA project floated the idea of having citizens apply for and carry a national ID card. Do you think this would be a good idea? Why or why not?

EXPLORING VISUAL IMAGES

Study the line drawing on the next page. What is the artist suggesting by having mirror-image figures, both holding their hands over the other's eyes? Do the human creatures look real or stylized? What implications does their appearance hold for the meaning of the drawing? What is the artist suggesting by the content of the buttons beside each face? Is the implied message of the drawing congruent with your own experiences with dealing with Internet security and privacy issues? Why or why not? Do you think this is an effective drawing to accompany a story about governmental and private-sector efforts to deal with Internet security issues? Why or why not? Write a reaction paper exploring your ideas regarding this visual.

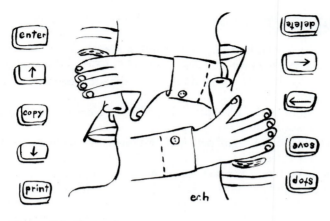

(*Source:* Eric Hanson)

Reading 5

This brief news article from the British Broadcasting Corporation was published on January 11, 2004. Keep in mind that the Republic of Cuba is a Communist nation; Fidel Castro has been its head of state since 1959. Note the terse journalistic style here, typical of the genre of the newswire release, which attempts to deliver "facts" as directly as possible.

"Cuba Cracks Down on Internet Use"

BBC News

A new law has been passed in Cuba which will make access to the internet more difficult for Cubans.

1   Only those authorised to use the internet from home like civil servants, party officials and doctors will be able to do so on a regular phone line.

2   The bill says the state telephone company Etecsa will use technical means to detect and impede access.

3   Correspondents say the law will affect thousands of Cubans who access the worldwide web from their homes.

It took effect on Saturday, according to a letter sent by Etecsa internet service E-net to customers.   4

The government says the move is necessary to "regulate dial-up access to internet navigation services, adopting measures that help protect against the taking of passwords, malicious acts, and the fraudulent and unauthorised use of this service".   5

Black market

The Cuban Government passed a decree last year that the internet could only be accessed using a more expensive telephone service charged in US dollars, not generally available to ordinary Cubans.   6

E-net customers who do not have the dollar phone service can still access the internet legally by buying special cards at Etecsa offices.   7

Some Cubans also can use international email and a government-controlled intranet at work and in schools.   8

But until now many people have been using computers and internet accounts borrowed or bought on the black market, and it is they who will be affected by the new law.   9

Blackout

The previous system allowing access to the web granted many Cubans a rare opportunity to observe western media and news reports.   10

Global television news channels are only available at luxury hotels which are off limits to Cuban tourists.   11

It is feared that as well as "blacking out" this window on the world, the new move to further limit web access could also damage Cuba's main source of foreign revenue: the tourism industry.   12

Thousands of ordinary Cubans have relied on the internet to advertise private accommodation for foreign tourists.   13

UNDERSTANDING THE AUTHOR'S IDEAS

1. According to the news story, why did the government of Cuba restrict its citizens' Internet access?
2. Prior to the new restrictions, how had ordinary citizens in Cuba been getting access to the Internet?
3. What does the article suggest will be the impact of the new restrictions on the tourism industry, and why?

EXPLORING YOUR OWN IDEAS

1. The fifth paragraph lists all the government's reasons for restricting access to the Internet. What do you think all the phrases in that paragraph actually mean?
2. Could similar restrictions ever be imposed on Internet access in the United States? Why or why not?
3. Suppose you agreed with the Cuban government's new policy on Internet access but were charged with establishing guidelines that would allow *exemptions* to the policy. What would those exemptions be, and why?
4. How much opportunity do U.S. citizens have to observe the workings of governments and societies in other countries via the Internet? How much do you think American citizens take advantage of these opportunities?

Reading 6

In the late 1990s, one of the major controversies involving the Internet was its use as a medium for downloading and sharing music files. Since professional musicians' work is copyrighted—they make their living from the royalties they receive from the sale of their recordings and their recordings' appearance on radio and television—this practice of downloading and sharing files constitutes a violation of federal law. McCollum's story in the Chronicle of Higher Education, *a weekly newspaper devoted to covering issues of importance to college and university administrators, faculty, and students, describes how one university, Carnegie Mellon in Pittsburgh, dealt with this issue.*

"How Forcefully Should Universities Enforce Copyright Laws on Audio Files?"

Kelly McCollum

Carnegie Mellon's search for MP3's pleases recording industry, but irks some students

1   Seventy-one students at Carnegie Mellon University got a lesson in copyright and computer ethics last month, after the university discovered that they had been distributing illegally copied MP3 audio files on the campus network. For college and university administrators, however, the lessons are more complicated.

Among students, MP3's are one of the year's hottest on-line trends, allowing   2
friends to trade songs digitally and music aficionados to search the Internet for rare
tracks by their favorite performers. But for recording artists, the format is a copyright-
infringement nightmare: Users can easily copy entire compact disks and serve them
up on the Net for anyone to download free. And the Recording Industry Association
of America has been aggressively pursuing copyright violations on campuses.

In the middle are university administrators. Few are eager to search students'   3
computers, but even fewer want to be sued because students are using their campus
networks in ways that violate copyright laws. And even though those laws make it
clear that responsible network administrators can't be held accountable for the behavior of every user, deans and campus-computing officials want to reduce illegal activity—and teach students ethics.

Network administrators at Carnegie Mellon say that is why they decided last   4
month to check the public folders of 250 student computers connected to the university's network. Dozens of the folders contained illegally copied MP3's, which were
accessible to about 11,000 users of the university's computer network, although not
necessarily to anyone outside the university.

Students who were caught making the files available to others on the campus net-   5
work lost their in-room Internet connections for the remainder of the semester,
meaning they must go to one of the university's computer labs when they need network access. Students who attended a 90-minute class on copyright got their sentences reduced to one month.

Carnegie Mellon's investigation, which came without warning to users, prompted   6
some students to complain about invasion of privacy and unfair punishment. But according to Paul G. Fowler, the university's associate dean of student affairs, the move
was meant to gauge just how significant a copyright-infringement problem the campus network faced. "It wasn't a crackdown. It wasn't some big caper," says Mr.
Fowler. "All we did was go in to take a look at the culture of our intranet."

Mr. Fowler says the search was prompted by a handful of complaints of copyright   7
violations the university had received from both on and off the campus. He adds that
administrators wanted to know whether the university needed to beef up its efforts at
educating students about copyrights. "We wanted to know if that's a good use of our
resources," he says. "We now know that it would be."

"We were expecting to find 5 or 10 machines. We found 71. Then we thought,   8
'Jeez—this is horrible.' I don't want all these students to lose network access for the
whole semester." Students were allowed to appeal their suspensions to Mr. Fowler.

Some of those students were sharing legal MP3's, like live performances by the   9
Dave Matthews Band, which expressly authorizes fans to record its shows and share
or trade the recordings. "They said, 'Dave Matthews said we could do it,'" says Mr.
Fowler. In two or three other cases, students who would have been put to undue
hardship by having their Internet access shut down, such as a student bedridden
with mononucleosis and strep throat, were let off the hook.

Carnegie Mellon's action was unusual—unless a copyright holder complains,   10
most universities don't go looking for trouble on their networks, even though it most
likely exists in the form of illegally copied MP3's and software. "We do not go trolling
for it," says Richard Fagen, director of information-technology services at the

California Institute of Technology. "You never want to do that."

11   "We certainly don't condone anything that's illegal or unethical, but you can only go so far," says Mr. Fagen. "We're not the cops, going around searching people's computers without any probable cause."

12   "We have a policy that makes it very clear that you can't violate the law using our networks," says Marjorie Hodges Shaw, director of the Computer Policy and Law Program at Cornell University. "But we do not monitor for illegal usage or for policy violations," she says.

13   Carnegie Mellon usually maintains a hands-off approach, too, says Mr. Fowler. "But the fact is that we've created this culture where students have told us that the intranet was free range. If that is in fact the culture, it would be hard for us to say, 'We didn't know students were sharing files left and right.' We could say that, but we'd be lying," he says.

14   What university officials know and when they know it matters because of the Digital Millennium Copyright Act, an Internet-age update to American copyright law that was passed last year. Under the act, "on-line service providers"—such as universities that offer Internet connections to students, or commercial providers like America Online—are relieved of some responsibility for copyright infringement by their users.

15   According to Arnold P. Lutzker, a lawyer who works with the American Library Association, the protection offered by the act means "you don't have to monitor, but you are required—if you have received notice—to act."

16   To qualify for the limited liability, explains Mr. Lutzker, an institution must first register itself as an on-line service provider, or O.S.P. A U.S. Copyright Office Web site (http://lcweb.loc.gov/copyright/onlinesp/) provides instructions for registering. Providers must also establish internal policies for dealing with copyright infringers.

17   The digital-millennium act, in fact, specifies how a service provider must respond when a copyright holder complains about a suspected infringement. The provider must shut off access to the infringing material and notify the user who posted it. The user can then appeal the shutoff and take up the matter with the copyright holder. As long as a university complies with those requirements, says Mr. Lutzker, it is probably free from liability for any given infringement. A detailed explanation of the provision is available on the A.L.A.'s Web site (http://www.ala.org/washoff/osp.html).

18   The law also includes a provision that limits an institution's responsibility for material posted by professors and graduate-student employees. "Typically an employer is liable for the actions of its employees, and this is a tweak on that," says Mr. Lutzker.

19   While the act's provisions can protect universities from getting sued for monetary damages if a student maintains an illegal MP3 archive, Mr. Lutzker warns that universities can still be liable if they are shown to be lax in discouraging copyright infringements. If an institution is the focus of repeated complaints, or if it creates an environment that is conducive to copyright infringement, a copyright holder might be able to sue to prevent future violations, he says.

20   Universities that receive reports of MP3-related copyright violations most often receive them from one entity—the Recording Industry Association of America.

21   The association, which represents record companies, works particularly hard to track

down illegal MP3's. The association has a staff of researchers who comb the Internet for sites that violate copyrights of its members. It has focused closely on academe.

Two years ago, when the association turned its attention toward colleges, "about 70 per cent of the infringing sites we found were on university networks," says Frank Creighton, a senior vice-president of the association who directs its anti-piracy efforts. At that time, Mr. Creighton says, the association began a campaign to educate students and universities about music copyrights. A handful of institutions, including Carnegie Mellon, helped design the campaign (http://www.soundbyting.com/). "Our tack has been to educate first, before we enforce," says Mr. Creighton.   22

"Now we're only finding about 30 per cent of the infringing sites on universities," he says. "We think that's largely due to not just the education campaign itself and students' actually getting the message, but also to the universities' understanding how big the problem is and putting in place their own procedures" to educate students and punish violators.   23

At the same time, the association has continued its practice of sending letters to universities whenever R.I.A.A. employees spot on-campus servers offering copyrighted music. Those letters—which must specify both the material in question and the server on which it resides—prompt most of the disciplinary actions taken by colleges and universities.   24

Mr. Fagen says Caltech, which has about 900 undergraduates, has received only three such complaints in recent years. Cornell has gotten 12 in the past year, says Ms. Hodges Shaw. And Carnegie Mellon has received about two dozen in total, says Mr. Fowler, adding: "That's not a huge number, but it's irritating to get them."   25

So far, every university the R.I.A.A. has contacted has responded by shutting down the infringing sites, says the association's Mr. Creighton. Even after an offending site is closed, the association still has the right to sue its creator for damages, but Mr. Creighton says that's rare.   26

"We think it's about education, so we're willing to give individuals or students that first pass. But if we do catch you doing it again, we have no alternative but to take the stance that you're thumbing your nose at us and you don't take us seriously, and there are potential civil and criminal remedies that we will invoke if we need to."   27

A university that didn't cooperate with a copyright holder's request would lose its limited liability under the copyright law, but that hasn't happened yet, says Mr. Creighton. "Can I say that somewhere down the road we're going to find a university that won't heed our warning? It's a possibility," he says. "And we hope we'd be able to negotiate that out of court first, before we had to go the route of actual litigation."   28

He acknowledges that universities' protected status has hindered the association's enforcement efforts. It has "led a lot of I.S.P.'s or universities not to scan their own networks for this infringing activity," he says. "It's actually worked against us in that sense."   29

"I absolutely applaud what Carnegie Mellon did and, in fact, we always ask universities for their help in seeking out those infringements and enforcing."   30

University officials, however, are quick to say they're not undertaking anti-infringement programs just to please the R.I.A.A.   31

"I'm no fan of the recording industry," says Carnegie Mellon's Mr. Fowler, "but our students need to understand that they're probably going to be out there creating   32 software someday that's going to make them a million dollars. If that software winds up in some shared community, their livelihood is jeopardized because people are sharing copyrighted material.

33   "That's going to be harmful to them," he continues. "So why shouldn't we afford the same opportunities to make a living to other members of our broader community as we would expect our students to have when they go on to make their millions?"

UNDERSTANDING THE AUTHOR'S IDEAS

1. The university administrator at Carnegie Mellon who led the investigation into illegal file sharing there was Paul G. Fowler, the associate dean of student affairs. How does Fowler explain the rationale for the investigation?
2. According to the story, Carnegie Mellon generally adopts a "hands-off" policy regarding the contents of students' computer files. What does Fowler's attitude toward this policy seem to be?
3. What is the Digital Millennium Copyright Act and how do its provisions affect the downloading and sharing of music files?
4. What has been the response of the Recording Industry Association of America to the occurrences of music downloading and sharing on university campuses?

EXPLORING YOUR OWN IDEAS

1. Do you believe network administrators at Carnegie Mellon violated the provisions of the Fourth Amendment? Why or why not?
2. Do you believe the punishment received by the Carnegie Mellon students was appropriate? Why or why not?
3. Does a college or university have a responsibility to teach its students about the ethics of Internet use? Why or why not?
4. The controversy over music downloading and file sharing has seemed to subside in recent years. Are there similar controversies involving Internet use and privacy that you believe are brewing and will come to the surface soon? If so, what are they?

Reading 7

Any new communications technology invariably changes not only who communicates with whom but also how they do so. When government-sponsored mail systems replaced private messengers, communications changed. When the telegraph replaced the Pony Express, communications changed. When the telephone replaced the telegraph, communications changed. And so on.

An article by John Schwartz from the January 3, 2004, New York Times *shows a distinctive change in family communications patterns brought about by one new bit of Internet technology, instant messaging.*

"That Parent-Child Conversation Is Becoming Instant, and Online"

John Schwartz

Nina Gordon types out an instant message and sends it. The data travels some 500 miles, from the computer in her living room in Queens to America Online's servers in Northern Virginia, and then to her son Schuyler's computer, which just happens to be in the next room—about 20 feet away from where she is sitting.   1

you hungry for dinner?   2

After a little online banter over dining options, her son, a 17-year-old with a wicked sense of humor and no shortage of attitude, sends his request: 3

an insty pizza and a beer   4

don't push your luck, comes the reply.   5

Instant messaging, long a part of teenagers' lives, is working its way into the broader fabric of the American family. The technology "has really grown up in the last 18 months," said Michael Gartenberg, vice president and research director at Jupiter Research. "It's certainly not just for kids anymore."   6

Almost three-quarters of all teenagers with online access use instant messaging and about half of all adults have tried the services, surveys show. Adults, who generally began using the services from AOL, Microsoft and Yahoo to stay in touch with co-workers during the day, Mr. Gartenberg said, are saying "this stuff I'm using for work is actually useful in my personal life as well."   7

Use among adults has grown to include friends and far-flung family members, particularly children away at college. AOL, which provides the most popular service, reports that more than one billion instant messages each day flow through its networks.   8

And now, as families own more than one computer, the machines spread beyond the den and home networks relying on wireless connections become increasingly popular, instant messaging is taking root within the home itself.   9

Although it might seem lazy or silly to send electronic messages instead of getting out of a chair and walking into the next room, some psychologists say that the role of the technology within families can be remarkably positive. In many cases, they say, the messages are helping to break down the interpersonal barriers that often prevent open communication.   10

"Conversation between parents and teenagers could be highly emotional and not necessarily productive," said Elisheva F. Gross, a psychology researcher at the Children's Digital Media Center at the University of California at Los Angeles. When young people are online, however, "it's their turf," she said. "It may be a way   11 for parents to communicate in a language and in a space that their children are more comfortable with."

12   Teenagers already use online communications to take on difficult topics with one another, said Katelyn McKenna, a research assistant professor in psychology at New York University. Preliminary results from a study she conducted last year, she said, suggest that "they are able to talk with one another about issues that bother them more readily online than when they are talking face to face."

13   Lissa Parsonnet said that her daughter, Dorrie, is sometimes more open to talking with her and her husband online about difficult subjects, like conflicts with friends, than in person.

14   "She talks to us as if we're people, not parents," she said.

15   Ms. Parsonnet, a psychotherapist, said that the online back channel strips away some of the parts of face-to-face communication that complicate matters: "They don't see your face turning red," she said. "They don't see you turning cross—all the things that will shut them up immediately."

16   Both instant messages and e-mail messages can help smooth things over after a fight, said Nora Gross, a 17-year-old in Manhattan who says that electronic communications have helped strengthen her relationship with her father. "I can remember a few times when we've had little blowups and sent apology letters over e-mail," she said. "We're both writers, so I guess it's easier for us to put our feelings into words through text."

17   While even quicker than e-mail, instant messages also have the advantage of not actually being instant, Ms. Parsonnet said, because the medium at least gives the user time to compose his or her thoughts and comments before hitting the button.

18   For users, instant-messaging software typically displays, in a small box on the computer screen, a "buddy list" of friends who are online at any given moment. Most instant messaging conversations are one-to-one, but it also possible to include several people in a group discussion—and to carry on multiple sessions with several people at once.

19   Ms. Parsonnet said that the instant messaging habit began naturally with Dorrie. One night, she wanted to ask Dorrie a question, but "I didn't want to go chasing her around the house." She didn't have to wander around the family's Short Hills, N.J., home, though, because "I could hear her instant message thing bleeping."

20   She signed on, saw that Dorrie was indeed online, and sent a note. "It was so easy," she recalled.

21   That ease of use is essential for adopting any new technology, said Michael Osterman, an industry analyst who studies the instant messaging market. The concept should even seem familiar to the many baby boomers who grew up in post-World War II suburban houses with built-in home intercom systems. But families rarely used the clunky devices to talk from room to room, he noted.

22   Instant messaging puts a much simpler, more effective intercom system at every set of fingertips. "It's an old idea that's been made practical," he said. "Instead of yelling downstairs, 'Hey, is there any fried chicken left?' you can I.M. downstairs.'"

Using instant messages to reach out to adolescents fits into the broad structure of   23
experimentation and adaptation that family therapists generally recommend, said A.
Rae Simpson, program director for parenting education and research at the M.I.T.
Center for Work, Family & Personal Life in Cambridge, Mass.

"People who are having difficulty communicating with each other write to each   24
other," Ms. Simpson said, similar to the way that many parents and adolescents find
they can talk more freely in the car than at home because they are not looking directly at each other. "It takes the intensity out of the eye-to-eye contact."

The uses of instant messages in the home can be banal, playful or profound. Lily   25
Mandlin, 15, who lives with her mother and two siblings in a four-bedroom apartment on Manhattan's Upper West Side, said that an instant message is sometimes
the best way to get her older brother to turn down his stereo.

"A little ping on the computer actually gets to him a lot quicker than screaming,   26
'Turn the music down!' " she said.

Mr. Gartenberg, the industry analyst, said, "There has been more than one time   27
when I have been checking something late at night and discovered one of the kids
was logged on. And I said, 'What are you doing? Go to bed!' "

Sometimes the messages are more, well, adult. Ms. Gordon, the Queens mother,   28
said that when she and her husband first got laptop computers with wireless cards,
they would even send messages to each other as they worked at home, sitting across
from each other in bed.

What messages would they send back and forth when they were sitting so close?   29

"Use your imagination," she said. "Sparks flying across the wireless network, so   30
to speak!"

Kathy Grace, a Web site designer in Austin, said that she is more likely to send in-   31
stant messages to her husband, Dennis, than to her daughter Ariel, because "we're
on different systems." Ariel is on AOL; Ms. Grace and her husband favor Microsoft
Messenger, which he uses at work.

Husband and wife will pop a message back and forth while she is working on the   32
laptop at the dining room table and he is using the bedroom PC, even though the
house is small, Ms. Grace said. "We keep the bedroom doors closed, and it's easier
than shouting," she said.

For all the advantages many families and experts see in instant messaging, some   33
adolescents say that they simply do not want their parents on their buddy list.

"People can be easily misunderstood online," one teenager, who asked that her name   34
not be used, wrote in an I.M. interview. "I am not as reserved when I talk to people online than in real life, so really, it would just exacerbate whatever problem was there."

Back at the Gordon home, the chatter is often just for the fun of wordplay—and   35
that, too, can strengthen the bond between generations.

It is another night, another dinner. Takeout seafood.   36

want another clam? Nina Gordon asks her son, eating in the next room.   37

i havent started the crab yet, he replies. A pun-fest ensues.   38

don't be crabby, she writes.   39

don't be coy, he replies.   40

never, she counters. oy, not coy.   41

42   While instant messages and e-mail may helpfully supplement face-to-face discussion, experts warn that it should not be relied on as the principal means of communication.

43   "The question is whether you can use it constructively, to bring it back to the face to face," said Sherry Turkle, director of the Initiative on Technology and Self at the Massachusetts Institute of Technology. If the conversation is strictly virtual, she said, "it's not so different from saying, 'I have a wonderful epistolary relationship with my husband, who I can't stand.'"

UNDERSTANDING THE AUTHOR'S IDEAS

1. According to the article, why do some psychologists think that communication via instant messaging may actually be better than face-to-face communication in some family situations?
2. What does Schwartz mean when he says that instant messages are not exactly instant?
3. Prior to instant messaging, what technologies were available to allow families to communicate from one room of a house to another?
4. According to the article, what are the different types of family relationships that are taking advantage of instant messaging?

EXPLORING YOUR OWN IDEAS

1. Commentators on technological change frequently claim that new technologies such as the Internet are damaging family values in America. Do you agree or disagree?
2. Are there issues of economic status and privilege inherent in this story? If so, what are they?
3. Why do you think some teenagers might not want their parents to be part of their instant messaging buddy lists?
4. Why do you think one particular use of instant messaging is for parents to keep students who have just gone off to college in touch with them?

UNIT WRITING ASSIGNMENT SUGGESTIONS

1. Consider the scope and pace of change that has occurred in your life because of the Internet and speculate about what effect the Internet might have on your life in the future. Write a **personal essay** reflecting your thoughts and speculations.
2. For a set period—for example, three consecutive days, or a week, or two weeks—keep track of all your interactions with the Internet. As you do so, keep a **journal** of your experiences.

3. Incorporating readings in this unit and others you may gather in your research, write a **stance or position paper** about some specific Internet privacy or security program and its relation to either the First Amendment to the U.S. Constitution, the Fourth Amendment, or both.

4. Write a **proposal** for a program or project that you believe would solve some issue involving the Internet and the copyright laws—for example, the illegal downloading and sharing of music files.

5. Keep track of the amount of "spam"—unsolicited, commercial e-mail—you receive during a set period, say, three days or a week. Write an **informative report** about what you record.

6. Conduct a detailed observation of someone—perhaps a young child or a senior citizen—learning to use the Internet for the first time, and write a **case study** based on your observations.

7. Research more information on the history and development of the Internet. Create an **annotated bibliography** for several aspects of this growing topic.

8. Read George Orwell's classic novel *1984* and write a **literary analysis essay** interpreting aspects of the novel from the perspective you've gained from these readings.

9. Conduct a **field observation** of the Internet habits of a select group of college students. Determine the types of functions they use and how frequently they use them. Draw conclusions about any general patterns that emerge.

10. For an interesting **Web-based assignment,** consult the newly created Web site www.whatsthedownload.com created by the music industry in response to the burning CDs craze. Study the Web site, identify its target audience, and analyze its appeals, summarizing its key arguments.

CREDITS

INDEX